JOHN RUFUS: THE *LIVES* OF PETER THE IBERIAN, THEODOSIUS OF JERUSALEM, AND THE MONK ROMANUS

Society of Biblical Literature

Writings from the Greco-Roman World

John T. Fitzgerald, General Editor

Number 24

JOHN RUFUS: THE *LIVES* OF PETER THE IBERIAN, THEODOSIUS OF JERUSALEM, AND THE MONK ROMANUS

Volume Editor
Sebastian P. Brock

John Rufus: The *Lives* of Peter the Iberian, Theodosius of Jerusalem, and the Monk Romanus

Edited and Translated with an Introduction and Notes by

Cornelia B. Horn

and

Robert R. Phenix Jr.

Society of Biblical Literature

Atlanta

JOHN RUFUS: THE *LIVES* OF PETER THE IBERIAN, THEODOSIUS OF JERUSALEM, AND THE MONK ROMANUS

Library of Congress Cataloging-in-Publication Data

John Rufus, Bishop of Maiuma, fl. 476-518.
[Vita Petri Iberi. English & Syriac]
The *Lives* of Peter the Iberian, Theodosius of Jerusalem, and the Monk Romanus / John Rufus ; translated with an introduction and notes by Cornelia B. Horn and Robert R. Phenix Jr.
p. cm. — (Writings from the Greco-Roman world ; v. 24)
Also published in hardback: Leiden ; Boston : Brill, 2008.
Includes bibliographical references and index.
ISBN 978-1-58983-200-8 (paper binding : alk. paper)
1. Petre, Iberieli, ca. 411-ca. 490. 2. Theodosius, Bishop of Jerusalem, fl. 450. 3. Romanus, Saint, martyr of Antioch, d 303? 4. Monasticism and religious orders–Iberia (Kingdom)–History–Early church, ca. 30-600. 5. Monasticism and religious orders–Palestine–History–Early church, ca. 30-600. I. Horn, Cornelia B. II. Phenix, Robert R. III. John Rufus, Bishop of Maiuma, fl. 476-518. De obitu Theodosii. English & Syriac. IV. Title.

BR1102.J64 2008
270.2092′2–dc22
[B] 2008017292

---

08 09 10 11 12 13 14 15 — 5 4 3 2 1

Printed in the United States of America on acid-free, recycled paper conforming to ANSI/NISO Z39.48-1992 (R1997) and ISO 9706:1994 standards for paper permanence.

Table of Contents

Preface vii

Abbreviations xi

Introduction xix

The Context of the History of Georgia from the Fourth to the Sixth Centuries xix

Christianity and Monasticism in Georgia in the Fourth and Fifth Centuries xxv

Peter's Genealogy in the *Life of Peter the Iberian*: Hagiographic Ancestry xxxiii

The History of the Christological Controversies and Their Context in Palestine from the Fourth to the Sixth Centuries xxxiii

Monasticism in Fifth-Century Palestine xlviii

On the Death of Theodosius liii

The Anti-Chalcedonian Defeat in Palestine liv

Authorship lviii

John Rufus lxii

Rhetoric and Genre in the *Life of Peter the Iberian* lxiii

Text-Critical Overview lxxi

Versions and Original Text lxxiii

Synopsis of the *Vita Petri Iberi* and the *De obitu Theodosii* lxxv

Outline of the *Vita Petri Iberi* lxxv

Outline of the *De obitu Theodosii* lxxxiv

Genealogical Tables of the Families of Peter the Iberian and Zuzo lxxxv

Chronological Timeline lxxxv

Texts and Translations

Life of Peter the Iberian 2

On the Death of Theodosius 282

Bibliography 303

Primary Sources: Editions and Translations 303

Secondary Sources and Reference Works 313

Preface

This book is the result of several years of labor in which there were many who had a share, those who kindly lent their time, knowledge, and sweat to help this work come into being, a work that spanned four cities and two continents. First, we graciously acknowledge the assistance of Sidney Griffith, David W. Johnson, and Monica Blanchard of the Catholic University in Washington, D.C. Working with them on Oriental Christian texts first in Syriac and Coptic as well as the history of Christianity in the Near East set the framework for inspiring Cornelia's interest in early and late antique asceticism in the Holy Land. The *Life of Peter the Iberian* formed the basis for Cornelia's dissertation on the history of the anti-Chalcedonian church in fifth-century Palestine. A substantially revised and reworked version of that earlier work was published in 2006 as *Asceticism and Christological Controversy in Fifth-Century Palestine: The Career of Peter the Iberian* (Oxford University Press).

An initial draft of the English translation of the works presented here saw the light of day while Cornelia held a Lady Davis Fellowship to study and conduct research for her dissertation in Jerusalem during 1998–99. The peaceful, quiet, truly monastic atmosphere at Mary Magdala Convent on the Mount of Olives, the abundant resources offered at the Hebrew University of Jerusalem, at the École Biblique et Archéologique, and at the Protestant Institute for Archaeology of the Holy Land, the stimulating contacts with scholars in Jerusalem such as Hanswulf Bloedhorn, Michael Stone, Brouria Bitton-Ashkelony, Aryeh Kofsky, Leah Di Segni, Yitzhar Hirschfeld, and David Satran, but also the challenges of everyday life in a city coveted and fought over by so many factions provided the necessary setting to enter into the mindset of the zealous, controversialist, and nevertheless also spiritual writer and historian John Rufus.

Work on the edition of the Syriac texts, however, began only when Robert and Cornelia both realized their shared dedication to matters of the Christian Orient. Robert carried the bulk of the work of establishing the Syriac text in comparison with and correction of the preceding *editiones principes*. Both commentary and introduction to the work reflect the great progress both Robert and Cornelia have made in becoming able to collaborate smoothly with one another.

We wish to record our thanks to Carl Griffin and Kristian Heal at Brigham Young University Press. They were the first to take an interest in publishing this work, when we still lived in St. Paul, Minnesota. Although in the end that collaboration was not meant to be, both of them provided valuable corrections to the typescript and other important assistance for which we are very grateful.

We express our gratitude to John Fitzgerald and Bob Buller of the Society of Biblical Literature, as well as to the members of the Editorial Board of the Writings from the Greco-Roman World series, for accepting this volume into their renowned series. Without their engagement, this volume would have remained in the dusty manuscript graveyard located on our hard drives. Given their support, however, we have good hopes of adding a companion volume of John Rufus's *Plerophoriae* to the present one, thus completing the presentation in Syriac and English of the *Opera Omnia* of what emerges to be the most influential anti-Chalcedonian historian of fifth- and early sixth-century Palestine.

Sebastian Brock graciously agreed to taking on the role of editor for the present volume. His well-known expertise in matters Syriac allowed him to provide many valuable corrections as well as welcome advice for improvement of the text and commentary. Our gratitude to him is profound. His contributions and the expert editorial and production work on the volume provided by Dr. Fitzgerald, Dr. Buller, and their staff allowed this volume to enter into the final stages of the collaboration history on this volume, finally achieved at the end of a long year of labor at our present location at Saint Louis University, St. Louis, Missouri. Our colleagues in the Department of Theological Studies here have made it a pleasant and fruitful one, with the reasonable expectation of many more to follow in the future. We are grateful to Aaron Overby for compiling the indices.

This work is dedicated in gratitude and with respect to our former teachers in the Department of Semitic and Egyptian Languages and Literatures at the Catholic University of America: †Dr. Michael P. O'Connor, Dr. Sidney H. Griffith, Dr. David W. Johnson, Dr. Douglas Gropp, Dr. Janet Timbie, and Dr. Monica

Blanchard. They introduced us to the languages, texts, methods, and ideas that make up the world of the ancient and early Christian Near East. Much of their inspiration has entered into this work and bears fruit in so much else of what we do.

Cornelia B. Horn and Robert R. Phenix Jr.
Saint Louis, Missouri
Feast of the Holy Cross, 14 September 2005

Abbreviations

In order to make the footnotes more compact, full bibliographical citations for individual works have been reserved for the bibliography at the end of this book. Throughout the footnotes, the template for citations is AUTHOR (or EDITOR), VOLUME:PAGE,LINE. Note that "VOLUME" and "LINE" are used only where applicable.

ABD	*The Anchor Bible Dictionary*. Edited by David Noel Freedman. 6 vols. New York: Doubleday, 1992.
ACO	*Acta conciliorum oecumenicorum*. Edited by Eduard Schwartz. 4 vols. in 17. Berlin: de Gruyter, 1914–.
ACW	Ancient Christian Writers
Amic.	Cicero, *De amicitia*
AnBoll	*Analecta Bollandiana*
ANF	*The Ante-Nicene Fathers: Translations of the Writings of the Fathers Down to A.D. 325*. Edited by Alexander Roberts and James Donaldson. 10 vols. Grand Rapids: Eerdmans, 1969–73.
ANRW	*Aufstieg und Niedergang der römischen Welt: Geschichte und Kultur Roms im Spiegel der neueren Forschung*. Edited by Hildegard Temporini and Wolfgang Haase. Berlin: de Gruyter, 1972–.
Ant.	Josephus, *Jewish Antiquities*
AOL	*Archives de l'Orient latin*
Apol.	Justin Martyr, *Apologia*
BASOR	*Bulletin of the American Schools of Oriental Research*
BBKL	*Biographisch-bibliographisches Kirchenlexikon*. Edited by Friedrich Wilhelm Bautz and Trautgott Bautz. Hamm: Bautz, 1975–.
BDEC	*The Blackwell Dictionary of Eastern Christianity*. Edited by Ken Parry, David J. Melling, Dimitri Brady, Sidney H. Griffith, and John F. Healey. Oxford: Blackwell, 1999.

BEATAJ	Beiträge zur Erforschung des Alten Testaments und des antiken Judentums
BEFAR	Bibliothèque des écoles françaises d'Athènes et de Rome
BEHE	Bibliothèque de l'École des Hautes Études
BELS	Bibliotheca Ephemerides liturgicae, Subsidia
BHG	*Bibliotheca hagiographica Graeca*. Edited by François Halkin. 3rd ed. 3 vols. Subsidia Hagiographica 8a. Brussels: Société des Bollandistes, 1957.
BHL	*Bibliotheca hagiographica Latina antiquae et mediae aetatis*. Subsidia Hagiographica 6. Brussels: Socii Bollandiani, 1898–1901.
BHO	*Bibliotheca hagiographica Orientalis*. Edited by Paul Peeters. Subsidia Hagiographica 10. Brussels: Imprimerie Catholique, 1910.
B.J.	Josephus, *Bellum Judaicum*
BJRL	*Bulletin of the John Rylands University Library of Manchester*
BM	British Museum
BNP	*Brill's New Pauly: Encyclopaedia of the Ancient World—Antiquity*. Edited by Hubert Cancik, Helmut Schneider, Christine F. Salazar, and David E. Orton. Leiden: Brill, 2002–.
Brockelmann	Carl Brockelmann, *Lexicon Syriacum*. 2nd ed. Halle: Niemeyer, 1928.
BTAVO	Beihefte zum Tübinger Atlas des vorderen Orients
ByzF	*Byzantinische Forschungen*
ByzZ	*Byzantinische Zeitschrift*
C. Ap.	Josephus, *Contra Apionem*
CCR	*Coptic Church Review*
CCSA	Corpus Christianorum, series apocryphorum
CCSL	Corpus Christianorum, series latina
CE	*The Coptic Encyclopedia*. Edited by Aziz S. Atiya. 8 vols. New York: Macmillan, 1991.
CH	*Church History*
Chron.	*Chronicle*
CMSBF	Collectio minor, Studium Biblicum Franciscanum
Const. ap.	*Constitutiones apostolicae*
CSCO	Corpus scriptorum christianorum orientalium

CSCO/Copt	Scriptores Coptici
CSEL	Corpus Scriptorum Ecclesiasticorum Latinorum
CSS	Cistercian Studies Series
CurBR	*Currents in Biblical Research*
DACL	*Dictionnaire d'archéologie chrétienne et de liturgie.* Edited by Fernand Cabrol and Henri Leclercq. 15 vols. Paris: Letouzey et Ané, 1907–51.
Dav.	John Chrysostom, *De Davide et Saule*
DEC	*Decrees of the Ecumenical Councils.* Edited by Norman P. Tanner. 2 vols. London: Sheed & Ward; Washington, D.C.: Georgetown University Press, 1990.
DECL	*Dictionary of Early Christian Literature.* Edited by Siegmar Döpp and Wilhelm Geerlings. Translated by Matthew O'Connell. New York: Crossroad, 2000.
DHGE	*Dictionnaire d'histoire et de géographie ecclésiastiques.* Edited by Roger Aubert. Paris: Letouzay et Ané, 1912–.
DOP	*Dumbarton Oaks Papers*
EECh	*Encyclopedia of the Early Church.* Edited by Angelo di Berardino. Translated by Adrian Walford. New York: Oxford University Press, 1992.
EncJud	*Encyclopedia Judaica.* 16 vols. Jerusalem: Encyclopaedia Judaica; New York: Macmillan, 1971–72.
EO	*Echos d'Orient*
Ep.	Pliny the Younger, *Epistulae*; Seneca, *Epistulae morales*
FC	Fathers of the Church
Fin.	Cicero, *De finibus*
GCS	Die griechischen christlichen Schriftsteller der ersten Jahrhunderte
Geogr.	Strabo, *Geographica*
GNO	Gregorii Nysseni opera
Gos. Heb.	*Gospel of the Hebrews*
GRBS	*Greek, Roman and Byzantine Studies*
Greg	*Gregorianum*
Hist. eccl.	*Historia ecclesiastica*
Hist. Laus.	Palladius, *Historia Lausiaca*

IEJ	*Israel Exploration Journal*
IKZ	*Internationale katholische Zeitschrift Communio*
Int	*Interpretation*
Irén	*Irénikon*
JA	*Journal asiatique*
JAC	*Jahrbuch für Antike und Christentum*
JECS	*Journal of Early Christian Studies*
JEastCS	*Journal of Eastern Christian Studies*
JEH	*Journal of Ecclesiastical History*
JK	Jaffé-Kaltenbrunner = *Regesta pontificum romanorum ab condita ecclesia ad annum post Christum natum MCXCVIII*. Edited by Philippus Jaffé, Samuel Loewenfeld, F. Kaltenbrunner, and P. Ewald. 2 vols. Leipzig: Veit, 1885–88.
JSJ	*Journal for the Study of Judaism in the Persian, Hellenistic and Roman Periods*
JSNTSup	Journal for the Study of the New Testament Supplement Series
JSOTSup	Journal for the Study of the Old Testament Supplement Series
JTS	*Journal of Theological Studies*
LCC	Library of Christian Classics
LCL	Loeb Classical Library
Leg.	Athenagoras, *Legatio pro Christianis*
LHR	Lectures on the History of Religions
LSJ	Liddell, Henry George, Robert Scott, and Henry Stuart Jones, *A Greek-English Lexicon*. 9th ed. with revised supplement. Oxford: Clarendon, 1996.
LTK	*Lexikon für Theologie und Kirche*. 3rd ed. Edited by Walter Kasper et al. 11 vols. Freiburg im Breisgau: Herder, 1993–2001.
LXX	Septuagint
Magn.	Ignatius of Antioch, *To the Magnesians*
Mart. Pal.	Eusebius of Caesarea, *De martyribus Palestinae*
MMAF	Mémoires publiés par les membres de la mission archéologique française au Caire
Mus	*Muséon*
NCE	*New Catholic Encyclopedia*. 2nd ed. 15 vols. Detroit: Thomson/Gale; Washington, D.C.: Catholic University of America, 2003.

NEAHL	*The New Encyclopedia of Archaeological Excavations in the Holy Land.* Edited by Ephraim Stern et al. 4 vols. Jerusalem: Israel Exploration Society and Carta; New York: Simon & Schuster, 1993.
NPNF	*A Select Library of Nicene and Post-Nicene Fathers of the Christian Church.* Edited by Philip Schaff and Henry Wace. 28 vols. in 2 series. Grand Rapids, Mich.: Eerdmans, 1978–79.
NS	new series
NTApoc	*New Testament Apocrypha.* Edited by Edgar Hennecke and Wilhelm Schneemelcher. 2nd ed. Translated by R. McL. Wilson. 2 vols. Louisville: Westminster John Knox, 1991.
OBC	Orientalia biblica et christiana
Obit. Theod.	*De obitu Theodosii*
OCA	Orientalia Christiana analecta
ODB	*The Oxford Dictionary of Byzantium.* Edited by Alexander P. Kazhdan et al. 3 vols. New York: Oxford University Press, 1991.
OLA	Orientalia Lovaniensia analecta
Onom.	*Onomasticon*
Orat.	Gregory Nazianzen. *Orationes*
OrChr	*Oriens christianus*
OS	*Ostkirchliche Studien*
ParOr	*Parole de l'Orient*
Payne Smith	Robert Payne Smith, *A Compendious Syriac Dictionary.* Edited by J. Payne Smith (Mrs. Margoliouth). Oxford: Clarendon, 1903. Repr., Oxford: Clarendon, 1994
PG	Patrologia graeca. Edited by Jacques-Paul Migne. 162 vols. Paris: Migne: 1857–86.
PGL	*A Patristic Greek Lexicon.* Edited by G. W. H. Lampe. Oxford: Clarendon, 1961.
Phld.	Ignatius of Antioch, *To the Philadelphians*
PL	Patrologia latina. Edited by Jacques-Paul Migne. 217 vols. Paris: Migne: 1844–64.
Pler.	*Plerophoriae*
PO	Patrologia orientalis
POC	*Proche Orient chrétien*
Pol.	Ignatius of Antioch, *To Polycarp*

PSBF	Publications of the Studium Biblicum Franciscanum
PW	*Paulys Real-Encyklopädie der classischen Altertumswissenschaft*. New edition by Georg Wissowa and Wilhelm Kroll. 50 vols. in 84 parts. Stuttgart: Metzler and Druckenmüller, 1894–1980.
R or Raabe	Richard Raabe, ed. and trans., *Petrus der Iberer: Ein Charakterbild zur Kirchen- und Sittengeschichte des 5. Jahrhunderts: Syrische Übersetzung einer um das Jahr 500 verfassten griechischen Biographie*. Leipzig: Hinrichs, 1895.
RAC	*Reallexikon für Antike und Christentum*. Edited by Theodor Klauser et al. Stuttgart: Hiersemann, 1941–.
SA	Studia anselmiana
SBLSP	Society of Biblical Literature Seminar Papers
SBLWGRW	Society of Biblical Literature Writings from the Greco-Roman World
SC	Sources chrétiennes
SEAug	Studia ephemeridis Augustinianum
StPatr	Studia patristica
Strom.	Clement of Alexandria, *Stromata*
Symp.	Plato, *Symposium*
TRE	*Theologische Realenzyklopädie*. Edited by Horst Robert Balz, Gerhard Krause, and Gerhard Müller. 36 vols. Berlin: de Gruyter, 1977–2004.
TRSR	Testi e ricerche di Scienze religiose
TS	Text and Studies
TS	*Theological Studies*
TTH	Translated Texts for Historians
TU	Texte und Untersuchungen
TUGAL	Texte und Untersuchungen zur Geschichte der altchristlichen Literatur
VC	*Vigiliae christianae*
VCSup	Supplements to Vigiliae christianae
Vir. ill.	Jerome, *De viris illustribus*
Vit. Const.	Eusebius of Caesarea, *Vita Constantini*
Vit. Cyr.	Cyril of Scythopolis, *Lives of the Monks of Palestine: Vita Cyriaci*

Vit. Euth.	Cyril of Scythopolis, *Lives of the Monks of Palestine: Vita Euthymii*
Vit. Mel.	Gerontius, *Vita S. Melaniae Junioris*
Vit. Pet.	*Vita Petri Iberi*
Vit. Sab.	Cyril of Scythopolis, *Lives of the Monks of Palestine: Vita Sabae*
Vit. Sev.	*Vita Severi*
Vit. Theod.	Cyril of Scythopolis, *Lives of the Monks of Palestine: Vita Theodosii*
ZAC	*Zeitschrift für Antikes Christentum/Journal of Ancient Christianity*
ZDPV	*Zeitschrift des Deutschen Palästina-Vereins*
ZKG	*Zeitschrift für Kirchengeschichte*
ZKT	*Zeitschrift für katholische Theologie*
ZNW	*Zeitschrift für die neutestamentliche Wissenschaft und die Kunde der älteren Kirche*

Introduction

The work of John Rufus, displayed in this book with two of the three texts that come down to us from his pen from late antique times,[1] was geared toward supporting the network of anti-Chaledonian Christians, ascetics as well as married laypeople, in fifth- and early sixth-century Palestine. Much of Rufus's work focused on his long-time friend and spiritual father, Peter the Iberian. It is the task of this introduction to provide readers with some of the historical, theological, and literary background that will facilitate their understanding of Rufus's portrayal of Peter the Iberian in the *Life of Peter the Iberian*, exploits that extended from his childhood in ancient Georgia, through his teenage years in Constantinople, his pilgrimage to Jerusalem and the Holy Land, his years as bishop of Maiuma, Gaza, his wanderings in Egypt, through Palestine, Arabia, and Phoenicia, and his final return to eternal rest in Maiuma, Gaza. Such a discussion of the relevant background and context will also allow readers better to appreciate Rufus's presentation in *On the Death of Theodosius* of Bishop Theodosius of Jerusalem, the challenger of Bishop Juvenal of Jerusalem, as well as of the Monk Romanus, the "Father of the Monks."

THE CONTEXT OF THE HISTORY OF GEORGIA FROM THE FOURTH TO THE SIXTH CENTURIES

The *Life of Peter the Iberian* begins with a Christian interpretation of the lives of Peter's parents and grandparents. This interpretation is set against the background of Georgian history in the fourth and fifth centuries of the Christian era. John Rufus wrote Peter the Iberian's *Life* for an audience that probably was ignorant of the political and religious history of Transcaucasia. The impact of the

[1] Next to the likely authorship of the *Vita Petri Iberi* and the *De obitu Theodosii*, both presented in this volume, John Rufus also is to be regarded as the author of the so-called *Plerophoriae*. Of these three works, the *Plerophoriae* was composed last. An English translation of the *Plerophoriae* by Cornelia Horn and Robert R. Phenix Jr. is in progress.

Life's protagonist and the "moral" of his tale can easily be grasped without any knowledge of Iberia. The lives and Christ-centered exploits of Peter's ancestors is Rufus's interpretation, which invites the reader to accept that Peter's spiritual authority is based on a religious piety that Peter somehow inherited from his parents and grandparents and that is thus "in the family." Yet for the modern reader who has the benefit of decades of archaeological and literary research, it is tempting to make use of this opportunity to better situate the "interpretation" of the first quarter of Rufus's work in what is known about the history and culture of Georgia in the period to which Rufus alludes.

Constant war between the Sassanid Persian Empire and the Roman Empire penetrated every aspect of life in the Caucasus, including Iberia. In the hands of the two imperial powers, religion formed one fundamental element in their caustic diplomacy with Iberia, Armenia, and other kingdoms of Transcaucasia. The religion of the Georgians wavered between the Christianity of the Roman Empire and the Zoroastrianism of the Persians.[2] While Georgia had a steadily growing Christian presence since the early fourth century, Zoroastrianism was at times in the fourth and fifth centuries embraced or enforced in Iberia.

The kingdom of Iberia has its origins in the second half of the first millennium B.C.E.[3] The political and social structures of the country during the lifetime of Peter the Iberian were already in place before the arrival of the first Christian missions in the early fourth century.[4] By that time, the medieval kingdom of Iberia was centered on the city of Mc'xet'a, which would later be the first seat of the head of the Georgian church. The people of Iberia, the *k'art'li*, formed the core of a nation, which at times was dominated by and at times dominated the other Caucasian nations to

[2] Günter Lanczkowski, "Iranische Religionen," *TRE* 16:247–58. For a study of influence of Zoroastrianism on a neighboring Christian people, see James A. Russell, *Zoroastrianism in Armenia* (Harvard Iranian Series 5; Cambridge: Harvard University Press, 1987).

[3] For a discussion of the early history of the Iberians and other proto-Georgians, see Cyril Toumanoff, *Studies in Christian Caucasian History* (Washington, D.C.: Georgetown University Press, 1963), 48–86.

[4] See ibid., 87. The Iberians had a system of dynastic monarchs already in place before the fall of the Achaemenid Empire in the late fourth century B.C.E.

its south, west, and east.[5] The *k'art'li* language became a vehicle of wider communication among Caucasian nations from the Middle Ages to the present, having been committed to writing sometime in the mid-fifth century.[6]

The other Georgian kingdoms were Albania and Colchis.[7] Albania emerged as an autonomous kingdom later than Iberia. Centered farther east and south from Iberia, it was subject to greater Iranian influence and enjoyed less autonomy than Iberia. After the third century, Albania was annexed at various times to either Persia or Iberia.

Colchis, later Lazica, along the Black Sea littoral, already had developed its social and political structures by the end of the second millennium B.C.E. but in the fourth century had been absorbed by the Roman Empire. Colchis had few natural barriers between itself and the encroaching Romans and was under greater Hellenistic influence than Iberia. Iberia (with or without Albania) is often called "Eastern Georgia" and Colchis, "Western Georgia."

Social development and political history in Iberia are better attested than for the other two kingdoms. Unfortunately, this evidence does not shed enough light on the fifth century to allow for a positive identification of Peter the Iberian with any onomastic evidence. There are only two works that provide a record of the early kings of Iberia, both attributed to the eighth-century Leontius, bishop of Ruisi (Mroveli): the first is the *History of the*

[5] For an explanation and discussion of the origins of the *k'art'li* and of Mc'xet'a, see ibid., 88 n. 120. For a helpful presentation of the main features of the history of Iberia, see Otar Lordkipanidse and Heinzgerd Brakmann, "Iberia II (Georgien)," *RAC* 17:12–106, here 16–70.

[6] On the origin of the Georgian alphabet, see Dee Ann Holisky, "The Georgian Alphabet," in *The World's Writing Systems* (ed. Peter T. Daniels and William Bright; New York: Oxford University Press, 1996), 364–69, especially 367–68; see also the bibliography there.

[7] The history of Colchis/Lazica is presented in Lordkipanidse and Brakmann, "Iberia II (Georgien)," 70–97.

Kings of K'art'li;[8] the second is a compilation called *The Conversion of K'art'li by Nino*,[9] which contains among its sources *The Primary History of K'art'li* and the *Royal Lists*.[10] The material and traditions that these works contain predates their relatively late attestation. Among other matters, these works demonstrate that the *K'art'li* dynasty became dominant at a relatively early date, claiming divine descent from the clan deity of the Iberians, *K'art'los*.[11] The autonomous kingdom of Iberia emerged first as a vassal of the Seleucid kingdom. The head of the Mc'xet'a dynasty bore the title "king of all Iberia," bestowed on Pharnabazus I after his liberation of Iberia from the Macedonian Empire in the late fourth century B.C.E.[12] Its autonomy waxed and waned with the shifting political and military dominance of the Caucasus between Parthian Persia and first the Seleucid and later the Roman Empires.

Iberia was not only subject to the expansionist policies of Rome and Persia. As an effect of the machinations of these two great powers, the borders of Iberia fluctuated depending on the relative strength of the Armenian dynasties to its south.[13] The weakening of the Arsacid dynasts of Armenia following the Sassanian victory in 363 C.E. was a period of Iberian expansion. The first Christian Iberian king, Mirian (Murabanes) III (284–361), was the head of one of the dynastic lines, the House of Mihrān, which was recognized by the Persian shah to be one of the Seven Great Houses of the Sassanid Empire. This implied that the House of Mihrān had married into the ruling Sassanid house of Irān. The head of another dynastic line from the same House of Mihrān, P'eroz, had in the meanwhile acquired control of Gogarene, a territory that vacillated between Iberian and Armenian

8 For an English translation of both the Georgian and the Armenian version, see Robert W. Thomson, *Rewriting Caucasian History: The Medieval Armenian Adaptation of the Georgian Chronicles* (Oxford Oriental Monographs; Oxford: Clarendon, 1996), 2–84. See also Toumanoff, *Studies in Christian Caucasian History*, 87.

9 For an English translation, see Thomson, *Rewriting Caucasian History*, 84–153.

10 Toumanoff, *Studies in Christian Caucasian History*, 87.

11 Ibid.

12 Ibid., 89; Lordkipanidse and Brakmann, "Iberia II (Georgien)," 17.

13 See Toumanoff, *Studies in Christian Caucasian History*, 186.

control. P'eroz also accepted Christianity and so frustrated Iranian influence in the Iberian kingdom.[14]

Names from the dynasty that ruled Gogarene before the House of Mihrān bear close resemblance to the names in the genealogy of the Syriac *Life of Peter the Iberian*. Many of these names reflect worship of the god Mithras. Rulers probably kept to names that were associated with their dynasty even after conversion to Christianity. The names that Rufus recounts in Peter the Iberian's genealogy have been found on monuments erected in Armazi, the center of pre-Christian religion in Iberia.[15] An inscription found in what is likely the oldest archaeologically preserved Georgian monastery in Palestine[16] contains the name "Buzmihr," which has been identified with the "Bosmarios (or Buzmirios)," Peter's father, in the Syriac *Life of Peter the Iberian*.[17] This "Buzmihr" of the inscription was one of the *vitaxas* of Gogarene. The *vitaxa* was a feudal dynast whose control over a piece of land was guaranteed in part by a king. Gogarene was located between the core Iberian lands around Mc'xet'a to the north and the Armenian kingdom to the south. The *vitaxas* of Gogarene were part of the Armenian kingdom until Gogarene was incorporated into Iberia in the mid-fourth century. Buzmihr was not "king of the Iberians," contrary to how the Syriac *Life of Peter the Iberian* styles him, but such confusion on the part of Rufus, who was no doubt unfamiliar with the dynastic/feudal system of K'art'li, is possible.[18] A Georgian inscription from the monastery

[14] Ibid., 187.

[15] For the genealogy of the *vitaxas* of Gogarene, see ibid., 260–62.

[16] Recent discoveries in Umm Lisan (also transcribed at times as Umm Leison) point to likely contemporaneous archaeological evidence for Georgian monastic life in the environs of Jerusalem. For further references, see Cornelia B. Horn, *Asceticism and Christological Controversy in Fifth-Century Palestine: The Career of Peter the Iberian*, (Oxford: Oxford University Press, 2006), 72, n. 111. See now also Tamila Mgaloblishvili, "An Unknown Georgian Monastery in the Holy Land," *ARAM* 18–19 (2006–2007): 527–539.

[17] See *Vit. Pet.* §§6, 14, 23–24, 118 (R 5, 8–9, 15–16, 86). In references to the *Vita Petri Iberi*, the number following the § sign pertains to the paragraph number supplied in both Syriac text and English translation below. We also provide in brackets reference to the page numbers of Richard Raabe's earlier edition of the Syriac text. For reference to this edition, see below, p. lxxi, n. 185. For further information here, see also Toumanoff, *Studies in Christian Caucasian History*, 260–61.

[18] So Toumanoff, *Studies in Christian Caucasian History*, 261.

Birru-l Qutt, in the Judean Desert,[19] southeast of Jerusalem and northeast of Bethlehem, has been offered as proof that Peter was a descendant of the *vitaxas* of Gogarene. Some scholars read the abbreviation WRZN, which is found as part of the inscription, as the name "Buzmihr," given that it appears with another name interpreted as "Maruan." In the Georgian *Life of Peter the Iberian* Peter's given name is indeed "Murvanos."[20]

Peter's paternal great-grandfather, Bakurios, was called the first Christian "king of the Iberians," against the better attested evidence that the first Christian Iberian king was Mirian III.[21] Varaz-Bak'ar or Varaz-Bakur (Latin: Aspacures III, 380–394), is attested in Leontius Mroveli's history. His second queen was the granddaughter of P'eroz *vitaxa* of Gogarene, the son-in-law of Mirian III.[22] If Varaz-Bak'ar or Varaz-Bakur is to be identified with the Bakurios of the *Life of Peter the Iberian*, it is possible that Rufus confused Bakurios with Mirian.

[19] Michel Tarchnishvili, "Le iscrizioni musive del monastero di Bir el-Qutt," in Virgilio Corbo, *Gli scavi di Kh. Siyar El Ghanam (Campo dei Pastori) e i monasteri dei dintorni* (Pubblicazioni dello Studium Biblicum Franciscanum 11; Jerusalem: Francescani, 1955), 135–39; see also Toumanoff, *Studies in Christian Caucasian History*, 261.

[20] See Ivane Lolashvili, არეოპაგიტული კრებული: დიონისე არეოპაგელი და პეტრე იბერიელი ძველქართულ მწერლობაში [*Areopagite Chronicle: Dionysius and Peter the Iberian in Classical Georgian Hagiography*] (Tbilisi: Mec'niereba, 1983), sect. 2, p. 119, and elsewhere.

[21] It is possible that the names "Mirian" and "Murvanos" are alternative forms of the same name. As indicated above, according to the "Georgian Life of Peter the Iberian," the name given to Peter was "Murvanos."

[22] Toumanoff, *Studies in Christian Caucasian History*, 262.

CHRISTIANITY AND MONASTICISM IN GEORGIA IN THE FOURTH AND FIFTH CENTURIES

The eighth-century Georgian writer Ioane Sabanidze indicated that Georgia had been Christian for five centuries or even longer.[23] According to the *Life of St. Nino*, Georgia accepted the Christian faith in the fourth century.[24] Other traditions indicate that Christianity had appeared in Armenia and Colchis in the first century,[25] although the claim to apostolic succession from the evangelical work of the apostle Andrew as it attaches to the Colchis-traditions was not fully developed until the eleventh century,[26] when the separation of Georgia from the apostolic patriarchate of Antioch was required due to practical difficulties of communication imposed by the Crusades. Little is known about the history, spiritual or otherwise, of Western Georgia, in the first five centuries C.E.

The development of Christianity in Iberia is better illumined in this period. In addition to the two hagiographic sources, that is, the *Martyrdom of Abo* and the *Life of St. Nino*, and paleographic evidence, hagiographic works attest, albeit indirectly, to the stages of Christianization in Georgia and its connection with the political flux of Persian and Roman hegemony. Two key

[23] The *Martyrdom of Abo* (see Karl Schultze, *Das Martyrium des heiligen Abo von Tiflis* [TU 28.4b; Leipzig: Hinrichs, 1905], 15) speaks of Georgian Christians in the eighth century whose ancestors had converted to the Christian faith already "five hundred years ago or even earlier." See also Alexandre Manvelichvili, *Histoire de Géorgie* (Paris: Nouvelles Éditions de la Toison d'Or, 1951), 91; and Lordkipanidse and Brakmann, "Iberia II (Georgien)," 40.

[24] During the reign of Emperor Constantine the Great, if one follows Greco-Roman historiography, or under Emperor Constantius II (337–361), according to the native sources. See Lordkipanidse and Brakmann, "Iberia II (Georgien)," 42 and 50–51.

[25] Archaeological evidence of burial customs as well as findings of Christian jewelry in graves (a silver ring depicting an anchor between two fish) point to the relatively early spread of Christianity in Iberia. See Lordkipanidse and Brakmann, "Iberia II (Georgien)," 40; for Colchis, ibid., 90.

[26] See ibid., 90; see also Francis Dvornik, *The Idea of Apostolicity in Byzantium and the Legend of the Apostle Andrew* (Dumbarton Oaks Studies 4; Cambridge: Harvard University Press, 1958), 210 and 262–63.

hagiographical sources are the *Life of St. Nino*[27] and the *Martyrdom of the Children of Kola.*

It is to Nino that the credit for the conversion of King Mirian III of Iberia is given. Nearly all details about her and her mission to Iberia come from her hagiographic witness. Nino, a virgin presumably from Cappadocia, is claimed to be the apostle to the Iberians and is the patron saint of Georgian Christians.[28] Whether or not all that has accreted to the memory of her life can be reduced to fact, her conversion of Queen Nana and of King Mirian was only the beginning of a very long process of Christianization. In that process, Georgian Christians had an interest in strengthening ties to the church in Jerusalem, which is reflected in a connection established in the *Life of St. Nino* between the saint and the bishop of Jerusalem.[29]

The *Martyrdom of the Nine Children of Kola* unfolds probably in the late fourth or early fifth century.[30] It recounts the story of pagan boys who decide to become Christians without parental permission, refuse to renounce their religion, and, in the end, receive martyrdom at the hands of their own parents.[31] The story,

[27] For an English translation of this text, see Margery Wardrop and James O. Wardrop, "Life of St. Nino," *Studia Biblica et Ecclesiastica* 5 (1903): 1–88.

[28] On St. Nino's efforts at Christianizing the Georgians, see the studies by Fairy von Lilienfeld, "Amt und geistliche Vollmacht der heiligen Nino, 'Apostel und Evangelist' von Ostgeorgien, nach den ältesten georgischen Quellen," in *Horizonte der Christenheit: Festschrift für Friedrich Heyer zu seinem 85. Geburtstag* (ed. Michael Kohlbacher and Markus Lesinski; Oikonomia 34; Erlangen: Lehrstuhl für Geschichte und Theologie des Christlichen Ostens, 1994), 224–49; and Cornelia B. Horn, "St. Nino and the Christianization of Pagan Georgia," *Medieval Encounters* 4 (1998): 242–64.

[29] There she is presented as the niece of the Patriarch of Jerusalem. See Wardrop and Wardrop, "Life of St. Nino," 7–10.

[30] For an English translation of the text, see David Marshall Lang, *Lives and Legends of the Georgian Saints* (London: Allen & Unwin; New York: Macmillan, 1956), 40–43.

[31] For a discussion of the martyrdom of children in early Christian times, see Cornelia Horn, "'Fathers and Mothers Shall Rise Up against Their Children and Kill Them': Martyrdom and Children in the Early Church," paper presented at the American Academy of Religion/Society of Biblical Literature Annual Meeting, Toronto, Canada, November 2002. See also the discussion in Cornelia Horn, "The Lives and Literary Roles of Children in Advancing Conversion to Christianity: Hagiography from the Caucasus in Late Antiquity and the Middle Ages," *Church History* 76.2 (2007), 262–297.

independent of hagiographical details designed to help Christians resist the Persians, reveals that pre-Christian religion remained alive well into the establishment of churches in Georgia.

A third work, the *Martyrdom of Shushanik*, attests to the impact of Persian hegemony on Iberia in the late fifth and early sixth centuries.[32] Before 483 C.E.,[33] Shushanik, the Christian wife of a Christian king of Iberia, was murdered for the faith by her husband, who converted to Zoroastrianism in order to secure an alliance with the Persian king.[34] The religion of Zoroastrianism, like Christianity in the Roman Empire after Constantine, had become a means of statecraft. To understand the connection between Zoroastrianism and Persian governance, one must understand the history of this *modus operandi* of Persian administration. Even by the sixth century, the impact of Zoroastrianism and the relative strength of Christianity in Iberia were not unequally matched.

In 224 C.E., Ardashir, a prince from the Fars province in Persia, completed his revolution of the Parthian Empire. A key element of the Sassanian formula for strengthening Persia was to enforce a single Persian culture and religion on all its subjects. Zoroastrianism, or Mazdaism, was revived as a religion of state. For Christians in Persia, this policy had limited impact, so long as Christianity remained a *religio illicita*, or illegal association, in the Roman Empire. In the aftermath of the Edict of Milan, however, things changed.[35]

[32] For an English translation of the *Martyrdom of Shushanik*, see Lang, *Lives and Legends*, 44–56.

[33] Lang (ibid., 44) states that Jacob of Tsurtav composed the *Martyrdom of Shushanik* between 476 and 483 C.E.

[34] On the role of gender in the Zoroastrian tradition, see the interesting study by Jamsheed K. Choksy, *Evil, Good and Gender: Facets of the Feminine in Zoroastrian Religious History* (Toronto Studies in Religion 28; New York: Lang, 2002).

[35] For discussion of the situation of Christians under the Sassanians, see Samuel Hugh Moffett, *A History of Christianity in Asia* (2 vols.; San Francisco: HarperSanFrancisco, 1992), 1:91–264; Sebastian P. Brock, "Christians in the Sasanian Empire: A Case of Divided Loyalties," in *Religion and National Identity. Papers Read at the Nineteenth Summer Meeting and the Twentieth Winter Meeting of the Ecclesiastical History Society* (ed. Stuart Mews; Studies in Church History 18; Oxford: Blackwell, 1982), 1–19, repr. as ch. 6 in Sebastian P. Brock, *Syriac Perspectives on Late Antiquity* (London: Variorum, 1984); and

Shah Yazdegerd II (438–457) undertook the complete subjugation of Armenia and Georgia.[36] Part of his policy was to assimilate their populations *in toto* to Zoroastrianism. Evidence for the effect of Yazdegerd's foreign policy comes from the *Martyrdom of Shushanik*. Varsken, prince of Georgia, embraced Zoroastrianism in the late fifth century. His wife, Shushanik, the daughter of the Armenian prince Vardan Mamikonean, refused to abjure Christ and was martyred for her conviction.[37] Yazdegerd was unable to subjugate either Armenia or Iberia. After Emperor Constantine I sanctioned Christian worship in 313, Persian shahs saw in their Christian subjects a liability. Christians in Persia were subject to intermittent persecutions and forced conversion to Zoroastrianism. For Aramean/Assyrian, Armenian, and Georgian Christians living in Persia, the decision of a shah to support (or at least not prevent) local persecution of Christians depended on political relations with Persia's archrival, Rome.[38]

The eastward creep of Roman hegemony since the third century was no better guarantor of freedom for its allies and vassals from its control than what the Persians offered. The Christian Armenian and Georgian kings attempted to extricate themselves from the Christian Roman Empire's influence. The independent kingdom of Lazica, formerly Colchis, had carved out a brief independence from its fellow Christian masters in the sixth century.[39]

A. V. Williams, "Zoroastrians and Christians in Sasanian Iran," *BJRL* 78 (1996): 37–53.

[36] See Wolfgang Hage, "Armenien I. Alte Kirche und Mittelalter," *TRE* 4:46; see also Russell, *Zoroastrianism in Armenia*, 115; Lordkipanidse and Brakmann ("Iberia II [Georgien]," 36) speak of "close relations" between Yazdegerd II and Iberia.

[37] For other female martyrs under Persian domination, see, e.g., the stories of Martha, Tarbo, Thekla, Anahid, Candida, and other Christian women associated with them. See the English translation of their martyrdom accounts in Sebastian P. Brock and Susan Ashbrook Harvey, *Holy Women of the Syrian Orient* (Transformation of the Classical Heritage 13; Berkeley and Los Angeles: University of California Press, 1998), ch. 3. For Candida, see Sebastian P. Brock, "A Martyr at the Sasanid Court under Vahran II: Candida," *AnBoll* 96 (1978): 167–81, repr. as ch. 9 in Brock, *Syriac Perspectives on Late Antiquity*.

[38] For some study of the Christian persecution in the Sassanid Empire, see also Josef Rist, "Die Verfolgung der Christen im spätantiken Sasanidenreich: Ursachen, Verlauf und Folgen," *OrChr* 80 (1996): 17–42; see also Brock, "Christians in the Sasanian Empire."

[39] Lordkipanidse and Brakmann, "Iberia II (Georgien)," 84–85.

Armenian as well as Georgian rulers attempted to secure local autonomy by playing the Romans off the Persians. After the Edict of Milan (313), the power of Georgian and Armenian vassal kings of the Sassanid Empire had gained some leverage in that the Romans had become their "co-religionists."

The *Life of Peter the Iberian* gives evidence of this policy with an example of politically motivated temperance of religion. The example of Bakurios in the *Life of Peter the Iberian* reflects the leverage Iberian kings were able to wield against both Rome and Persia. Georgian kings were responsible for supplying troops for the Persian army, under the command of their king. This allowed the Georgians to play Rome off Persia in pursuit of the path of greatest independence. When Bakurios, Peter's maternal grandfather and king of the Iberians, refused to worship the rising sun while on campaign with the Persian shah and his generals on the grounds that he worshiped the one who created the sun, we are told the shah was forced to temporize. "What can we do to him?" "It is Bakurios, and we are in need of him" (*Vit. Pet.* §13 [R 8]). The Persians could not take for granted the allegiance of Christian allies on their Roman frontier, yet neither could the Romans. Peter's encounter with the court of Theodosius II was as a hostage, guaranteeing Georgia would not ally the strength of their arms or provide assistance to the Persians (§§24 [R 15–16] and 29 [R 20]).

Political alliance between Georgia and Persia is also evident in the relationship between the Georgian and Persian Churches. The Council of Seleucia-Ctesiphon (410) assembled to provide a framework for the autonomy of the church in Persia.[40] The Sassanid kings had learned from their experience in the fourth century that persecution was a not entirely successful strategy for assimilating its Christian subjects to Zoroastrianism. Perhaps fearing that Christian martyrdom in Persia might have the effect of converting Persians to Christianity, as it did in the Roman Empire, the Sassanids attempted to allow the Christians to form a distinct Christian church in Persia that would be independent of patriarchal jurisdictions in Constantinople and Antioch. The activities

[40] Complementary to the following discussion, see also Wilhelm Baum and Dietmar W. Winkler, *The Church of the East: A Concise History* (London: Routledge, 2003), 7–41.

and allegiance of such a church reduced the uncertainty of the loyalty of its Christian subjects.[41]

Until 410 C.E., the Christian church of Persia was under the jurisdiction of the apostolic see of Antioch. Due to the incessant war between Persia and Rome, communication with Antioch was subject to disruption. Zoroastrian persecution in the fourth century had left the church in need of hierarchs, schools, and churches. The council of 410 was called in part to draft canons for the governance of the church in Persia without recourse to Antioch. To this council, which formed the canonical foundation of the church of the East, the church in Georgia sent at least one representative.[42] After the christological controversies of the fifth century, Georgia and Armenia accepted the decisions of the Council of Ephesus (431) and hence came to identify with the church in the Roman Empire. Those theologians and scholars in the Roman Empire who rejected the theological and disciplinary decisions of Ephesus were expelled from the Roman Empire on charges of heresy and sedition. Many of the most influential of these theologians were Syriac speakers, who were warmly received during the fifth and sixth centuries by the persecuted Syriac-speaking Christians of Persia. Whatever the claims of the orthodoxy of these scholars and bishops, their influence caused the Persian church never to accept the decisions of the Council of Ephesus, marking the emergence of the Assyrian Apostolic Church of the East as a distinct ecclesiastical entity. This break of the church in the Roman Empire was consistent with the Persian Empire's desire to isolate its Christian church from the church of its Roman enemy.

Unable to secure Iberia militarily, the Persians soon began a persecution of Christians. After the death of Aspacures III, the Iberian kings Pharsamanios and Bosmarios (ca. 395–416) appealed to Rome, and Rome was able to repel the Persians momentarily. Following this, as surety that the Iberian throne would not be swayed to the Persians, it is likely that the young prince Peter was given as a hostage to the court of Theodosius II (*Vit. Pet.* §24 [R 15–16]).

[41] See the problematic discussed in Brock, "Christians in the Sasanian Empire."

[42] See Julius Aßfalg and David Marshall Lang, "Georgien," *TRE* 12:391.

After Peter's arrival in Constantinople, the narrative of the *Life of Peter the Iberian* leaves the history of Georgia behind. The only allusion to Georgia is the mention of letters that Peter refused to write to or receive from any members of his family or from acquaintances back home for fear of losing his ascetic discipline (*Vit. Pet.* §19 [R 12]). Yet developments in Georgia took a decisive turn in the mid-fifth century. King Vaxt'ang Gorgasali (447–522) united Iberia and Lazica into a powerful kingdom.[43] While this kingdom did not survive him, Gorgasali's reforms of Georgian administration and of the organization of the Georgian church had far reaching effects, which would bear fruit in the powerful Christian kingdom of Georgia in the twelfth through fifteenth centuries.

Before Gorgasali's union of Eastern and Western Georgia, the Georgian church had been united under a single catholicos already in the fifth century. Gorgasali decided that so long as the Georgian catholicos was subordinate to bishops in the Roman Empire, Georgia could not be independent of Constantinople's influence. Byzantium's model of the state made the emperor God's instrument for the protection of the church. The Patriarch was the emperor's high priest. Gorgasali reasoned that his independence from Rome (and Persia) rested with an independent church, of which he, like the Roman emperor and the Persian shah, would be its God-mandated protector. Gorgasali moved the seat of the catholicos from the old see of Mc'xet'a to his capital, Tbilisi. A similar understanding of church independence as a necessary condition for national independence was also reached by the Armenians in the same period.[44]

Georgia, like Armenia, rejected the Council of Chalcedon (451 C.E.). For reasons that appear to be as much political as theological, after 583 Georgia changed its mind and accepted the theological and canonical decisions of Chalcedon. After the death of King Bakur III in 580, Iberia became a vassal of the Persian

43 For the feats of King Vaxt'ang Gorgasali, see the account provided by Juansheri in his *Life of Vaxt'ang Gorgasali*. Ed. Alexandre Sardzveladze, Zurab Sardzveladze, and Tamar Xazomia, ცხოვრება ვახტანგ გორგასლისა [*Life of Vakhtang Gorgasali*] (Tbilisi: Mecniereba, 1986). For an English translation of the Georgian and Armenian witnesses, see Thomson, *Rewriting Caucasian History*, 153–251.

44 See Hage, "Armenien I," 46.

shah. It was remarked that in the fifth century there was an intervening shift of Georgian alliance with the Romans, as Peter was given as a hostage to Theodosius II by his father Bosmarios, who "preferred the friendship of the Romans as Christians rather than the assistance of the impious Persians" (*Vit. Pet.* §24 [R 16]). Granted that this comment occurs in an anti-Chalcedonian text, yet even there it speaks to a pre-Chalcedonian situation, still unencumbered by the context of christological struggles. What was of interest were politically advantageous alliances. In the sixth century, Persian pressure continued to force Georgia to seek Roman protection, the price for which eventually was adoption of the Chalcedonian Christianity of the Roman emperor.[45] In 606 C.E., Catholicos Kyrion II formally embraced Chalcedon. The anti-Chalcedonian Armenian hierarchs excommunicated the Georgian hierarchy at the Synod of Dvin in 608. The Armenians had been able to maintain their independence from virtually every Christian church in a unique way. They were anti-Chalcedonian but accepted the formulation of a one-nature Christology proposed by Julian of Halicarnassus.[46] The rest of the anti-Chalcedonian world adopted the formulation of Julian's one-time friend-turned-archrival, Severus of Antioch (512–518).[47] Armenia was able to sidestep Roman hegemony on the one hand and influence from its Georgian political rivals on the other.

45 For some discussion that adherence to Chalcedon had become a matter of Byzantine patriotism and identity in Constantinople, see W. H. C. Frend, *The Rise of the Monophysite Movement: Chapters in the History of the Church in the Fifth and Sixth Centuries* (Cambridge: Cambridge University Press, 1972), 172.

46 Julian of Halicarnassus's theology is characterized by his view that Christ's body was incorruptible. See Frend, *Rise of the Monophysite Movement*, 253–63; see also René Draguet, *Julien d'Halicarnasse et sa controverse avec Sévère d'Antioche sur l'incorruptibilité du corps du Christ: Étude d'histoire littéraire et doctrinale suivie des Fragments dogmatiques de Julien* (Leuven: Smeesters, 1924).

47 Severus of Antioch refuted the theology of Julian of Halicarnassus explicitly. These works were edited by A. Sanda, *Severi Antiiulianistica* (Beirut: Typographia Catholica, 1931). For a study of the controversy, see Draguet, *Julien d'Halicarnasse*. For a critique of Draguet's study, see Martin Jugie, *Julien d'Halicarnasse et Sévère d'Antioche (controverse sur la passibilité du corps de Jésus-Christ): La doctrine du péché original chez les pères grecs* (Paris: Feron-Vrau, 1925). For more recent studies of the context of Julian's theology, see, e.g., Katherine Adshead, "Justinian and Aphthartodocetism," in *Ethnicity and Culture in Late Antiquity* (ed. Stephen Mitchell and Geoffrey Greatrex; London: Duckworth; Swansea: Classical Press of Wales, 2000), 331–36.

PETER'S GENEALOGY IN THE *LIFE OF PETER THE IBERIAN*: HAGIOGRAPHIC ANCESTRY

The interpretation that the *Life of Peter the Iberian* offers with its detailed genealogy of Peter makes the claim that Peter's spiritual authority was based on the religion of his parents, grandparents, and relatives.[48] The genealogy presents Peter's resistance to Chalcedon as the spiritual heritage of his faithful parents and grandparents, who were believers before the controversies of Nestorius of Constantinople and Cyril of Alexandria. At the time that Rufus composed this work, the Roman emperor had become identified, at least by those in the East, with the Chalcedonian definition. Byzantine patriotism identified a Chalcedonian emperor and empire, perhaps out of proportion to the merits of the council's theological and canonical definitions, with peace and security against all that plagued the Byzantine consciousness, real or imagined. The story of the *Life of Peter the Iberian* favors neither the Persian nor the Roman emperors, but the inconsistent treatment of each is designed to create of Peter a character through whom Rufus inspires his readers to resist the pressure to enter into communion with the Chalcedonian establishment.

THE HISTORY OF THE CHRISTOLOGICAL CONTROVERSIES AND THEIR CONTEXT IN PALESTINE FROM THE FOURTH TO THE SIXTH CENTURIES

After Peter's encounter with the piety of Emperor Theodosius II and Empress Eudocia at the imperial court in Constantinople,[49] it is the history of the christological controversy, especially on the stage of Palestine and to a lesser extent of Egypt, that forms the object of Rufus's attention in his portrait of Peter. Rufus's interpretation of the events before, during, and after Chalcedon in Palestine and Egypt offers the literary lens through which the reader views Peter. Through sketches of Peter's miracles

48 See also Horn, *Asceticism and Christological Controversy*, 50–59.

49 For a fuller discussion of Eudocia's support of Peter and his anti-Chalcedonian network, see Cornelia Horn, "Empress Eudocia and the Monk Peter the Iberian: Patronage, Pilgrimage, and the Love of a Foster-Mother in Fifth-Century Palestine," *ByzF* 28 (2004): 197–213.

and ascetic athleticism, Rufus recounts the events that in the end essentially extinguished anti-Chalcedonian Christianity from Palestine until it availed itself of the new political climate created by the Arab conquest of the region in the 630s.[50]

The controversies that led to the Council of Chalcedon had a permanent effect on Christianity. Christianity in the Eastern Roman Empire would be split, while new challenges in the governance of the church, of the authority and jurisdiction of patriarchal sees, would be entwined with the theological controversies and the increasingly different military and political experiences of Old and New Rome. The christological controversy that consumed Christians East and West in the fifth century was a continuation of the fourth-century controversies over the Christian concept of a Triune Godhead.[51] However, the political and ecclesiastical forces of the Roman Empire had rapidly changed in the intervening years between the Council of Constantinople I in 381 and that of Ephesus in 431. These changes were the result of the response of the empire to Christianity and of the church to a Christian Roman emperor. The christological controversies of the fifth century were not the product of political or ecclesiastical crises, but the chief players in the decades-long drama were not immune to these "temporal" realities either. The prerogatives and authority of ancient sees, the spiritual authority of monastics, and the tension of acquired authority of Constantinople as "New Rome" could not be disentangled from the motivations of the chief combatants and architects of these theological controversies. Moreover, language and ethnic identity played then, as it does

[50] Indispensable to this survey is Frend, *Rise of the Monophysite Movement*, especially 6–49.

[51] The councils of Nicaea (325) and Constantinople I (381) sought to clarify the Christian understanding of the Trinity. For helpful discussions of the development of the Trinitarian doctrine in the early Church, see Franz Courth, *Trinität in der Schrift und Patristik* (Handbuch der Dogmengeschichte 2.1a; Freiburg: Herder, 1988). See also G. L. Prestige, *God in Patristic Thought* (2nd ed.; London: SPCK, 1952); R. P. C. Hanson, *The Search for the Christian Doctrine of God: The Arian Controversy 318–381* (Edinburgh: T&T Clark, 1988); and Basil Studer, *Gott und unsere Erlösung im Glauben der Alten Kirche* (Düsseldorf: Patmos, 1985). Comments in anti-Chalcedonian documents indicate that the opponents of Chalcedon feared the council had turned the Trinitarian concept of God de facto into a quaternian one. For comments, see Horn, *Asceticism and Christological Controversy*, 259, n. 156, with further references.

now, a secondary although critical role in the final stages of this conflict,[52] when the anti-Chalcedonian churches were organized around ancient patriarchates that also reflected quite naturally the linguistic and "ethnic" boundaries of Armenians, Georgians, Copts, Syro-Arameans, Nubians, and Ethiopians.

The opening volley of this controversy is typically dated to 428 C.E. Nestorius, archbishop of Constantinople (consecrated 28 April 428), was reported to have proclaimed from the pulpit that Mary did not give birth to God but to Christ.[53] Nestorius, in conflict with the imperial ladies like his distinguished and controversial predecessor John Chrysostom,[54] may have found the piety that was in vogue at the court, primarily with Empress Pulcheria, to smack of Origenism.[55]

[52] A. H. M. Jones ("Were Ancient Heresies National or Social Movements in Disguise?" *JTS* 10 [1959]: 280–98) provoked a considerable amount of discussion of whether or not nationalistic tendencies were operative in theological controversies of the ancient Church.

[53] In *Pler.* 1 (Nau and Brière, 12), John Rufus reports that Nestorius proclaimed Mary had given birth "to an instrument of God." For the brilliant reply, delivered by Proclus of Cyzicus, later to become bishop of Constantinople, see his homily "On the Holy Virgin Theotokos Delivered While Nestorius Was Seated in the Great Church of Constantinople" (Constas, 136–47). For a helpful discussion of the events during this controversy as well as the larger context, see ch. 2 of Constas, *Proclus of Constantinople.*

[54] On the conflict between John Chrysostom and Empress Aelia Eudoxia, see Kenneth G. Holum, *Theodosian Empresses: Women and Imperial Dominion in Late Antiquity* (Berkeley and Los Angeles: University of California Press, 1982), 70–78. For Chrysostom's involvement in the Origenist controversy, see the comments in Elizabeth A. Clark, *The Origenist Controversy: The Cultural Construction of an Early Christian Debate* (Princeton: Princeton University Press, 1992), 21–25 and 46–47.

[55] Pulcheria's claims of having given birth to God appear to have been grounded in a spirituality that also is reflected in Origen's writings. Hugo Rahner ("Die Gottesgeburt: Die Lehre der Kirchenväter von der Geburt Christi im Herzen der Gläubigen," *ZKT* 59 [1935]: 333–418, here 351–58) provides ample documention for Origen's development of the theme of the birth of God in the human believer. The connections between the Origenist controversy and the christological controversies of the fifth and sixth centuries have not yet been subjected to a comprehensive investigation. More recently, Daniël Hombergen (*The Second Origenist Controversy: A New Perspective on Cyril of Scythopolis' Monastic Biographies as Historical Sources for Sixth-Century Origenism* [SA 132; Rome: Pontificio Ateneo S. Anselmo, 2001]) has approached aspects of the question for a sixth-century, Palestinian setting.

The *Letter to Cosmas* recounts an incident between Nestorius and Empress Pulcheria, which if true sets this debate in some relief.[56] Pulcheria had claimed the right to receive communion in the sanctuary with the clergy. Nestorius attempted to forbid her from continuing her idiosyncratic practice.[57] When Pulcheria argued that she was entitled to receive communion in the sanctuary because she had given birth to God, Nestorius drove her away with the reply, "You? You have given birth to Satan!"[58] Had Nestorius been a more careful student of the fate of Chrysostom in that one's battle with Pulcheria's mother, Eudoxia, he might have found a more efficient diplomacy.

Nestorius had been educated by Theodore of Mopsuestia, John Chysostom's friend and colleague.[59] Theodore of Mopsuestia (d. 428) emphasized a careful appreciation of biblical texts on their own terms.[60] Origen's students, far less capable than their teacher in formulating their master's complex theology and

[56] *Letter to Cosmas* 8 ("Histoire de Nestorius d'après la letter à Cosme et l'hymne de Sliba de Mansouriya. Part I. La Lettre à Cosme," in François Nau, ed. and trans., *Documents pour servir à l'histoire de l'église nestorienne: Textes syriaques* [PO 13.2; Paris: Firmin-Didot, 1919], 278,12–279,12); see also Holum, *Theodosian Empresses*, 153.

[57] Next to the clergy, only the emperor enjoyed the privilege of receiving communion in the sanctuary, a privilege that Pulcheria had extended to herself.

[58] *Letter to Cosmas* 8 (Nau, *Documents pour servir à l'histoire*, 279,9).

[59] In Antioch, both Theodore of Mopsuestia and John Chrysostom had been students of Libanius, the pagan rhetor, and of Diodore of Tarsus. Nestorius received his theological education under Theodore. After his death, Theodore would be implicated by association and condemned at the Council of Constantinople in 553. For a well-balanced, recent study of Theodore's christological thought, see Frederick G. McLeod, "Theodore of Mopsuestia Revisited," *TS* 61 (2000): 447–480; and now also idem, *The Roles of Christ's Humanity in Salvation: Insights from Theodore of Mopsuestia* (Washington, D.C.: Catholic University of America Press, 2005). See also Peter Bruns, *Den Menschen mit dem Himmel verbinden: Eine Studie zu den katechetischen Homilien des Theodor von Mopsuestia* (CSCO 549; Subsidia 89; Leuven: Peeters, 1995).

[60] See also Peter Bruns, "Zum Offenbarungsverständnis des Theodor von Mopsuestia im Zwölfprophetenkommentar," in *Athanasius and His Opponents, Cappadocian Fathers, Other Greek writers after Nicaea* (vol. 4 of *Studia patristica: Papers Presented at the Twelfth International Conference on Patristic Studies Held in Oxford, 1995*; ed. Elizabeth A. Livingstone; StPatr 32; Leuven: Peeters, 1997), 272–77; and John O'Keefe, "'A Letter That Killeth': Toward a Reassessment of Antiochene Exegesis, or Diodore, Theodore, and Theodoret on the Psalms," *JECS* 8 (2000): 83–104.

approach to Scripture, seized on Origen's more speculative and allegorical methods of biblical interpretation.[61] In fact, the "literal" and the "allegorical" methods (as well as others) were prevalent in all schools of Christian theology, even if individual theologians showed a predilection for a certain method over others.

Nestorius brought irrevocably onto the stage of history what might have been dismissed as a petty sacristy squabble between a strong-headed Antiochene monk and a vain empress. Like Chrysostom, Nestorius depicted Mary in a manner that, taken out of context, would be deprecating, in order to drive home his argument against the misguided piety of the empress and her courtiers. To disabuse Pulcheria of the notion that she had somehow given birth to God within her, Nestorius argued that not even Mary could make that claim. Not even Mary was *theotokos*, that is, "birthgiver of God." It was perhaps too strong a rhetorical flourish for the context of a public assembly. One cannot be certain that Nestorius was attempting to use such a public occasion to make a profound theological statement. For his unwavering opposition to the empress, the former bishop John Chrysostom had been exiled. Yet whereas John was not called the "Golden-Mouthed" without good reason, Nestorius proved less diplomatic and less theologically astute. From the pulpit he declared that Mary was the birthgiver not of God but of Christ.

Nestorius's statement would not necessarily have had such great impact without a simmering theological problem arising from the formulation of the Christian faith at the Council of Nicaea in 325 C.E. The council had stipulated that the Son of God

[61] The most prominent student of Origen's work whose writings influenced the Origenist controversy was Evagrius of Pontus. For studies of aspects of Evagrius's reading of the scriptures, see, e.g., George C. Berthold, "History and Exegesis in Evagrius and Maximus," in *Origeniana Quarta* (ed. Robert J. Daley; Innsbruck: Tyrolia, 1987), 390–404; Luke Dysinger, "The Significance of Psalmody in the Mystical Theology of Evagrius of Pontus," in *Biblica et Apocrypha, Ascetica, Liturgica* (vol. 2 of *Studia patristica: Papers Presented at the Twelfth International Conference on Patristic Studies Held in Oxford, 1995*; ed. Elizabeth A. Livingstone; StPatr 30; Leuven: Peeters, 1997), 176–82; and idem, "The Logoi of Providence and Judgement in the Exegetical Writings of Evagrius Ponticus," in *Cappadocian Writers, Other Greek Writers* (vol. 4 of *Studia patristica: Papers Presented at the Thirteenth International Conference on Patristic Studies Held in Oxford, 1999*; ed. M. F. Miles and E. J. Yarnold; StPatr 37; Leuven: Peeters, 2001), 462–71.

was ὁμοούσιος τῷ πατρί, "consubstantial to (God) the Father."[62] This was the reply to the claims of Arius, a priest in Alexandria, according to whom the Son of God could not have been consubstantial with the Father and at the same time have become incarnate in the flesh. For Arius, the Son of God was the first of all creatures but a creature nevertheless, created like all other matter.[63] The Council of Nicaea rejected this view in no uncertain terms,[64] stipulating that the Son is consubstantial (*homoousios*) and thus also co-eternal with the Father.

Yet this did not explain how the divinity of the second person of the Trinity could remain consubstantial to the Father during the incarnation in the flesh in the person of Jesus of Nazareth. Even Athanasius, the Alexandrian champion of the orthodoxy of Nicaea, was unable to resolve this difficulty.[65] His supporter, Apollinaris, the bishop of Laodicea,[66] resolved this problem by asserting that in Jesus of Nazareth the human rational soul was replaced by the second person of the Trinity. Jesus the Christ was a single nature, a single essence, or hypostasis, after the incarnation, "one nature made flesh."[67] This phrase became the rallying

[62] *Ekthesis of the 318 Fathers of Nicaea* (*DEC* 1:5): πιστεύομεν . . . εἰς ἕνα κύριον Ἰησοῦν Χριστὸν ὁμοούσιον τῷ πατρί.

[63] See, e.g., *Confession of the Arians, Addressed to Alexander of Alexandria* (Edward Rochie Hardy, ed., *Christology of the Later Fathers* [LCC 3; Philadelphia: Westminster, 1954], 332–34, here especially 333).

[64] At the end of the Creed of Nicaea, the representatives of the church added the following anathemas: "And those who say 'there once was when he was not,' and 'before he was begotten he was not,' and that he came to be from things that were not, or from another hypostasis or substance, affirming that the Son of God is subject to change or alteration—those the catholic and apostolic church anathematises" (*DEC* 1:5).

[65] See his *Letter to Bishop Epictetus of Corinth* from ca. 371. See also Frend, *Rise of the Monophysite Movement*, 13.

[66] Apollinaris (ca. 315–392), bishop of Laodicea, was initially on good terms with Athanasius of Alexandria. His theological construct of the unity of Christ as consisting of a human body in which the Logos held the place of the human soul was condemned at the First Council of Constantinople (381). See also Ekkehard Mühlenberg, *Apollinaris von Laodicea* (Göttingen: Vandenhoeck & Ruprecht, 1969); and idem, "Apollinaris," *TRE* 3:362–71.

[67] μία φύσις σεσαρκωμένη. See Hans Lietzmann, *Apollinaris von Laodicea und seine Schule: Texte und Untersuchungen* (Tübingen: Mohr Siebeck, 1904), 206,28 and 251,1.

cry of Cyril and later of the anti-Chalcedonians such as Philoxenus of Mabbug and Severus of Antioch.[68]

Opposed to this view were certain influential theologians in the see of Antioch, notable among them being Theodore of Mopsuestia, but also Diodore of Tarsus, Theodore's teacher. The solution to the problem that Theodore and Diodore espoused was to claim that the human and divine natures were harmoniously united without change into a single person, or *prosōpon*.

In an attempt to resolve the central matter of defining the interaction of humanity and divinity in Christ, a question that the Council of Nicaea and subsequent theologians had been unable to address successfully, Emperor Theodosius I (379–395) summoned a second general council to gather in Constantinople in 381. It reiterated the condemnation of Arius and condemned the teachings of Apollinaris, including his followers in the list of heretics.[69] In effect, the doctrinal wrangling of the previous decades over the relationship of the Son to the Father had really only resolved that the Father, Son, and, in the end, also the Holy Spirit should be called "persons." A second ecclesiastical canon of Constantinople I accorded the archbishop of Constantinople a rank second in honor only to Old Rome.[70] These two decisions were to become inextricable points of contention in various forms well into the seventh century and beyond. Nestorius's remark that Mary was not the birthgiver of God (*theotokos*), but the birthgiver of Christ (*Christotokos*) was the occasion for a confrontation between rival theological solutions to the Trinitarian controversy. It also provided the opportunity for the aggressive attempt by the bishop of Alexandria to secure for that see an undisputed primacy in the Christian world.

[68] Apollinaris's formulation underlies Cyril of Alexandria's phrase of the "one nature of the Logos made flesh," the heart of Cyril's christological formulation. Cyril, however, did not realize that he had accepted Apollinaris's words; rather, he was falling prey to forgeries of Apollinaris's texts that were circulated under Athanasius's name. See also Paul Galtier, "Saint Cyril et Apollinaire," *Greg* 37 (1956): 584–609. On the influence of the phrase on later authors, see also Mühlenberg, "Apollinaris," 370.

[69] Canon 1 (*DEC* 1:31).

[70] Canon 3 (*DEC* 1:32).

The most violent reaction against Nestorius came from Bishop Cyril of Alexandria (412–444).[71] His complicity in the torture-murder of the pagan philosopher Hypatia in 415 demonstrated that he was unscrupulously zealous of his interests.[72] He was also a praeternaturally gifted theologian, a gift that he applied with vigor to prove Nestorius and his supporters were heretics in the same mold as the Arians. Cyril was as astute a politician as he was a theologian. Moreover, his rivalry with John Chrysostom was not well hidden. It was his predecessor and uncle, Theophilus of Alexandria (385–412),[73] who between 402 and 404 succeeded in having Chrysostom sent into exile.[74] Even if apocryphal, the report illustrates Cyril's defense of the prerogatives of his see against those of Constantinople.

Neither Rome nor Alexandria had been at all satisfied with canon 3 of the Council of Constantinople, which stated, "Because it is New Rome, the bishop of Constantinople is to enjoy the privileges of honor after the bishop of Rome."[75] Byzantium had been a suffragan see of Heracleia[76] until Constantine established it as his capital on 8 November 324.[77] Alexandria claimed its apostolicity

[71] For a study of the christological controversy surrounding Nestorius's teaching and written from a perspective that focuses on Cyril of Alexandria, see John A. McGuckin, *St. Cyril of Alexandria: The Christological Controversy: Its History, Theology, and Texts* (VCSup 23; Leiden: Brill, 1994).

[72] On Cyril's involvement, see Aziz S. Atiya, "Cyril I, Saint," *CE* 3:672.

[73] With vibrant and perhaps somewhat misguided energy, Theophilus turned first against pagans and pagan shrines, destroying at least large sections of the Serapeum and its library in 391 (but see below, *Vit. Pet.* §99 [R 72], which would evidence the continued existence of the Serapeum also during the later half of the fifth century; see also Horn, *Asceticism and Christological Controversy*, 179), and in later years against the so-called Origenists by way of harrassing and persecuting a group of ascetics known as the Tall Brothers. His struggle against Constantinople and thus against John Chrysostom was ongoing. See also Tito Orlandi, "John Chrysostom, Saint," *CE* 5:1357; and Aziz S. Atiya, "Origenist Controversies," *CE* 6:1855–56.

[74] Donald B. Spanel, "Theophilus," *CE* 7:2250–51; see also above, p. xxxv, n. 54.

[75] Canon 3 of the Council of Constantinople I (*DEC* 1:32).

[76] See Timothy E. Gregory, "Heracleia," *ODB* 2:915.

[77] Although the city was dedicated only on 11 May 330. See Timothy E. Gregory and Anthony Cutler, "Constantine the Great," *ODB* 1:499.

from Saint Mark and indeed from Christ himself.[78] The church in Egypt was proud to be heir to the tradition and early veneration of the event of the flight of the Holy Family to Egyptian lands (Matt 2:13–21). In addition, Alexandria had been a center of Christian learning at least from the time of Pantaenus and Clement of Alexandria. Origen, whose disciples were not trusted in Antioch, had been perhaps its greatest headmaster.[79]

More than this, Christians in Egypt had suffered extensively during the Roman persecutions. As late as 344, persecution was vigorous in Egypt.[80] Indeed, the Egyptian church so heavily identifies with its witness against the Roman emperor that year 1 of its church calendar corresponds to the first year of the reign of Diocletian (284–305), whose persecution of Christians was particularly pronounced in Egypt. The Coptic church reckons the years from this event A(nno) M(artyrum), "from the year of the martyrs."[81] It was unthinkable that the prestige of a church with such witness should be usurped at the whim of a Roman emperor who was not even baptized. Old Rome was in a position simply to refuse to accept canon 3 as valid, as it claimed for itself the honor of the ancient Roman capital, where the Senate continued to meet.[82] Alexandria was in a more difficult position. Unlike Old Rome, it was more closely integrated into the economy of the eastern Mediterranean and was less remote physically and culturally from Constantinople and Antioch than Rome. Constantinople depended on the grain shipment from Alexandria. There was little that Rome could offer the East until the dominance of Germanic political powers gave Rome a bargaining chip against the Roman emperor. Episodes in the history of the christological controversy

78 For a treatise on the priesthood of Christ and subsequently an account of Saint Mark as the first bishop of Alexandria, see Sawîrus (Severus) ibn al-Muqaffaᶜ, *History of the Patriarchs of the Coptic Church* (Evetts, 1:120–34, 135–48). For the importance of Mark in the mind of John Rufus, see also *Vit. Pet.* §62 (R 44).

79 For studies of the catechetical school of Alexandria, see Aziz S. Atiya, "Catechetical School of Alexandria," *CE* 2:469–73, with bibliography.

80 See Heinz Heinen, "Persecutions," *CE* 6:1935–38, here 1937.

81 For a discussion of the eras in use in Alexandria and of the origin of the Coptic calendar, see Aelred Cody, "Calendar, Coptic," *CE* 2:433–36, here 434.

82 See Ralph W. Mathisen, "Senate," in *Late Antiquity: A Guide to the Postclassical World* (ed. G. W. Bowersock, Peter Brown, and Oleg Grabar; Cambridge: Harvard University Press, 1999), 689–90.

demonstrate that, without the support of the emperor, Rome's ability to wield any influence in ecclesiastical affairs in the East was practically nil.[83]

To make matters worse, there was a simmering feud between Antioch and Alexandria over the ecclesiastical jurisdiction of Palestine. Until Constantine, Palestine and Jerusalem were not only ignored but also denigrated. For Christians, the true Jerusalem was the heavenly Jerusalem, the eschatological kingdom of God that Jesus had come to proclaim.[84] It was the inhabitants of Jerusalem who had crucified the Messiah of God. Christ's resurrection and ascension into heaven were interpreted as signs that God had once and for all forsaken his city. Anti-Jewish sentiment was part of this anti-Jerusalem position. The slanderous opinion of much of the pre-Constantinian church was that only Jews who rejected the Messiah still worshiped in Jerusalem.

Constantine and his mother Helena inaugurated the settlement of Palestine by Christians and promoted a renewed veneration for the places associated with biblical persons and events, but none more important than the sites of the crucifixion, burial, and resurrection of Jesus.[85] The construction of churches and shrines became a way for the rich of the Roman Empire to secure their heavenly treasure by spending their earthly chattels to build "the city of God on earth." Many of the pilgrims stayed

[83] See the discussion of Pope Leo I's desperate and vain attempts to defend his theology and authority in the face of Dioscorus's usurpation of ecclesiastical privilege in Frend, *Rise of the Monophysite Movement*, 156.

[84] For a developed discussion of the place of the notion of a "Holy Land" in the early Christian mind, see Robert L. Wilken, *The Land Called Holy: Palestine in Christian History and Thought* (New Haven: Yale University Press, 1992); see also idem, "Heiliges Land," *TRE* 14:684–94.

[85] For a discussion of Helena's contribution to the Christianization of the landscape of the Holy Land, see Edward Yarnold, "Who Planned the Churches at the Christian Holy Places in the Holy Land?" in *Historica, theologica, gnostica, biblica* (vol. 1 of *Papers of the Ninth International Conference on Patristic Studies, Oxford, 1983*; ed. Elizabeth A. Livingstone; StPatr 18.1; Kalamazoo, Mich.: Cistercian, 1985), 105–9. See also Kenneth G. Holum, "Hadrian and St Helena: Imperial Travel and the Origins of Christian Holy Land Pilgrimage," in *The Blessings of Pilgrimage* (ed. Robert Ousterhout; Illinois Byzantine Studies; Urbana: University of Illinois Press, 1990), 66–81.

on for life.[86] With the ascendancy of Christian asceticism, Palestine became a magnet for new monastic foundations under the patronage and protection of benefactors in Constantinople. The *Life of Peter the Iberian* indicates that Emperor Theodosius II had encouraged the settlement of Jerusalem and Palestine by granting ownership of any unclaimed real estate and that Peter and John took advantage of this policy to establish a *xenodocheion*, or inn, for pilgrims in Jerusalem (see *Vit. Pet.* §§64–67 [R 44–47]). Of course, "unclaimed" in this case meant "unclaimed by another Christian party." Jews and Samaritans were not accorded much attention in this imperial policy. It is possible that the intermittent rebellions of Samaritans and Jews in Palestine were in part responses of the native landowners to this usurpation of their property.[87] These rebellions were always crushed by harsh Roman reprisals. As late as the time of the reign of Emperor Justinian (527–565), Samaritans were agitating against what in their eyes had become the simple elimination of non-Christians from Palestine.[88]

Cyril had composed three letters stating the problem with Nestorius's statement. To the third letter he had appended twelve anathemas that had been ratified by the bishops of Egypt before they were sent to Nestorius.[89] Yet Cyril had also unwittingly made use of material that was taken from the writings of Apollinaris, who had been condemned at the Council of Constantinople in 381.[90] John, bishop of Antioch,[91] recognized the source of Cyril's

[86] Aryeh Kofsky ("Peter the Iberian: Pilgrimage, Monasticism and Ecclesiastical Politics in Byzantine Palestine," *Liber Annuus* 47 [1997], 209), has spoken of "one-way pilgrims." See also Horn, *Asceticism and Christological Controversy*, 252.

[87] For evidence of bloody conflicts involving Samaritans, see also *Pler.* 10.

[88] Uprisings of the Samaritans occurred in 453 under Juvenal and again in the sixth century. See Frend, *Rise of the Monophysite Movement*, 152; and Nathan Schur, *History of the Samaritans* (BEATAJ 18; Frankfurt am Main: Lang, 1989), 82–91. For an uprising in 529–530 C.E., see also Cyril of Scythopolis, *Vit. Sab.* 70 (Schwartz, 172; Price, 181–82).

[89] For the text of these anathemas, see *DEC* 1:59–61.

[90] See above, p. xxxviii with n. 66.

[91] John was bishop of Antioch from 428 to 442. A helpful and clear precis of his life and work is presented in S. Müller-Abels, "John of Antioch," *DECL*, 326.

writings and condemned them as consistent with the Apollinarian heresy. At the Council of Ephesus, which was called in 431 to decide Nestorius's fate, John of Antioch condemned Cyril and his supporters. The imperial judge of the council sided with John. Cyril's response was to bribe the imperial court, and, with the support of Pulcheria, John's condemnation was rejected. In the end, the council condemned Nestorius, "the new Judas," and deposed him on 22 June 431.[92] A synodical letter also deposed John of Antioch together with about thirty other Eastern bishops.[93] Cyril had scored an everlasting triumph for the orthodoxy of his writings.

Two years after the council, John of Antioch and Cyril of Alexandria reached an agreement regarding the need to acknowledge the full humanity of Christ. The Formula of Reunion of 433 pushed Cyril to public confession of precisely that while it required of John an acknowledgment of potential dangers inherent in a divisive formulation of a Christology in two natures.[94] Yet while Cyril gained prestige through this compromise, which established peace between these two church leaders for a while, John's influence subsequently declined.

Cyril's thought would become the standard of orthodoxy at the Council of Chalcedon in 451. After a period of relative harmony between the competing theological and ecclesiastical interests of Antioch, Alexandria, Rome, and Constantinople, the balance of power was tipped in Rome's favor with the accession to the chair of Peter of one of the most able and energetic defenders of its claims to primacy, Leo I, in August 440.[95] In turn, Cyril's

[92] See *ACO* 1.1.2:54. See also Frend, *Rise of the Monophysite Movement*, 18. John Rufus readily adopted the medium of references to Jesus' betrayer Judas as tool in his polemics against Nestorius and the adherents of Chalcedon, whom he saw as followers of Nestorius. See, e.g., *Vit. Pet.* §§47, 76, 83, 179 (R 32, 52, 58, 135); *Pler.* 16, 17, and 25. Rufus's polemic will be discussed in the introduction to the reedition and English translation of John Rufus's *Plerophoriae*, a work in progress by Horn and Phenix.

[93] See *DEC* 1:62–63.

[94] For the text of the Formula of Reunion, see *DEC* 1:70–74.

[95] On Leo I, see Trevor Jalland, *The Life and Times of Leo the Great* (London: SPCK, 1941); Leo J. McGovern, *The Ecclesiology of Saint Leo the Great* (Rome: Pontificia Università Gregoriana, 1957); Basil Studer, "Leo der Grosse und der Primat des römischen Bischofs," in *Unterwegs zur Einheit: Festschrift für Heinrich Stirnimann* (ed. Johannes Brantschen and Pietro

successor in June 444 was his fearsome archdeacon Dioscorus.[96] In Antioch and Constantinople, the less able Domnus and Flavian assumed their respective patriarchal dignities.[97]

For the remainder of Theodosius's reign, the ascendancy of Dioscorus over the other patriarchal sees was virtually unchecked. Theodosius supported Dioscorus's decision to eliminate once and for all the vestiges of a two-nature Christology and to establish the primacy of Alexandria. By October 449, he had succeeded in accomplishing both.

Yet his triumph was short lived. Theodosius died unexpectedly on 28 July 450.[98] His sister Pulcheria, whose influence in the court had dramatically increased, acted immediately. Her motivations for opposing Dioscorus and his allies in Constantinople were not difficult to understand. As a result of the Council of Ephesus II (the "Robber Synod"),[99] Dioscorus had deposed the bishop Flavian of Constantinople on charges of misconduct in the handling of the trial of Eutyches. Anatolius, Dioscorus's *apocrisarius*, or personal representative to the emperor, was appointed bishop of Constantinople in his place.[100] At the end of the council, Theodosius had requested Dioscorus to make known the results of the synod to all the bishops of the empire in an encyclical letter.[101] Dioscorus had effectively usurped the prestige of Constantinople and become the only power remaining on the field.

Selvatico; Fribourg: Universitätsverlag, 1980), 617–30; and Walter Ullmann, "Leo I and the Theme of Papal Primacy," *JTS* 11 (1960): 25–51.

96 See Theopistus, *Vita Dioscori* (Nau, 5–108, 241–310); see also Martiniano P. Roncaglia, "Dioscorus I," *CE* 3:912–15.

97 Domnus was bishop of Antioch from 441 to 449. Flavian held the see of Constantinople from 446 to 449.

98 For comments on Theodosius's death, afterlife, as well as situations that almost killed him, see *Pler.* 27, 32, 36, and 35. See also Timothy E. Gregory and Anthony Cutler, "Theodosios II," *ODB* 3:2051–52.

99 Pope Leo I labeled the Council of Ephesus II as *latrocinium*, or "Robber Synod," in a letter to Pulcheria from 20 July 451. See also Frend, *Rise of the Monophysite Movement*, 44.

100 See Martin Jugie, "9. Anatole," *DHGE* 2:1497–1500.

101 See Johannes Paul Gotthilf Flemming, ed., *Akten der ephesinischen Synode vom Jahre 449* (Abhandlungen der Königlichen Gesellschaft der Wissenschaften zu Göttingen, Philologisch-historische Klasse NS 15; Göttingen: Weidmann, 1917), 151–55; and Frend, *Rise of the Monophysite Movement*, 43.

Pulcheria chose as her consort Marcian and at once began to purge the court of Theodosius's officials. Flavian's body, which had been buried in exile, was returned to Constantinople and his name rehabilitated. In 451 Marcian called for a general council that after some delay convened in Chalcedon on 8 October.[102] Dioscorus arrived early with his Egyptian bishops and excommunicated Pope Leo. Yet the other two main bishops, Juvenal of Jerusalem and Anatolius of Constantinople, did not support this excommunication.[103] At the "Robber Synod" Juvenal had sided with Dioscorus; now, despite his promises to his monks in Palestine,[104] Juvenal threw his allegiance with Anatolius. Chalcedon recognized the system of apostolic sees that was outlined in canon 3 of the Council of Constantinople in 381.[105] It codified the system of patriarchates,[106] primarily in order to resolve jurisdictional disputes between Constantinople, Alexandria, and Antioch.[107] The council's elevation of the see of Jerusalem to a patriarchate no doubt was the fulfillment of a promise made to elicit Juvenal's support.[108] Dioscorus was deposed from his see, although not condemned as a heretic. It was the end of the meteoric rise and chaotic villainy of Dioscorus. His successors did not wield the same power, and eventually Egypt preserved its primacy over its

[102] On the reasons for the delay and the plea of Pope Leo I that the council be postponed, see Leo the Great, *Letter* 26 (PL 54:747B). See also Frend, *Rise of the Monophysite Movement*, 38.

[103] Up to the present, the normative study of Juvenal of Jerusalem remains the article by Ernest Honigmann, "Juvenal of Jerusalem," *DOP* 5 (1950): 211–79.

[104] Anti-Chalcedonian literature emphasizes Juvenal's promises to the monks of Palestine given before his departure to Chalcedon. See, e.g., *Pler.* 25.

[105] See above, p. xl–xli.

[106] Technically, the title "patriarch" was applied to the bishops of Rome, Constantinople, Alexandria, Antioch, and Jerusalem in the sixth century under Emperor Justinian I (*Novellae* 123.3; Rudolf Schöll and Wilhelm Kroll, eds., *Corpus Juris Civilis* [6th ed.; Berlin: Weidmann, 1954], 3:597–98). See also Aristeides Papadakis and Alexander Kazhdan, "Patriarchates," *ODB* 3:1599–1600.

[107] In particular, the conflicting claims of Alexandria and Constantinople over Nubia and Ethiopia. See Frend, *Rise of the Monophysite Movement*, 15.

[108] On this tactic to win Juvenal's support, see also the critical comments in Zachariah Rhetor, *Chron.* 3.3 (Brooks, 1:155–57; Hamilton and Brooks, 49–50); see also below, *Vit. Pet.* §76 (R 52). Until then Jerusalem had been a suffragan see of Caesarea Maritima.

own bishops at the expense of remaining in communion with Old and New Rome and with Jerusalem.

The heart of the matter was the statement of the relationship between Christ's human and divine natures. The council received the christological formulation advanced by the indefatigable Pope Leo. A letter addressed to Bishop Flavian of Constantinople and known to posterity as the *Tome of Leo* interpreted Cyril's Christology as implying that the two natures were inseparably joined in a single hypostasis, each nature retaining its own properties without change.[109] This difficult formula would be rejected outright by Dioscorus's supporters who defined orthodoxy as strict adherence to Cyril's formulation. Chalcedon in its turn held that Leo's formula indeed did express the teaching of Cyril and was rightfully included in the doctrinal definition of the council.[110]

Yet even those who were present and agreed with Leo's interpretations of Cyril disagreed over what Chalcedon had in fact achieved. For many of the Eastern bishops, the council was not a new statement of faith but an interpretation of Nicaea and Ephesus. For Leo, the council was a binding declaration that was not negotiable. In addition, later popes interpreted Chalcedon's acceptance of Leo's interpretation of Cyril's doctrine as an assent to the bishop of Rome's primacy of magisterium and primacy of place in the organization of the church.[111] These differences continued to widen in the subsequent centuries, exacerbated by the different political fortunes of east and west. The origins of the schism of 1054 are present already in the aftermath of Chalcedon. This primacy of Old Rome was bolstered by monasteries and bishops who, during the chaos of the Acacian schism (484–518), severed communion with Constantinople and Antioch. It is this event that perhaps served as precedent for the establishment

[109] For the *Tome of Leo*, see Leo, *Epistula* 28 (JK 423 = *Collectio Novariensis de re Eutychis* 5, *ACO* 2.2.1:24,15–33,2). See *Gestorum Chalcedonensium versio a Rustico edita*, act. II [III], 20, *ACO* 2.3.2:14,27–30 [273,27–30]). For an English translation, see Hardy, *Christology of the Later Fathers*, 360–70. See also Horn, *Asceticism and Christological Controversy*, 332.

[110] In the minds of the people, Leo's and Cyril's proclamations melted into one. Both leaders spoke of the same faith. See Frend, *Rise of the Monophysite Movement*, 142.

[111] For an insightful discussion of Leo the Great's establishment of papal power, see Ullmann, "Leo I and the Theme of Papal Primacy."

of communion between the Maronite Antiochene patriarchate and Rome in the course of the thirteenth-fifteenth centuries.[112]

In Palestine in the latter sixth century, the monks and Christian faithful were clearly on the side of Chalcedon and, more importantly, accepted Leo's interpretation of Chalcedon as universally binding. Yet in the fifth century, many of the monks at first had greeted the return of their bishop Juvenal from Chalcedon with hostility. According to anti-Chalcedonian sources from the ascetic milieu, the monks confronted Juvenal and accused him of breaking his solemn vow not to allow any novelties to be mixed with the pure faith of Nicaea. As Juvenal refused to take back his signature to the Chalcedonian tome, the monks elected one from among their midst, the monk Theodosius, as a rival bishop of Jerusalem. John Rufus's works are among our best sources on that schism. In the end, it was short-lived, since within a year Marcian had offered Juvenal the services of the Roman army. That intermezzo nevertheless was fundamental in establishing the beginnings of an anti-Chalcedonian hierarchy and ultimately an independent anti-Chalcedonian church.[113]

In Palestine, perhaps more than elsewhere, the acceptance of Chalcedon was guided by prestigious monastic foundations. They were both independent of local authority and distant enough from their Constantinopolitan patrons to come to a decision about the matter of the Council on its own terms.

MONASTICISM IN FIFTH-CENTURY PALESTINE

Christian life in Palestine was distinguished by two important areas of monastic settlement: the Judean Desert and the somewhat more densely populated Gaza region. In both instances, relative proximity to an urban center, Jerusalem and Gaza, defined the ascetic experience: in the case of the Judean Desert by way of the

[112] For an excellent study of the earlier history of the Maronites, see Harald Suermann, *Die Gründungsgeschichte der Maronitischen Kirche* (OBC 10; Wiesbaden: Harrassowitz, 1998).

[113] See the brief discussion in Horn, *Asceticism and Christological Controversy*, 86–88. For further work on the origins of the Syrian Orthodox Church more particularly, see now also the work by Volker Menze, "The Making of a Church: the Syrian Orthodox in the Shadow of Byzantium and the Papacy," Ph.D. thesis (Princeton University, 2004).

ascetic's relative distance to urban life: in the case of Gaza by way of greater proximity. The ascetic population of the Judean Desert cast their lot with the Chalcedonians, whereas the Gaza region, owing to the strong Egyptian influence of its monastic origins,[114] remained an island of supporters of the anti-Chalcedonian confession until sometime after the death of Peter the Iberian in 491, probably until the second decade of the sixth century.

Gaza and its littoral extending to the south were divided between the Roman provinces of Augustamnica and Palaestina. Augustamnica extended from Gaza to the Nile Delta and was considered a part of Egypt.[115] Eremitic monasticism in Gaza first appeared in the early fourth century. The first witness to monasticism in Gaza is Jerome's *Life of Hilarion.*[116] Jerome borrowed heavily from a Latin translation of the *Life of Anthony* in order to demonstrate that Hilarion had surpassed Anthony in every virtue.[117] It is difficult to sort out from Jerome's literary constructions the details of fourth-century Gazan monasticism. There is not even much agreement on the reliability of Jerome's textual witness. Also, it is known that Jerome never met Hilarion.[118]

One point of the development of ascetic lifestyles to which the *Life of Hilaron* attests is that Hilarion's first dwelling was eremitic. Only out of necessity did he become the abbot of a cenobitic establishment sometime during the reign of Constantius (337–361).[119] While this development seems to be the norm for other centers of monasticism and indeed is also attested in the *Life of Anthony*, Jerome's mention of Hilarion's monastic establishment during the mid-fourth century would be less a literary

[114] For a study of the Egyptian influence on Palestinian monasticism, see Samuel Rubenson, "The Egyptian Relations of Early Palestinian Monasticism," in *The Christian Heritage in the Holy Land* (ed. A. G. O'Mahony, G. Gunner, and K. Hintlian; London: Scorpion Cavendish, 1995), 35–46.

[115] For a brief overview of individual monks in the region, see Brouria Bitton-Ashkelony and Aryeh Kofsky, "Gazan Monasticism in the Fourth-Sixth Centuries: From Anchoritic to Cenobitic," *POC* 50 (2000): 14–62.

[116] See Jerome, *Vita Hilarionis* (PL 23:29–54; Ewald, 245–80).

[117] Bitton-Ashkelony and Kofsky, "Gazan Monasticism," 20; see 19 for a long list of parallel motifs and claims shared between the *Life of Hilarion* and the *Life of Anthony*.

[118] For a discussion of Jerome's possible sources, see ibid., 21.

[119] Ibid., 22.

comparison to Anthony than one of the facts around which Jerome wove his edifying story.[120]

Other details from Sozomen's *Historia ecclesiastica* reveal that Maiuma, Peter the Iberian's see and final resting place, continued to be a center for cenobitic monasticism.[121] Many of Hilarion's disciples, known by name from Sozomen's historiography, continued the work of their elder.[122] Rufus explicitly connected Peter the Iberian with Hilarion by claiming Peter as the successor to the founder of ascetic life at Gaza.[123]

At the time Peter the Iberian arrived in Maiuma, monastic institutions had been founded that attracted learned monks from Egypt and Syria, who in turn contributed to establishing Gaza as a center of scholarship. Silvanus, some of whose sayings are recorded in the *Apophthegmata Patrum*, founded a coenobium in Gaza at the end of the fourth century that has left evidence of the scholarship of its inhabitants.[124] In the fifth century, one of Silvanus's disciples, the hermit Zeno (d. 451), whom the *Life of Peter the Iberian* mentions,[125] is said to have had contact with the philosopher Aeneas of Gaza.[126] The *Life of Peter the Iberian* recounts that Peter and John sought Zeno's advice pertaining to the monastic life (*Vit. Pet.* §72 [R 49]). Not uncommonly for the Palestinian ascetic milieu that is characterized by a dominance of

[120] Jerome's *Life of Hilarion* may have been one of the sources for Sozomen's brief biography of Hilarion in his *Historia ecclesiastica* (book 3). See ibid., 25.

[121] According to *Vit. Pet.* §75 (R 51), when Peter the Iberian arrived in the region he joined an already-existing monastic community under the leadership of Abba Irenion.

[122] Bitton-Ashkelony and Kofsky, "Gazan Monasticism," 26–27.

[123] *Vit. Pet.* §137 (R 101). See also the discussion in Cornelia Horn, "Peter the Iberian and Palestinian Anti-Chalcedonian Monasticism in Fifth- and Early Sixth-Century Gaza," *ARAM* 15 (2003): 113–15.

[124] For a study of Abba Silvanus and his followers, see M. Van Parys, "Abba Silvain et ses disciples, une famille monastique entre Scété et la Palestine à la fin du IVe et dans la premiere moitié du Ve siècles," *Irén* 61 (1988): 315–31 and 451–80. See also the comments in Bitton-Ashkelony and Kofsky, "Gazan Monasticism," 28.

[125] *Vit. Pet.* §§68, 71–75 (R 47, 49–51); see also *Pler.* 8, 13, and 52.

[126] For discussion and references, see Horn, *Asceticism and Christological Controversy*, 156–157; and Bitton-Ashkelony and Kofsky, "Gazan Monasticism," 29.

the master-disciple model, Zeno became their spiritual guide.[127]

Monasticism in Palestine after Chalcedon was not changed in substance by the decrees of the council *per se*. The administration and population of the monasteries and *lavrai*[128] had been in the hands of foreigners inspired to visit the Holy Land as pilgrims and then encouraged by Constantine and his successors to settle Palestine. The effect this had on the indigenous population, which into the sixth century were largely Jews and Samaritans, must have been perceived as something of an occupation or an enforced redistribution of landed property. The *Life of Peter the Iberian* refers to an edict of Theodosius II that permitted monks, but seemingly also any visitor to the Holy City, to claim any piece of land in Jerusalem for the purpose of constructing on it a building or religious institution (*Vit. Pet.* 64 [R 44–45]), provided that the land was not already owned. While such a law might sound considerate, it was hardly in the interest of protecting the local population, since "owner" would easily be construed as coextensive with "Christian."

Monastic foundations had to rely for their well-being on imperial benevolence and rich benefactors, most of whom resided far from Palestine. The dependence of these and nearly all of the churches and shrines on benefactors and pilgrims was the same before and after Chalcedon. As acceptance of Chalcedon became a matter of national interest for many of the influential in Constantinople from the time of Justin I (518–527), it is natural that those institutions that depended on their largesse would sway with them.

[127] For a study of the relationships between ascetics in the Gaza area, see also Jennifer Hevelone-Harper, "Letters to the Great Old Man: Monks, Laity, and Spiritual Authority in Sixth-Century Gaza" (Ph. D. diss., Princeton University, 2000), published as eadem, *Disciples of the Desert: Monks, Laity, and Spiritual Authority in Sixth-Century Gaza* (Baltimore: Johns Hopkins University Press, 2005); and John Chryssavgis, "Abba Isaiah of Scetis: Aspects of Spiritual Direction," in *Ascetica, Gnostica, Liturgica, Orientalia* (vol. 2 of *Studia patristica: Papers Presented at the Thirteenth International Conference on Patristic Studies Held in Oxford, 1999*; ed. M. F. Miles and E. J. Yarnold; StPatr 35; Leuven: Peeters, 2001), 30–40.

[128] *Lavrai* are an organizational form of ascetic life typical of Palestine. The individual cells of the monks are arranged around a central open space, allowing the ascetics to join eremitical and cenobitic forms of life.

Pilgrims were an important source of revenue and prestige for monastics and the maintenance of holy sites.[129] The centrality of pilgrims and pilgrimage in the *Life of Peter the Iberian* can hardly be overstated.[130] Peter and his followers, who undergo forced peripatetic exile rather than submit to communion with the Chalcedonian bishop of Jerusalem, their multifaceted adventures on their pilgrimage, and their travel tours form the bulk of the narrative.

The spiritual interpretation of pilgrimage that Rufus presented in this text even turned Peter into a traveling holy site.[131] Anti-Chalcedonians felt they were barred from many of the churches, especially at places where Chalcedonians formed the majority of the worshiping community. Their monasteries were forced either to recognize Chalcedon and enter into communion with Juvenal and his Chalcedonian successors or to be disbanded. In order to be able to hold on to a rightful claim to "holy places," Rufus provided a new interpretation of the events as well as of the definition of "holy place," a definition that suited the actual circumstances of the anti-Chalcedonian experience in Palestine. According to that newly defined understanding, holy places were holy only if the bishop and the believers worshiping there were orthodox, that is, anti-Chalcedonian. In other words, it was faith, not possession of a building or even of relics, that conferred holiness and spiritual authority. Thus Rufus portrayed Peter as a holy man who was holy for defying Chalcedon, the bishops, and the emperor, and this holiness was manifest wherever he traveled.

[129] For a discussion of the economic situation of the Holy Land during the relevant time period, see Michael Avi-Yonah, "The Economics of Byzantine Palestine," *IEJ* 8 (1958): 39–51.

[130] See Horn, *Asceticism and Christological Controversy*, 226–331. For a complementary discussion of Peter the Iberian as pilgrim, see also Brouria Bitton-Ashkelony, "פטרוס האיברי עולה לרגל [The Pilgrim Peter the Iberian]," *Cathedra* 91 (1999): 97–112; eadem, "*Imitatio Mosis* and Pilgrimage in the Life of Peter the Iberian," in *Christian Gaza in Late Antiquity* (Jerusalem Studies in Religion and Culture 3; ed. Brouria Bitton-Ashkelony and Arieh Kofsky; Leiden and Boston: Brill, 2004), 108–31.

[131] For a discussion, see Cornelia Horn, "Transgressing Claims to Sacred Space: The Advantage of Portable Relics in the Christological Conflict in Fifth Century A.D. Syria-Palestine," paper delivered at the American Academy of Religion/Society of Biblical Literature Annual Meeting, Atlanta, November 2003.

Consequently, Peter had to be shown as an associate of the great travelers of the Bible: Moses, Jesus, and Paul; thus he was manifested as the sole true heir to the biblical and apostolic tradition.

On the Death of Theodosius

The short piece appended to the *Life of Peter the Iberian* is a brief story of the death of the first (and last) anti-Chalcedonian bishop of Jerusalem, Theodosius (451–453). Included in this work is also a short notice on the monk Romanus, who figures prominently in the early life of Peter. Textual evidence suggests that *On the Death of Theodosius* was not composed as an afterthought or in response to an event subsequent to Rufus's work on the *Life of Peter the Iberian* but that the two texts were conceived as a single work in two parts. Rufus promises in the *Life* to recount the story of Theodosius "at the end, when it pleases God" (*Vit. Pet.* §88 [R 62]). At the beginning of his account of Theodosius's death, Rufus gives as reason for his writing that he "remember[ed] that [he] promised in the previous matters to relate the manner of the death of the blessed Theodosius."[132] The promise in the *Life* and the recollection of that promise at the beginning of the second work contain a similar Syriac expression translated "the manner of his death/his falling asleep."[133] Moreover, given the pressing position anti-Chalcedonians were in throughout the Roman Empire during the time Rufus was writing, it is more likely that Rufus penned the two works at the same time. In the two manuscripts containing the *Life of Peter the Iberian*, *On the Death of Theodosius* immediately follows the *Life*. As mentioned above, only after the complete collection did the scribe place the *finis* to the entire collection, suggesting that the texts were transmitted to his day as a two-part work.

Following Juvenal's return to office by imperial force in 453, Theodosius was sent into exile in Egypt. For reasons that are not certain, although plausibly either to mediate a dispute between two anti-Chalcedonians or to gain the support of the influential

[132] *Obit. Theod.* §1 (Brooks, 1:21; also edited and translated below, p. 282–283). References to the *De obitu Theodosii* indicate the paragraph number of the Syriac text and the English translation below, followed in brackets by a reference to the respective page numbers in Brooks's edition.

[133] *Vit. Pet.* §88 (R 62): ܙܢܐ ܕܡܘܬܗ; *Obit. Theod.* §1 (B 21): ܙܢܐ ܕܫܘܢܝܗ.

Symeon Stylites, Theodosius traveled to Antioch. He was recognized at the city gates, arrested, and brought to Constantinople at the order of Emperor Marcian. When Marcian was unable to win him over, Theodosius was confined to the Chalcedonian monastery of St. Dios. Unyielding to the abbot's pressure to accept Chacledon, Theodosius was imprisoned in a narrow, unheated cell during winter. Due to exposure, malnourishment, and other tortures, Theodosius became severely ill. At the death of Marcian, in 457 Emperor Leo remanded Theodosius into the custody of anti-Chalcedonians in the monastery of Sykai, on the other side of the Golden Horn, where he died after a few days. His body was spirited away to Cyprus to prevent it from falling into Chalcedonian hands.

This work concludes with a brief life of the monk Romanus. Under the empress Eudocia's patronage, Romanus had founded an anti-Chalcedonian monastery at Eleutheropolis. Even after Eudocia entered into communion with Juvenal as ransom for Constantinople's support in rescuing her family in Rome, she still protected Romanus and gave support to other anti-Chalcedonians until her death in 460.

THE ANTI-CHALCEDONIAN DEFEAT IN PALESTINE

Anti-Chalcedonian witness in Palestine was rapidly declining by the time Rufus composed the *Life of Peter the Iberian.* In contrast, there was almost no alternative to anti-Chalcedonian doctrine in Egypt, and the see of Antioch maintained a significant anti-Chalcedonian church down to and after the Arab invasion of the 630s. Frend gives three reasons for the success of the Chalcedonian definition in the institutions and piety of Christians in Palestine.[134] The first is that the status of Jerusalem as a patriarchate depended on the validity of the decrees and canons of the Council of Chalcedon. Before this council, Jerusalem had been a suffragan see of the metropolitan of Caesarea Maritima. Emperor Marcian granted the bishop of Jerusalem the title of patriarch to enlist his support at the council. Second, the religious churches and monastic foundations, as well as the infrastructure in support of the pilgrimage trade, depended on the support of the wealthy

[134] Frend, *Rise of the Monophysite Movement*, 151–54.

and the nobles in Constantinople. Constantine's decision to encourage Christian settlement in Jerusalem and its environs had attracted a large number of monks from every corner of the empire and beyond. Since a great many of the leaders of the monasteries were not from Palestine, their assessment of the Chalcedonian decision was different from the reception in culturally and ethnically homogenous Egypt. They could accept or reject its decree without betraying loyalty to a nation or clan. Finally, the rural population was in the majority Jews and Samaritans, who were opposed to Christian settlement on their land and were ready to rise in force against what they no doubt perceived as occupation. There was a Samaritan uprising against the opponents of Juvenal in 453,[135] and Samaritan rebellions under Zeno and Justinian are also recorded. At the same time, the monks of the *lavrai* were more isolated from these conflicts, were predominantly Greek-speaking, and more readily identified with the ecclesiastical establishment in Jerusalem as well as with the pro-Chalcedonian world outside of Palestine than with the locals. This was in large measure because they depended on Constantinople for monetary support and protection. In his *Life of Sabas*, Cyril of Scythopolis, a Chalcedonian, writes in the sixth century that Christians in Palestine are "reduced [in number] and preyed upon."[136] The tide seems to have turned against anti-Chalcedonians when with her death they lost the support of Empress Eudocia, who had been a strong force of the anti-Juvenal party.[137]

[135] *Pler.* 10. See also the discussion in Horn, *Asceticism and Christological Controversy*, 336.

[136] Cyril of Scythopolis, *Vit. Sab.* 72 (Schwartz, 175,12–13; Price, 184, translation modified); see also Frend, *Rise of the Monophysite Movement*, 153 n 2.

[137] See *Pler.* 20 and 25. On Empress Eudocia's patronage of the anti-Chalcedonian movement in Palestine, see Horn, "Empress Eudocia and the Monk Peter." The Chalcedonian side also knew to employ Eudocia for their own purposes. According to a reconstruction that favors the Chalcedonian accounts, one might say that, when Eudocia's daughter and granddaughters in Rome were taken hostage by the Vandal king Gaiseric, Eudocia's family in Constantinople forced her to accept Juvenal in exchange for their help against Gaiseric. She immediately restored communion with Juvenal, and after her death in 460, Palestine accepted Marcian's council. That then would have been the motivation for Peter the Iberian to withdraw to Egypt.

As the *Life of Peter the Iberian* recounts, Peter eventually returned to Maiuma. Yet no longer was the impact of anti-Chalcedonians to be felt in Palestine. The *Life of Peter the Iberian* reports that Isaiah, the Egyptian monk who had settled in the Gaza region and who was to become the spiritual companion of Peter, had support in Constantinople.[138] The adoption of Zeno's *Henotikon* had held in Palestine,[139] and the patriarch of Jerusalem remained in communion with the capital. Yet the interpretation of the *Henotikon* in a strictly Chalcedonian manner was taking firmer root in the new *lavrai* founded in Jerusalem and Palestine.[140] In 494, the Chalcedonian defender Sabas, who founded the great *lavra* in the Wadi Kidron as well as many other smaller houses,[141] became archimandrite of all *lavrai* in Palestine at the appointment of Sallustius the patriarch of Jerusalem (486–494).[142] Peter's followers were increasingly isolated after Sabas's appointment. The decline and ultimate extinction of the number of anti-Chalcedonian holdouts in Palestine seems to have been unstoppable. Despite the embattled Emperor Zeno's earlier

[138] According to the anti-Chalcedonian tradition, both Peter the Iberian and Abba Isaiah resisted Zeno's *Henotikon*. The question of Abba Isaiah's precise theological adherence is relatively undecided, some claiming him as a Chalcedonian, others arguing in favor of him holding a one-nature Christology. Isaiah gained fame as spiritual advisor. For a recent English translation of the spiritual homilies of Abba Isaiah, see John Chryssavgis and Pachomios (Robert) Penkett, trans., *Abba Isaiah of Scetis: Ascetic Discourses* (CSS 150; Kalamazoo, Mich.: Cistercian, 2002). For details on editions of the text of these homilies or discourses, see below, 202 n. 4.

[139] Zeno ruled the Byzantine Empire from 474 to 491. The *Henotikon*, which he issued, attempted to reconcile Chalcedonians and anti-Chalcedonians on the basis of doctrinal formulations reached before Chalcedon. For the text of Zeno's *Henotikon*, see Evagrius Scholasticus, *Hist. eccl.* 3.14 (Bidez and Parmentier, 111,1–114,5; Whitby, 147–49; see also Frend, *Rise of the Monophysite Movement*, 362–66). For a discussion of the historical context, see Frend, *Rise of the Monophysite Movement*, ch. 4.

[140] Frend, *Rise of the Monophysite Movement*, 189.

[141] For a study of the material witness to Sabas's ascetic and monastic endeavors, see Joseph Patrich, *Sabas, Leader of Palestinian Monasticism: A Comparative Study in Eastern Monasticism, Fourth to Seventh Centuries* (Dumbarton Oaks Studies 32; Washington, D.C.: Dumbarton Oaks Research Library and Collection, 1995).

[142] See Cyril of Scythopolis, *Vit. Sab.* 30 (Schwartz, 115,15–25; Price, 124–25); see also Frend, *Rise of the Monophysite Movement*, 189.

attempted patronage of Peter at the end of his *imperium*, Palestine was lost to the anti-Chalcedonians.

Peter's importance for the anti-Chalcedonians in the sees of Alexandria and especially Antioch was greater than in Palestine. Severus of Antioch saw in Peter a model to be imitated.[143] It appears to have been the resolve of Peter and John Rufus (among others) against Chalcedon that persuaded Severus to abandon his law studies, take up the monastic habit, and write in defense of the anti-Chalcedonian cause. Indeed, it is possible that Severus and Peter met in Beirut around 488 C.E., when Peter is dated to have visited there "on travels" (*Vit. Pet.* §§149–152 [R 112–14]). Beirut had a well-known school of law, and Peter made many recruits from among its students.[144]

After the exile of Patriarch Severus from Antioch in 518, the first signs of a final schism were apparent. When Emperor Anastasius (491–518) died the same year, there was a reaction against the *Henotikon.* Emperor Justin I ended any pretensions at compromise. Anti-Chalcedonian bishops in all parts of the empire except Egypt were forcibly removed, although in some instances the natural tenure of the anti-Chalcedonian bishop was allowed to end before replacing him with a Chalcedonian. Persecution of anti-Chalcedonians was rampant. Entire metropolitan provinces were purged of bishops. In 521 the persecution was put into force systematically in all the East except Egypt. Anti-Chalcedonians were grossly mistreated by the Chalcedonian bishops. Yet even after the appointment of the Chalcedonian Ephrem as patriarch of Antioch (527–545),[145] Severus in exile was as vigorous as during the time when he was still in possession of his see. The persecution of the anti-Chalcedonians resulted in a shortage of bishops. Severus

143 See, e.g., Severus of Antioch, *Letters* 5.11 (Brooks, 1.2:370, 2.2:328).

144 For a more detailed discussion, see Horn, "Peter the Iberian and Palestinian Anti-Chalcedonian Monasticism," 117–20.

145 On Ephrem of Antioch's theology, see Theresia Hainthaler, "Ephraem von Antiochien und sein Neuchalcedonismus," in *Augustine and His Opponents, Jerome, Other Latin Fathers after Nicaea, Orientalia* (vol. 5 of *Studia patristica: Papers Presented at the Twelfth International Conference on Patristic Studies Held in Oxford, 1995*; ed. Elizabeth A. Livingstone; StPatr 33; Leuven: Peeters, 1997), 524–29.

took steps toward consecrating a separate hierarchy for the anti-Chalcedonians by allowing John, bishop of Tella (519–538),[146] to ordain clergy for the dire need of the anti-Chalcedonian faithful of Syria, Armenia, and Arabia. Severus thus continued what had begun earlier already under Theodosius of Jerusalem.[147]

The controversy had been settled against Chalcedon in Egypt and in favor of Chalcedon in Palestine, Asia Minor, and Europe. Only southern Anatolia and Syria remained divided. The situation was unresolved at the time of the Arab conquest of Syria in the 630s, which removed these lands from the hands of the Byzantines. Over the next century, the last effects of Chalcedon were worked out in Syria. With the ʿAbbasid establishment of Baghdād as their capital in 750 and the subordination of most Christians under the authority of the patriarch of the Church of the East, the matter of open conflict came to a close.

In Georgia, the effects of persecution as well as war with the Persians swayed the church to accept Chalcedon by 583. In 606 the Georgian Catholicos Kyrion II ratified this decision. The *Life of Peter* was rewritten for his fellow Georgians to cast him as a champion of the Chalcedonian cause in Palestine. Peter's work and influence as anti-Chalcedonian appear to have lived on in Egypt and throughout Syria, but from his native Georgia to Constantinople and to Palestine even his identity succumbed to Justinian's enforcement of Chalcedonian doctrine.

AUTHORSHIP

It is a reasonable assumption that the author of the *Life of Peter the Iberian*, *On the Death of Theodosius*, and the *Plerophoriae* is John Rufus.[148] Establishing Rufus as the author of these works is difficult, since the manuscripts of the first two works do not ascribe

[146] On John of Tella, see the account by John of Ephesus, "Life of John of Tella," in *Lives of the Eastern Saints* (Brooks, 2:524–25). For a *Life of John of Tella* written by one of his disciples, see also Elias, *Life of Bishop John of Tella* (Brooks, 1:29–95 [Syriac] and 2:21–60 [Latin]).

[147] See William H. C. Frend, *The Rise of Christianity* (Philadelphia: Fortress, 1984), 837–48; see also the comments in Horn, *Asceticism and Christological Controversy*, 106–111.

[148] On John Rufus, see Eduard Schwartz, *Johannes Rufus, ein monophysitischer Schriftsteller* (Sitzungsberichte der Heidelberger Akademie der

these works to anyone. Likewise, Evagrius Scholasticus, whose *Historia ecclesiastica* mentions episodes that occur in the *Life of Peter the Iberian*, does not name their source.

Despite the evidence from the *Life of Peter the Iberian* that the author must have known Peter intimately, alternative authors might be discussed. A potential candidate is a certain Theodore mentioned as a close acquaintance of Peter. This Theodore, however, is also identified as a close acquaintance of the narrator of the events and so cannot be the author. It is likely that this Theodore was one of Rufus's sources. Having left Rufus in Beirut and written to him from Maiuma, Theodore "urged him in letters to come and visit and gain profit from the saints in Palestine, especially from the great Peter [the Iberian], the living martyr" (*Vit. Pet.* §112 [R 82]). Raabe's textual emendation and complicated reconstruction of the text, which at times seems to confuse Theodore and the author of the text, in the end cannot overcome the natural conclusion from the text that Theodore was an acquaintance of both Peter and John Rufus.[149]

Zachariah Rhetor, who between 500 and 519 penned books 3–6 of what is now preserved in the eighth-century *Chronicle* that bears his name, might be posited as another alternative to Rufus.[150] In each of these four books Zachariah Rhetor narrates details about Peter the Iberian, some of which are unique to Zachariah's pen. Zachariah inserts notices concerning Peter in his other works, biographies of Severus of Antioch and of Abba Isaiah of Gaza.[151] Zachariah was probably a native of Gaza, and his father's house was located near Peter's Maiuma monastery.[152]

Wissenschaften, Philosophisch-Historische Klasse 1912.16; Heidelberg: Winter, 1912); Horn, *Asceticism and Christological Controversy*, 4–12 *et passim*. J.-M. Sauget and T. Orlandi ("John of Maiuma [John Rufus]," *EECh*, 445–46) express hesitations and situate the author in the circle of Rufus's followers.

149 See the discussion in Horn, *Asceticism and Christological Controversy*, 33.

150 For references to editions of Zachariah's works, see above, p. xlvi, n. 108.

151 See Zachariah Rhetor, *Vit. Sev.* (Kugener, 7–115; an English translation by Jan-Eric Steppa is in preparation). For the *Life of Abba Isaiah*, see Zachariah Rhetor, *Vita Isaiae* (Brooks, 1:3–16 [Syriac], 2:3–10 [Latin]). An English translation is in progress.

152 See Zachariah Rhetor, *Vit. Sev.* 88 (Kugener, 88,9).

On the one hand, there is no evidence from other sources that Zachariah and Peter met. On the other hand, Zachariah expresses at the outset of his *Life of Isaiah* his admiration for Abba Isaiah, Abba Theodore, and "the blessed Peter," probably Peter the Iberian, and advertises his written treatment of each of these men.[153] Did Zachariah Rhetor write a *Life* of Peter the Iberian? To the above evidence from Zachariah's *opera*, scholars have added that the disposition of MS Sachau 321 implies that a second story of Peter the Iberian was copied after the first, but the three folios containing it are missing. Indeed, *On the Death of Theodosius* breaks off in mid-sentence, and it has been suggested that there are three folios missing. The manuscript resumes with a short fragment, followed by the scribe's statement: "The account about Peter the Iberian is completed."[154] The short fragment gives more evidence about Gregory Nazianzen than Peter the Iberian: "yet already also with vain praises, from which shameful passions tend to arise. And they took this bond of temporary silence in order to be cleansed by it and to learn, as Gregory [Nazianzen] says, 'the measure of speech and silence.'"[155] Brooks argued that the fragment followed by the closing statement of the scribe implies that the fragment is the end of another *Life* of Peter, which he attributed to Zachariah. Others have then concluded that the fragment also ought to be connected with the "Georgian Life of Peter the Iberian."[156] There is no material evidence for assigning this fragment to any author, and the final statement could just as easily have been a notice on the collection of texts about Peter the Iberian and his close associates. It is equally possible that the short missing text was a later *Life* of John Rufus.

In addition to the Syriac *Life of Peter the Iberian*, there is extant a work in Georgian entitled *C'xovreba Petre Iverisa.*[157] The

[153] Zachariah Rhetor, *Vita Isaiae* 3–4 (Brooks, 1:3–4 [Syriac], 2:3 [Latin]).

[154] Ibid., 1:18 (Syriac) and 2:12 (Latin).

[155] Ibid., 1:18 (Syriac) and 2:12 (Latin). See also the discussion in Horn, *Asceticism and Christological Controversy*, ch. 1.

[156] See the discussion in David Marshall Lang, "Peter the Iberian and His Biographers," *JEH* 2 (1951): 158–68.

[157] See Lolashvili, *Areopagituli krebuli*. The Georgian text had been already edited and translated into Russian by Nikola(i) Y. Marr, ed. and trans., "ცხოვრება პეტრე იბერისა [*Life of Peter the Iberian*]," *Pravoslavnyy Palestinskiy Sbornik*, 47 = 16.2 (1896): 1–78 (Georgian text), 81–115 (Russian translation).

monk Makarios wrote that he translated from the Syriac *Life of Peter the Iberian* written by a certain Zachariah, "a disciple of Peter the Georgian."[158] Under Makarios's hand, Peter becomes a Chalcedonian saint, and the entire story is retold with a pro-Chalcedonian interpretation. The family names of Peter's lineage are also altered. Most striking is that Peter's name from birth in the Syriac *Life of Peter the Iberian* was Nabarnugios, which Makarios alters to Murvanos.[159] Makarios's work also contains an introduction and conclusion not found in the Syriac *Life of Peter the Iberian.* The Syriac and Georgian texts are obviously more closely related than either one to the details unique to Zachariah's *Chronicle.* Makarios's attribution of the Syriac *Life of Peter the Iberian* to Zachariah could be the result of confusion, the same manner of mistake that assigned to Zachariah Rhetor the books of the *Chronicle* other than those he contributed. The date of the *C'xovreba Petre Iverisa* is at least from the period following the acceptance of Chalcedon and the break with the Armenian church undertaken by the Georgian Catholicos Kyrion II in 606. This distance between the time of Peter and the completion of the *C'xovreba* and the complex circumstances in which it was written could account for the attribution to Zachariah, aided by Zachariah's favorable inclination toward Chalcedon toward the end of his life. Given that the essential anti-Chalcedonian interpretation tying together the Syriac *Life of Peter the Iberian* has been reversed in the Georgian *C'xovreba Petre Iverisa,* such a work would not have been attributed to an anti-Chalcedonian such as John Rufus. While Zachariah Rhetor displayed anti-Chalcedonian inclinations in his earlier work, he concluded his life as Chalcedonian bishop of Melitene, and thus Zachariah would have been a favorable choice for a Chalcedonian Georgian in search of a possible author. In the end, these data can neither rule out John Rufus as author of the text underlying the "Georgian Life of Peter the Iberian" nor suggest conclusively a more plausible option.

158 Marr, "ცხოვრება პეტრე იბერისა," 53. See also Marr's introduction, 20.
159 For a discussion of this name, see p. xxiv above.

John Rufus

Almost the only sources of information about John Rufus are his own works. There is little mention of him elsewhere.[160] In the *Life of Peter the Iberian*, Rufus appears briefly in two passages. In the first, the author indicates that he was ordained in Antioch during the reign of Emperor Basiliscus, that is, before August 476, when the anti-Chalcedonian patriarch of Antioch Peter II, also known as Peter the Fuller (bishop, 468–488), had returned from exile to his see (*Vit. Pet.* §106 [R 79]). It is during his patriarchate that the Chalcedonian and anti-Chalcedonian parties in the see of Antioch permanently separated. The second passage recounts how the author of the *Life of Peter the Iberian* met the protagonist of his story (*Vit. Pet.* §§111–115 (R 81–83)]). The author was living in Antioch during the patriarchate of the Chalcedonian Calendion (481–484). The *Plerophoriae* indicates that Rufus was a native of the Roman province of Arabia (*Pler.* 22), which extended east of the Jordan and whose capital was Bostra. The section of the *Life of Peter the Iberian* that narrates Peter's travels in Arabia reveals a detailed knowledge of this region.[161] Rufus must have been one of Peter's closest allies. Peter undertook this journey late in his life, time enough to have befriended Rufus, who could have acted as Peter's guide.

There is little other information about John revealed in either the *Life of Peter the Iberian* or the *Plerophoriae*.[162] In part this was probably to protect himself from persecution during the reign of Emperor Justin I (517–523). Since the author was one of the few prominent ascetics in Palestine who rejected Chalcedon, it was assumed that audiences would have known their source without his name appearing on the document. Monastic piety is another plausible explanation, and indeed the work contains language that both

[160] Zachariah Rhetor drops a few comments about him in *Vita Severi*. The announcement of priestly ordination pertaining to John the Eunuch at *Pler.* 5 appears to be unrelated to immediate ordination events in John Rufus's life.

[161] For a discussion of their activities in the region, see Cornelia Horn, "A Chapter in the Pre-history of the Christological Controversies in Arabic: Readings from the Works of John Rufus," *ParOr* 30 (2005): 133–56.

[162] For a fuller discussion of John Rufus as the one who spoke the mind of the anti-Chalcedonian community on the world around them, see Jan-Eric Steppa, *John Rufus and the World Vision of Anti-Chalcedonian Culture* (Gorgias Dissertations: Ancient Christian Studies 1; Piscataway, N.J.: Gorgias, 2002).

knows the rhetoric and reveals the author's humility. Very likely Rufus was well-known to anti-Chalcedonians in Syria and Palestine.

RHETORIC AND GENRE IN THE *LIFE OF PETER THE IBERIAN*

In arrangement, figures, themes, and style, the *Life of Peter the Iberian* reflects the rhetorical training of its author, John Rufus, who almost certainly composed this work to praise Peter on the occasion of the first anniversary of his death. In this respect, the *Sitz im Leben* of this work has parallels with the *Life of Rabbula of Edessa*, composed around 437 C.E. Furthermore, there are parallels of rhetorical influence in each of these two works. One important difference is that the audience of the *Life of Peter the Iberian* consisted of Greek-speaking monks, members of Peter's monastery or of monastic daughter foundations established by the first generation of spiritual children, and that this work is therefore probably a translation from Greek into Syriac. The *Life of Rabbula of Edessa*, on the other hand, is a genuine Syriac work. Although composed earlier than the *Life of Peter the Iberian*, it evinces a stage of development that is consistent with the increasing influence of Greek literature on all Syriac literary genres in the course of the fifth century.

That John Rufus had received training in law is suggested by the *Life of Peter the Iberian* itself. The episode of Peter's sudden departure from his itinerary for Tyre in response to a divine vision, in which God told Peter to fetch for him "market loaves," clearly points to the central importance of a circle of students of law within the community of Peter's disciples. The reference to "market loaves" is used as a metaphor for lawyers, called "market men," as Rufus explains (*Vit. Pet.* §150 [R 113]). At this time Rufus had already been a companion on Peter's journeys. His attention to the scene of recruitment of young lawyers, however, may very well imply that Rufus himself had a vital connection to this profession. That law-school students such as Severus of Antioch down the road associated with Peter's disciples also helps one to understand the relevance of the episode.

Rufus's likely association with the legal profession in some form or another, even if only by way of contact with fellow academic students in this branch of training, implies that before accepting the monastic habit Rufus also had a solid training in rhetoric, which was the instrument of courtroom procedure in antiquity. Greek rhetoric in the practice of law evolved with the establishment of jury courts and thus originated almost a millennium earlier than Rufus's lifetime, roughly during the early sixth century B.C.E. and in the context of Solon's legal reform.[163] Solon's judicial system became the model for the Romans, the Byzantines, and the West. Rhetoric remained at the heart of this institution in late antiquity.

Rhetorical theory in the Roman world appeared for the first time already full-grown in 90 B.C.E. and reached its apogee with Cicero (108–44 B.C.E.), after whom Roman rhetoric declined. The Roman emperors imposed an autocracy that drastically curtailed debate on substantial issues of policy. At the same time that restrictions on free debate pushed rhetoric into decline, it became the central discipline of Roman education.[164] The *Institutio oratoria* of Quintillian (ca. 35–84 C.E.) describes the system of rhetorical education in Rome that remained in place for the next five centuries. This combination of the decline of public debate and the rise of rhetoric to central importance in education contributed to the increasing influence of rhetoric in other literary forms, such as poetry, biography, and the novel.

[163] For an accessible overview of the history of rhetoric and its place in the establishment of the Athenian state, see James J. Murphy and Richard A. Katula, with Forbes I. Hill and Donovan J. Ochs, *A Synoptic History of Classical Rhetoric* (3rd ed.; Mahwah, N.J.: Hermagoras, 2003), 7–9, 26 *et passim*. Other works on the history of law and rhetoric include Kathleen Freeman, *The Murder of Herodes* (New York: Norton, 1963). Helpful general works on the history of rhetoric include George Kennedy, *The Art of Persuasion in Greece* (Princeton: Princeton University Press, 1963); idem, *Classical Rhetoric and Its Christian and Secular Traditions from Ancient to Modern Times* (2nd ed.; Chapel Hill: University of North Carolina Press, 1999); idem, *A New History of Classical Rhetoric* (Princeton: Princeton University Press, 1994); and Thomas Cole, *The Origins of Rhetoric in Ancient Greece* (Baltimore: Johns Hopkins University Press, 1991).

[164] Murphy and Katula, *Synoptic History of Classical Rhetoric*, 202–3; see also Donald Lemen Clark, *Rhetoric in Greco-Roman Education* (New York: Columbia University Press, 1957), 216 and 265.

John Rufus's rhetorical education would have encompassed not only the creation of speeches. Education in rhetoric required other exercises, such as creating descriptive narratives, which would serve a biographer or encomiast well. Augustine's Christian apology for the adoption of rhetoric "to argue for the good" was already passé for the Greek-speaking East. For example, New Testament authors incorporated rhetoric into their arguments and their depiction of the lives of Jesus and the apostles.[165] There were a number of centers of rhetoric in Syria, most notably Antioch, the home of John Chrysostom and his teacher, Libanius.[166] Apamea boasted a school whose curriculum may have left its mark on at least one fifth-century Syriac writer, John of Apamea.[167] In Palestine, the rhetorical schools in Gaza were esteemed in the fourth century. Suppressed by Porphyry, the bishop of Gaza, in the early fifth century for their support of classical religion, they

[165] For recent studies of rhetorical dimensions of the Gospels, see C. Clifton Black, *The Rhetoric of the Gospel: Theological Artistry in the Gospels and Acts* (St. Louis: Chalice, 2001); Amos N. Wilder, *Early Christian Rhetoric: The Language of the Gospel* (Peabody, Mass.: Hendrickson, 1999); and Richard A. Burridge, "The Gospels and Acts," in *Handbook of Classical Rhetoric in the Hellenistic Period, 330 BC–AD 400* (ed. Stanley E. Porter; Leiden: Brill, 1997), 507–53.

[166] The relationship between rhetoric and politics in the life and work of Libanius was subjected to investigation in Hans-Ulrich Wiemer, *Libanios und Julian: Studien zum Verhältnis von Rhetorik und Politik im vierten Jahrhundert n. Chr.* (Vestigia 46; Munich: Beck, 1995). See also Craig A. Gibson, "The Agenda of Libanius' Hypotheses to Demosthenes," *GRBS* 40 (1999): 171–202. For the influence of Libanius on John Chrysostom, see, e.g., the studies by David G. Hunter, "Libanius and John Chrysostom: New Thoughts on an Old Problem," in *Cappadocian Fathers, Chrysostom and His Greek Contemporaries, Augustine, Donatism, and Pelagianism* (vol. 4 of *Papers Presented to the Tenth International Conference on Patristic Studies Held in Oxford, 1987*; ed. Elizabeth A. Livingstone; StPatr 22; Leuven: Peeters, 1989), 129–35; idem, "Preaching and Propaganda in Fourth Century Antioch: John Chrysostom's Homilies on the Statues," in *Preaching in the Patristic Age: Studies in Honour of Walter J. Burghardt* (ed. David G. Hunter; New York: Paulist, 1989), 119–38; idem, "Borrowings from Libanius in the *Comparatio Regis et monachi* of St. John Chrysostom," *JTS* NS 39 (1988): 525–31; as well as Julia Alissandratos, "The Structure of the Funeral Oration in John Chrysostom's 'Eulogy of Meletius,'" *Byzantine Studies* 7 (1980): 182–98.

[167] On John of Apamea, see Karl Pinggéra, "Johannes von Apamea," *BBKL* 23:737–41. Peter Bruns ("John of Apamea," *DECL*, 326) dates him to the sixth century.

returned to their former prominence in the late fifth and early sixth centuries.[168] It seems that the period in which the *Life of Peter the Iberian* unfolds was one of temporary decline for the school in Gaza. It cannot be determined whether Peter as bishop was in part responsible for this decline. Perhaps the upheaval in Gaza to which the *Life of Peter the Iberian* attests was a significant factor.

In form, the *Life of Peter the Iberian* shows many features of the encomium, a speech of praise that exercised a special influence on biography.[169] The encomium presented the virtues of its subject through elaboration of family, birth, education, and heroic deeds, called *topoi*. Rufus has greatly expanded the *topos* of the subject's origins, illustrating the nobility and virtue of both parental lines.[170] Although an audience might expect some elaboration of the subject's genealogy, Rufus's expansion on this theme seems to run beyond the accustomed length, so much so that Rufus felt the need to offer his audience an explanation for his lengthy stories about Peter's forbearers. There is quite little, if anything, mentioned about Peter's education, which is not surprising, given that he left Iberia as a hostage at the age of twelve.[171] Encomia often epitomize the subject's education with one line,[172] so this

[168] On the history of rhetoric in Gaza, see George A. Kennedy, *Greek Rhetoric under Christian Emperors* (Princeton: Princeton University Press, 1983), 169–77.

[169] Biography was not one of the subjects of the school curriculum. Along with history, encomium was one of the most important genres for the development of biography. See Richard A. Burridge, "Biography," in Porter, *Handbook of Classical Rhetoric*, 371–91, here 374–78. Early Jewish and Christian literature features examples of biographies written in the style of encomia. See, e.g., Jerome H. Neyrey, "Josephus' Vita and the *Encomium*: A Native Model of Personality," *JSJ* 25 (1994): 177–206; and Maged S. Mikhail and Tim Vivian, "Zacharias of Sakhâ: An *Encomium* on the Life of John the Little," *CCR* 18 (1997): 1–64.

[170] See *Vit. Pet.* §§6–19 (R 5–12). Elaboration of genealogy was not unheard of in encomia and was standard in the biographies of political figures or military heroes.

[171] Note, however, that the later *Georgian Life of Peter the Iberian* is concerned with pointing to Peter's early schooling in Georgia. See Horn, *Asceticism and Christological Controversy*, ch. 2.

[172] For an example of Syriac literature influenced by Greek rhetoric, see the *Life of Rabbula* (J. Josephus Overbeck, ed., *S. Ephraemi Syri, Rabulae episcopi Edesseni, Balaei aliorumque opera selecta* [Oxford: Clarendon, 1865], 160; our translation): "while growing up he was educated in the literature of the

brevity could be a matter of rhetorical form rather than of Rufus's limited knowledge of Peter's youth.

One characteristic of the *Life of Peter the Iberian* is that it follows through with a chronological framework from the beginning to the end. Not an insignificant portion of that framework consists of miracles proving Peter's authority. This feature marks a difference from the *Life of Rabbula*: after Rabbula's consecration to the episcopacy, the author sets aside the chronological narrative in order to speak of the various areas of the bishop's activity arranged more or less topically. In the *Life of Peter the Iberian*, in contrast, the chronological element is set up as background. Many of the events narrated take place between Easter and Pentecost of subsequent years. In classical novels, chronology is a secondary matter.[173]

The importance of miracles as the seal of divine approval for the anti-Chalcedonian movement takes a literary shape that resembles the classical aretalogy, or tales of miracles demonstrating the power of the gods over humans. Aretalogy certainly is incorporated into the Gospel accounts but also is to be found in

Greeks as a member of the wealthy nobles of their city, Qenneshrin." Other examples from biographical arrangement are conveniently collected in Burridge, "Biography," 379–80; on the *topos* of the subject's education, see 383.

173 The novel *Historia Apollonii Regis Tyri* or *History of Apollonius*, much read in Byzantium and Western Europe in the Middle Ages, disregards "external" chronology: an important character, Athenagoras, is presented to be at once a young man and nevertheless old enough to have a daughter the same age as his romantic interest, Tarsia. See Tomas Hägg, *The Novel in Antiquity* (Oxford: Blackwell, 1983), 152.

the apocryphal Acts of the Apostles.[174] While not a part of either classical biography or the novel per se, aretalogy, as well as rhetoric, had influence on them. Classical novels and romances were also fond of the *Reisefabulistik*, fantastic voyages, occasions for demonstrating the virtue and heroism of the travelers.[175] The (apocryphal) Acts of the Apostles contain numerous elements of the characteristic presentation of such a preference for stories of a hero's journeys.[176]

The tales of Peter's wanderings recount natural and divine wonders in the confines of the "Holy Land" while incorporating aretalogy. Rufus speaks of the sites (and sights) he "witnesses" with Peter as ܬܕܡܪܬܐ, *tedmərātā*, "wonders." While it is not the land of the Lotus eaters of Ulysses, Rufus projects the fascination with the strange and distant into the hagiographical landscape of the Palestinian "near abroad": a statue of Emperor Julian chasing Peter in Egypt (*Vit. Pet.* §100 [R 73]); the resting place of Moses revealed on Mount Pisgah (§118 [R 85]); the natural wonder of the well-tempered bath in the Syrian Desert (§123 [R 91]). In each place Peter manifests the power of God and the divine approval that this power bestows. To be sure, the narration of Israel in the wilderness in the Pentateuch and the conquest of the land in the

[174] On aretalogy in Christian literature, see, e.g., Francesco Corsaro, "Elementi romanzeschi e aretalogia negli Atti apocrifi di Paolo e Tecla: codici e strutture formali," in *La narrativa cristiana antica: codici narrativi, strutture formali, schemi retorici: XXIII Incontro di studiosi dell'antichità cristiana, Roma, 5–7 maggio 1994* (ed. Salvatore Pricoco, Paolo Siniscalco, and Gianna Dareggi; SEAug 50; Rome: Institutum Patristicum Augustinianum, 1995), 77–90; and David R. Cartlidge, "Transfigurations of Metamorphosis Traditions in the Acts of John, Thomas, and Peter," *Semeia* 38 (1986): 53–66. For aretalogy in other early Christian literature, see, e.g., Wolfgang Fauth, "Pythagoras, Jesus von Nazareth und der Helios-Apollon des Julianus Apostata: zu Eigentümlichkeiten der spätantiken Pythagoras-Aretalogie," *ZNW* 78 (1987): 24–48. For a study that favors classification as *chreiae* over that of aretalogies of some of the relevant texts, see Phillip Sigal, "Manifestations of Hellenistic Historiography in Select Judaic Literature," in *Society of Biblical Literature 1984 Seminar Papers* (SBLSP 23; Chico, Calif.: Scholars Press, 1984), 161–85.

[175] Hägg, *Novel in Antiquity*, 117–18.

[176] For an overview of rhetoric in the Christian apocrypha generally, see Richard I. Pervo, "Rhetoric in the Christian Apocrypha," in Porter, *Handbook of Classical Rhetoric*, 793–805, which focuses on the *Acts of Thomas*, *Acts of Paul*, *Acts of Peter*, *Acts of John*, and *Acts of Andrew*, with a brief bibliography on the topic.

book of Joshua or the tours and miracles of Jesus in Samaria and Judea might also have been *Vorbilder* for Rufus, yet such accounts do not exhaust the well from which he drew his inspiration.

If these genres hint at the classical literary motifs at work in Rufus's imagination, then rhetoric was the means Rufus employed to express them. A prominent rhetorical figure is the biblical citation, a commonplace of Christian hagiography borrowed from the Christian exegetical homily.[177] The *prooemion* of the *Life of Peter the Iberian* begins with a citation from Hebrews, and the narrator introduces his work as an imperfect attempt to obey this command, an exhortation through the example of the speaker. To emphasize the virtue of the subject, citations are often chained together in short, impetuous *cola*, reflecting the "Asianic" rhetorical style, which in the original Greek might have had the features of consonance and rhythmic arrangement as well.[178]

The translator of the *Life of Peter the Iberian* reflects many fifth-century elements of Syriac literature.[179] Where original compositions in Syriac such as the *Life of Rabbula of Edessa*, composed even earlier than the *Life of Peter the Iberian*, render, for example, the Greek ξενοδοχεῖον by ܟܣܢܘܕܟܝܢ,[180] the Syriac *Life of Peter the Iberian* renders the sense of the word by ܒܝܬ ܩܘܒܠܐ ܕܐܟܣܢ̈ܝܐ instead (*Vit. Pet.* §19 [R 12]). Quite frequently, however, one finds in the Syriac *Life of Peter the Iberian* Greek words taken over almost in transcription into the Syriac.[181] While some

177 On rhetoric in the Christian exegetical homily see Folker Siegert, "Homily and Panegyrical Sermon," in Porter, *Handbook of Classical Rhetoric*, 421–43.

178 Asianism was a derogatory term first applied to orators such as Cicero by the proponents of Atticism. Asianism and Atticism both defined a spectrum of rhetorical style that persisted to the late Byzantine period. See "Asianism" in David E. Aune, *The Westminster Dictionary of New Testament and Early Christian Literature and Rhetoric* (Louisville: Westminster John Knox, 2003), 65–66. For a study of the characterization of John Chrysostom's rhetorical style as Asianic, see P. J. Ryan, "Chrysostom: A Derived Stylist?" *VC* 36 (1982): 5–14.

179 One example from the lexicon that argues against a pre-sixth century translation into Syriac is the expression *ketābê kahanāyê*, meaning the Bible, but literally, the expression means "priestly books." See *Vit. Pet.* §21 (R 14). This expression is not attested in any dated manuscript before the sixth century.

180 *Life of Rabbula* (Overbeck, *S. Ephraemi Syri*, 182, 202, and 203).

181 For the presence of Greek vocabulary in Syriac, see also Sebastian P. Brock, "Greek Words in Syriac: Some General Features," *Scripta Classica Israelica* 15 (1996), 251–262, repr. as ch. 15 in Sebastian Brock, *From Ephrem*

of these may have already passed into the Syriac language, there are many calques noted by Raabe that have been preserved in the notes to the present edition and translation. Overall, the Syriac translation has sought to preserve also the rhetorical style of the original Greek syntax, which as such is an important element of style. It is possible that the translator recognized these rhetorical forms and thus felt inspired or compelled to preserve them.[182] Again, the *Life of Rabbula* imitates Greek rhetorical style even in the features of its syntax. Preservation of such details in the *Life of Peter the Iberian* reflects the steadily increasing influence of classical rhetoric on Syriac prose in the fifth century.[183]

to Romanos: Interactions between Syriac and Greek in Late Antiquity (Aldershot: Ashgate, 1999).

[182] Translation techniques from Greek into Syriac have been the subject of several studies. For a limited sample of examples, see Harald Suermann, "Die Übersetzung des Probus und eine Theorie zur Geschichte der syrischen Übersetzung griechischer Texte," *OrChr* 74 (1990): 103–14; Lionel R. Wickham, "Translation Techniques Greek/Syriac and Syriac/English," in *V. Symposium Syriacum, 1988, Katholieke Universiteit, Leuven, 29–31 Août 1988* (ed. René Lavenant; OCA 236; Rome: Pontificium Institutum Studiorum Orientalium, 1988), 345–53; Sebastian P. Brock, "Towards a History of Syriac Translation Technique," in *III. Symposium Syriacum, 1980: les contacts du monde syriaque avec les autres cultures, Goslar 7–11 Septembre 1980* (ed. René Lavenant, OCA 221; Rome: Pontificium Institutum Studiorum Orientalium, 1983), 1–14, repr. as ch. 10 in Sebastian P. Brock, *Studies in Syriac Christianity: History, Literature, and Theology* (Hampshire, Great Britain: Variorum, 1992); and idem, "Aspects of Translation Technique in Antiquity," *GRBS* 20 (1979): 69–87, reprinted as ch. 3 in Brock, *Syriac Perspectives on Late Antiquity*. For a discussion of issues in the process of translating Scripture from Greek into Syriac, see the helpful contribution by Sebastian P. Brock, "Translating the New Testament into Syriac (Classical and Modern)," in *Interpretation of the Bible: The International Symposium in Slovenia* (ed. Joze Krasovec; JSOTSup 289; Sheffield: Sheffield Academic Press, 1998), 371–85.

[183] The field of study of the influence of Greek rhetoric on Syriac literature is still wide open. Pioneering studies have been contributed in the form of a Zürich *Habilitationsschrift* by Leo Haefeli, *Stilmittel bei Afrahat dem persischen Weisen* (Leipziger semitistische Studien NS 4; Leipzig: Hinrichs, 1932; repr., Leipzig: Zentralantiquariat der DDR, 1968). Rhetorical analysis of the twelve Syriac hymns ascribed to Balai can be found in Robert R. Phenix Jr., "A Critical Investigation of Twelve Syriac Verse Homilies on Joseph (Genesis 37–50) Attributed to Balai (Fifth-Century A.D.)" (Ph. D. diss., Eberhard-Karls University, Tübingen, Germany, 2005), to appear in Studien und Texte des antiken Christentums, Mohr-Siebeck, 2008.

The literal character of the translation from Greek into Syriac of the *Life of Peter the Iberian* is reflected in several points on the level of the word. The translator did not attempt to change the biblical citations to reflect the Peshitta. All citations are slavish translations of the Greek. Many nouns are kept in their Greek forms. Finally, there also is some evidence of glossing, such as in the form of the Greek word *basternion*, which is preceded in the Syriac by a gloss explaining this to be the throne in which Eudocia traveled (*Vit. Pet.* §12 [R 7]).

TEXT-CRITICAL OVERVIEW

There are two extant manuscripts for both the *Life of Peter the Iberian* and for *On the Death of Theodosius*, one kept in Berlin and one preserved in the British Museum in London. The basis for Richard Raabe's *editio princeps* and German translation of the *Life of Peter the Iberian* was a manuscript collected by Eduard Sachau and later acquired by the Staatsbibliothek zu Berlin: Stiftung Preußischer Kulturbesitz: Orientabteilung.[184] In 741 C.E. a scribe completed what is known to Western scholars as Sachau MS No. 321.[185] In this collection the *Life of Peter the Iberian* occupies folios 68 verso through 103 recto. From folio 103 recto, column b, to folio 104 verso one can find most of the text of *On the Death of Theodosius*.[186] The final section, amounting to a little more than a page of printed text in Brooks's *editio princeps* of the work, is missing. The bottom edges of this Sachau MS 321 suffered moisture damage, and on many pages the ink is faded.

In his comments accompanying his edition of the Syriac *Life of Peter the Iberian*, Raabe rightly remarked that it was a felicitous accident that this work was preserved in another manuscript

[184] Richard Raabe, ed. and trans., *Petrus der Iberer: Ein Charakterbild zur Kirchen- und Sittengeschichte des 5. Jahrhunderts; syrische Übersetzung einer um das Jahr 500 verfassten griechischen Biographie* (Leipzig: Hinrichs, 1895).

[185] Referenced in the following as MS Sachau 321. It is also referred to as "MS 26 (Sachau 321)" in the catalogue. See Eduard Sachau, *Verzeichniss der syrischen Handschriften* (2 parts; vol.–23 of *Die Handschriften-Verzeichnisse der Königlichen Bibliothek zu Berlin*; Berlin: Ascher, 1899), 1:94 and 96.

[186] Sachau (*Verzeichniss der syrischen handschriften*, 96) does not identify the existence of the *De obitu Theodosii* as a separate text but assumes the respective pages of the manuscript under the text of *Vita Petri Iberi*.

now property of the British Museum, MS BM Add. 12,174, folios 48 recto through 78 verso.[187] That same manuscript preserves the complete text of the *On the Death of Theodosius* on folios 141 recto to 142 verso.[188] According to William Wright's *Catalogue of the Syriac Manuscripts in the British Museum*, MS BM Add. 12,174 is of later provenance; a notice dates its completion to 1197 in the monastery of Mar Barsauma in Melitene.[189]

Raabe used MS BM Add. 12,174 to supplement the damaged portions of MS Sachau 321. Where there are variant readings, MS Sachau 321, the older manuscript, generally preserves the better reading, although occasionally Raabe found it necessary to follow MS BM Add. 12,174. In Raabe's apparatus, MS Sachau 321 is labeled "A" and MS BM Add. 12,174 appears under the *siglum* "B."[190] It is worthwhile to convey Raabe's own general observations on these texts. Our own examination of these manuscripts against Raabe's printed edition and notes agrees with his careful work in many, nearly every instance. We have established our Syriac text on the basis of a comparison of microfilms of the original manuscripts with Raabe's printed edition. We have essentially adopted Raabe's edition, except for the few instances where we corrected some of his readings. Therefore we have not included in our own edition, except where appropriate, Raabe's apparatus. We have followed the same procedure in establishing our Syriac text of the *On the Death of Theodosius*, adopting Brooks's edition and correcting his reading where our own study of the manuscript evidence required us to do so.

It is necessary to remark that Raabe's analysis of the language of the two manuscripts that contain the *Life of Peter the Iberian* depends on his view that they are translations into Syriac, either from Greek or from Coptic. His reasons for this will be taken up below but include primarily the syntax of the documents and the relatively frequent occurrence of loanwords.

[187] See Raabe, *Petrus der Iberer*, vi.

[188] See also William Wright, *Catalogue of the Syriac Manuscripts in the British Museum* (3 vols.; London: British Museum, 1870–72), 1126.

[189] Ibid., 1123–24, 1137. On the monastery of Barsauma, see also Ernest Honigmann, *Le couvent de Barsauma et le patriarcat Jacobite d'Antioche et de Syrie* (CSCO 146; Subsidia 7; Leuven: Durbecq, 1967).

[190] See Raabe, *Petrus der Iberer*, vi.

Manuscripts Sachau 321 and BM Add. 12,174 agree in all basic points and in most details. The differences between the two are primarily orthographic, but they also extend beyond the usual domain of variant spellings of proper nouns and the transcription of Greek loanwords. There are synonymic correspondences, as well as in MS Sachau 321 a difference in the usage of the conjunction ܘ (*wa*) and the relative pronoun ܕ (*da*). In those parts of the text attested only in MS BM Add. 12,174, there are sporadic syntactic differences. Raabe argues that these reflect different translation techniques and concludes that the differences MS BM Add. 12,174 exhibits suggest that it was a copy of a Syriac *Vorlage*. This *Vorlage* was in a relatively poor condition so that the copyist misread nearly every instance of its divergence from MS Sachau 321. Raabe conjectured that the synonyms were the result of substituting words in current Syriac usage to replace those that had fallen out of use. Syntactic differences also suggest that the copyist attempted to conform the highly graecized syntax of his *Vorlage* (which is represented more faithfully by MS Sachau 321) to the syntactic rules and style of Syriac prose.

There is evidence that the condition of MS BM Add. 12,174 has deteriorated in the time since Raabe. Primarily, the damage to the lower margins has been exacerbated, making less of the text legible.[191]

Versions and Original Text

In addition to the Syriac *Life of Peter the Iberian*, which MS Sachau 321 and MS BM Add. 12,174 attest, there is extant only one other version of the story of the life of Peter the Iberian in Classical Georgian, which was treated above in the discussion on the authorship of the Syriac *Life of Peter the Iberian*. Fragments of what is sometimes identified as a Coptic *Life of Peter the Iberian* in fact belong to a *Life of Timothy Aelurus*.[192]

[191] Our investigation of both manuscripts was not firsthand but relied on microfilm copies, which are almost certainly not faithful to the ink-on-paper contrast of the originals. It is possible that MS BM Add. 12,174 is more legible than the photos on microfilm suggest.

[192] See the photographs and subtitle—"Codex showing the life of Peter the Iberian. Courtesy The Metropolitan Museum of Art, New York"—that accompany the articles "Codex" and "Codex Alexandrinus" in *CE* 2:567. See

The *Life of Peter the Iberian* preserved in Syriac translation is the oldest of the extant versions, a translation of a Greek original.[193] The Syriac *Life of Rabbula*, bishop of Edessa (411–438), likewise shows Greek influence in its syntax and rhetorical construction,[194] yet it is very unlikely that it is a translation from a Greek original. The influence of Greek letters on Syriac only increased over time, exerting force on Syriac writing well after the dominance of Arabic, which had its beginning in the eighth century. Thus, the character of the Syriac *Life of Peter the Iberian* reflecting Greek influence could either be the result of the text being a translation from Greek or could just as easily be ascribed to the Greek-Syriac diglossia of its author, who would have been a representative of the broader sociolinguistic situation in Syria, Palestine, and Mesopotamia in the sixth century.

Raabe also assumed a Greek original but only reported in support of this claim that the *Life of Peter the Iberian* contains syntactic as well as onomastic evidence to that effect. Discussion of the first category of evidence would require a lengthy study. Thus this question is set aside here with the notice that, while there are constructions that arguably reflect the constraints of Greek prose, these could just as easily have been the result of the sociolinguistic parameters in which Syriac was being composed in much of Syria and Palestine. Syriac was written in the Christian milieu in many instances in an environment where Greek was also an important

the discussion of the text fragments in Hugh Gerard Evelyn-White, *New Coptic Texts from the Monastery of Saint Macarius* (part 1 of *The Monasteries of the Wadi ʿn Natrûn*; New York: Metropolitan Museum of Art, 1926), pl. VIII, English translation numbered XXXI on 164–67. See also Horn, *Asceticism and Christological Controversy*, 13 note 12.

193 In light of *Hist. eccl.* 2.5, 8; 3.33 (Bidez and Parmentier, 56; Whitby, 85), Evagrius Scholasticus appears to have had access to the Greek text.

194 For an edition of the *Life of Rabbula*, see Overbeck, *S. Ephraemi Syri*, 159–209. An English translation by Cornelia B. Horn and Robert R. Phenix Jr. is forthcoming in the SBLWGRW series (Atlanta: Society of Biblical Literature). For a study of the rhetorical form characterizing the introduction to the *Life of Rabbula*, see Robert R. Phenix Jr., "Kunstprosaische Elemente in der *Vita Rabbulae*: Ein Blick auf das Encomium an den Helden," in *Die Suryoye und ihre Umwelt: Viertes deutsches Syrologen-Symposium in Trier 2004: Festgabe Wolfgang Hage zum 70. Geburtstag* (ed. Martin Tamcke and Andreas Heinz; Studien zur Orientalischen Kirchengeschichte 36; Münster: LIT, 2005), 281–93.

language.[195] After the rise of the Seleucid kingdom after Alexander's death (during the night from 10 to 11 June 323 B.C.E.), Greek was established as a language of cultural, economic, and political importance in Mesopotamia, Syria, and Palestine, where Aramaic had been at least since the Neo-Babylonian Empire (618–536 B.C.E.) the dominant language of wider communication. Syriac, the dialect of Aramaic spoken originally in northern Mesopotamia around the cities of Edessa and Nisibis, was to become the dominant language in much of Southwest Asia already by the fourth century C.E. With the rise of Christianity and the spread of Syriac as its chief vehicle in Mesopotamia, Persia, and Syria, Christian theology in Greek gave that language a renewed prestige among Syriac authors. Fluent knowledge of Greek became essential for scholars in the Syriac world, and its prestige influenced as much the Syriac language as it did the thought of the authors who used Syriac to express themselves.

SYNOPSIS OF THE *VITA PETRI IBERI* AND THE *DE OBITU THEODOSII*

Outline of the Vita Petri Iberi

The *Life of Peter the Iberian* follows the classical arrangement of biography. The author begins by presenting the reason for which the *Life* is worthy to be written and heard (§§1–2). The author then presents Peter's nationality and the origin of his monastic name Peter in two short sections that stress the Christianity of the Iberians and Peter the Iberian's imitation of the apostle Peter, "the Rock" of the faith (§§3–5). Next the reader learns of Peter's family and lineage, the two key themes of which are his royalty and the Christian righteousness expressed via the ascetic piety of his parents, grandparents, and nurse (§§6–19). Peter is the "rose blossom that sprang up from such a holy root," a phrase that introduces a section of praise for Peter and his holy way of life (§20).[196] The

[195] See Sebastian P. Brock, "Syriac Culture, 337–425," in *The Late Empire, A.D. 337–425* (vol. 13 of *The Cambridge Ancient History*; ed. Averil Cameron and Peter Garnsey; Cambridge: Cambridge University Press, 1998), 708–19.

[196] A similar expression is used in the *Life of Rabbula* (Overbeck, *S. Ephraemi Syri*, 160; our translation). After introducing the temperaments of

author follows this with a *captatio benevolentiae*, exhorting the audience to imitate Peter's ascetic virtues, which are presented in a series of quotations from the Pauline letters and Matthew (§21). The author concludes the introduction with a statement that Peter was chosen for the honor that he received before his birth (§22) and presents a story in which Peter's birth is announced to his father Bosmarios, here employing citations from the annunciation to Mary in Luke 1 (§23).

The author then confirms Peter's precocious asceticism and spiritual wisdom as a child and a diplomatic hostage at the court of Emperor Theodosius II of Constantinople with several stories of the miracles that Peter performed as a child as well as the devilish temptations that he overcame (§§24–30). Next Peter meets his lifelong fellow ascetic, John, and the two of them devise a plan to run off to Jerusalem to dedicate their lives to God in ascetic holiness (§31). Peter and John escape at night from the royal court through the agency of the Persian martyrs whose relics Peter and John constantly venerated. Their destination: Jerusalem (§§32–33).

Peter and John carried the reliquary containing the bones of the martyrs through Asia Minor (§34), while the Holy Spirit made known their arrival in all the cities along their journey (§35). They were mistaken for runaway slaves and captured by a tax collector in one of the cities but were set free when the martyrs appeared to the tax collector in a dream (§§36–37). At last the youths arrived in Jerusalem in great joy and reverence (§38) and were received by Melania the Younger, her husband Pinianus, and her mother Albina, founders of monasteries for men and women whose story the author briefly recounts (§§39–41). Melania the Elder (§42) and Poemenia, the founder of the Church of the Ascension (§43), also receive brief mention.

The two saints became novices in the monastery for men on the Mount of Olives and received the monastic habit from Gerontius, the abbot of the monastery, whose holiness and ascetic miracles are recounted (§§44–48). The two saints are presented

Rabbula's parents, his strong-willed pagan father with connections to the emperor Julian and his equally resolute Christian mother, who strove constantly to convert her husband to Christianity, the author begins the narration of the events of Rabbula's life proper with the statement "From them was born the most heroic Rabbula, a zealot, a second Josiah, if this likeness by which we paint the honor of the saint is adequate."

as having had opportunity for contact with Cyril of Alexandria, who came to Jerusalem to perform the deposition of the relics of the Persian martyrs that were in Peter and John's possession (§49). From the author's perspective, Peter and John grew in spiritual athleticism in Jerusalem (§§50–51). Peter sought to imitate the blessed Passarion, the founder of a monastery for men distinguished by its unceasing services of prayer and hymnody (§52). Yet the devil afflicted Peter with a debilitating illness. After Peter rejected the devil's temptation, Christ showed him a vision in which monks were chanting psalms, and he promised Peter that he would establish a monastery through him (§53).

The author then begins to relate the story of how Peter moved from Jerusalem to Gaza (§54) but breaks off instead and retells the various miracles and signs that God worked through Peter and John, portents that foretold the coming events surrounding the Council of Chalcedon and its aftermath (§§55–62). Eventually the author returns to the subject of Peter's arrival in Gaza (§63).

Peter had built in Jerusalem a solitary monastery near the "Tower of David" (§64). When a dispute arose with the neighbor concerning the property line, words came to blows, and the neighbor punched John in his face. Yet John and Peter understood the beating as a share in Christ's own sufferings, and the next day God struck their bellicose neighbor (§65). Although without funds, Peter and John turned their monastery into a hostel and received pilgrims (§§66–67), but the abbot Zeno convinced them to return to the discipline of monastic life, and thus they entered a monastery (§§68–69). After proving themselves through asceticism and obedience, Zeno granted them permission to return to their own dwelling in Jerusalem (§70). Empress Eudocia, the wife of Theodosius II, whom Peter and John had known at the court, sought them out for spiritual guidance, yet at Zeno's advice Peter and John fled from her to avoid temptation, and they seem to have handed over their monastery to other monks (§71).

Finally the two arrived in a monastery in Gaza (§72). Peter's ordination to the priesthood is foretold (§73), after Juvenal of Jerusalem had tried to ordain him already in Jerusalem (§74). In the end, Paul, Juvenal's nephew and the bishop of Gaza, tricked Peter into ordination, yet Peter refrained from all ministry until his ordination to the episcopacy seven years later (§75).

Next the author sets the background to the events following the Council of Chalcedon. With Juvenal definitively accepting the decrees of the council, the anti-Chalcedonian bishops of Palestine, as well as Archbishop Dioscorus of Alexandria, went into exile (§§76–77). The inhabitants of Maiuma, Gaza, forcibly brought Peter to Theodosius, the anti-Chalcedonian bishop of Jerusalem, to be ordained as their bishop. Warned in a vision not to flee, Peter continued to resist serving at the altar until popular pressure won the day, and in the end a eucharistic service confirmed Peter's worthiness (§§78–80).

Peter remained in Gaza for six months, after which time the emperor issued a decree that all anti-Chalcedonian bishops were to agree to the decisions of Chalcedon or vacate their sees (§81). With the blessing of Theodosius of Jerusalem, Peter fled to Alexandria (§82). During the slaying of Dioscorus's partisans in the theater (§83), Peter saw a vision of the souls of these newly departed martyrs (§84). Proterius, the pro-Chalcedonian bishop of Alexandria, in vain sent men to kill Peter (§85). Instead, Peter arrived in Oxyrhynchos in the Upper Thebaid (§§86–87), where through heavenly guidance he denounced all the errors contained in the decree of Chalcedon (§88). Meanwhile, Dioscorus died in exile (§89). Proterius continued the persecution of anti-Chalcedonian Christians in Egypt. After Emperor Marcian had died (§90), Peter returned to Alexandria. While the city rejoiced over Marcian's death, the monks there, headed by Longinus, arranged for Timothy Aelurus to be ordained bishop of Alexandria, an act performed by Peter the Iberian and Eusebius of Pelusium (§91). Proterius ratchetted up his persecution, plunging Alexandria into violent confusion (§§92–94). With Proterius murdered by one of his guards, the frenzied crowds treated his corpse with the utmost disrespect (§95). All the while Emperor Leo commanded that Timothy should be enthroned as Proterius's successor. After seven years, Timothy was forced into exile in Gangra (§97). Since another bishop Timothy (Salophaciolus), a pro-Chalcedonian, was appointed, Peter remained in Egypt to minister to the anti-Chalcedonian Christians (§98). During the remainder of his time there, Peter experienced several miracles that confirmed the truth of the anti-Chalcedonian position and Peter's sanctity (§§99–104).

Satisfied that the threat against the anti-Chalcedonian Christians had come to an end, Peter returned to Palestine and settled in the vicinity of Ashkelon. While there, he attracted many novices and traveled extensively throughout the region to minister to the anti-Chalcedonian Christians (§105). At the ascension to the throne of Emperor Basiliscus, anti-Chalcedonian bishops were restored to their sees, first among them Timothy Aelurus of Alexandria (§106). The author of the *Vita Petri Iberi* alludes to his own ordination to the priesthood and that he was living in Antioch (§107) when Emperor Zeno came to power and reversed Basiliscus's decrees (§108). Despite Timothy Aelurus urging him to come back to Egypt, Peter had declined, citing his spiritual needs and those of the Christians of Palestine as the reason (§109). Timothy died just before he was to go into exile (§110). Peter remained in Palestine to resist the Chalcedonian hierarchs (§111).

Theodore, a lawyer living in Antioch and an acquaintance of the author of the *Vita Petri Iberi*, had fled to Palestine to escape the pro-Chalcedonian bishop Calendion and to become one of Peter's disciples (§112). In elliptical speech, the author states that this Theodore had convinced him to join him in Palestine and likewise become part of the circle of Peter's disciples (§§113–115).

A lengthy account of Peter's first journey throughout Palestine follows (§§116–164), with miracles recounted at every stage. The author speaks of Peter's gastro-intestinal ailment for which he sought aid at several of the hot springs east of Jerusalem (§§116–117). Peter set out to bathe in the spring at Livias, in Arabia, near Madeba,[197] and then moved on to Baʾar. En route he and his troupe passed by Mount Pisgah, where the Christians had erected a church to commemorate the tomb of Moses. Peter fondly recollected an earlier meeting with an ascetic on this mountain, at

[197] On Madeba and the famous Madeba Map, a mosaic kept in the Greek Orthodox Church of St. George, Madeba, Jordan, which details many of the sites frequently visited by Christian pilgrims to the Middle East, see Herbert Donner, *The Mosaic Map of Madaba: An Introductory Guide* (Kampen: Kok Pharos, 1992); and Michele Piccirillo, *Chiese e Mosaici di Madaba* (Collectio maior 34; Jerusalem: Franciscan Printing Press, 1989). For an attractive presentation of the Madeba mosaic map and discussion of recent excavations and archaeological surveys in the area, see Michele Piccirillo and Eugenio Alliata, eds., *The Madaba Map Centenary 1897–1997: Travelling through the Byzantine Umayyad Period* (Collectio maior 40; Jerusalem: Studium Biblicum Franciscanum, 1999).

which time the ascetic foretold the Council of Chalcedon and Peter's future episcopacy (§§118–119). The site provided the ideal setting to instruct the disciples with a story of the miraculous revelation of the tomb of Moses (§§120–121).

Having successfully prayed and ended a drought in Madeba shortly before Pentecost (§122), Peter arrived in Baʾar with the magistrates and citizens of Madeba in tow. The stifling heat that normally prevented the citizens from using the baths was suddenly cooled (§123) and a fire that threatened to destroy their property was quickly extinguished through Peter's intercession (§124). The infestations of flies that normally surrounded the baths were nowhere to be seen while Peter was present (§125). In addition, the author recounts the "miracle" of the hot and cold running water that created a temperate bath there (§126).

After the Feast of the Ascension, Peter and company returned to Madeba, where Peter's prayers granted a sterile woman offspring (§127) and reconciled another couple also by promising them children (§128). A dreadful vision Peter received foreshadowed and warned of the events following the Council of Chalcedon (§129).

The group departed from Madeba after a few days and traveled to Batmin, where they celebrated Pentecost before returning to Jerusalem (§130). However, the tribune Elijah persuaded Peter to remain in the mountains on account of the heat (§131). The author conveys Elijah's story of how Peter had healed his ears (§132). Elijah himself conducted Peter to the village of Beth Tafsha, five miles north of Jerusalem, to spend the rest of the summer there; at that site also a small fish-pond miraculously returned sufficient food for the saint (§133).

Later Peter joined the rest of his disciples in the low country, having been seen beforehand by a monk who in a vision realized that Peter had been constantly visiting the holy sites of Jerusalem all over the summer, albeit at night (§§134–135). Peter then left his disciples in the plain and made further excursions (§136). Dionysios, a lawyer in Gaza, asked Peter to live with him in Magdal Tutha, near the church of Saint Hilarion south of the city. Peter blessed the lawyer's vineyards so that they bore a great abundance of good wine (§137). While Peter was in the area, Abba Isaiah the Egyptian was also dwelling nearby in Beth Daltha. The author recounts the spiritual bond that formed between Peter and Abba

Isaiah (§§138–139). At the time, Emperor Zeno summoned both Peter and Abba Isaiah to Constantinople, on account of the miracles that each had been performing. Distressed at the thought of meeting the pro-Chalcedonian Zeno, Peter sent off a petition to Zeno pretentiously pleading that on account of old age the two of them could not make the journey. He quickly decided to lay low in Phoenicia until his contacts in Constantinople had persuaded Zeno to rescind his summons (§140).

En route through Phoenicia, Peter arrived at the city of Arca, near Tripoli, and his disciples traveled from near Jerusalem to join him there. The magistrate Maximus welcomed Peter on order from Saint Andrew, but the pro-Chalcedonian bishop of the city forced them to leave (§140). Peter fled the city and caught up with his disciples, and they all went to Orthosias on the sea, where they spent the winter in a salt depot. Peter recruited numerous anti-Chalcedonian disciples in Arca and Orthosias (§141). At the time of their stay in the region, a gardener living close to the salt depot saw in a dream a revelation of the martyrs Lucas, Phocas, Romanus, and their companions and discovered their burial site (§§142–144). Guided by Peter, he told the local bishop, who came and had the relics unearthed; after the Feast of Pascha, the bishop deposited their relics in the *martyrion* of Sergius and Bacchus. Additional signs and wonders followed (§145).

After Pentecost, Peter and his disciples traveled to Tripoli, where they were guests on the estate of the *comes* Apringius, just outside the city. Here Peter received word from Zeno that he did not have to travel to Constantinople (§146), while one of the brethren witnessed a miracle at the *martyrion* of St. Leontius (§§147–148).

Peter grew anxious to return to Gaza, knowing that his death was close at hand. As he prepared to depart from Tripoli by ship, he suddenly changed his mind and decided instead to go to Beirut (§149). However, his disciples boarded the ship and sailed to Long Village, where they stayed with the family of Basilides, one of Peter's monks. In the meantime, the author recounts how a vision had induced Peter to abandon his plans and instead win souls among the law students in Beirut, a task at which he proved rather successful (§§150–152).

Eventually Peter caught up again with the rest of his disciples in Long Village and traveled on to Tyre (§153), where he recruited the Jewish girl Eugenia into his circle of followers (§154). Magistrates from Beirut and Tyre came to receive his blessing, and Peter exhorted them to good works worthy of the faith (§155). In his instructions, Peter gave them three commandments that ensure salvation: until the end of their lives, they should adhere to the orthodox faith; they should always speak the truth; and they should remain far from all fornication and lasciviousness (§§156–157).

Next Peter came to Ptolemaïs, where he attracted a certain Aaron to the monastic life, and eventually he moved on to Caesarea, where the other brethren had been waiting for him (§§158–159). The author presents a digression on the abbot Gregory and the blessed Sabina, whose convent the aforementioned Eugenia of Tyre entered (§160). Abba Gregory received Peter and remained with him until they arrived in Caesarea (§161).

After celebrating Pascha and Pentecost in Caesarea, the group journeyed on to Ashdod, where they stayed in a poor and miserable dwelling on the shore (§162). All of Peter's acquaintances from Maiuma and Gaza as well as from Ashdod came out to meet him (§163). They attempted to persuade him to return to Gaza, but he rejected this entreaty, knowing that his death was near and desiring to die as a foreigner in a strange land (§164).

The last section of the *Vita Petri Iberi* recounts Peter's final days and the events following his death (§§165–193). After a brief introduction to this section (§165), the author tells that Peter fell ill and made out a will while still in Ashdod (§166). The announcement of the death of Abba Isaiah reached him there as well, and Peter expected that his own turn had come (§§167–168). Abba Isaiah's successor, Abba Peter the priest, visited Peter the Iberian's disciples and recounted the wondrous death of Abba Isaiah (§169).

Having moved from Ashdod to the fortress in Jamnia with Peter, Peter the Iberian's disciples witnessed many miracles and exorcisms, including the healing of a Jewish fisherman (§170). At the time of the commemoration of the death of John the Eunuch, Peter's companion, a shortage of fish was relieved by a miracle (§171). Peter's last walk to his deathbed is recounted in poignant detail (§172). First the imminent death of Peter the Iberian was revealed to one of his disciples, Abba Sana, who saw the heavenly council debating whether Peter should be released from his tribulations in this world or remain to strengthen the orthodox in their time of need (§§173–174). Then Peter celebrated the commemoration of John (§175). The author of the *Vita Petri Iberi* recounts the contents of Peter's will and identifies the four heirs whom he appointed (§176).[198] Peter was to see one last vision, the contents of which are not divulged, and then he was ready to die (§177).

At the time of his death, with Peter were Abba John, his heir, and a few of his closest disciples, to whom Peter entrusted the authority of the monastery (§178). The author then states that Peter called the brethren together and gave them their final instructions before his death: they were to avoid all heresies, especially that of the Chalcedonians; they were to have faith and were to preserve their chastity (§179).[199] On the night of Peter's death, the priest Athanasius from Egypt saw a vision of the eulogy in heaven for Peter the Iberian, given by Peter of Alexandria (§180). The disciples fasted the whole day, and around dinnertime Peter gave the brethren his last blessing; the priest Abba Gregory closed Peter's eyes (§181).

Abba Gregory and a few disciples prepared Peter's body for burial, clothing it in his vestments and placing it in the church, where they spent the night keeping vigil (§182). After the eucharistic service offered on Peter's behalf, some of his disciples took his body secretly to Maiuma to be entombed in his old monastery (§§183–184). Other disciples remained in Jamnia. At dinner, Abba Maxos revealed to them visions that he had seen on two occasions while standing beside Peter as he performed the divine liturgy (§§185–187).

Before dawn, Abba Gregory deposed Peter's body in a sarcophagus under the altar in the church of his monastery in Maiuma, next to the bodies of John the Eunuch and Abraham of Athrib, whose connection with Peter the author recounts (§188). The people of Maiuma, learning of the death of Peter, ran to his tomb and, discovering that his body had already been buried, venerated his sarcophagus and prepared to perform vigils for the next seven days (§§189–190). Since the church was too small to accommodate all the pilgrims who had come, the brethren, led by Theodore, eventually undertook the renovation of the monastery, which was completed in time for the translation of Peter's relics

[198] This seems to be a different will from the one he made out in Ashdod.

[199] Much of §§165–193 is told out of sequence, with repetitions, as though it were a harmonization of different accounts.

to a place under the altar on the first anniversary of his death (§§191–192). The author concludes with the dates on which the memorials of Peter's death, translation, and burials are celebrated (§193).

Outline of the De obitu Theodosii

Following the *Vita Petri Iberi*, the manuscript continues with the account of the deaths of Theodosius of Jerusalem and Abba Romanus. The author recalls the promise he had made in the *Vita Petri Iberi* to recount Theodosius's death (§1). Theodosius of Jerusalem had been driven out by Emperor Marcian and had gone into hiding in Egypt while Romanus was imprisoned in Antioch (§2). A conflict between Romanus and a certain Timothy, who is otherwise not mentioned by John Rufus, attracted the attention of Theodosius. He traveled to Antioch to attempt to mediate the dispute and to visit Simeon the Stylite (§3). However, Theodosius was caught near Antioch (§4), and Marcian commanded that he be taken to Constantinople. Failing to persuade Theodosius to abandon his opposition to Chalcedon, Marcian had him imprisoned in a cell filled with lime during the winter, without allowing any visitors (§5). After Marcian had died, Emperor Leo was informed that Theodosius was at his end, and he permitted Theodosius to be taken to Sykai, where he died shortly thereafter (§6). In a vision, Peter saw Theodosius being translated to heaven. In Sykai, the brethren quickly took Theodosius's body out of the city by ship and buried him in Cyprus, in an anti-Chalcedonian monastery; Theodosius is commemorated on the day after James, the first bishop of Jerusalem (§7).

Meanwhile, Romanus spent five years in exile, during which time his grace and eloquence converted many to oppose Chalcedon (§8). While Romanus was in exile, a famine gripped Palestine, and the inhabitants turned against Juvenal, the pro-Chalcedonian bishop of Jerusalem. Juvenal petitioned Marcian through Empress Eudocia to permit Romanus to return from Antioch. Permission was granted, and he settled in Eleutheropolis because his monastery in Tekoa was under Juvenal's jurisdiction. He established a new monastery in the village of Kefar Turban, where he died (§9). He was buried under the altar of the church of the prophet Zachariah in a natural cave that miraculously opened from the solid rock (§10). The author concludes with the date of the commemoration of Romanus and of Passarion, whose hostel had been the inspiration for Peter and John to build their own monastery in Jerusalem (§§11–13).

GENEALOGICAL TABLES OF THE FAMILIES OF PETER THE IBERIAN AND ZUZO

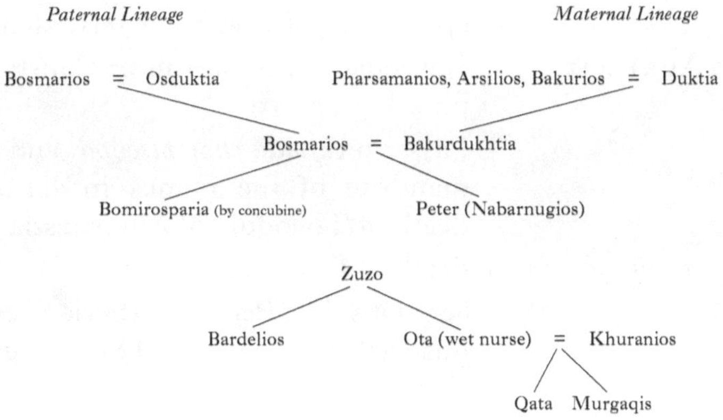

CHRONOLOGICAL TIMELINE

284–361	reign of Mirian III, the first Christian king of Iberia
315–392	lifetime of Apollinaris of Laodicea
325	Council of Nicaea I (First Ecumenical Council)
379–395	reign of Emperor Theodosius I
380–394	reign of Aspacures III of Iberia
381	Council of Constantinople I (Second Ecumenical Council)
382	birth of Melania the Younger
385–412	episcopacy of Theophilus of Alexandria
ca. 395	birth of Abba Gerontius of Jerusalem
402–404	John Chrysostom of Constantinople sent into exile
407	death of John Chrysostom
410	Council of Seleucia-Ctesiphon; establishment of autonomous Christian church in Persia

412–444	episcopacy of Cyril of Alexandria
ca. 413/417	birth of Peter the Iberian (subsequent calculations are based on 417)
415	torture and murder of the philosopher Hypatia with the involvement of Cyril
417	arrival of Melania the Younger in Jerusalem
422–458	episcopacy of Juvenal of Jerusalem
428 (10 Apr.)–431	episcopacy of Nestorius of Constantinople
428	Passarion made *chorepiscopos* and archimandrite of the monks in Jerusalem; death of Theodore of Mopsuestia
428/29 or 429/30 (win.)	death of Passarion
429	at age twelve, Peter the Iberian sent as a hostage to the court of Theodosius II at Constantinople
430	Abba Isaiah heard of the anti-Chalcedonian prophetic announcement made by Abba Paul of Thebes
431	Council of Ephesus (Third Ecumenical Council)
431 (22 Jun.)	Nestorius deposed at first "Cyrillian" session of Council of Ephesus
437	upon Theodosius II's invitation, Melania the Younger visited Constantinople, where she may also have met Peter the Iberian
437 (Feb.)	Melania returned to Jerusalem from her visit to Constantinople
437	Peter the Iberian, now twenty, and John the Eunuch escaped from Constantinople and went on a pilgrimage to the Holy Land; entered Melania's monastery on the Mount of Olives
438–457	reign of Yazdegerd II of Persia
438	First pilgrimage of Empress Eudocia to Jerusalem

438 (15 Mar.)	Empress Eudocia invited Cyril of Alexandria to come to Jerusalem for the consecration of the Church of St. Stephen
438 (16 Mar.)	at Eudocia's request, Cyril of Alexandria deposited the relics of the Forty Martyrs of Sebaste (Armenia) and a relic of St. Stephen in a *martyrion* on the Mount of Olives; at that occasion, also the Persian martyrs' relics that Peter had brought from Constantinople were deposited
439	death of Melania the Younger
440–461	episcopacy of Pope Leo the Great
440–468	episcopacy of Basil of Seleucia
440–521	lifetime of Philoxenus of Mabbugh
441–442	Empress Eudocia settled at Jerusalem while Peter avoided visiting her
444	Peter left Jerusalem and settled in the Gaza area
445/446	Peter the Iberian's ordination to the priesthood by Paul of Maiuma
445/446	death of Theodotus, the outspoken anti-Nestorian bishop of Ancyra, who wrote a multivolume work against Nestorius
446	death of Proclus, bishop of Constantinople; displayed an anti-Nestorian theological mindset; coined the Theopaschite formula *unus e Trinitate passus*
446–449	episcopacy of Flavian of Constantinople
447–522	reign of Vakht'ang Gorgasali of Iberia and Lazica
448	Synod of Constantinople
449 (13 Jun.)	Pope Leo the Great wrote *Tome* to Flavian of Constantinople
449	Second Council of Ephesus ("the Robber Council"), at which Juvenal of Jerusalem and twenty-one Palestinian bishops supported Dioscorus, Cyril of Alexandria's successor

450 (Apr.)	death of Bishop Flavian of Constantinople from beatings at the Robber Council of Ephesus; Anatolius becomes bishop of Constantinople
450 (16 Jul.)	*Tome of Leo* sent to Anatolius of Constantinople
450 (28 Jul.)	death of Emperor Theodosius II
450 (25 Aug.)–457	Emperor Marcian, husband of Pulcheria, ruler of Eastern Roman Empire
450 (21 Oct.)	Anatolius of Constantinople signed the *Tome of Leo*
451	Council of Chalcedon (Fourth Ecumenical Council), at which Jerusalem was granted the status of patriarchate; the Chalcedonian Martyrius fled from Egypt to the Judean Desert; rejection of Council of Chalcedon by some in the Holy Land against the position taken by Juvenal of Jerusalem; death of the hermit Zeno
ca. 451	death of Nestorius at the Great Oasis (Upper Egypt)
after 451	death of Hesychius of Jerusalem
451–453	Theodosius functioned as anti-Chalcedonian bishop of Jerusalem
451–521	lifetime of Jacob of Sarug
452–453	Juvenal of Jerusalem cast out from his see; gathered forces in Constantinople; beginnings of anti-Chalcedonian church in Palestine
452/453	Peter the Iberian consecrated as bishop; began his priestly activities only after his reordination to the priesthood also at the hands of Theodosius of Jerusalem
452 (25 Nov.)	Letter 109 of Pope Leo to Bishop Julian of Cos concerning the rebellious monks in Palestine
453 (Jun.)	Letter 123 of Pope Leo to Empress Eudocia concerning the rebellious monks in Palestine

453 (Aug.)	Chalcedonian Bishop Juvenal returned to Jerusalem with army to crush the anti-Chalcedonian rebellion
453	Jerusalem briefly has two functioning bishops: the Chalcedonian Juvenal and the anti-Chalcedonian Theodosius
ca. 453–457	Theodosius of Jerusalem captured at Antioch; taken to Constantinople at the order of Emperor Marcian; imprisoned in Dios monastery; eventually died there
454 (4 Sep.)	Letter 139 of Pope Leo to Juvenal of Jerusalem concerning religious practices in holy places
455	Peter the Iberian left for Egypt
456	influx of monks from Asia Minor into Palestine, among them the famous monk Sabas
457–474	reign of Emperor Leo; champion of Chalcedon
457	anti-Chalcedonian Theodosius of Jerusalem left his exile in Egypt and headed to Antioch in order to solve a dispute there; later captured at Antioch and taken to Constantinople at the order of Emperor Leo
457–460, 475–477	episcopacy of Timothy Aelurus
459–478	Patriarch Anastasius of Jerusalem, a Chalcedonian; under influence of Emperor Basiliscus subscribed to *Encyclical*; gained him repudiation under Emperor Zeno
460 (20 Oct.)	death of anti-Chalcedonian Empress Eudocia
465–538	lifetime of Severus of Antioch
468–470	Peter the Fuller's insertion of the words "who was crucified for us" into the Trisagion troparion
474–475, 476–491	reign of Emperor Zeno

475 (Jan.)–summer 476	reign of Emperor Flavius Basiliscus; at this time Peter the Fuller was archbishop of Antioch; Basiliscus supported anti-Chalcedonians; he reestablished Timothy Aelurus as anti-Chalcedonian bishop of Alexandria
475–476	Basiliscus issued *Encyclical*, which annulled the decisions of Chalcedon
475	Peter returned to the Holy Land near Ashkelon
475–before August 476	John Rufus ordained as a priest in Antioch
476	Zeno overthrew Basiliscus and annulled his *Encyclical*
476	Peter Fuller, anti-Chalcedonian bishop of Antioch, just returned from exile and, as a consequence of Zeno's actions, had to leave again
476	death of anti-Chalcedonian bishop Timothy Aelurus
477	second exile of Bishop Peter the Fuller under Emperor Zeno
478–486	episcopacy of Martyrius, Chalcedonian bishop of Jerusalem, as the successor of Athanasius of Jerusalem
479–484	Calendion as bishop of Antioch, a Chalcedonian supporter
479	Martyrius, the new Patriarch of Jerusalem, achieved a union between Chalcedonian and anti-Chalcedonian sides in Palestine; reconciled with some anti-Chalcedonians; was successful by way of compromise
480–485	death of Abba Gerontius
481	Zeno invited Peter the Iberian and Abba Isaiah to Constantinople in order to "convert" them; Peter fled to regions of *Palaestina*, *Arabia*, *Phoenicia*
482/484 (13 Dec.)	martyrdom of Shushanik, Georgian princess

482	Zeno issued *Henotikon* as a document of reconciliation between Chalcedonians and anti-Chalcedonians
482–565	lifetime of Emperor Justinian I, supporter of Theopaschitism
484–518	Acacian schism
485	Peter the Fuller regained the Patriarchate of Antioch
485–488	Peter the Iberian lived in close proximity to Abba Isaiah's monastery in Beth Daltha in a village known as Magdal Tutha
486	Severus, monk and future anti-Chalcedonian patriarch of Antioch, took up studies of law in Beirut
488	Severus of Antioch was baptized in *martyrion* of Leontius of Tripoli in Phoenicia; probable year of meeting between him and Peter the Iberian
ca. 490s	biography of Peter the Iberian composed by Zacharias Rhetor/Scholasticus
490–570s	lifetime of John Philoponos
490	Severus of Antioch visited Jerusalem; came under influence of Peter's ascetic heritage; founded an anti-Chalcedonian monastery near that of Peter's
491 (11 Aug.)	death of Abba Isaiah
491	death of Peter the Iberian in Jamnia
491–518	reign of Emperor Anastasius, who succeeded to the throne of Zeno and gave full freedom to the anti-Chalcedonians
492–494	new movement of Chalcedonian defenders championed their cause in the Holy Land
492	by a common vote the monks Sabas and Theodosius (both Chalcedonians) elected as archimandrites for the *lavrai* and *coenobia*
494–513	patriarchate of Elias of Jerusalem

495	foundation of a guest-house of Mar Sabas's *lavra* in Jerusalem
498–514	Pope Symmachus of Rome
ca. 500	John Rufus wrote the *Vita Petri Iberi*
512 (8 or 16 Nov.)–518	Severus served as anti-Chalcedonian patriarch of Antioch instead of the deposed Flavian
512–518	anti-Chalcedonian triumph in Palestine
519–538	episcopacy of John of Tella
521	persecution of anti-Chalcedonians, except in Egypt
527–565	reign of Emperor Justinian I
527–545	episcopacy of Ephrem of Antioch
553	Second Council of Constantinople (Fifth Ecumenical Council)
580	Iberia became a vassal of the Persian shah
608	Georgian church under Bishop Kyrion II reversed its position: accepted Chalcedon and separated from the Armenian church
741	date of MS Sachau 321, which includes the *Vita Petri Iberi*
787	Second Council of Nicaea (Seventh Ecumenical Council)
875	date of writing of MS BM Add. 14,650, which contains Syriac text of *Plerophoriae*
ninth–tenth centuries	time during which MS BM Add. 14,631, which preserves the *Plerophoriae*, was copied

Account of the Way of Life of the Holy Peter the Iberian, Bishop, Approved Confessor, and Ascetic of Our Lord

Text and Translation

—

On the Memory of How the Blessed Theodosius, Bishop of Jerusalem, Departed to Our Lord

Text and Translation

ܬܫܥܝܬܐ ܕܕܘܒܪܘ̈ܗܝ ܕܩܕܝܫܐ ܦܛܪܘܣ
ܐܝܒܪܝܐ ܐܦܝܣܩܘܦܐ ܘܡܘܕܝܢܐ ܒܚܝܪܐ
ܘܡܘܬܐ ܕܗ̈ܘܢ

(§1) [R 3] ܕܐܬܕܟܪܘ ܠܡܕܒܪ̈ܢܐ ܕܝܠܢ: ܗܢ ܦܘܠܘܣ ܫܠܝܚܐ ܐܠܗܝܐ ܦܩܕܢ. ܟܕ ܐܡܪ ܗܟܢܐ. ܐܬܕܟܪܘ ܠܡܕܒ̈ܪܢܝܟܘܢ: ܗܠܝܢ ܕܡܠܠܘ ܥܡܟܘܢ ܡܠܬܐ ܕܐܠܗܐ. ܗܢܘܢ ܕܟܕ ܡܬܒܩܝܢ ܐܢܬܘܢ ܒܫܘܠܡܐ ܕܕܘܒܪ̈ܝܗܘܢ ܐܬܕܡܘ ܒܗܝܡܢܘܬܗܘܢ ܀

(§2) ܐܝܟ ܗܿܝ ܡܟܝܠ ܕܫܘܕܥܬܐ ܒܐܝܬܐ ܦܪܝܫܝܢ ܚܢܢ ܘܕܫܦܝܪܐ ܠܐܠܗܐ: ܘܦܘܩܕܢܐ ܫܠܝܚܝܐ ܡܫܡܠܝܢ ܚܢܢ. ܗܕܐ ܒܝܕ ܥܘܗܕܢܐ ܡܬܬܒܥܝܢ ܚܢܢ ܕܗܕܐ ܢܥܒܕ. ܐܝܟ ܕܒܫܪ̈ܪܐ ܠܗ̇: ܐܘܪܚܐ ܪܒܬܐ ܕܦܘܪܩܢܐ ܐܚܝܕܐ ܠܡܬܚ̈ܪܐ: ܗܠܝܢ ܕܡܫ̈ܠܡܬܐ ܓܠܝܢ ܘܕܢܬܕܡܘܢ ܫܘܝܢ: ܕܒܪ̈ܐ ܡܬܚܙܝܢ ܕܗܢܘܢ ܕܒܐܠܗܐ ܗܘܘ ܬܝ̈ܒܐ. ܠܐ ܕܝܢ

[1] "Approved" here translates ܒܚܝܪܐ, which in early Christian discourse in Syriac not infrequently is used as honorary title for ascetics.

[2] The title is part of the transmission history of the text. See MS Sachau 321, folio 68 verso, bottom of the right-hand column, partly legible; MS BM Add 12,174, folio 48b, clearly legible. For discussion, see Cornelia Horn, "Beyond Theology: The Career of Peter the Iberian in the Christological Controversies of Fifth- and Sixth-Century Palestine" (Ph. D. diss., The Catholic University of America, 2001), 7 and n. 17; see also more recently Horn, *Asceticism and Christological Controversy*, 14–15.

[3] Square brackets include page references to Richard Raabe's edition of the *Vita Petri Iberi*.

[4] Heb 13:7: Μνημονεύετε τῶν ἡγουμένων ὑμῶν, οἵτινες ἐλάλησαν ὑμῖν τὸν λόγον τοῦ θεοῦ, ὧν ἀναθεωροῦντες τὴν ἔκβασιν τῆς ἀναστροφῆς μιμεῖσθε τὴν πίστιν. The Syriac version of the scriptural verse differs from the Greek version most importantly in the connotations its rendering of the Greek suggests for the phrase "outcome of the way of life," ܫܘܠܡܐ ܕܕܘܒܪ̈ܐ. ܕܘܒܪ̈ܐ designates the art of ascetic practices that are unto salvation as well as a "way of life" in a cultural or philosophical context. For a Christian monastic audience, this word would

Account of the Way of Life of the Holy Peter the Iberian, Bishop, Approved[1] Confessor, and Ascetic of Our Lord[2]

[R 3] (§1)[3] We are commanded by the divine Apostle Paul to remember our leaders when he says the following, "Remember your leaders, those who spoke with you the word of God. Just as you have observed the perfection of their way of life, imitate their faith!"[4]

(§2) So we are now repaying a just debt[5] and one that is well-pleasing to God,[6] while fulfilling the apostolic command.[7] Furthermore, we are required to do this with care,[8] for truly the excellent way of life of those who led others toward God is a great path of salvation for those disciples who are zealous[9] for what is

have strong overtones of ascetic practice. ܫܘܠܡܐ can mean at once the end of a period of time, such as a lifetime, or the completion of something, but also consummation or perfection. For other instances of the use of Heb 13:7 in early Christian, ascetic, anti-Chalcedonian literature, see, e.g., Stephen of Heracleopolis, *Panegyric on Apollo*: ⲡⲁⲓ ⲉⲧϫⲱ ⲙⲙⲟⲥ ϫⲉⲁⲣⲓⲡⲙⲉⲉⲩⲉ ⲛⲛⲉⲓⲛⲛⲟϭ (Kuhn, 1:34,24); "For I did not write these things as though telling you his life, since I am not fit for this sort of undertaking, but I did this as though fulfilling the apostolic command of him who says: *Remember your great ones*. For he whom we honour is truly great in heaven and upon earth" (2:26,19).

5 Allusion to Matt 6:12b.

6 1 Thess 2:4.

7 Possibly an allusion to Col 3:20.

8 Heb 3:12.

9 It is instructive to note the frequency (more than 50 times) of occurrences of the words "zealous" or "zeal" throughout the text. Underlying this emphasis seems to be an interest on the part of the author to stress the dedication of anti-Chalcedonians to the cause of the true faith, manifested in proper practices as much as in right belief.

ܠܗ ܕܡܕܒܪܢܐ ܟܠܗܘܢ. ܐܠܐ ܘܕܪܥܝܐ ܛܒܐ. ܘܕܐܒܐ ܪܚܡ ܝܠܕܐ.
ܘܕܐܦܝܣܩܘܦܐ ܚܝܠܐ. ܘܕܡܕܒܪܢܐ ܕܕܚܠܬ ܐܠܗܐ ܘܡܗܕܝܢܐ ܕܫܒ̈ܝܠ
ܦ̈ܘܩܕܢܐ. ܠܡܗܕܝܢܐ ܘܢܦܫܗ ܣܡ ܠܗ. ܗܘ ܕܫܘܐܠܬ ܪܚܝܡ ܠܟܠܢ.
ܘܠܗ ܕܐܡܪ ܘܠܗܠܝܢ ܕܫܡܥܝܢ ܒܗ ܒܡܡܠܬܐ. ܐܝܟܢܐ ܕܟܠܗ
ܫܘܒܚܬܐ ܢܬܠ. ܕܟܠܝܠܐ ܘܡܫܒܚܐ ܕܬܫܒܘܚܬܐ ܢܣܒ: ܒܗ ܟܠ
ܬ̈ܠܘܬܗ ܡܫܒ̈ܚܬܐ ܬܬܠܝܢ ܚܢܢ. ܘܐܦ ܠܗ ܐܝܟ ܕܫܘܒܚܐ. ܐܠܐ [R 4]
ܒܫܘܪܝܬܗ ܕܟܬܒܐ ܫܘܒܚܐ ܕܚܝܒܝܢ ܚܢܢ ܢܦܪܘܥ܀

(§3) ܪܫܐ ܕܝܢ ܒܟܠܗܝܢ ܕܬܫܒܘܚܬܐ ܕܡܛܠܬܗ. ܫܘܪܝܐ ܕܝܠܝܕܘܬ
ܫܪܒܬܗ. ܡܛܠ ܗܘ ܕܐܦܢܝܐ ܠܫܘܬܐܣܬ. ܕܐܠܗܐ ܒܪܐ ܕܐܝ̈ܒܪܝܐ.
ܘܒܪܐ ܕܐܝ̈ܒܪܝܐ ܡܠܟܝܢ. ܘܡܢ ܓܢܣܐ ܡܠܟܝܐ ܘܡܠܟܘܬܐ ܒܡܫܝܚܐ܀

(§4) ܐܬܪܐ ܗܘ ܡܢ ܓܒܠ ܐܝܬܘܗܝ ܗܘܐ ܠܡܠܟܐ ܦܪܘܣ. ܐܬܪܐ
ܕܐܝܒܪܝܐ. ܡܫܡܗܐ ܕܗܘܢ ܒܪܒܢܐ. ܕܠܘܬ ܡܕܢܚ ܫܡܫܐ ܗܘܝܢ.

[1] Allusion to Tit 2:14.
[2] Allusion to Ps 119:35.
[3] John 10:11, 14; 1 Pet 5:4.
[4] The Syriac ܪܚܡ ܝܠܕܐ may translate the Greek φιλόστοργος (Raabe, 13 n. 6).
[5] 1 Pet 2:25.
[6] 1 John 4:15; Rom 15:9, 14:11.
[7] For the implied allusion to the crown of glory, see 1 Pet 5:4.

good[1] and who delight in imitating it.[2] Now placed before us is not only the memory of a leader but also of a good shepherd,[3] and the love of a compassionate[4] father; of a holy bishop,[5] of a confessor of the fear of God,[6] and of a martyr many times over,[7] one equally beloved by all, both speaker and hearers alike. As befitting great cheer, let us take up the word and the renowned report[8] concerning him, placing our trust in his holy prayers.[9] Although it is not as it deserves,[10] **[R 4]** we shall willingly repay the debt as far as we are able.[11]

(§3) We begin his story with the genealogical origin[12] of his family, because it has been fittingly said, "God is with the generation of the righteous,"[13] "the generation of the righteous is blessed,"[14] and, "they are a chosen race" and "a priestly kingdom."[15]

(§4) Now, the country of the blessed Peter was the famous country of the Iberians, those northerners[16] set toward the rising

[8] Probably based on the Greek idiom λόγον καὶ ἀκοήν; see Heb 11:2, 11:39, 1 Tim 3:7.

[9] Phlm 1:22.

[10] Cf. Eph 2:9; Gal 2:16.

[11] 1 Tim 5:4.

[12] Matt 1:1.

[13] Ps 14:5.

[14] Ps 112:2.

[15] 1 Pet 2:9, see Exod 19:6, 23:22 (LXX).

[16] The Syriac ܓܪܒܝܐ may translate the Greek ἀρκτικοί (Raabe, 14 n. 4).

ܕܡܬܚܬܫ ܒܟܠܗܝܢ ܥܡ ܙ̈ܕܝܩܐ ܘܦܪ̈ܫܐ. ܟܕ ܢܦܩ ܟܠ ܚܕ ܡܢܗܘܢ
ܕܒܬܠܐ ܕܝܠܗ ܢܚܙܘܗܝ، ܠܐܬܪܐ: ܒܪܚܡܬܐ ܠܘܬ ܒܡܕܝܢܬܐ.
(§5) ܐܝܟ ܠܒܢܝܐ ܕܝܢ ܕܐܬܪܗܘܢ ܕܝܠܗܘܢ܆ ܡܕܝܢ ܐܝܬ ܗܘܐ ܠܗ
ܫܡܐ ܢܒܪܢܘܓܝܘܣ. ܟܕ ܕܝܢ ܐܫܬܘܝ ܠܐܣܟܝܡܐ ܩܕܝܫܐ ܕܕ̈ܝܪܝܐ.
ܗܝܕܝܢ ܐܬܝܗܒ ܠܗ ܫܡܐ ܦܛܪܘܣ. ܒܫܡܐ ܕܪܝܫܐ ܕܫ̈ܠܝܚܐ.
ܟܕ ܡܢ ܡܦܘܚܝܬܐ ܐܠܗܝܬܐ ܒܟܪ ܐܝܟ ܕܐܡܪܐ ܡܬܚܫܒ ܐܢܐ:
ܐܬܬܘܝܒ ܐܫܡܗܬܐ ܗ̇ܢܘܢ ܕܢܗܘܐ ܠܗ ܐܣܟܝܡܐ ܩܕܝܫܐ. ܡܛܠ
ܕܟܠܢܫ ܗܘܐ ܕܢܛܪ ܒܕܘܒܪܗ ܘܒܬܘܠܘܬܗ، ܘܒܦܐܪܫܘܬܐ ܕܡܫܝܚܘܬܗ:
ܗ̇ܝ، ܕܡܢܗ ܕܐܠܗܐ ܐܬܓܠܝܬ ܠܗ. ܕܡܛܠܬܗ̇ ܘܦܪܘܣܘ ܗܘܐ ܕܝܢ
ܟܐܦܐ ܫܡܗ ܗ̇ܘ. ܘܥܠ ܗܕܐ ܟܐܦܐ ܠܒܪܬܐ ܬܒ̈ܝܪܬܐ ܫܡܥܘܢ
ܫܬܐܣܗ. ܟܕ ܐܡܪ ܠܘܬܗ ܡܪܢܐ. ܐܢܬ ܗܘ ܟܐܦܐ ܘܥܠ ܗܕܐ
ܟܐܦܐ ܐܒܢܝܗ̇ ܠܥܕܬܝ، ܘܬܪ̈ܥܐ ܕܫܝܘܠ ܠܐ ܢܚܣܢܘܢܗ̇: ܘܐܬܠ ܠܟ
ܩ̈ܠܝܕܐ ܕܡܠܟܘܬܐ ܕܫܡܝܐ. ܘܡܕܡ ܕܬܐܣܘܪ ܒܐܪܥܐ ܢܗܘܐ ܐܣܝܪ
ܒܫܡܝܐ. ܘܡܕܡ ܕܬܫܪܐ ܒܐܪܥܐ ܢܗܘܐ [R 5] ܫܪܐ ܒܫܡܝܐ܀
(§6) ܕܦܛܪܘܣ ܗܘ ܡܟܝܠ ܛܘܒܢܐ ܐܒܐ ܕܝܠܢ ܘܐܦܝܣܩܘܦܐ: ܐܒܘܗܝ،
ܐܝܬܘܗܝ، ܗܘܐ ܒܘܣܡܪܝܘܣ ܡܠܟܐ ܕܐܝܒܪ̈ܝܐ. ܐܒܐ ܕܝܢ ܕܐܒܘܗܝ:
ܒܘܣܡܪܝܘܣ. ܐܡܗ ܕܝܢ ܒܩܘܪܘܦܝܐ. ܐܡܐ ܕܝܢ ܕܐܡܗ̇ ܡܪܝܬܐ
ܕܘܩܛܝܐ. ܘܐܚܘܗ̇ ܡܢ ܐܡܐ ܙܟܐ ܒܩܘܪܘܣ. ܒܥܠܗ̇ ܕܕܘܩܛܝܐ.
ܗ̇ܘ ܕܡܕܒܪܢܐ ܕܗ̇ܢܘܢ ܕܐܬܟܠܗ ܒܗ ܐܬܪܐ: ܡܠܟܐ ܒܪܫܦܝܪܐ

[1] The land of the Iberians had as borders Colchis in the west, the Caucasus in the north, Albania in the east (not to be confused with modern-day Albania in southeastern Europe; for a description of the ancient Albanians and their land, see Strabo, *Geogr.* 11.4.1–8 [Jones, 5:222–31]), and Armenia in the south. In antiquity, the country of the Iberians was known as *Iberia secunda*, literally "the second Iberia"; the ancients referred to Hibernia (Spain) as *Iberia prima*, i.e., "the first Iberia." For Strabo's description of Iberia, see *Geogr.* 11.3.1–6 (Jones, 5:216–21). Today the country of the Iberians is called Georgia.

[2] For a good summary of the constant struggles and military alliances between Iberia, Byzantium, and Persia, see Lordkipanidse and Brakmann, "Iberia II (Georgien)."

[3] *Vit. Pet.* §48 (R 32) recounts that Abba Gerontios gave Nabarnugios this new name, Peter.

of the sun[1] who are constantly fighting against the Romans and the Persians, each of whom is anxious to make the country [of Iberia] its own through a friendly alliance.[2]

(§5) In the language of their country, he first had the name Nabarnugios. Yet when he was deigned worthy of the holy habit of the monks, then the name Peter was [given] to him instead, being the name of the chief of the apostles.[3] Those fathers who gave him the holy habit were doubtless moved by divine inspiration, I believe, because he was to become zealous in his way of life, in his practices, and in the boldness of his faith, which had been entrusted to him by God, on account of which our Lord aforetime also named Peter "the Rock."[4] Upon this rock he founded the orthodox church, when he spoke to him saying, "You are 'the Rock,' and upon this rock I will build my church, and the gates of Sheol shall not prevail against it. I will give you the keys of the kingdom of heaven: whatever you will bind on earth will be bound in heaven, and whatever you will loose on earth will **[R 5]** be loosened in heaven."[5]

(§6) The father of our blessed father and bishop Peter was Bosmarios, king of the Iberians; his father's father was also Bosmarios;[6] his mother, Bakurduktia; his mother's mother, the holy Duktia. His maternal grandfather was the great Bakurios, the husband of Duktia [and] the first Christian king who ruled

[4] The Syriac text creates the impression that the apostle Peter and Peter the Iberian almost merge into one. It is not easy to differentiate which statements are to be ascribed to one and which to the other. Whether or not the underlying Greek also employed such ambiguity cannot be decided. As a feature of the Syriac text, however, the merging of different figures into one is reminiscent of what also happens in Syriac prose and poetic compositions with regard to the presentation of the different biblical Marys, who are seemingly confounded with one another.

[5] Matt 16:18–19.

[6] Raabe (15 n. 1) commented already that the manuscript witness for the name of Peter's father is not stable. See, e.g., below, *Vit. Pet.* §118 (R 86), which has ܢܒܪܘܢܘܓܝܘܣ ܒܪܗ ܕܒܘܣܡܘܪܝܘܣ ܒܪ ܒܘܣܪܘܡܝܘܣ i.e., literally "Nabronugios the son of Bosmorios son of Bosromios."

ܗܘ̣ܐ: ܘܠܟܠܗ ܗܘ ܒܒܢܝܐ ܗܕܐ، ܠܘܬ ܕܫܠܚ ܐܠܗܐ: ܗ̇ܢܘܢ ܕܒܗ
ܟܠܗܘܢ ܡ̈ܠܟܐ ܘܡ̈ܠܟܬܐ ܕܐܒ̈ܗܬܐ ܗ̣ܘܘ. ܒܗ̇ܝ ܕܡܬܝܪܬ ܬܘܒ
ܡܢܗ̇ ܘܡܠܟܘܬܐ ܕܫܡܝܐ. ܡܫܝܚܬܗ ܕܝܢ ܗ̇ܝ ܐܡܐ: ܐܘܕܘܩܣܝܐ
ܐܢܬܬܐ ܗ̇ܝ ܕܒܘܣܡܪܝܘܣ. ܐܡܐ ܕܝܢ ܕܒܘܣܡܪܝܘܣ ܐܒܘܗܝ܀
ܦܪܣܡܢܝܘܣ ܕܝܢ ܐܒܘܗܝ، ܗܘܐ ܐܚܐ: ܕܐܘܕܘܩܣܝܐ ܡܫܝܚܬܗ ܗ̇ܝ
ܐܒܐ ܗ̇ܘ ܕܒܪ ܡܫܒܚܐܝܬ ܐܒܘܗܝ، ܗܘܐ ܠܘܬ ܐܪܩܕܝܘܣ ܡ̇ܠܟܐ
ܕܪ̈ܘܡܝܐ: ܘܐܝܩܪܐ ܕܪܒ ܚܝܠܐ ܐܝܬ ܗܘܐ ܠܗ: ܘܪ̈ܫܝܬܐ ܡ̇ܠܬܐ
ܗܘܐ. ܠܫܪܪܬܐ ܕܢ ܡܢ ܡܫܝܚܘܬܐ ܕܐܘܪܬܕܘܟܣܝܐ ܐܝܬܝܗ ܕܐܪܩܕܝܘܣ
ܓ̣ܙܪ: ܘܐܫܟܚ ܕܢܬܦܪܫ. ܘܠܠܐܝܬ ܠܐܬܪܗ ܫܕܪ. ܘܟܕ ܐܡܠܟ ܥܠ
ܐܝܒܪ̈ܝܐ: ܘܠܗܘ̈ܢܝܐ ܣܘܪ̈ܝܐ ܥܒܕ ܒܗܘܢ: ܕܩ̈ܕܡܝܐ ܐܒܗ̈ܬܗܘܢ
ܕܐܝܒܪ̈ܝܐ: ܟܠܬܐ ܕܒ̈ܢܝܬܐ ܩ̣ܕܡܝܬܐ ܗܘܐ. ܠܗܠܝܢ ܕܡܫܒܚܝܢ
ܠܢܘܗܪܐ.

(§7) ܠܗܢܐ ܕܝܢ ܒܘܣܡܪܝܘܣ ܡܫܝܚܗ ܕܗܢ ܐܡܐ ܕܛܘܒܢܐ ܦܛܪܘܣ.
ܐܚܐ ܐܝܬ ܗܘܐ ܠܗ ܘܫܡܗ ܐܪܣܝܠܝܘܣ. ܗ̇ܘ ܕܒܪ ܥܡ ܒܘܣܡܪܝܘܣ
ܘܒܣܡܪܝܘܣ ܒܡܫܡܫܘܬܐ ܦܪ: ܡܢ ܒܬܪ ܕܪܫܝܢܘܬܐ ܕܐܝܒܪ̈ܝܐ. [R 6]
ܒܬܠܬܐ ܘܒܬܠܗ ܫܘܒܚܬܐ ܠܫ̈ܡܗܝ، ܓ̇ܠܐ.

(§8) ܐܢ̈ܫܐ ܕܝܢ ܫ̈ܠܝܬܐ ܠܛܘܒܢܐ ܦܛܪܘܣ ܠܐ ܗܘܐ ܠܗ. ܒܠܚܘܕ

[1] For a discussion of Peter's parents, see Horn, *Asceticism and Christological Controversy*, 50–58. See also Paulus Peeters, "Les débuts du christianisme en Géorgie d'après les sources hagiographiques," *AnBoll* 50 (1932): 5–58, here 54–58; Toumanoff, *Studies in Christian Caucasian History*, 260–61; Cyril Toumanoff, *Les Maisons princières géorgiennes de l'Empire de Russie* (Rome: Toumanoff, 1983); and, for a slightly altered English translation of the introduction to that study, idem, "The Princely Nobility of Georgia," in *From Byzantium to Iran: Armenian Studies in Honour of Nina G. Garsoïan* (ed. Jean Pierre Mahé and Robert W. Thomson; Atlanta: Scholars Press, 1997), 37–46.

[2] A P'arsman, one of the sons of Varaz-Bak'ar, is mentioned in *The Conversion of K'art'li by Nino* 135 (Thomson, *Rewriting Caucasian History*, 149). His mother was the granddaughter of P'eroz. For a discussion of the episode involving Eudoxia, Arsilios, and Pharsamanios, see Peeters, "Les débuts du Christianisme en Géorgie," 56–57.

[3] Arcadius was ruler of the Byzantine Empire from 395 to 408 C.E.

[4] The Syriac ܗܘܐ ܡ̇ܠܬܐ ܕܪ̈ܫܝܬܐ may translate the Greek τὰ πρῶτα φέρεσθαι or ἀποφέρεσθαι (see Raabe, 15 n. 2), for which Raabe also refers to related parallel expressions in Eusebius of Caesarea, *Hist. eccl.*

that country,[1] having led that whole nation to the fear of God. Although each of them were kings and queens of the Iberians, they in turn also acquired through virtue the kingdom of heaven. His paternal grandmother, Bosmarios's wife, Osduktia, [was] the mother of his father Bosmarios. The brother of Osduktia, his paternal grandmother, was Pharsamanios,[2] the one who was held in glory at [the court of] Arcadius, emperor of the Romans,[3] having both the honor of a military leader and of the first honors.[4] Subsequently, after Pharsamanios had fled from the injury of Eudoxia, wife of Arcadius,[5] and was able to hide himself, he hastily returned to his country. Once he became king over the Iberians and had brought along with him the White Huns who are the neighbors of the Iberians,[6] he was the cause of many evils for those who are subject to the Romans.

(§7) The great Bakurios, the maternal grandfather of the blessed Peter, had as a brother the holy Arsilios.[7] When this one had grown old with Bakurios and Bosmarios and had reached old age during the time of his rule of the Iberians,[8] **[R 6]** he completed his life in virginity and in great holiness.

(§8) Blessed Peter had no full siblings, but only a paternal sis-

7.32.23 and 8.14.2 (Schwartz and Mommsen, 2:726,24–25 [ἀπεφέρετο τὰ πρῶτα τῆς ἐπιστήμης] and 2:780,1–2 [τῶν τὰ πρῶτα τῆς Ῥωμαίων συγκλήτου βουλῆς ἀπενηνεγμένων]). Sebastian Brock also alerted us to the similar expression below at *Vit. Pet.* §39 (R 27) p. 53, n. 7.

[5] Perhaps Rufus hoped his audience would also recall the story of Joseph and Potiphar's wife at Gen 39. See also the comment by Schwartz, *Johannes Rufus*, 27.

[6] The White Huns (Hephtalites) were the northern neighbors of the Iberians. See Knud Hannestad, "Les relations de Byzance avec la Transcaucasie et l'Asie Centrale aux ve et vi^e^ siècles," *Byzantion* 25–27 (1955–57): 435 n. 7, 436 with n. 5.

[7] Moses of Khoren (ca. 407–492), *History of the Armenians* 3.60 (Thomson, 333), mentions that at the time of Mesrop's sending out of pupils to Byzantium and Edessa as translators of Greek and Syriac literature into Armenian, "a certain Ardzil was king of Georgia." The *Georgian Chronicle* (Qauxč'išvili, 91) features a certain King Arčil (422–432 C.E.).

[8] According to Strabo, *Geogr.* 11.3.6 (Jones, 5:220), κατ' ἀγχιστείαν τε καὶ ἡλικίαν τὸν πρεσβύτατον. The Iberians accorded the kingship to men of highest age. See also Raabe, 15 n. 5.

ܕܝܢ ܚܬܐ ܡܢ ܐܒܼܐ ܡܢ ܕܪܘܒܬܐ ܕܫܡܗ̇ ܒܡܢܝܪܘܣܦܘܪܐ. ܒܛܘܣܐ
ܕܚܬܐ ܚܬܬܐ ܠܗ ܐܬܝܗܒܼܬ ܒܪܒܝܐ ܕܐܒܘܗܝ.

(§9) ܐܢܬܬܐ ܕܝܢ ܡܕܝܢܬܐ ܘܡܫܡܫܢܝܬܐ ܕܫܡܗ̇ ܙܘܙܘ. ܪܒܼܬ ܠܦܛܪܘܣ.
ܒܪ ܒܪܒܝܬ ܥܒܪܐ ܐܝܬܘܗܝ. ܘܠܘܬܗ̇ ܦܠܛ ܗܘܐ. ܕܠܐ ܢܬܝܕܥ
ܡܚܪܝܐ ܠܦܪ̈ܣܝܐ. ܕܡܛܠ ܗܕܐ ܘܕܝܢ ܦ̈ܠܛܝܐ. ܥܕܪ ܐܢܛܝܓܕܐ.
ܒܬܪܗ̇ ܕܝܢ ܕܗܕܐ ܕܡܬܦܪܢܣܐ ܐܘܠܦܢܐ. ܡܪܒܝܢܝܬܐ ܗܘܬ ܕܛܠܝܐ.
ܗ̇, ܕܐܦ ܐܢܘܬܗ̇ ܒܪ ܠܘܬܐ ܐܝܬܘܗܝ ܗܘܐ. ܒܟܠܗ̇ ܕܝܢ ܕܗܕܐ
ܐܝܬܘܗܝ ܗܘܐ. ܒܡܪܐܝܢܘܣ. ܐܢܫܐ ܕܝܢ ܚܬܝܬ ܒܪܕܝܢܘܣ. ܒܢ̈ܝܗܘܢ
ܕܝܢ: ܡܠܟܐ ܘܡܦܪ̈ܢܣܢܘܬܐ. ܒܢ̈ܝ ܬܪܒܝܬܐ ܘܒܢ̈ܝ ܡܫܡܫܢܘܬܐ ܐܝܬܝܗܘܢ
ܗܘܘ ܕܛܠܝܐ.

(§10) ܘܠܐ ܐܝܟ ܡܢ ܙܥܘܪܘܬ ܢܦܫܐ. ܡܬܪܘܬ ܡܠܬܐ ܚܫܘܒ ܠܗܢܐ
ܬܢܝܐ ܕ̈ܡܠܟܐ. ܠܘ ܓܝܪ ܦܪܗܣܝܐ ܠܗܠܝܢ ܐܬܚܫܒܢ. ܐܠܐ ܡܛܠ
ܕܗ̇ܘ ܐܟܐ ܙܢܐ ܫܘܒܐ ܘܢܘܣ ܐܠܗܐ ܐܝܟ ܕܟܬܝܪܐ: ܒܪ ܠܟܠܗܘܢ
ܗܠܝܢ ܫ̈ܡܗܐ ܐܚܝܕܐ ܡܚܒܫ. ܒܝܕ ܢܡܘܣܐ ܒܢܝܬܐ. ܒܢܡܘܣܐ
ܕܫܡܬܐ. ܒܟܬܒܐ ܡ̈ܫܝܚܬܐ ܕܝܘܡܐ. ܕܒܪܝܗܘܢ ܡܫܡܠܝܐ ܗܘܐ.
ܒܪ ܗܢܐ ܦܘܪܒܢܐ ܦܪܒ ܠܗܘܢ ܫܠܦ ܥܠܬܐ ܗ̇, ܕܫܒܘ ܠܗ: ܗ̇,
ܕܝܗܒܐ ܠܗ ܕܢܒܠܘܢ ܠܒܠܟܐ. ܘܡܛܠܗܕܐ ܕܘܕܡܐ ܢܫܒܝܢ ܘܚܝܝܢ
ܡܝ̈ܬܐ: ܕܗܠܝܢ ܕܗܘ ܢܣܒ ܕܢܦܩ ܠܡܕܝܢܬܐ. ܘܡܢܝܗܘܢ ܗܟܢܐ
ܕܐܝܟ ܗܢܐ ܡܘܬ: ܕܗ̇ܘܢ ܘܢܣܒ ܠܐ ܢܒܥܘܪ ܒܥܘܕܪܢܐ. ܐܝܬ ܓܝܪ

[1] For a biblical parallel, consider Isaac, who had a stepbrother in Ishmael, son of Abram and his concubine Hagar; see Gen 16.

[2] In light of the fact that the young boy Peter will be handed over to the Eastern Roman Emperor Theodosius II as a hostage only a little later on, the present comment points to the rivalry between the Persians and the Byzantines, a struggle during which the Iberians seem to have found ways, even if only small ones, to assert their independent right to action.

[3] It was common practice for wealthy families in the early Christian world to have their offspring reared by wet-nurses and foster-parents. See, e.g., Basil of Caesarea, *Letter* 37 (Deferrari, 192–95; Way, 1:83), where Basil speaks of the son of his old wet-nurse. References to other examples are provided in the discussion presented in Suzanne Dixon, *The Roman Mother* (Norman: Oklahoma University Press, 1988), 120–29; see also eadem, *The Roman Family* (Baltimore: Johns Hopkins University Press, 1992), 119, and the literature cited there.

ter from a concubine whose name [was] Bomirosparia.[1] In accord with his father's wish, she was considered [as holding] the rank of a full sister to him.

(§9) It was a holy and famous woman, whose name was Zuzo, who raised Peter. While he was still an infant he was hidden in her house, in order not to be given as a hostage to the Persians, who many times sent messengers for this purpose.[2] This woman's daughter was called Ota. She was the foster-mother of the blessed one and also gave him suck when he was a baby.[3] Her husband was Khuranios; her full brother [was] Bardelios. Their sons Qata and Murgaqis were foster-children and of the same age as the blessed one.

(§10) No one out of faintheartedness[4] should think that this reciting of names is wordiness, for we recorded these not without reason. This affectionately loving and God-loving[5] father, as he truly is, would join all these names together once a year on the Saturday in the middle week of the Fast[6] to celebrate their commemoration as their recompense for the quiet life that they had conferred upon him and that he had chosen for himself so as to cast off the world.[7] For this reason we insignificant ones also thought it right that we should not fail to commemorate those whom he

[4] The Syriac ܙܥܘܪܘܬ ܢܦܫܐ may translate the Greek μικροψυχία (Raabe, 16 n. 1).

[5] The Syriac ܪܚܝܡ ܚܘܒܐ ܘܪܚܝܡ ܐܠܗܐ may translate the Greek φιλόστοργός και φιλόθεος (see also Raabe, 16 nn. 2 and 3).

[6] Presumably in the middle of Great Lent, the period of fasting observed in preparation for Easter; probably on one of the Saturdays on which the departed faithful are commemorated by name at the Divine Liturgy. Thus one might conclude that this event probably took place on the third Saturday of Lent, on which commemorations of the dead still take place in Orthodox churches.

[7] Here the author comments on the ideal of ascetic withdrawal into a life of quietness that Peter chose for himself. In the course of the *Vita Petri Iberi* Rufus shows how Peter's responsibilities as bishop and leader of anti-Chalcedonians in Egypt, Palestine, Arabia, and Phoenicia repeatedly frustrated his longing for that ascetic ideal. See also below *Vit. Pet.* §138 (R 103).

ܐܬܐ. ܘܕܪ̈ܘܫܬܐ ܢܐܬܘܢ ܕܢܣܩ ܡܠܬ̈ܗܐ. ܟܕ ܥܒܕܝܢ ܬܫܡܫܬܐ
ܕܟܠܠ ܗܠܝܢ.

(§11) ܪܒܐ ܕܝܢ ܒܩܘܪܣܘܦ [R 7] ܗܘ̇ ܕܡܕܒܪܢܐ ܕܡ̈ܠܟܐ ܕܐܝܒܪ̈ܝܐ
ܗܘ̣ܐ ܒܦܘܠܝܛܝܐ. ܘܕܦܘܠܝܛܝܐ ܒܬܪ ܘܠܟܗ ܕܗܢܐ. ܠܕܐܝܟ ܗܢܐ
ܪܘܡܐ ܕܕܫܠܬ ܐܠܗܐ ܡܛܠܗ. ܘܠܡܫܪܬܐ ܘܕܘܒܪ̈ܐ ܕܟܡܫܝܚܐ.
ܐܝܟܢܐ ܕܟܕ ܡ̈ܠܟܐ ܐܝܬܝܗܘܢ ܟܕ ܡܬܠܟܝܢ. ܫ̈ܢܝܐ ܕܕܝܪܘܬܐ
ܢܛܝܪܘܢ ܘܢܐܣܘܢ. ܟܕ ܟܝܢ ܟܘܢܐܝܬ ܥܠܝܗܘܢ ܠܫ̈ܪܕܐ ܬܪ̈ܝܗܘܢ
ܥܠܝܡܘܬܐ ܠܓܒܬܐ. ܐܪܝܫܘ ܡܢ ܫܘܬܦܘܬܐ ܒܡܪܝܬܐ. ܟܕ ܗܘ̇ܝܬ
ܠܗܘܢ ܠܝܠܕܘܬ ܒ̈ܢܝܐ ܕܐܬܝܗܒܬ ܠܗܘܢ. ܘܗܘ̇ ܗ̇ܘ ܡܗܝܡܢܐ
ܒܩܘܪܣܘܦ. ܟܕ ܠܪ̈ܘܡܐ ܘܠܬ̈ܫܒܘܚܬܐ ܘܠܝܬ̈ܝܪܘܬܐ ܢܣܒ ܢܦܫܗ. ܬܠܬ
ܫ̈ܢܝܢ ܒܥܒܕܬܐ ܗ̇ܘ ܕܐܝܬܘܗܝ، ܟܕ ܗܘܐ ܒܪܬܐ ܕܡܕܝܢܬܐ. ܘܟܕ
ܒܝܫܬܐ ܬܫܡܫܬܐ ܦܬܝܓܪ ܥܒܕ ܗܘܐ. ܠܐ ܠܐ[1] ܡܥܒܕ ܗܘܐ ܗܘܐ
ܕܟܠܦܠܟ ܕܠܘܗ ܒܥܠܡܐ ܬܫܠܡܐ ܢܩܝܐ. ܘܟܕ ܠܗܠܝܢ ܒܩܘܦܝܢܐ ܐܢܝܢ
ܗܘܐ: ܗ̣ܘ ܘ̈ܠܠܘܬܐ ܡܟܠ ܗܘܐ ܠܡܢܬ ܬܫܡܫܬܐ ܕܡܢܗ ܐܬܝܒܪ.
ܘܠܗܘܢ ܕܐܬܬ ܙܒܢ ܗܘܘ. ܗ̣ܘ ܗܘ̇ ܕܠܟܠܐ ܟܐܝܕܘܗܝ، ܡܟܠ ܗܘܐ.

(§12) ܗ̣ܘ ܕܝܢ ܠܦܟܝܬܘܬܐ ܕܩܘܡܝܐ: ܒܬܪ ܘܠܟܗ ܕܗܢܐ ܘܒܬܪ ܠܒܝܫܗ:
ܟܕ ܟܠܗ ܝܟܬܐ ܡܠܟܝܐ ܐܘܪܟܝܬ ܡܢܗ̇: ܘܗܩܐ ܗ̣ܘ، ܠܗ̇ ܐܠܒܫܬ:
ܘܠܦܘܪܝܢ ܕܝܠܗ̇ ܗܘ̇ ܕܡܬܩܪܐ ܒܡܦܪܢܝ. ܠܟܠܗ ܗܘ̇ ܕܗܢܐ
ܡܬܪ̈ܝܬܐ ܙܒܢܬ. ܘܦܠܓܬ ܠܡ̈ܣܟܢܐ. ܘܟܕ ܥ̈ܒܕܐ ܘܐ̈ܡܗܬܐ ܦ̈ܠܚܐ

[1] MS B reads only ܠܐ.

[2] One gets the impression that the author comments on a practice still current among Peter's ascetic followers at the time of the composition of the *Vita Petri Iberi*.

[3] See "the root of Jesse" in Isa 11:1, 10, quoted in Rom 15:12.

[4] To provide the opportunity for such an increase in virtue seems to have been a motive for writing the *Vita Petri Iberi*.

[5] The Syriac has the plural noun ܡ̈ܠܟܐ "kings" to cover both.

[6] See 1 Cor 7:5 (allusion).

[7] The Syriac ܝܠܕܘܬ ܒ̈ܢܝܐ may translate the Greek τεκνογονία (Raabe, 17 n. 1).

[8] The early Christian ideal of married life included the restriction of sexual encounter of the couple to times when procreation was desired. Ample evidence from writers of the tradition can be found, e.g., Justin Martyr, *1*

thought worthy of a memorial[2] and from whom a flower such as him had sprouted forth.[3] It is certain that the lovers of virtue will gain enormously when they hear their story.[4]

(§11) The great Bakurios, **[R 7]** the first Christian king of the Iberians, and his wife Duktia attained such a height of the fear of God, of virtue, and of ascetic ways of life in Christ that, even though they were king and queen,[5] while still reigning they sought to live and did live lives of monasticism. For when the two together had reached a satisfactory mutual agreement,[6] they abandoned carnal intercourse, since the begetting of children,[7] which already had been granted to them, was sufficient for them.[8] Indeed, the faithful Bakurios would give himself over to fasting, prayer, and the giving of alms, [even] sweeping the church of the city three times a week with his own hands. Because he was very lavish[9] in love of the poor, he did not consider it unfitting to have various cooked meals made in his palace, which he would carry in large baskets, bringing them at night to the house for the poor that had been built by him, and those who were lying there the king fed with his own hands.

(§12) The blessed Duktia, his wife and partner in his zeal, cast off from herself all royal ornament and clothed herself in sackcloth.[10] She even sold her sedan chair,[11] called a "basternion,"[12] all [her] gold[13] and pearls, and distributed [the money] to the poor.

Apol. 29 (Wartelle, 136–37; Cyril R. Richardson, ed. and trans., *Early Christian Fathers* [LCC 1; New York: Westminster, 1953; repr., New York: Simon & Schuster, 1996], 260); Athenagoras, *Leg.* 33 (Pouderon, 197–99; Richardson, *Early Christian Fathers*, 303, 336–38); Clement of Alexandria, *Strom.* 2.18, 23 (Stählin, 2:160,14–16 and 188,26–27; Ferguson, 217 and 249); 6.12 (Stählin, 2:482, 7–8; *ANF* 2:503): ἀδελφὴ δὲ τούτῳ ἡ γυνὴ μετὰ τὴν παιδοποιίαν, ὡς καὶ ὁμοπατρία; *Const. ap.* 6.29 (Metzger, 2:386–89; *ANF* 7:463).

9 The Syriac may translate the Greek ὑπερβάλλων (Raabe, 17 n. 2).

10 A biblical sign of repentance. See, e.g., Jonah 3:5–8.

11 The Syriac transliterates the Greek φορεῖον.

12 The Syriac transliterates the Greek βαστέρνιον and βαστέρνον, "closed litter." See LSJ, 310. The term is used for a covered vehicle used by women.

13 The Syriac may translate the Greek χρυσός (Raabe, 17 n. 4).

ܚܬܝܬܐ ܗܘܬ ܒܨܘ̈ܡܐ ܘܒܨ̈ܠܘܬܐ܆ ܠܒܥܘܬܐ ܕܐܝܟ ܗܕܐ ܥܓܠܬ
ܡܢ ܡܪܢ܆ ܐܝܟܢܐ ܕܐܝ̈ܕܝܗ̇ ܒܠܚܘܕ ܬܣܝܡ ܘܬܫܬܡܠܐ ܐܣܝܘܬܐ.

(§13) ܡܛܠ ܕܝܢ ܕܒܪܐ ܒܣܘܪܝܣ ܗ̇ܘ ܕܗܘ̣ܐ ܒܙ̈ܒܢܝܗ̇ ܕܗܕܐ܆ [R 8]
ܥܡܐ ܕܠܐ ܢܓܪܪ ܗܕܐ ܬܫܥܝܬܐ. ܥܡ ܡܫܪ̈ܝܬܗ ܠܒܪ ܐܣܛܪ̈ܛܝܐ܆
ܘܟܠܝܠܐ ܕܡܘܕܝܢܘܬܐ ܒܗ ܦܠܛ. ܟܠܗ ܕܝܢ ܒܙ̈ܒܢܝܗ̇ ܘܕܣܗܕܘܬܐ.
ܟܕ ܓܒܪ ܚܕ ܡܠܟܐ ܕܦܪ̈ܣܝܐ ܟܕ ܐܙܠ ܗܘܐ ܠܩܪܒܐ܆ ܐܝܟ ܡܢ
ܕܢܩܘܡ ܗܘܐ ܠܗ ܡܠܟܐ ܕܥܒܕܐ ܒܟܢܫܗ܆ ܘܐܝܟ ܕܒ ܚܠܡܗ܆ ܟܕ ܒܝܢܐ
ܕܡܚܙܐ ܕܕܒܝܢ ܥܒܕܐ܆ ܗ̇ܘ ܡܠܟܐ ܘܚܠܡܗ ܕܟܪ ܫ̈ܠܝܚܐ ܘܡ̈ܗܘܦܠܐ܆
ܘܡܛ̈ܦܠܐ ܘܚܠܡܗ ܙ̈ܘܕܒܢܐ܆ ܡܢ ܥܠܝܐ ܥܡܘܪܘ ܢܒܝܬܘ ܡܢ ܙ̈ܕܝܩܐ
ܘܠܥܡ̈ܡܐ ܗܘܕܘ܆ ܒܬܪ ܗ̇ܘ ܟܕ ܢܬܒ ܒܠ ܗܘܣܦܝܗ. ܘܟܕ ܗܕܐ
ܐܬܐܡܪܬ ܠܡܠܟܐ ܡܢ ܗܪ̈ܦܐ ܐܣ̈ܝܐ܆ ܟܕ ܡܢ ܡܕܡܡܗܘ, ܗ̇ܘ
ܒܣܘܪܝܣ܆ ܘܐܫܬܐܠ ܕܐ ܥܪܝܪܬܐ ܐܝܬܝܗ̇ ܗܕܐ ܕܐܬܐܡܪܬ
ܡܛܠܬܗ܆ ܒܡ ܦܐܪܣܝܐ ܐܝܟ ܡܢ ܟܠܗ ܚܝܠܐ܆ ܗ̇ܘ ܕܒܪ ܠܒܢܗ
ܥܪܝܪܬ ܕܕܝܢܐ ܘܕܬܠܬܐ ܬ̈ܠܝܐ ܕܫܒܚܘܗܝ܆ ܕܐܝܟ ܒܪܦܠܘܣܐ
ܐܢܬ, ܘܠܐ ܥܠܝܟ ܠܝ܆ ܕܟܕ ܥܒܕ ܐܝܟ ܠܗ̇ ܕܐܬܬܘܗܝ, ܒܠܒܘܕܘܗܝ,
ܐܠܗܐ ܥܪܝܪܐ ܘܟܪܘܝܐ ܕܟܠ. ܠܟܪܝܬܐ ܕܠܗ ܐܘܣܦܪܕ܆ ܗ̇,
ܕܠܫܡܫܬܐ ܕܠܐ ܘܕܚܠܡܘ ܫ̈ܒܝܐ ܐܬܦܪܬ ܕܐܬܒܗܪ. ܐܝܟܢܐ ܕܟܕ
ܦܩܕ ܐܬܕܢܪ ܡܠܟܐ܆ ܘܟܢ ܦܐܪܣܝܐ ܕܠܗ ܐܬܟܣܝ܆ ܢܬܦܩܝ

[1] Although miracles of healing are more numerous than grains of sand on the beach in early Christian literature, laying on of hands, without any further specification, is not that frequently the medium by which these miracles are worked. "Laying on of hands" in early Christian texts more often refers to the act of transmitting the grace of the Holy Spirit and to ordaining members of the clergy. Thus Rufus's depiction of Duktia makes her out to be a specially gifted person indeed.

[2] See 1 Cor 9:25; 1 Thess 2:19; 2 Tim 4:8; Jas 1:12; 1 Pet 5:4. The crown of confessorship or martyrdom was the first prize an early Christian could hope to obtain in his or her struggle for perfection. References to this crown can be found, e.g., in LSJ, 1042; *PGL*, 1258. See, e.g., Clement of Rome, *2 Clem.* 7.3 (Kirsopp Lake, ed. and trans., *The Apostolic Fathers* [2 vols.; LCL; Cambridge Harvard University Press, 1970], 1:138–39): "Let us run the straight course, the immortal contest, and let many of us sail to it, and contend, that we may also receive the crown, and if we cannot all receive the crown, let us at least come near to it"; John Chrysostom, *Dav.* 2.2 (PG 54:688–90). For a discussion of the centrality of the notion of martyrdom in the *Vita Petri Iberi*, see Cornelia Horn, "Weaving the Pilgrim's Crown: John Rufus's View of Peter the Iberian's Journeys in Late Antique Palestine," *JEastCS* 56 (2004): 171–90.

On many occasions when she prolonged [her periods of] fasting and prayers, she received from our Lord such grace that she would merely lay her hands on [someone] and accomplish healing.[1]

(§13) [Again,] concerning the great Bakurios, her husband, **[R 8]** it is appropriate that we would not pass over this story. For along with his other virtues, he once also wove the crown of confessorship, or rather, as he would have wanted, even of martyrdom.[2] Once he was going to war alongside the emperor of the Persians[3] as one who had made a covenant of peace with him and as his general. When he saw that as soon as the sun arose, the emperor and all his generals, consuls,[4] and satraps, as well as all the nobility,[5] suddenly leapt down[6] from their horses and worshiped the sun,[7] he himself remained sitting on his horse. When this was told to the emperor by the other satraps, Bakurios stood before him and was asked if what had been told about him was true. He who was truly a sharer in the zeal of Daniel and his three young friends[8] shouted out with confidence in front of the whole army, "I am a Christian, and it is not lawful for me that I should foresake the one who alone is the true God and Creator of all to worship his creature, created to give light for the service of myself and of all human beings."[9] The emperor, even though he was very

[3] Presumably Shapur II (309–379).

[4] The Syriac transliterates the Greek ὑπατός. Observation made by Sidney H. Griffith in *marginalia* to the text, abbreviated as "Griffith, *marginalia*" in the following.

[5] The Syriac may translate the Greek μεγιστᾶνες (Raabe, 17 n. 6).

[6] The Syriac has a syndetic hendiadys: "jumped up and got down."

[7] Zoroastrianism/Mazdaism was the official religion of the Sassanian Empire and the traditional religion of Persia in ancient and late antique times. The Zoroastrian worldview is built around a god of light (Ohrmazd, Ahura Mazda) and a god of darkness (Ahriman, Angra Mainyu) who are in combat with one another, creating good and evil. The principle deities of the Zoroastrian pantheon enthroned among the Sassanians also included the sun-god Mithra and the fire-god Adhur. See Speros Vryonis and Alexander Kazhdan, "Zoroastrianism," *ODB* 3:2230–31; idem, "Sasanians," *ODB* 3:1845–46; Jarnsheed K. Choksy, "Zoroaster" and "Zoroastrianism," in Bowersock, Brown, and Grabar, *Late Antiquity*, 754–55 and 755–57; and Frank R. Trombley, "Mithraism," *ODB* 2:1385–86.

[8] See Dan 3:16–18.

[9] See Gen 1:14.

ܘܒܣܟܐܝܬ ܠܘܬ ܗܠܝܢ ܕܟܠܗ ܢܐܡܪ܆ ܒܩܘܪܝܘܣ ܐܬܘܗܝ ܘܡܗܝܡܢ ܚܠܘܗܝ܆ ܡܢܐ ܡܫܒܚܝܢ ܕܢܒܥܐ ܠܗ. ܘܗܠܝܢ ܡܢ ܡܢܬܐ ܡܢ ܢܟ̈ܣܐ ܕܒܩܘܪܝܘܣ.

(§14) ܐܪܣܠܝܘܣ ܕܝܢ ܐܚܘܗܝ܆ ܚܬܝܬܐ ܕܗܘܝܐ. ܗ̇ܘ ܕܡܢ ܠܟܠ ܐܡܪܝܢ܆ ܕܒܫܡܫܘܬܐ ܘܒܒܘܠܘܬܐ ܪܒܐ ܡܠܟܘܬܐ ܕܐܝܒܪ̈ܝܐ܆ ܒܗ ܒܘܣܡܪܝܘܣ ܐܒܘܗܝ܆ [R 9] ܕܦܛܪܘܣ ܕܝܠܢ܆ ܗ̇ܘ ܕܐܦ ܢܒܪܢܘܓܝܘܣ. ܟܕ ܦܠܛ ܐܦܝܣܘܗܝ܆ ܘܐܬܚܦܛܘ ܠܗ ܟܪ̈ܝܐ ܙ̈ܥܘܪܐ ܕܐܬܪܐ܆ ܕܢܕܘܟ ܡܛܠ ܠܢܕܘܬ ܒ̈ܢܝܐ ܘܡܘܠܟܐ ܕܡܠܟܘܬܐ܆ ܟܕ ܐܬܐ ܠܗ ܐܢܬܬܐ ܡܢ ܒܢܬܐ ܕܡܠܟܘܬܐ܆ ܗ̇ܝ ܠܘܬܗ̇ ܒܬܘܠܬܐ. ܟܕ ܚܠܦ ܕܝܢ ܕܡܕܡ ܕܒܗܬܬܐ ܚܒܪܬ܆ ܘܗ̇ܝ ܫܦܝܪܐ ܗܘܬ ܟܕ ܢܟܦܐܝܬ ܐܬܪܒܝܬ ܡܢܗ. ܠܚ̇ܬܬܐ ܕܝܢ ܝ̈ܕܗ ܡܢ ܒܠܥ ܠܗ̇ܘ ܪܥܝܢܐ܆ ܐܦ ܠܡܒܝܢܘܬܐ ܘܠܢܟܦܘܬܐ ܡܫܝܚܐܝܬ ܕܦܝܠܘܣܘܦܝܐ܆ ܐܡܪ ܠܘܬܗ. ܗܐ ܡܫܒܚܢܐ ܠܝ ܢܦܫܝ ܘܕܡܝ. ܗܐ ܙܥܘܪܐ ܘܢܩܫܬ ܦܘܡ ܡܠܠܐܝܬ܆ ܘܠܐ ܬܘܒ ܒܗܢܐ ܐܬܪܐ ܕܕܠܒܐ ܬܗܘܐ ܒܫܐܝܬ. ܘܕܡܝ ܢܬܩܒܠ ܟܠ. ܘܟܕ ܠܗ̇ܘ ܡܢܐ ܫܪܝܗ܆ ܒܬܪܝܢ ܐܡܪ ܠܐܢܬܬܗ. ܡܛܠ ܕܨܒܝܬܝ[1] ܗܕܐ܆ ܠܐ ܡܥܪܐ ܓܪܐ ܐܢܐ ܠܟܝ. ܘܠܐ ܠܒܗܬܬܟܝ ܫܒܩ ܐܢܐ. ܡܗܝܡܢ ܐܢܐ ܕܝܢ ܒܒܪܗ ܕܐܠܗܐ܆ ܗ̇ܘ ܕܠܡܣܘܡܗ ܠܟܠܡܘܬ܆ ܕܢܒܥܐ ܕܬܩ̈ܠܒܐ ܢܒܕ ܣܒܪ܆ ܘܗܒܢܐ ܢܬܠܠܡ ܒܡܪܒ. ܘܡܣܪܐ ܗ̇ܝ ܠܘܬܠܬܐ ܕܗ̇ܘ ܢܒܥܐ ܒܒܪ̈ܐ ܗܘܬ. ܘܐܬܪܐ ܗ̇ܘ ܕܐܬܚܙܝܬ ܒܪܣܡܗ̇ ܒܪ ܦܪ܆ ܒ̈ܬܘܠܬܐ܆ ܡܢܗܪܐܝܬ ܡܬܟܠܠܝܢ ܗܘܘ ܫ̈ܢܝܗ̇ ܘܒܣܪܗ̇. ܘܟܠܗ ܗܢܐ. ܐܝܟܢܐ ܕܟ̈ܢܘܫܬܐ ܢܦܫܐ ܘܒܡܫܟܢܐ ܬܗܘܐ ܡܬܗܦܟܐ. ܐܠܐ ܠܒܝܫ ܕܗ̇ܘ ܙܕܝܩܐ܆ ܬܘܒ ܡܢ ܠܒܬܪ ܦܘܪܢܣܐ ܝܠܕ. ܟܕ ܡܬܪܕܝܐ ܒܪ ܡܢ ܡܫܝܚܘܬܐ ܐܠܗܝܬܐ܆ ܘܠܡܬܬܢܨܚܢܘܬܐ ܐܬܬ ܕܢܦܘܪ̈ܬܐ ܘܒܡܬܬܢܨܚܢܘܬܐ ܡܫܝܚܝܬܐ ܗܘܬ. ܡܪܢܐܝܬ ܡܬܬܚܝܣܢܐ [R 10] ܗܘܬ. ܟܕ ܐܬܚܒܪܬ ܠܘܬ ܡܫܬܘܕܥܢܘܬܐ ܘܠܡܬܬܢܨܚܢܘܬܐ ܘܢܟܦܐ

[1] MS A has ܕܨܒܝܬ printed in the text. Grammatically, however, it must be ܕܨܒܝܬܝ for the 2fs perf., as MS B has.

[2] Rufinus of Aquileia, *Hist. eccl.* 10.11 (Schwartz and Mommsen, 2:973–76; Amidon, 20–23), provides an account of the conversion of Iberia as told to him by "that most faithful man Bacurius, the king of that nation who in our realm held the rank of *comes domesticorum* and whose chief concern was for religion and truth" (Amidon, 23) and a man employed in military service in Palestine in the 390s. This passage indicates that individuals could be considered "kings" or "princes" of the Georgians/Iberians who were not exercising the royal office in a straightforwardly monarchical way.

amazed and dumbfounded by his boldness, turned around and secretly said to his own people, "It is Bakurios, and we are in need of him. What can we do to him?" These are [only] some of the heroic deeds of Bakurios.

(§14) Arsilios, his full brother, whom we mentioned above, governed in old age and in virginity the kingdom of the Iberians together with Bosmarios,[2] the father **[R 9]** of our Peter, who also [is named] Nabarnugios.[3] The ruling men of the country strongly urged him, entreating him to marry for the sake of begetting sons and the succession of the kingdom. When they brought to him a wife of royal descent, he remained a virgin toward her. He learned that she had done something shameful, although she denied [it] when she was gently accused by him. Finally he hunted down the unsuspecting criminal. Oh the humility and great gentleness of philosophy![4] He said to him, "Behold, your pledge is your life and your blood. Now quickly leave with provisions and money for expenses. Do not abide in this country lest you die in an evil way and your blood be reckoned against me." When he had dismissed him in this way, he afterwards said to his wife, "Because you have done this, I will not dismiss you nor will I mock at your shame. Yet I have faith in the Son of God, whose law you have abused, that he will cause your genitals to breed[5] worms, and thus your flesh will be consumed." Immediately this chaste man's curse became deed. The area below her belly became putrid with worms, [and] her life and her flesh were miserably consumed, to such an extent that she was changed into dried bones and skin.[6] But the zeal of that just man again begat redemption from the curse. She was chastened by the divine scourge, came to recognition of the offense, was greatly repentant, and groaned bitterly. **[R 10]** She turned

[3] See above, *Vit. Pet.* §5 (R 4).

[4] It is not uncommon in early Christian texts to find direct comparison and identification between the ideals of the philosophic and the ascetic life.

[5] The Syriac ܢܒܥ may translate the Greek βρύειν, "to swell, to be full to bursting" (see Raabe, 18 n. 2).

[6] Dried bones and skin can appear in ascetic texts as an outer sign of a perfected ascetic, e.g., *Vit. Pet.* §116 (R 83), describing Peter. At the present instance one gets the impression that through the curse an ascetic appearance was forced upon the woman.

ܕܠܟܐ ܗܘܐ ܠܘܬܗ ܐܬܬ܂ ܐܝܟܢܐ ܕܓܠܝܐܝܬ ܐܫܬܕܪܐ ܢܦܫܗ̇ ܡܕܡ
ܬܪܥܐ ܕܕܝܪܐ܂ ܘܡܕܡ ܟܠܗ ܬܓܠܐ ܣܝܒܬܐ܂ ܘܠܟܠܗܘܢ ܬܬܟܫܦ܂
ܕܢܘܦܩܘܢ ܠܟܠ ܡܢܗ̇܂ ܟܕ ܐܝܬܝܗ̇ ܡܩܪܒܬܐ ܘܡܓܪܒܬܐ ܘܡܩܒܠܢܝܬܐ
ܕܐܠܗܐ܂ ܘܫܘܕܐ ܕܒܢܝܢܫܐ ܦܪܝܐ ܗܘܬ ܢܦܫܗ̇܂ ܘܡܬܠܗܕܐ ܠܟܠܢܫ
ܐܝܟܢܐ܆ ܠܘܬ ܣܘܥܪܢܐ ܘܕ̈ܘܟܪܢܐ ܘܡܬܦܝܣܢܘܬܐ ܚܝܐ܂ ܘܟܕ ܗ̇ܘܐ
ܝܘܡܐ ܒܐܝܠܐܝܬ ܡܢ ܟܠܗ ܒܟܝܗ̇܆ ܘܬܟܫܦܬܐ ܣܓܝܐܬܐ ܡܢ
ܕܝܪܐ܆ ܒܬܡ ܐܡܝܢܘܬܐ ܘܕܡ̈ܥܐ ܘܐܬܬܢܝܚܘܬܐ ܕܢܦܫܗ̇܆ ܐܬܬܦܝܣܬ
ܡܢ ܡܫܟܢܘܬܐ܂ ܘܡܟܝܢܐ ܗܘ̣ܬ ܡܕܝܫܬܐ ܒܬܪ ܗܠܝܢ܆ ܟܕ ܕܡܟܝܪܐ
ܡܫܝܚܬܐ ܘܒܝܘܬܐ܂ ܐܝܟܢܐ ܕܠܦܘܩܕܢ̣ܐ ܘܬܝܒܘܬܐ ܬܗܘܐ ܠܟܠܢܫ܂
ܕܐܘܪܝܢܐ ܕܠܒܘܬܐ ܘܕܦܘܪܩܢܐ܂

(§15) ܗ̣ܘ ܕܝܢ ܗܘܐ ܡܗܝܡܢܐ ܐܪܣܛܘܠܐܘܣ ܡܢ ܕܒܬܪܗ ܡܫܝܚܬܐ܆
ܟܠܗ̇ ܗܕܐ ܠܒܥܘܬܐ ܘܦܪܗܣܝܐ ܐܚܝܕ ܠܘܬ ܐܠܗܐ܂ ܐܝܟܢܐ
ܕܐܬܘ̈ܬܐ ܢܒܥ ܟܕ ܬܠ̈ܝܬܗ܂ ܐܝܟ ܕܗ̇ܘ ܠܒܥܘܬܐ ܐܚܐ ܕܠܝ܆ ܟܕ
ܡܥܕܪ ܠܗ ܕܓܠܝܐܝܬ ܐܡܪܗ܂ ܟܕ ܡܬܟܠܝܐ ܗܘܐ ܕܝܢ ܟܠ ܐܝܟܢܐ܆
ܘܒܠܦ ܡܛܠ ܠܒܥܘܬܐ ܦܛܪܘܣ ܕܐܝܟ ܡܢ ܟܠܗܝܢ܆ ܘܡܥܕܪܢܝܬܐ
ܡܕܝܫܬܐ ܒܟܬܒ̈ܐ܆ ܘܬܡܢ ܕܒܬܪ ܕܕܝܢܘܬܐ ܡܬܟܝܢܘܬܐ܆ ܐܝܟܢܐ ܕܟܕ
ܙܕܝܩܐ ܡܠܬܐ ܟܕ ܐܠܗܐ ܡܫܝܚܐ܆ ܥܠܝܗ̇ ܠܗ ܟܕ ܐܡܪ܂ ܡܛܠ
ܕܐܬܒ̣ܝ܆ ܠܒܥܘܬܗܘܢ܂ ܠܗ̇ܘ ܕܐܝܬ ܠܗ ܙܕܩܐ ܡܢܗܘܢ܆ ܘܟܕ ܟܠܬܐ
ܒܐܘܪܫܠܡ܆ ܐܝܟܢܐ ܕܐܝܬ ܠܝ ܐܝܬ܂ ܡܦܝܣ ܐܝܟܢܐ ܠܝ ܒܪ܆ ܕܬܬܠܟܐ
ܟܠܝ܆ ܐܝܟܢܐ ܕܟܕ [R 11] ܬ̈ܠܬܝܢ ܐܚܝܕ ܙܒܢܐ܂ ܘܡܛܠ ܕܕܟܪܐ
ܐܝܬ ܠܦܓܥܐ ܪܘܚܢܝܐ ܕܐܪܥܐ܆ ܗܠܝܢ ܪ̈ܫܝܐ ܡܢܝܚܢܘܬܐ
ܘܡܗ̈ܝܡܢܐ܆ ܕܢܒܥܘܢ ܠܗܘܢ ܙܕܩܐ ܘܡܥܕܪܢܘܬܐ܆ ܗܠܝܢ ܦܪ̈ܝܫܬܐ
ܕܒܠܒܐ܆ ܗܠܝܢ ܕܠܘܬ ܦܘܪܩܢܐ[1] ܘܡܗܝܡܢܘܬܐ ܡܫܟܠܠܬܐ ܢܛܪܘܢ܆
ܗ̣ܘ ܡܕܝ̈ܢܝ܆ ܚܫܝ̈ܟܬܐ ܐܡܝܢ ܠܗ̇ ܐܝܟ ܡ̇ܠܟܐ ܕܒܪ܂ ܕܫܡܫܬܐ

[1] Raabe misprints ܦܘܪܓܐ ("tower") here.

[2] The confession of one's sin was largely a public phenomenon in early Christianity. For a discussion of penance in the early church, see Karl Rahner, *Theological Investigations 15: Penance in the Early Church* (New York: Crossroad, 1982).

[3] For the account of the life in the desert of another radically repentant female sinner, see the story of a certain Maria that circulated among ascetics in Palestine and that was put into writing around the middle of the sixth century by Cyril of Scythopolis, *Vit. Cyr.* 18–19 (Schwartz, 233,4–234,23; Price, 256–58).

herself to confession and came to repentance and to such wholehearted contrition that she publicly threw herself down in front of the door of the church, revealing her sin in front of everyone.[2] She begged everyone to trample on her, calling herself a despicable whore, an adulteress, an enemy of God, and the shame of humanity. By this she moved all to pity, tears, and compassion. Since everyone fasted together and the church earnestly interceded on her behalf with persistance, tears, and groans, she was healed from the affliction. Moreover, through a virtuous way of life and asceticism she became so holy following these [events] that she became for everyone a model and an example of the way of grace and salvation.[3]

(§15) The faithful Arsilios, on account of his virtuous way of life, found such grace and confidence toward God that he would work signs through his prayers, as our blessed father attested, affirming it without deception. During his reign over the Iberians he learned that the blessed Peter had separated from the world to dwell in the Holy City and was practicing there the way of life of monasticism—as the course of the narrative will make clear, with the help of God. He sent to him saying, "As it is written, 'Blessed is he who has seed in Zion and sons of [his] house in Jerusalem.'[4] Even as we have you, I make petition to you, my son, to pray for me so that through **[R 11]** your prayers I may find mercy." Although it is the custom of many of the great ones of the earth, [who are] pleasure-seekers and careless, to appoint for themselves male and female singers, those vanities of the world, to sing for pleasure[5] and corrupting delight,[6] he, like King David, appointed for

Benedicta Ward (*Harlots of the Desert: A Study of Repentance in Early Monastic Sources* [CSS 106; Kalamazoo, Mich.: Cistercian, 1987], 28–29) also has a translation of the relevant passage. It is not unlikely that Rufus and the anti-Chalcedonian monks in Maiuma, Gaza, would have been familiar with Mary's story and thus would have been able to compare Arsilios's wife to her.

[4] Isa 31:9 (LXX).

[5] Raabe misread the Syriac ܦܘܪܓܝܐ ("pleasure") and wrote ܦܘܪܓܐ ("tower") instead.

[6] Possibly in reference to Exod 32:4, 6 (1 Cor 10:7) or 1 Sam 30:16.

ܘܒܟܠܗܝܢ ܩ̈ܠܐ ܩ̈ܕܝܫܬܐ ܕܐܠܗܐ ܡܙܡܪܝܢ. ܐܝܟܢܐ ܕܐܦ ܒܪܬܐ:
ܠܐ ܬܗܘܐ ܡܫܠܡܐ ܡܕܡ ܦܠܓܝܢ ܕܝܠܗ.
(§16) ܐܘܕܘܩܝܐ ܕܝܢ: ܡܫܒܚܬܗ ܕܐܦ ܐܡܐ ܕܛܘܒܢܐ ܦܛܪܘܣ.
ܒܠܗ ܗܢܐ ܐܝܬܝܗ̇ ܗܘܬ ܩܕܝܫܬܐ. ܐܝܟܢܐ ܕܐܦ ܒܬܪ ܡܘܬܗ̇. ܒܪ
ܡܬܒܝܢܐ ܗܘܬ ܕܒܗܬܐ ܡܕܡ ܕܡܦܪܬܐ. ܘܐܡܝܢܐܝܬ ܡܢ ܙܘܓܐ
ܢܦܠܐ ܗܘܬ. ܒܪ ܐܝܬܘ ܦܓܪܗ̇ ܘܩܒܪܗ ܬܡܢ ܐܝܟ ܕܫܐܠ ܡܢ ܩ̈ܕܝܫܐ.
(§17) ܡܣܒܪܐ ܥܠܬ ܡܩܦܠܬܐ. ܠܘܒܠܝܢܝܬܐ ܕܝܢ ܘܗܘ ܗ̇ܝ ܕܐܙܒܢܬ
ܠܘܒܠܢܐ. ܩܕܝܫܬܐ ܕܐܝܟ ܗܕܐ ܗܘܬ. ܐܝܟܢܐ ܕܒܪ ܫܒܪܐ
ܐܝܬܘܗܝ ܗܘܐ: ܘܒܐܪܝܢ ܕܢܓܝܪ ܗܘܐ. ܘܩܒܠ ܩܘܛܠܢܐ ܡܬܪ̈ܚܡܢܘܗܝ
ܕ̈ܪܚܡܐ. ܒܪ ܦܝܫܐ ܒܠܠܝܐ ܘܗܠܝܢ ܐܡܪܐ ܗܘܬ ܒܒܪܬ ܩܠܐ
ܐܝܪܝܬܐ. ܡܪܝ ܝܫܘܥ. ܐܠܗܝ ܘܡܫܝܚܐ ܢܫܐ ܕܝܠܝ. ܐܬܪܚܡ ܥܠܝ.
ܘܒܪ ܒܝܢ ܗܢܐ ܘܗܟܢܐ: ܘܒܠܚܘܕ ܐܘܟܝ. ܗ̇ܝ ܠܘܒܠܝܢܝܬܐ ܕܗܟܢܬ ܒܪ
ܡܬܒܪܟܐ ܒܒܝܬܗ̇: ܕܐܝܬܘܗܝ ܗܘܐ ܕܐܬܒܢܐ ܩ̈ܘܝܡܐ. ܘܠܒܬ ܠܚܘܕ
ܡܢ ܐܩܠܝܡܐ ܘܐܘܒܠܬ ܒܪ ܐܚܪܬܐ ܒܦܪܪܣܝܐ. ܡܪܝܐ: ܒܪܝ
ܐܝܟܢܐ ܦܠܚܬ ܠܝ. ܘܫܘܦ ܟܠܝ ܘܟܠ ܩܢܝ. ܘܠܐ ܫܒܩܬ ܒܟܘܬܗ̇
ܕܢܚܣܪ ܒܗܬܗ̇ ܡܕܡ. ܒܪ ܚܙܐ ܗܘ̣ ܘܗܟܢܐ ܠܩܛܝܠܐܝܬ ܐܢܕܝܢ ܗܘܝ.
(§18) ܐܝܬ ܗܘܐ [R 12] ܕܝܢ ܕܒܗ̇، ܡܕܝܢܬܐ ܒܪܢܫܐ ܐܚܕ ܡܢ ܗܠܝܢ
ܢܒ̈ܝܐ. ܢܟܝܠܐ ܘܕܩܛܠܐ ܢܚܒܠ ܗܘܐ. ܘܒܪ ܘܩܒܠ ܩܘܛܠܐ
ܐܬܪܓܝ ܒܢܘܗܝ. ܠܐ ܡܗܘܡܢܐ ܗܘܐ ܡܢ ܢܚܘܬܗ. ܒܪ ܪܓܠܬ ܕܝܢ ܗ̇ܝ.
ܡܢ ܟܠ ܣܒܠܬ ܢܘܪܐ ܡܢ ܥܡܠܝ ܘܠܒܠܗܝܢ ܢ̈ܦܠܬܗ ܕܐܦ ܒܪܘ ܡܪܝܢ
ܗ̇ܘ ܠܫܪܪܐ ܐܒܠܬ. ܒܪܬܗ̇ ܕܝܢ ܕܗܕܐ ܕܡܬܩܪܝܐ ܗܘܬ ܐܘܠܝܐ.

[1] See 2 Sam 6:5.

[2] This could be counted as an instance of the so-called "Jesus Prayer" ("Lord Jesus Christ, son of God, have mercy on me [a sinner]"; see Irénée Hausherr, *The Name of Jesus* [trans. Charles Cummings; CSS 44; Kalamazoo, Mich.: Cistercian, 1978], 266). On 99–100 Hausherr discusses passages in the *Vit. Pet.* §§38, 53, and 147 (R 27, 35–36, 110) that contain the key words "Jesus," "Christ," and "sinner," sometimes in a prayer context, yet he does not notice the present instance, which is the clearest example of a person, and a layperson at that, actually praying a form of the "Jesus Prayer."

himself singers of sacred things,[1] who were singing the holy words of God at meals and on every occasion, so that his palace was not at all different from a church.

(§16) Osduktia, the paternal grandmother of the blessed Peter, was so holy in every [respect] that after her death, when a guard post that was under construction was collapsing during an earthquake, it ceased collapsing immediately when her body was brought out and laid there like that of one of the saints.

(§17) The blessed Zuzo who reared the blessed one was so holy that when Peter was an infant, while he was sleeping at her side, she would often drench him with tears when she rose up at night and was saying the following words in the Iberian language: "Lord Jesus, my God and Giver of my life, have mercy on me!"[2] Once when there was an earthquake and everything was shaking, while the blessed one was running about in her house, which had eight apses,[3] she held on to each of the pillars[4] and cried out[5] with boldness,[6] "Lord, see how I have served you, and spare me and my children!" Her prayer did not allow her house to suffer any loss, although this earthquake ruined many at that time.

(§18) [Again,] there was **[R 12]** in that city a man from among the notables, [one who was] avaricious and who did wrong against many. Although he had been scolded by her many times, he did not turn away from his avarice. [At last,] when she prayed, fire at once descended from heaven and devoured all his fields, which

[3] Literally, "which was of eight apses." The Syriac renders the Greek κογχή, "mussel," "shelly marble," or a "niche" or "apse." See LSJ, 966. *PGL* (759) notes that Eusebius of Caesarea employed the word in reference to the "apse" of a church.

[4] The Syriac may translate the Greek στῦλος; Griffith, *marginalia*.

[5] For a scriptural context for the imagery of "earthquake" and "pillars," see Ps 75:3; Job 9:6; 26:11.

[6] The Syriac transliterates the Greek παρρησία.

ܗܝ، ܕܐܦ ܡܪܚܡܢܘܬܗ ܕܐܘܪܚܝܐ ܗ̣ܘܬ. ܒܠܚܘܕ ܘܩܝܡܘܬܗ̇ ܒܡܫܝܚܘܬܐ
ܘܒܨܘ̈ܡܐ ܘܒܨ̈ܠܘܬܐ ܐܦܩܬ.

(§19) ܐܡܗ ܕܝܢ ܕܡܕܝܢܬܐ ܐܝܟܐ ܕܐܝܬ ܒܡܘܪܕܘܦܘܠܝܣܐ܆ ܡܢ ܒܬܪ ܡܘܬܗ ܕܒܥܠܗ̇ ܐܪܡܠܘܬܐ ܓ̇ܒܬ. ܘܟܕ ܠܐ ܐܬܡܟܪܬ ܕܠܓܒܪܐ ܕܬܪ̈ܝܢ ܬܗܘܐ܆ ܒܨܘ̈ܡܐ ܘܒܨ̈ܠܘܬܐ ܐܡܝܢܐ ܗܘܬ. ܟܕ ܠܐ ܡܒܛܠ ܦܠܚܐ ܕܡܕܒܪܢܘܬܐ ܠܓܒܪܝ، ܐܠܐ ܟܕ ܒܡܘܬ̈ܪܐ ܕܠܗ̇ ܐܝܟܢܐ ܕܢܫ̈ܐ ܕܕܝܪ̈ܘܬܐ ܬܬܐܢܝܚ܆ ܒܝܬ ܡܘܟܠܐ ܕܐܟܣ̈ܢܝܐ܆ ܘܒܝܬ ܒܪ̈ܢܫܐ ܒܠܚܘܕܝܗ̇ ܒܢܬ. ܠܗܕܐ ܟܕ ܥܒܕ ܐܘܪܚܐ ܕܐܝܢܐ ܕܐܬܐܬܐ ܘܬܫܡܫܬܗ، ܚܙܬ ܠܦܘܣܦܘܪ ܕܐܠܗܐ ܢܒܝܐ ܦܪܘܦܘܣ. ܘܗ̇ܝ ܟܕ ܗܕܐ ܒܠܒܗ̇ ܠܐ ܡܟܠ ܐܬܬ. ܐܠܐ ܘܠܐ ܗܘ ܐܝܟ ܐܣܓܝ ܡܬܚܫܒܐ ܡܢ ܟܕ ܥܒܠ ܐܫܬܡܫܬܐ ܕܕܝܪܘܬܐ܆ ܕܢܬܬܒܥ ܠܐܚܐ ܡܢ ܕܠܗ̇. ܐܘ ܕܢܦܩܠ ܠܐܬܪ̈ܚܬܐ ܡܢ ܐܚܐ. ܘܗܕܐ ܗ̣ܘ ܐܬܓܠܝܬ ܠܝ ܘܩܒܠܝܢ ܩܘܪܒܢܐ.

(§20) ܟܕ ܡܢ ܒܬܪܐ ܡܕܝܢܬܐ ܕܐܝܟ ܗܢܐ܆ ܘܡܢ ܐܒܗ̈ܬܐ ܡܕ̈ܝܢܬܐ ܕܐܝܟ ܗܠܝܢ܆ ܡܚܒܒܐ ܕܦܘܪܕܐ ܥܒܕ܆ ܗ̇ܘ ܐܘܪܚܝܐ ܡܕܝܢܬܐ ܦܠܘܪܘܣ. ܘܡܢ ܡܪ̈ܟܒܢܐ ܕܫ̈ܠܝ ܐܠܗܐ ܕܐܝܟ ܗܠܝܢ ܐܬܬܪܝ. ܘܕܦܐܝܬ ܘܒܫܘܒܬ ܘܐܢܐ ܕܗܠܝܢ ܕܐܒܘܗܝ، ܘܪܒܘܬܗ، ܗ̇ܘ ܗܘܐ ܡܬܐܬܐ ܠܒܢܝܢܐ ܐܝܟ ܕܟܬܝܒ܆ ܡܢܗܪܐ ܡܕܝܢܬܐ ܘܡܢܗܪ ܠܟܘܪܗ. ܘܡܬܠܒܒ ܠܟܠ ܚܕ̈ܕܐ ܙܪܥܐ. ܕܢܦܓܥ ܒܗܘ ܕܡܫܝܚܐ. ܘܢܦܫܗ ܘܒܢܘܗܝ ܠܡܫܡܫܘܬܐ ܬܪܝܨ̈ܬܐ ܫܡܫܝܢܐ. ܡܛܠ ܒܠܚܘܕ ܚܕ ܐܚܪܢܐ ܘܡܢ ܫܪܒܬܗ ܘܡܕܒܪܐ ܠܫܡܫܘܬܗ ܐܚܪܢܬܐ. ܗ̇ܘ ܟܕ ܗܘ ܒܬܪ ܬܠܡܝܕܐ [R 13] ܕܩܠܝܠܝܐ

[1] See also Judg 15:1–8.

[2] Already in the classical world, women who remained widows after the deaths of their first husband, who thus were *univira* (espoused only once), were idealized. Early Christian authors advised women to strive for that ideal as well. For a helpful discussion, see Marjorie Lightman and William Zeisel, "Univira: An Example of Continuity and Change in Roman Society," *CH* 46 (1977): 19–32; see also Gillian Clark, *Women in Late Antiquity: Pagan and Christian Lifestyles* (Oxford: Oxford University Press, 1994), 19–20.

[3] The Syriac ܒܝܬ ܡܘܟܠܐ ܕܐܟܣ̈ܢܝܐ may render the Greek ξενοδοχεῖον (see Raabe, 20 n. 2). The existence of guest houses in which strangers could find rest was of particular significance for minority groups such as anti-Chalcedonians in Palestine whose members repeatedly had to hide from persecutions they felt they experienced at the hands of Chalcedonians.

[4] The name could refer to the island of Cyprus as well as to the Herodian fortress Kypros in the Judean Desert. It is more likely that Peter took off to a secure place in the Judean Desert, i.e., to Kypros. For a fuller development of

indeed were quite ready to be harvested.[1] Moreover [Zuzo]'s daughter, who was called Ota and who was the blessed one's nurse, spent all her days in holiness, in fasting, and in prayer.

(§19) Our holy father's mother Bakurduktia remained a widow after the death of her husband. She did not consent to become [a wife] to a second husband[2] but rather was persistent in fasting and prayer. No longer inclined to dwell in the city, but desiring [instead] to live a life of monasticism in her villages, she built in every place a guesthouse for strangers[3] and a house for the sick. When the blessed one heard that she was about to come and visit him, he fled to Kypros,[4] so that he would not see her face. When she learned this, she did not come again. He was never willing, ever since he received the monastic habit, to write to one of his own or to receive letters from anyone, and he had told us this many times.[5]

(§20) The blessed, holy Peter, the rose blossom that sprang up from such a holy root and from such holy forefathers[6] and that was brought up by such God-fearing foster-parents, became, righteously and in the manner of those who begat him and brought him up, a chosen vessel just as it is written, "honored, hallowed, and one who is useful for his Lord," and "one who is ready for every good work,"[7] to bear the name of Christ[8] and to hold in honor and preach the orthodox faith before all men,[9] from his youth until his last breath, himself remaining a disciple **[R 13]** and a faithful

the argument, see Cornelia Horn, "Peter the Iberian and Monastic Settlement of the Herodian Fortress of Kypros," work in progress.

5 If Peter indeed displayed such an attitude, he served Rufus well as a model of a monk who practiced fully the ideal of completely cutting himself off from any ties to family and relatives and thus living as a stranger. The pursuit of *xeniteia*, the ideal of living as a stranger, was a formative force in early Christian ascetic life in the east. See, e.g., the discussion by Antoine Guillaumont, "Le dépaysement comme forme d'ascèse dans le monachisme ancien," *Annuaire de l'École pratique des hautes études, Section des sciences religieuses* 76 (1968–69): 31–58, repr. in idem, *Aux origines du monachisme chrétien: Pour une phénoménologie du monachisme* (Spiritualité Orientale 30; Paris: Abbaye de Bellefontaine, 1979), 89–116. Also see Horn, *Asceticism and Christological Controversy*, 230 *et passim*.

6 See Isa 11:1; 10; Rom 15:12. Also see above *Vit. Pet.* §10 (R 6).

7 2 Tim 2:21.

8 2 Tim 2:19.

9 Matt 10:32; Luke 12:8.

ܘܡܕܒܪܢܘܬܐ ܫܠܝܚܝܬܐ. ܟܕ ܒܟܠܗܝܢ ܫܩܝܠ ܨܠܝܒܗ ܕܡܫܝܚܐ. ܘܡܠܝܐ
ܡܢ ܪܘܚܐ ܩܕܝܫܐ. ܘܟܕ ܓܡܝܪܘܬܗ ܘܫܘܠܡܗ: ܠܩܘ̈ܒܠܐ ܐܬܐ ܛܪ.
ܠܡܬܕܒܪܢܘܬܗ ܕܡܫܝܚܐ ܘܕܐܘܢܓܠܝܘܢ. ܟܕ ܛܘܦܣܐ ܝܗܒ
ܢܦܫܗ ܕܟܠ ܛܒܬܐ ܘܕܘܒܪܐ ܡܫܬܪܐ: ܐܝܟ ܡܪܕܝܘܬܐ ܥܠܝܢܝܬܐ.
ܒܡܠܬܐ. ܒܗܘܦܟܐ. ܒܚܘܒܐ. ܒܗܝܡܢܘܬܐ. ܒܕܟܝܘܬܐ. ܘܡܫܝܢܘܬܐ
ܢܟܦܘܬܐ ܕܗܝܡܢܘܬܐ ܬܪܝܨܬ ܫܘܒܚܐ.܀ ܘܐܬܟܠ ܥܠ ܗ̇ܘ ܗܘܐ ܥܘܕܪܐ
ܒܛܠܝܘܬܗ ܩܕ̈ܝܫܬܐ. ܐܝܟ ܢܘܚ ܒܕܪܗ. ܟܕ ܡܐܟܘܬܐ ܟܠܦܢܝܐ
ܐܚܪܢܐ ܕܡܪܕܘܬܐ ܢܕܐ ܗܘܬ.܀

(§21) ܐܠܐ ܡܝܬܪ̈ܬܗ ܡܢ ܡܩ̈ܒܠܬܐ ܘܕܟܐܠܗܐ: ܘܕܒܘܪ̈ܘܗܝ,
ܐܘܓ̈ܠܢܐ ܕܟܠ ܡܘܡܬܐ ܕܠܗ ܪܫܐܝܬ ܡܬܒܝܢܝܢ ܗܘܘ: ܘܒܛܝܒܘܬܐ
ܐܠܗܝܬܐ ܒܗܘܢ ܪܚܡ ܗܘܘ: ܠܗ ܕܡܫܒܠܢܘܬܐ ܘܕܡܕܒܪܢܘܬܐ ܕܩ̈ܠܐ
ܕܝܠܗ ܐܬܠܝܗ̇: ܢܦܫܐ ܕܦܬܐܝܬ ܢܚܬܒ ܘܠܬܚܬܐ ܢܫܠܡ. ܕܢܠ ܐܒܐ
ܚܙܐ ܕܠܡܐ ܟܕ ܒܬܚܘܡܐ ܕܠܐ ܣܟܐ ܘܕܠܐ ܚܒܝܐ ܕܬܘܪ̈ܘܗܝ,
ܐܗܠܝܟ. ܟܕ ܠܐ ܡܢܦܣܐܝܬ[1] ܘܠܐ ܡܬܨܝܕܢܐܝܬ ܐܝܬ ܠܗ ܕܐܣܝܐ.
ܕܡܢ ܓ̈ܦܟܐ ܕܓ̈ܠܠܐ ܕܠܒܘܬܐ ܕܢܦܫܐ ܠܗ ܐܬܦܢܝܘ ܘܐܬܠܒܒ.
ܘܡܛܠ ܚܦܝܛܘܬܐ ܕܠܗ ܘܡܣܝܒܪܢܘܬܐ: ܫܘܦܪܢܐ ܕܐܣܟܡܐ ܡܝܬܪܘܬܐ.
ܡܢ ܗܪܟܐ ܟܠܗ̇ ܡܢ ܕܒܪ̈ܘܗܝ, ܕܗ̇ܘ ܘܩ̈ܘܒܠܘܗܝ: ܕܟܢ̈ܫܐ ܡܫ̈ܠܡܐ
ܘܬܪ̈ܝܢܐ ܘܡܣܟܢ̈ܐ. ܕܟܕ ܠܚܘܒܐ ܕܐܠܗܐ ܐܬܦܢܘ. ܒܢܝܢܘܬܐ

[1] MS B has ܡܦܝܣܐܝܬ, which Raabe adopts. MS A has a lacuna here.

[2] Thus gaining apostolic authority that allowed him to lead his followers, even against the wishes of an ecclesiastical hierarchy.

[3] This is the first occurrence of the phrase "carrying the cross of Christ," which in Rufus's works becomes a characteristic description of the anti-Chalcedonian ascetic. For a fuller discussion of the significance of the cross in the spirituality of the anti-Chalcedonian ascetic community in fifth- and early sixth-century Palestine, see Horn, *Asceticism and Christological Controversy*, 338–342.

[4] Note the imagery of "catching." This theme is relevant at several other instances throughout the *Vita Petri Iberi*. See, e.g., below at §§153, 154 (R 115). Peter is portrayed as a "fisher of men," in allusion to Matt 4:19 and Mark 1:17.

[5] 1 Tim 4:12.

[6] See Exod 13:25.

[7] One is reminded of the saying ascribed to Abba Hilarion: "From Palestine, Abba Hilarion went to the mountain to Abba Anthony. Abba Anthony said to him, 'You are welcome, torch which awakens the day.' Abba Hilarion said, 'Peace to you, pillar of light, giving light to the world.'" See *Apophthegmata Patrum, Abba Hilarion* 1 in Benedicta Ward, trans., *The Sayings of the Desert*

imitator of the apostles,[2] always carrying the cross of Christ[3] and being full of the Holy Spirit. Through his grace and power he snatched many for obedience to Christ and the gospel,[4] himself giving an example of such goodness and of a virtuous way of life according to the apostolic exhortation: "in word, in manner of life, in love, in faith, in purity."[5] [He was] a shining pillar[6] of the orthodox faith,[7] and for all civilization he was a fortress[8] through his holy prayers, in the likeness of Noah when the ark was rolling on the last deluge of chastisement.[9]

(§21) But it is not for the weakness and poverty of our words to dare to complete the task of describing at length his truly manifold and godly virtues and his evangelical way of life, manifested at every stage of his life in a special way and increasing within him by divine grace.[10] For I fear, lest when I walk on the endless and bottomless depth[11] of his right actions, since I am unexperienced and unable to swim, I will be shipwrecked and drowned by the floods of the waves of grace that are attached to him and because of my feebleness and weakness [such] excellence should suffer harm.[12] Each one of his customs and his gifts [were such] that they showed themselves by the grace of God at different times, [in different] ways[13] and deeds, in asceticism and in Naziriteship,[14] and, to

Fathers: The Alphabetical Collection (rev. ed.; Kalamazoo, Mich.: Cistercian, 1984), 111.

[8] See Ps 18:2.

[9] See Gen 7. Here one may catch a glimpse of a layer of apocalyptic expectation that appears to have characterized the way in which anti-Chalcedonians in Palestine saw the world around them and their own role within it during the fifth and sixth centuries. Rufus's later text, the *Plerophoriae*, is even richer in imagery like this. For a discussion of the role of signs and revelations in that later part of Rufus's work, see Steppa, *John Rufus and the World Vision*, 113–41.

[10] Possibly allusions to Luke 2:53.

[11] The Syriac ܠܐ ܥܒܪܐ may translate the Greek ἄβυσσος (Raabe, 21 n. 3).

[12] Allusions to Mark 14:28–31 (6:45–52; John 6:15–21).

[13] See Heb 1:1.

[14] For a discussion of this form of asceticism, see Horn, *Asceticism and Christological Controversy*, 194–96 *et passim*; idem, "Beyond Theology," ch. 3. See also *Vit. Pet.* §28 (R 19).

ܘܒܚܝܪܘܬܐ. ܘܕܫܠܝܚܐܝܬ ܐܡܪ: ܒܫܢ̈ܩܐ. ܒܐܢܢ̈ܩܣ. ܒܐܓ̈ܘܢܐ.
ܒܪ̈ܕܘܦܝܐ. ܒܟܒ̈ܠܐ. ܒܫܓ̈ܘܫܝܐ. ܒܫܗܪ̈ܐ. ܒܐܣ̈ܪܐ. ܒܡܬܟܬ̈ܫܢܐ.
ܒܐܓ̈ܘܢܐ ܕܡܛܐ ܠܕܡܐ. ܠܐ ܠܘܬ ܣܓܝܐܬܐ ܒܠܚܘܕ:: ܘܠܐ ܠܘܬ
ܕܡܐ ܘܒܣܪܐ: ܐܠܐ ܠܘܬ ܐܪ̈ܟܘܣ ܘܫܘ̈ܠܛܢܐ. [R 14] ܠܘܬ ܐܚ̈ܝܕܝ,
ܥܠܡܐ ܕܚܫܘܟܐ ܗܢܐ. ܠܘܬ ܪ̈ܘܚܐ ܕܒܝܫܘܬܐ. ܒܡܫܡܫܢܘܬܐ
ܦܓ̈ܥܐܬܐ. ܒܚܝܠܐ ܕܐܬܘ̈ܬܐ ܘܕܬܕܡܪ̈ܬܐ ܘܕܐܣܘ̈ܬܐ. ܒܚܝܠܐ
ܕܪܘܚܐ ܩܕܝܫܐ. ܒܝܕ ܙܝ̈ܢܐ ܕܙܕܝܩܘܬܐ: ܗܠܝܢ ܕܝܡܝܢܐ ܘܕܣܡܠܐ.
ܒܫܘܒܚܐ ܘܒܨܥܪܐ. ܒܛܘܪ̈ܦܐ ܘܒܡܫܩܠܘܬܐ. ܐܝܟ ܠܐ ܝܕܝܥܐ ܟܕ
ܘܝܕܝܥ ܗܘܐ. ܘܠܐܠܗܐ ܒܠܚܘܕܘܗܝ, ܝܕܝܥ ܗܘܐ ܟܡܐ ܕܙܕܩ ܗܘܐ
ܕܢܬܝܕܥ. ܐܝܟ ܡܝܬ ܗܘܐ ܠܡܚܙܝܐ ܚܝ ܗܘܐ ܕܝܢ ܒܟܠܝܘܡ ܘܪܬܚ
ܒܪܘܚܐ. ܐܝܟ ܡܬܪܕܝܢܐ ܕܝܢ. ܠܦ̈ܓܥܐܐ ܕܝܢ ܡܬܚܙܐ ܗܘܐ. ܟܕ
ܠܢܦ̈ܫܬܐ ܘܠܦܓ̈ܪܐ ܗܘܐ ܡܬܐܣܝܐ ܕܐܢܫ ܠܟܠܢܫ ܡܢܗܘܢ.
ܐܝܟ ܕܒܕܡ ܠܘܬ ܠܗ̇ ܘܠܒܕܡ ܐܚܪܢ. ܠܐ ܒܠܚܘܕ ܥܠ ܐܪܥܐ:
ܐܠܐ ܘܒܐܘܪ̈ܚܐ ܕܒܝܡܐ. ܗܟܢ ܟܕ ܐܝܬ ܗܘܐ ܠܗ ܗܘ ܫܘ̈ܡܗܬܐ
ܕܫܘ̈ܡܗܐ. ܐܡܪܐ ܕܠܒܝܫ ܐܢܬܘܗܝ, ܗܘܐ ܠܟܘ ܠܗ ܘܐܬܕܒܪܬܗ ܘܕܒܘܪܗ.
ܗܠܝܢ ܘܒܠܗܝܢ ܕܠܗܠܝܢ ܢܦܩ. ܕܟܕ ܠܒܥܘܬܐ ܕܡܫܝܚܐ ܕܚܕܬ ܗܘܐ
ܒܗ. ܠܘܬ ܠܒܝܫܐ ܘܦܘܪܝܘܢܐ ܕܦܓ̈ܥܐܐ ܡܬܟܠܝܢܐܝܬ ܐܬܬܒܪ̈ܝܘ[1]
ܡܢܗ. ܒܟܠ ܡܕܡ ܐܝܟ ܕܫܬܝܩܐܝܬ ܘܫܪܝܪܐܝܬ ܐܬܚܙܝ. ܘܐܝܟ
ܕܒܫܝܢܘܬܐ ܐܢܝܕܐ: ܥܒܕ ܐܢܐ. ܘܡܫܬܪܝܐ ܐܝܟ ܠܪ̈ܘܚܢܝܐ ܕܗܠܝܢ.

[1] So MS B. MS A and Raabe have ܐܬܬܒܪ̈ܝ,.

[2] ܫܠܝܚܐܝܬ needs to be understood as refering to the Apostle, not merely as "barely." See Payne Smith, 580.

[3] The Syriac transliterates the Greek ἀνάγκη.

[4] The Syriac transliterates the Greek ἀγών.

[5] See 2 Cor 6:4–5.

[6] The Syriac transliterates the Greek ἀρχαί (Raabe, 22 n. 2).

[7] The Syriac ܫܘ̈ܠܛܢܐ may translate the Greek ἐξουσίαι (Raabe, 22 n. 3).

[8] The Syriac ܐܚ̈ܝܕܝ, ܥܠܡܐ may translate the Greek κοσμοκράτορες (Raabe, 22 n. 4).

[9] Eph 6:12.

[10] Rom 15:19.

[11] See 2 Cor 6:8; Rom 15:19.

[12] See 2 Cor 6:9.

speak in the manner of the Apostle,[2] "in afflictions, in necessities,[3] in sufferings, in persecutions, in labors, in fasts, in vigils, in struggles, in fights, in contests[4] unto blood, not only against sin"[5] and "not [only] against flesh and blood but against princes[6] and authorities,[7] **[R 14]** against the rulers[8] of this dark age, against the spirits of evil,"[9] "in many [expressions of] trust, in the power of signs and wonders and healings,"[10] "in the power of the Holy Spirit, with the weapons of righteousness, those of the right hand and of the left, in honor and in shame, in slander and in good reports."[11] For he was "as one who is unknown and one who is known,"[12] but "he was known to his God alone,"[13] "as much as he ought to be known."[14] He was as one dead to the flesh,[15] but was alive always and fervent in the spirit.[16] For though poor, he enriched many because he was nourishing souls and bodies with nourishment suited to each one of them. Although he had nothing, he possessed everything,[17] not only on earth but also in the storehouses that are in heaven.[18] For there he had treasures stored up, where at every moment were his heart, his mind, and his manner of life.[19] These [things] and all that are like them, that through the grace of Christ dwelling in him were sublimely directed by him toward the zeal and salvation of many,[20] I leave aside because I am not able to explain accurately and truthfully nor to write as in a story.[21] I refer their friends to the mouths of all those who from the beginning were [among the] saints, the ones who have heard

13 See Gal 4:9.
14 See 1 Cor 8:2–3.
15 See Col 2:13.
16 See Rom 8:10–12.
17 See 2 Cor 6:10.
18 See Matt 6:20. See also the incident below, *Vit. Pet.* §67 (R 46–47).
19 See Matt 6:21.
20 See 2 Tim 3:15.
21 The meaning of the Syriac word ܬܫܥܝܬܐ ranges from "relation, narration, account" to "story, history, biography." See Payne Smith, 623. The same word is also used in the title of the present work.

ܠܘܬ ܦܘܩܕܢܐ ܕܟܠܗܘܢ ܗܠܝܢ ܕܗܢ ܡܕܝܢ ܗܘܘ ܒܗ[1] ܡܕܒܪܢܐ. ܗܢܘܢ
ܕܗܢ ܗܠܝܢ ܕܩ̈ܢܝܢ ܦܘܠܚܢܐ ܥܒܕܗ. ܗܠܝܢ ܕܐܝܟ ܕܒܟܬ̈ܒܐ ܟܗ̈ܢܝܐ
ܟܬܝܒܢ. ܗܟܝܠ ܐܢܐ ܕܢܕܪܝܢ. ܘܫܬܡܠܐ ܕܒܝܬܐ ܕܡܢܗܘܢ ܘܦܘܬܪܐ.
ܒܟܠܕܘܟܝܢ ܚܢܐ ܠܚ̈ܬܢܐ. ܘܚܕ ܐܝܟ ܠܐ ܡܫܬܐܠ: ܡܛܠ ܕܠܚܒܘܬܐ
ܐܠܗܝܬܐ ܡܬܬܟ̈ܪܝܢ. ܘܠܐ ܐܝܟ ܠܐ ܢܗܒܝܢ ܠܗܠܝܢ ܕܡܬܐܡ̈ܪܢ.
ܐܠܐ ܡܬܐܠܠܝܢ ܕܩ̈ܪܝܢ ܡܢ ܥܙܪܐ ܢܗܘܐ ܕܥܒܕ. ܐܢܐ ܚܢܐ ܙܒܢܐ
ܐܘ ܡܠܬܐ ܕܢܬܒܥܐ ܢܦܩܘ [R 15] ܫܬܐܬܐ: ܗܠܝܢ ܕܟܐܢ̈ܘܬܗ،
ܘܒܗܘܢ ܠܚܒܘܬܐ ܕܡܫܝܚܐ ܗܕܪܬ. ܠܘܬ ܦܘܪܢܣܐ ܗ̇ܝ ܐܝܟ ܕܐܡ̇ܪܬ
ܘܡܬܦܪ̈ܢܣܘܬܐ ܕܗ̇ܢܘܢ. ܗ̇ܕܝܢ ܒܠܒ̈ܘܬܐ ܒܠܚܘܕܝܗܘܢ: ܕܐܝܟܢ ܕܩܦܠܐܐ:
ܠܘܬ ܡܘܬܒܐ ܘܕܝܢܐ ܘܥܘܕܪܐ ܕܡܫܝܚܘܬܐ ܬܪܝܨܬ ܥܘܗܕܢܐ.
ܘܕܒܬܐ ܡܐܬܘܬܝܢ ܕܟܠܗ. ܕܗ̇ܝ ܕܐܝܬ ܟܗܢܐ ܘܪܝܫܐ ܐܦܝܣܩܘܦܐ.
(§22) ܘܟܐܢܐ ܙܒܢ: ܘܠܐ ܐܝܟ ܐܝܟ ܗܢܘܢ ܙܢ̈ܝܢ ܒܬ̈ܠܬܐ ܢܐܡܪ.
ܡܢ ܢܦܫܗ ܢܦܩ ܘܣܠܩ ܐܡܪܐ ܕܐܝܟ ܗܢܐ. ܐܠܐ ܒܗ ܐܬܚܙܝ ܡܢ
ܠܚܒܘܬܐ ܕܟܠ. ܡܢܬܐ ܡܕܡ ܐܠܗܝܬܐ ܘܥܒܕܬ ܠܬܕܡܘܪܬܐ: ܗ̇ܝ
ܕܐܦܠܐ ܒܗ ܡܣܘܪܗܘܢ ܐܢܐ ܒܝܕܐ ܕܐܚܪ̈ܢܝܢ. ܐܠܐ ܬܢܐܬ
ܐܝܟ ܕܒܝܕܐ ܒܗ ܠܗܕܡܐ ܐܦܣܩܘܦܐ: ܒܗ ܡܠܠ ܠܟܠ ܠܘܬ ܥܘܪܢܐ
ܕܠܗ ܚܣܠܬܐ ܐܢܐ ܠܟܠܬܐ. ܒܕܡܘܬܐ ܚܢܐ ܕܢܝܚ ܐܒܗ̈ܬܐ
ܐܒܗܝܢ. ܘܐܦ ܗܘ ܡܢ ܡܠܟܝܢܐ ܐܬܒܠ ܘܐܬܠ. ܠܝܢܐ ܕܝܢ
ܒܦܬܘܪܬ ܘܒܢܐ ܢܬܚܒܝ ܒܗ ܘܟܘܪܬܐ܀
(§23) ܒܗ ܡܦܝܢ ܒܡܘܣܬܪܢܘܣ ܐܚܘܗܝ ܕܗܢܐ ܡܢ ܦܘܐܣܛܘܠܘܢ[2]

[1] So MS B. MS A has a lacuna here, and Raabe omits this word.

[2] Raabe's emendation of the transliteration. MS A reads ܦܘܐܣܛܘܠܘܢ; MS B reads ܦܘܣܛܘܠܘܢ.

[3] The anecdotes and apophthegmata-like traditions passed on among the anti-Chalcedonians in Syria-Palestine and gathered in part in the *Plerophoriae* contain many instances that attest to such an intense oral tradition. See, e.g., *Pler.* 1, 10, 12, 17, 18, 20, 31, and many other instances. See also below *Vit. Pet.* §§32, 80, and 115 (R 22, 56, 83). For an edition of the Syriac text and French translation of John Rufus's *Plerophoriae*, see Nau and Brière, *Jean Rufus, évêque de Maïouma*.

[4] Syr., ܟܬ̈ܒܐ ܟܗ̈ܢܝܐ, lit. "priestly books."

[5] See Luke 4:37.

[6] See Rom 10:20; Isa 65:1.

[7] Or, "better suited for us."

[8] See 1 Cor 14:12.

[9] Both terms, "high priest" with stronger Old Testament allusions and

them many times.[3] I advise that we follow closely these [accounts] as though they were written in the holy books,[4] so that we might be filled with the knowledge and the benefit that is from them. For they are renowned in every place,[5] and without anyone's asking they are proclaimed by divine grace itself.[6] No one fails to believe these [things] that are said but rather holds that [the things] he hears are less than the truth. For what time or word would be sufficient[7] to relate **[R 15]** accurately these [deeds] that the grace of Christ performed through him and with him for the salvation and the boldness of those who desire to be zealous for the good, as I have said, than the many [deeds he worked] for the establishment and edification and confirmation of the orthodox faith and his catholic church,[8] of which [Grace] set him up as high priest[9] and shepherd?[10]

(§22) How [did this take place]? May no one, like those lovers of accusations,[11] say, "Of his own accord he took and seized such an honor." He was called by grace from on high, a calling at once divine and marvelous, which not even in haste I could pass over but rather I will recount it briefly, as far as possible, while taking the story a little further back to its beginning. For in the likeness of the patriarch Isaac, he too was conceived and born on account of a promise,[12] the manner [of which] we will relate briefly at an appropriate time.[13]

(§23) Once, when his father Bosmarios was returning from

"shepherd" with more of a New Testament ring, point toward Peter's later function as bishop of Maiuma and ultimately as anti-Chalcedonian bishop in Palestine. For his ordination as bishop, see below *Vit. Pet.* §§75, 78–79 (R 51, 53–55).

[10] See 1 Pet 2:25.

[11] The Syriac may render the Greek φιλεγκλήμονες (Raabe, 23 n. 4).

[12] See Gen 15.

[13] The Syriac ܒܦܘܪܣ ܬܘܪ ܕܦܐܝܐ translates the Greek ἐν εὐκαιρίᾳ (Raabe, 23 n. 5).This reference seems to indicate a natural break in the flow of the text. It appears as if the narrator interrupted his account and continued the narrative with the following incident at another occasion, not immediately during the same session. Instances like this one (see, e.g., also *Vit. Pet.* §§114–115 [R 83]) support the assumption that the written form of the *Vita Petri Iberi* grew out of an originally oral account. See the comments in Horn, "Beyond Theology," 26.

ܡܕܡ ܕܢܐܬܐ ܠܡܕܝܢܬܐ. ܩܪܝܒ ܠܐܪܓܠܝܬܐ ܕܐܝܬ ܒܡܪܓܝܬܐ. ܟܕ
ܦܓܥ ܙܕܝܩܐ: ܘܡܒܪܟܬܐ ܕܐܘܪܚܐ ܟܠܗ. ܘܟܕ ܐܬܐܠܨ ܕܢܫܪܐ ܥܠ
ܦܘܪܘܣ: ܘܡܫܪܝܢܬܐ ܗܘܬ. ܢܦܩܐ ܠܐܦܝ ܕܐܡܪ ܠܗ: ܒܦܘܪܣܛܝܢܐ: ܗܘܐ
ܗ̇ܘܐ ܠܝ ܡܬܒܪܟܢܐ ܢܘܗܪܐ. ܐܠܐ ܩܘܡ ܥܒܘܪ ܘܟܘܠ ܠܥܡܟ.
ܘܣܓܝ ܠܐܢܬܬܟ: ܘܬܒܛܢ. ܘܬܐܠܕ ܠܟ ܒܪܐ. ܗ̇ܘ ܕܢܗܘܐ ܡܫܡܫ
ܩܕܡ ܐܠܗܐ ܘܩܕܡ ܒܢܝ̈ܢܫܐ.

(§24) ܟܕ ܗܟܝܠ ܒܫܠܡܘܬܐ ܐܠܗܝܬܐ ܕܐܝܟ ܗܕܐ ܐܬܓܠܝ ܘܐܬܒܠ.
ܘܐܬܪܒܝ: ܟܕ ܕܟܝܠ ܐܝܬܘܗܝ، ܗܘܐ ܒܡܘܡܬܗ ܒܪ ܬܪܬܥܣܪܐ ܫܢ̈ܝܢ:
ܗܟܢܪܐ ܐܫܬܕܪ [R 16] ܠܪܚܡ ܠܐܠܗܐ ܘܒܣܝܠܝܐ ܬܐܘܕܘܣܝܘܣ
ܘܒܪܗ ܡܠܟܐ ܕܪ̈ܗܘܡܝܐ. ܘܟܕ ܩ̈ܦܠܐܬܐ ܡܟܠ ܗܕܐ ܐܦܝܣ ܟܕ
ܡܫܕܪ ܐܟ̈ܬܒܐ: ܡܫܬܕܪ ܡܢ ܒܡܣܪܝܘܣ ܐܒܘܗ،: ܕܡܟܠܝܢ ܗܘܐ
ܗ̇ܘ ܕܒܢܐ ܥܠ ܐܬܪܐ ܕܐܝ̈ܒܪܝܐ. ܟܕ ܩܕܡ ܢܦ̇ܩ ܡܠܗ ܢܣܡܘܬܐ
ܕܪ̈ܘܡܝܐ ܐܝܟ ܒܪ̈ܗܘܡܝܐ: ܠܒܪ ܡܢ ܡܕܒܪܢܘܬܐ ܕܦܪ̈ܣܝܐ ܙ̈ܥܘܪܐ.
ܡܫܬܕܪ ܕܝܢ ܥܡ ܙܘܓܐ ܦܠܛܝܢܐ̈ ܘܐܢܫܪܐ.

(§25) ܘܟܕ ܐܬܐ ܠܘܬ ܦܠܛܝܢ ܬܐܘܕܘܣܝܘܣ: ܘܡܟܝܟܐܝܬ ܡܠܟܐ
ܐܬܩܒܠ: ܘܐܝܟ ܒܪܐ ܡܬܪܒܝܐ ܗܘܐ ܡܠܟܐ ܘܡܬܢܟܦ: ܟܕ ܢܦܩ

[1] The Syriac transliterates the Greek προάστειον, "suburban farm" or "estate." See Payne Smith, 463; Raabe, 23 n. 6. See also Raabe, *Vit. Pet.* 15, line 15, who emends the transliteration (MS A: ܦܪܘܐܣܛܝܘܢ; MS B: ܦܪܘܣܛܝܘܢ) to ܦܪܘܐܣܛܝܘܢ.

[2] The spelling ܐܪܓܠܝܬܐ in MS Sachau 321, folio 71 recto, is rare.

[3] The Syriac may translate the Greek δίοδος (Raabe, 23 n. 7).

[4] See Josh 1:2.

[5] See Luke 1:31.

[6] See 1 Sam 2:26.

[7] See Luke 2:42.

[8] Also known as Theodosius II, Eastern Roman emperor from 408 to 450 C.E. As the son of Arcadius (395–408), he was proclaimed Augustus on 10 January 402, briefly after his birth, but became emperor only after his father's death. Throughout his reign Theodosius was strongly influenced not only by prefects and chamberlains at his court (e.g., the prefect Anthemius or the chamberlain Chrysaphius) but also by his sister Pulcheria and his wife Athenais, better known by her baptismal name, Eudocia. Theodosius II is probably most famous for his codification of Roman law in the *Codex Theodosianus* (438 C.E.).

one [of his] estate[s][1] to come to town, he arrived at a torrent[2] that lay across [his route. The water had risen] to a high flood and prevented [him] from crossing[3] the path. While he was compelled to stop on its bank and was worried, he saw a man who said to him, "Bosmarios, behold, you can cross the river. Get up, cross,[4] enter into your house, and know your wife. She will conceive and bear you a son,[5] who will be honored before God and before men."[6]

(§24) Having then been conceived, born, and reared in such divine grace, while [Peter] was but twelve years of age,[7] he was sent [as] a hostage **[R 16]** to the God-fearing and Christian Theodosius the Younger, emperor of the Romans.[8] Sending messengers, [Theodosius] had very much pressed the matter. Thus [Peter] was sent with great pomp and honor by his father Bosmarios, who was reigning at the time over the country of the Iberians, because [Bosmarios] preferred the friendship of the Romans as Christians rather than the assistance of the impious Persians.[9]

(§25) [Peter] came to the blessed Theodosius and was received by him affectionately and was raised and loved by him like

For a contemporary portrait of Theodosius II, see Socrates Scholasticus, *Hist. eccl.* 6.23–7.48 (PG 67:729–842; Hansen and Širinjan, 347–95; Zenos, 2:153–78).

[9] For discussion of the relationship between the Persians and the Byzantines at the time and the Georgians sandwiched in between them, see above, pp. xxii–xxiii; see also Charles Burney and David Marshall Lang, *The Peoples of the Hills: Ancient Ararat and Caucasus* (History of Civilization; London: Weidenfeld & Nicolson, 1971); Ivane A. Yavaȟišvili, ქართველის ერის ისტორია [*History of the Georgian People*] (4 vols; Tibilisi: Stalinis saxelobis T'bilisis saxelmcip'o universitetis gamomc'emloba, 1941–51); Ernest Honigmann, *Die Ostgrenze des byzantinischen Reiches: Von 363 bis 1071, nach griechischen, arabischen, syrischen und armenischen Quellen* (Corpus Bruxellense Historiae Byzantinae 3; Brussels: Éditions de l'Institut de Philologie et d'Histoire Orientales, 1935); Manvelichvili, *Histoire de Géorgie*; Gregor Paradze, "Probleme der ältesten Kirchengeschichte Georgiens," *OrChr* 29 (1932): 153–71; Cyrill Toumanoff, "Christian Caucasia between Byzantium and Iran," *Traditio: Studies in Ancient Medieval Thought and Religion* 10 (1954): 109–89; see also Aßfalg and Lang, "Georgien," 12:389–396; and Lordkipanidse and Brakmann, "Iberia II (Georgien)," especially 16–37.

ܚܦܝܛܘܬܐ ܕܡܛܠ ܕܢܒܠܬ ܐܠܗܐ ܘܪܚܡܬ ܡܫܝܚܐ ܕܫܠܝܚܐ:
ܘܕܐܘܕܘܟܣܝܐ ܡܠܟܬܐ ܒܪܬ ܙܘܓܗ ܘܒܪܬ ܠܒܝܗ: ܘܕܓܒܪ̈ܐ ܘܕܢܫ̈ܐ
ܕܡܫܡܫܝܢ ܠܗܘܢ. ܘܐܬܝܪܐܬ ܕܐܘ̈ܠܘܓܝܐ ܗ̇ܢܘ ܕܡܬܩܪܝܢ
ܡܘܡܠ̈ܐ: ܐܝܬܝܗܘܢ ܗܘܘ ܓܝܪ ܒܠܗܘܢ ܕܚܕܪܝܢ ܐܝܟ ܕܒܕܝܪܐ
ܒܟܠܝܘܡ: ܒܨ̈ܠܘܬܐ ܘܒܬܫܒ̈ܚܬܐ ܕܠܠܝܐ: ܘܒܐܚܪ̈ܢܝܬܐ
ܗܠܝܢ ܕܩ̈ܕܝܫܝܢ ܠܐܠܗܐ: ܐܬܚܘܠ ܒܠܒܢܐ. ܘܟܕ ܐܬܐ ܠܗ ܒܡܬܐܬ
ܡܢ ܐܒ̈ܗܘܗܝ، ܪܚܡܬ ܐܠܗܐ: ܐܝܟ ܒܠܝܘܢܘܬܐ ܕܝܘܪܐ. ܠܗܕܐ
ܒܥ̈ܦܠܬܐ ܘܒܚܘܒܘܬܐ ܟܠ ܝܘܡ ܒܝܘܡ ܡܪܒܐ ܗܘܐ ܒܚܦܝܛܘܬܐ.
ܒܕܡܐ ܕܒܠܚܘܕܘܬܐ ܪܒܬܐ ܘܡܠܘܬܐ ܕܠܒܘܫܬܐ ܡܫܝܚܝܬܐ ܠܢܦܫܗ
ܫܩܠ. ܟܕ ܡܢ ܠܒܪ ܗ̇ܘ ܥܠ ܓܘܫܡܗ: ܠܒܘܫܐ ܕܗܕܪܐ ܠܒܝܫ ܗܘܐ.
ܡܢ ܠܓܘ ܕܝܢ ܠܒܘܫܐ ܡܕܡ ܚܫܝܢܐ ܘܡܦܪܓܠܐ ܬܚܝܬ ܗܘܐ.
ܕܝܠܫܬܐ ܒܬܪܘܬܗ. ܡܐܒܠܘܬܗ ܕܝܢ ܐܝܬܝܗ̇ ܗܘܬ: ܗ̇ܝ ܕܐܝܬ
ܗܘܐ ܠܕܝܢܐ ܘܠܬܫܡ̈ܫܬܗ، ܘܡܕܒܪܐ ܒܡܫܡܫܢܘܬܐ ܕܒܬܪܬܐ. ܘܚܕܐ
ܠܬܠܬܐ ܒܫܢܝܢ [R 17] ܘܠܐܪܒܥܐ ܗܕܐ ܓܡܠ ܗܘܐ. ܐܝܬ ܕܝܢ
ܐܡܬܝ، ܘܚܕܐ ܠܟܠܬܐ ܕܫܡܬܐ. ܐܝܟ ܕܠܡܫܡܫܢܐ ܕܡܫܡܫܐ ܕܪܚܡ
ܡܪܘܬܐ: ܘܕܘܒܪ̈ܐ ܠܗ ܡܬܚܫܒܐ ܕܫܡܝܐ. ܬܫܡܫܬܐ ܕܝܢ: ܐܪܥܝܐ
ܐܝܬܝܗ̇ ܗܘܬ: ܠܡ̇ܠܟܐ ܫܠܝܛܐ ܘܐܚܝܕܐ. ܟܕ ܡܫܒܚܐ ܕܝܢ ܡܕܒܪ̈ܐ
ܗܘܐ ܢܦܫܗ: ܘܡܬܕܒܪܢܐ ܗܘܐ ܡܢ ܟܠ ܦܠܚܘܬܐ ܕܡܫܡܫܐ ܘܪܘܚܢܐ:
ܘܡܫܡܫܢܘܬܐ ܪܒܐ ܗܘܐ: ܣ̇ܥܪܐ ܗܘܐ ܡܫܟܚܐ ܕܐܠܗܐ ܘܚܝܠܐ ܡܢ ܪܘܚܐ
ܩܕܝܫܐ. ܘܗܢܐ ܟܠܗ: ܐܝܟܢܐ ܕܒܡܠܟܘܬܐ ܐܠܗܝܬܐ ܟܕ ܒܟܠ
ܓܠܝܢܐ ܐܝܬܘܗܝ، ܐܦܝܘܬܐ ܩ̈ܠܝܠܬܐ ܘܐܬܬ̈ܥܝܪܬܐ ܘܫܦܝܠܐ ܙܥܘܪܐ.
ܘܗ̇ܘ ܒܟܠܝܘܡ ܒܐܝ̈ܕܘܗܝ، ܢܬܦܠܚ. ܘܡܛܠ ܕܠܐ ܠܓܒܪ ܐܦܩ

[1] Theodosius II had two girls with Eudocia. There is some dispute concerning his fathering a little boy who passed away at young age. See the discussion in R. Scharf, "Die 'Apfel-Affäre' oder gab es einen Kaiser Arcadius II?" *ByzZ* 83 (1990): 435–50. See also Horn, "Empress Eudocia and the Monk Peter the Iberian."

[2] Although the Syriac here has her name as "Eudoxia," at all other instances it is "Eudocia."

[3] The author clearly portrays Eudocia in a positive light. For a discussion of her sustained support of the anti-Chalcedonian movement, see Horn, "Empress Eudocia and the Monk Peter the Iberian."

a son.[1] He witnessed the diligence on account of the fear of God and the love of Christ of the emperor, of Eudocia,[2] the empress, his wife and the companion of his zeal,[3] of the men and women serving them, and especially of the eunuchs,[4] who are called *cubicularii*.[5] For they were all living in the palace as in a monastery,[6] with prayers, fasts, night services, and the other [exercises] that are pleasing to God, [and Peter] became inflamed with zeal. Having had at home from his parents the love of God like a spark of fire, he constantly stoked [these] sparks day by day, with diligence, through courses of asceticism[7] and self-denial, until the great flame and the fire of heavenly grace filled his soul. Underneath he was clothed with a hair shirt against his body, but on the outside he was clad in a splendid and shining garment to hide his virtue. His food was that which Daniel and his friends had,[8] and this in small measure, and he ate it once every three or four **[R 17]** days, occasionally only once a week. He loved discipline in order to subjugate the flesh and its disorderly joys. The earth was a bed for the young and tender king, and while he conducted himself so and was purified from every defilement of the flesh and of the spirit[9] and was growing in age, he became a temple of God and full of the Holy Spirit.[10] All of this was in such a way that through divine grace, while he was still a child, many healings and signs and

4 The Syriac transliterates the Greek εὐνοῦχοι. Eunuchs, i.e., castrated male persons, were appointed to take charge of the women at court.

5 I.e., chamberlains. The Syriac transliterates the Latin *cubicularii*. Chamberlains, often eunuchs, functioned as personal attendants at the court. Through their immediate access to persons of power, many of them were able to exert influence on ecclesiastical and state politics.

6 See also Socrates Scholasticus, *Hist. eccl.* 7.22.4–5 (PG 67:785; Hansen and Širinjan, 368), who knows about Theodosius that he rendered his "palace little different from a monastery [οὐκ ἀλλοιότερα δὲ ἀσκητηρίου κατέστησε τὰ βασίλεια]."

7 Literally, "advancement."

8 See Dan 1:12.

9 2 Cor 7:1.

10 See 1 Cor 3:16.

ܠܬ̈ܡܘܢܝܐ܆ ܟܕ ܥܒܕ ܐܝܟ ܗܠܝܢ ܐܣܝ̈ܘܬܐ܆ ܚܙܐ ܡܢܗܝܢ ܠܩܘܕܡ
ܐܘܚܕ܆ ܕܡܦܩܐ ܕܠܒܠܗܝܢ ܠܒܪ܀

(§26) ܓܪ̈ܡܐ ܕܝܢ ܕܩܕ̈ܝܫܐ ܡܕ̈ܝܢܐ ܐܝܬ ܗܘܐ ܠܗ܆ ܕܐܬܐܝܗܘܢ
ܗܘܘ ܦܬ̈ܘܪܐ ܒܟܣܦܐ. ܕܫܬܐܝܬ ܬܘܒܠܐ ܗ̇ܢܘܢ ܐܬܕܪܘ ܗܘܘ.
ܗ̇ܢܘܢ ܕܒܟܠ ܡܢ ܡܫܠܡܢܘܬܗ ܕܦܘܠܚܢܐ ܘܒܝܪܐ܆ ܘܡ̈ܫܡܫܢܘܗܝ
ܡܬܚܪܡܝܢ ܣܝܢ܆ ܘܕܒܪ̈ܝܫܘܗܝ ܡܫܬܟܚܝܢ܆ ܘܦܩܘܕܘܬܗܘܢ ܦܬܝܚ ܣܝܢ.
ܗܠܝܢ ܒܦܪܕܣܐ ܒܐܝܢܐ ܡܒܣܡ ܗܘܘ ܠܗ܆ ܟܕ ܒܡܫܠܡܢܐ ܐܒܐ
ܕܡܬܒܝܢܐ ܗܘܐ. ܘܬܡܢ ܕܢܚܝܢ ܗܘܐ ܡܕܒܪܢܘܗܝ ܥܠ ܐܘܪܚܐ.
ܘܬܫܡܫܬܐ ܐܠܗܝܬܐ ܡܫܡܠܝܐ ܗܘܐ܆ ܟܕ ܢܗ̈ܪܐ ܘܒܣܡ̈ܐ
ܘܬܫܒܚܬܐ ܘܒܥܘܬܐ. ܘܟܕ ܒܠܗ ܐܘܪܚܐ ܘܚܝܠܐ ܡܡܪܢ ܗܘܐ
ܠܗܘܢ܆ ܚܙܐ ܗܘܐ [R 18] ܠܗܘܢ ܒܠܚܘܕܝܬ ܘܐܦܝ̈ܢ ܩܕ̈ܝܫܐ. ܟܕ
ܡܢܗܪ̈ܝܢ ܒܗܘܢ ܘܥܡܪܝܢ ܥܡܗ ܘܡܠܠܝܢ ܥܡܗ.

(§27) ܒܬܪ ܗܟܝܠ ܟܕ ܫܠܡ ܒܐܬܪܐ ܡܕܝܢܬܐ ܕܒܝܬ ܕܝܢܐ: ܕܟܕ
ܠܟܠܗܘܢ ܡܫܬܠܛܢܘ ܡܠܟܐ ܥܘܠܐ: ܘܢܝܫܘܢ ܠܡܠܟܐ ܘܕܝܬܝܩܘܢ
ܡܢ ܥܕ̈ܢܐ܆ ܗܘ ܟܕ ܚܙܐ ܢܦܫܗ ܒܡܫܠܡܢܐ ܕܩܫܝܪܐ܆ ܒܠܗ ܝܘܬܐ
ܥܒܕ ܗܘܐ ܗܘ ܒܐܝܕ̈ܘܗܝ، ܕܗ̇ܘ ܒܫܬ ܝܘܡܬܐ. ܟܕ ܥܒܪ ܠܐܦ̈ܝ
ܘܠܬܠܬܐ. ܠܐܘܪܚܐ ܕܝܢ ܒܝܬ ܘܐܫܬܘܕ. ܢܦܩܐܝܬ ܗܟܝܠ ܟܕ ܡܛܝܠܐ
ܩܛܝܢܬܐ ܐܫܬܘܕ: ܘܡܢܗ ܒܡܫܠܡܢܐ ܫܠܡܐ. ܘܟܕ ܫܕܪ ܠܗܬ
ܡܠܟܘܬܐ ܕܠܗ܆ ܦܩܕ ܕܢܐܬܐ ܠܗ ܡܫܝܚܐ ܠܕܠܡܐ ܕܢܗܪܐ. ܗܘ ܕܝܢ
ܟܕ ܐܫܬܘܕ ܥܠ ܕܠܐ ܡܐܘܪܚܐ ܗܠܝܢ ܕܡܠܟܐ: ܘܢܝܚ ܕܢܝܚܘܗܝ،
ܐܒܘܗ ܕܗܠܝܢ ܬ̈ܘܪܒܐ ܕܥܒܕܐ: ܡܠܦ ܕܝܢ ܟܕ ܡܢܗ ܕܐܬܠܡܝܕܐ

[1] Here Rufus portrays Peter the Iberian as a wonder-worker already at a young age.

[2] I.e., they had suffered martyrdom. The Greek noun μάρτυς from which the English word "martyr" is derived, means "witness." The Greek verb μαρτυρέω means "to testify" or "to give witness."

[3] Peter was in the possession of relics, i.e., bones, of martyrs, perhaps of the martyrs of Karkha d^{e}Beth Ṣ^{e}lokh. According to a tradition preserved in Coptic, he had with him relics of Jacobus Intercissus, also known as St. James the Cut-Up, who suffered martyrdom in 421 in Beth Lāpat (modern Khorramabad, Iran) under Bahrām V. For an appendix to the Coptic *passio* of Jacobus Intercissus that details this tradition concerning Peter the Iberian, see Giuseppe Balestri and Henri Hyvernat, eds., *Acta Martyrum* (4 vols.; CSCO 43–44, 86, 125; CSCO/Copt 3–4, 6, 13; Leuven: Durbecq, 1951–55), 2:50–61 (Coptic), 4:35–42 (Latin). For a fuller discussion of the role of relics in the *Vita Petri Iberi*, see Horn, "Transgressing Claims to Sacred Space"; idem, "Weaving the

even great miracles were accomplished in the palace through his hands.[1] In order not to detract the hearers entirely, omitting the rest I will put forward one of them, sufficient to confirm them all.

(§26) He possessed the bones of [some] holy martyrs, Persians by race, who in those times had truly borne witness[2] [and] whose names we still mention, whose memorial services we keep and [whose] martyrdoms we read according to the tradition and the custom of the blessed one.[3] These [bones] he placed with honor in a shrine[4] in the bed-chamber[5] where he was leading the ascetic life. There he would sleep in front of them on the ground[6] and perform the divine services with lights, incense, hymns of praise, and intercessions.[7] While offering honor and what is pleasing to them, many times he saw **[R 18]** them openly chanting [psalms], keeping vigil, and praying with him.

(§27) Now when the holy feast of Epiphany came, [a time] when custom requires all the senators[8] both to visit the emperor and to be visited by one another, he shut himself up in the bed-chamber of the martyrs. He completely decorated this house of prayer with his [own] hands, wiping clean the walls and the ceiling [and] even sweeping and washing the floor.[9] Then, after he had thus washed several lamps[10] and had polished [them] diligently, he hung [them] up. He sent for his storekeeper,[11] ordering [him] to bring him oil to light the lamps.[12] But [the storekeeper] was angry that [Peter] was not mindful of the things of the world, being anxious to see him [become] like the rest of the nobility.

Pilgrim's Crown." See also the comments in Horn, *Asceticism and Christological Controversy*, 66–69 *et passim*.

[4] I.e., in a reliquary.

[5] The Syriac transliterates the Greek κοιτών (Raabe, 25 n. 1).

[6] See 1 Sam 3:3.

[7] These special instructions for how to perform the divine service are still part of the Typikon for feasts of major saints.

[8] The Syriac transliterates the Greek συγκλητικός (Griffith, *marginalia*).

[9] Note how Peter is presented as imitating and surpassing the work of cleaning sacred space, modeled for him by his maternal grandfather, Bakurios. See above, *Vit. Pet.* §11 (R 7).

[10] The Syriac transliterates the Greek ἡ κανδῆλα (*PGL*, 700) or κανδήλη (LSJ, 874). See also Raabe, 25 n. 2, who derives the word from the Latin *candela*.

[11] The Syriac transliterates the Greek κελλαρίτης (Raabe, 25 n. 3).

[12] Literally, "for the flame of the lights."

ܐܬܬܟܒ݂. ܠܫܥܬܐ ܐܬܬܦܝܣ. ܟܕ ܐܡܪ. ܒ̈ܢܝܢ ܗܕ̈ܪܐ ܕܡܬܠܗܝܐ
ܘܕܐܬܪܗ ܘܕܝܠܗ. ܕܟܕ ܐܫܬܪܪ ܡܢܗܘܢ܆ ܐܝܟ ܕܠܐܝܡܪܐ ܘܫܘܒܚܐ
ܡܠܟܐ ܠܘܬ ܕܘܪ̈ܡܝܐ܆ ܕܢܦܩ ܢܓܕܐ ܕܢܗܘܐ. ܘܠܐ ܟܠ ܕܢܦܩܝܢ ܣܝܡ
ܠܗ ܢܓܕ ܕܗ̈ܘܐ. ܘܠܐ ܢܓܕܐ ܕܢܣܪ ܡܥܝܢܐ. ܗܘ ܕܝܢ ܠܡܠܟܐ ܡܕܝܢܐ
ܘܦܠܣܛܝܢܐ ܟܕ ܐܪܓܫ ܒܡܥܒܕܢܘܬܐ ܕܒܥܠܕܒܒܐ܆ ܫܬܬܘܬܐ
ܐܘܟܠܬܐ܆ ܒܡܫܝܚܘܬܐ ܘܒܨܠܘܬ ܪܘܚܐ ܒܩܘܡܬܐ ܕܐܝܟ ܗܕܐ
ܗܝ. ܘܠܡܘܟܟܐ ܐܗܦܟܗ ܠܘܬ ܓܠܘܬܐ. ܘܟܕ ܪܬܚ ܒܡܗܝܡܢܘܬܐ
ܘܒܪܘܚܐ܆ ܘܩܪܐ ܠܬܠܬܐ ܕܗܠܝܢ ܡܕ̈ܝܢܐ܆ ܟܕ ܫܠܡ ܗܘ ܪܡܫܐ ܕܝܠܗ
ܕܨܦܪܐ܆ ܟܕ ܒܥܕ̈ܢܐ [R 19] ܒܠܚܘܕ ܕܠܐ ܡܫܚܐ ܠܟܠܗܘܢ ܡܕ̈ܝܢܬܐ
ܐܚܝܕ ܐܢܘܢ. ܘܗܠܝܢ ܥܒܕܐ ܢܦ̈ܫܬܐ ܕܒܐܝܕܐ ܡܕܝܢܐ܆ ܕܠܐ ܥܠܬܐ
ܠܠܒܐ ܘܐܬܡܟܟܐ ܟܕ ܕܠܩ ܒܗܪ̈. ܗܝ ܕܟܕ ܐܫܬܒܩ ܠܚܠܒܐ.
ܘܠܟܠܗܘܢ ܗܢܘܢ ܕܝܠܗ ܘܠܣܘܢܩܠܝܬܗ܆ ܠܟܠܗܘܢ ܠܡܬܒܗܐ ܐܬܬܐ.
ܐܚܪܢܐ ܕܦܓܥܬܐ ܠܐܬܬܐ ܢܬܘܢ܆ ܠܘܬ ܗ̇ܝ ܕܢܬܒܢܘܢ ܒܕܘܒܪ̈ܗ
ܘܒܢܝܘܬܗ. ܘܫܘܟܢܐ ܕܠܐ ܐܝܟ ܕܗܠܝܢ ܕܐܝܟ ܗܢܝܢ܆ ܕܒܥܒܗ
ܡܬܒܢܝܢ ܘܩܝܡܝܢ ܠܗ ܒܥܒܕܐ ܠܘܬܗ ܐܬܟܢܫܘ.
(§28) ܡܬܠܗܕܐ ܗܟܝܠ ܒܚܕ ܡܢ ܝܘ̈ܡܬܐ. ܟܕ ܩܐܡ ܒܨܠܘܬܗܘܢ
ܘܡܫܠܠ ܒܡܘܡܘܢ ܗܠܝܢ ܕܦܘܪܫܢܗܘܢ܆ ܡܢ ܥܠܝܐ ܢܚܬ ܠܒܢ

[1] I.e., διάβολος, the accuser.

[2] We owe this translation to Derwas J. Chitty, "Peter the Iberian" (draft of English translation of the Syriac *Life of Peter the Iberian*; unpublished manuscript kept at the Library of the House of St. Gregory and St. Macrina, Oxford, 1967), 12.

[3] Almost following the advice of Evagrius of Pontus, who, e.g., in his *Praktikos* 15 states that "[t]urbid anger is calmed by the singing of Psalms, by patience and almsgiving [θυμὸν δὲ καταπαύει κυκώμενον ψαλμῳδία καὶ μακροθυμία καὶ ἔλεος]" (Guillaumont and Guillaumont, 536; Bamberger, 20; for a more recent translation of the relevant passage, see also Sinkewicz, 100). Also note Evagrius's more developed comments on the relationship between anger and prayer in his *Chapters on Prayer* 20–27 (PG 79:1171–73; Bamberger, 58–59; Sinkewicz, 195). Of interest is Columba Stewart, "Evagrius Ponticus on Prayer and Anger," in *Religions of Late Antiquity in Practice* (ed. Richard Valantasis; Princeton: Princeton University Press, 22), 65–81.

[4] I.e., the martyrs whose relics Peter prepared to venerate.

[5] Another miracle occurring in the context of blessings on oil or water for liturgical use in early Christian literature was worked through the prayers

Impelled by the devil,[1] [the storekeeper] turned in fury saying, "[Too] strong [are] the expectations that both his country and ours have for him, that although he was sent by them for honor and royal glory to the Romans, he should want to become a monk! He will make all of us who are counting on him miserable!" and he refused to send any oil. The holy boy-philosopher,[2] being aware of this instigation of the adversary, showed at such a [young] age an evangelical sincerity with serenity and long-suffering [that] he turned anger to prayer.[3] Fervent in faith and in the Spirit, he called upon the prayers of those saints.[4] When the evening of the vigil came, he **[R 19]** furnished all the lamps with water alone instead of oil [and] lit [them]. Once lit, they remained [burning] night and day without ceasing during the seven days of the holy feast.[5] When the emperor and all his [courtiers] and the Senate heard this, it was a marvel to them all, so that many came to desire to be moved with zeal by his way of life and by his asceticism.[6] It was no small number [that] gathered to him from among those who were so inclined to practice asceticism with him and [who] were equal to him in zeal.

(§28) One day while he was standing with them and was speaking with them [about] the [matter] of their salvation,[7] he

of Bishop Narcissus of Jerusalem and recounted by Eusebius of Caesarea, *Hist. eccl.* 6.9.3 (Schwartz and Mommsen, 2:538). Going beyond what is stated here in the *Vita Petri Iberi*, in Narcissus's miracle, explicitly "the nature of the water was changed into that of oil [ἐξ ὕδατος εἰς ἐλαίου ποιότητα τήν φύσιν]," to be used for the lamps of the church. See the comment at Raabe, 26 n. 1. For an example of a further miracle related to the provision of oil in times of need, even if not in a liturgical context, yet still in an ascetic context in Palestine, see Antony of Choziba, *Vita Sancti Georgii Chozebitae* 37 (Houze, 136,11–13; Vivian, 97), where a "vat of oil" blessed by George of Choziba remained full for three weeks. See also Yizhar Hirschfeld, *The Judean Desert Monasteries in the Byzantine Period* (New Haven: Yale University Press, 1992), 100.

[6] Note *Pler.* 37 (Nau and Brière, 86), as well as the ascetic influence of the deacon Basil on the young Peter in Constantinople; see *Pler.* 35 (Nau and Brière, 78).

[7] Notice the connection established here between the one who lives the ascetic life and the expertise he gains concerning the knowledge necessary for salvation.

ܒܢܝܬܗܘܢ ܒܐܣܟܡܐ ܕܢܙܝܪܐ. ܘܟܕ ܢܦܠ ܫܓܫܐ ܠܗ̇ ܠܟܢ
ܬ̈ܠܡܘܗܝ. ܟܕ ܐܡܪ ܠܐ ܚܙܝܬܘܢ. ܐܠܐ ܐ݇ ܗ̇ܘ ܒܠܫܢܗܘܢ. ܟܕ ܦ̇ܬܚܐ
ܘܐܡܪ ܥܡ ܚܒܝܢܐ ܘܕܡ̈ܟܐ. ܡܪܝ ܘܐܠܗܝ.. ܗ̇ܘ ܕܝܢ ܫܓܪ ܗܘܐ.
ܕܐܦ ܡܠܝ ܐܣܝܐ ܫܦܝܪ ܗܘܐ. ܡܠܝ ܕܝܢ: ܠܐ ܚܙܘ. ܐܠܐ ܗ̇ܘ
ܒܠܫܢܗܘܢ ܚܙܐ. ܐܝܟܢܐ ܕܒܠܥܗܘܢ ܗ̇ܢܘܢ ܕܠܗܬܗ. ܟܕ ܡܬܒܩܐ
ܙܒܢܐ ܘܒܕܝܠܬܐ ܒܪܬܬܐ ܗ̇ܘܐ: ܟܕ ܢ̇ܚܡܘܗܝ ܠܣܘܦܐ ܐܠܗܝܐ
ܕܐܬܝܗܒ ܠܗ: ܢܬܢܪܐ ܢܬܢܗܘܢ ܠܛܠܝܢܗܘܢ ܐܠܗܝܐ ܘܠܣܘܟܗܘܢ.
ܡܛܠܗܕܐ ܘܗܘܐ ܠܗܘܢ ܒܓܘ ܒܟܠܗܐ ܘܥܠܘ ܐܣܟܡܐ
ܟܠܗ ܕܗܘܐ ܗ̇ܘ ܕܢܙܝܪܐ. ܗ̇ܢܘ ܕܐܦ ܥܡ̈ܗܘܢ ܐܡܪ ܗܘܐ
ܠܝ. ܕܒܗܘܢ ܐܬܬܘܗܝ ܗܘܐ: ܘܠܒܫ ܠܐܠܗܐ ܬܐܘܕܘܛܐ ܕܢܙܝܪܐ
ܘܐܚ̈ܘܗܝ. ܦܘܠܘܣ ܘܦܘܪܦܘܪܝܘܣ. ܥܬ̈ܝܪܐ ܒܐܘܠܦܢܐ. ܘܡ̈ܢܝܐ
ܐܝܬܝܗܘܢ ܗܘܘ. [R 20] ܘܐܦܝܣܩܘ̈ܦܐ ܕܐܘܣܝܐ ܡܠܟܝܬܐ. ܐܠܐ
ܡܠܝ ܗ̇ ܘܒܝܬܐܪܝܐ ܠܒܪ ܡܢ ܩܘܣܛܢܛܝܢܐ: ܕܪ̈ܡܘܟܘܗܝ، ܕܐܬܒܢܝܐ
ܟܕ ܛܠܝܐ ܐܬܝܗܘܢ: ܘܒܛܠܝܘ ܡܬܕܪܝܢ ܒܟܘܪܐ ܐܬܐܬܗ ܐܬܬܐܢܝܣ܀
(§29) ܟܕ ܡܬܚܫܒ ܗܘܐ ܕܝܢ ܒܡܘܡܕܬܐ ܘܒܪܘܚܬܐ ܐܠܗܝܬܐ:[1]
ܘܡܫ̈ܡܫܢܐ ܣܓܝ ܗܘܐ ܒܠܒܗ ܐܝܟ ܡܠܬܐ ܕܢܒܝܐ ܒܡ̈ܣܝܢܬܐ
ܕܝܘܝܕ: ܘܢܘܗܪܐ ܡܢ ܢܘܗܪܐ ܡܢܠܦ ܗܘܐ: ܕܢܬܪ ܙܡ ܘܬܘܪ ܟܠܐ.
ܐܬܪ̈ܟܢ ܕܢܦܩ ܡܢ ܟܠܗܐ ܘܡܢ ܡܘܫܦܬܗ: ܘܢܪܗܛ ܠܘܬ ܗ̇ܝ
ܡܕܝܢܬܐ ܕܬܪ̈ܬܐ. ܗ̇ܝ ܕܐܬܝܗ̇ ܐܬܚܪܝܬܐ. ܘܟܕ ܩ̈ܪܝܒ

[1] MS B does not have ܐܠܗܝܬܐ but after ܘܒܪܘܚܬܐ inserts the following: ܢܘܗܪܢܝܬܐ: ܘܡܒܪܟܐ ܗܘܐ ܐܡܝܢܐܝܬ ܒܠܒܗ ܠܬܫܒܘܚܬܐ ܕܢܘܪܐ ܐܠܗܝܬܐ ܘܡܫܒ̈ܚܢܐ ...

[2] The term "Nazirite" describes a person who lives according to ascetic rules, set down in the vow of holiness known as the Nazirite vow in Num 6. The rules required abstention from all grape products, unrestricted growth of body hair, and avoidance of contact with corpses. According to the Scriptures, Israelites could take this vow for a limited period of time or for life (for the latter, see Samson at Judg 13:4–7; 16:17; more generally Amos 2:11–12). See above, *Vit. Pet.* §21 (R 13).

[3] See John 20:28.

[4] See Payne Smith, 235.

[5] It is not impossible that this Theodotus could be identified with Theodotus of Ancyra, who was bishop until sometime before 446. Formerly a friend of Nestorius, Theodotus became one of his strongest opponents at the Council of Ephesus in 431. He also was a member of the delegation sent

suddenly saw our Lord among them in the habit of a Nazirite.[2] He fell down, worshiped him, [and] grasped his feet, although no one saw him but he alone. He cried out and said with weeping and tears, "My Lord and my God!"[3] Although he thought that those others could also see [him], they could not, and only he saw [our Lord], so that all who [were] with him [were] greatly amazed, afraid, and trembling. After they had learned of the divine vision that had appeared to him, they increased their divine zeal and their love. On account of this [event], a multitude of them renounced the world and took the habit after he had become a monk. He told us their names also: among them was the God-clad[4] monk Theodotus[5] and his brothers Proclus[6] and Sophronius,[7] of an illustrious office, [who were] architects **[R 20]** and stewards[8] of the royal estate.[9] Indeed, these are but a few of the many gifts of the blessed one while he had been a child and was living in the palace, [which] we have narrated in passing.

(§29) While he was growing up in age and in divine love[10] and was making ascents in his heart[11] according to the word of David, the singer of sacred [psalms], and was exchanging fire for fire, higher and clearer, he yearned to depart afar from the world and from its vanity[12] and to hasten to the first of virtues, which

to Theodosius II to report about the events at Ephesus. Proclus of Constantinople is known to have consecrated Theodotus's successor. See Josef Rist, "Theodotus von Ankyra," *BBKL* 11:997–99; Peter Bruns, "Theodotus of Ancyra," *DECL*, 570. We owe the pointer to Theodotus to Griffith, *marginalia*.

6 This Proclus might be identical with Proclus, archbishop of Constantinople, 434–446.

7 We have not been able to identify this Sophronius any further.

8 The Syriac transliterates the Greek ἐπίτροπος, "procurator, steward." See also *Vit. Pet.* §166 (R 123) as well as Ignatius of Antioch, *Pol.* 8.2 (Camelot, 155; Richardson, *Early Christian Fathers*, 120), where "epitropus" could be a personal name or could be used as the title of the widow's husband.

9 The Syriac transliterates the Greek οὐσία here in the secondary meaning of "wealth, substance, estate, income." See Payne Smith, 7.

10 See Luke 1:80, 2:40. MS B (BM 12,174) adds "... [and in] spiritual [love] and was adding continually every day to the grace of divine fire, and was placing..."

11 Ps 84:5 (83:5 [LXX]). See also Pss 120–134 (119–133 [LXX]).

12 See 2 Pet 2:20.

ܩ̈ܛܠܐ ܗܟܢܐ ܕܢܒܥܘܢ ܠܗ ܐܒܘܗܝ. ܟܕ ܐܬܠܡܕ ܢ̈ܝܪܐ ܘܕܘܒܪܐ
ܡܬܬܘܕܝܢ ܗܘܘ. ܘܐܝܟܢܐ ܟܬܝܒܐ ܕܠܡ: ܓܒ̈ܪܐ ܟܠܗ ܐܡܪ ܐܢܐ:
ܗ̇ܘܢ ܠܚܫ̈ܝ ܬܘ̈ܟܠܐ ܕܡܢܝܚ ܠܗ: ܠܡܫܡܠܐ ܕܐܝܟ ܗܕܐ ܐܬܘ: ܡܢ
ܗܢܐܬܐ ܕܠܘܬܗ. ܐܝܟܢܐ ܕܐܬܝܢ ܩ̈ܛܠܐ ܢܗܘܘܢ ܕܡܫܬܥܝܢܘܬ
ܢܡܠܠܘܢܗ̇. ܘܐܠܘ ܠܐ ܡܫܬܪܪܬܐ ܟܠܗܘܢ ܕܡܪܝܐ ܟܠܗ̇. ܐܬܬܘ
ܘܫܒܪܘ[1] ܡܛܝܘܬܗܘܢ. ܠܘ ܕܝܢ ܟܠܗܘܢ. ܐܠܐ ܘܪܒܠ ܠܐܠܗܐ
ܬܐܘܕܘܣܝܘܣ ܡܠܟܐ. ܟܕ ܚܙܐ ܕܐܝܟ ܡܗܕܪܐ ܢܛܪܘܗܝ: ܕܕܠܡܐ
ܟܕ ܡܬܬܟܪܟ ܠܗ ܡܢ ܗ̇ܘ ܒܥܠܗ: ܘܠܐ ܡܫܡܫ ܠܗ ܐܝܟ ܕܡܒܠܥ:
ܒܬܠܡܝܕܘܬܐ ܘܡܫܡܫܢܘܬܐ ܚܠܦ ܙܒܢܐ ܘܡܕܒܪܢܘܬܐ ܢܓܕ ܐܢܘܢ. ܟܕ
ܩܢܝܗ̇ ܠܘܬܗ: ܘܡܠܠܬܗ̇ ܕܗܕܐ ܕܒܩ ܠܗ. ܒܢܘܟܪܝܘܬܐ ܩܣܢܝܐܬܐ
ܐܡܝܢ ܗܘܐ ܠܗ. ܕܠܐ ܡܫܬܐܠܢܘܬ ܢܕܘܡ.

(§30) ܐܠܐ ܘܠܐ ܡܕܡ ܐܚܪܬ [R 21] ܕܚܫܒܬ ܡܢ ܚܠܡܗ ܕܡܫܝܚܐ.
ܘܠܐ ܕܚܙܝܢ ܡܢ ܚܘܒܐ ܕܠܗ ܕܕܒܩܬ ܒܢܦܫܗ ܠܗ. ܗ̇ܘ ܕܡܢ
ܥܕܪܘܬܗ ܫܒܩܗ ܐܝܟ ܕܠܥܡܘܐܝܠ. ܘܪܚܡܗ ܐܝܟ ܕܠܐܣܪܐܝܠ.
ܘܐܝܟ ܕܠܝܘܣܦ ܗܟܢܐ ܐܦ ܠܗ. ܐܝܟ ܕܠܒܪܝܐ ܚܡܪܐ ܗܘܐ
ܠܗ ܘܡܢܛܪ. ܗ̇ܘ ܕܠܢܛܪܗ ܠܟܠܢܐ ܕܡܟܠ ܐܣܟܡܐ ܕܕܝܪܝܘܬܐ
ܠܒܪܐ ܐܒܐ. ܟܐܒܕܐ ܚܠܬܝܬܐ ܘܟܕܪܟܐ ܪܟܐ. ܟܕ ܐܬܩ̈ܬܐ
ܘܬܕܡܪ̈ܬܐ. ܐܝܟ ܕܢܦܠ ܒܗ ܠܐܣܪܐܝܠ. ܡܢ ܦܪܥܘܬܐ ܕܡܨܪ̈ܝܐ.
ܘܠܐܪܥܐ ܕܡܘܠܟܢܐ ܐܒܠ. ܗ̇ܝ ܕܡܪܕܝܐ ܚܠܒܐ ܘܕܒܫܐ. ܟܕ
ܡܕܒܪܐ ܕܪܘܚܢܝܐ ܘܡܢ̈ܗܪܢܝܐ ܘܢܦܘܪܐ ܘܟܒܪ ܠܘܬܐ ܐܚܝܕ ܠܗ̇
ܠܩܘܪܐ ܩܕ̈ܝܫܐ. ܘܠܡ ܕܢܦܪ ܡܢܗ ܡܬܬܚܝܕ ܗܘܘ. ܒܟܐ ܓܒܪ
ܕܢܫܟܚܬܐ ܕܪܘܚܢܝܐ ܕܡܢ ܟܠܟܐ ܠܗ ܡܫܠܡܟܐ ܗܘܬ. ܩ̈ܕܡܐ
ܘܩܢ̈ܝܢܐ ܡܕܪ̈ܝܢܘ ܕܗܠܝܢ ܟܢܟܢܝܢ ܗܘܘ ܠܗ ܡܢ ܗܕܐ. ܟܕ

[1] So MS B. MS A and Raabe have ܘܫܒܪܘ ܐܬܘܬܗܘܢ.

[2] The Syriac transliterates the Greek ξενιτεία. MS Sachau 321 reads "foreign [fem. sing.]"; BM Add 12,174 has the better reading, which is translated above. On the centrality of the concept of pilgrimage in the ascetic spirituality of Peter the Iberian, see Horn, *Asceticism and Christological Controversy*, ch. 4. For a study of the notion of *xeniteia*, or estrangement, in ascetic literature, see also Guillaumont, "Le dépaysement comme forme d'ascèse"; and Daniel Caner, *Wandering, Begging Monks: Spiritual Authority and the Promotion of Monasticism in Late Antiquity* (Berkeley and Los Angeles: University of California Press, 2002), 24–30.

is pilgrimage.[2] Although he often attempted to flee, he could not, since the devil and the demons were aware [of his attempts].[3] Men of his household, his slaves, I mean, the bodyguards[4] who escorted him, became so angered out of hatred for him that many times they secretly attempted to murder him. Had it not been for the Lord's protection [, which] alone hindered [them], they would have committed and accomplished their audacity. Moreover, the God-fearing Emperor Theodosius was anxious to keep [him] as a hostage, lest if [the child] were demanded back by his people and he [could] not present him as he had received him, he might make them foes and enemies instead of friends and allies. For this reason, [the emperor] summoned him and threatened him, and he was held in tight custody, so that he could not flee secretly.

(§30) However, there is nothing **[R 21]** mightier than the power of Christ and no[thing] more fervent than the love of those who love him purely. He who from his childhood had cherished him like Samuel and shepherded him like Israel and like Joseph[5] thus continued to lead and guard him like a sheep. He who brought his good desire for the monastic habit to fulfillment with a mighty hand and a stretched-out arm,[6] through signs and wonders, as he once snatched Israel from the tyranny of the Egyptians and brought [them] into the Land of the Promise flowing with milk and honey,[7] raised up for him as helpers of his flight, as guides, as watchmen, and as companions those holy martyrs who were well served by him.[8] For as much as the desire for flight from the world inflamed him, demons and men, [who are] their

[3] The author either intends to characterize the following "men of his household, his slaves," as "demons" or to say that "the devil and the demons" perceived and made known Peter's attempts at flight to his servants, a thought more clearly expressed in the emendation adopted in MS BM Add 12,174, fol. 52 recto.

[4] Literally, "spear-bearers," for Greek δορυφόροι (Raabe, 27 n. 4).

[5] For a discussion of these allusions to Old Testament figures, see Horn, "Beyond Theology," 247; and Horn, *Asceticism and Christological Controversy*, 180–181.

[6] See Deut 11:2; Ps 135:12.

[7] Exod 3:8, 17; 13:5; 33:3; Lev 20:24; Num 13:27 *et alibi*.

[8] See, e.g., Matt 3:17; 12:18; 17:5.

ܒܪܐܬ ܢܛܪܝܢ ܗܘܘ ܒܡܗܝܪܘܬܐ. ܠܡܠܠܘܬܗ ܘܠܡܫܡܥܬܗ. ܘܠܬܟܫܦܬܗ ܘܠܫܘ̈ܥܒܕܗ.

(§31) ܘܟܕ ܐܫܟܚ ܠܗ̇ܘ ܕܡܢ ܐܠܗܐ ܐܬܝܗܒ ܠܗ. ܠܛܘܒܢܐ ܝܘܚܢ ܐܘܢܘܟܘܣܐ: ܒܪ ܢܫ̈ܘܗܝ ܘܒܪ ܛܟܣܗ: ܘܕܝܠܗ ܐܟܘܬܐ ܠܗ ܒܪܒܝܬܐ ܕܦ̈ܐܝܐ ܕܠܒܠܗ: ܘܡܕܒܪܢܐ ܕܐܘܪܚܐ ܕܠܗܕܐ ܡܫܝܚܐ. ܗ̇ܘ ܕܐܬܝܗܒ ܗܘܐ ܒܝܘܡܘܗܝ ܡܢ ܐܬܪܐ ܕܠܙܩܝܐ.[1] ܕܒܟܠܗ̇ ܕܣܒܠܬ ܐܠܗܐ ܘܒܢܝܚܘܬܐ ܘܒܦܘܬܐ: ܘܡܫܝܚܘܬܐ ܘܡܟܝܟܘܬܐ ܡܫܡܠܝܬ ܗܘܐ. ܟܕ ܠܗܢܐ ܟܡܐ ܚܙܐ: ܘܒܐܘܪܚܐ ܕܝܘܡܐ ܚܕܐ ܘܐܘܕܥܗ ܠܗ: ܐܝܟ ܦܘܠܘܣ [R 22] ܠܒܪܢܫܐ. ܟܡܐ ܡܬܢܨܚ ܡܠܘܟܐ ܘܒܪ ܠܘܬܐ. ܕܒܪܘܡܐ ܕܦܘܪܣܐ. ܘܡܛܠ ܕܝܕܥ ܕܡܢ ܡܒܪܝܢܘܬܐ ܕܐܒ̈ܗܐ ܐܬܝܠܝܕ. ܗ̇ܝ ܕܠܐ ܢܬܛܠܩܘܢ ܢܘ̈ܡܘܣܘܗܝ. ܐܠܐ ܢܬܢܛܪܘܢ ܡܬܕܒܪܝܢ ܘܡܬܓܠܝܢ. ܫܩܠܗ ܠܗ ܠܗܘܢ ܥܡܗ. ܗ̇ܘ ܕܡܪܕܘܬܐ: ܐܝܟܐ ܕܡܟܝܢ ܗܘܘ ܒܢ̈ܝ ܢܫܘܗܝ ܕܡ̈ܕܝܐ ܦ̈ܪܝܫܐ. ܘܟܕ ܬܪ̈ܝܢܘܗܝ ܐܟܠܘ ܕ̈ܝܢܘܗܝ ܠܟܠ ܡܢ ܗܠܝܢ ܒܪ̈ܢܫܐ: ܘܐܬܐ ܡܠܠܘ ܥܡ ܫ̈ܕܪܐ. ܡܟܝܠ ܒܓܢܐ ܬܘܒ. ܡܛܠ ܕܟܢܐ ܘܝܘܢܐ ܕܒܪܘܡܝܐ. ܘܡܟܝܠ ܐܝܟ ܠܐ ܝܕܥ ܘܠܐ ܐܘܪܚ. ܘܠܐ ܦ̈ܐܪܐ ܘܠܐ ܚ̈ܝܘܬܐ. ܒܕܡܐ ܕܠܥܡܠܐ ܢܦܩ ܫܘܥܒܕܐ.

(§32) ܟܕ ܗ̇ܢܘܢ ܦܪ̈ܝܫܐ. ܫܩܠܗ ܐܝܟ ܢܘܚܠܠܐ ܕܠܐ ܟܕܢܐ. ܟܢܫ ܡܠܦܢ̈ܘܬܐ ܕܐܝܟ ܗܠܝܢ. ܒܡܕܒܪܢܘܬܐ ܡܠܟܝܬܐ ܕܟܠܗ̇ ܗܕܐ ܘܕܐܝܟ ܗܕܐ. ܗܠܝܢ ܕܐܦ ܡܠܘ ܠܒ̈ܬܘܗܝ ܠܒܝܬ ܡܠܟܘܬܐ ܘܡܫܝܚܘܬܐ ܘܡܠܟܐ. ܫܪܝ ܗܘܘ ܠܗܘܢ ܒܪ ܐܝܟ ܕܒ̈ܬܝܢ ܦܠܚ̈ܐ ܥܡܟܬ: ܟܕ ܗܘ ܛܘܒܢܐ ܡܫܝܚܐ ܗܘܐ ܠܡܫܡܫܘ̈ܗܝ: ܗ̇ܢܘܢ ܕܐܦ ܢܐܬܘܢ

[1] So MS B. MS A and Raabe read ܕܠܐܘܕܝܩܝܐ "from (the city of) the Laodiceans."

[2] See above, *Vit. Pet.* §30 (R 21).

[3] A marginal note that is only in MS Sachau 321, fol. 72 verso, states, "This John received the blessed Peter from the [baptismal] font." This comment may indicate that John the Eunuch was Peter the Iberian's godfather. John the Eunuch is mentioned once in *Pler.* 5 (Nau and Brière, 16).

[4] Since the Syriac ܕܠܙܝܩܝܐ in MS Sachau 321 fol. 72 verso is written without *syame*, indicating the singular, against Raabe's emendation, the reading of MS BM Add 12,174 fol. 52 recto ܕܠܙܝܩܝܐ "Lazica" seems more fitting as an identifier of a land or place that is not specifically called a city. For his name, ܡܬܪܐܕܦܠܘܣ, see also *Vit. Pet.* §40 (R 29). Thus against Raabe (28) and Chitty ("Peter the Iberian," 14), who appears to have followed Raabe, one ought to assume that John the Eunuch was a Lezghian, a native of one of the

helpers,[2] were hindering him from this by watching vigilantly [and] with caution his coming in and his going out, his wishes and his thoughts.

(§31) [Peter had also] found the one who was given to him by God, the blessed John the Eunuch,[3] the sharer of his customs and his zeal, and one who was equal to him in desire for eternal life and a helper on the way that leads to it. He was by his race from the land of Lazica[4] [and] was adorned with all fear of God, dignity, chastity, faith, and humility.[5] [Peter] took him [along] with him and joined him to himself through the bond of love. As Paul [had done with] **[R 22]** Barnabas,[6] he treated him [as] an advisor and a companion in the flight of salvation. Since he knew that through the action of the demons their plans would not be hidden but would become known and be revealed by those [watching him], he took John with him to that shrine wherein the bones of the holy martyrs were deposited. While both of them leaned their heads over those bones, they talked there with one another. Once they had agreed on the time and manner of the flight, no one [else] knew nor made [it] known, neither demons nor men, until the plan came to fulfillment.

(§32) These holy martyrs took them in watches of the dead of night[7] through the royal city, which [was] completely [quiet].[8] They filled their hearts with great courage and strength, for [Peter and John] saw them as a cloud or a pillar of fire,[9] as I heard many times when the blessed one recounted [it] to his most in-

peoples of the Caucasus. This also seems to fit well with the author's emphasis on John the Eunuch being a "sharer of [Peter's] customs," just mentioned in the text, although this may also refer to Peter's ascetic habits.

5 1 Tim 6:11.

6 For the close collaboration of Paul and Barnabas, see Acts 13 and 14. They finally parted ways (see Acts 15:36–41).

7 The Syriac ܠܠܝܐ ܕܠܐ ܥܕܢܐ may translate the Greek phrase νὺξ ἄκαιρος (Raabe, 28 n. 1). Raabe also referred to Zachariah's use of that expression at three instances. See Zachariah Scholasticus, *Vit. Sev.* 58 (fol. 121 recto col. 2), 71 (fol. 124 verso col. 1), and 84 (fol. 127 verso col. 1) (Kugener, 58,13, 71,12, and 84,12).

8 Literally, "which [was] all of this and like this," possibly rendering a Greek expression τοσαύτη καὶ τοιαύτη (Raabe, 28 n. 2).

9 See Exod 13:21.

ܡܫܒܚܝܢ ܗܘܘ ܡܢ ܬܫ̈ܒܚܬܐ ܕܐܝܟ ܗܠܝܢ܆ ܐܒܘܐ ܕܒܢܝܐ ܐܘ
ܒܥܘܕܐ ܕܢܘܗܪܐ܆ ܕܒܫܘܒܚܐ ܡܕܡܝܢ ܗܘܘ ܙܕܩܝܢ ܡܕܡܝܢܘܗܝ ܘܡܗܕܪܝܢ
ܠܗܘܢ. ܐܘ ܠܐܬܕܡܪܘܬܐ. ܡܫܒܚܝܢ ܗܘܘ ܘܡܪܢܢܝܢ ܒܫܘܝܘܬ ܒܪܬ
ܩܠܐ ܡܕܡ܆ ܒܡܠܐ ܕܡܠܝܨ ܘܒܠܐ܆ ܬܫܒܘܚܬܐ ܗܕܐ ܐܠܗܝܬܐ.
ܕܗܝ ܕܐܦ ܬ̈ܠܬܐ ܕܠܗ ܩܢ̈ܘܡ ܐܝܬ. ܐܝܬܝܗܘܢ ܚܕ ܗܠܝܢ. ܒܬܪ
ܠܡܫܝܚܐ܆ ܘܒܪܗ܆ ܢܘܗܪܐ ܕܡܢ ܢܘܗܪܐ. ܘܫܘܒܚܐ ܠܗ ܡܬܪܬܝܢܐ.
ܘܠܗܠܝܢ ܕܚܙܝܢ ܠܗ ܦܘܪܫܢܐ ܕܐܒܗ̈ܬܐ ܗܘܐ. ܒܗܢܐ ܗܘܐ ܕܝܢ ܗܘ
ܠܩܒܠܐ ܘܠܗ ܠܠܗ ܕܠܗ ܬܫܒܘܚܬܐ. [R 23] ܘܠܐ ܫܠܝܢ ܗܘܘ ܡܢ
ܕܒܘܬܪܝܢ ܡܕܝܢܬܐ ܒܠܚܘܕܝܗ܆ ܒܕ ܦܩܕܝܢ ܗܘܘ ܐܚܪܢܝܢ ܡܕܡܝܢܘܗܝ
ܗ̇ܢܘܢ ܩܫ̈ܝܫܐ ܡܕܝܢܬܐ ܘܡܙܗܪܝܢ ܠܗܘܢ܆ ܒܕܡܐ ܕܢܦܩܘ ܠܡܕܝܢܬܐ.

(§33) ܘܟܕ ܢܦܩ ܕܒܝܬ ܡܠܟܘܬܐ ܗܘܐ ܡܫܠ܆ ܠܡܥܠܬܐ ܕܡܠܘܬܐ ܒܗ ܐܠܦܐ.
ܘܬܩܢ ܒܕ ܟܕ ܒܕܪܝܫܗܘܢ ܘܫܘܟܢܗܘܢ ܕܩܘܕܫܐ ܐܫܟܚܘ܆ ܡܕܝܢܬܐ
ܒܢܦܘ. ܒܕ ܕܢܦܠ ܕܝܢ܆ ܕܕܠܡܐ ܒܕ ܕܪܕܦ ܒܬܪܗܘܢ܆ ܐܘ ܒܕ ܡܬܝܕܥܝܢ
ܒܕܘܟܬܐ ܗܝ ܕܡܬܩܪܝܐ ܩܠܝܐ ܢܬܛܫܘܢ܆ ܐܬܒܛܠܘ ܗܘܘ
ܒܬܪ ܬܪ̈ܬܝܢ ܘܠܬ̈ܠܬ ܕܡܕܝܢܬܐ ܡܢ ܒܬܪ ܡܩܒܠܝܢܗܘܢ܆ ܐܝܟ
ܕܠܒܬܠܗܘܢ ܬܠܬܐ ܝܘ̈ܡܬܐ܆ ܐܫܟܚܘ ܐܚܪܢܐ ܡܫܟܢܐ ܘܫܦܝܐ
ܠܓܢ̈ܒܐ ܠܒܝܬ. ܘܒܬܪ ܫܢ̈ܝܗ ܕܐܠܗܐ ܗ̇ܘ ܕܒܝܬܗܘܢ ܐܝܟ ܗܘܐ
ܘܡܗܕܪܐ ܠܗܘܢ܆ ܐܬܒܛܠܘ ܕܠܐ ܢܬܝܕܥܘܢ܆ ܡܢ ܗܠܝܢ ܕܝܕܥܝܢ
ܒܐܘܪܚܐ ܘܡܩܡܩܝܢ ܡܠܠܘܢ.

(§34) ܘܡܒܠ ܡܢ ܬܡܢ ܥܕܡܐ ܠܝܘܦܐ ܘܩܪ̈ܝܬܐ ܫ̈ܠܒܐ. ܘܟܕ
ܐܬܪܐ ܕܡܩܦܘܣ܆ ܫܘܩܠܐ ܕܠܗܘܢ ܒܕܝܘ ܬܪ̈ܝܗܘܢ ܒܠܚܘܕܝܗܘܢ܆
ܒܡ ܫܘܕܪܐ ܩܫ̈ܝܫܐ ܗܘ ܕܐܬܝܬܘܗܝ ܗܘܘ ܢܛܪ̈ܝܗܘܢ ܘܩܕܡ

[1] The Syriac ܒܫܘܝܘܬ ܒܪܬ ܩܠܐ ܡܕܡ may translate the Greek ἐν ὁμοφωνίᾳ τινί (Raabe, 29 n. 1).

[2] The Syriac ܬܫܒܘܚܬܐ may render the Greek δοξολογία.

[3] Note the reference to the wording of the Nicene Creed. See *Ekthesis of the 318 Fathers* (i.e., the Nicene Creed; *DEC* 1:5). At *Pler.* 37 (Nau and Brière, 86–87) Rufus reports Peter's account of a vision of the Trinity in a wheel of incomprehensible light that he had had during his early years in Constantinople. For a fuller discussion, see Horn, *Asceticism and Christological Controversy*, 261–262 and 395.

[4] Literally, "openly."

[5] Peter and John seem to have left Constantinople shortly after 437. See the discussion in Paul Devos, "Quand Pierre l'Ibère vint-il à Jérusalem," *AnBoll* 86 (1968): 344, 347; and Horn, "Beyond Theology," 52. The distance between the Great Palace of Theodosius and the harbor was relatively

timate friends, who also were able to profit from such accounts. They went [and] journeyed before them in the darkness to guide them. Oh the wonder! With a certain harmony[1] [and] in a voice that was fitting and sweet [the martyrs] were praising and singing this divine doxology,[2] the words of which I also [will] set down as follows: "Seek Christ, and behold the Light from Light,[3] the incomprehensible glory. For those who seek him, he is the rewarder of the wage." The blessed one [always] remembered the melody of that doxology. **[R 23]** The holy martyrs were before them, walking ahead of them and guiding them, [and] they did not cease singing aloud[4] in this way until they reached the harbor.[5]

(§33) Knowing that they were now in watchful care, [Peter and John] confidently sought a ship. When again through the aid and the support of the martyrs they found [one], they boarded [it] immediately. They were [still] afraid they might be caught by [those] pursuing them or [that] they might be recognized in the place called "the Straits,"[6] because the gates and the harbors of the city were guarded for three days after their exit in search for them. So they put on other clothing that was poor and typical for slaves. By the protection of God who was going with them and guiding them, they were able not to be recognized by those [who were] sitting in "the Straits" and [who] were on the lookout for them.

(§34) From there they left the journey by sea and walked on foot.[7] They made their course through the mainland of Asia Minor,[8] the two of them alone with the holy martyrs who were their

short. For an instructive discussion of the neighborhoods of Constantinople that immediately benefited from a location at the seaside, see Paul Magdalino, "The Maritime Neighborhoods of Constantinople: Commercial and Residential Functions, Sixth to Twelfth Centuries," *DOP* 54 (23): 209–26.

[6] The Syriac transliterates the Greek Στενόν, a name used for the Straits of the Bosphorus, the waters between the harbor of Constantinople and the Black Sea. Raabe (29 n. 2) notes that the frequent limitation of this term to the European side of the Straits of the Bosphorus does not seem to have been part of Rufus's conception.

[7] Peter and John seemed to have taken a night ferry over the Bosphoros.

[8] The Syriac expression ܐܬܪܐ ܕܗܦܝܪܘܣ partially translates and partially transliterates the Greek γῆ ἤπειρος (Raabe, 29 n. 3), an expression referring to "the Continent," understood as the mainland of Asia Minor.

ܠܘܬܗܘܢ. ܟܕ ܠܓܒܝܢ ܓܪ̈ܡܝܗܘܢ ܡܫܡܪ̈ܐ ܒܓܠܘܣܩܘܡܐ ܝܩܘܪܐ
ܕܕܗܒܐ܆ ܐܝܟܢܐ ܕܡܫܟܢܐ ܪܒܐ ܠܡܘܫܐ ܕܐܠܗܐ ܡܢ ܟܪ̈ܘܒܐ.
ܠܓܒܝܢ ܗܘܘ ܕܝܢ ܘܬܟܠܐ ܝܩܘܪܐ ܕܒܘܣܡܝܢ ܐܘܢܓܠܝܛܐ ܒܠܚܘܕ.
ܗܘܐ ܡܟܝܠܐ ܗܘܬ܆ ܡܢܬܐ ܡܢ ܩܝܣܐ ܕܨܠܝܒܐ ܩܕܝܫܐ ܘܡܣܡܪܐ
ܘܦܪܘܣܐ. ܕܒܗ ܡܬܢܛܪܝܢ ܗܘܘ܆ ܘܐܬܘ̈ܬܐ ܦܪ̈ܝܫܬܐ ܘܚ̈ܝܠܐ ܕܠܐ
ܡܬܡܢܝܢ ܗܘ, ܒܗ ܡܕܝܢ. ܟܕ ܡܥܕܪܢܘܬܐ ܢܚܬܐ ܢܦܩܐ ܒܗ ܠܦܘܪܩܢܗܘܢ
ܘܠܟܐ̈ܒܝܗܘܢ. ܒܬܪܟܢ [R 24] ܟܕ ܟܠܗ ܥܒܕܬܐ ܕܡܫܩܠܬܐ ܒܐܘܪܚܐ
ܗ̇, ܡܢܬܐ ܕܨܠܝܒܐ ܟܕ ܡܬܕܒܪܐ ܡܫܝܚܐ ܥܩܒܐܝܬ. ܘܒܠܗ ܗܘܐ܆
ܐܝܟܢܐ ܕܒܐܪ̈ܚܬܗܘܢ ܢܦܠܘܢ܆ ܘܢܬܥܣܘܢ ܐܩ̈ܝܗܘܢ. ܘܦܓܪ̈ܝܗܘܢ.
ܘܒܕܒܠ ܬܘܒ ܢܬܐܪܬ ܢܬܦܩܕ ܡܫܝܚܐ. ܘܗܕܡ̇ ܐܪܐ ܐܬܐܬܗ
ܗ̇, ܕܦ̇ܪܐ ܢܒܝܐ ܡܫܝܚܐ ܕܫܪܝܘܬܐ܆ ܠܡܫܡܠܝܘܬܗ̇ ܘܫܠܡܐ ܕܪܘܚܐ
ܡܫܬܡܠܝܐ܆ ܕܢܕܪܐ ܗܘܬ ܘܬܪܘܪܐ ܥܡ ܫܠܡܗ ܕܨܠܝܒܐ܆ ܗ̇ܘ ܕܢܦܩܘ
ܕܢܦܠܘܢ ܗ̇ܘܢ ܡܫܝ̈ܚܐ܆ ܘܠܐܠܗܐ ܕܐܬܓܠܝ ܢܦܩܘܢ ܚܘܫܒܢܐܝܬ.
ܟܕ ܠܫܘܫܘܬܗܘܢ ܬܠܝ ܡܪܟܒܐ ܗܘܬ܆ ܘܡܦܩܕܐ ܟܕ ܐܬܚܡ̈ܬܐ
ܕܕܐܝܟ ܗܠܝܢ.

(§35) ܗ̣ܝ, ܕܝܢ ܗܕܐ ܘܟܕ܆ ܗܘ̈ܕܪܐ ܡܕ̈ܝܫܐ ܡܣܘܒܐ ܗܘܬ
ܠܡܬܬܚܝܗܘܢ. ܟܕ ܒܪ ܕܕܪ̈ܝܢ ܗܘܐ ܒܐܘܪܚܐ܆ ܘܚܒܪ̈ܝܢ ܗܘܘ ܟܠ
ܐܬܪ̈ܘܬܐ ܘܡܕܝ̈ܢܬܐ ܘܩܘܪ̈ܝܐ܆ ܘܠܐ ܢܟ̈ܪܐ ܐܬܚܙܝܘܢ ܗܘܘ ܗ̣ܝ܆
ܠܡܥܡܪ̈ܝܗܘܢ ܕܐܬܪ̈ܘܬܐ ܘܠܗ̇ܘܢ ܕܕܝܪ̈ܝܢ ܒܗܘܢ܆ ܡܥܡܕܝܢ ܗܘܘ
ܒܫܘܒܚܗ ܕܕܘܒܪܬܐ ܠܒܪ ܡܢ ܬܪ̈ܒܐ ܘܠܒܪ ܡܢ ܡܟܠܬܐ܆ ܒܢܝ̈ܐ
ܕܚܠܬܐ ܘܕܝ̈ܪܝܐ ܘܕܝ̈ܢܐ ܥܡ ܦܘܪ̈ܫܐ ܘܠܡܦܩܕܐ܆ ܐܝܟ ܡ̇ܢ
ܕܠܗܘܪ̈ܒܐ ܕܫܘ̈ܕܪܐ ܢܦܫܝ܆ ܘܠܒܪ ܡܢ ܥܘܡܪܐ ܢܬܒܝ. ܘܠܗ̇ܘܢ
ܕܟܠܝܢ ܡܫܐܠܝܢ܆ ܕܐܝܟܢܐ ܐܝܬܝܗܘܢ. ܘܡܢܘ ܐܝܬܝܗܘܢ܆ ܗ̇ܢܘܢ
ܕܠܓܒܝܢ ܒܓܪ̈ܡܐ ܕܣܗ̈ܕܐ ܡܫ̈ܝܚܐ. ܐܡܪܝܢ ܗܘܘ ܒܪ܆ ܕܒܡܫܟܢܐ
ܕܐܬܚܙܝ ܚܕ ܐܢܫ̈ܝܢ ܡܢܗܘܢ܆ ܟܕ ܡܫܦܠܝܢ ܘܦܩܕܝܢ ܕܢܩܘܡ
ܠܦܘܪܢܣܗܘܢ. ܐܝܟܢܐ ܕܟܕ ܦܘܫ ܐܬܕ̈ܒܪܘ ܒܩܝܒܘܛܘܬܗ ܕܡܪܢ

[1] The Syriac word transliterates the Greek γλωσσόκονον. Payne Smith (70) translates it as "case, money-box, coffin," or a case wherein the remains of saints were preserved, i.e., "shrine, reliquary."

[2] See Eusebius of Caesarea, *Hist. eccl.* 1.2.4 (Schwartz and Mommsen, 2:12,9 [ὁ μέγας Μωυσῆς]). See also Raabe, 29 n. 4; E. Becker, "Konstantin der Grosse, der 'neue Moses,'" *ZKG* 31 (1910): 161–71.

[3] The Syriac word transliterates the Greek κιβωτός.

guardians and companions. They carried their precious bones in a little gold reliquary,[1] [just] as the great[2] Moses [carried] the ark[3] of God with the cherubim.[4] Besides this, they carried only the little book of John the Evangelist, in which was fastened a part of the wood of the holy, precious, and saving cross, by which they were guarded. Our Lord showed many signs and not a few powerful deeds: by it he gave a quiet energy to reassure them and console them. This piece **[R 24]** of the cross let oil flow forth in abundance continually for a whole week on the journey, to such an extent that they would receive [it] in their hands and anoint their faces and their bodies and yet again more oil would gush forth. This is indeed what the prophet calls the "oil of gladness."[5] It is the grace and power of the Holy Spirit, who rejoices and exults in the power of the cross,[6] which these saints set out to carry. They cheerfully cleaved to the God who was crucified, while she [the Holy Spirit] increased their cheerfulness more and raised [it up] through such amazing [signs].[7]

(§35) She also made manifest their arrival [in towns along the way] through [the presence of] the holy martyrs. While traveling on [their] way and passing through regions, cities, and villages, completely unknown to the inhabitants of the regions and to those who traveled with them, they found in many places outside the gates and outside the entrances gatherings of children, of men, and of women with branches and torches who had come out to meet the martyrs. Sitting outside the [city] walls, [those waiting for them] asked people entering [the city], "Where are they, and who are they who bear the bones of the holy martyrs?" For they [also] said, "Yesterday some of their company arrived [to] announce and to command [us], 'Go out to meet them!' " Thus, while they were

[4] Exod 25:10–22; 37:1–9

[5] Isa 61:3. The Syriac ܡܫܚܐ ܕܚܕܘܬܐ translates the Greek ἄλειμμα εὐφροσύνης (Raabe, 30 n. 2).

[6] See 1 Cor 1:18.

[7] Note that the Holy Spirit is conceived of as feminine here. The Greek original of the *Vita Petri Iberi* would have used πνεῦμα, the grammatical gender of which is neuter. For a discussion of early examples of the use of feminine language for the Holy Spirit in the Syriac tradition, see Sebastian P. Brock, "The Holy Spirit as Feminine in Early Syriac Literature," in *After Eve: Women, Theology and the Christian Tradition* (ed. J. Martin Soskice; London: Marshall Pickering, 1990), 73–88.

ܕܡܛܠܬܗܘܢ܆ ܘܝܬܝܪ ܗܘܬ ܠܗܘܢ ܚܘܣܝܘܬܐ ܘܡܥܕܪܢܘܬܐ ܕܠܟܐ܂
ܕܠܠܐܬ ܘܕܠܐ ܒܟܠܐ ܙܒܢ ܗܘܘ ܥܡ ܠܒܣܝܡܘܬܐ [R 25] ܘܚܕܘܬܐ܂
ܐܝܟ ܗܿܝ ܕܥܡ ܐܒ̈ܗܐ ܕܐܝܟ ܗܕܐ ܡܫܬܘܬܦܝܢ ܗܘܘ.
(§36) ܐܚܐ ܕܝܢ ܡܢ ܗܠܝܢ ܕܡܬܡܪܝܢ ܒܪ ܐܬܪ̈ܐ ܕܝܗܒ ܒܡܫܠܡܢܐ܂ ܟܕ
ܐܬܪܝܢ ܐܝܬܝܗܘܢ ܒܐܘܪܚܐ܆ ܘܐܡܪܝ ܕܢܦܩܘ ܒܪ̈ܘܡܐ ܐܬܝܢܗܘܢ܆
ܘܦܠܓ ܕܐܬܥܡܠܘܬܗ ܘܠܒܪܘܬܗ ܢܦܩ ܐܢܘܢ܆ ܟܕ ܒܪܫܠܬܐ ܘܒܓܢܒܘܬܐ
ܐܢܫ ܙܒܢܝܢ܆ ܦܩܕ ܕܢܐܙܠܘܢ ܠܒܝܬܗ. ܗܢܘܢ ܕܝܢ ܢܦܩܘܗܝ
ܡܢܐ ܠܒܪ ܒܠܚܘܕ ܗܘܘ ܕܢܦܩܘܢ܆ ܕܐܝܟ ܒܢ̈ܝܐ ܐܟܣܢܝܐ
ܘܡܣ̈ܟܢܐ ܕܒܬܪ ܗܘܘ. ܐܠܐ ܕܒܢ̈ܝܢܗܘܢ ܢܦܠܘܢ ܠܘܬ ܠܘܬ ܡܪܢܐ.
ܘܠܘܩܒܠܗܘܢ ܢܦܩܘܢ ܘܢܣܒܘܢ ܠܒܝܬܝ̈ܗܘܢ ܡܫܟ̈ܢܐ ܗܘܐ ܡܪܢܝܐ. ܗܘܝܘ
ܕܒܗ ܟܠܠܐ ܐܬܐ ܠܘܬܗ ܕܒܪܢܐ܆ ܒܡ ܒܡܐܬܪܐ ܩܠܝܡܐܐ. ܟܕ
ܒܘܚܡܢ ܫܟܠܐ ܡܫܟܠܐ܆ ܠܗ ܘܠܟܠܗ ܒܝܬܗ܆ ܐ ܗܘ ܕܠܐ ܢܦܪܐ
ܐܢܘܢ ܠܛܠܠܐ ܒܠܠܚܐ. ܐܝܟ ܕܠܐܒ̈ܗܐ ܕܐܠܗܐ. ܘܕܒܗ ܡܥܒܕܝܢ
ܘܠܘܬܗ ܡܫܡܫܝܢ. ܘܟܕ ܒܬܪܗܘܢ ܕܟܐܝܢܐ ܢܦܪܐ ܐܢܘܢ. ܐܦ
ܒܬܪ ܟܕ ܒܪܫܠܬܐ ܘܒܪܬܘܬܐ ܗܘܐ܆ ܡܫܪܐ ܦܪܡ ܒܦܪܘܪܐ܆ ܘܟܕ ܢܦܠ
ܥܠ ܐܦܘ̈ܗܝ ܘܡܕܡܝܢܘܢ܆ ܢܦܫ ܗܘܐ ܠܗܘܢ ܪܘܚܐ. ܘܟܕ ܦܠܓ
ܐܦܝܗ ܐܢܘܢ ܕܢܣܬܘܪܘܢ ܒܐܬܪܗ܆ ܟܕ ܡܫܬܘܕܐ ܠܗܘܢ ܕܝܗܒܐ
ܠܗܘܢ ܕܢܪܐ܆ ܘܕܟܠܠܬܐ ܕܦܘܩܐ ܫܐܠܡ ܠܗ܆ ܘܕܟܠܗ ܢܦܫܐ ܡܦܪܓ
ܠܗܘܢ܆ ܒܪܢܐ ܒܬܪ ܡܬܪܬܝܢܐ ܐܬܬܘܗܝ ܗܘܐ ܒܡܗ ܐܬܪܐ܆ ܟܕ ܠܐ
ܐܬܬܦܝܣ ܠܗ܆ ܒܡ ܐܡܪܐ ܩܠܝܡܐܐ ܘܢܩܝܫܐ ܒܪܝܐ ܐܢܘܢ܆ ܐܝܟ
ܕܠܒܪ̈ܝܐ ܘܡܒܪܕܢܐ܆ ܗܘ ܕܥܡ ܦܪܡ ܗܢ ܦܩܪ ܕܡܒܪܐ ܢܣܒ ܗܘܐ ܠܗܘܢ.
(§37) ܟܕ ܗܒܢܐ ܗܟܝܠ ܡܫܪܐܝܬ ܘܒܫܕܪܘܬܐ ܐܬܪܘܬܐ ܐܟܣܢܝܐ܆ [R 26]
ܘܐܬܪܐܬ ܙܟܘ ܒܗܘܢ ܙܒܢܬܐ ܘܫܒܥܐ ܕܠܘܬ ܡܪܢ܆ ܘܡܫܡܫܢܘܬܐ
ܕܒܩܕܫܐ ܡܪ̈ܢܝܐ܆ ܘܕܒܠܗ ܐܘܪܚܐ ܘܒܟܠ ܕܘܟܐ܆ ܒܕܐܝܟ ܗܕܐ
ܢܦܩܬܐ ܘܫܘܪܬܐ ܘܡܡܪܝܢܘܬܐ ܕܐܠܗܐ ܡܬܚܫܒܝܢ ܗܘܘ܆ ܐܟܚܕܐ
ܕܬܠܝܒܝܢ ܒܠܒܗܘܢ ܡܠܬܗ ܕܡܫܝܚܐ܆ ܐܝܟ ܢܘܪܐ ܕܡܫܬܥܪ ܡܢܗ܆
ܘܠܦܪܘܩܗܘܢ ܡܣܒܒ܆ ܦܬܘ ܒܒܩܘܗܝ ܘܡܚܦܠ ܠܗܘܢ܆ ܘܩܛܠ ܠܗܘܢ
ܒܠ ܒܡܫܟܢܐ ܕܐܒܘܗܝ܆ ܡܪܢܐ ܒܠܫܘܕܗܘܢ܆ ܙܒܢ ܐܢܘܢ܆ ܘܠܬܐ ܗܘܐ
ܒܒܣܡܘܢ ܐܠܗܐ ܢܡܒܪܟܢܐ܆ ܫܕܪ ܐܢܘܢ ܘܙܕܩܐ ܐܢܘܢ܆ ܘܢܛܪ

1 Raabe conjectures that the Syriac ܒܪܐܕܪܐ transliterates the Greek πάρεδροι and questions if the original Syriac word was not ܦܪܐܕܪܘ (Raabe, 25 n. 5).

greatly awestruck at the care of our Lord for them, the cheerfulness and steadfastness of their heart also increased. Easily and without trouble they traveled with courage **[R 25]** and joy, as people who were protected by such a hand.

(§36) A man from among those called tax-collectors,[1] who [was] well-known in the government, came upon them on the road. Thinking they were fugitive slaves, he sought to take them into his service and enslave [them].[2] Terrifying their thoughts with fear and threat, he commanded [them] to come with him. They followed him, led like foreign slaves and captives. What else could they do but to lift their eyes up to the Lord and cry out in their heart[s] and call upon their guardians, the holy martyrs? That very same night [the martyrs] attacked the [tax-collector] with many reproaches, threatening him and all his house with utter destruction if he would not let these young men go in peace as men of God who take refuge in him and hasten to him. When they had made him ready to let them go in honor, in fear and in trembling he apologized to them immediately at first dawn, falling down on his face before them. [He tried] hard [to] persuade them to stay on his land, promising to build them a monastery, to endow it with sufficient income, and to offer them every pleasure, for he was a wealthy man in that country. When they did not consent to [his suggestion], he who earlier on had been so ambitious to become their master dismissed them as though [they were his own] lords and benefactors with many honors and appeasements.[3]

(§37) When they were released with honor by this miracle, **[R 26]** they cultivated in themselves more and more the affection and love for our Lord and faith in the holy martyrs. On the whole journey in every place they were taking delight in such care and [acts of] protection and guidance from God that the word[s] of Moses applied to them, "Like the eagle who protects its nest and cherishes its nestlings, it spreads out its wings and takes them and carries them on the strength of its feathers."[4] "The Lord alone led them, and there was no alien god with them."[5] He encom-

[2] Literally, "enslave [them] to him."
[3] See Exod 11:2–3; Ezra 1:6.
[4] Deut 32:11.
[5] Deut 32:12.

ܐܢܘܢ ܐܝܟ ܒܒܬܐ ܕܥܝܢܐ: ܣܦܩܐ ܥܒܕ ܐܢܘܢ ܒܐܘܪܚܐ:
ܐܣܩ ܘܐܘܬܒ ܐܢܘܢ ܥܠ ܚܣܢܗ ܕܐܪܥܐ ܩܕܝܫܬܐ. ܟܕ ܚܕ̈ܝܢ
ܐܚܝܕܐ ܘܪܘܡ. ܐܝܟ ܐܘܪܚܐ ܕܒܡܘܪܬܐ. ܡܢ ܪܗܘܡܐ ܚܕܬܐ
ܥܕܡܐ ܠܐܘܪܫܠܡ ܡܪ̈ܕܝܬܐ ܥܒܕܘ. ܟܕ ܡܢ ܐܟܣܢܝܐ ܒܠܥܕ
ܐܟܣܢܝܐ ܡܫܠܦܝܢ. ܘܡܢ ܠܐ ܢܘ̈ܒܪܐ ܠܐ ܢܘ̈ܒܪܐ. ܘܡܢ ܚܘܒܐ
ܕܐܬܚܙܝ ܗܘܐ ܒܗܘܢ. ܟܕ ܚܒܝܒ ܒܠܥܕ ܘܡܫܟܢܐ ܠܡܫܠܡܘܬܐ ܕܡܢ
ܡܪ̈ܕܝܬܐ ܕܐܘܪܚܐ.

(§38) ܟܕ ܕܝܢ ܒܩܘܪܒܐ ܗܘܘ: ܕܐܘܪܫܠܡ ܡܕܝܢܬܐ ܩܕܝܫܬܐ: ܗ̇ܝ
ܕܪܫܡܐ ܗܘܬ ܠܗܘܢ: ܘܚܙܘ ܡܢ ܪܘܡܐ ܕܐܝܬ ܠܩܘܒܠܗ̇ ܥܠ ܣܡܟܐ
ܐܦ̈ܛܘܬܐ: ܕܐܝܟ ܕܢܒܗ ܕܡܫܟܢܐ ܡܟܪܘܡ ܬܠܝܠܐ ܪ̇ܡܐ ܕܒ̈ܝܬܐ
ܡܕ̈ܝܢܐ ܘܦ̈ܠܛܝܐ: ܗ̇ܘ ܕܝܠܒܟܐ ܦܪܘܣܐ ܘܡܣܟ̈ܢܐ: ܕܡܒܚܬܐ
ܡܕܝܢܬܐ: ܬܘܒ ܕܝܢ ܘܕܣܘܠܡܐ ܣܒܝܪܐ ܕܒܠܦܪܐ ܕܠܩܘܒܠܗ̇:
ܘܪܘܒܐܝܬ ܐܘܚܕܘ: ܟܕ ܡܠܬܐ ܗ̇ܝ ܢܒܝܘܬܐ ܡܫܬܡܠܝܐ: ܗܐ ܝܗܘܢ
[R 27] ܡܕܝܢܬܐ ܕܦܘܪܩܢ: ܒܢ̈ܝܟܝ ܢܬ̈ܘܢ ܠܐܘܪܫܠܡ: ܘܡܫܒܚܐ
ܘܡܘܒܠ ܠܛܒܘܬܐ ܐܝܟ ܚܠܡܘܢ ܐܣܘܣܐ ܠܡܫܒܚܐ ܗ̇ܘ ܕܐܣܝܡ
ܠܗܘܢ: ܠܗ̇ܘ ܕܒܪܐ ܘܐܣܦ ܗ̇ܘܕ, ܘܡܫܘܒ ܐܢܘܢ. ܟܕ ܚܙܘ ܢܦܫܗܘܢ
ܥܠ ܐܦ̈ܝܗܘܢ. ܠܐ ܫܠܝܘ ܡܢ ܕܦܩܕܝܢ ܡܢ ܠܥܠ ܗ̇ܘ ܪ̇ܘܡܐ. ܘܥܠ
ܒܪ̈ܟܝܗܘܢ ܢܦܠܘ. ܘܣܓܕܘܬ ܒܩ̈ܦܘܬܗܘܢ ܘܒܟܢ̈ܝܬܗܘܢ ܫܐܠܝܢ

[1] Deut 32:10.

[2] The Syriac ܣܦܩܐ ܥܒܕ may translate the Greek αὐτάρκησεν of Deut 32:11 (LXX). See also Raabe, 31 n. 2.

[3] See Deut 32:13. For the development of the use of the term "Holy Land" in early Christianity, see Wilken, *The Land Called Holy*; idem, "Heiliges Land."

[4] Νέα Ῥώμη, or "New Rome," was part of the official name by which Constantinople was known.

[5] Chitty ("Peter the Iberian," 18) translates "five furlongs." A *stadium* equals 125 Roman steps, which equals one eighth of a Roman mile, which measured 4,856–5,4 feet, or 1,480–1,520 meters. Thus they were about 1 km (or 0.6 miles) outside of Jerusalem.

[6] Literally, "houses."

[7] I.e., the Church of the Resurrection, a building sponsored by Emperor Constantine. See Eusebius, *Vit. Const.* 3.26–40 (Schwartz and Mommsen, 2:95–101; Richardson, 1:527–30). Within Christian tradition the church is known

passed them and went before them and "guarded them like the apple of [his] eye."[1] He made them sure[2] of their path and made them ascend to dwell in the stronghold of the Holy Land.[3] Rejoicing together and exulting as if it were a short trip, they made the journey from New Rome[4] to Jerusalem, hourly exchanging one foreign home for another and people who knew [them] not for people who knew [them] not. The love that was growing hot within them at all times [was] secretly consoling [them] in [their] weakness caused by the journey.

(§38) When they were in the neighborhood of Jerusalem, the holy city beloved to them, they saw from atop a hill about five stadia[5] away, like the flashing of the sunrise, the high roof of the holy and worshipful churches,[6] that of the saving and worshipful Cross, of the holy Anastasis,[7] and again of the worshipful Ascension, which [is] on the mountain opposite it.[8] They cried out aloud, fulfilling that prophetic word, "Behold, Zion, **[R 27]** the city of our salvation. Your eyes shall see Jerusalem."[9] They sent up praise and thanksgiving as their strength allowed to Christ whom they loved, to him who called them, brought them out, guided them, and preserved them. They cast themselves upon their faces [and] did not cease worshiping from on that height. Crawling

either as the Church of the Holy Sepulcher or the Church of the Resurrection. The latter name appears to be more commonly known in Eastern Christian communities, while Western Christians tend to use the first.

[8] I.e., on the Mount of Olives. Eusebius, *Vit. Const.* 3.43 (Schwartz and Mommsen, 2:101–2; Richardson, 1:530–31), commented on how Constantine's mother, Queen Helena, was responsible for the erection of the Church of the Ascension over a cave that was believed to be a site where Jesus taught his disciples. The pilgrim Egeria saw that building and is a witness to the name "Eleona Church" for it, nowadays known as the Church of the Pater Noster. See, e.g., Egeria, *Diary* 30.2; 35.4 (Franceschini and Weber, 77 and 79; Gingras, 104 and 108). The place from which the Lord ascended into heaven was marked by the so-called Imbomon or Inbomon, which was erected as a church before 378 C.E. by the wealthy Roman lady Poemenia (see *Vit. Pet.* §43 [R 30]). When Rufus speaks of the Church of the Ascension, he does not have in mind the building erected by Queen Helena that was ultimately destroyed by the Persians in 610, but rather Poemenia's foundation.

[9] Isa 33:20.

ܥܠܡܐ ܕܗܘ̇ ܐܪܥܐ ܩܕܝܫܬܐ. ܠܦܠܪܘܦܘܪܝܐ ܕܫܘܡܠܝܐ ܕܡܠܟܘܬܐ
ܗܘܬ ܒܗܘܢ. ܒܪܡܫܐ ܕܠܓܘ ܡܢ ܥܘܪܐ ܩܕܝ̈ܫܐ ܗ̣ܘܘ. ܘܠܗ̇ ܠܒܣܝܣ
ܕܝܠܒܟܐ ܡܚܡܪܐ ܚܒܘܫܐ. ܐܡ̇ܪ ܐܢܐ ܠܓܓܘܠܬܐ ܩܕܝܫܬܐ ܘܩܒܪܬܐ
ܩܕܝܫܬܐ. ܟܕ ܢܕܝܢ[1] ܐܚܝܕܐ ܘܚܒܝܢ. ܘܚܕܝܢ ܘܡܫܒܚܝܢ ܘܪ̇ܘܝܢ.
ܐܝܟ ܡܢ ܕܡܟܠܗܘܢ ܡܢ ܒܕܘ ܠܫܥܒܕ. ܗ̇ܘ ܕܪܫܝܡ ܠܗܘܢ. ܘܒܟܡܐ
ܡܟܝܠ ܒܟܬܝܒ ܒܫܥܬܐ.

(§39) ܘܡܛܠ ܕܐ̇ܦܣܘܣ ܠܡܠܬܐ: ܟܕ ܥ̇ܕܡ ܐܢܐ ܦܓ̈ܥܬܐ: ܐܠܗܐ
ܗ̇ܘ ܕܢܛܪ ܘܫܒܘܩ ܐܢܘܢ: ܟܕ ܐܒܗ̈ܝܐ ܐܝܬܝܗܘܢ ܘܠܐ ܡܬܚ̈ܫܒܐ
ܒܗܠܝܢ ܕܚܙ̈ܝܬܐ ܩܕ̈ܝܫܬܐ: ܦܘ ܗ̇ܕܐ، ܐܢܘܢ ܠܗܬ ܡܩ̈ܕܠ ܐܒܗ̈ܝܐ
ܠܒ̈ܢܐ. ܘܡܫ̈ܠܦܢܐ ܘܡܕܒܪ̈ܢܐ ܕܪܓܠܗܘܢ ܩܕܝܫܬܐ: ܟܕ ܢܦ̣ܩ ܠܒܪ
ܠܗܘܢ ܡܡܠܠܢܘܬܐ ܛܒܬܐ. ܐܡ̇ܪ ܐܢܐ ܕܝܢ ܠܛܘܒܢܝܘܬܐ ܡܐܠܝܢܐ
ܗ̇ܝ ܕܪܡܥܠܬܐ. ܗ̇ܝ ܕܒܗ ܦܢܝܢܘܣ ܒܟܠܗ̇. ܘܒܗ ܐܠܒܝܢܐ ܐܡܗ̇.
ܗ̇ܢܘܢ ܕܪ̈ܥܝܬܐ ܚ̇ܠܛܝܢ ܗܘܘ ܕܣܘܢܩܠܝܛܘܣ ܕܪܘܡܝ. ܘܒܓܢܣܐ
ܘܒܝܘܬܪܐ ܘܒܫܘܒܚܐ: ܘܒܟܠܗ̇ ܡܦܪܓܘܬܐ ܕܗܠܝܢ ܕܥܬܝܪܐ
ܐܝܬܝܗܘܢ ܗܘܘ: ܐܚܝܢܐ ܕܐܦ ܒܓܢܣܐ ܕܡܠܟܘܬܐ ܡܫܬܘܕܥܝܢ
ܗܘܘ: ܟܕ ܠܡܫܝܚܐ ܐܚܘܗ ܒܪܫܡܬܐ ܥܬܝܪܬܐ: ܘܐܬܬ ܡܢ ܟܠܗܝܢ
ܠܗ [R 28] ܢܦ̇ܩܘ. ܘܫܒܩܘ ܠܗܘܢ ܒܥܘܬܪܐ ܗ̇ܘ ܕܗܘܐ ܠܗ ܘܐܚܝܢܘܬܐ
ܡܟܬܪ: ܝܠܕ ܗ̇ܘ ܕܪܕܐ ܘܡܬܓܢܪ ܘܡܬܢܨܚ: ܘܟܠ ܟܠܗܝܢ
ܚ̣ܙܘ. ܢܦܫܗܘܢ. ܟܕ ܡܫܠܡܝܢܘܬ ܥܠܝܗܘܢ ܠܟܠܒܐ. ܟܕ ܗܘ̇ܓܝܐ
ܡܢ ܕܗܠܝܢ ܕܐܝܬ ܗܘܐ ܠܗܘܢ: ܗܠܝܢ ܕܦ̈ܩܝܕܝܢ ܗܘܘ: ܠܡ̈ܫܡܫܢܐ
ܘܠܡ̈ܣܟܢܐ ܗܠܝܢ ܕܐܝܬܝܗܘܢ ܗܘܘ ܒܟܠܕܘܟ ܒܪܫܝܢܘܬܐ ܕܪ̈ܘܚܐ.

[1] Raabe misprints سام here.

[2] The Syriac transliterates the Greek πληροφορία, "assurance." Occurrences of this word or closely related terms throughout the text are significant for grasping the author's purpose in writing. The usage of this term throughout the *Vita Petri Iberi* also closely connects the present text to Rufus's second major work, *Plerophoriae*.

[3] The Syriac word transliterates the Greek βάσις.

[4] That the author uses the personal name "Jesus" points to an intensified religious experience and a sense of closeness to Christ on the part of the young men. Hausherr (*The Name of Jesus*, 100) even sees it as an instance that characterizes Nabarnugios and Mithridatos as young men who are equal in standing to the martyrs because of their familiarity and experience of personal closeness

on their knees, they greeted continuously with their lips and with their eyes this holy land with full assurance[2] of the love that was kindled in them until they were inside the holy walls and embraced the foot[3] of the venerable cross. (I am speaking of the holy Golgotha and the holy Anastasis.) They were rejoicing and weeping and confessing and praising and exulting, like people who already had received Jesus,[4] whom they loved, and who henceforth were dwelling with him in heaven.[5]

(§39) To cut [my] word[s] short, leaving out many [things], God, who guarded and preserved them because they were strangers and inexperienced in these holy places, led them to good hosts of pilgrims, to teachers, and to helpers of their holy desire. He prepared for them beforehand a good hostess. I refer to the blessed Melania,[6] that Roman [lady] who with Pinianus her husband and with Albina her mother held first rank in the Senate of Rome,[7] in family, wealth, glory, and all the rest of splendor, even so that they had a link to the imperial family. Since they loved Christ with true affection and valued him more than **[R 28]** anything, they also laid up for themselves the wealth that stays and always remains, instead of that which flows [away], is snatched away, is corrupted, and corrupts.[8] Despising all these [things], they adhered to him, stripping off the world completely. The greater part, indeed, of the things they had that were easy [to divide], they distributed [as alms] to the poor and needy everywhere in the empire of the Romans and

to Christ. Here their experience is compared to that of those entering paradise and thus constitutes a good example of realized eschatology.

[5] One catches a glimpse here of one of the possible interpretations of Jerusalem as a prefiguration of heaven.

[6] Melania was born around 382 C.E. The daughter of Publicola, Melania fled with her husband Pinianus from Italy before the Vandals invaded it in 410, and lived for several years in Thagaste, North Africa. From there she withdrew to Jerusalem in 417, where she died in 439. On Melania, see the biography by her protegé Abbot Gerontius, *Vita S. Melaniae Junioris* (Gorce). For an English translation, see Elizabeth A. Clark, *The Life of Melania the Younger: Introduction, Translation, and Commentary* (New York: Mellen, 1984).

[7] See also Zachariah Rhetor, *Vit. Sev.* 17 (fol. 111 recto col. 2; Kugener, 17,3).

[8] 1 Tim 6:10; 2 Tim 3:2; Matt 6:24; Luke 16:9–13; see also Heb 13:5.

ܘܐܦ ܩ̈ܪܝܬܐ ܡܕ̈ܝܢܐ ܘܡܕ̈ܝܢܬܐ ܦܠܓܗ. ܟܠܗܝܢ ܕܝܢ ܗܠܝܢ ܕܥܘܬܪܐ ܗܘ
ܥܒܕܘ ܘܐܝܟ ܕܠܐ ܚܒܪܘ: ܘܟܠܗܘܢ ܕܝܢ ܐܬܬܢܝܘ ܚܕܐܟܚܕܐ.
ܠܘܬ ܡܣܟ̈ܢܘܬܗ ܐܝܟ ܠܡܕ̈ܝܢܬܐ ܡܕ̈ܝܢܬܐ. ܠܗ̇، ܕܒܪ ܐܬܬܐ ܘܐܚܘܗ
ܒܥܘܬܪܐ ܕܐܠܗܐ. ܗܕܐ ܒܡܘܪܐ ܙܥܘܪܐ ܘܡܠܝܐ، ܒܢ̈ܝܫܐ: ܐܝܟܢܐ
ܒܠܒܪܐ ܡܕܝܢܐ ܕܝܗܘܕܐ. ܥܠ ܛܘܪ ܫܠܝܡܐ ܡܕܝܢܐ ܚܕ ܡܢ ܕܓܒܪ̈ܐ:
ܐܣܝܪܐ ܕܝܢ ܕܢ̈ܫܐ. ܘܡܠܠܬܐ ܠܬܪ̈ܝܗܘܢ ܗܟܢ. ܠܡܫܒܘܚܬܐ
ܘܠܡܫܠܡܐ ܕܐܠܗܐ. ܘܠܡܫܒܠܐ ܘܦܘܪܫܢܐ ܕܢ̈ܫܝܬܐ ܩ̈ܕܝܫܬܐ:
ܕܗܢܘܢ ܕܡܛܠ ܦܘܪܫܢܗܘܢ ܐܬܝܢ ܠܗܝܢ. ܘܒܗ ܒܗܘܢ ܚܕܪܝܢ ܗܘܘ
ܡܫܒܚܐ: ܒܟܠܗ̇ ܚܝܒܘܬܐ ܘܫܠܡܘܬܐ ܘܚܝܪܘܬܐ ܘܡܣܝܒܪܢܘܬܐ:
ܐܟܘܬ ܫܦܝܪܐ ܡܬܚܫܒܝܢ ܗܘܘ: ܟܕ ܡܫܡܫܝܢ ܗܘܘ ܢܦܫܗܘܢ.
ܐܦ ܒܗ ܒܐܡܫܝܚܐ. ܐܦ ܓܒܪ ܡܢ ܟ̈ܠܠܐ ܦܬܚܝܢܐ ܐܢܬܘܬܗ،
ܗܘܐ ܠܡܫܡܫܘܗܝ. ܠܡܫܡܫ ܡܫܡܫܢܐ ܘܡܦܠܚܐ. ܘܟܕ ܠܒܪܐ ܫܬܝܬܐ
ܕܝܠܕܘܬܐ ܕܒܥܡ ܡܫܝܚܐ ܢܦܩ: ܡܢ ܦܠܚܝܐ ܕܐܝܪ̈ܘܢܝܗܘܢ
ܬܪܘܬܐ ܕܡܫܠܡܘܬܗ ܕܦܓܪܐ ܟܠܗܘܢ ܡܬܦܪܫܝܢ ܗܘܘ. ܟܕ ܦܫܝܛܘ
ܟܕ ܗܟܠ ܗܘܐ ܡܛܠܐ ܥܠ ܟ̈ܬܦܬܗ ܡܢ ܡܕܒܪܐ ܡܢ ܪܘܡܐ.
ܘܡܫܘܚܐ ܟܕ ܗܘܐ ܕܠܐ ܡܫܚܠܦܬܐ. ܟܕ ܕܝܢ ܠܡܫܡܠܝܘܬܐ: [R 29]

[1] On the phenomenal wealth that Melania and her husband possessed, see Gerontius, *Vit. Mel.* 15–19 (Gorce, 156–66; Clark, 38–43); see also José M. Blazquez, "Las posesiones de Melania la Joven," in *Historiam Pictura Refert: Miscellanea in onore di Padre Alejandro Recio Veganzones, OFM* (ed. Josep Marti-i-Aixala, Eugenio Alliata, and Fabrizio Bisconti; Rome: Pontificio Istituto Archeologia Cristiana, 1994), 67–80.

[2] Phil 3:8.

[3] An important reference documenting the existence of double monasteries in the early church. For a recent study of the development of such double monasteries, see Daniel F. Stramara, "Double Monasticism in the Greek East, Fourth through Eighth Centuries," *JECS* 6 (1998): 269–312.

in the holy churches and in the monasteries as well.[1] They left everything else behind and reckoned [it] as dung,[2] [and] girding themselves lovingly with the cross of our Lord, they came to the Holy City to adore it. When they had come and [since they] loved dwelling there, they established two large and populous [monastic] dwellings, one for men, one for women,[3] on the holy Mount of Olives by the side of the holy Ascension.[4] For both they set up an endowment for the glory[5] and praise of God and for the reception and salvation of the souls of those many who go there for their salvation.[6] Dwelling in them in quiet, they were fighting the good fight[7] in complete self-denial, quietness, Naziriteship,[8] and humility, making themselves poor in [their monastic] habit as well. For even their clothing was from crushed straw, humble and worthless. And keeping[9] the approved yoke of the crucifixion with Christ,[10] they were achieving daily from their hands' work the nourishment of the body's weakness: Pinianus would carry sticks on his shoulders from the far desert and would sell [them] in the

[4] The monasteries were located between Poemenia's Church of the Ascension and the Eleona Church. Melania the Elder already had built a monastery in Jerusalem in 379. See Palladius, *Hist. Laus.* 46.5 (Butler, 2:135; Meyer, 124).

[5] The Syriac text uses ܬܫܒܘ as abbreviation for ܬܫܒܘܚܬܐ.

[6] Note how the monastic life is here understood as one of the significant ways of obtaining salvation.

[7] See 2 Tim 4:7.

[8] See also *Vit. Pet.* §§21, 28, 50, 69, 138 (R 13, 19, 33, 47, 102).

[9] The Syriac ܢܛܪܝܢ may translate the Greek φυλάσσοντες (Raabe, 33 n. 6).

[10] See Matt 11:29–30.

ܒܝܕ ܦܘܠܚܢܐ ܕܒܥܡܪܐ ܒܥܡܠܐ ܗܘܬ܂ ܘܡܢ ܗܢܐ ܢܦܫܬܐ ܒܝܬܝܪ̈ܬܐ
ܕܬܪܣܝܬܗ̇ ܡܥܠܝܐ ܗܘܬ܂ ܕܫܪܟܐ ܠܣܢܝܩܐ ܦܠܓܐ ܗܘܬ.

(§40) ܗܕܐ ܗܟܝܠ ܒܕ ܥܒܕܬ ܡܐܬܝܬܐ ܕܠܐܘܪܫܠܡ ܕܦܛܪܘܣ
ܘܕܝܘܚܢܢ ܛܘ̈ܒܢܐ ܡܫ̈ܝܚܐ܃ ܗܢܘܢ ܕܝܢ ܕܒܢܘܗܝ ܘܡܬܠܡܕ̈ܘܗܝ ܕܦܛܪܘܣ
ܩܠܝ̈ܠܐ ܕܐܬܪ̈ܘܬܗܘܢ ܡܬܩܢܝܢ ܗܘܘ܃ ܘܒܠܒܗܬ ܕܓܒܗ ܐܬܚܡܗܘܢ ܘܡܢ
ܐܚܪܐ܂ ܣܓܝܐܬ ܡܓܠܬ ܐܢܘܢ. ܐܦ ܠܒܪ ܐܬܒܢܝܬ܃ ܕܒܕ ܒܢܝܢ
ܐܬܬ ܠܒܢܝ̈ܢܐ ܡܠܒܫܬܐ ܕܡܣܛܝܛܘܣܐ܂ ܗܕܐ ܣܢܝܬ ܗܘܬ ܠܛܘܒܢܐ
ܦܛܪܘܣ܂ ܒܕ ܒܕܒܠ ܛܘܒܢܐ ܡܠܒܫܬ ܡܫܬܒܚܐ ܗܘܐ. ܘܐܬܒܛܠܬܗ
ܗܘܬ ܦܘܩ. ܕܣܝܬܗ ܕܛܘܒܢܬܐ ܕܡܫܝܚܐ ܡܢ ܛܘܒܢܘܬܗ ܐܝܬ ܗܘܐ
ܒܠܗܝ܂ ܐܝܬܘܗܝ ܗܘܐ ܓܒܪ ܐܝܟ ܕܐܡܪܬ ܡܢ ܥܒܪܘܬܗ܂ ܪܚܡ
ܠܐܠܗܐ.

(§41) ܒܠܬܐ ܕܝܢ ܡܐܬܝܬܗ ܕܛܘܒܢܬܐ ܡܐܠܝܢܐ ܕܠܡܕܒܪܝܬ
ܡܠܟܘܬܐ܂ ܐܬܝܢܗ̇ ܗܘܬ ܗܕܐ. ܬܐܘܕܘܣܝܘܣ ܡܠܟܐ ܕܝܢ
ܠܐܠܗܐ܂ ܒܕ ܐܬܬ ܐܘܕ ܠܘܬܗ ܡܢ ܩܕܝܫܐ ܕܘܟܬܐ܃ ܕܐܬܬܪܝܪ ܡܢ
ܘܠܛܘܒܢܘܬܗ ܡܠܟܐ܃ ܕܢܬܒܪܟ ܠܗ ܠܒܪܬܗ ܕܛܘܒܢܐ ܬܐܘܕܘܣܝܘܣ܃
ܘܐܬܝܗܘܢ ܗܘܐ ܗܢܐ ܒܪ ܚܝܠܗ ܕܗܕܝܪܬܐ ܡܐܠܝܢܐ܃ ܘܒܕܒܠ ܠܐ
ܡܫܬܦܝܐ ܐܝܬܘܗܝ ܗܘܐ ܕܛܘܒܢܬܐ ܕܒܪܘܚܢܝܐ܃ ܘܐܬܪܪܬ

[1] The image of "working in wool" is closely related to "weaving," a notion that served early Christian authors as one of the possible metaphors to describe the incarnation, in which the Word of God wove for himself a body. In antiquity, the task of "weaving" was one of the main areas of women's work. The themes of weaving, women, and incarnation were featured prominently, e.g., in the homilies of Proclus of Constantinople (see, e.g., the discussion in Nicholas Constas, "Weaving the Body of God: Proclus of Constantinople, the Theotokos, and the Loom of the Flesh," *JECS* 3 [1995]: 169–94; Constas, *Proclus of Constantinople*, ch. 6) and in the poetry of Ephraem the Syrian (see, e.g., the discussion in Kathleen McVey, "Ephrem The Syrian's Use of Female Metaphors to Describe the Deity," *ZAC* 5 [2001]: 276–79). As traditions developed, references to the image of "wool" came to express ascetic identity even in cross-cultural and cross-religious dimensions. From wool being an identifier of ascetics who wore a simple woolen garement, Sufi mystics in Islamic traditions are named directly in reference to that term, *suf* being the word for "wool."

[2] See Acts 20:34–35; 1 Cor 4:12; 9:13–15, 18; 1 Thess 2:9; 2 Thess 3:7–9.

[3] With the example of Pinianus and Melania, who despite their ascetic commitment labored manually in order to sustain themselves, Rufus provides the anti-Chalcedonian ascetic community with a model to be followed. Here a properly balanced ascetic life is one that includes manual labor, especially since the surplus of the labor can help to alleviate the needs of the poor. For a rebuttal

market without shame; the blessed [Melania] **[R 29]** labored in the work of wool[1] and from this supplied the humble need of her sustenance.[2] The rest she distributed to the needy.[3]

(§40) When [Melania] heard of the arrival of the holy youths Peter and John in Jerusalem—at that time they were [still] called Nabarnugios and Mithridatos[4] in the languages of their countries[5]—and learned who they were and from where [they came], she received them joyfully. She remembered that she once went to the royal city of Constantine [and] had seen the blessed Peter there,[6] when he was still a little boy, being brought up like a king. She loved him much, for she saw that the grace of Christ was upon him from his youth. For from his childhood he was, as I have said, dear to God.[7]

(§41) The occasion of the blessed Melania's coming to the royal city was as follows. To the God-fearing Emperor Theodosius came a man from the nobles of Rome who had been sent by Emperor Valentinian[8] to espouse to him the daughter of the blessed Theodosius.[9] [The man] was a family member of the holy Melania, and he had not yet taken part in the grace of the Chris-

of ascetics who avoided manual labor, see, e.g., Augustine, *De opere monachorum* (Zycha, 5.3:529–96; Muldowney, 323–94). See also the comments in Caner, *Wandering, Begging Monks*, 22–24, 117–20, and several other passages (see index "manual labor"). For a voice from the East, see Gregory of Nyssa, *De pauperibus amandis* (van Heck).

[4] The name is related to that of Mithra, the Persian god of light.

[5] See also *Vit. Pet.* §§5, 14 (R 4, 9).

[6] This took place in 424 or 437 C.E.

[7] See above, *Vit. Pet.* §30 (R 21).

[8] I.e., Emperor Valentinian III (425–455). Born in 419 as the son of Constantius III and Galla Placidia, Valentinian became emperor in 425, yet for many years his mother effectively ran the affairs of the empire in his stead.

[9] The young princess's name was Licinia Eudocia. Some speculate that at the time of the visit of the Roman noble man she was just two years old, having been born in 422. Thus the visitor effectively only arranged for the engagement of the couple. It seems more reasonable, however, to assume that Melania visited Constantinople in the year in which the actual marriage took place. The wedding ceremony occurred on 29 October 437. Rufus may have conflated the two events: the visit for the purpose of converting Valentinian's messenger, and the visit at the occasion of the wedding. See also Gerontius, *Vit. Mel.* 50–56 (Gorce, 224–39; Clark, 64–69).

ܕܢܝܚܗ̇ ܠܛܘܒܢܝܬܐ ܡܐܠܢܝܐ: ܘܐܬܐܡܪ، ܕܗܘܪܐ ܒܪܘܡܝܢܐ: ܐ
ܗ̣ܘ ܕܩܒܠ ܒܗ̇ ܘܫܡܥ ܡܢܗ̇ ܡܠܬܐ ܕܦܘܪܩܢܐ܆ ܟܕ ܥܕܪ ܐܝܟ
ܕܐܡܪܝܢ ܗ̣ܘ ܙܢܐ ܠܡܫܝܚܝܐ ܦܠܓܐ܆ ܐܦܝܣܗ̇ ܠܗ̇ ܠܛܘܒܢܝܬܐ
ܕܬܐܬܐ ܒܪܡܫܐ ܠܡܕܝܢܬܐ [R 30] ܡܠܟܬܐ ܡܛܠ ܦܘܪܩܢܐ ܕܢܦܫܐ.
ܗ̇ܝ، ܕܟܕ ܐܬܬ ܘܟܕ ܛܠܝܘܬܐ ܐܪܡܠܘܬܐ ܕܟܒܪܬܐ ܗܘܬ ܒܗ̇:
ܡܗܝܡܢܐ ܘܟܪܝܣܛܝܢܐ ܡܫܡܠܝܐ ܒܕܒܪܬܗ̇: ܘܠܐܚܪ̈ܢܐ ܩ̈ܠܝܠܐ
ܚܒܝܬ: ܘܠܘܬ ܕܘܒܪܐ ܐܠܗܝܐ ܕܕܡܐ ܠܕܝܠܗ̇ ܢܓܫܬ: ܘܠܪܚܡܬܗ̇
ܕܛܘܒܢܐ ܦܠܘܪܘܣ ܗܢܝ ܐܚܬܗ ܠܗ ܠܒܢܗ̇. ܡܩܪܒܐ ܗܘܬ ܠܡܕܝܢܬܐ
ܡܢܫܬܐ. ܟܕ ܐܚܝܕܐ ܗܘܬ ܕܟܪܗ̇ ܡܕܝܢܬܐ ܘܒܝܬܘܬܗ̇.
(§42) ܡܛܠ ܕܝܢ ܕܐܦ ܐܢܬܬܐ ܡܐܠܢܝܐ ܐܝܬ ܗܘܬ[1] ܠܐܦܪܘܢܝܣ:
ܡܢ ܒ̈ܢܝܐ ܕܪ̈ܘܡܝܐ: ܕܐܦ ܗ̣ܘ ܫܠܝܡܬ ܗܘܬ ܠܟܠܗܐ ܘܫܩܠܬ
ܐܘܡܢܘܬܐ. ܘܙܦ ܠܡܕܒܪ ܕܝܗ̇، ܡܢ ܡܕܝܢܬܐ ܐܬܠܝܗ ܗܘܬ: ܗܕܐ ܕܝܢ
ܐܢܬܬܐ. ܗ̇ܝ، ܕܡܟܠܬ ܠܡ̈ܫܝܚܐ.
(§43) ܗܘܬ ܕܝܢ ܐܢܬܬܐ ܡܢ ܩܕܡ ܗܠܝܢ ܬܪ̈ܬܝܢ: ܡܫܡܫܢܝܬܐ ܒܟܢܫܐ
ܘܒܬܘܠܬܐ. ܢܟܦܬܐ ܣܓܝ ܘܕܚܠܬ ܐܠܗܐ. ܕܫܡܗ̇ ܦܘܡܦܝܢܐ. ܗ̇ܝ،
ܕܐܚܝܕܐ ܕܬܓܪܐ: ܒܪ̈ܘܡܝܬܐ ܡܢܫܬܐ ܘܩܕܝܫܬܐ. ܕܒܪܘܡܝ̈ܢܗ̇ ܕܗ̇ܝ،
ܘܒܝܘܡܗ̇ ܠܒ̈ܢܝ ܗܠܝܢ ܕܐܫܬܩܦܘ. ܗ̇ܝ، ܕܐܦ ܠܒܪܬܐ ܕܦܘܠܝܛܐ
ܡܢܫܐ ܒܝܬ ܘܐܓܪܬ ܒ̈ܢܝܢܐ. ܘܠܦܬܟܪܐ ܕܐܝܬ ܗܘܐ ܒܦܠܘܪܐ

[1] Raabe misreads ܗܘܐ.

[2] I.e., he was not baptized.

[3] A noteworthy incident of evangelistic and/or missionary activity on the part of a woman. See also Palladius, *Hist. Laus.* 54.4 (Butler, 2:146–47; Meyer, 135), concerning the success of her relative, Melania the Elder, in converting Apronius, the pagan husband of Melania the Elder's niece Avita. The passage allows one to perceive different degrees of individuals' affiliation with the Christian community.

[4] I.e., Melania the Elder (ca. 342-ca. 410). She was the paternal grandmother of Melania the Younger. On Melania the Elder, see Palladius, *Hist. Laus.* 46, 54–55 (Butler, 2:134–36, 146–49; Meyer, 123–25, 134–36, 136–37). A Roman lady of immense wealth, she was widowed in her early twenties (ca. 365) and subsequently became a model of asceticism. She left the Eternal City, visited Egypt and its ascetic heroes (ca. 372), and eventually settled in Palestine.

tians.[2] He yearned to see the blessed Melania and promised to become a Christian if he met her and heard from her the word of salvation. So the Christ-loving emperor sent [for her], as I have said. He persuaded the blessed [lady] to come to the royal **[R 30]** city for the sake of the salvation of a soul. When she had come and through the divine grace dwelling in her had made him a believer and a complete Christian,[3] she edified many others and enkindled [them] to the divine way of life similar to her own. Having further aroused the desire of the blessed Peter toward her zeal, she returned again to the Holy City, taking up her former way of life and her asceticism.

(§42) There was another Melania in Jerusalem, also from the nobles of the Romans, who also had renounced the world and taken the [monastic] habit. It should be known that this [Melania], indeed, was the earlier one,[4] while ours who received the saints [was] the latter.

(§43) Before these two was another [woman], famous by lineage and wealth, of great modesty and God-fearing, whose name [was] Poemenia,[5] who loved to dwell in the holy and worshipful places, so that by her ways of life and by her love those who were named [above] were made zealous.[6] It was she who built the Church of the Holy Ascension and surrounded [it with] build-

Through her close friendship with Rufinus of Aquileia, she eventually incurred Jerome's wrath in the course of the Origenist controversy.

[5] On Poemenia, see Palladius, *Hist. Laus.* 35.14 (Butler, 2:106; Meyer, 103); Emile Amélineau, *Monuments pour servir à l'histoire de l'Égypte Chrétienne aux IVe, V^e, VIe et VIIe siècles* (2 vols.; MMAF 4.1–2; Paris: Leroux, 1888–95), 2:650–65 ("Vie de Jean de Lycopolis"), here 664–65. Paul Devos ("La 'Servante de Dieu' Poemenia d'après Pallade, la tradition Copte et Jean Rufus," *AnBoll* 87 [1969]: 189–208) established, among other things, that the Poemenia featured in the *Life of John of Lycopolis* is the same as the one in the works of John Rufus. See also E. D. Hunt, *Holy Land Pilgrimage in the Later Roman Empire AD 312–460* (Oxford: Clarendon, 1982), 47, 76–78, 160–63; and J. R. Martindale, *The Prosopography of the Later Roman Empire*, vol. 2: *AD 395–527* (Cambridge: Cambridge University Press, 1980), 894–95.

[6] According to Rufus, Melania the Elder and Melania the Younger desired to imitate the intensively ascetic and pilgrim way of life of Poemenia.

ܕܡܬܩܪܐ ܕܓܪܙܝܡ ܕܒܫܡܪܝܢ: ܕܒܕܒܝܠ ܡܠܟ ܗܘܐ: ܘܡܕܒܚܐ ܠܗܘ
ܘܟܠܐ ܡܫܬܠܛ. ܗܘܐ ܡܢ ܒܥܘܪܐ ܕܗܘ ܐܬܪ̈ܐ ܗܫܒܬ.

(§44) ܗܕܐ ܗܟܝܠ ܡܐܠܢܝܐ ܐܚܪܬܐ. ܐܢܬܬܗ ܕܦܝܢܝܢܘܣ ܘܒܪܬܗ
ܕܐܠܒܝܢܐ ܐܢܬܬܗ ܗ̇ܝ ܕܠܗܘܢ ܩܕ̈ܝܫܐ ܒܣܕܘܬܐ ܡܓܠܬ. ܐܝܟ
ܕܠܬ̈ܝܢܐ ܫܬ̈ܝܒܐ. ܟܕ ܓܝܪ ܠܘܬܗ̇ ܐܬܦܢܝܘ. ܗܢܝܢ ܘܬ̈ܠܦܘܣܐ
ܕܕܘܒܪܐ ܕܒܘܣܡܬܐ ܐܬܡܣܪܘ ܒܡܗܡܪܐ ܗ̇ܘ ܕܓܒܪܐ. ܐܟܚܕܐ ܕܝܢ
ܘܠܐܣܟܡܐ ܕܝܚܝܕܘܬܐ [R 31] ܐܫܬܘܝܘ ܡܢ ܐܒ̈ܗܐ ܡܕ̈ܒܪܢܐ: ܡܢ
ܡܕܒܪܐ ܘܦܠܚܐ ܠܓܪܘܢܛܝܘܣ. ܕܐܝܬܘܗܝ ܗܘܐ ܡܕܒܪܐ ܘܪܝܫ ܕܝܪܐ
ܕܦܠܓܐ ܡܕܒܪܐ ܕܕ̈ܝܪܬܐ.

(§45) ܐܦ ܓܝܪ ܗܢܐ ܠܓܪܘܢܛܝܘܣ: ܗ̇ܘ ܕܦܠܚܢܐ ܡܠܬܐ
ܕܡܠܠܬܗ: ܕܐܝܬܘܗܝ ܗܘܐ ܒܗܝܡܢܘܬܗ ܐܘܪܬܕܘܟܣܐ: ܟܕ ܒܕܒܝܠ
ܠܦܠܐ ܐܝܬܘܗܝ ܗܘܐ: ܠܡܫܡܫܢܘܬܐ ܕܦܘܪܬܐ ܐܫܬܘܝ ܡܢ ܡܕܒܪܢܘܬܐ
ܡܐܠܒܝܢܐ: ܘܗ̣ܘ ܒܠܒܗ̇ ܕܗܕܐ. ܘܟܕ ܠܘܬܗܘܢ ܗ̣ܘ ܐܬܩܪܒ
ܡܕܝܢܬܐ: ܘܕܝܟܪ ܠܗ̇ܠܟܐ ܗܘܐ. ܐܬܒܝ ܠܗܘܢ ܕܦܩܐ: ܕܐܦ
ܒܐܣܟܡܐ ܗܢܐ ܕܕܝܪܝܘܬܐ ܢܬܦܬܦ: ܐܝܟ ܗ̇ܝ ܕܐܝܬ ܠܗ
ܕܢܣܒ ܘܡܕܒܪܐ ܘܝܢܐ. ܘܟܕ ܫܠܡܘܗܝ ܬܪ̈ܝܗܘܢ ܒܠܫܢܕܝܗܘܢ:
ܘܐܘܠܦܘܗܝ ܠܡܪܗ ܡܕܝܢܐ ܕܦܘܪܗ: ܘܡܫܡܫ ܩܫ̈ܝܫܐ ܕܐܣܟܡܐ ܥܠ

1 See above, *Vit. Pet.* §38 (R 26).

2 Although Rufus might express anti-Samaritan polemic, Hadrian (11 August 117–31 December 137) had rebuilt the temple of Zeus on the ruins of the old Samaritan temple. Antiochus IV Epiphanes (175–164) had first built a temple to Zeus on this location (2 Macc 6:3; Josephus, *Ant.* 11.257–264).

3 Mount Gerizim was the center of worship of the Samaritans. See below, *Vit. Pet.* §166 (R 123).

4 Archaeological excavations have revealed the foundations of a church on top of the mountain. See Itzhak Magen, "Gerizim, Mount," *NEAHL* 2:490–492; Jeffrey K. Lott, "Gerizim, Mount," *ABD* 2:993.

5 Literally, "that other Melania."

6 Albina was the daughter-in-law of Melania the Elder.

7 Melania the Younger was mother of two children, first of a daughter, then of a son. According to Gerontius, *Vit. Mel.* 5–6 (Gorce, 134–36; Clark, 29–30), both children died at a young age.

8 Literally, "head of a monastery." The title "abbot" could be applied to any monk who was in a position of authority. Abbots of especially important monasteries might alternatively be called "archimandrites." In Palestine, a tradition developed according to which two abbots or archimandrites were

ings.[1] She demolished the idol[2] that was on the mountain called Gerizim,[3] in Samaria, which was still standing and until that time was worshiped by the inhabitants of that region.[4]

(§44) The later Melania,[5] the wife of Pinianus and the daughter of Albina,[6] was the one who received these saints with joy like beloved sons.[7] For having been received by her, there they were also conferred with honor through the examples of the ascetic ways of life in the men's monastery. At the same time they were esteemed worthy of the habit of the solitary life **[R 31]** from the holy hands of the holy and famous Gerontius, who was the priest and archimandrite[8] of the holy Mount of Olives.[9]

(§45) This Gerontius, who was famous in his reputation and by family a Jerusalemite, while still a child was accepted for the service of watchman by the holy Melania and her husband. When he had grown up with them in a manner holy and pleasing to God, he appeared to them worthy to partake of the sacred habit of monasticism, as one whose way of life and manner are suitable for it. The two of them alone took him to the Holy Sepulcher of our Savior and placed the garments of the [monastic] habit on the holy

installed, one as the archimandrite of the cenobitic monks, one as the archimandrite of the anchoritic monks. According to Cyril of Scythopolis, *Vit. Euth.* 27 (Schwartz, 42,10–15; Price, 38) Gerontius and Elpidius, the successors of Passarion, were the archimandrites of the Palestinian monks at the time of Theodosius of Jerusalem. Eventually Gerontius was replaced as head of the cenobitic monks of the Holy City. See Cyril of Scythopolis, *Vit. Theod.* 4 (Schwartz, 239,4–6; Price, 265). See also David J. Melling, "Archimandrite," *BDEC*, 42.

[9] On the importance of Gerontius as the one who initiated Peter and John the Eunuch into the ascetic life, see below *Vit. Pet.* §48 (R 32); on his exemplary fasting, see *Pler.* 41. Gerontius was one of the few staunch anti-Chalcedonians who did not reconcile with Juvenal of Jerusalem when he violently reclaimed the bishop's throne of the Holy City from Theodosius in 452 C.E. For the Chalcedonian evaluation of Gerontius, see the following *vitae* by Cyril of Scythopolis: *Vit. Euth.* 27, 30, 43, 45 (Schwartz, 42,13–14, 49,8–10, 62,19–63.2, 67,14–17; Price, 38, 46, 59, and 64); *Vit. Sab.* 30, 38 (Schwartz, 115,2–3, 127,19; Price, 124, 136); *Vit. Theod.* 4 (Schwartz, 239,6; Price, 265). Some discussion of his role can be found in Lorenzo Perrone, *La chiesa di Palestina e le controversie cristologiche: Dal concilio di Efeso (431) al secondo concilio di Costantinopoli (553)* (TRSR 18; Brescia: Paideia, 1980), 112–13. Gerontius is also the likely author of the *Life of Melania the Younger*.

ܟܐܦܐ ܩܕܝܫܬܐ܂ ܐܝܟ ܕܗܘ ܐܒܘܗܝ ܕܒܢ̈ܝ ܐܠܗܝܐ. ܟܕ ܫܐܠ[1]
ܕܢܬܠܡ ܠܗ ܒܗ ܠܒܘܫܐ ܒܡܫܝܚܐ ܗܠܝܢ ܬܠܬ. ܗܝܡܢܘܬܐ ܬܪܝܨܬܐ
ܘܩܕܝܫܘܬܐ ܘܕܕܡ̈ܟܐ.

(§46) ܘܗܟܢܐ ܠܬܠܬܝܗܘܢ ܐܫܬܘܝ. ܘܡܝܬܪܐܝܬ ܠܛܘܒܢܘܬܐ ܗ̇ܝ
ܕܕܡ̈ܟܐ. ܐܝܟܢܐ ܕܟܕ ܐܬܬܦܝܣܘ ܡܫܝܚܐ ܐܟܣܢܝܐ ܘܪܝܫ ܕܝܪܐ
ܟܠܘܪܐ ܩܕܝܫܐ ܕܝܬ̈ܪܐ: ܘܕܒܡܪ̈ܐ ܕܒܗ̇ ܘܪ̈ܝܫܝ ܦ̈ܠܝܟܐ ܒܝܕ
ܢܦܩܐ ܒܫܒܬܐ. ܬܠܬܐ ܒܢ̈ܝܐ ܕܬܫܒܘܚܬܐ ܐܠܗܝܬܐ ܡܬܩܒܠܐ
ܗܘܬ. ܘܡܬܪܐܝܬ ܒܐܕܒܟܐ ܩܕܝܫܐ. ܟܠܘܪܐ ܩܕܝܫܐ ܚܕ.. ܘܒܗ̇ܘ
ܒܡܪܐ ܕܟܪܢܐ ܚܕ.. ܘܬܘܒ ܒܗ̇ܘ ܒܡܪܐ ܕܝܫܘܥ ܚܕ.. ܒܗܠܝܢ ܓܝܪ
ܦ̈ܬܟܐ ܕܝܪ̈ܚܐ: ܒܠܚܘܕ ܡܩܪܒܐ ܗܘܐ ܒܝܫܐ ܘܬܫܡܫܬܐ ܕܝܠܝܬܐ
ܠܬܒܥܘܬܐ ܡܐܠܝܬܐ. ܐܝܟ ܒܥܕܐ ܕܒܕܬܐ ܕܪܘܡܝ. ܘܒܟܠ ܚܕ ܡܢ
ܗܠܝܢ ܒܝ̈ܫܐ ܟܕ ܡܩܪܒܐ [R 32] ܗܘܐ ܒܬܫܡܫܬܐ ܩܕܝܫܬܐ: ܗܟܢܐ
ܕܠܐ ܫܠܝܐ ܒܕܡܥܐ ܠܫܘܠܡܐ ܐܦܢ ܗܘܐ ܕܪ̈ܒܟܐ: ܒܗ ܒܐܒܐ
ܘܫܘܡܐ ܕܠܒܐ: ܐܝܟܢܐ ܕܠܐ ܐܢܫ ܡܢ ܗ̇ܘ ܕܒܫܝܡ ܡܫܡܫ ܗܘܐ
ܕܠܒܘܢ ܢܦܫܗ. ܟܕ ܟܠܗ ܒܘܫܝܐ ܒܬܬܘܣܬܐ ܐܬܬܘܗܝ ܗܘܘ.
ܘܒܟܠܬܐ ܘܒܬܟܫܦܬܐ ܡܫܬܠܡܝܢ ܗܘܘ. ܘܕܪ̈ܟܐ ܒܕܡܘܬܗ ܐܫܕܝܢ
ܗܘܘ.

(§47) ܡܛܠ ܗܕܐ ܘܕܒܐܝܬ ܟܕ ܠܬܒܥܘܬܐ ܕܐܝܟ ܗܕܐ ܐܫܬܘܝ.
ܕܢܗܘܐ ܠܗ̇ ܠܗܕܐ ܘܒܗ ܫܘܠܡܐ ܚܘ. ܟܕ ܐܕܪܟ ܒܪ ܠܢ̈ܒܝܐ
ܕܡܪܘܬܐ: ܕܒܡܪܐ ܕܩܘܪܒܐ ܕܟܠܗܘܢܐ: ܘܠܒܝܐ ܗܡܕܢܐ ܚܘ̇
ܒܗܘܢ: ܒܕܡܐ ܠܩܘܪܒܐ ܘܠܟܢܝܫ ܚܘܫܒܐ ܘܦܬ̈ܓܡܐ ܕܩܘܡ ܕܝ̈ܢܐ:
ܘܒܠܠܐ ܕܟܪܘܢܘܬܐ ܦܠܪ܂ ܗܟܢܐ ܐܫܬܟܠ. ܘܟܕ ܦܠܓ ܐܬܦܠܣ

[1] MS B reads ܫܐܠ.

[2] In the context of the present work, the holy rock is to be understood as the rock of Golgotha, i.e., the rock formation on which the cross had been erected on which Christ died. See also below, *Vit. Pet.* §56 (R 38).

[3] With the reading ܫܐܠ as found in MS B. According to MS A, one ought to read "while he asked."

[4] Most recently, Daniel Callam ("The Frequency of Mass in the Latin Church ca. 400," *TS* 45 [1984]: 619–21) questions, not whether Melania had the Eucharist celebrated daily in her monastery, but whether indeed this custom was one of Roman or perhaps rather of North African origin.

[5] Liturgical celebrations did not require a silent inactivity on the part of the attendant laity.

rock.[2] They clothed him as from the hands of our Lord, while they asked[3] that there would be bestowed upon him together with the sacred garment these three [gifts]: right faith, holiness, and tears.

(§46) He was esteemed worthy of these three, and especially of the grace of tears. When he had been appointed simultaneously as priest and as abbot of the holy Mount of Olives and of the monasteries on it, often he would celebrate three gatherings of the divine service in a single day, and especially on the holy Sunday: one on the holy mountain, and one in the monastery for men, and again one in the monastery for women. On the remaining days, he celebrated daily a gathering and a private service for the blessed Melania according to the custom of the Church of Rome.[4] In each liturgy, when he had begun **[R 32]** the holy service, he shed tears ceaselessly until the end with grief and anguish of heart such that no one of those assembled could control himself, while all [the members of] the congregation were in penitence and empassioned with gasping and groans[5] were shedding tears like him.[6]

(§47) Therefore it was fitting that having been deemed worthy of such a grace he should show a worthy end. For he came to be perfected[7] in the time of the rebellion, of the transgression[8] of the Council of Chalcedon, during which he showed martyr-like zeal,[9] having been placed in chains, imprisoned, and having stood before judges, thus weaving the crown of confessorship. Although he

[6] Tears are understood as a sign of repentance. The centrality of *penthos*, or "contrition" and "repentance," in Eastern Christian spirituality and asceticism has been studied by Irénée Hausherr, *Penthos: The Doctrine of Compunction in the Christian East* (trans. Anselm Hufstader; CSS 53; Kalamazoo, Mich.: Cistercian, 1982). See also Barbara Müller, "Die Tränen der Wüstenväter: Das Penthos in den *Apophthegmata Patrum*," *OS* 46 (1997): 281–313; and Francis Leduc, "Penthos et larmes dans l'œuvre de saint Jean Chrysostome," *POC* 41 (1991): 220–57.

[7] I.e., he completed his life.

[8] The Syriac ܥܒܘܪܝܐ may translate the Greek παράβασις or παρανομία (Raabe, 36 n. 2).

[9] For the centrality of the image of "martyr" for anti-Chalcedonians in Palestine in their assessment of their situation, see Horn, "Weaving the Pilgrim's Crown."

ܡܢ ܕ̈ܝܢܐ: ܗܢܘܢ ܦܪ̈ܨܘܦܐ ܡ̈ܫܒܚܐ ܩ̈ܠܝܠܐ: ܕܒܠܚܘܕ ܢܫܬܘܕܐ
ܕܢܚܠܠ ܥܡ ܝܘܒܢܐܠܝܘܣ ܒܦܘܪܐ ܒܪ. ܠܐ ܡܫܬܘܬܦ ܥܡܗ· ܘܢܬܒܪܐ
ܡܢ ܐܘܠܝܢܐ· ܘܠܐ ܗܘ ܐܝܟܢܐ. ܐܠܐ ܐܡܪ· ܚܣ ܠܝ ܡܢ ܡܪܝܐ
ܕܐܚܙܐ ܦܪ̈ܨܘܦܐ ܕܝܗܘܕܐ ܡܫܠܡܢܐ.

(§48) ܐܚ̈ܘܗܝ ܕܗܢܐ ܢܣܒ ܐܣܟܝܡܐ ܠܐܒ̈ܗܬܐ ܕܝܠܗ· ܠܦܛܪܘܣ
ܘܠܚܘܣܢ. ܘܗܘ ܥܒܕ ܠܗܘܢ ܚ̈ܫܐ ܗܠܝܢ· ܚܠܦ ܚ̈ܫܐ ܕܗܘ̈ܝ
ܗܘܘ ܠܗܘܢ ܡܢ ܐܒܗ̈ܬܗܘܢ.

(§49) ܐܝܟܢܐ ܕܡܚܒܠ ܚ̈ܝܝܢ ܗܘܘ ܒܓܠܝܐ· ܘܡܬܦܫܝܢ ܗܘܘ
ܡܫܬܪܘܬܐ ܕܝܘܢܝܘܬܐ. ܒܡܘܪܐ ܗܘ ܕܚܒܪܐ ܐܝܟܢܐ ܕܦܪܚܬ
ܐܦܪܚܬ· ܘܗܘ ܕܡܢ ܠܐܢܛܝܦܛܪܘܣ ܪܫ ܕܝܪܐ ܐܒܘܬܗ ܗܘܐ. ܬܘܒ
ܡܚܠ ܗܦܟ ܘܡܪ̈ܥܐ ܡܣܝܒܐ ܕܗܠܝܢ ܗܘܕ̈ܐ ܩ̈ܕܝܫܐ. ܡܗ̈ܕܝܢܐ
ܓ̈ܒܐ ܘܩ̈ܢܝ ܠܬܘܗܘܢ· ܡܢ ܪ̈ܘܚܐ ܕܗܠܝܢ ܐܘܪܚܝܢ ܗܘܕ̈ܐ [R 33]
ܦܓ̈ܪܐ ܕܡܣܟ̈ܢܐ. ܒܪ ܩܘܪܠܗܘܣ ܢܣܒܐ ܘܦܠܚܘܬܐ ܘܪܕܝܐ

[1] The Syriac transliterates the Greek πρόσωπα.

[2] Given the relatively close relationship between the sound-pattern of the names "Juvenal" and "Julian," it is most likely that by speaking of "Juvenal the apostate" Rufus also intended his audience to be reminded of "Julian the Apostate" as a figure who held a central place in early Christian polemics. See also below, *Vit. Pet.* §100 (R 73) with p. 151, n. 4; *Pler.* 25 (Nau and Brière, 61). Julian was Roman emperor between the years 361 and 363. Having grown up in a Christian environment and having received an education in the Christian faith as well, Julian privately rejected Christianity around 351. On his accession to the imperial throne he initiated reforms in the realm of politics, economy, and religion that were also geared toward promoting religious toleration and the revival of pagan religious practices. When Julian died in battle against the Persians on 26 June 363, Christian authors such as Ephraem the Syrian could not help but vengefully interpret his defeat as God's punishment. See, e.g., Ephraem the Syrian, *Hymns against Julian* (Beck, 1:71–91 [Syriac], 2:64–86 [German]; Lieu, 89–128; also McVey, 226–57). For more recent monographic studies of Emperor Julian in English, see, e.g., Robert Browning, *The Emperor Julian* (Berkeley and Los Angeles: University of California Press, 1975); Glen W. Bowersock, *Julian the Apostate* (Cambridge: Harvard University Press, 1978); and Polymnia Athanassiadi-Fowden, *Julian and Hellenism: An Intellectual Biography* (Oxford: Clarendon, 1981).

[3] I.e., even if he would not receive the Eucharist from him and thus would not be in doctrinal and sacramental communion with him.

often was urged by rulers and by many illustrious persons[1] to consent merely to speak with Juvenal the apostate[2] even if he would not communicate with him,[3] and [so] be relieved from [his] distress, he never once consented, but said, "The Lord forbid that I should see the face of Judas the betrayer!"[4]

(§48) [Gerontius's] hands gave the [monastic] habit to our fathers, Peter and John, and he gave them these names in exchange for the names which had been chosen for them by their [own] countries.[5]

(§49) Now [in the place] where they were dwelling in quiet, setting a pattern[6] of the utmost height of asceticism in that monastery for men, as I have said before, in which this Gerontius was abbot,[7] there they laid down the precious bones of these holy martyrs, their good guides and companions,[8] alongside the bones of the famous forty **[R 33]** martyrs of Sebaste,[9] while the holy and

[4] A reference to Judas Iscariot, the disciple of Jesus who betrayed him. See Matt 26:14–16, 21–25, 45–50; 27:3–10; Mark 14:10, 17–21, 43–46; Luke 22:3–6, 21–23, 47–48; John 13:2, 18, 21–30; 18:2–5; Acts 1:16–20, 25.

[5] Nabarnugios was named Peter and Mithridatos was named John, known as John the Eunuch. See above, *Vit. Pet.* §§5, 14, 40 (R 4, 9, 29). See also below, *Vit. Pet.* §118 (R 86).

[6] The Syriac may translate the Greek τυποῦν or ὑποτυποῦν (Raabe, 37 n. 1).

[7] See above *Vit. Pet.* §§39, 44 (R 28, 31).

[8] See *Vit. Pet.* §§26–27, 30, 31, 32, 33 ("the holy martyrs who were their guardians and companions"), 35, 36 (R 17–19, 21, 22, 23, 24, 25).

[9] See *BHO* 712–17; *BHG* 1201–8n. These martyrs are said to have been executed in Sebaste, Armenia, under Licinius (308–324 C.E.), co-emperor with Constantine and responsible for the eastern Roman Empire before his defeat. Brief accounts and eulogies are presented in Sozomen, *Hist. eccl.* 9.2 (PG 67:1597–1601; Bidez and Hansen, 392–94; Hartranft, *NPNF* 2/2:420–21); Basil of Caesarea, *In quadraginta martyres Sebastenses* (PG 31:508–25); and Gregory of Nyssa, *Encomium in xl martyres* 1 and 2 (PG 46:749–88; Lendle, 137–42, 145–56, 159–69). See also the text and English translation of the so-called *Testament of the Forty Martyrs of Sebaste* in Herbert Musurillo, *The Acts of the Christian Martyrs* (Oxford: Clarendon, 1972), 354–61. See also Alexander Kazhdan and Nancy Patterson Ševčenko, "Forty Martyrs of Sebasteia," *ODB* 2:799–800.

ܕܐܦܝ̈ܣܩܘܦܐ ܕܐܠܟܣܢܕܪܝܐ: ܩܕܫ ܫܘܪܝܗܘܢ ܕܗܠܝܢ. ܟܕ ܐܬܬܦܝܣ
ܓܒܪܐ ܗܢܐ ܡܢ ܗܿܝ ܡܗܝܡܢܬܐ ܘܬܪܝܨܬ ܫܘܒܚܐ ܐܘܕܘܩܝܐ
ܡܠܟܬܐ: ܕܢܐܬܐ ܡܛܠ ܣܝܡܐ ܕܓܪ̈ܡܐ ܩܕ̈ܝܫܐ ܕܐܣܛܦܢܘܣ
ܡܫܒܚܐ ܘܡܫܠܡ ܒܟܠ: ܪܝܫܐ ܕܣܗ̈ܕܐ ܘܪܝܫܐ ܕܡܫܡܫ̈ܢܐ: ܘܐܝܟܢܐ
ܒܚܕ ܕܗܝܟܠܐ ܦܐܝܐ ܕܒܢܬ ܠܒܪ ܡܢ ܬܪ̈ܥܐ ܓܪ̈ܒܝܝܐ ܕܡܕܝܢܬܐ
ܩܕܝܫܬܐ: ܗܢܝܐܬ ܡܫܠܡܬܗ ܠܡܪܬܐ. ܘܟܕ ܐܬܐ ܥܡ ܣܘܓܐܐ
ܕܐܦܝ̈ܣܩܘܦܐ ܕܟܠܗ ܐܓܩܢܝܐ: ܘܣܝܡܐ ܕܓܪ̈ܡܐ ܩܕ̈ܝܫܐ
ܕܪܝܫܐ ܕܣܗ̈ܕܐ ܥܒܝܕܬ ܒܚܕ: ܒܫܒܥܣܪܐ ܒܐܝܪ ܢܝܣܢ: ܒܬܪܥܝܢ
ܡܚܕܐ ܒܐܣܬܒܚܘܪܐ ܒܗ ܒܢܝܣܐ: ܟܕ ܐܬܬܦܝܣ ܡܢ ܩܕܝܫܬܐ
ܡܐܠܝܢܐ: ܐܦ ܗܟܢܐ ܕܗܘܐ ܩܕܝܫܐ ܦܛܪܘܣ ܘܕܐܪܚܡ ܣܗ̈ܕܐ
ܗܘܘ ܚܕ ܟܠܘܪܐ ܕܢܘ̈ܪܬܐ: ܒܗܝܟܠܐ ܒܢܝܢܐ ܕܐܦ ܗܘ ܐܬܬܣܝܡ

[1] Cyril was bishop of Alexandria from 412 to 444. One of the most influential theologians and ecclesiastical politicians of the early church, Cyril was instrumental in the condemnation of Nestorius of Constantinople at the Council of Ephesus in 431. The literature on Cyril is vast. See, e.g., McGuckin, *St. Cyril of Alexandria*; and, more recently, Thomas G. Weinandy and Daniel A. Keating, eds., *The Theology of St. Cyril of Alexandria: A Critical Appreciation* (London: T&T Clark, 2003).

[2] See Acts 7:54–60.

[3] The Syriac transliterates the Greek ἐγκαίνια (Raabe, 37 n. 4), describing a festival of dedication or consecration.

[4] The reference is to the Church of St. Stephen's, located just outside the Old City of Jerusalem, to the north of the Damascus Gate, which until the fourteenth century was known as St. Stephen's Gate. See Klaus Bieberstein and Hanswulf Bloedhorn, *Jerusalem: Grundzüge der Baugeschichte vom Chalkolithikum bis zur Frühzeit der osmanischen Herrschaft* (3 vols.; BTAVO B/100.1–3; Wiesbaden: Reichert, 1994), 2:231–36, who also conveniently list relevant archaeological literature. According to tradition, the priest Lucian discovered the relics of St. Stephen in Kefar Gamala in 415. Subsequently, the

blessed Cyril, archbishop of Alexandria, served [the liturgy at] their deposition.[1] For when [Cyril] was persuaded by the believing and orthodox Empress Eudocia to come for the deposition of the precious bones of the glorious and all-praised Stephen, the first of the martyrs and the first of the deacons,[2] and to conduct the consecration[3] of the beautiful temple that she had built outside the northern gates of the Holy City,[4] he gladly accepted the invitation.[5] He came with a multitude of bishops from all of Egypt and magnificently conducted the deposition of the holy bones of the first of the martyrs on the fifteenth of the month of Iyor.[6] Immediately afterwards, on the sixteenth of that month, persuaded by the holy Melania, he also conducted the deposition of the holy Persian martyrs and of the forty martyrs with them on the Mount

precious find was transferred to the Church of Sion in Jerusalem. Eventually a Church of St. Stephen's was erected, to which relics of the saint were transferred. See now also Paul Devos, "L'année de la dédicace de Saint-Étienne à Jérusalem: 439," *AnBoll* 105 (1987): 265–79. Empress Eudocia herself was buried on the grounds of the Church of St. Stephen's. The original buildings sponsored by Eudocia were destroyed most likely in the course of the violence under Caliph Hārūn ar-Rašīd between 809 and 813 C.E. Today's church and monastery complex, used by the Dominican Fathers, also house the famous École Biblique Française.

[5] For a study of Cyril's direct contact with Palestine, see F. M. Abel, "Saint Cyrille d'Alexandrie dans ses rapports avec la Palestine," in *Kyrilliana: Spicilegia edita Sancti Cyrilli Alexandrini XV recurrente saeculo: Études variées à l'occasion du XVe centenaire de Saint Cyrille d'Alexandrie (444–1944)* (Cairo: Editions du Scribe Egyptien S.A.E., 1947), 203–30.

[6] By the fifth century, Iyor corresponds exactly with the Julian calendar May. Thus the deposition took place on 15 May. Raabe (37 n. 5) discusses the seemingly conflicting events of both Eudocia's and Melania's presence in the Holy City at the same time for the events recounted. Also see the discussion in Horn, "Empress Eudocia and the Monk Peter the Iberian."

ܢܨܝܚܐܝܬ ܡܢܗ ܕܠܗ̇ ܕܐܘܕܘܩܝܐ ܡܠܟܬܐ. ܐܝܟ ܕܡܫܪܪ ܘܡܠܟܬܐ
ܕܪܚܝܡ ܗܘܐ ܥܠ ܐܣܛܘܐ.

(§50) ܐܠܐ ܠܘܬ ܗܝ ܕܡܫܬܡܥܐ ܠܝ ܢܦܫܐ. ܒܪ ܗܟܢܐ ܗܘܐ ܗܟܝܠ ܐܬܦܢܝ،
ܠܐܘܪܫܠܡ ܛܘܒܢܐ ܗܘ ܐܒܐ ܓܘܢܝܐ ܕܝܠܢ: ܒܪ ܗܘܐ ܗܟܝܠ ܡܢ ܒܬܪ
ܕܒܢܐ ܗܘܐ ܠܗ ܒܥܘܡܪܐ ܠܒܝܬ ܩܒܪܐ: ܒܗ ܒܪ ܦܠܣܛܝܢ ܘܬܒ ܚܘܝ:
ܘܬܡܢ ܡܟܝܠ ܒܫܠܝܐ ܒܬܪ ܗܘܐ: ܘܕܘܒܪܐ ܕܢܦܫܐ ܠܐܘܪܫܠܡ
ܡܫܝܢܐ ܗܘܐ: ܒܪ ܢܝܢܐܝܬ ܘܫܦܝܪ ܒܝܘܡܬܐ ܗܘ ܠܗ ܡܕܒܪ
ܗܘܐ: ܘܠܡܫܡܫܘܬ ܦܘܪܕܝܣܐ ܕܒܡܨܪܐ ܕܠܝܠ ܠܩܘܪܒܢܐ ܗܘ ܕܡܫܝܚ
ܠܡܣܒܠ [R 34] ܪܘܚܝܐ: ܘܠܡܫܝܚܘܗ ܡܢܘܪܐ ܗܘ ܒܠܒܘܫܐ ܕܐܠܗܐ:
ܘܕܠܐ ܡܫܚܢ ܕܢܬܟܒܪ ܠܫܡܝܫܐ ܕܐܠܗܐ: ܒܚܘܒܐ ܘܒܚܝܠܐ
ܘܒܡܬܒܪܢܐ ܕܟܠ ܐܪܒܥܐ ܘܒܥܡܪܐ: ܘܒܗܠܝܢ ܕܘܒܪܐ ܩܕܝܫܐ ܡܬܒܪ
ܗܘܐ ܘܡܬܒܪ ܗܘܐ. ܟܠܗ ܗܢܐ ܚܙܝܢ ܗܘܐ ܠܟܢܘܫܬܐ. ܒܪܚܡܐ
ܕܢܦܫܗ ܠܡܫܝܚܘܬܐ ܕܥܒܕܐ ܕܛܝܒܘܬܐ. ܘܠܫܠܡܘܬܐ ܕܬܫܥܐ ܕܟܝܢ.
ܘܒܡܫܡܫܢܘܬܐ ܡܟܝܠ ܢܦܫܗ ܗܘܐ ܕܢܬܦܢܐ ܠܐܘܪܫܠܡ. ܘܒܡܬܐܪܐ
ܕܐܒܝܐ. ܘܢܬܬܠܛ ܥܠ ܒܗܝܪܐ. ܟܠܗ ܕܝܢ ܠܡܕܐ ܫܠܡܘܬܐ ܐܝܬܘܗܝ ܠܗ

[1] This inscription has not yet been rediscovered. For the date of 13 October, the eighth-century *Jerusalem Georgian Lectionary*, entry 1295 (Tarchnischvili, 1:53 [Georgian], 2:44 [Latin]) notes the feast of the deposition of the forty martyrs of Sebaste in a monastery founded by a certain priest Paul. If there is any connection between that monastery, the "venerable temple" for which Eudocia provided splendid furnishings, and a monastery of St. Quaranta mentioned in the *Commemoratorium de casis Dei vel monasteriis* (ca. 809) (Tobler and Molinier, 301–5) and in Anastasius Vardapet's list of monasteries (see L. Alishan, "Les LXX couvents arméniens de Jérusalem," *AOL* 2 [B] [1884]: 394–99; Avedis Krikor Sanjian, "Anastas Vardapet's List of Armenian Monasteries in Seventh-Century Jerusalem: A Critical Examination," *Mus* 82 [1969]: 265–92), connected in some way with the Armenian community of the Holy Land remains to be determined. See also Bieberstein and Bloedhorn, *Jerusalem*, 3:416.

[2] Such a comment could also have functioned to regain and refocus the attention of the audience on an account that was to be delivered in parts over several days.

[3] See above *Vit. Pet.* §§42, 44, 48 (R 30–31, 32). Note Rufus's choice of establishing ascetic and monastic orthodoxy for Peter and John the Eunuch

of Olives in the venerable temple that was furnished splendidly by Empress Eudocia herself, as the inscription incised on the wall there declares.[1]

(§50) But let us return to what we set out to do.[2] Our common father had been deemed worthy of the holy [monastic] habit,[3] having already at that very time passed beyond the age of twenty years,[4] and with his fellow-soldier[5] John was henceforth dwelling there in quiet and displaying a way of life appropriate to his [monastic] habit. Carrying himself like a Nazirite in great asceticism,[6] he subdued and subjected to severity the bridle of the flesh, which has a tendency [to give] offense[7] and which stands against **[R 34]** the spirit,[8] and [also] his rebellious will, that enemy of God,[9] which also cannot subject itself to the law of God.[10] Through hunger and through thirst and through a bed on the ground and through vigil, and through these harsh ways of life, he extended all this [effort] toward asceticism until he inflicted severe pain to the commotion of the impulses of [his] youth and quenched the flame of the passions.[11] Then with ease he was devoting [himself] to be reconciled to the spirit,[12] to be engaged

through his impressive account of Gerontius's initiation into the monastic life, which, it is to be understood, carried on into the asceticism of the two young men.

[4] Rufus's emphasis on Peter's age suggests a concern for a minimum age for monastic initiation.

[5] For other instances of the use of the image of the soldier in descriptions of ascetics, see also *Life of Rabbula* (Overbeck, 159; Horn and Phenix, forthcoming in SBLWGRW).

[6] See above, *Vit. Pet.* §39 (R 28), for other references to this form of asceticism within this text.

[7] Jas 3:2.

[8] Gal 5:17.

[9] Rom 8:7a.

[10] Rom 8:7b.

[11] See Eph 6:16; Prov 24:20. One of the most influential early Christian texts detailing the working of the passions and providing advice on how to fight them is Evagrius of Pontus, *Praktikos*.

[12] See 2 Cor 5:20.

ܬܪ̈ܬܝܗܘܢ. ܟܕ ܒܓܠܕܐ ܢܒܝܫܐ ܘܓܪ̈ܡܐ: ܠܗ̇، ܚܠܝܨܘܬܐ ܟܝܢܝܬܐ
ܘܫܦܝܪܘܬ ܓܘܫܡܐ ܚܒܝ. ܐܝܟܢܐ ܕܐܦ ܟܕܘ ܢܗܘܐ ܟܦܦ. ܟܕ ܡܪܝܡ
ܡܢ ܦܓܪܢܘܬܐ ܕܓܒܪܘܬܐ ܘܡܢ ܚܝܠܘܬܐ ܟܝܢܝܬܐ. ܗ̇ܘ ܕܡܕܡܐܬ
ܦܓܪ ܚܠܝܡ ܗܘܐ. ܘܦܓܪ ܫܦܝܪ ܗܘܐ ܒܪܒܘܬܐ ܕܓܘܫܡܐ.
ܕܡܟܐ ܡܚܝܠ ܕܕ̈ܪܐ ܘܡܟܝܟܐ ܐܓܘ̈ܢܐ

(§51) ܘܡܟܝܟܐ ܬܟܘ̈ܫܐ ܗܢܘܢ: ܟܕ ܕܠܐ ܥܠܝܒܐ ܠܘܩܒܠ ܐܬܠܘܦܪ̈ܐ
ܡܬܟܬܫ ܗܘܐ: ܘܠܘܩܒܠ ܫ̈ܐܕܐ ܕܟܠܗ ܙܘ̈ܢܐ ܕܟܒܝܫܘܬܐ: ܟܠܠܐ:
ܒܐܝܡܡܐ: ܠܘ ܒܚܠ̈ܡܐ ܒܠܚܘܕ ܘܒܦܢܛܣܝ̈ܣ: ܐܠܐ ܐܦ ܗ̇ܝ
ܕܡܬܐܡܪܐ: ܐܝܕܐ ܠܘܬ ܐܢܫܐ ܘܦܪܨܘܦܐܝܬ. ܟܕ ܐܡܝܢܐܝܬ ܡܚܝܐ
ܗܘܐ ܘܐܬܐ ܠܡܕܒܪܐ ܕܢܘܚ ܪܗܛܐ ܡܕܒܪܐ: ܗ̇ܘ ܕܡܕܒܪܢܐ ܗܘܐ
ܪܫܐ ܘܡܠܦܢܐ ܕܕܐܝܟ ܗܢܐ ܕܡܒܪܐ ܐܘܢܓܠܝܐ. ܐܡܪ ܐܢܐ ܕܝܢ
ܠܗ̇ܘ ܕܡܬܚܙܝ ܚܕ. ܘܢܘܕܝ: ܘܐܬܐ ܠܕܘܟܬܗ ܚܕܐ ܗܘܐ: ܟܕ ܠܚܘܕܘܗܝ،
ܥܡ ܐܠܗܐ ܒܠܚܘܕܘܗܝ، ܡܬܚܒܠܐ ܗܘܐ: ܘܐܓܘܢܐ ܕܡܬܚܬܪܘܬܐ
[R 35] ܢܛܪ ܚܛܝܬܐܝܬ ܟܕ ܗܘܐ ܒܒܪܝܬܐ: ܘܠܐܝܢܐ ܒܥܘܕܪܢܐ
ܘܒܡܠܐܐ ܡܢ ܐܠܗܐ ܐܬܥܫܢ، ܘܠܐ ܕܡܫܠܡܘܬܐ ܕܟܠܬ ܐܬܬܗ̇

[1] Ps 118:97 and 99. The Syriac transliterates the Greek θεωρία (Raabe, 38 n. 1). Payne Smith (602) allows for a broad range of meanings, from "philosophical speculation, theory; method of study, observation, research," to "spiritual contemplation, intution, ecstasy," and more. Raabe's emphasis on scholarly or scientific inquiry in his translation of the term as "wissenschaftliche Untersuchung" implies a concern on his part with the question of the relationship between theology and science and the question of theology as a science.

[2] The advanced ascetic is here portrayed as defying any natural and biological strength and beauty of the physical body. Peter Brown (*The Body and Society: Men, Women and Sexual Renunciation in Early Christianity* [LHR 13; New York: Columbia University Press, 1988]) explores questions of the body in early Christian contexts quite well.

[3] Note the emphasis on imagery taken from the fields of athletics and war. For the fight against the demons, see, as the most influential text, Athanasius of Alexandria, *Vita Antonii* (Bartelink; Gregg, 29–99).

[4] See Rev 12:10.

[5] The Syriac transliterates the Greek φαντασίαι (Raabe, 38 n. 3).

[6] For the example of the anti-Chalcedonian ascetic woman Miqa, who according to Rufus fought directly and physically with the devil, see *Pler.* 43.

[7] I.e., John the Baptist.

[8] See Matt 3:1–7; Mark 1:2–8; Luke 3:3–14; John 1:6–9. John the Baptist's message is predominantly one of repentance. In the early Christian church,

in contemplation,[1] and to have dominion over the flesh. Yet he would rather bring the two of them [flesh and spirit] into one harmony, when he enclosed that great strength and the beauty of the body in dried-up skin and bones, so that he who before was very healthy and was very radiant in the majesty of [his] body would already be crookbacked [and] bowed down from the multitude of contemptible things [he endured] and from great asceticism.[2]

(§51) How many wrestling matches and how many contests and how many temptations he endured, ceaselessly fighting against the devil and against his demons,[3] the spirits of evil, by night and by day,[4] not only in dreams and in imagination[5] but, as it is said, hand to hand and personally,[6] continually moving [from one place to another until he finally] came to the desert of John the Forerunner,[7] who was the first chief and teacher of such an evangelical way of life[8]—I mean, however, that [desert] that extends[9] to the Jordan.[10] There he led his way of life, conversing with God alone[11] and manfully conducting the contest[12] **[R 35]** of virtue with [ever] greater diligence. Of what help and consolation from God he was deemed worthy lies neither with the weakness of

John the Baptist was seen as one of the ideal models of the ascetic life. See, e.g., for the Syriac ascetic tradition, Shafiq AbouZayd, *Ihidayutha: A Study of the Life of Singleness in the Syrian Orient: From Ignatius of Antioch to Chalcedon 451 A.D.* (Oxford: ARAM Society for Syro-Mesopotamian Studies, 1993), 126–27, as well as the depiction on the title page. A fuller study of John the Baptist as a model for ascetics in early Christianity is a *desideratum*.

9 The Syriac may render the Greek διέτεινε (Raabe, 38 n. 5).

10 The *Georgian Life of Peter the Iberian* lays greater emphasis on the time Peter spent in the Judean Desert. For references, see Horn, *Asceticism and Christological Controversy*, 203. For another occasion when Peter visited the Judean Desert, see *Vit. Pet.* §19 (R 12). When Peter went on his pilgrimage to Mount Nebo during his early years in Jerusalem as well as when he went to visit that site again, he probably also traveled through the Judean Desert. See *Vit. Pet.* §118 (R 85).

11 Literally, "only with God alone." Note the emphasis on solitude. Also at other instances Rufus portrays Peter as showing a preference for withdrawing from contact with fellow humans and enjoying the solitary life possible in asceticism. See, e.g., *Pler.* 2, 10, and 56.

12 Note again the emphasis on the Pauline language of athletic competition.

ܕܬܠܬ. ܘܠܐ ܗܝ̇ ܡܫܟܚܘܬܗ ܕܝܠܢܐ ܡܣܦܩܐ. ܡܛܠܗܕܐ ܗܘ̇
ܠܩ̈ܠܝܠܐܬܐ ܣܐܡ ܐܢܐ: ܗ̇ܝ ܕܐܦ ܠܡܬܪܐܬ ܣܘܢܐ ܠܫܡܘܥܝܢܐ
ܘܠܬܫܒܘܚܬܐ: ܕܢܬܝܒܬ ܠܗ ܒܥܘܕܪܢܐ. ܗܘ ܩܒܠ ܐܣܟܝܡܐ: ܕܐܠܝܢ
ܨܒܐ ܐܢܐ ܕܐܚܘܐ. ܠܬܫܥܝܬܐ ܗ̇ܝ ܕܗܠܝܢ ܕܐܫܬܥܝܘ. ܠܡܘܬܪܢܐ ܕܝܢ
ܕܗܠܝܢ ܕܫܡܥܝܢ.

(§52) ܗܘ ܢܒܝܐ ܚܢܢ ܠܛܘܒܢܐ ܦܣܪܝܘܢ: ܠܗܘ ܕܩ̇ܕܡ ܪ̇ܝܫ ܡ̈ܣܟܢܐ
ܘܪܝܫ ܐܟ̈ܣܢܝܐ: ܕܗܘ ܥܒܕܗ ܕܡܠܟܘܬܗ ܕܒܐܠܗܐ ܘܐܬܩ̈ܢܬܗ: ܒܝܬ
ܡ̈ܣܟܢܐ ܒܢܐ ܠܒܪ ܡܢ ܬܪ̈ܥܐ ܡܕ̈ܝܢܝܐ ܕܡܕܝܢܬܐ: ܠܢܝܚܐ
ܘܠܒܘܝܐܐ ܕܗ̇ܢܘܢ ܕܡܢ ܡܫܠܡܘܬܐ ܕܘܐܝܬ ܡܬܟܫܝܢ ܦܓ̈ܪܝܗܘܢ:
ܘܠܗܘܢ ܡܢ ܥܘܪ̈ܢܐ ܕܝܢ ܕܝܠܗܘܢ ܡܕܒܪܬܐ: ܒܡܕܪܐ ܪܒܐ ܘܦܐܝܐ
ܐܩܝܡ: ܠܬܫܡܫܬܐ ܘܠܝܘܩܪܐ ܕܗܢܘܢ ܕܐܡܣܟܢܐܝܬ ܕܠܐ ܥܠܝܠܐ
ܡܫܒܚܝܢ ܠܡܪܝܐ: ܐܬܬܪܝܒ ܕܐܦ ܗܘ ܡܕܒܪܢܐ ܕܗܘܐ ܠܒܝܬܐ
ܢܗܘܐ. ܘܗܘ ܗܘܐ ܒܦܘܫܗ ܕܒܡܕܒܪܢܘܬܗ ܕܡܪܢܐ ܢܒܝܐ ܒܠܬܐ: ܘܢܦܫܗ
ܛܒ ܡܚܝܠܐ ܢܒܝܐ ܕܕܢܝܐ ܩܕܝܫܐ ܕܡܫܒܚܝܢ ܠܡܪܝܐ:

(§53) ܗܘܝܢ ܕܢܬܪܐ ܒܡܕܒܪܐ: ܐܬܚܫܒ ܗܘ ܒܡܘܪܝܐ ܒܗܘܐ ܢܦܠ.

[1] That certain time limits were placed on Rufus's recounting supports the thesis that the setting for the delivery of this account also had an oral character. His vocabulary choices of "setting down" and "listening" point to both an oral context and a context of written composition.

[2] Passarion had great influence on the monastic body in Palestine. From complementary but later Chalcedonian sources one can learn that, according to Cyril of Scythopolis, *Vit. Euth.* 16 (Schwartz, 26,18–19; Price, 22), Passarion was "rural bishop and archimandrite of the monks" of Palestine. The monks of his monastery included a certain Anastasius, keeper of the sacred vessels of the Church of the Resurrection (*Vit. Euth.* 22 [Schwartz, 35,1–5; Price, 30–31]). His immediate successor Elpidius shared the office of abbot of the monks of Palestine with Gerontius (see *Vit. Euth.* 27 [Schwartz, 42,12–14; Price, 38]). For a discussion of the significance of Passarion as a model for Peter the Iberian, see Horn, "Beyond Theology," 134–42. In the *Obit. Theod.* §9 (B 26–27), Rufus records that Passarion died "on the 25th of the second Teshrin," i.e., in November, a few years after Abba Romanus had passed away.

[3] The ruins of the monastery of Passarion have not yet been discovered. Bieberstein and Bloedhorn (*Jerusalem*, 3:413) think that it was located in the vicinity of Mount Zion, i.e., close to the Church of Zion. For arguments to the contrary, see Horn, "Beyond Theology," 140 and n. 216.

our word to describe [it] nor [in] the measure of time [available to the audience to] receive it. Although I am therefore leaving aside many things, I think it is necessary to set down something especially worthy of remembrance and of narration that happened to him at the beginning when he received the [monastic] habit, as an example of what is omitted for the profit of those who are listening.[1]

(§52) The blessed Passarion,[2] that great lover of the poor and lover of strangers, besides his other godly virtues and righteous acts, built a house for the poor outside the eastern gates of the city for the rest and consolation of those whose bodies were wretchedly afflicted by weakness. He also erected inside the [city] walls of holy Zion a great and comely monastery[3] for the service and for the chanting [of psalms] of those who continuously without ceasing are praising the Lord.[4] When [Peter] saw this [foundation of Passarion's], he longed to become an imitator of this good thing. He made up his mind that with the help of the Lord he would build a house[5] and would there establish a certain number of holy monks to praise the Lord.[6]

(§53) However, before he could begin with the work he be-

[4] Such emphasis on uninterrupted praise and worship of God that even continues throughout the night is best known in connection with the monastery of the so-called Akoimetai, or "Sleepless Ones," in Constantinople. Yet Jerusalem had its own group of zealously dedicated worshipers, known as Spoudaioi, literally, "the Zealous Ones." According to Cyril of Scythopolis, *Vit. Theod.* 1 (Schwartz, 236,13; Price, 262), already during the reign of Emperor Marcian the young Theodosius was able to join a group of Spoudaioi who had a monastery near the Tower of David. For further evidence and studies, see S. Pétridès, "Le Monastère des Spoudaei à Jérusalem et les Spoudaei de Constantinople," *EO* 4 (1900–1901): 225–31. For a discussion of the related group of the Philoponoi in Egypt and Beirut, see idem, "Spoudaei et Philopones," *EO* 7 (1904): 341–48; and Siméon Vailhé, "Les Philopones d'Oxyrhynque au IVe siècle," *EO* 14 (1911), 277–278.

[5] I.e., a church.

[6] This emphasis on a desire to "praise the Lord" suggests a connection between Peter's monastery and the spirituality practiced among the Spoudaioi, and even Philoponoi.

ܘܟܕ ܒܗ ܙܒܢܐ ܗܘܐ ܡܫܟܚܬ. ܚܙܐ ܠܐܬܠܡܝ̈ܕܐ ܕܩܐܡ ܠܘܩܒܠܗ.
ܒܪ ܒܠܐܝܬ ܡܪܚܝܢ ܘܡܬܚܝܣ ܘܐܡܪ. ܗܐ ܚܙܝ ܡܪܝܐ ܥܒܕ ܠܝ ܘܗ̇ܘ
ܕܐܡܪ ܐܢܬ. ܚܙܝ ܐܠܗܐ ܐܡܝܢܐ ܗ̇ܘ ܘܗܘ ܕܠܗ ܐܬܢܩܦܬ. ܘܡܛܠܬܗ
ܟܠܗܝܢ ܫܒܩܬ. ܘܗܫܐ ܐܡܪ ܡܠܬܐ ܡܕܡ ܠܘܬܗ ܘܐܓܗܐ. ܗ̣ܘ ܗܘ
ܕܝܢ ܒܪ ܢܦܫ ܒܗ ܘܐܬܟܪܝ: [R 36] ܐܝܟ ܗ̇ܘ ܕܪ̈ܚܡܝܢ ܩ̈ܢܝܢܐ ܥܬܝܪ
ܗܘܐ ܒܫܢܝܐ ܕܒܡܕܝܢܬܗ ܐܡܪ ܠܘܬܗ. ܡܛܠ ܢܦܫܟ ܕܝܠܟ: ܐܡܪ
ܐܢܬ ܒܠܒܐ ܠܒܝܬܐ ܘܒܡܕܝܢܬܐ: ܚܙܐ ܒܗ ܐܠܗܐ ܘܡܬܒܪܢܐ.
ܒܒܪܐ ܕܝܠܟ ܚܠܝܢ ܐܢܬ ܠܝ ܕܐܫܦܘܪ. ܢܛܠܝܢ ܫܠܡ ܕܡܫܝܚܐ.
ܘܡܫܪܐ ܕܫܒܩ ܫܒܘܬ ܕܡܫܝܚܐ: ܒܪ ܐܝܟ ܬܢܢܐ ܐܫܬܪܝ. ܗ̣ܘ ܒܝܫܐ
ܠܐ ܡܬܚܫܒܐ ܗ̣ܘܐ. ܘܡܚܠ ܥܙ ܕܢܒܚܐ ܗ̣ܘ ܦܛܪܘܣ. ܘܒܗ
ܕܫ̈ܒܩܐ ܡܬܢ̈ܬܐ ܘܬܐܬܚ̈ܝܬܐ ܢܦܪܐ ܠܡܪܝܐ. ܗ̇ܘ ܕܒܪ ܡܣܒܪܐ ܐܬܚܝܕ
ܠܗ ܐܝܟ ܗ̇ܘ ܕܒܠܒܒܐ: ܕܒܪ ܒܪܒܠ ܡܬܠܠ ܐܢܬ: ܐܡܪ ܕܗܘܐ ܐܢܐ
ܡܪܒ ܐܢܐ. ܐܡܪ ܠܘܬܗ. ܡܢܐ ܠܝ. ܠܡܢܐ ܡܬܡܛܦܐ ܠܝ ܐܒܘܪ
ܢܦܫܐ. ܠܐ ܢܕܥ ܐܢܬ ܕܪ̈ܚܡܐ ܘܪܚܡܬܐ ܫܘܠܛܢܐ ܐܢܬ ܠܝ: ܘܟܐܪ̈ܝ
ܐܢܬܘܢ ܗ̇ܘ ܕܐܬܐܢܐ ܗ̇ܘ ܕܐܬܡܚܬ. ܐ ܕܝܢ ܡܬܠܠܗܕܐ ܒܪܢܐ
ܠܝ: ܟܠ ܕܠܐ ܐܡܪܬ ܕܐܬܒܥܠܐ ܢܕܪܝܢ ܘܫܪܟܐ ܗ̇ܘ ܕܐܩܒܠܬ:
ܕܐܟܢܐ ܠܝ ܡܚܠܐ ܐܝܟ ܕܡܕܒܪ ܒܟܠܬ. ܐܠܐ ܒܚܝ̈ܠܝ ܘܒܪܝ. ܘܒܕ
ܚܪ ܐܝܟ ܕܠܘܬ ܫܡܫܐ. ܒܪܐ ܒܙܬܐ ܡܕܡ ܫܦܝܪܬܐ ܘܫܒܝܚܬܐ
ܕܚܠܝܐ ܢܗܝܪܐ ܘܡܫܒܚܐ. ܘܒܗ ܐܝܟ ܕܒܣܪܪܐ ܡܢܗܘܢ ܘܠܐ
ܐܝܟ ܕܟ̈ܘܪܐ ܒܠܐܝܬ. ܘܡܫܬܫܢ ܘܡܬܒܪܢ ܐܝܟ ܫܡܫܐ

[1] Although the motif of being stricken by disease is sometimes used as an indicator of the presence of heresy or unbelief (see, e.g., *Pler.* 14: "For the Nestorians are sick with the sickness of the Jews"; see also *Pler.* 22), here the emphasis is on the devil's attack and temptation. Within the corpus of writings that can be attributed to John Rufus, the motif of "disease" is used sometimes but not predominantly in connection with heresy. See also Steppa, *John Rufus and the World Vision*, 158.

[2] See Matt 19:16–22; Mark 10:17–22; Luke 18:18–25.

[3] Encouraging Peter to speak out against God, Satan invites Peter to become like him, an "accuser" or "slanderer" of God. See also Matt 4:8–9; Luke 4:7–8.

[4] The Syriac may render the Greek ἐμπνεῖν (Raabe, 39 n. 2).

[5] Note how, through the use of the possessive pronoun and the personal

came weak, falling into an obstinate illness.[1] While he was lying severly [stricken], he saw the devil standing opposite him, [who] openly mocked and reviled [him] and said, "Behold, see what he has done to you, he whom you love! See where he has placed you, he to whom you were joined and for whose sake you have left everything![2] Speak any word against him right now and be free!"[3] But while [Peter] breathed[4] at him and was greatly agitated **[R 36]** as one who many times had experience of [the devil's] shamelessness, he said to him, "You are speaking about my Jesus,[5] [you] defiled and shameless dog,[6] contending against God[7] and being a blasphemer! You advise me to do your work! May the power of Christ bring you to nought!" As soon as the Evil One heard the name of Christ, he was dissolved like smoke and disappeared.[8] After this Peter began to weep and with bitter tears and groans to call out to the Lord, who immediately appeared to him as it is written, " 'While you are still speaking,' he is saying, 'behold, I am near.' "[9] He said to him, "What is [wrong] with you? Why are you weary, [you] discouraged [one]? Do you not know that I have the power over life and death[10] and [that] it is in my hands whether you live or die? If you are grieved because I did not grant that you should fulfill your vow and the covenant that you promised, to build me a temple as you desired [to do] before, lift up your eyes and see!" He looked up as though to heaven [and] saw a church, beautiful and magnificent, full of light and glory. Standing in it as in a row, not openly in choirs, were men, about fifty in num-

name Jesus, Rufus here portrays Peter as a young man who has reached an intimate level of personal relationship with Christ.

[6] In Semitic cultural settings, dogs are customarily regarded as filthy and dirty animals.

[7] Here Peter realizes the essence of Satan as that of the one who does not obey God's will but speaks out against God.

[8] Hausherr (*The Name of Jesus*, 99) quotes from this section of the *Vita Petri Iberi* as an instance of effective prayer addressed to Jesus Christ. See also *Pler.* 43, where Miqa likewise relies on the power of the name of Christ. See also *Vit. Pet.* §17 (R 11).

[9] See Isa 58:9. See also *Vit. Pet.* §124 (R 92), where the same verse is used again.

[10] With this comment Christ emphasizes his divine power.

ܟܗ̈ܢܝܢ ܡܟܗܢܢܐ. ܘܩܠܐ ܗܘܐ ܠܘܬܗ ܟܕ ܐܡܪ: ܗܢܐ ܒܪܬܐ ܗ̇ܝ
ܕܐܫܬܘܕܝܬ ܕܬܬܝܗܒ ܠܟ. ܗܕܐ ܘܗܠܝܢ ܕܚܙܝܬ: ܡܛܠ ܠܐ ܬܦܢܐ
ܠܝ. ܘܟܕ ܗܠܝܢ ܐܡܪ: ܥܒܪ ܡܢ ܠܘܬܗ ܡܠܐܟܐ. ܗܘ ܕܝܢ ܟܕ ܗܘ̣ܐ:
ܘܒܚܙܘܬܐ ܗܕܐ: ܬܘܒ ܡܬܚܙܝܬ ܐܬܓܠܝ ܚܝܠܐ ܘܫܘܒܚܘܬܐ
ܘܡܫܡܫܢܘܬܐ. ܘܟܕ ܚܙܐ ܟܕ ܡܢ ܗܘܐ ܚܘܪܐ ܦܠܢܦܘܪܬܐ ܗܘܐ.
[R 37] ܗܘܝܐ ܚܙܐ ܕܢܩܫܘܢ ܘܢܙܡܪܘܢ ܐܢ̈ܫܐ ܗܠܝܢ ܕܟܗܢܘ: ܟܕ
ܫܪܪܐ ܫܪܝܪܐ ܡܫܒܚܝܢ. ܘܡܩ̈ܠܠܝܢ ܠܗ ܒܟܢܫܐ ܠܡܫܒܚܐ:
(§54) ܗܘ ܗܢܐ ܓܒܪܐ ܗܘܝ ܘܐܬܚܙܝ ܡܢ ܐܢ̈ܫܐ ܕܠܗ. ܐܠܐ
ܕܢܒܝܐ ܟܠ ܗܠܝܢ ܕܫܪܒܐ ܕܐܫܬܡܥܬܐ ܐܠܝܐ. ܘܟܕ ܡܬܚܫܚ ܚܝ
ܒܡܠܐ ܕܡܢܝܐ ܒܬܘܪ̈ܬܐ: ܡܢ ܐܒܗܐ ܕܫܡܫܝܢ ܠܟܠܬܐ. ܬܘܒ
ܢܦܩܘܢ ܢܦܩ. ܒܗܘܕܝܢ ܚܕ ܥܣܪ ܕܐܫܬܘܕܝܢ ܚܕ ܕܟܕ. ܐܠܗܐ ܢܠܦ:
ܕܐܡܪܢܐ ܡܢ ܐܘܪܫܠܡ ܢܠܦ ܕܗܘܠܐ: ܘܐܬܐ ܠܒܪ ܒܐܬܪܐ ܕܒܪܐ

[1] Any future discussion of the question of whether either Peter the Iberian or John Rufus is to be identified with the author of the *Corpus Dionysiacum* will have to consider this vision and decide whether this may have been the event or one of the events through which Pseudo-Dionysius gained his insights into the ecclesiastical hierarchies. The thesis of Peter the Iberian's authorship of the Areopagite's work was proposed first and independently of one another by Shalva I. Nuc'ubize and Ernest Honigmann. For fuller bibliographical information pertaining to this discussion, see Horn, *Asceticism and Christological Controversy*, 167. See also *Vit. Pet.* §173 (R 131).

[2] In its directness and from the perspective of an anti-Chalcedonian author writing at the turn of the fifth to the sixth century, such a comment might have to be taken as a pointer to the establishment of a renewed, and consequently also separate, church, separate from the local hierarchy in Jerusalem. Note in the following the emphasis on "chanting" and overall on dedicated service to God, most prominently but not exclusively in the form of asceticism. Thus Peter the Iberian emerges as the renewer, if not even the founder, of the new, and implied "true," church, a church that is truly "orthodox" in the sense that "right praise" is given to God.

[3] Through the emphasis on praising God in song and worship, in this

ber, serving and chanting [psalms].[1] A voice [came] to him saying, "Here is the church that you promised to build me![2] Here are those who chant [psalms]! So then, do not be grieved!" When he had said these [things], the Lord departed from him. Worshiping and being joyous, he was again filled more and more with power, cheerfulness, and faith.[3] Since he was fully assured[4] by this vision, **[R 37]** he arranged that those brothers with him should stand and chant [psalms] in like manner, ordered in rows.[5] By his prayers this order[6] has remained and is kept by his brethren until today.[7]

(§54) Yet it is necessary to return to the rest of the story and, employing as few words as possible, to turn and take up again from where we left off.[8] For we recall that we promised by the help of God to teach how he moved [his] dwelling place from Jerusalem and came to live in the region of the city of Gaza, which is at

context Rufus effectively portrays Peter as featuring and thus modeling a type of spirituality that shares significant elements with forms of worship practiced in more modern Pentecostal and charismatic movements. That this does not have to turn into dissolute behavior is fittingly stressed by references to order.

4 Note that the Syriac transliterates πληροφορηθῆναι. The frequent use of forms of πληροφορία and its derivatives in both the *Vita Petri Iberi* and the *Plerophoriae* could be a further indicator of the common authorship of the different works by John Rufus, a point that is not weakened by the fact that we have access to the works only in Syriac translation, no longer in the original Greek, since it is not unlikely that the Syriac continuously transliterates the Greek vocabulary in these instances.

5 The second ܣܕܪܐ is attested in both manuscripts. The "row" may refer to the order in which the monks lined up in rows.

6 The Syriac transliterates here as in the previous sentence the Greek τάξις and forms thereof.

7 I.e., the time of Rufus's composition of the *Vita Petri Iberi*. The description is a good example of an aetiology.

8 The author had not really indicated such intentions in writing further above. For similar comments that connect individual narrative portions of the text with one another, see also *Vit. Pet.* §50 (R 33).

ܡܕܝܢܬܐ ܕܟܠ ܓܢܣ ܢܫܐ܆ ܐܝܟܢܐ ܕܐܦ ܠܡܫܘܠܡܘܬܐ ܐܫܬܘܝ܂
ܘܠܬܪܬܐ ܠܬܪܥܘܬ ܟܗܢܘܬܐ. ܒܬܫܡܫܬܐ ܕܟܗܢܘܬܐ ܐܠܗܝܬܐ܀

(§55) ܐܘܪܫܠܡ ܡܕܝܢܬܐ ܩܕܝܫܬܐ܆ ܡܕܝܢܬܗ ܕܡܠܟܐ ܪܒܐ܆ ܕܒܗ̇ ܪܐܙܐ ܦܪܘܩܝܐ ܕܥܠܡܐ ܫܟܠ ܐܬܓܡܪ܆ ܟܕ ܕܢܚܗ ܕܐܠܗܐ ܘܦܪܘܩ ܡܫܝܚܐ܆ ܒܗ̇ ܡܢ ܩܕܡ ܐܬܓܒܪܬ ܡܢ ܪ̈ܘܡܝܐ܆ ܡܢ ܒܬܪ ܡܪܕܘܬܐ ܕܝܗ̈ܘܕܝܐ ܕܥܠ ܡܫܝܚܐ܆ ܐܝܟ ܩܕܝܫܘܬ ܫܪ̈ܟܐ ܕܥܠܡܐ ܢܦ̈ܩܐ܆ ܘܐܝܟ ܓܙܪ ܕܝܢܐ ܕܠܗ ܕܡܫܝܚܐ܆ ܠܚܪܒܬܐ ܡܫܕܪܐ ܐܬܝܗܒܬ ܘܐܬܓܒܪܬ ܬܘܒ ܦܬܐܝܬ܆ ܒܝ̈ܘܡܘܗܝ ܕܩܘܣܛܢܛܝܢܘܣ ܡܠܟܐ ܪܚܡ ܠܡܫܝܚܐ ܘܡܗܝܡܢܐ܆ ܗܘ ܐܒܐ ܘܦܛܪܝܪܟܐ ܕܟܠܗܘܢ ̈ܡܠܟܐ ܒ̈ܣܝܠܐ܆ ܗܘ ܕܒܙܪܥܐ ܓܒܝܐ ܕܘܝܕ ܢܨܝܚܐ. ܘܡܢ ܕܫܠܛ ܐܠܗܐ ܐܡܪܗ ܠܦܘܠܚܢܘܬܐ ܗܕܐ. ܗ̇ܝ ܕܦܩܕ ܠܗ ܠܡܠܟܬܐ ܘܡܪܬܐ ܐܡܗ ܩܕܝܫܬܐ.

(§56) ܗܕܐ ܓܝܪ ܡܠܟܬܐ ܪܚܡܬ ܐܠܗܐ܆ ܟܕ ܒܗܝܡܢܘܬܐ ܫܡܝܢܬܐ ܕܕܚܠܬ ܐܠܗܐ ܘܒܛܝܒܘܬܐ ܐܠܗܝܐ [R 38] ܡܫܪܪܐ܆ ܘܡܬܕܒܪܢܝܬܐ ܘܒܪ ܛܝܒܘܬܐ ܐܝܬ ܠܗ̇ ܒܗ̇. ܠܐ ܡܣܒܪܬ[1] ܕܗ̇ܝ ܒܡܘܡܬܗ̇ ܕܐܬܬܐ ܠܬܘܕܝܬܐ

[1] So MS B. MS A and Raabe have ܐܣܒܪܬܝ.

[2] Raabe reconstructs the underlying Greek as τὸ παραθαλάσσιον Γάζη (40 n. 1). For the location of Maiuma and further references to relevant literature on the city, see Yoram Tsafrir, Leah Di Segni, and Judith Green, *Tabula Imperii Romani: Iudaea-Palaestina: Eretz Israel in the Hellenistic, Roman and Byzantine Periods* (Jerusalem: Israel Academy of Sciences and Humanities, 1994), 175.

[3] I.e., of the episcopate.

[4] More literally, the Syriac means "rising" (of the sun) and in a metaphorical sense "manifestation" and "epiphany." See Payne Smith, 95.

[5] The author states that the Romans completely destroyed Jerusalem and implies that Constantine was the first to rebuild the city. Earlier sources indicate otherwise. Jerusalem was damaged, perhaps severely, in 70 C.E., when general (later emperor) Titus captured the Jerusalem temple. Emperor Hadrian visited Jerusalem in 129–130 C.E. and decided to rebuild the city as a Greco-Roman one, which precipitated the Second Jewish War (or Bar Kokhba Revolt) in 132–135. Rome tried to keep Jews out of the city by means of Hadrian's "death edict," not by deliberately destroying the city. Hadrian wanted it as a pagan glory, not as a desolated city. It is uncertain whether Jerusalem was de-

the seashore,[2] how he was esteemed worthy of the priesthood and eventually of the high priesthood[3] by the election of divine grace.

(§55) Jerusalem, the Holy City, the city of the Great King, in which the mystery of the salvation of the whole earth was wrought by the manifestation[4] of our God and Savior, Christ, having of old been utterly destroyed by the Romans,[5] after the effrontery of the Jews against Christ, according to the predictions of all the prophets and according to the sentence of Christ himself,[6] was finally built up anew and was [re]inhabited more fully in the times of Constantine, the Christ-loving and believing emperor, the father and patriarch of all the Christian kings, who in truth was chosen [as a] new David and by his God-fearing mother the blessed Helena who was equal to him in zeal and [who was] indeed his true mother.[7]

(§56) This God-loving queen, confirmed in the fervent faith of the fear of God and in divine **[R 38]** zeal and having her son [as] helper and sharer in [her] zeal, did not neglect to come in person

stroyed in 132–135. Sources earlier than John Rufus, particularly Cassius Dio, do not state that the anti-Roman forces destroyed the city, which was under Roman control. Moreover, there is no archaeological or numismatic evidence to support this assertion. The Bar Kokhba letters do not provide clear evidence to resolve this ambiguity. The only unequivocal statements on the fate of Jerusalem come from Christian sources in late antiquity, during or after the reign of Constantine. The Christian polemic concerning the "Christian" settlement of Jerusalem, and therefore the exclusive right of Christians to colonize the city, sharply increased during and after the reign of Emperor Julian (361–363), who attempted to rebuild the Jewish temple in Jerusalem. John Rufus's remarks in this passage are quite consistent with this post-Constantinian Christian understanding of the destruction of Jerusalem as an act of supersession, granting the right of habitation of the city to Christians exclusively. See Brian W. Jones, "Hadrian," *ABD* 3:17–18.

6 See Mark 13:1–2; Luke 21:5–6.

7 Helena, probably a native of Drepanum, a town later renamed Helenopolis in her honor, was the concubine of Constantius Chlorus, who divorced her after becoming Caesar in 292 C.E., in order to marry, for political reasons, the step-daughter of Augustus Maximian, Theodora. The *Vita Petri Iberi* here reflects traces of an ancient discussion concerning Constantine's legitimacy and Helena's moral character.

ܡ̈ܕܝܢܬܐ ܕܩܘܕܫܐ. ܘܡܕ ܡܛܬ ܗܝ ܟܕ ܒܥܬ ܘܐܫܟܚܬ ܒܟܘܪ̈ܝܐ
ܐܠܗܐ: ܠܨܠܝܒܐ ܦܪܘܩܝܐ ܕܐܙܕܩܦ ܡܫܝܚܐ. ܘܒܢܬ ܗ̇ܘܬ ܠܗ̈ܝܟܠܬܐ
ܘܠܐܩ̈ܘܬܐ ܕܢܦ̈ܫܬܐ ܘܕܩ̈ܒܪܐ ܠܟܠܗ̇ ܐܬܪ. ܕܢܠܦܫܗ̇ ܐܦ ܐܬܦ̇ܩܕ.
ܘܡܢ ܒܬܪܟܢ ܐܫܬܟܚܬ ܠܒܪ̱ ܩ̈ܠܝܬܐ ܙܘ̈ܪܒܐ ܘܦܐܝ̈ܢ ܠܐܠܗܐ.
ܘܗ̈ܝܟܠܐ ܦܐܝ̈ܐ. ܟܠ ܡܢܗ ܐܠܗܝܐ ܕܒܪ̱. ܘܡܒܪܟܬܐ ܡܕܝܢܬܐ
ܕܐܘܪܫܠܡ ܠܡܫܠܡܢܘܬܐ ܗܝܟܠܬܐ: ܗ̇ܝ، ܕܐܝܬܝܗ̇ ܩܘܕܫ ܩܘܕ̈ܫܝܢ ܥܬܝܪܐ.
ܘܡܕܒܚܐ ܥܬ̈ܝܪܐ: ܗ̇ܘ ܕܐܙܕܝܢܬ ܡܢ ܡܕܡ ܡܢ ܢܒܝܐ ܡܘܫܐ ܐܬܟܪܝ
ܦܬܓܡ ܐܬܪܓܡ. ܡܢ ܟܐ̈ܦܐ ܠܐ ܦܣ̈ܝܩܬܐ ܘܠܐ ܦܠ̈ܝܫܬܐ. ܕܡܢ
ܚܝܠܐ ܫ̈ܪܝܪ. ܐܝܟܐ ܠܒܪ̱ ܐܢܫܝܐ ܕܐܝܟ ܗܘܢ. ܐܠܐ ܗܘܐ
ܡܕܒܚܐ ܒܠܚܘܕܘܗܝ، ܐܝܟ ܕܟܬܝܒ ܡܕܒܚܐ ܕܩܘܕܫܐ ܠܐ
ܡܬܦܠܚܐ. ܘܦܣܘܩܐ ܘܦܘܠܚܢܐ ܠܐ ܡܩܒܠ. ܕܟܠܗܘܢ، ܗ̇ܘ ܐܒܢܐ
ܥ̈ܬܝܪܐ ܕܐܠܗܐ ܐܬܢܓܕ ܘܐܬܦܪܣ. ܗ̇ܘ ܕܢܓܠ ܫܠܝܛܘܬܗ ܕܟܠܟܐ.
(§57) ܡܛܠ ܕܝܢ ܕܠܡܕܒܪܐ ܡܠܬܐ ܐܬܬ ܠܝ. ܘܒܡܗܕܝܢܐ ܒܓܕܝܢ
ܕܐܠܟܐ ܗܝܓܪܐ: ܕܙܕܩܐ ܢܫܒ ܐܢܐ. ܕܬܪܐ ܡܕܡ ܘܬܕܡܘܪܬܐ
ܐܬܪܐ ܘܕܚܝܠܬܐ: ܕܡܛܠ ܚܝܠܗ ܐܠܗܐ ܡܕܡܗܘܢ، ܕܠܒܘܟܐ ܗܘܬ.
ܠܬܫܒܘܚܬܐ ܕܐܠܗܐ ܘܠܦܘܪܩܢܐ ܕܡܫܪܐ ܕܪ̈ܘܚܢܝܐ.
ܘܠܬܫܡܫܬܐ ܘܠܡܫܪ̈ܝܢܘܬܐ ܕܡܫܝܚܘܬܗ̱. ܐܦܢܝ ܒܡܠܬܐ ܘܠܡܟܬܒܬܐ

1 On Helena's pilgrimage travel to Jerusalem in 326, see Eusebius, *Vit. Const.* 3.42 (Schwartz and Mommsen, 2:101; Richardson, 1:530).

2 In his account of Helena's pilgrimage to Jerusalem, Eusebius does not mention her finding the cross. Cyril of Jerusalem (ca. 349–387), writing about twenty-five years after Helena's visit, appears to be the first one to speak of finding the cross. That story was frequently told afterwards. See, e.g., the *Inventio Sanctae Crucis* (Cyriacus Legend) in Drijvers and Drijvers. See also Jan Willem Drijvers, *Helena Augusta: The Mother of Constantine the Great and the Legend of Her Finding of the True Cross* (Leiden: Brill, 1992).

3 According to the legend of the finding of the cross, the relics were identified by a healing miracle worked through it.

4 Helena was expressly responsible for the building of the Church of the Nativity in Bethlehem and the Church of the Ascension on the Mount of Olives. See Eusebius, *Vit. Const.* 3.43 (Schwartz and Mommsen, 2:101–2; Richardson, 1:530–31).

5 While Eusebius (*Vit. Const.* 3.25–40 [Schwartz and Mommsen, 2:94–101; Richardson, 1:526–30]) details at length Constantine's efforts in building

to the holy places of Christ.[1] First she searched for and by divine help found the saving wood of the precious cross[2] and set it up for worship and for healing of soul and body for all the world,[3] for whose sake he had been nailed [to it]. She later erected great and God-befitting churches for our Lord[4] and beautiful shrines over the divine tomb of our Lord, at the holy place of the Skull, the worshipful Golgotha,[5] which is the true holy of holies and the true altar, from of old by a mystic symbol[6] announced and prefigured by the prophet Moses, constructed by nature from rocks, uncut and unhewn.[7] For what other [altar] is like this [one], except this altar alone?[8] It is truly the altar of the indivisible Christ, accepting neither cutting nor division, upon which the true Lamb of God was slain and offered up,[9] who bears the sin of the world.[10]

(§57) Because our account has come to this point and we have made mention of the worshipful cross, I think it is right that I place into the account and bring forward publicly a certain mystic symbol,[11] a great and awesome wonder that because of the blessed one's divine power occurred in his presence for the glory of God,

the Church of the Holy Sepulcher, at *Vit. Const.* 3.42 (Schwartz and Mommsen, 2:101; Richardson, 1:530) it becomes clear that Helena was at least equally involved in it, even giving the initial impetus for it.

6 The Syriac translator here has in mind the concept of ܪܐܙܐ, "mystery" or "symbol," which comprises the notions of both μυστήριον and σύμβολον. For discussion of the Syriac concept, see Edmund Beck, "Symbolum-Mysterium bei Aphrahat und Ephräm," *OrChr* 42 (1958): 19–40; Robert Murray, "The Theory of Symbolism in St. Ephrem's Theology," *ParOr* 6 (1975): 1–20.

7 See Exod 20:25; Deut 27:5–6.

8 Not challenging the uniqueness of the present site, also note the text's emphasis on the altar consecrated by St. Mark at *Vit. Pet.* §61, 62 (R 43, 44).

9 Early Christian biblical interpretation customarily sees Christ's sacrifice on the cross prefigured in the lamb whose slaughter was connected with the celebration of Passover. See Exod 12:3–13; John 1:36; 1 Cor 5:7; 1 Pet 1:19; and Rev 4:1–5:14; 7:14.

10 On the relevance of this passage in the context of the Chalcedonian/anti-Chalcedonian struggle over the holy places, see Horn, *Asceticism and Christological Controversy*, 352–53 *et passim*.

11 The Syriac text again employs the concept of *rāzā*.

ܐܢܬܬܐ. ܕܗ̇ܝ ܕܟܕ ܫܡܗܪܐ ܘܥܬܝܪܐ ܗ̇ܘ ܗܘܐ ܗܘ [R 39] ܠܡܠܟܘܬܐ: ܗ̇ܘ
ܒܗ̇ܝ ܕܫܪܝܪ̈ܬܐ ܡܗܝܡܢܐ ܐܝܟ ܕܠܝ. ܗ̇ܘ ܗܘ ܐܦ ܐܫܬܟܚ ܘܒ̈ܣܝܡ
ܦܓ̈ܥܬܐ ܘܡܕܡ ܦܓ̈ܥܬܐ. ܟܕ ܡܬܬܦܝܣ ܠܢܒܝܐ ܕܐܡܪ: ܘܚܘܘ
ܒܥܡ̈ܡܐ ܥܒ̈ܕܘܗܝ. ܘܐܫܬܥܘ ܒܟܠܗܝܢ ܬܕܡܪ̈ܬܗ. ܘܐܫܬܒܚܘ ܒܫܡܗ
ܩܕܝܫܐ. ܐܬܕܟܪܘ ܬܕܡܪ̈ܬܗ ܗܠܝܢ ܕܥܒܕ.. ܟܕ ܓܝܪ ܠܠܝܘܣܐ
ܐܝܬܘܗܝ, ܗܘܐ ܒܪܚܒܠ. ܘܟܠܠܝܢ ܡܬܪܟܐ ܗܘܐ ܠܘܬ ܠܡܠܟܘܬܐ
ܬܐܘܕܘܣܝܘܣ ܡܠܟܐ. ܐܬܩܒܝ, ܕܡܠܬܐ ܕܡܠܟܐ ܢܩܒ. ܡܢ ܡܠܝ̈ܗܘ
ܗܠܝܢ ܕܐܡܪܬ ܚܕܐ ܐܬܬܐ ܡܢ ܐܘܪܫܠܡ ܠܟܢܫܗ ܕܡܠܟܐ. ܘܡܚܬܡ
ܠܗ ܒܡܕ̈ܒܪܬܐ. ܘܠܗܕܐ. ܟܕ ܒܡܕܝܢܬܐ ܘܡܕܝܢܬܐ ܠܓܒܪ: ܕܩܘܣܛܢܛܝܢܐ
ܢܗܪܐ ܒܪܗ̇. ܢܦܩܘ ܘܡܫܬܪܝܐ ܘܡܫܪܝܐܬ. ܘܟܕ ܗܟܢ̇ ܒܡܦܠܦܢܝܢ
ܕܕܗܒܐ: ܘܟܠ ܚܕ ܒܥܒܕܐ ܥܬܝܕܬ ܕܝܢ ܒܟܠܐܕܐ ܢܗ̈ܪܐ ܡܫܬܐ
ܗܘܐ ܠܗ̇: ܟܕ ܡܬܚܙܝܢ ܗܘܘ ܘܢܦܩ ܗܘܐ ܠܗ̇: ܬܘܒ ܗܟܢܐ ܗܘܐ
ܠܗ̇ ܒܪܘܚܬܗ.

(§58) ܒܬܪ ܗܠܝܢ ܒܝܘܡ ܚܕ ܡܢ ܝܘ̈ܡܬܐ ܟܕ ܥܒܪ ܗܘܐ. ܟܕ ܢܦܠ ܟܠ
ܐܦܩܗܘ, ܘܢܫܡܗ̇ ܘܐܬܟܢܝ: ܦܢܐ ܠܐܚܪ ܡܢ ܗܠܝܢ ܘܡܟܝܠܬܐ ܗܠܝܢ
ܕܒܥܒܗ. ܗ̇ܘ ܕܢܦܩ ܡܗܝܡܢܐ ܘܢܦܩ ܒܢܦܫܐ ܡܢ ܗܠܝܢ ܐܚܪ̈ܢܐ
ܐܚܪ ܗܘܐ ܠܗ: ܕܗܕܝܢ ܒܠܒܘܕܗ, ܐܫܬܟܚ ܠܘܬܗ. ܘܫܠܛܗ ܕܐܦ
ܗ̇ܘ ܒܦܓܪ ܘܢܦܫܐ. ܟܕ ܕܝܢ ܦ̇ܢܐ ܗ̇ܘ: ܘܐܬܐ ܕܢܦܩ ܐܦܩܗܘ, ܟܠ
ܗ̇ܝ, ܡܫܬܐ ܡܕܝܢܬܐ ܘܢܦܩܢ: ܟܕ ܡܟܪܟܐ ܐܟܚܕܐ ܕܦܓܥܬ ܐܡܪܬ
ܒܡܪܘܬܐ ܘܒܗ̇ܘ ܦܘܠܚܢܐ. ܗܦ̇ܟ ܡܢ ܥܠ ܗܘܢܐ ܫܘܪܬܐ. ܘܟܕ ܦܪܝܫ

[1] Note again that the "assurance" is also a reference to the key theme of the *Plerophories*. See also *Vit. Pet.* §38 (R 27).

[2] The author here provides a concise statement regarding the threefold purpose of miracles that happen through or in connection with a holy man (or woman).

[3] This comment allows one to catch a glimpse of a strongly oral setting out of which portions of the present narrative emerged. One finds numerous parallels to such an oral context also in the *Plerophoriae*.

[4] Ps 105:1–5.

[5] The Syriac transliterates the Greek παλάτιον.

[6] Modern excavations have brought to light a splendid mosaic pavement of the *chrysotriclinium*, the throne room of the Great Palace. The imperial palace stood on the territory now occupied by the Blue Mosque and the adjacent Cankurtaran neighborhood, extending to the sea. The mosaic depictions include lush scenes of wildlife and pastoral settings. The mosaics, which had fallen into decay, were restored in 1892 by the Austrian Academy of Science.

for the assurance of the hope of the Christians,[1] and for the support and the stability of our faith.[2] To this event the blessed one, this trustworthy son of truth, our father, **[R 39]** was a witness and [moreover] an eyewitness. He told [it] many times to many,[3] being obedient to the prophet who says, "Show forth among the peoples his great deeds and tell all his wonders and glory in his holy name: bring to remembrance his amazing deeds that he has done!"[4] When he was still a little boy being raised in the palace[5] of the blessed Emperor Theodosius,[6] he managed to receive a particle of the cross from the clergy who, according to custom, used to come from Jerusalem in the emperor's honor to bring him "blessings."[7] He covered it in a [little bit of] wax,[8] which he wrapped up in a clean cloth[9] to keep it secure and with honor, and placed it in a golden box.[10] Every Sunday, and especially on solemn feasts, he would take it out, and, having blessed himself with it and kissed it, he would return it again to its place.

(§58) Once on one of the days when he did this, when he had fallen on his face, had kissed it, and had blessed himself, he called a man from among those chamberlains[11] who were with him, one whom he thought more trustworthy and on more familiar [terms] than the rest [and] who at that time was alone with him. [Peter] urged him to worship [the particle of the cross] and be blessed [by it]. Yet when he approached and came to touch his lips to[12] the holy particle and be blessed, although as I said before, it was

Today they are accessible to the public *in situ* in the Mosaic Museum built above them.

7 The Syriac seems to translate the Greek εὐλογίαι (Raabe, 41 n. 3), a term used for tokens pilgrims brought back from holy places. A token that had come into physical contact with the holy place was thought to convey the same grace and blessing attached to the original site.

8 Syriac transliterates the Greek κηρός.

9 Raabe translates ܦܘܠܣܝܐ as "cloth," and we follow him here. According to Brockelmann (573), one might also translate the word as "pergamentum."

10 The Syriac ܩܡܦܛܪܝܐ transliterates the Greek κάμπτρια. The variant reading in MS BM Add. 12,174 has ܩܘܡܝܛܪܝܘܢ, transliterating the Greek κοιμητήριον, i.e., "cemetery, burial-place" (see Raabe, 42 n. 2).

11 The Syriac transliterates the Latin *cubicularius* via the Greek κουβικουλάριος (see also *PGL*, 772).

12 Literally, "put his face upon."

ܡܢ ܐܒ̈ܗܘܗܝ ܕܡܫܝܚܐ: ܡܬܟܪܟܐ ܗܘܬ ܒܟܢܫܬܐ [R 40] ܟܕ ܦܪܚܐ
ܘܒܝܢܐ ܡܦܣܝܢܐ. ܘܟܕ ܗܕܐ ܚ̇ܙܐ ܗ̣ܘܬ: ܒܬܡܗܐ ܗܘܐ ܗ̣ܘ ܠܛܘܒܢܐ
ܘܐܡܪ. ܘܟܕ ܡܫܘܪ: ܡܬܟܪܟܢ ܗܘܐ ܘܪܗ̇ܛ ܒܟܢܫܬܐ ܟܕ ܦܪܚܐ
ܕܢܠܒܫܝܘܗ̇ ܠܗ̇ ܠܗܘܢܐ. ܗ̇ܝ ܕܝܢ ܟܕ ܚܝ̣ ܚܘܬܐ ܐܬܦܫܚܬ ܠܗ̇ ܡܦܣܝܢܐ:
ܠܐ ܡܬܚܫܚܫܬܐ ܗ̣ܘܬ: ܘܠܐ ܬܘܒ ܐܬܚܙܝܬ ܒܬܪ ܗܟܢ ܗ̇ܝ ܡܚܠܬܐ:
ܥܡ ܗ̇ܝ ܡܪܘܬܐ ܘܦܘܠܚܢܐ. ܗ̇ܘ ܕܝܢ ܟܠܒܬܐ ܐܝܟ ܕܐܕܪܟ ܠܚܝܬܐ
ܘܗ̣ܘ ܠܛܘܒܢܐ. ܗ̇ܝ ܕܠܐ ܓܘܦܐ ܗܘܐ ܗ̇ܘ ܠܛܠܝܐ ܐܢܬܬܗ̇ ܗܘܬ.
ܒܕܫܬ ܒܢܐ ܕܠܐ ܕܓܠܐ ܗܘܐ ܡܢ ܠܦܠ̈ܓܐ. ܕܕܡܟܐ ܕܝܢ ܠܗܕܐ:

(§59) ܘܬܕܡܘܪܬܐ ܐܚܪܬܐ ܐܫܬܥܝ ܗ̣ܘ ܛܘܒܢܐ: ܡܛܠ ܚܝܠܗ̇
ܕܓܓܠܘܬܐ ܡܪܫܥܬܐ: ܘܕܛܝܒܘܬܐ ܐܠܗܝܬܐ ܕܡܛܫܝܐ ܒܗ̇. ܟܕ
ܚܙܝܬܐ ܒܝܘܡ ܡܥܠܬܐ ܢܦܩܬ ܠܐܦ̈ܘܗܝ ܕܛܘܒܢܐ ܢܘܚ ܐܘܡܟܣܐ:
ܘܠܟܠܗ ܦܪ̈ܨܘܦܗ ܪܚܝܐ ܗܘܬ: ܒܟܘܡܬܐ ܐܬܬܫܝܗܘܢ ܘܗܘܘ ܬܘ̈ܪܝܗܘܢ.
ܘܟܕ ܣܦܪ ܚܙܐ ܗܘܐ ܠܗܘܢ: ܘܡܬܚܫܕ ܗ̣ܘ ܛܘܒܢܐ ܢܘܚ: ܐܦ
ܕܬܬܒܝܐ ܠܬ̈ܢܝܢܐ: ܟܕ ܚܒܝܫ ܒܪܘܬܐ: ܘܐܝܟܐ ܗܘܬ ܠܠܩ̈ܘܬܗܘܢ:
ܟܕ ܠܘܬ ܢܦܫܗ ܗ̣ܘܐ ܗ̣ܘ ܡܬܡܟܟܢܐ ܦܠܚܘܗ: ܘܟܪܘܝܐ ܘܟܪܝܬܐ
ܐܠܗܐ ܪܚ̇ܡ: ܕܒܪܗ̇ ܒܠܠܝܐ ܠܛܘܒܢܐ ܢܘܚ: ܘܐܪܓܒ ܬܪ̈ܝܗܘܢ
ܠܡܫܟܬܐ ܡܪܫܥܬܐ. ܘܟܕ ܫܠܘܗ ܠܕܘܟܬܐ ܕܓܓܠܘܬܐ ܡܪܫܥܬܐ ܡܢ
ܒܟܠܐ ܒܪܒܝܫܐ: ܐܝܟ ܗ̇ܝ ܕܡܫܠܝܐ ܗ̣ܝ ܕܡܟܘܬܐ ܘܡܚܦܛܢܐ: ܣܒܒ
ܒܘܪܟܐ. ܟܕ ܡܦܣܣ ܠܒܪ ܒܕ̈ܡܟܐ ܡܪ̈ܝܪܬܐ ܘܟܐܒ̈ܢܝܬܐ. ܘܟܕ
ܥܡܠܘܗܝ ܠܘܬܐ: ܘܡܫܟܘ ܘܡܪܟܘ ܕܢܣܒܪܘ ܠܟܐܦܐ ܡܣܒܪܢܘܬܐ
ܕܓܓܠܘܬܐ ܡܪܫܥܬܐ: ܒܢܐ ܗ̣ܘ ܠܛܘܒܢܐ ܢܘܚ [R 41] ܐܝܟ
ܕܕܡܘܬܐ ܕܐܕܢܐ: ܕܢܦܩܬ ܡܢ ܬܡܢ ܘܡܦܪܬ ܠܦܬܗ: ܘܚܦܪܬ ܠܟܠܗ
ܦܪ̈ܨܘܦܗ. ܘܟܕ ܗ̣ܘܐ ܦܪ̈ܝܐ ܐܫܬܥܝ ܕܕܟܝܐ ܟܠܗ: ܟܕ ܠܝܬ ܚܡܬܐ

[1] The white dove is here used as a symbol of purity. For a fuller discussion, see Horn, *Asceticism and Christological Controversy*, 361, 377.

[2] Note the play on words in Syriac: ܡܟܪܟܐ ("wrapped up") and ܡܬܟܪܟܐ ("circling around").

[3] For another scene that portrays Peter as superior to a person affected by impurity, see the account of his encounter with the *decurion* outside of Caesarea Maritima (*Pler.* 56).

[4] For the Syriac ܚܫܚܫܬܐ, Payne Smith (136) suggests "scab," "ring-

wrapped up in wax and cloth, it suddenly became a white dove,[1] and flying from the hands of the saint, it circled around[2] the house, **[R 40]** fluttering and seeking an exit. The blessed one was amazed and cried out when this happened. He jumped up and ran about the house trying to catch the dove, but it found for itself an exit through a window and vanished. Henceforth the particle with the wax and cloth was never seen again. The reason [for all this], as the blessed one understood the vision, was that the young [chamberlain] was not worthy, for it happened [to be] that he had been made impure by defilements.[3]

(§59) The blessed one also recounted a similar miracle concerning the power of the holy Golgotha and of the divine grace hidden in it. Once a severe eruption[4] broke out on the face of the blessed John the Eunuch and was consuming[5] his whole face, distressing both [of them]. It was very painful for them:[6] the blessed John [was] ashamed even to be seen by anyone.[7] As [their] anxiety gained strength and was consuming their hearts, the believing Peter, coming to himself[8] and being fervent in spirit and divine fervor, took the blessed John by night to the holy Anastasis.[9] When they had gone up to the place of the holy Golgotha on the northern side, a place quiet and hidden, they knelt down, beseeching our Lord with bitter tears and groans. When after completing [their] prayer they got up and approached the worshipful rock of the holy Golgotha for worship, the blessed John saw **[R 41]** [something] like a hand come out from there, approach

worm," or "lichen." John the Eunuch appears to have been affected with a kind of herpes.

5 More literally even "feeding on."

6 Peter and John the Eunuch are presented as the closest friends who suffered physically for one another.

7 In biblical and early Christian times, disease was seen as the result of sin. Thus suffering from disease also caused feelings of shame in the sick person.

8 The Syriac seems to translate the Greek phrase παρ' ἑαυτῷ γενέσθαι (Raabe, 42 n. 3).

9 I.e., to the Church of the Resurrection.

ܐܘ ܦܠܛܐ ܕܗܘܿ ܒܐܒܐ. ܘܡܠܝܢ ܗܿܝ ܠܬܫܒܘܚܬܐ ܕܫܠܝܚܐ ܐܠܗܝܐ
ܕܐ̈ܠܗܐ ܡܕܝܢܐ: ܘܠܦܠܝܪܘܦܘܪܝܐ ܕܗܒܢ̈. ܕܢܦܩܐ ܕܝܢ ܢܣܒ ܐܢܐ
ܗܿ ܒܕܒܓܘܬܐ:

(§60) ܘܐܚܪܬܐ ܬܕܡܘܪܬܐ ܕܓ̈ܕܫܬ ܠܘܬܗ ܕܠܝܗ ܕܠܛܘܒܢܐ ܗܘܝܢ
ܒܝ̈ܬܝܐ ܐܚܪ̈ܢܐ: ܐܦ ܠܗܕܐ ܬܡܝܗܬܐ. ܠܬܫܒܘܚܬܐ ܕܫܡܝܗܘܢ
ܕܠܘܬ ܚ̈ܕܪܐ: ܘܕܡܗܝܡܢܘܬܗܘܢ. ܕܠܘܬ ܐܠܗܐ ܘܦܐܪܗܣܝܐ ܕܠܘܬܗ.
ܒܬܪ ܚܕ ܒܪ ܐܬܪܗ ܗܿܘ ܠܛܘܒܢܐ ܗܘܝܢ ܒܡܕܝܢܬܐ ܡܥܠܐ ܐܬܒܢܐ
ܕܐܬܦܫܩ ܒܠܘܩܘܗܝ: ܘܗܿܘ ܐܒܐ ܦܛܪܘܣ ܦܿܩܕ ܐܬܒܢܝ ܗܘܐ: ܘܕܠܐ
ܥܠܝܐ ܡܬܚܫܒ ܗܘܐ ܠܡܪܢܐ ܡܛܠ ܚܘܠܡܢܘܗܝ. ܐܬܐ ܠܗ ܡܠܐ
ܕܐܡܪ: ܐܬܠܒܒ. ܗܐ ܐܦ ܚܘܠܡܢܐ ܢܣܒ ܐܢܐ ܠܗ ܡܛܠ
ܒܗܘܬܟ. ܘܡܚܘܣ ܐܢܐ ܥܠ ܚ̈ܝܘܗܝ. ܬܬܒܣܪܐ ܥ̈ܒܕܐ ܐܚܪ̈ܢܝܬܐ.
ܗܿܝ ܕܐܦ ܗܘܬ. ܘܗܕܝܢ ܕܐܬܚܒܫܐ: ܒܪ ܐܬܡܠܟ ܘܥܒ̈ܪ ܕܢܛܝܠ. ܥܒ̈ܪ
ܦܓܪܗ ܕܢܬܒܠܩ ܩ̈ܠܦܐ ܒܚ̈ܫܬܐ: ܡܢ ܠܦܘ̈ܩܘܗܝ ܒܕܡܐ ܠܡܕܠܗ.
ܘܒܪ ܡܚܡܝܢ ܒܠܘܗܝ: ܕܕܠܒܐ ܒܪ ܡܚܠܝܢ ܗܿܘ ܘܡܠܦܐ ܢܫܒܠ
ܐܦ ܠܦܪ̈ܘܩܘܗܝ. ܬܘܒ ܒܪ ܣܦܝܠܐܝܬ ܐܬܦܪܥ ܘܢܓܠ ܗܿܘ ܐܒܐ
ܦܛܪܘܣ. ܠܐ ܡܚܝܠ ܢܦܓܥ ܠܡܕܠܗ. ܒܪ ܐܬܒܠܩ ܕܝܢ. ܗܿܘ ܦܓܪܗ
ܘܒܣܪܗ. ܐܝܟ ܕܥܒܪܐ ܕܠܒܪ ܡܫܚܐ. ܘܒܬܪ ܩܠܝܠ ܡܚܒܐ ܠܐ ܕܒܝܐ
ܗܘܬ. ܐܝܟ ܕܠܐ ܢܥܒܕ ܕܡܕܡ ܕܓ̈ܢܝܐ ܘܒܕܝܕ ܢܓܠܠ. ܒܪ ܚܿܒܪ
ܕܝܢ ܣܕ ܡܢ ܚ̈ܕܪܐ ܕ̈ܒܝܐ: [R 42] ܡܦܝܣ ܗܘܐ ܠܗ ܗܿܘ ܐܒܐ
ܦܛܪܘܣ: ܐܝܟ ܕܡܢ ܦܠܝܪܘܦܘܪܝܐ ܐܠܗܝܬܐ: ܕܢܒܕܩ ܠܗܘܢ ܡܘܪܒܐ
ܡܕܝܢܐ. ܐܬܝܩܘ ܗܘܘ ܒܪ ܬܘ̈ܪܗܘܢ ܠܐܘܪܚܐ ܕܒܡܘܬܐ. ܗܿܘ
ܕܝܢ ܠܛܘܒܢܐ ܦܛܪܘܣ. ܘܢܦܩܬ ܒܡܘܬܐ. ܗܿܘ ܕܝܢ ܒܪ ܒܐܬܝܬ

ⁱ An image of the "hand of God" over the Israelites during the exodus was discovered in the synagogue of Dura Europos; see Carl H. Kraeling, *The Synagogue* (New Haven: Yale University Press, 1956; repr., New York: Ktav, 1979), plate LIII. Similarly, the Church of San Vitale in Ravenna has a depiction of two scenes in a single composition, those of Abel and Melchizedek presenting sacrificial offerings to two altars, above which an outstretched hand is depicted as extending down to receive them. See Giuseppe Bovini, *Ravenna Mosaics* (Greenwich, Conn.: New York Graphic Society, 1956), 44. A very clear depiction of the relevant detail may be found in Leonard von Matt and Giuseppe Bovini, *Ravenna* (New York: Abrams, 1973), plate 77, p. 121.

[2] The Syriac transliterates the Greek πληροφορία.

[3] The Syriac transliterates the Greek παρρησία.

his face, and wipe his whole face clean.[1] At dawn, [his face] was found completely pure, without injury or defilement from the disease. Those [signs] surely [happened] for the demonstration of the divine power of the holy cross and for the assurance[2] of our hope.

(§60) Another miracle, like this one, I suppose, that happened to the same blessed John on other occasions I will attach to this account for the demonstration of their love for each other and of their faith in God and boldness[3] toward him. Once when the blessed John had fallen sick with a severe infirmity,[4] so that [all hope] concerning him was lost, Abba Peter was very despondent and did not cease making supplication to the Lord on behalf of his recovery. [Then] a voice came to him saying "Take heart! Behold, I shall grant him recovery because of your request: I am adding twelve more years to his life." And so it happened. Following [this there occurred another] wonder. When he recovered his health and began to grow strong, his body began to husk off thick scales from his [toe-]nails to his neck. When they were all distressed that perhaps, if this scaling should continue, it would also spoil his face, again Abba Peter earnestly made supplication and prayed, [and] thus the [affliction] did not spread beyond his neck. When he was healed, his body and his flesh were like that of a newborn infant,[5] and his voice was so unintelligible that he could say nothing clear or intelligible.[6] When one of the solemn feasts arrived, **[R 42]** Abba Peter persuaded him, as if from divine assurance, to perform for them the holy oblation,[7] for both of them had been esteemed worthy of the honor of the priesthood

[4] From the presentation of John the Eunuch as having previously been affected by skin disease (*Vit. Pet.* §59 [R 40]) and as having fallen sick again at this instance, one might conclude that he suffered from ill health, affecting in particular his outer appearance. One might also see this presentation as being in support of Rufus's characterization of John the Eunuch as a visionary, given that people of weak physical health not infrequently appear to be more in tune with the spiritual realm.

[5] See also 2 Kgs 5:14.

[6] John the Eunuch's healing process is depicted as an experience of rebirth. His restored body and voice showed the signs of a merely babbling infant. That this state was brought about by Peter's prayers would have signalled to the anti-Chalcedonian audience the effectiveness and initiatory quality of Peter's intercession.

[7] I.e., the Eucharist.

ܡܫܬܐܠ ܗܘܐ ܐܝܟ ܠܐ ܒܫܠܠܐ ܘܐܝܟ ܡܢ ܕܠܐ ܡܢܝܐ ܗܘܐ܆ ܟܬܪ
ܗܘ ܐܝܟܢܐ ܦܛܪܘܗ. ܟܕ ܡܦܝܣ ܘܡܫܬܦܠ. ܟܕ ܐܡܪ ܕܠܐ ܐܠܝܐ
ܕܬܡܟܐ. ܐܠܐ ܟܕܗ ܠܟܠܐ ܫܩܠܐ ܠܬܠܬܐ. ܘܟܕ ܫܬܡܫ ܚܝ ܚܕ
ܫܒܩ ܐܠܗܐ. ܟܕ ܕܝܢ ܐܬܦܢܝ ܐܬܬܦܝܣ. ܘܟܕ ܩܡ ܩܕܡ ܡܕܒܚܐ
ܩܕܝܫܐ܆ ܘܓܢܕܐܝܬ ܘܒܕܚܠܬܐ ܐܡܪ ܠܘܬ ܚܕܐ ܫܠܡܐ ܠܟܠܟܘܢ܆
ܘܗܒܐ ܠܟܠܗ ܩܘܪܒܐ ܩܕܝܫܐ ܫܟܠ. ܘܟܕ ܡܬܕܟܪ ܢܦܫ ܡܢ ܐܠܗܐ
ܟܬܪ ܥܠܗ ܩܕܡܝܬܐ܆ ܐܝܟ ܗܘ ܕܠܐ ܡܬܚܙܐ ܐܬܦܢܝܗ܆ ܟܬܪ ܘܡܢ
ܟܬܪ ܫܦܝܪ ܡܬܠܠܐ ܟܠܗ ܘܒܢܐ ܕܫܪܟܐ܀

(§61) ܒܚܕ ܗܢܐ ܙܒܢܐ ܢܘܚܝ. ܟܕ ܒܚܙܘܐ ܗܘܐ ܟܠܗܘܢ
ܢܦܠܬܐ܆ ܬܠܬܐ ܥܒܕ ܒܗܘ ܚܙܘܐ. ܟܕ ܟܡ ܐܝܟ ܗܘ ܠܐ ܡܠܠ.
ܫܪܐ ܗܘܐ ܕܝܢ ܠܡܬܚܙܝܘ ܕܫܠܝܐ ܘܡܫܬܠܡܢܐ ܕܬܪܬܝܢ ܕܡܢ. ܟܕ
ܫܡܝܐ ܡܢ ܥܠ ܦܬܝܚܝܢ ܗܘܘ܆ ܘܠܩܪܢܬܐ ܕܬܪܥܝܢ. ܠܬܪܥܐ ܕܬܒܝܠ.
ܠܡܘܠܦ ܐܘܩܝܢܘܣ ܐܘܟܝܬ ܚܠܦܐ. ܠܟܠܗܘܢ ܕܒܟܠ ܢܘܗܪܐ
ܘܪܘܚܢܘܬܐ ܕܠܘܩܒܠ ܘܚܒܝܒܘܬܐ ܘܫܝܢܐ. ܠܡܠܐܟܐ ܕܩܕܡܝܢ
ܪܘܚܢܝܢ. ܘܠܚܝܠܘܬܐ ܩܕܝܫܐ ܕܫܡܝܐ ܥܠܝܐ. ܠܡܠܐܟܐ. ܠܬܪܝܢ
ܡܠܐܟܐ. ܠܫܠܝܛܢܐ. ܠܡܪܘܬܐ. ܠܫܘܒܚܐ. ܠܚܝܠܘܬܐ ܕܫܡܝܐ
ܩܕܝܫܐ. ܕܟܪܘܒܐ. ܕܣܪܦܐ. ܠܟܘܪܣܐ ܠܡܪܟܒܬܐ. ܘܟܬܪ
ܟܠܗܘܢ ܠܐܬܪܐ ܡܫܒܚܬܐ [R 43] ܘܦܪܘܫܬܐ ܕܠܓܡܐ ܡܪܝܐ.
ܘܟܠܗ ܠܡܪܢܐ ܦܪܘܩܐ ܘܡܫܝܚܐ. ܕܢܚܙܐ ܘܐܬܐ ܒܝܗ ܬܫܒܘܚܬܐ
ܐܒܗܬܐ. ܘܫܠܡ ܠܐ ܡܬܡܠܠܢܐ. ܠܡܘܫܒܬܐ ܕܚܣܝܕܝܢ. ܘܠܟܠܗ
ܕܒܢܐ ܐܠܗܐ ܘܕܫܠܝܐ. ܗܘ ܕܢܝܢ ܩܕܡ ܘܟܝܢ ܦܓܪܐ ܟܕ ܢܦܫܐ
ܩܕܝܫܐ. ܘܡܘܬܐ ܕܢܦܫܐ ܘܦܪܘܫܐ ܦܪܡ ܐܘܟܝܬ ܠܝ ܠܡܘܕܝܬܐ.

[1] I.e., of the episcopate. The following event took place after 451.

[2] See Matt 6:5–13.

[3] The attempt to identify Peter the Iberian with the author of the Pseudo-Dionysian corpus rests also on acknowledging a parallel between the following vision and the conception of the heavenly hierarchy as found in the Areopagite's work. As author, Peter would have written down what John the Eunuch would have shared with him about his vision. Also contrast the following with the more fearful, negative depiction of the signs of the *parousia* found in *Pler.* 10.

[4] See Rev 4:1; Mark 1:10; Acts 7:56; Ezek 1:1.

[5] See Rev 4:1; 1 Cor 15:52

[6] See Joel 2:10.

[7] See Joel 2:10; 2 Pet 3:10, 12. The Syriac translates the Greek στοιχεῖον.

[8] Literally, "change." The experience of intensive light accompanied the transfiguration of Christ in the Scriptures (Matt 17:2, 5; Mark 9:3; Luke 9:29).

[and] the blessed Peter also of the high priesthood.[1] [John] sensibly declined as incapable of speech and [thus] unable [to do it]. Yet Abba Peter persisted, persuading and urging [him], saying, "It is not necessary for you to speak aloud, but perform the prayers inside [your] heart, for even when we are silent, God hears."[2] Being compelled, [John] consented. He stood in front of the holy altar and clearly and intelligibly said to the people, "Peace be with all of you!" and thus celebrated the entire holy oblation. Having received anew from God his former voice as if he had never fallen sick, he remained articulate for all the rest [of his life].

(§61) Once this blessed John beheld in a vision, for three whole days without talking to anyone at all, the fearful and glorious Second Coming of our Lord,[3] the heavens suddenly being opened[4] and the horns summoning,[5] the quakings of the earth,[6] the transformation of the elements,[7] that is, the transfiguration,[8] everything full of light and the perturbation of confusion and trembling and commotion, angels immediately preceding and the first orders[9] of the heavenly hosts, angels, archangels, powers,[10] dominions,[11] glories;[12] the orders[13] of the holy apostles, of the prophets, of the martyrs, of the righteous; cherubim, seraphim,[14] and after all of them the worshipful and **[R 43]** saving sign[15] of the cross of the Lord;[16] and the Lord himself, Savior and Christ, raised up and coming with the Father's glory[17] and ineffable power. [He saw] the thrones prepared[18] and the divine and fearful tribunal, which from of old and many times through the holy prophets and by the Judge and Savior himself was announced to

9 The Syriac transliterates the Greek τάξις.

10 The Syriac translates the Greek ἐξουσίαι (Raabe, 44 n. 5). See also Eph 3:10; 6:12.

11 The Syriac translates the Greek κυριότητες (Raabe, 44 n. 6). See Col 1:16.

12 The Syriac translates the Greek δόξαι (Raabe, 44 n. 7). See Col 1:16.

13 The Syriac transliterates the Greek τάξις.

14 It is especially this moment of emphasis on heavenly order in the events that John the Eunuch sees in his vision that may lead one to note a parallel to the heavenly realm as described by Pseudo-Dionysius's mystagogy.

15 See Matt 24:30.

16 Literally, "of the dominical cross."

17 Matt 24:30.

18 See Rev 11:16; 20:4; see also Dan 7.

ܚܙܐ ܠܗܘ ܗܘܐ ܕܝܢ܆ ܕܚܙ. ܒܠܠܝܐ. ܡܕܒܪܐ ܕܩܐܡ ܥܠ ܐܪܒܥܐ܆
ܕܟܠܡܕܡ ܕܚܝ̈ܐ ܕܒܪܒܝܠ ܘܗܫܐ ܢܗܪ ܠܘܬܢ܆ ܕܟܠܗܘܢ ܬܪ̈ܝܗܘܢ
ܡܫܡܫܝܢ ܗܘܘ. ܘܠܘܬܗ̇ ܣܓܕܬܐ ܕܕܝ̈ܪܐ ܩܕ̈ܝܫܐ ܕܝܪ̈ܝܗܘܢ، ܡܢܟܝܢ܆
ܘܟܠܫ. ܡܫܡܫܘܢ ܐܝܟ ܫܘܦܪܗ. ܘܗܘܐ ܡܢ ܥܠܝܐ ܩܠܐ ܕܡܬܢܝܬܐ
ܘܫܘܒܚܐ ܕܐܦܘܠܘܓܝܐ ܘܐܝܟ ܕܡܘܬܐ ܕܟܢ̈ܫܐ ܕܩܕ̈ܝܫܐ܆ ܘܫܦܝܪ
ܡܢ ܗ̇ܘ ܡܕܒܪܐ ܠܗܠܝܢ ܩܕ̈ܝܫܐ ܕܡܢܟܝܢ ܠܘܬܗ̇ ܠܐܘܪܚܗ ܕܡܢ.
ܒܪ. ܥܡܠ ܗܒܠ ܬܠܬܐ ܫܥ̈ܬܐ ܒܫܘܐ ܕܐܝܟ ܗܢܐ܆ ܘܫܒܩ ܙܐܪܐ
ܐܣ̈ܝܐ ܩܒܝܠܐ ܕܠܐ ܥܠܝܦ ܠܒܪܢܫܐ ܕܢܛܠܠ܆ ܟܕ ܗܠܝܢ ܒܪ. ܐܬܐ
ܠܘܬ ܢܦܫܗ܆ ܟܕ ܕܝܢ ܒܪ. ܬܘܒ ܐܝܟ ܬܠܬܝܢ ܫܥ̈ܬܐ. ܒܪ. ܠܐ ܪ̈ܒܐ
ܕܢܛܠܠ ܥܡ ܐܚܐ ܡܕܡ. ܡܬܐܠܨ ܕܝܢ ܐܦܠܐ ܡܨܝ̈ܐ ܗܘܐ. ܟܠܗ ܫܢ̈ܝ
ܬܡܢ ܐܒܗܘܗܝ ܗܘܐ ܒܬܪܟܢܘܬܗ܆ ܘܠܐ ܡܛܠ ܟܠ ܐܪܒܥܐ ܗܦܟܝ
ܗܘܐ ܕܫܢܝ. ܗ̇ܘܐ ܕܝܢ ܦܪ̈ܘܩܗ ܐܝܟ ܦܪܘܩܐ ܕܥܠܡܐ. ܘܟܠܗ
ܕܡܘܬܗ ܐܪܙܬܐ ܐܢܬܬܗ ܗܘܬ ܡܢ ܗ̇، ܐܢܫ̈ܝܬܐ. ܐܠܐ ܗܘܢܐ
ܚܘܐ ܡܢ ܠܫܪܬܐ ܗܘܬ ܟܠܗ ܙܒܢܐ ܩܕܝܫܬܐ.

(§62) ܡܛܠ ܕܝܢ ܕܠܡܕܒܪܐ ܐܬܟܬܫܬ܆ ܠܐ ܫܦܝܪܐ ܐܢܐ ܐܬܐ
ܕܡܘܬ ܒܗ ܒܪ. ܡܬܦܪܫ܆ ܐܝܟ ܕܗܘ ܠܦܪܢܐ ܦܪܘܣܐ ܘܩܕܡ ܩܝܡܬܐ
[R 44] ܐܫܬܟܚ ܠܝ. ܒܪ. ܥܠܘ ܒܪ ܡܢ ܒܬܪܝܢ ܒܩ̈ܝܢܐ ܕܡܕܒܪܘܬܐ
ܒܠܡܕܘܫܬܐ܆ ܘܒܐܠܗܘܬܢܐ ܡܕܒܪܝܢ ܗܘܘ܆ ܬܡܢ ܒܡܕܒܪܗܘܢ، ܠܗܢܐ
ܡܕܒܪܐ ܩܕܝܫܐ. ܘܒܪ. ܡܬܦܪܫ܆ ܒܢܐ ܗܘ ܠܦܪܢܐ ܠܐܠܗܐ ܟܠܗ̇ܘܬ܆
ܠܩܕܝܫܐ ܡܢܘܩܘ ܐܘܠܘܓܝܐ ܕܩܐܡ ܘܫܡܥ ܠܗ. ܘܡܬܠܠܗܕܐ
ܬܫܡܫܬܐ ܕܐܝܟ ܗܠܝܢ ܘܫܠܡܐ ܦܘܠܝܐ ܘܐܦܘܡܬܐ ܒܐܪ̈ܕܘܗܝ،
ܫܟܝܢܬ ܠܦܪܘܬܐ܆ ܗܠܝܢ ܕܠܐ ܡܨܝܐ ܕܢܟܬܫܐ ܢܦܫܝ. ܘܡܬܠܠܗܝܢ

[1] See Matt 25:31–46.

[2] This refers to a time and setting contemporary to Rufus. At the same time, it is a reference to a moment of divine authorization and confirmation for the practices of worship and consequently of belief of the anti-Chalcedonian community. The author claims that anti-Chalcedonian liturgy, certainly as celebrated in ascetic settings, mirrors the heavenly liturgy.

[3] Evagrius of Pontus, *Praktikos*, introductory letter (Guillaumont and Guillaumont, 490–91; Bamberger, 14), explained that the monks "carry a staff that is the tree of life that affords secure footing to those who hold on to it. It allows them to support themselves upon it as upon the Lord." Thus the monks' staff can function as a sign of their attempt to hold on to the right, life-giving faith.

[4] 1 Thess 4:16–17.

us beforehand as a testimony.[1] He saw only one altar, standing on the earth, in every [detail] like the one that still to this moment we keep,[2] at which both of them were serving, and a multitude of holy monks who were standing around it, each one of them holding his staff.[3] Behold, suddenly [there were] blasts of horns and commotions of the elements, and as it were clouds flew [down] and snatched away from that altar those saints who were standing by it [to take them away] to the meeting with our Lord.[4] When he had in this way completed three days in such a vision and had seen many other mysteries about which a human being may not speak, when he came to himself afterwards, he remained for about thirty days as one dazed, not wanting to say anything to anyone, or rather he was unable to [speak], for in his mind he was wholly there [at the scene of the vision], and he was supposing that he was no longer dwelling on earth. His face was like the face of an angel, and his whole appearance was different from that of a human being.[5] This vision indeed took place a long time later, at the end [of his life].[6]

(§62) Since I have mentioned the altar, I shall not hide the sign that took place on it when it was consecrated, as the blessed Peter related to us **[R 44]** many times.[7] When they departed later during the Chalcedonian rebellion[8] and were dwelling in Alexandria, there they made this holy altar. At its consecration the blessed one clearly saw St. Mark the Evangelist, who was standing [there to] consecrate it. On account of this, grace accomplished such wonders[9] and [so] many works of power and healings by

[5] Exod 34:29–35.

[6] Given that the miracle of healing that restored John the Eunuch to infant-like health occurred after 451 and that twelve years were added to his life, the vision appears to have taken place before, certainly not much later than, 463 C.E. John the Eunuch was buried in Peter the Iberian's monastery between Gaza and Maiuma. See *Vit. Pet.* §188 (R 142). Regular commemorations of him were celebrated in the monastery as well. See *Vit. Pet.* §171 (R 127).

[7] This comment supports the assumption that much of the material gathered in the present text, and presumably in other works by John Rufus, originates in an oral tradition initiated by Peter the Iberian.

[8] The Syriac word could also be translated as "chastisement" or "persecution."

[9] See Eph 3:7.

ܘܠܐ ܚܝܠܐ ܐܝܬ ܠܝ. ܘܠܐ ܙܒܢܐ ܕܒܐܝܕܐ ܒܐܝܕܐ ܢܐܡܪ. ܐܠܐ
ܗܢܐ ܚܘܐ ܗ̇ܝ ܐܢܫ ܕܐܡܪܬ: ܠܫܪܟܐ ܟܕ ܡܕܒܪ ܒܐܠܗܘܬܐ:
ܘܚܠܦ ܐܘܪܬܕܘܟܣܝܐ ܕܪܕܝܦ ܐܬܟܠܠ.

(§63) ܚܕ ܕܝܢ ܟܕ ܥܘܕܝܢ ܡܬܚܠܡ ܚܢ: ܢܦܩܢܐ ܠܐܘܪܚܐ ܕܢܦܩܝܢ ܡܢ
ܬܫܒܚܬܢ. ܟܕ ܡܫܠܡܝܢ ܚܢ ܚܠܬܐ ܗ̇ܝ ܕܐܘܩܝܬ ܐܝܟ ܠܡܕܝܢܬܐ ܗ̇ܘ
ܕܒܢܝܬ ܠܘܬ ܠܡܕܝܢܬܐ: ܐܢܚܢܐ ܕܟܕ ܚܙܝܢ ܐܬܕܒܪܢ ܒܥܠܝܬܐ
ܕܐܢܬܘܢ ܠܡܘܬܐ.

(§64) ܗ̇ܝ ܗܟܝܠ ܡܕܝܢܬܐ ܩܕܝܫܬܐ ܐܘܪܫܠܡ: ܟܕ ܗܟܢܐ ܡܟܠܬ
ܕܐܬܦܟܢܐ ܡܕܢܚ: ܡܢ ܩܘܦܠܝܢܘܣ ܡܠܟܐ ܕܪܗܘܡܝܐ: ܘܚܪܒܬ
ܒ̈ܢܝ ܐܢܫܐ ܘܕܠܐ ܥܡܪܐ ܐܫܬܒܩܬ ܗ̇ܘܬ ܒܙܒܢ ܒܥܘܪܢܐ: ܟܕ ܥܡܪܐ
ܡܕܒܪܢܐ ܐܬܦܬܚܬ ܡܢ ܕܘܡܝܢܐ. ܠܡܥܒܪ ܡܠܠ ܟ̈ܠܬܐ ܘܒܡܥܘܪܐ ܐܝܬ
ܗܘܐ ܒܗ̇. ܟܕ ܚܙܝܢ ܗܟܢܐ ܡܠܝܢ ܕܥܪ ܒܚܝ̈ܠܐ ܘܐܦܝܣܩܘܦܐ ܕܐܝܬܘܗܝ
ܒܬܪܟܢ ܒܐܘܪܫܠܡ: ܕܡܫܝܚܐ ܕܒܥܘܪܐ ܢܦܩܘ ܒܡܕܝܢܬܐ:
ܘܡܫܝܚܐ ܕܩܢܝܢܐ ܢܦܩܘ ܥܡܠܝܢܐ ܠܟܠ ܕܡܥܠܐ ܘܡܢܝܢܐ:
ܕܒܐܝܕܐ ܕܗ̇ܝ ܡܕܝܢܬܐ ܕܡܕܝܢܬܐ: ܟܠ ܕܘܟܬܐ [R 45] ܕܐܬܦܪܫܐ ܠܗ:
ܢܦܩ ܡܢ ܕܠܐ ܠܡܣܒ ܘܢܒܝܐ ܒܗ̇ ܡܕܒܪܐ. ܗܢܝܢ ܗܟܝܠ ܐܦ
ܠܡܒܢܐ ܦܠܛܪܘܢ: ܠܟܠ ܠܘܬ ܢܦܫܗ ܩܕܝܫܬܐ: ܒܗ̇ܘ ܕܡܬܦܪܫܐ
ܡܛܠ ܕܕܘܝܕ ܢܒܝܐ[1] ܚܙܐ ܠܗ ܕܘܟܬܐ: ܘܒܢܐ ܒܗ̇ ܕܢܐ. ܗ̇ܝ
ܕܐܦ ܗܘܬܐ ܒܟܠ ܡܬܦܪܫܐ ܕܐܢܝ̈ܫܐ. ܘܡܛܠ ܡܢ ܗܟܠܐ. ܡܢ

[1] Here MS A reads ܢܒ݁ܝܐ, while MS B has ܢܒܝܐ, which Raabe does not note but which is to be preferred, not only for syntactical reasons. Without access to the manuscript, Griffith, *marginalia*, also suggested ܢܒܝܐ as the better reading.

[2] Literally, "be contained by a number." See John 21:25.

[3] The author's choice of the verb "speak" instead of "write" supports the thesis that the original *Sitz im Leben* of the *Vita Petri Iberi* was in an oral setting. Only in a second step does the author seem to have put to paper what he had originally already passed on in oral narrative.

[4] See above, *Vit. Pet.* §54 (R 37).

[5] See below, *Vit. Pet.* §§74–75 (R 50–51).

[6] For an account of the destruction of Jerusalem at the hands of the Romans, see Josephus, *B.J.* 7.1.1 (Thackeray, 3:504–5). For a discussion of the correlation of literary and archaeological evidence regarding the physical structures of Jerusalem, see Bieberstein and Bloedhorn, *Jerusalem*, 1:108–28, 142–53.

means of it that they cannot be counted,[2] and we have neither strength nor time to speak one by one about them.[3] This vision, as I have said, was revealed at the end, when they were dwelling in Alexandria and were being persecuted for orthodoxy.

(§63) Having fulfilled our promise, let us return to our account where we left off[4] to divulge the reason that brought them to the monastery between Gaza and Maiuma, [from] where, while dwelling [there], they were led away by force to come to the priesthood.[5]

(§64) When it was rebuilt by the Christian Emperor Constantine, the Holy City, Jerusalem, at first was still sparsely populated and had no [city] wall, since the first [city] wall had been destroyed by the Romans.[6] There were but a few houses and [few] inhabitants.[7] Thus, when the high priests and bishops, who later on were in Jerusalem,[8] desired that a multitude of inhabitants should dwell in the city and that a multitude of buildings should be built, they gave authority to anyone who wished and who was able to take any **[R 45]** spot he pleased without payment [and] without price in any part of the city in order to build thereon a dwelling. At that time the blessed Peter also chose for himself a place up toward the [Church of the] Holy Zion, in what is called the "Tower of David," the prophet.[9] He built therein a monastery that still [stands] to this day,[10] called "the Monastery of the Iberians."[11] It

See also p. 79, n. 5 above for a discussion of the evidence concerning the destruction of Jerusalem.

[7] Literally, "inhabitants in it."

[8] Cyril, John, and Juvenal were the three most significant bishops of the Holy City during those years. Cyril became bishop of Jerusalem in 350. John occupied the episcopal throne of Jerusalem from 386 to 417. Juvenal was bishop of Jerusalem from 422 to 458.

[9] Although MS A clearly reads ܢܒܚܐ, we follow here the reading of MS B, ܢܒܝܐ.

[10] Literally, "hour" or "time."

[11] Literally, "that of the Iberians." This monastery is not to be confused with the Monastery of the Holy Cross, located just outside the Old City in the western part of Jerusalem. For a long time of its history, the Monastery of the Holy Cross was in the possession of the Iberians. Today it belongs to the Greek Patriarchate of Jerusalem.

ܕܐܬܐ ܠܝܗܘܢ ܡܕܝܢܬܐ܆ ܡܢ ܬܪܥܐ ܕܕܘܝܕ ܕܠܗ ܕܡܓܕܠܐ. ܘܒܗ
ܒܢܐ ܗܘܐ ܒܥܘܡܪܐ ܥܡ ܢܘܚ ܪ ܫܘܒܚܗ.

(§65) ܐܬܐ ܕܝܢ ܕܢܬܚܒܫ ܬܡܢ. ܟܕ ܚܙܐ ܠܗ ܠܕܘܟܬܐ ܠܐ ܚܒܪ
ܐܢܐ. ܐܬܬܝܗ ܕܝܢ ܗܕܐ܆ ܐܝܟ ܡܢ ܢ̈ܒܝܐ ܕܡܠܦܢܘܬܗ ܫܒܒܐ
ܗܘܐ ܠܗܘܢ. ܗܘ ܕܐܦ ܗܘ ܟܕ ܥܒܠ ܕܘܟܬܐ܆ ܒܚܕ ܒܢܝܢܐ
ܬܡܢ. ܟܕ ܗܘܐ ܕܝܢ ܚܙܝܢܐ ܡܛܠ ܬܘܡܟܐ ܐܚܝܢܐ ܕܓܪܫܐ
ܠܫ̈ܡܝܐ܆ ܗܘ ܐܚܐ ܦܛܪܘܣ ܒܥܠܡܐ ܐܬܘܗܝ ܗܘܐ ܒܥܠܡܬܐ. ܗܘ
ܢܘܚ ܐܘܢܘܡܣܐ ܟܕ ܐܫܬܟܚ ܠܒܪ ܠܗܬ ܩܛܠܐ܆ ܡܩܒܠ ܗܘܐ
ܒܝܚܐܝܬ ܘܡܫܡܫܢܐܝܬ ܠܗ. ܕܐܝܟ ܗܢܐ ܐܬܘܗܝ ܗܘܐ ܒܢܝܢܗ.
ܕܡܫܡܫܢܘܬܗ ܕܩܘܫܐ ܡܬܕܡܪܐ ܗܘܐ. ܗܘ ܕܝܢ ܕܫܡܥܘܢ ܗܘܐ܆
ܐܝܟ ܗܘ ܕܡܫܬܐܠ ܒܟܠ ܕܗܘܝ ܐܦܝ ܠܡܘܠܕܗ. ܫܩܠܗ ܒܠ ܦܘܡܗ
ܢܛܠܬܐܝܬ ܠܗ ܠܛܘܒܢܐ. ܟܕ ܐܬܕܟܪ ܠܡܫܡܫܢܘܬܗ ܕܩܘܦܐ. ܗܘ ܕܝܢ
ܟܕ ܥܠܒ ܘܦܠܚ ܒܐܝܕ ܠܗ܆ ܟܕ ܡܕܡ ܗܘ ܠܐ ܦܠܚ܆ ܐܠܐ ܕܫܒܩ
ܠܩܛܠܐ ܘܠܗ ܟܕ ܡܠܐ ܣܓܝܐܐ܆ ܒܠ ܠܘܬ ܐܚܐ ܦܛܪܘܣ ܠܓܘ܆ ܟܕ
ܠܦܘܡ ܠܒܝܬ ܒܐܝܕܗ ܘܡܫܡܠ. ܐܬܬܝܗ ܗܘܬ ܕܒܐܒܐ ܗ̇ܝ ܡܫܝܚܘܬܐ.
ܟܕ ܫܡܥ ܕܝܢ ܬܪ̈ܝܗܘܢ ܒܘܪܟܐ܆ ܘܫܩܠ ܠܡܫܘܬܐ ܫܡܕܝܢ ܗܘܘ
ܠܡܪܢ܆ ܗܘ ܕܐܫܒܗ܆ ܐܝܟ ܠܫܘܬܦܘܬܐ ܕܫܘ̈ܦܘܗܝ.. ܘܟܕ ܡܕܡ ܠܐ
ܐܡܪ ܠܘܬ ܗܘ܆ ܘܗܠܝܢ ܕܚܙܝ ܒܠܘ ܡܢ [R 46] ܒܚܙ̈ܘܗܝ܆ ܐܬܦܠܓܘ
ܕܫܒܘܢ ܢܐܘܠܘܢ ܡܢ ܗ̇ܝ ܕܗܘܬܐ. ܘܠܦܘܬܗ ܕܗܘܡܐ ܐܚܪܢܐ ܗܘ
ܫܦܝܐ ܐܬܩܕܪ ܡܒܠܬܐ܆ ܟܕ ܠܝܬ ܗܘܐ ܠܗ ܡܕܡ ܡܢ ܡܕܡ ܕܟܒܪ.
ܐܝܟܢܐ ܕܬܬܒܪܟ ܗܕܐ ܠܟܠܗܘܢ ܚܒܘܪ̈ܘܗܝ ܕܐܘܪܫܠܡ܆ ܕܡܛܠ

[1] The monastery built by Peter was located in the immediate vicinity of what today is known as the Anglican Christ Church, thus in the neighborhood of the "Tower of David." For a fuller discussion of the archaeological evidence, see Bieberstein and Bloedhorn, *Jerusalem*, 2:170–71; Horn, *Asceticism and Christological Controversy*, 285 *et passim*.

[2] Palestinian asceticism is characterized by pairs of monks living closely together and sharing their experience in a common life. Often, but not necessar-

is located on the left, as one is coming to holy Zion from the second gate of the same tower.[1] There he dwelt in quiet together with John, the companion of his quiet [life].[2]

(§65) The sign that took place there as they were building [their monastic dwelling] place I will not omit. It was the [following]. A well-known man from among the clergy was their neighbor, who also had staked out a place and [erected] a building there. One day, as happens with neighbors, when a dispute about the boundary [occurred], Abba Peter was in quiet in [his] cell, while John the Eunuch happened to be outside with the laborers, [trying to] persuade this [man] gently and humbly, as was his custom, who in his humility was like Moses.[3] The wrongdoer, as though he had suffered grievances because he [John the Eunuch] at all contradicted him, struck the blessed one hard on his cheek, being like the servant of Caiaphas.[4] Although he was hit and in great pain, [John] made no reply at all, but leaving the laborers and this [man] full of anger, he went inside to Abba Peter, holding his cheek with his hand and crying for help, since this blow was painful. The two of them knelt down and praised our Lord with thanksgiving that he had deigned them worthy of participation in his beatings. He did not say anything to this [man], and those who were building went in from **[R 46]** their work and got ready to depart from that place. The next morning that headstrong [man] was dead and buried, although he [had suffered from] no

ily, a given ascetic pair constitutes a teacher-disciple relationship. The example of Peter the Iberian and John the Eunuch fits in very well with this.

[3] Later anti-Chalcedonian literature continues this characterization of Moses as "meek." See, e.g., Stephen of Heracleopolis, *Panegyric on Apollo* (Kuhn, 1:2,22–23 [Coptic], 2:2,14 [English]), who describes Archimandrite Apollo as exibhiting the "meekness and lack of vindictiveness of Moses and David."

[4] See Matt 26:67.

ܓܒܪܐ ܕܗܘܐ ܠܗܠܝܢ ܩܕܝܫܐ܇ ܗܘ ܕܐܝܟܢܐ ܐܠܗܐ ܠܐ ܐܓܪ ܪܘܚܗ.
ܗܘ ܕܒܟܠܗܝܢ ܡܨܥܪ ܗܘܐ ܠܗܘܢ.

(§66) ܟܕ ܦܫܘ ܗܟܝܠ ܬܠܡܝܕܘܗܝ ܒܠܚܘܕܝܗܘܢ ܒܗܿ ܕܒܩܠܝܬܐ܆ ܘܐܝܬ
ܗܘܐ ܠܗܘܢ ܒܕܚܠܬ ܒܣܘܦܩܐ ܕܢܦܩ ܠܗܘܢ܆ ܡܢ ܗܿܘ ܕܐܫܬܒܩܘ ܕܟܕ.
ܢܦܩܘ ܢܣܒܘܢ. ܟܕ ܡܢ ܓܙܘ ܘܫܟܚܘܗ ܟܠ ܕܐܝܬ ܠܕܝܪܐ ܩܕܝܫܐ
ܘܠܡܣܟܢܐ ܦܠܓܘ. ܐܬܢܫܒܘ ܕܒܗܿܘ ܕܦܩ ܬܐܓܘܪܬܐ ܠܓܡܠܐ
ܐܬܐܓܪܘ. ܘܠܐܟܣܢܝܐ ܘܠܡܣܟܢܐ ܕܡܢ ܟܠܕܘܟ ܐܬܝܢ ܠܗܓܕܝܬܐ
ܕܕܘܟܝܬܐ ܩܕܝܫܬܐ܇ ܢܦܠܘܢ ܘܢܣܒܘܢ. ܟܕ ܗܦܟܘ ܗܟܝܠ ܡܕܝܢܬܐ
ܦܩܕܐܝܬ܇ ܡܦܠܓܝܢ ܗܘܘ ܐܟܣܢܝܐ ܐܒܪܗܡܐܝܬ܇ ܗܠܝܢ ܐܟܣܢܝܐ
ܘܬܘܬܒܐ. ܘܕܠܐ ܡܢܝܢ ܠܓܒܪ ܒܬܫܒܘܚܬܐ ܕܐܝܟ ܗܠܝܢ. ܐܡܝܢܐ
ܕܬܓܒܪ ܐܢܝܢ ܩܛܠܐ. ܕܐܦ ܒܫܢܬܐ ܦܬܘܪܐ ܒܝܫ. ܘܗܘܐ ܢܗܘܐ
ܐܝܬ ܠܗܘܢ. ܘܬܐܪܐܝܬ ܒܟܐܪܐ ܢܕܝܐ. ܘܒܕ ܕܐܝܟ ܗܟܢ
ܐܬܝܗܘܢ܇ ܗܿܘܢ ܒܠܚܘܕܝܗܘܢ ܡܬܟܪܟܝܢ ܗܘܘ ܠܗܘܢ. ܟܕ ܒܟܪ̈ܝܬܐ
ܢܦܩܝܢ ܗܘܘ ܗܿܢܘܢ. ܐܟܚܕܐ ܗܘܬ ܠܒܪ ܠܡܕܝܢܬܐ ܕܐܝܟܐ ܣܘܣܝܬܐ
ܕܢܦܫܐ. ܘܣܓܝܐ ܕܡܫܟܚܐ ܕܒܝܫ ܡܬܩܢܝܢ ܗܘܘ. ܘܡܬܟܢܫܝܢ ܗܘܘ
ܒܬܕܡܘܪܬܐ.

(§67) ܘܡܕܒܪ ܒܗܘܢ ܟܕ ܒܢܫܐ ܕܐܟܣܢܝܐ ܐܬܟܢܫܘ ܠܘܬܗܘܢ܇
ܢܦܩ ܠܗܘܢ ܣܘܡܟܐ. ܘܟܕ ܙܒܢܐ ܐܠܨ ܗܘܐ܇ ܒܟܪܝܘܬܐ ܗܿܘܘ.
ܒܠܚܘܕ ܪܐܙܐܝܬ ܦܪܚܝܢ ܗܘܘ ܠܘܬ ܐܠܗܐ܇ ܟܕ ܡܬܟܢܫܝܢ ܗܘܘ
ܡܢ ܚܫܘܟܐ ܕܢܫܡܝܢ ܗܘܘ ܐܟܣܢܝܐ. ܟܕ ܒܠܗ ܕܝܢ ܠܐܦܣܬܘܩܐ
ܕܢܦܩܘܢ܆ ܕܕܠܩܐ ܡܕܡ ܥܛܝܢܐ ܡܢ ܚܫܘܟܐ ܐܬܓܠܝ ܘܦܩ܇
[R 47] ܒܠܗܘܢ ܡܐܢܐ ܕܓܠܐ ܒܠܚܘܕ ܡܢܗܘܢ ܐܫܬܟܚ ܐܕܝܫܐ ܗܿܘ
ܕܡܢܗܘܢ ܐܬܘܗܝ ܗܘܐ ܕܝܠܗ.

(§68) ܟܕ ܕܝܢ ܙܒܢܐ ܗܦܟܐ ܒܥܠܠܐ܇ ܟܕ ܗܟܝܠ ܡܦܠܓܝܢ ܗܘܘ

[1] Literally, "evil."

[2] Note the apocalyptic, somewhat threatening overtones in Rufus's text, who is signaling to his audience that God will also not be patient with those insulting anti-Chalcedonian saints at the time Rufus is writing the *Vita Petri Iberi*.

[3] Literally, "remained for them."

[4] The Syriac renders the Greek ξένοι (Raabe, 47 n. 1).

[5] See Gen 18:1–8. For a fuller discussion of Abraham as an exemplary model of hospitality for Peter the Iberian, see Horn, *Asceticism and Christological Controversy*, 275–77.

[6] The Syriac may render the Greek πάροικοι (Raabe, 47 n. 3).

illness[1] before this. [Thus] it became known to all the inhabitants of Jerusalem that, because of the insult done to those saints, God the Judge who was always helping them had not been patient.[2]

(§66) Thus the two of them lived alone in that place and still had the money that remained[3] from what they had been able to take when they left [Constantinople]. Although they already had distributed the greater part of it in every place to holy monks and to the poor, with the rest they planned to conduct good business, receiving and refreshing the pilgrims and the poor who were coming from everywhere to worship in the holy places. While they were thus able to provide enough for [their] necessities, they received pilgrims[4] in Abrahamic manner,[5] they [who themselves were] pilgrims and foreigners[6] and who had no experience at all in such services. Many times it happened that they would have as many as ten tables [for serving] in one day, particularly on solemn feasts. They alone waited[7] on them, [even] though they were [also] observing the vigil [of night prayers], for the cheerfulness of soul and the love of Christ by whom they were strengthened and comforted in a wonderful way were victorious over the weakness of [their] nature.

(§67) Once when a multitude of pilgrims had come together at their place, they found themselves lacking in supplies. As time was pressing, they began crying out in their heart secretly to God, ashamed by the hardship[8] [with] which the pilgrims were wearing [them] out. When they entered the pantry[9] to search if perhaps anything needful had been forgotten and remained, **[R 47]** each of the vessels was found full with that kind [of food] that earlier had been stored in it.[10]

(§68) After they had been engaged in receiving pilgrims

[7] The underlying Greek might have been μόνοι ὑπηρέτουν (Raabe, 47 n. 4).

[8] The underlying Greek might have been θλῖψις (Raabe, 47 n. 5).

[9] The Syriac transliterates the Greek ἀποθήκη, "granary," "magazine," or "storehouse."

[10] Literally, "that had belonged to it from earlier on." For comparable accounts of miraculous provisions of food, see also Besa, *Vita Sinuthii Archimandritae* 27–28, 139–143 (Leipoldt and Crum, 21, 61–63; Bell, 50–51, 81–82).

ܐܟܣܢܝܐ܂ ܠܣܢܐܬܐ ܡܛܠܝ ܐܝܟ ܕܝܢ ܩܪܝܒܐ ܣܓܝܐܐ ܘܛܠܝܐ܂ ܗܘ ܕܐܝܬܘܗܝ ܗܘܐ ܬܠܡܝܕܐ ܕܐܒܐ ܣܝܠܘܢܐ܂ ܗܘ ܕܐܦ ܒܡܠܘܗܝ ܠܚܒܝܒ ܗܘܐ܂ ܘܐܬܘ ܒܥܠܘ ܠܟܘܡܪܐ܂ ܘܐܬܪ ܢܬܕܪܫܘܢ ܒܗ܂ ܫܘܒܪܐ ܘܡܟܝܟܘܬܐ܂ ܟܕ ܐܡܪ ܠܗܘܢ܂ ܕܗܫܐ ܕܓܒܪܬܘܢ ܘܛܠܝܐ ܕܐܟܣܢܝܐ܂ ܠܐ ܡܫܟܚ ܦܠܚܢܐ ܕܢܘܟܪܝܘܬܐ܂ ܟܕ ܡܬܕܪܝܢ ܐܢܘܢ ܕܝܢ ܒܟܘܡܪܐ܂ ܗܕܐ ܐܪܐ ܚܢܝ ܐܢܫܝܢ ܕܐܝܬܝܢ ܟܘܡܪܐ܂ ܠܗܠܝܢ ܕܒܟܠ ܠܟܠܗܝܢ ܐܬܝܗܘܢ ܒܟܘܡܪܘܬܐ܂

(§69) ܟܕ ܓܠܘ ܗܟܝܠ ܠܚܕ ܡܢ ܟܘܡܪܐ ܩܕܝܫܐ ܒܟܠܗ ܡܫܬܡܫܢܘܬܐ ܘܫܥܒܕܐ ܘܚܪܘܬܐ ܡܕܒܪܝܢ ܗܘܘ ܢܦܫܗܘܢ܂ ܐܡܝܢܐ ܕܐܬܠܡܝܕܐ ܟܕ ܠܐ ܦܣܩܝ ܠܬܫܬܬܐ ܕܚܒܘܬܗܘܢ܂ ܐܬܬܢܝܚ ܕܢܝܚ ܐܒܘܗܝ ܡܢ ܐܝܟ ܕܒܝܘܬܗܘܢ ܘܪܘܚܢܘܬܗܘܢ܂ ܟܕ ܡܬܦܩܕ ܠܗܘܢ ܢܫܩܘܬܐ ܡܫܠܡܐ܂ ܐܦ ܕܝܢ ܒܬܪ ܡܢ ܢܝܚܬܐ܂ ܟܕ ܦܐܫ ܒܡܕܒܪܐ ܘܓܢܐ ܥܡ ܐܚܐ ܐܚܪܐ ܦܛܪܘܣ܂ ܒܗ ܠܗ ܕܡܘܬܗ܂ ܐܝܟܢܐ ܕܥܠܝܡܐ ܘܦܫ ܦܐܝܐ܂ ܗܘ ܕܝܢ ܟܕ ܒܠܚܘܕܘܗܝ ܒܝܬܐ ܠܦܠܣܛܝܢܐ܂ ܘܠܗ ܠܣܛܪܐ ܕܐܘܡܢܘܬܐ ܣܠܩ܂ ܒܗ ܐܩܝܡܘܗܝ܂ ܟܕ ܠܓܒܐ ܘܠܓܒܐ ܡܬܗܦܟ ܗܘܐ܂ ܟܕ ܡܬܕܪܟܝܢ ܕܝܢ ܐܚܐ ܘܡܬܦܫܩܝܢ ܕܡܢܐ ܗܝ܂ ܟܕ ܐܬܝܗ ܓܠܬܐ܂ ܘܓܒܐ ܒܡܠܬܐ ܙܥܘܪܐ ܟܕ ܐܡܪ܂ ܡܪܝ ܫܡܥܬ ܐܢܫ ܡܢ ܦܘܡ ܚܬܢܝ܂ ܗܕܐ ܕܒܗ ܥܡܪܬܐ ܘܢܝܚܘܬܐ܂ ܘܚܕܝܘܬܐ ܕܗܕܐ ܦܠܣܛܝܢܐ܂ ܘܡܫܡܫܝܢ ܠܗ ܢܦܫܐ܂ ܟܕ ܫܡܥ ܕܝܢ ܗܘ ܒܝܫܐ ܫܡܗ ܕܦܘܡܗ܂ ܡܚܕܐ ܠܐ ܡܬܚܙܝܢܐ ܗܘܐ܂

[1] On Zeno, see also *Pler.* 8 and possibly 52. *Apophthegmata Patrum* preserves eight sayings by Abba Zeno. For an English translation, see Ward, *Sayings of the Desert Fathers*, 65–67.

[2] Toward the end of the fourth century, a certain Abba Silvanus is attested at Gerar. *Apophthegmata Patrum* contains twelve sayings attributed to Abba Silvanus. For an English translation, see Ward, *Sayings of the Desert Fathers*, 222–24. For a specialized study, see van Parys, "Abba Silvain et ses disciples," 315–31, 451–80. On ascetic life at Gerar and environs, see also Sozomen, *Hist. eccl.* 9.17 (PG 67:1627–30; Bidez and Hansen, 407–8; Hartranft, 2:427).

[3] Literally, "performed."

[4] Advance in the ascetic life was usually achieved by first living in a community setting before the more advanced individual would strive to live a solitary life. Although the reference to children may be understood as a reference to Peter's and John's relatively young age, the presence of children in monasteries was not unheard of. See, e.g., Abba Poemen, who lived at Scetis with his two brothers, the younger of whom appears to have been staying with

for quite some time, eventually the holy Zeno,[1] the hermit and prophet who was a disciple of the great Silvanus[2] and who was renowned everywhere, advised them to enter again a [cenobitic] monastery and to receive further training through obedience and humility, saying to them, "Now that you have become experienced in[3] the reception of pilgrims, come, labor [in] the monastic way of life, [and] be instructed in a [cenobitic] monastery, for this is more profitable for those who are still children in age."[4]

(§69) Once they had entered one of the holy monasteries, they exercised themselves in all attentiveness, obedience, and Naziriteship,[5] so that the devil, since he could not bear the sincerity of their asceticism, acted cunningly to drag them down from the quality of their asceticism and of their good disposition,[6] by devising for them manifold temptations.[7] One day, when Abba Peter was standing in the choir and chanting with the brethren, [the devil] revealed to him a very beautiful naked woman in front of his eyes.[8] Although only[9] he [could] see the apparition,[10] he knew the vision was unchaste [and so] covered his face, turning hither and thither. The brethren were amazed and wondered what the cause of this [behavior] was. He cried out in a loud voice, saying, "Our Lord, Jesus,[11] remove this shameful and impure image and the abomination of this apparition from before my eyes and let me be by myself!" When the Evil One heard the name of our Savior, he immediately disappeared.

them while still a young boy. See *Apophthegmata Patrum*, Abba Poemen 180 (Ward, *Sayings of the Desert Fathers*, 222).

5 See above, *Vit. Pet.* §21 (R 13), with further references.

6 Literally, "cheerfulness."

7 Note that, although Rufus refers to "manifold" temptations, he goes on merely to single out one type, that of sexual temptations.

8 Literally, "in front of him."

9 The underlying Greek might have been μόνος. See Raabe, 48 n. 2.

10 The Syriac transliterates the Greek φαντασία, for the rendering of which Payne Smith (450) suggests, among others, "display," "ostentation," "imagination," or also "fancy," "phantasm," and "apparition."

11 Rufus presents Peter as entertaining a highly personalized relationship with Christ, given that Peter repeatedly addresses him as "Jesus." See also *Vit. Pet.* §53 (R 36).

(§70) ܟܕ ܥܒܪܘ ܕܝܢ ܙܒܢܐ ܒܗܘܢܐ ܐܝܟ ܡܠܟܐ ܕܡܫܝܚܐ ܐܝܠܝܢ܇
ܘܐܬܘ ܟܕ ܢܕܥܬܗ ܦܝܫܘ [R 48] ܠܒܪܝܗܘܢ܇ ܘܒܡܕܝܢܬܐ ܩܕܝܫܬܐ
ܒܥܠܝܬܐ ܫܪܝܢ ܗܘܘ. ܟܕ ܠܐ ܡܟܝܠ ܐܦ ܒܗ ܒܕܡܘܬܐ ܡܦܠܚܝܢ
ܗܘܘ ܐܟܣܢܝܐ. ܐܘܦ ܗܘܐ ܠܗ ܓܒܪ ܗܘ ܒܡܫܟܢ ܟܕ ܫܦܝܪ
ܐܬܦܪܣ. ܒܥܢܘܬܐ ܕܝܢ ܪܒܬܐ ܘܒܕܘܒܪܐ ܡܫܝܐ܇ ܫܪܝܢ ܠܗܘܢ
ܚܫܘܫ ܗܘܘ.

(§71) ܐܠܐ ܠܐ ܐܫܬܒܩ ܕܢܦܩܘܢ ܙܒܢܐ ܬܘܒ ܒܡܕܝܪܝܗܘܢ ܢܡܘܣܐ.
ܐܘܕܘܩܝܐ ܡܠܟܬܐ ܗܝ܂ ܕܐܬܬܝܗ ܗܘܬ ܐܢܬܬܗ ܕܡܠܟܐ ܡܗܝܡܢܐ
ܬܐܘܕܘܣܝܘܣ ܙܥܘܪܐ܆ ܟܕ ܠܡܬܢܐ ܫܩܠܬ ܕܡܐܠܝܢܐ ܗܝ܂ ܕܦܩܕܬ
ܐܬܐܡܪܬ ܗܘܬ ܡܢܗ. ܐܬܬܚܪܬ ܐܦ ܗܝ܂ ܠܥܠܝܬܐ ܘܠܡܕܝܢܬܐ
ܕܡܕܝܢܬܐ ܩܕܝܫܬܐ. ܐܝܟ ܗܝ ܕܐܬܡܗܐ ܦܪܘܫܐ܆ ܕܗܝ܂ ܒܥܘܡܩܗ
ܬܗܘܐ ܦܓܪܐ ܠܒܢܫܐ ܦܪܘܫܐ ܕܫܠܡܝܢ܆ ܕܡܫܝܚܐ ܡܠܟܐ
ܕܐܬܡܫܚܬܐ. ܟܕ ܕܝܢ ܡܠܟܬܐ ܡܗܝܡܢܬܐ܆ ܟܕ ܒܠܚܘܕ ܡܪ̈ܝܢܬܐ
ܒܓܒܪܬ ܐܪܥܐ܆ ܘܠܡܕܝܢܬܐ ܩܕܝܫܬܐ ܗܝ܂ ܕܐܬܐܪܟܐ ܗܘܬ ܐܬܬ܆
ܘܠܡܓܒܪܬܐ ܐܫܬܘܬܗ. ܟܕ ܠܦܩܬ ܕܝܢ ܕܐܦܠܐ ܦܠܛܪܘܣ ܬܘܒ ܚܕܪܐ܆
ܒܝܬ ܕܐܬܒܢܝܘܗܝ ܒܦܣܝܩܘܬܐ. ܐܝܟ ܡܪܥܝܬܗ ܕܒܪܫܒܬ ܚܘܒܐ
ܗܘܬ ܠܗ ܐܡܐ ܒܩܘܠܛܠܝܢ. ܗܝ ܕܝܢ ܡܕܡܟܢܬܐ ܡܩܒܠ ܗܘܐ
ܕܢܫܬܒܩ. ܕܗܝ ܡܠܬܗ ܠܐ ܢܦܩ. ܡܛܠ ܕܢܗܘܐ ܕܐ ܗܘܐ. ܟܕ
ܕܝܢ ܗܝ܂ ܚܙܬܗ ܟܕ ܐܡܪܬ܆ ܕܐ ܠܐ ܚܕܐ ܗܝ ܕܐܬܒܪܬܐ ܐܝܠܝܢ܇
ܗܝ܂ ܡܬܠܦܪܘܣ ܐܚܬܐ ܠܘܬܗ܆ ܟܕ ܟܬܒܬܐ ܕܡܥܒܪܬܐ ܗܝ ܬܗܘ
ܬܚܒܪ ܠܗ ܝܗܒ ܩܕܝܫܬܐ. ܟܕ ܕܒܠ ܗܝ ܢܘܪܐ ܘܗܝ ܚܣܡܐ
ܕܩܪ̈ܝܫܐ܆ ܢܦܩ ܚܕܐ ܙܢ ܘܡܛܠ ܒܗܝܢ. ܘܟܕ ܐܬܦܢܝܬ ܒܗ ܡܛܠ

[1] The text does not specify exactly where Peter the Iberian and John the Eunuch stayed during that time. Abba Zeno lived at Kefar She'artha (see *Vit. Pet.* §73 [R 50]).

[2] More literally, "with his knowledge."

[3] The Syriac might render the Greek ἡ κατοικία αὐτῶν and thus allude to Acts 17:26. See also Raabe, 48 n. 5.

[4] See above, *Vit. Pet.* §§39–46 (R 27–31).

[5] On that journey she visited Antioch, where she was celebrated as a gifted poetess.

[6] Other reasons advanced for Eudocia's pilgrimage include her desire to offer prayer and thanksgiving to God for the well-being of her daughter Licinia Eudoxia.

[7] Compare the visit of a Roman lady of senatorial rank to Abba Arsenius.

(§70) After they had spent time in the [cenobitic] monastery[1] following the advice of the holy Zeno, with his consent[2] they returned again **[R 48]** to their monastery and dwelt in quiet in the Holy City. Thenceforth they did not receive pilgrims in [their former] manner, as there was not enough money for it, since it had been well distributed. [Instead,] they wore themselves out in great asceticism and in harsh ways of life.

(§71) Yet it was not ordained that they should dwell[3] there for long. Empress Eudocia, who had been the wife of the believing Emperor Theodosius the Younger, having taken up the zeal of Melania, whom we mentioned earlier,[4] also yearned for quietude and to dwell in the Holy City, in order to be close to and to worship in person the saving passions of Christ, the King of Glory, [which he had suffered] for our sake. She made a journey carried about like a queen through all the cities[5] and came to the Holy City, for which she had a longing, and was esteemed worthy of worshiping [there].[6] When she learned that Abba Peter dwelt there, she anxiously sought to see him[7] as his foster-mother, because with loving affection[8] she had been a mother to him in the palace.[9] At first he asked to be allowed not to leave his cell, because he judged [it] a temptation.[10] She persisted, saying that if he did not wish to come to her, she by all means would come to him, being prepared to make [her] journey from where she stayed[11] to the holy [Church of] Zion. He [relented and] came out once and spoke with her because he feared the burdens and the envy of people. When

See *Apophthegmata Patrum*, Arsenius 28 (Ward, *Sayings of the Desert Fathers*, 13–14).

[8] The Syriac might render the Greek φιλοστοργία. See Raabe, 49 n. 1.

[9] Given that other historical sources portray Pulcheria as having taken on the role of a mother for her imperial siblings (see, e.g., Sozomen, *Hist. eccl.* 9.1), Rufus's emphasis on Eudocia's maternal concerns might arise from an attempt to contrast the Chalcedonian supporter with Eudocia as a caregiver of the leader of the later anti-Chalcedonians. For fuller discussion, see Horn, "Empress Eudocia and the Monk Peter the Iberian."

[10] Note again that temptation is closely connected to fear of potential contact with a woman.

[11] Instead of "from where she stayed," a more literal translation would be "from there."

ܒܝܫܘܬܗ ܦܪܗܣܝܐ: ܘܡܟܝܟܘܬܗ ܘܢܟܦܘܬܗ ܘܐܦ ܒܫܡܠܝܘܬܗ܂ ܫܡܥ
ܡܢܗ܂ ܕܬܠܡܝܕܝܢ ܒܪ܆ ܡܛܠ ܕܐܬܚܙܝܬ [R 49] ܚܙܝܬ ܠܝ܂ ܐܬܬܕܟܪܬ
ܠܡܠܬܟܝ ܡܫܝܚܝܬܐ܂ ܗܘ ܕܝܢ ܚܒܝܒܐ ܘܐܡܪ ܠܗ܂ ܐܢܐ ܦܪܪܗܣܝܐ
ܐܝܬ ܠܗ ܠܫܠܡܐ ܕܢܦܠܐ܂ ܗܘ ܕܝܢ ܐܡܪܬ ܠܗ܂ ܬܫܬܡܫܝܢ ܟܠ ܙܒܢ
ܒܪܝ܂ ܘܡܗܝܡܢܐ ܒܗ ܦܬܚܐ ܠܡܠܬܗ ܒܠܒܐ ܐܬܚܘܬܗ ܗܘܐ܂ ܒܗ ܕܝܢ
ܬܘܒ ܐܬܪܬ ܒܗ ܡܬܐܡܢܐ ܕܬܐܬܐ ܠܘܬܗ܂ ܡܫܪܝܐ ܙܕܩ ܠܘܬ
ܡܫܝܢܐ ܐܝܟ ܢܦܫܐ ܗܘ ܕܦܪܝܫ ܐܡܪܬ܂ ܘܐܡܝܢ ܕܐܝܬ ܗܘܐ ܠܗ
ܒܪܝܟ ܟܠܐ ܠܗ ܚܘܫܒܘܗܝ܆ ܒܟܠ ܐܦ ܓܒܪ ܒܥܡܗ ܡܬܕܒܪ ܗܘܐ܂
ܫܡܥ ܡܢܗ܂ ܫܘܒ ܢܦܫܝ܂ ܡܗܝܡܢܐ ܡܫܬܠ ܒܗ ܐܬܬܦܝܣ
ܠܡܠܬܗ܂ ܒܗ ܫܡܥ ܠܐܘܪܫܠܡ ܡܕܝܢܬܐ ܡܫܝܚܐ: ܘܕܝܢܗ ܫܡܥܗ̇
ܠܐܚܝܢ ܕܐܦ ܗܘܢ ܥܠܝܗ ܠܒܠܒܐ܂ ܐܝܟܐ ܕܐܝܬ ܚܒܪ ܒܡܘܫܐ܂
(§72) ܕܐܝܬ ܒܝܬ ܐܝܟ ܠܡܕܝܢܬܐ ܘܟܘܪܬܐ ܕܡܬܦܪܢܣܐ ܡܘܡܟܐ܂
ܕܡܠܝܐ ܗܘܐ ܒܗܘ ܙܒܢܐ܆ ܦܠܓܐ ܕܡܕܝܢܬܐ ܡܫܝܚܝܐ ܕܝܢܝܐ ܕܓܝܒܘ
ܘܡܫܬܡܥܝܢ܂ ܐܬܬܢܚ ܗܘܬ ܗܘ ܕܝܢ ܡܕܒܪܢܘܬܐ ܕܥܡܗ ܕܠܗܘ
ܐܬܪܐ܂ ܕܡܚܘܝܐ ܐܠܗܘܬܐ܂ ܕܐܠܗܐ ܗܘ ܚܫܒ ܒܟܠ ܘܡܫܘܦܐ
ܕܢܩܫܬ܂ ܕܦܪܝܩ ܙܒܢ ܠܗ̇ ܡܕܝܢܬܐ ܕܟܠ ܗܦܟ ܒܢܚܐ ܘܦܫܛ
ܒܫܠܝܐ܂ ܘܐܦ ܒܫܝܢܐ ܘܐܦܝܣܩܘܦܐ ܕܓܒܝ ܠܗ܂ ܒܙܒܢܐ
ܬܪܝܢ ܕܡܕܝܢܬܐ܂ ܕܫܒܩ ܟܠ ܒܢܝܢܐ ܕܐܢܫ ܗܘܐ܂ ܡܕܒܪܢܐ

[1] Compare Luke 10:42.

[2] The Syriac transliterates the Greek παρρησία. The usage of the term "boldness [of speech]" in Rufus's work is a characteristic of the authority gained by anti-Chalcedonian ascetics. John Rufus might have had in mind the use of this term in the Pauline literature. The term παρρησία is widely used in secular and Christian literature in antiquity. For helpful studies, see, e.g., G. Bartelink, "Quelques observations sur παρρησία dans la littérature paléo-chrétienne," in *Græcitas et latinitas christianorum primæva: Studia ad sermonem christianum primævum pertinentia: Supplementa* (Nijmegen: Dekker & van de Vegt, 1968), 3:7–57; and Erik Peterson, "Zur Bedeutungsgeschichte von παρρησία," in *Reinhold Seeberg Festschrift* (ed. Wilhelm Koepp; Leipzig: Scholl, 1929), 283–97. For a discussion of the relevance of the term in contemporary Chalcedonian literature in Palestine, see Hombergen, *The Second Origenist Controversy*, 108–12.

[3] This comment indicates that part of Peter's reluctance to meet with Eudocia was grounded in his fear to be caught up in activity and lose his ascetic quietness. See also *Vit. Pet.* §§138, 144 (R 103, 108).

[4] More literally, "again."

[5] The journey would have taken some time, given that Peter came from Jerusalem and Zeno was living in Kefar She'artha.

[6] One might also translate "preserve." See Payne Smith, 564.

she noticed in him his great serenity, his humility, his modesty, and also his wisdom, he heard her say, "Blessed are you, my son, because you have chosen **[R 49]** the good [portion] for yourself.[1] Remember me in your holy prayers!" He replied, "What boldness [of speech][2] does a sinner have to pray?" She said to him, "Your sins [be] upon my head, my son!" He then returned to his cell and remained in quiet.[3] On another occasion[4] she persisted, ardently desiring to come to him. Immediately he ran to the holy Zeno, the prophet, who was mentioned earlier.[5] As was his custom, he [Peter] revealed to him his thoughts, for he routinely discussed [matters] with him. He [Peter] heard from him [Zeno], "Rescue,[6] rescue your soul!" Thus obeying his advice, he left Jerusalem the Holy City and also handed over[7] his monastery to men who likewise had also cast off the world.

(§72) He came to dwell in the community that is between Gaza and the little town called Maiuma,[8] which at that time was full of many holy men, monks bearing their cross.[9] His migration to this place was guided by the divine care of God, the all-wise one and the guardian of our souls, who prepared in advance for this town, on the seashore and very Christian,[10] a high priest and bishop, one who was worthy of it [that is, of the episcopacy].[11] Especially in the time of the rebellion [this town] was in need of such

7 Literally, "left."

8 See also Theodosius, *De situ terrae sanctae* 3 (Geyer, 116,18–19): "Inter Ascalonam et Gazam civitates duas, id est Antedona et Maioma."

9 See Matt 19:21; Mark 10:21; Luke 14:33. While the command to carry one's cross was addressed to all Christians who wanted to follow Christ, and while ascetics, independent of their precise doctrinal affiliation, understood their ascetic efforts as ways of "carrying the cross," the connection between asceticism and the cross became a significantly differentiating mark of anti-Chalcedonian asceticism in Palestine. See Horn, *Asceticism and Christological Controversy*, 350–51.

10 The inhabitants of the port city of Maiuma adopted the Christian faith more readily and in larger numbers than their neighbors in Gaza. For the account of the Christianization of the region, including the resistance encountered in Gaza, see Mark the Deacon, *Vita Porphyrii Gazensis* (Grégoire and Kugener; Hill; for a recent abbreviated translation of important sections of the text into English, see Rapp, 53–75).

11 Rufus's audience would likely have heard a comment like that at the same time also as polemic against Juvenal of Jerusalem.

ܕܕܚܠܬ ܐܠܗܐ. ܘܟܗܢܐ ܐܡܝܢܐ ܘܫܠܝܚܐ ܕܡܦܝܣܢܘܬܐ ܬܪܝܨܬܐ
ܥܒܘܕܐ. ܘܐܝܟܢܐ ܕܫܠܦ ܢܦܫ̈ܬܗ. ܕܐܝܬ ܠܗ ܦܐܪܪܗܣܝܐ
ܡܬܟܠܢܘܬܐ ܠܘܬ ܡܪܢ ܕܢܚܘܣ ܥܠ ܚܛܗ̈ܐ ܕܥܡܐ ܐܝܟ ܕܟܬܝܒ.
ܘܕܡܟܝܟ ܕܚܫ ܥܡ ܡܚܝܠܘܬܢ̈. ܟܕ ܗ̇ܘ ܕܒܟܠܡ ܡܬܢܣܐ ܥܡܢ.
(§73) ܟܕ ܗܟܢܐ ܗܟܝܠ ܒܗܢܐ ܒܢܝܫܐ ܥܒܪ ܗܘܐ. ܐܡܝܢܐܝܬ
ܐܬܐ [R 50] ܗܘܐ ܚܕ ܒܢܝܢ ܒܪ ܩܠܝܬܗ ܠܘܬ ܐܒܘܢ ܩܕܝܫܐ.
ܘܗ̇ܘ ܙܒܢܐ ܥܒܪ ܗܘܐ ܒܟܦܪ ܣܥܪܬܐ ܩܪܝܬܐ. ܥܠ ܡܣܟܢܘܬܗ̈
ܡܬܐ̈ܠܐ ܡܢ ܟܐܒܐ. ܘܟܠܗܘܢ ܗ̈ܕܡܘܗܝ ܒܗܘܢ ܡܬܕܪܫ ܗܘܐ. ܘܬܘܒ
ܠܘܬ ܐܣܟܝܡܐܝܬ ܡܬܬܪܝܨ ܗܘܐ ܐܘܪܚܐ ܕܡܛܘܪܬܐ ܕܒܐܠܗܐ.
ܦܓܪ ܐܬܪܨ ܗܘܐ ܡܢܗ. ܘܡܢ ܟܘܡܪܘܬܗ ܢܦܩ ܗܘܐ. ܡܬܬܟܪܐ
ܗܘܐ ܗܟܝܠ ܗ̇ܘ ܦܓܪܐ. ܕܒܬܪ ܟܕ ܐܬܐ ܠܘܬܗ: ܚܙܐ ܗܘܐ ܗ̇ܘ
ܩܕܝܫܐ ܒܗܘ ܠܦܓܪܐ. ܘܟܕ ܐܬܩܪܒ ܠܘܬܗ: ܐܡܪ ܠܗ. ܦܓܪܐ. ܘܟܕ
ܥܢܐ ܒܫܠܡ ܐܒܐ: ܬܘܒ ܐܬܩܪܒ ܘܐܡܪ ܠܗ ܦܓܪܐ. ܘܒܙ̈ܒܢܬܐ ܕܬܠܬ
ܒܗ̇ ܒܙܒܢܬܐ. ܟܕ ܕܝܢ ܐܬܕܡܪܬ ܘܐܬܬܢܝܬ ܒܗ̇ ܐܡܪܬ ܠܗ. ܫܒܘܩ ܠܝ
ܡܪܝ: ܐܒܐ. ܠܐ ܝܕܥ ܐܢܐ ܕܠܡܢܐ ܐܢܬ ܘܫܐܠܐ: ܘܐܡܪ. ܐܝܢ.
ܐܝܢ. ܫܒܘܩ ܠܝ. ܘܟܕ ܚܙܐ ܦܓܪܐ ܝܠܕ. ܘܡܢ ܟܠܗ ܥ̈ܒܕܐ ܒ̈ܝܫܐ:
ܗ̣ܘܬ ܗܘܬ ܒܬܝܒܘܬܐ ܕܠܗ. ܘܟܐܢܐ ܗܘܐ. ܘܗ̇ܘ ܟܕ ܕܐܦܠܐ
ܗܕܐ ܒܫܠܡܐ ܢܦܩ.
(§74) ܟܕ ܒܕܒܠ ܥܒܪ ܗܘܐ ܗ̇ܘ ܒܡܕܒܪܐ ܩܕܝܫܬܐ: ܘܫ̈ܒܝܠ
ܩܫܝܐ ܗܟܝܠ ܒܟܢܝܫܘܬܗ. ܗ̇ܘ ܕܗ̇ܢܘܢ ܐܦܝܣܩܘܦܐ ܐܝܬ ܗܘܐ
ܠܗ: ܕܟܪܘܦܘܣܝܢܐ ܒܕܪܝܫܘܬܗ: ܠܐ ܐܬܚܙܝ. ܟܕ ܐܠܗܐ ܡܦܢܐ
ܗܘܐ ܠܗ. ܘܗܢܐ ܟܠܗ ܟܕ ܒܝܫܐ ܡܫܬܐܠܐ ܗܘܐ ܒܝܗܘ
ܩܕܝܫܬܐ. ܗܟܝܠ ܒܟܢܝܫܘܬܗ ܕܢܣܒ ܐܬܥܝܕ ܬܘܦܣܐ ܘܢܛܘܦܣܘܗܝ,
ܡܢ ܩܠܝܬܗ ܕܩܪܝܒܐ ܗܘܬ ܠܬܡܢ. ܘܟܕ ܚܙܝܢ ܗܘܘ ܕܢܐܬܐ:

[1] One might also translate "messenger" or "envoy." By describing Peter in both religious terms and the language of secular representation, Rufus's depiction of him carries political overtones. Raabe (51 n. 1) sees a parallel to Heb 3:1, although 2 Cor 5:18–20 is perhaps also implied here.

[2] See Heb 4:16; 5:3.

[3] See Heb 4:15.

[4] See Heb 5:3.

[5] Literally, "village of barley." For further references, see Tsafrir, Di Segni, and Green, *Tabula Imperii Romani*, 165.

a man, [one who was] at once a helper of the fear of God, a preacher and guardian of the orthodox faith, and an ambassador[1] on behalf of our souls, [who] possessed boldness before our Lord to [gain] pardon for the sins of the people,[2] as it is written, one able to suffer for our weakness,[3] in that he always makes supplication for us.[4]

(§73) While dwelling in this community, he would frequently come **[R 50]** with his cell-companion John to the holy Zeno, who at that time was dwelling in the village of Kefar She'artha,[5] about fifteen miles from Gaza, in order to discuss with him all his thoughts and to make straight [his] path of virtue in God [with] greater fervor.[6] [Peter] was much beloved by him [Zeno] and received [some] of his grace. The blessed one used to recount [to us],[7] "Once, when I came to him, the holy Zeno was standing for prayer. He turned to me and said to me, 'Pray!' When I remained silent, again he turned and said to me, 'Pray!' [He did this] three times in all. But I, amazed and worked up at this, said to him, 'Forgive me, my lord, Abba, do you not know that I am a layman and a sinner?' He said, 'Yes, yes, forgive me!' And when he had performed the prayer, he sat down."[8] Seven days later his [Peter's] own ordination[9] took place—and in what manner! It is fitting therefore that we should not pass this over in silence either.

(§74) When he [Peter] was still dwelling in the Holy City, Juvenal, who at that time was his bishop, many times attempted to ordain him and could not, since God was protecting him. [Juvenal tried] so hard [that] when a liturgy was being celebrated in the [Church of the] holy Zion, Juvenal dared to send select [men] to take him by force from his cell, which was nearby. When they

[6] Raabe (51 n. 6) suggests that the underlying Greek said κατεύθυνε θερμότερον τὴν τῆς ἀρετῆς ὁδόν.

[7] Rufus is recording what he had put to memory from Peter the Iberian's accounts of events in his life. Note that Peter seemed customarily to have talked about what had happened to him in earlier years.

[8] For a similar scene, see below, *Vit. Pet.* §118 (R 86).

[9] The Syriac transliterates the Greek χειροτονία. The genuine Syriac expression would have been ܣܝܡ ܐܝܕܐ. See Payne Smith, 213. Note that the Greek emphasizes the "stretching out" of the hand, while the Syriac has in view the "laying on" of the hand.

ܐܬܚܙܝ، ܠܗ ܡܠܐܟܐ ܘܐܡܪ ܠܗ. ܗܐ ܕܢܫܬܡܥܘܢ ܠܟܪܘܙܘܬܟ
ܐܢܫܝܢ. ܐܠܐ ܩܘܡ ܥܪܘܩ ܡܢ ܗܪܟܐ. ܘܟܕ ܗܟܢܐ ܥܒܕ. ܬܘܒ
ܚܦܝܛܐܝܬ ܢܛܪ ܗܘܐ ܢܦܫܗ.

(§75) ܟܕ ܗܟܝܠ ܥܒܪ ܒܐܬܪܐ ܕܗܣܘܡܟܐ. ܐܦܝܣܩܘܦܐ
[R 51] ܐܝܬܘܗܝ، ܗܘܐ ܗܝܕܝܢ ܕܗ، ܕܥܕܬܐ ܦܘܠܘܣ ܒܪ ܐܚܘܗܝ،
ܕܝܘܒܢܠܝܘܣ. ܫܠܚ ܠܗ ܕܒܫܘܪܝܐ ܕܡܟܘܪܝܗ ܕܐܬܡܢ. ܡܛܠܬܐ ܢܦܩ
ܗܘܐ ܠܗ ܗܘ ܦܘܠܘܣ ܠܛܘܒܢܐ ܦܛܪܘܣ. ܕܐܬܟܡܗ ܗܘܐ ܕܠܐ
ܢܣܝܡ ܟܠܗ، ܐܒܪܐ. ܟܕ ܗܘܬ ܗܫܝܪܘܬܗ ܕܐܦܝܣܩܘܦܐ ܩܕܝܫܐ:
ܕܒܡܕܝܢܬܐ ܕܟܘܦܪ ܗܘܕܐ ܥܒܪ ܕܒܡܬܐ. ܠܝܕ ܡܢ ܗܢܘܢ ܟܠܒܐ
ܪܐܙܐ. ܘܩܦܣܐ ܠܗ ܕܟܪܘܙܘܬܐ ܢܟܪ.. ܗܘ ܕܝܢ ܟܕ ܢܦܩ ܟܣܗ
ܡܕܝܢܬܐ ܠܛܘܒܢܐ ܐܢܝܢܘܢ ܪܫܝܢܐ ܗܘ ܕܟܡܪܐ: ܕܐܝܬܘܗܝ،
ܗܘܐ ܟܪ ܚܢܝܢܐ ܘܫܟܟܐ ܘܚܣܝܪܐ ܕܗܠܝܢ ܩܪܝܫܐ: ܟܕ ܗܢܐ ܟܠܐ
ܡܫܟܢܘܬܐ ܢܦܠ ܡܢܥܠ. ܘܟܪܘܙܘܬܗ ܟܕܪ ܩܫܝܫܐ ܠܬܪܝܗܘܢ:
ܟܡ ܡܛܪܐ ܣܓܝܐܐ ܘܟܢܝܫܘܬܐ. ܗܢܝܢ ܟܕ ܐܬܟܢܫܘ ܦܛܪܘܣ:
ܐܫܬܟܚ ܠܡܕܝܢܬ ܢܕܒܬܐ ܘܟܢܘܫܬܐ ܕܡܕܝܢܬܐ ܘܫܘ. ܟܕ ܗܘ ܘܟܕ
ܗܟܢܐ ܦܩܕ ܗܢܘܢ ܐܒܪܐ: ܫܩܠ ܩܢܘܡ ܦܛܪ ܟܕ ܠܐ ܝܕܥܐ ܕܐܬܥܒܕ
ܒܐܫܬܡܫܘܬܐ ܟܗܢܘܬܐ. ܟܕܡܐ ܕܐܦ ܠܐܝܩܪܐ ܕܐܦܝܣܩܘܦܘܬܐ
ܐܬܩܪܝ: ܒܝܕܐ ܕܡܪܕܘܬܐ ܘܕܒܘܪܐ ܕܟܠܗܘܢܐ.

(§76) ܟܕ ܚܪ ܐܫܬܪܝ ܒܟܠܗܘܢ ܒܟܘܪܐ ܕܟܢܫܬܐ: ܕܟܠܗܘܢ
ܡܠܝܢ ܐܦܝܣܩܘܦܐ ܡܕܝܢܬܐ: ܘܫܪܪܐ ܕܛܘܒܢܐ ܪܫܝܐ ܕܠܐܘܢ:

[1] See Matt 2:13. One could compare the flight of the Holy Family to Egypt.

[2] I.e., not to ordain him.

[3] Many saints and martyrs carried the name "Victor." The present Victor might be identified with Victor Stratelates, son of Romanus. See Michel van Esbroeck, "Victor Stratelates, Saint. Coptic Tradition," *CE* 7:2303–5; and Khalil Samir, "Victor Stratelates, Saint. The Copto-Arabic Tradition," *CE* 7:2305–8. The sixth-century Madeba Map pin-points the location of a

were about to arrive, an angel appeared to [Peter], saying "Behold, they are coming to take you for ordination: Get up and flee from here!"[1] [So Peter] fled and guarded himself [thenceforth] with [even] greater care.

(§75) While he was dwelling in the region of Maiuma, Paul, **[R 51]** the nephew of Juvenal, was bishop of that place. Not long after Peter had settled there, Paul sent [his] guarantee to the blessed Peter, who had asked him not to lay hand[s] on him.[2] Now, there occurred a synod of many bishops on the memorial [day] of Victor, the martyr of fair victory.[3] [There Paul] revealed [his] secret to one of them [i.e., one of those bishops present] and persuaded him to perform the ordination. That [bishop], however, took with him as helper the blessed Irenion, the abbot of the monastery, an intimate acquaintance and also a revered neighbor of these saints; using him he suddenly and unsuspectedly fell [upon them] and performed the ordination of both of them to priests with much force and resistance. When Peter later recalled [that event], he understood the foreknowledge and prophecy of the holy Zeno. Still, even though he had thus received the laying on of hand[s], for seven years he remained[4] unwilling to consider [himself as] in the priestly ministry, until he was also esteemed worthy of the honor of the episcopate in the time of the rebellion and transgression in Chalcedon.

(§76) When the rejection [of the faith] by the signature[s] of all those rebellious bishops, the ratification of the wicked *Tome*

shrine or church dedicated to St. Victor in the vicinity of Maiuma. For a discussion of the archaeological evidence and possible connection of that saint to the anti-Chalcedonian milieu, see Horn, "Peter the Iberian and Palestinian Anti-Chalcedonian Monasticism," 125–26; eadem, *Asceticism and Christological Controversy*, 213, 215.

[4] This information allows one to conclude that Peter was ordained to the priesthood in 445/446, assuming that his elevation to the episcopacy under Theodosius took place in 452/453.

ܘܣܘܕܬܐ ܕܝܘ̈ܠܦܢܐ ܒܝ̈ܫܬܐ ܕܢܣܛܘܪܝܘܣ: ܕܕܝܘܣܩܘܪܘܣ ܡ̇ܢ ܕܝܢ
ܐܦܝ̈ܣܩܘܦܐ ܕܐܓܘܦܛܘܣ. ܘܦܠܚܢܐ ܕܕܝܪ̈ܐ ܘܡܬܟܬܫܢܐ ܕܣܠܩ
ܕܣܠܩܬ ܐܠܗܐ: ܐܫܬܕܪ، ܠܐܟܣܘܪܝܐ. ܟܕ ܠܐ ܨܒܐ ܕܢܫܠܡ
ܠܛܘܡܣܐ. ܬܐܘܕܘܪܝܛܘܣ ܕܝܢ ܘܡܫܒܚܐ: ܗ̇ܘ ܕܡܢܗܘܢ ܕܗܠܝܢ
ܕܗܘܐ ܡܢ ܒܪܘ. ܚܒܝܫܐ ܗܘܬ ܡܐܬܪܗܘܣ ܕܠܗܘܢ. ܘܡܫܢܝܢ
ܡܛܠ ܟܠܝܘܬܐ ܕܪܘܫܥܗ: ܕܠܐ ܕܝܢܐ ܐܬܡܟܠܘ. ܘܦܠܒܝܢܘܣ
ܗ̇ܘ ܕܗ̣ܘܐ ܐܦܝܣܩܘܦܐ ܕܩܘܣܛܢܛܝܢܘܦܘܠܝܣ. ܕܡܛܠܬܗ̇ ܕܗܕܐ
ܠܐܬܐ ܗܘܬ ܡܐܬܪܗܘܣ ܕܠܗܘܢ. ܡܢ [R 52] ܒܬܪ ܣܗܕܘܬܗ ܗܦܟܘ
ܐܚܠܦܗ، ܘܝܘܒܢܠܝܘܣ ܕܝܢ ܗ̇ܘ ܕܡܬܐܡܪ ܪܫ ܟܘ̈ܡܪܐ ܕܐܘܪܫܠܡ:
ܟܕ ܫܠܡ ܠܟܢܝ ܢܚܘܣܐ ܘܐܘܕܝ ܒܗ ܐܒܕܐ: ܘܠܡܕܝܢܬܐ ܕܩܘܕܫܐ

[1] The *Tome of Leo* refers to the letter sent by Pope Leo the Great (440–461) to Bishop Flavian of Constantinople (447–449) in 449. The letter set out in detail why Leo opposed Eutyches' teaching that the person of the incarnate Christ consisted only of one, namely, the divine, nature. Leo formulated in the letter that Christ's one person was composed of two natures, one divine and one human. That formulation eventually was accepted as binding by the Council of Chalcedon. For reference to the critical edition of the text of the *Tome of Leo*, see above, xlvii n. 109.

[2] Nestorius was bishop of Constantinople from 428 to 431. His refusal to allow veneration of Mary as *Theotokos*, i.e., literally "God-bearer" or "Mother of God," caused great uproar. Eventually Nestorius was deposed by the Council of Ephesus in 431, for allegedly teaching that Christ was a "mere man," and was sent into exile. When the Council of Chalcedon formulated that Christ was "one person in two natures," Nestorius felt vindicated. Thinking along the same lines, anti-Chalcedonians opposed the council of 451 because they felt that it had revived Nestorius's teachings.

[3] Dioscorus was bishop of Alexandria from 444 to 451. In 449 he presided over the so-called "Robber Council" that worked toward the restoration of Eutyches and the deposition of Flavian of Constantinople. Flavian, who refused to sign the synod's declaration, died from beatings he received only a few days after the conclusion of the synod. Because of disorder that Dioscorus caused, he was deposed at the Council of Chalcedon in 451 and exiled to Gangra in Paphlagonia (also see *Vit. Pet.* §89 [R 62]). Among anti-Chalcedonians, Dioscorus continued to be venerated as a martyr. For an anti-Chalcedonian account of his life, see Theopistus's *Life of Dioscorus* (Nau, 5–108, 241–310).

[4] The Syriac transliterates the Greek ἐξορία.

of Leo,[1] and the renewal of the wicked teachings of Nestorius[2] were proclaimed everywhere, [it happened] that Dioscorus,[3] head of the bishops of Egypt, being both a zealous [defender] of the truth and a fighter on behalf of the fear of God, was cast into exile[4] as long as he was unwilling to consent to the ungodliness.[5] Theodoret[6] and Ibas,[7] whose deposition[8] already had been brought about by these same men and [who] had been put under anathema because [their beliefs] revealed [Nestorius's] ungodliness, were accepted without trial.[9] [Even a]fter [his] death, they again took in Flavian, bishop of Constantinople, whose deposition **[R 52]** had taken place for this [same] reason. Juvenal, however, who was called[10] high priest of Jerusalem, having consented to

[5] On Rufus's portrayal of Dioscorus, see also *Vit. Pet.* §§83, 89, 97 (R 58, 62, 70); and *Pler.* 7, 14, 16, 21, 25, 59, 66, 68, and 69.

[6] Theodoret was bishop of Cyrrhus from 423 to 457/8 or 460 or 466. In the christological conflict between Nestorius and Cyril of Alexandria, he defended a two-nature Christology, in line with many other theologians from Antioch's area of influence. Deposed and exiled by Dioscorus and the Robber Council in 449, Theodoret was restored to his see in 451. Together with Theodore of Mopsuestia and Ibas of Edessa, Theodoret was the third of the *Three Chapters* who were anathematized in 553 under Emperor Justinian. Not all of Theodoret's writings were condemned, only works in which he opposed Cyril of Alexandria and the Council of Ephesus. Much of his work on biblical commentary and asceticism has survived. See, e.g., Robert C. Hill, trans., *Theodoret of Cyrus: Commentary on Daniel* (SBLWGRW 7; Atlanta: Society of Biblical Literature, 2006).

[7] Ibas was bishop of Edessa from 435 to 449 and again from 451 to 457. Based on the views he expressed in his famous letter to Mari, a bishop in Persia, Ibas was attacked for holding Nestorian convictions. The so-called Robber Council of 449 condemned him, whereas the Council of Chalcedon restored him to his office. Ibas's letter was finally condemned as one of the *Three Chapters* by the Second Council of Constantinople in 553. Yet the position Ibas advanced appears to have been one of mediation between Nestorianism and the orthodoxy promoted by Chalcedon.

[8] The Syriac transliterates the Greek καθαίρεσις, which Payne Smith (524) translates as "deposition, degradation from office."

[9] At the Council of Chalcedon.

[10] Note how the author here is challenging Juvenal's claim to the bishop's throne of the Holy City.

ܡܫܠܡܢܐ ܒܪܡ ܢܦܩ܇ ܦܓܥ ܒܗ ܪܘܚܐ ܣܛܢܝܐ. ܟܕ ܝܗܒ ܦܘܡܗ ܕܢܫܡ
ܠܣܘܢܗܕܘܣ ܐܝܟ ܠܗܿ ܕܡܬܐܡܪ ܠܗܝܡܢܘܬܐ ܕܠܐܘܢ. ܘܠܛܘܡܣܐ
ܕܟܡ ܚܠܫ. ܘܦܩܕ ܠܟܠܗܘܢ ܠܟܗ̈ܢܘܗܝ ܘܠܕܝܪ̈ܝܐ ܕܦܠܣܛܝܢܐ ܟܕ ܐܡܪ.
ܕܢܩܒܠܘܢ ܐܝܬܘܗܝ ܘܕܢܫܡܥܘܢ ܢܦܫܐ ܬܘܕܝܬܐ ܕܐܝܬ ܒܗ܇ ܘܗܘ
ܕܝܠܦ ܠܗ܇ ܘܗܐ ܠܗ ܕܢܬܦܪ.

(§77) ܘܟܕ ܗܠܝܢ ܐܫܬܡܥ ܗܘ,[1] ܠܟܠܗܘܢ ܘܠܕܝܪ̈ܝܐ ܘܡܗܝ̈ܡܢܐ
ܕܦܠܣܛܝܢܐ܇ ܟܕ ܡܬܬܙܝܥܝܢ ܒܛܢܢܐ ܐܠܗܝܐ. ܠܘܩܕܡ ܢܦܩܘ
ܠܐܘܪܚܗ ܕܗܿܘ ܡܚܒܠܢܘܬܗ ܠܐܘܪܫܠܡ. ܘܦܓܥܘ ܐܬܚܒܩܘ ܠܗ
ܕܢܬܦܢܐ ܠܟܠܗܘܢ܆ ܘܢܫܠܐ ܠܪܥܝܐ ܘܬܬܟܬܫ ܥܠ ܫܪܪܐ. ܟܕ ܠܐ
ܐܬܦܢܝܘ. ܐܬܟܢܫܘ ܐܟܚܕܐ ܠܡܕܝܢܬܐ ܩܕܝܫܬܐ܇ ܟܕ ܐܝܬ ܠܗܘܢ
ܒܡܨܥܬܗܘܢ ܠܒܪܢܫܐ ܡܫܒܚܐ܇ ܗܿܘ ܕܐܬܦܩܕ ܒܗ ܗ̇ܘ ܡܢ
ܪ̈ܫܝܥܐ. ܡܚܕܐ ܕܝܢ ܠܥܕܪܐ ܕܝܠܗ ܘܠܡܕܝܢܬܗ ܬܪܝܨܬ ܫܘܒܚܐ܇ ܗܿܘ
ܕܦܪܩܗ ܒܕܡܗ. ܘܟܕ ܡܢ ܠܒܘܬܗ ܡܬܢܦܫܝܢ܇ ܘܐܝܟ ܒܥܝܢܘܗܝ
ܘܐܦܝ̈ܣܩܘܦܐ ܐܪܬܘܕܘܟܣܘ ܫ̈ܪܝܪܐ. ܘܩܕܝܫܐ ܪ̈ܗܒܢܐ ܐܝܟ
ܕܕܝܪ̈ܝܐ. ܟܕ ܚܙܘ ܠܛܘܒܢܐ ܬܐܘܕܘܣܝܘܣ ܡܢ ܬܐܟܠܬܐ ܩܕܝܫܐ܇
ܓܒܪܐ ܕܒܕܘܒܪ̈ܐ ܕܕܝܠܬܐ ܡܢ ܠܛܘܒܢܘܬܗ ܐܬܟܢܫܘ܆ ܘܒܟܠܗܘܢ
ܡܗܝܡܢܬܐ ܕܕܝܠܗ ܡܢܝܐ ܡܚܝܐ. ܘܡܢ ܒܗܘ ܐܟܘܬܐ ܩܛ̈ܠܐ.
ܘܗܢ ܒܗܝܡܢܘܬܐ ܪ̈ܥܝܬܐ ܢܒܘ܆ ܥܠ ܡܫܝܚܘܬܗ ܬܪܝܨܬ ܫܘܒܚܐ.

[1] MS A has a lacuna here. MS B and Raabe read ܗܘܐ.

[2] I.e., Juvenal signed the documents of Chalcedon. For references to his signature to the texts, see Horn, *Asceticism and Christological Controversy*, 80–81.

[3] On Judas's betrayal of Jesus, see Matt 26:14–16, 20–25, 47–50; 27:3–5; Mark 14:10–11, 18–21, 42–45; Luke 22:3–6, 21–23, 47–48. According to Zachariah Rhetor, *Chron.* 3.3 (Brooks, 1:155–57; Hamilton and Brooks, 49–50), imperial flattery, pressure, and the promise "that he would give the three provinces of Palestine to the honor of the See of Jerusalem" (Brooks, 1:156,18–19; Hamilton and Brooks, 49) motivated Juvenal to set his signature to the documents of Chalcedon.

[4] For Simon the Magician, see Acts 8:9–24. In early Christian literature, Simon the Magician is regarded as the arch-heretic. See also *Pler.* 20, 25.

[5] Anti-Chalcedonian polemic employed anti-Jewish language to express its contempt of the teachings of Chalcedon, which from an anti-Chalcedonian perspective employed again the same disbelief concerning Christ's divinity that Jews had shown and continued to show. See also *Pler.* 14, 20, 25, 63.

the transgression of the law and set [his] hand to it,[2] and preferring the portion of Judas the betrayer,[3] returned with much pomp, even though before going up to the council he had rejected what is called the *Tome of Leo*, scoffing at the ungodliness that is in it and testifying to all the clergy and monks in Palestine, saying, "It is Jewish," and, "In it is Simon the Magician's opinion,"[4] and, "He who consents to it deserves to be circumcised."[5]

(§77) When these things were heard by the clergy and the holy monks in Palestine, being agitated by divine zeal they first went out to confront Juvenal on the road.[6] They very earnestly entreated him to remember his words and to reject the ungodliness and to fight on behalf of the truth. When he was not persuaded,[7] they gathered together in the Holy City, having our Lord Jesus Christ in their midst,[8] who was denied by the godless ones but who helps his truth and his orthodox church, which he has redeemed by his blood.[9] Inspired by his grace and having with them both zealous orthodox bishops[10] and the holy Romanus, the father of the monks,[11] they chose the blessed Theodosius[12] from the holy rank,[13] a man who from his childhood pursued with diligence the ways of life of monasticism and [who] was adorned with all the gifts of the fear of the Lord. He already had proven himself in

6 For a further description of that same event, see also *Pler.* 10, 56.

7 Zachariah Rhetor, *Chron.* 3.3 (Brooks, 1:157; Hamilton and Brooks, 50): "[Juvenal] showed himself like Pilate, saying, 'What I have written, I have written.' "

8 See Matt 18:20.

9 1 Pet 1:18–19.

10 These seem to have been bishops of Palestine who did not go with Juvenal to the Council of Chalcedon and who were later not replaced by anti-Chalcedonian bishops selected by Theodosius.

11 On Romanus, see below, *Obit. Theod.* §§2, 8–12 (B 21, 25–27). See also *Pler.* 10, 25, 39, 87. Romanus shares the title "father of the monks" with Longinus (*Vit. Pet.* §91 [R 64–65]), Hilarion (§137 [R 101]), and Abba Isaiah (§§167–168 [R 124]).

12 On Theodosius, see below, *Obit. Theod.* §§1–7 (B 21–25). See also *Pler.* 25, 29, 54, 56, 91. For Theodosius's ascension to the episcopal throne of Jerusalem and his tenure, see Horn, *Asceticism and Christological Controversy*, 85–92. For a discussion of Theodosius's career, see Perrone, *La chiesa di Palestina*, 89–103, 114–16.

13 The Syriac transliterates the Greek τάγμα.

ܐܦܝܣܩܘܦܗܘܢ، ܕܪ̈ܗܒܢܐ ܘܪ̈ܘܚܢܐ ܕܡܕܝܢܬܐ ܩܕܝܫܬܐ ܐܘܪܫܠܡ. ܗܘ
ܕܗ̣ ܢܦܫ ܒܡܘܬܐ ܡܢ ܐܠܗܐ: ܒܡܫܒܠܢܘܬܐ ܟܠܗ̇ ܚܝܦܘܬܐ
[R 53] ܘܫܘܠܛܢܐ ܥܒܕ ܗܘܐ. ܕܒܢ̈ܬܐ ܕܬܫܘܬܗܘܢ، ܕܕܒܝܬܐ
ܬܬܒܪ ܗܝܡܢܘܬܐ ܫܠܝܚܝܬܐ. ܟܕ ܟܒܫܐ ܗܘܐ ܡܢ ܬܐܟܒܐ
ܕܕ̈ܝܢܐ ܡܪ̈ܝܪܐ ܘܥ̈ܡܠܝ ܢܦܫܐ: ܒܢ̈ܝܐ ܡܪ̈ܝܪܐ ܗܢܘܢ ܕܬܬܪܐܬ
ܡܬܬܗܕܝܢ ܒܟܠܗ ܕܗܢܐ ܐܘܪܫܠܡ ܘܗܝܡܢܘܬܐ ܕܠܐ ܡܘܡ.
ܠܗܠܝܢ ܒܟܘܪ̈ܐܦܝܣܩܘܦܐ ܥܒܕ. ܐܦ̈ܝܣܩܘܦܐ ܘܩܫ̈ܝܫܐ. ܠܟܠ ܕܝܢ ܡܕܝܢܬܐ
ܗܘ ܕܐܠܝܨ ܗܘܐ ܠܗ̇ ܥܕܪܐ. ܟܕ ܗ̣ܘ ܒܥܬܐ ܕܟܠ ܡܕܝܢܬܐ ܒܒܪ.
ܗܘܐ ܦܘܩܕܢܐ ܘܠܗ̇ܘ ܕܡܬܒܥܐ ܡܢܗܘܢ. ܗܘܝܐ ܗܘ ܡܢ ܟܠܗ̇
ܫܘܬܐ ܘܝܘܪܐ ܡܬܦܪܫܝܢ. ܟܕ ܒܪ ܒܟܘܪ̈ܐܦܝܣܩܘܦܐ ܥܒܕ ܗܘܐ: ܗܘ
ܦܠܢܛܪܐ ܒܬܪ ܠܐ ܕܗܘܬ ܡܦܩܕ ܗܘܐ ܠܗܘܢ ܠܗ̇ܘܢ
ܕܒܟܘܪ̈ܐܦܝܣܩܘܦܘܬܐ ܗܘܢ: ܟܕ ܐܡܪ. ܕܗܘܝܐ ܒܟܘܪ̈ܐܦܝܣܩܘܦܐ ܥܒܕ.
ܐܝܟ ܠܒܗܘܢ: ܘܒܢ̈ܝܐ ܕܗܝܡܢܘܬܐ ܬܪܝܨܬ ܫܠܝܚܝܐ. ܗܘ ܟܕ ܙܒܢ
ܥܠ ܐܦܝܣܩܘܦܐ ܕܕܐܝܟ ܗܠܝܢ ܗܘܢ.
(§78) ܗ̇ܝܕܝܢ ܡܚܝܠ ܚܒܪܐ ܕܡܘܬܐ ܕܒܟܘܪܐ: ܟܕ ܡܬܬܒܥܝܢ ܡܢ
ܒܢܝܐ ܐܠܗܝܐ: ܘܢܕܝܢ ܠܗ ܠܝܘܒܢܐ ܦܠܛܘܣ ܡܢ ܙܒܢܐ ܗܟܢܐ
ܕܠܘܬܗܘܢ ܚܒܪ ܗܘܐ: ܘܟܠ ܐܕܝܢܐ ܕܡܬܒܪܬܐ ܡܢܘܬܐ: ܡܥܕܐ
ܟܕ ܙܒܢܐ ܟܠܗ ܒܡܟܐ ܠܐܬܪܐ ܕܚܒܪ ܗܘܐ ܒܥܠܡܬܐ ܣܠܩܘܗܝ،

[1] Underlying the Syriac expression may be the Greek ἐπεδείξατο ἀγῶνας. See Raabe, 53 n. 6.

[2] Pulcheria, "Letter to Strategios, Governor of Bithynia" (*ACO* 2.1.1:29; 2.3.1:21), constitutes evidence for the presence of monks from Palestine at the council. See also Horn, *Asceticism and Christological Controversy*, 79.

[3] I.e., the real source of authority for Theodosius's actions is his being empowered by God. Rufus likewise presents Peter the Iberian as relying directly on God as the ultimate source of authority. See the discussion in Horn, *Asceticism and Christological Controversy*, 142–43.

[4] Literally, "under him."

[5] That concern for purity of faith was central to the anti-Chalcedonian opposition to Chalcedon is well illustrated also at *Pler.* 18.

[6] Compare Eusebius of Caesarea, *Hist. eccl.* 7.32 (Schwartz and Mommsen, 2:730,6–7): πολιτείας εὐαγγελικῆς.

[7] One notices here the first institutional actions of the establishment of a separate anti-Chalcedonian church in Palestine. See the comments in Horn, *Asceticism and Christological Controversy*, 86–88.

many contests on behalf of the orthodox faith,[1] including in the godless synod.[2] They appointed him high priest and shepherd of the Holy City, Jerusalem. Having received the priesthood from God,[3] he worked with all diligence, **[R 53]** attention, and care so that in the churches under his authority[4] the apostolic faith should be kept pure.[5] He chose from the rank of the holy and cross-bearing monks holy men who were especially confirmed in every evangelical way of life[6] and blameless in faith, [and] ordained them bishops[7] and martyrs.[8] After the people of each city themselves had cast a vote,[9] he sent to each city the one who was suitable for it and whom they [the people] had chosen,[10] [and] each was received with all joy and exultation. When he was performing the ordination, with a loud voice this patriarch[11] bore witness to those who were being ordained, saying, "I am ordaining you martyrs and preachers of the orthodox faith, for this time requires such bishops."[12]

(§78) At that time then, the inhabitants of Maiuma, Gaza,[13] at once ran as a whole people to where the blessed Peter was dwelling in quiet, since they were moved by divine power and had known him [during] the long period while he was dwelling with

[8] I.e., witnesses for the faith. The Syriac translates the Greek for either μάρτυρες or ὁμόλογοι, the former being the term more commonly rendered by the Syriac word.

[9] The Syriac seems to transliterate the Greek ψήφισμα. See Payne Smith, 452, according to which ܦܣܝܦܝܣܡܐ can also be translated as "decree" or "act."

[10] In the early church, the voice of the laity had greater weight in electing a new bishop.

[11] The Syriac transliterates the Greek πατριάρχης. That term came into usage in the Christian realm only after the Council of Chalcedon. Rufus here identifies Theodosius of Jerusalem with that title, although he uses it interchangeably with "archbishop" (see *Vit. Pet.* §79 [R 55]). Among the Jews, the title "patriarch" or *nasi* was used for the *ethnarchos* of the Jews until 425 C.E., when it was abolished by the Roman authorities.

[12] For a discussion of the centrality of language of persecution and martyrdom in Rufus's work, see Horn, "Weaving the Pilgrim's Crown."

[13] The Greek may have formulated ὁ Μαϊουμᾶς Γάζης. See Raabe, 54 n. 5.

ܒܗ. ܩ̈ܠܝܬܐ ܡܢ ܐܬܬܚܕܬ ܠܦܘܠܚܢܗܘܢ. ܘܬܪ̈ܥܐ ܐܚܝܕ ܘܐܘܪܓ. ܒܗ
ܒܝܐ ܕܐܝܟ ܚ̈ܢܘܩܐ ܐܬܐ ܠܘܬܗ. ܒܬܪ ܕܝܢ ܒܗ ܩܠܝܠܐ ܩܠܝܬܐ
ܘܢܘܟܐ: ܗ̣ܘ ܒܒܝܬܐ ܕܒܘܪܗ، ܘܠܒܝܫܗ، ܘܟܠܗܠܝܢ ܦܘܫܗܘܢ. ܘܒܗ
ܩܠܝܬܐ ܕܢܫܝܐ ܕ̈ܝܪܝܐ: ܘܗ̣ܘ ܠܦܘܪܩ ܘܒܝܬܐ ܩܠܝܬܐ ܐܝܟ ܕܒܝܬܐ
ܒܗܘ ܕܢܦܩ ܠܗܘܢ. ܐܬܬܘܗܝ، ܠܟܢܫܬܐ ܡܕܝܢܬܐ: ܕܬܡܢ ܡܢ
ܪ̈ܒܝܢܐ ܕܒܢܘܬܐ ܒܗܘܢ ܠܟܢܫܐ ܕܠܗܘܢ ܘܐܦܝܣܩܘܦܐ. ܒܗ
ܕܝܢ ܒܐܘܪܚܐ ܪ̈ܒܝܢ ܗܘܘ: ܘܡܢ ܒܗ ܪܡܫܐ ܦ̇ܢܝܢ ܗܘܐ. ܐܬܐ
ܠܡܕܝܢܬܐ ܕܡܬܩܪܝܐ ܣܘܟܐ. [R 54] ܗܝ ܕܝܢ ܡܢ ܒܦܘܬܗܐ ܕܟܠ
ܚܢܝܢ ܒܝܘ. ܠܗ ܕܝܢ ܠܡܪܢܐ: ܒܠܬܐ ܡܕܡ ܚܠܝܐ ܕܠܗ ܕܒܪܝܬܐ
ܚܕܝܘ ܕܒܪܬܐ: ܒܗ ܗܝ ܕܝܢ ܕܡܢ ܕܐܬܩܘܢܗ، ܘܒܗ ܦܠܛ ܠܠܝܐ:
ܘܡܢ ܣܘܟܘܗܝ، ܐܠܝܢ ܗܘܐ ܘܐܟܠ ܠܗ ܠܒܗ: ܒܕܠܝܬ ܚܘܪ ܡܢ
ܢܘܪܐ ܐܚܪܢܐ ܕܦܪܝܫܬ ܐܚܪܬ: ܘܕܠܐ ܥܘܕ ܠܐܝܣܪܐ ܕܒܗܘܢܬܐ
ܢܣܒ ܗܘܐ ܗ̣ܘ ܠܗ: ܐܬܢܣܒ ܕܢܦܩܬ ܡܬܪܐܬ ܐ ܐܠܝܐ: ܐܘ
ܕܢܦܠ ܡܘܒܠܐ ܕܐܝܟ ܗܕܐ. ܘܒܗ ܥܒܬܐ ܕܠܐ ܥܒܬܐ ܐܬܬܚܕܬ:
ܘܟܠܗܘܢ ܠܟܝܢ ܡܢ ܒܟܠܐ ܕܐܘܪܚܐ: ܘܡܢ ܥܒܬܐ ܐܒܝܕܝܢ: ܥܡܠ
ܡܢ ܗܠܝܢ ܕܢܬܪܝܢ ܠܗ ܕܢܦܫܗܘܢ ܠܗ: ܕܢܦܩ ܠܕܘܟܬܐ ܕܐܟܪܐ ܕܗܘܕܡ
ܚܠܒܬܐ: ܐܝܟ ܕܠܡܫܝܚܬܐ ܦܪܘܫܬܐ. ܘܒܗ ܗ̇ܝ ܐܦܣܘܣ: ܘܢܦܩ
ܒܠܝܠܘܗܝ: ܙܒܢ ܕܢܒܙܐ ܢܦܫܗ ܡܢ ܙܘܥܐ: ܠܕܘܟܬܐ ܕܒܐܦܩܐ

1 For a fuller discussion of Peter the Iberian's role as bishop of Maiuma, see Horn, *Asceticism and Christological Controversy*, 89–91.

2 Contrast the different behavior Jesus displayed at the time of his arrest: Matt 26:51–55; Mark 14:47–49; Luke 22:49–53; John 18:4–11. For a recent study of the motif of resistance against ordination in early Christian literature, see G. Schöllgen, "Flucht vor dem Bischofamt: Anlässe und Motive," paper delivered at the Fourteenth International Conference on Patristic Studies, Oxford, August 2003.

3 The Syriac transliterates the Greek λεκτίκιον. See Payne Smith, 245, suggesting as translation "litter," "bier," "pyx," or "portable altar."

4 I.e., they expected that Theodosius of Jerusalem would ordain Peter as bishop for Maiuma.

5 Sokha (Khirbet Shuwaikah) was located between Eleutheropolis and Jerusalem, nine miles away from Eleutheropolis. See also Eusebius, *Onom.* (Klostermann, 156,18–20; Freeman-Grenville, Chapman, and Taylor, 86): Σοκχώ. κῶμαί εἰσι δύο. ἀνιόντων ἀπὸ Ἐλευθεροπόλεως εἰς Αἰλίαν, ἐν τῷ ἐνάτῳ

them and [was] manifesting every kind of virtue.[1] They took him by force, despite [the fact that] he struggled very much against them and shut and barred the doors when he saw that they were coming upon him like robbers.[2] Nevertheless, with great force and love this people carried him and put him on a litter,[3] while a multitude of the well-known officials, the clergy, and many people who imitated and followed [after] them, brought him to the Holy City so that there they would be counted worthy of their shepherd and bishop by the high priest of the priesthood.[4] While they were traveling on the road and evening was already approaching, they came to a village called Sokha.[5] **[R 54]** They took lodging in inns[6] nearby, but the saint they made lodge in the upper chamber of a house in the village itself, together with some who were able to guard him. In the middle of the night, tormented by his thoughts and eating up his heart because he had always fled from honor, as I have said before, and considering himself unworthy of the honor of the priesthood, he very much had in mind to die if necessary rather than to accept such a burden. In the dead of night,[7] while all of them were wearied from the hardship of the journey and were overcome by sleep, he asked those who were guarding him to allow him to go out on the balcony[8] in front of the upper chamber to relieve a bodily need. When they let [him go] and he had gone

σημείῳ, ἡ μὲν ἀνωτέρα, ἡ δὲ κατωτέρα, Σοκχὼθ χρηματίζουσαι. φυλῆς Ἰούδα: "Sokhō. There are two unwalled villages, going out from Eleutheropolis toward Aelia [i.e., Jerusalem] at the ninth marker; one that is higher up and one that is below; [also] called Sokkheth. [Both are located within the territory of the] tribe of Judah." For further references, see Tsafrir, Di Segni, and Green, *Tabula Imperii Romani*, 234; see also Pietro A. Kaswalder, *Onomastica Biblica: Fonti scritte e ricerca archeologica* (CMSBF 40; Jerusalem: Franciscan Printing Press, 2002), 283.

[6] The Syriac renders the Greek πανδοκίον or πανδοχεῖον, which Payne Smith (440) suggests can refer to an "inn," "tavern," or "hostelry." See also *PGL*, 1001, 1002.

[7] Literally, "when the hour came, which [is] not the hour." The Syriac seems to translate the Greek ὥρα ἄωρος = ἀωρία, which has been understood as μεσονύκτιον. See Raabe, 55 n. 3. See also *Vit. Pet.* §32 (R 22).

[8] Literally, "to a place of the roof."

ܕܐܚܬ ܠܬܚܬ. ܟܕ ܡܫܕܠ ܕܫܕܐ ܡܢ ܬܪ̈ܬܝܢ ܟܪ̈ܥܐ. ܐܦ ܕܡܢ
ܠܦܛܪܘܣ ܕܢܥܪܘܩ. ܐܦ ܟܕ ܡܫܬܪܚ. ܘܠܐ ܢܚܫܚܐ ܗܘ̇ܐ: ܢܫܬܠܡ ܡܢ
ܦܛܪܐ ܕܪ̈ܥܘܬܢ ܕܕܒܪܝܢ ܠܗ. ܟܕ ܕܝܢ ܟܠܬ. ܗܘܐ ܕܗܘܐ ܢܓܕܝ: ܗܘ̇ܝܐ
ܘܠܐ ܠܗܬܡ ܕܐܡܪ. ܦܛܪܐ ܦܛܪܐ. ܐܢ ܗܕܐ ܬܥܒܕ: ܠܝܬ ܠܟ
ܡܢܬܐ ܥܡܝ. ܘܗܟܢܐ ܟܕ ܐܬܓܠܝ ܡܢ ܫܡܝܐ: ܐܬܕܪܟ ܠܐܘܪܫܠܡ.
ܘܟܕ ܩ̈ܛܝܠܬܐ ܟܢ ܗܘܬ ܥܒ̈ܕ: ܘܠܢܦܫܗ ܡܦܛܪ ܗܘܐ: ܘܡܬܠܬܐ
ܩ̈ܛܝܠܬܐ ܡܚܫܒ ܗܘܐ: ܕܐܟܪ̈ܝܗܘܬ ܕܠܐ ܫܘܐ ܠܟܗܢܘܬܐ ܡܫܡܫ
ܗܘܐ ܕܡܚܘܝܐ ܢܦܫܗ: ܘܠܗ̇ܘ ܕܒܥܠ ܗܘܐ ܕܒܪܘܦܣܝܐ ܢܚܒܘܗܝ،
ܡܫܡܫ ܗܘܐ.

(§79) ܒܬܪ ܟܕ ܡܢܗ ܕܐܦܝܣܩܘܦܘܬܐ ܐܠܗܝܬܐ ܦܫܩܐ ܘܒܪܘܦܣܝܐ
ܡܛܠ. ܐܟܠܐ ܗܟܝܠ ܣ̈ܓܝܐ ܕܢܦܩܘ. ܐܠܐ ܟܕ ܗܘܬܐ ܒܗܝܠܬܐ
ܐܬܒܥܝܘ. ܠܐ ܠܗܘܢ ܡܟܝܠ [R 55] ܠܬܫܡܫܬܐ. ܟܕ ܟܠܗܘܢ ܡܦܝܣܝܢ
ܘܡܬܟܬܫܝܢ ܗܘܘ ܘܗ̇ܘ ܒܐܦܝܣܩܘܦܘܬܐ. ܟܕ ܟܕܐ ܬܘܒ ܕܡܢܗ ܕܒܬܪ ܩܠܐ
ܐܠܗܝܬܐ ܐܬܚܙܝ ܠܗ ܘܐܬܦܩܕ ܠܗ. ܘܗܟܢܐ ܟܕ ܟܢܫܐ ܡܬܪܥܠܐ
ܒܟܪܝܘܬܐ ܡܙܝܥܬܐ ܗ̇ܘ ܕܡܬܒܪܝܢ ܫܠܝܚܐ: ܗܘ ܡܢ ܢܦܫܗ ܟܕ.
ܟܠܗܘܢ ܡܬܒܪܝܢ ܘܡܬܟܬܫܝܢ. ܢܦܩ ܟܕ ܪܗܛ. ܘܐܬܛܫܝ ܥܡ ܙܢ

[1] See Matt 4:5–6; Luke 4:9–10.

[2] Early Christian canons stipulate that in certain cases a physically impaired person cannot be ordained. See, e.g., *Canons of Nicaea*, canon 1 (Henry R. Percival, *The Seven Ecumenical Councils of the Undivided Church: Their Canons and Dogmatic Decrees* [NPNF 2/14; Grand Rapids: Eerdmans, 1979], 8); *Arabic Canons of Nicaea*, canon 1 (Percival, *Seven Ecumenical Councils*, 46); *Apostolic Canons* 22 and 23 (Percival, *Seven Ecumenical Councils*, 595); see also *Canons of Nicaea*, canon 9 (Percival, *Seven Ecumenical Councils*, 23).

[3] The repetition of the name "Peter" could be an allusion to John 21:15–17, where Jesus repeatedly asks Simon Peter whether he loves him.

[4] See John 13:8.

[5] According to Zachariah Rhetor, *Chron*. 3.4 (Brooks, 1:158–59; Hamilton and Brooks, 51–52), Peter accused himself of being a heretic.

[6] That Rufus here speaks of "priesthood" and not of "episcopate" re-

out alone, he ran to throw himself from the height [on]to a rocky place below,[1] expecting that one of two things would happen: either he would escape by all [possible] means, or, being maimed and [therefore] unfit,[2] he would be released from the coercion of [his captors], who were taking him [for ordination]. [Just] when he was about to [jump], a voice came to him saying, "Peter, Peter,[3] if you do this, you [will] have no part with me!"[4] Thus, being prevented from [his] attempt, he was taken to Jerusalem. There he stirred up many [charges], accused himself,[5] and called forth several objections by which he hoped to demonstrate that he was unworthy for the priesthood.[6] He even called to witness [against him] the one who was about to ordain him.

(§79) Nevertheless, although he received from divine grace itself the decree and ordination,[7] not even then did he wish to serve. Rather, he shut himself up in the priest's residence.[8] From the first, he refused to accept **[R 55]** [the task of conducting] the [eucharistic] service, although everyone, even the patriarch[9] himself, was persuading and earnestly entreating [him], until he was again threatened and commanded by the divine voice. When the [eucharistic] service was celebrated in the holy church of what is

flects his idea that Peter did not accept the previous ordination at the hands of Juvenal's nephew Paul, then bishop of Maiuma, and of Abba Irenion as valid. Only when Peter was ordained as bishop by Theodosius of Jerusalem did he also become validly ordained as priest.

7 Note again how God's power and grace are considered to be the ultimate source of authority.

8 Literally, "the priestly place." Likely a reference to a separate house set aside for the use of the priest. That separate place was located in or in the neighborhood of Jerusalem. If Rufus intended to speak of the sacristy of a given church, he could have chosen a distinct word for that.

9 The titles "patriarch" and "archbishop" are used interchangeably in this text, reflecting the still relatively novel introduction of the first title into the early Christian vocabulary used for members of the hierarchy. See also *Vit. Pet.* §78 (R 53) with p. 113, n. 11.

ܐܦܝ̈ܣܩܘܦܐ ܘܥܡ ܐܦܝ̈ܣܩܘܦܐ ܕܫܪ̈ܒܐ. ܟܕ ܢܦܩܘ ܠܡܩܒܠܗ
ܟܠܗܘܢ. ܒܚܕܘܬܐ ܘܪܘܙܐ ܘܒܙܡܝܪ̈ܬܐ ܘܡܫܒܚܝܢ ܗܘܘ ܠܐܠܗܐ.
ܐܚܝܕܝܢ ܗܘܘ ܕܝܢ ܒܒܥܘܬܐ ܣܓܝܐܬܐ܆ ܘܒܡܕܪ̈ܫܬܐ. ܕܕܠܒܪܐ ܗ̣ܘ
ܡܒܬܐܠܝܢܘܬܐ ܒܠܒܬܐ ܬܗܘܐ ܕܒܫܠܐ ܕܩܕܝܫܬܐ. ܟܕ ܕܝܢ ܐܬܐ
ܠܒܝܬܐ ܩܕܝܫܬܐ ܕܫܝܠܘܚܐ. ܟܕ ܡܢ ܟܠܗܘܢ ܡܬܕܚܩ܁ ܢܦܩ ܟܠ
ܬܪܘܣܦ ܒܫܒܒܐ ܟܐܒ ܢܘܚܐ. ܟܕ ܒܐܪܐ ܪܒܐ ܘܡܪܫܐ ܘܡܫܝܚܐ
ܘܫ̈ܒܐ ܗ̣ܘܐ ܠܢܦ̈ܫܬܐ ܕܟܠܗܘܢ. ܘܟܕ ܡܦܪܣܗ ܒܟܠܐ܁ ܘܟܠܫ
ܡܬܪܚܩ ܗܘܐ ܕܝܢ ܐܝ̈ܕܘܗܝ ܩ̈ܕܝܫܬܐ ܢܫܬܘܦ ܠܬܐܪܐ ܦ̈ܘܡܐ.
ܬܘܒ ܡܢ ܢܟܦܘܬܐ ܣܓܝܐܬܐ ܡܬܬܚܙܐ ܗܘܐ܁ ܕܗ̣ܘ ܢܦܩ. ܐܠܐ
ܘܟܕ ܠܗܘܢ ܠܐܦܝ̈ܣܩܘܦܐ ܘܠܩܠܝ̈ܪܝܩܐ ܡܦܣ ܗܘܐ܆ ܕܐܦ ܬܫܡ̈ܫܬܐ
ܩ̈ܕܝܫܬܐ ܢܫܠܡܘܢ܆ ܠܐ ܠܡܩܡ ܝܓܠܐ ܕܢܦܩܘܢ ܩܕܡ ܡܕܒܚܐ ܩܕܝܫܐ
ܘܐܘܪܫܠܡ ܩܕܝܫܬܐ ܢܒܛܠܐ܁ ܒܟܡܐ ܕܐܫܬܝܩ ܗܘ ܒܥܕܬܐ ܘܠܐ
ܘܐܩܪ̈ܒܘܗܝ܁ ܕܐܦ ܫܢܝܐ ܗܘܬ. ܕܟܣܝܘܬܐ ܡܬܢܟܦ. ܘܐܬܡܠܟ ܟܕ
ܚܙܡܢ܁ ܕܢܩܕܘܢ ܠܗ ܘܠܥܕܬܐ܁ ܐܝܟ ܕܠܐ ܢܫܠܠܐ ܠܗܘܢ ܚܝܐ.
ܘܗܟܢܐ ܟܕ ܐܬܦܢܝ̱ ܡܢ ܩܕܡ ܡܕܒܚܐ ܩܕܝܫܐ.܀

(§80) ܗܠܝܢ ܕܝܢ ܡܘܕܥ ܗ̇ܘ ܕܬܪܬܐ ܢܦܪܐ. ܙܟܘܬ ܫܟܒܘܪܬܐ ܕܝܢ
ܕܐܠܗܐ ܘܪܘܚܢ̈ܐ ܐܢܫܘܬܗ ܘܢܝܚܘܬܗ ܒܐܝܪܢܣܝܐ ܬܬܒܪ ܘܬܬܦܪܥ
[R 56] ܒܝܠܕܘܬܗ. ܠܦܢܝܐ ܘܠܫܝܪܝܐ ܕܡ̈ܫܡܫܢܐ. ܘܠܡܣܟ̈ܢܐ
ܕܗܝܡܢܘܬܐ ܬܪܝܨܬ ܫܘܒܚܐ. ܗܠܝܢ ܟܕ ܕܝܢ ܫܡܥܝܢ: ܘܗܢ ܒܪܬ
ܘܠܐ ܕܠܗ ܕܡܠܟܐ ܐܬܬܦܝܣܘ: ܘܗܢ ܩ̈ܠܝܬܐ ܗܠܝܢ ܕܗܕܝܢ
ܡܕܒܪܝܢ ܗܘܘ ܘܒܗܘܢ ܡܟܗܢܝܢ ܗܘܘ܁ ܠܐ ܡܫܟܚܝܢ ܚܢ ܕܢܫܬܘܩ. ܡܛܠ
ܒܪ ܕܠܐ ܒܪܒܝܠ ܟܕ ܠܒܠܝܐܬ ܬܪܥܐ ܗܘܐ ܠܬܐ̈ܢܬܐ ܩܕܝܫܬܐ: ܘܠܐ
ܦܪܩ ܐܬܬܚܙܝ: ܡܢ ܥܠ ܐܬܐܠܝ ܕܢܦܩ ܩܕܡ ܡܕܒܚܐ: ܘܬܫܡܫܬܐ

[1] This refers to the church built at the Pool of Shiloah (today known as *Birkat Silwan*). Before 451, Empress Eudocia had a basilica erected at the site. That building is represented on the Madeba Map (ca. 575). Antoninus Martyr (sixth century C.E.) also saw a church and a pool there. See Antoninus Placentinus, *Itinerarium* 24–25 (Geyer, 141–42). Today a mosque, built after 1896, is standing over the site of the ancient Byzantine remains. See Bieberstein and Bloedhorn, *Jerusalem*, 3:22–23; W. Harold Mare, "Siloam, Pool of," *ABD* 6:24–26; idem, *The Archaeology of the Jerusalem Area* (Grand Rapids: Baker, 1987), 241–43; Hillel Geva and Michael Avi-Yonah, "Jerusalem. The Byzantine Period," *NEAEHL* 2:772–73, with comments on "The Church of Siloam"; and Robert Wenning, "Schiloach," *LTK* 9:145.

[2] Literally, "he himself."

[3] I. e., in August.

called Shiloah,[1] Peter[2] ran out, leaving everyone amazed and astounded. They were gathered with the archbishop and with the rest of the bishops when they all came out toward him in joy and exultation and with marvel, praising God. For they were seized in great distress and in anxiety that perhaps this refusal should be a cause of offense to many. Yet once he had arrived at the holy Church of Maiuma, being carried about by all, he sat on the throne on the seventh of the month of Ab,[3] when there took place a great, holy, and heavenly feast and life for the souls of each of them. The people hurried and everyone desired earnestly to partake of the saving mysteries[4] from his holy hands. [Yet] again out of great modesty he demurred from making the oblation himself. Even though he was giving assent to the bishops and the clergy to celebrate the holy services, he [himself] at first was not willing to stand before the holy altar and celebrate the holy Eucharist until the people became vexed and indignant and anticipated what was in fact true: that he was contemplating flight.[5] They ran [after him], threatening to set him and the church on fire if he would not celebrate the [eucharistic] service for them.[6] Being so compelled, he stood before the holy altar.

(§80) May he who has understanding understand [what follows] from here on.[7] May the greatness of God's care and his love for humanity and his power be preached with freedom [of speech] and be declared **[R 56]** everywhere for the conviction and confirmation of the believers and for the establishment of the orthodox faith! We cannot remain silent [about] those things that we have heard[8] and [about which] we were instructed by the utterance of the blessed one and by many of those who at that time were near [to him] and were serving as priests with him. Although he was

[4] I.e., receive the Eucharist consecrated by Peter. Reception of the consecrated eucharistic gifts from the hands of Peter became a unifying moment of the anti-Chalcedonian community in Palestine.

[5] Much of Peter's traveling can be characterized as a reaction in response to threat or as an attempt to escape an oppressing situation. Thus the motif of flight is significant throughout the *Vita Petri Iberi*.

[6] Here one catches a glimpse of the often and readily violent nature of human interactions in situations of conflict within the early Christian world.

[7] See Matt 19:12.

[8] See 1 John 1:1–3.

ܡܕܝܢܬܐ ܢܨܝܚܬܐ: ܒܗ ܕܫܠܝܬܐ ܗܦܟܐܬܐ ܘܣܘܪܕܪܐ ܘܪܬܝܬܐ: ܒܪ
ܡܫܡܫ ܠܘܬܗ ܘܐܬܪܝܡ ܡܢ ܩܠܝܪܘܣ: ܕܡܫܡܫܝܢ ܕܢܬܗܕܘܢ ܐܢ ܗܘ
ܕܡܢ ܗܠܝܢ ܕܙ̈ܕܩܢ ܢܬܒܪܘܢ܆ ܟܕ ܡܠܐܟܐ ܚܙܝܐ ܘܩܒܠ ܦܘܬܐ ܕܪܘܚܐ
ܩܕܝܫܐ: ܘܟܠܗ ܐܢܐܦܘܪܐ ܫܡܠܝ܆ ܟܕ ܐܬܐ ܠܘܬ ܩܨܝܐ ܕܣܒܠܐ
ܕܠܚܡܐ: ܒܗ ܟܠܗ ܫܒܚܬܐ ܘܥܘܩܐ ܕܠܒܐ ܘܕܡ̈ܥܐ ܩ̈ܒܠܐܬܐ:
ܐܝܟ ܕܐܦܠ ܗܘܐ ܠܗ ܒܢܝܐ܆ ܟܠܗ ܗܘܐ ܓܒܪ ܕܗܟܢܐ ܟܕ ܓܢܐ܆
ܐܚܪܢܐ ܕܟܠܗ ܦܬܘܪܐ ܡܕܒܚܐ ܢܬܪܘܦ. ܘܗ̇ܘ ܟܕ ܐܬܬܘܗ ܘܒܪܬܝܬܐ
ܗܘ̣ܐ ܥܠ ܠܒܣܬܪܗ܆ ܘܠܐ ܡܫܟܚ ܐܡܪܝܢ ܕܢܬܩܪܒ܆ ܠܡܕܒܚܐ ܕܗܠܝܢ
ܠܫܘܒܚܐ ܕܫܪܒܐ. ܘܟܕ ܡܬܦܪܣ ܗܘܐ ܐܬܦܠܝ܆ ܘܣܝܡܗ ܠܡܪܝܐ
ܕܡܚܐ ܥܠ ܓܒܗ. ܘܡܠܒܒ ܠܗ ܘܐܡܪ ܠܘܬܗ. ܐܦܝܣܩܘܦܐ ܡܢܝ
ܠܐ ܬܕܚܠ. ܡܛܠ ܫܘܒܚܐ ܕܝܠܟ ܚܕܪܬ ܗܕܐ܆ ܘܠܐ ܡܛܠ ܗ̇ܘ ܕܝܠܟ.
ܕܢܐܠܦ ܟܠ ܐܢܫ ܕܐܝܟܢܐ ܐܬܘܗܝ ܕܚܝܠܐ܆ ܘܡܢܘ ܐܬܬܝܗܘܢ ܗܠܝܢ
ܕܡܫܡܫܝܢܬܐ ܬܪܝܨܬ ܫܘܒܚܐ ܐܝܬܝܗ. ܗ̇ܝ ܡܛܠ ܬܕܡܘܪܬܐ ܕܗܕܝܢ
ܗ̇ܘܬ. ܒܫܘܡܠܐ ܕܟܠܗ ܡܬܬܢܝܚ ܒܗܕܐ ܠܫܘܡܥܐ.
(§81) ܟܕ ܗܘ܆ ܗܟܝܠ ܒܒܪܬܐ ܡܕܝܢܬܐ ܕܟܠܗ [R 57] ܐܝܟ ܕܒܢܐ
ܕܫܬܐ ܫ̈ܢܝܢ܆ ܟܕ ܟܠܗܘܢ ܡܕܒܪܢܐܝܬ ܘܕܝ̈ܪܝܢ ܘܒܗܘܢ ܠܦܘܠܚܐ
ܠܡܕܒܪ̈ܢܘܬܗ ܕܡܫܝܚܐ ܡܕܒܪܢܝܬܐ: ܥܠ ܥܘܕܪܢ ܓܒܝܢܐ ܕܐܠܗܐ
ܘܡܫܡܫܢܘܬܐ ܕܡܛܠ ܙܟ ܒܬܒܐ ܕܐܝܟ ܗܢܐ: ܘܐܝܟ ܕܒܡܠܐܟܐ
ܐܫܬܪܝ ܠܗ ܘܦܠܓ ܒܪܘܚܗ ܘܒܢܦܫܗ. ܐܟܠܡܢܝܐ ܗ̇ܘ ܡܬܚܒܫ
ܒܗ ܐܠܗܐ ܘܢܫܡܥܐ: ܗ̇ܘ ܡܬܚܫܒܢܐ ܡܕܒܪܢܐ ܘܡܫܠܡܢܐ ܘܫܡܫܐ
ܕܡܬܚܫܒܢܐ. ܟܕ ܠܐ ܡܫܬܪܒ ܠܡܢܐ ܒܠܗ ܥܘܒܕܐ ܕܐܠܗܐ:
ܘܦܘܪܫܢܐ ܕܬܫܡܫܬܐ ܢܩܝܐ: ܟܕ ܕܚܝܠ ܕܕܠܚܐ ܡܦܩܕܢܐ ܢܗܘܐ:
ܕܐܝܦܘܬܐ ܕܒܠܒܐ ܐܬܛܝܒܬ ܒܟܠܡܘܬܐ ܠܗܘܒܠ ܕܝܒܠܐ ܐܠܗܐ:

[1] Rufus here captures the sense of awesomeness and reverence with which Peter approached the Eucharist, and which would be expected of his followers in the anti-Chalcedonian community as well.

[2] Literally, "if any of those things that are right."

[3] Note the separate mention of the *epiklesis*, the prayer asking for the descent of the Holy Spirit, who transforms the gifts of bread and wine into the body and blood of Christ. The invocation of the Holy Spirit continues to be a distinguishing mark of Eastern Christian liturgies.

[4] For other eucharistic miracles, see, e.g., *Pler.* 10, 65, 70, 77, 86.

[5] Henry Chadwick ("Eucharist and Christology in the Nestorian Controversy," *JTS* NS 2 (1951): 145–64) has shown the centrality of questions of

not yet reciting well the holy prayers and had not previously studied them, he was suddenly forced to stand in front of the altar and celebrate the holy service with great fear, terror, and trembling,[1] while some members of the clergy stood by him to remind [him] if he should leave out anything necessary.[2] When the moment arrived, he made the invocation of the Holy Spirit and completed the whole [prayer of the] Eucharist.[3] When he came to the fearful breaking of the bread, with all groaning and anguish of heart and many tears, as was his custom, so much blood burst forth when he broke [it], so that the holy table was sprinkled all over.[4] He was astounded and in trembling and drew back, no longer daring to apply himself to the breaking of the rest of the [loaves of] bread. He quickly turned and saw the Lord standing at his side, encouraging him and saying to him, "Bishop, break [it]! Do not be afraid! I did this for the sake of my glory and not for yours, so that everyone may learn where the truth is and who possesses the orthodox faith."[5] This miracle that took place at that time is [still] recounted by everyone's mouth to today.

(§81) [Peter] stayed in his holy church **[R 57]** for a time of about six months, while everyone was feasting and leaping for joy and calling the inhabitants of the city of Maiuma blessed because of the good pleasure of God and the protecting care of such a high priest. They were holding him up like an angel and were hanging on his compassion and on his love. [But] the devil, [who] fights against God and is envious,[6] that first rebel[7] and adviser and patron of rebels,[8] because he could not endure to see such great praise of God and the salvation of humans because he was afraid that perhaps there would be a reversal[9] [of the deed] that [his] diligence had contrived in writing at Chalcedon against the fear of

soteriology and the sacraments for the christological controversies of the early fifth century.

[6] The underlying Greek text may have formulated θεομάχος καὶ βάσκανος. See Raabe, 57 n. 2.

[7] The underlying Greek may have used the term ἀποστάτης. See Raabe, 57 n. 3. See also below the expression for "rebellious dragon," *Vit. Pet.* §88 (R 62).

[8] Here Rufus also implies that the Chalcedonians are to be regarded as disciples of Satan.

[9] The Syriac seems to translate the Greek μεταβολή. See Raabe, 58 n. 1.

ܬܘܒ ܟܕ ܥܠ ܒܡܠܟܐ ܗܘ ܕܗܕܝܢ ܐܝܟ ܗܘܐ: ܘܡܠܟܐܝܬ ܥܒܕ
ܗܘܐ ܠܦܘܩܕܢܘܗܝ܆ ܡܚܕܐ ܠܗ ܟܕ ܦܘܩܕܢܐ ܡܠܟܝܐ܆ ܠܪ̈ܫܝ ܟܢܘ̈ܫܐ
ܦܩܕ ܕܪ̈ܝܫܐ ܘܡܪ̈ܝܫܐ ܐܬܪ̈ܘܬܐ ܕܕܚܠܬ ܐܠܗܐ܆ ܗܢܘܢ ܕܐܬܬܩܝܡܘ ܡܢ
ܬܐܘܕܘܣܝܘܣ ܪܒܐ ܘܡܠܝܣܝܐ ܪܫ ܟܗ̈ܢܐ: ܒܟܠܗܝܢ ܡ̈ܕܝܢܬܐ
ܕܦܠܣܛܝܢܐ ܢܬܪ̈ܕܘܢ ܡܢ ܟܘܪ̈ܣܘܬܗܘܢ܆ ܘܐܢ ܗܘ ܕܠܐ ܢܨܒܘܢ
ܒܡܠ̈ܬܐ ܢܦܩܘܢ܆ ܘܒܣܝܦܐ ܢܬܩܛܠܘܢ. ܗܘ ܕܝܢ ܪܫ ܕܟܘ̈ܡܪܬܐ
ܬܐܘܕܘܣܝܘܣ܆ ܐܝܟܐ ܕܗܘ ܕܡܫܬܐܠ܆ ܫܘܒܚܐ ܕܪܫܘܬܗ ܢܣܒܘܠ܆ ܟܕ
ܗܘ ܕܡܬܢܛܪܐ ܗܘܐ ܡܢܗ ܕܡܠܟܐ ܦܘܪܩܢܐ ܐܦ ܠܟܠܗܘܢ܆ ܟܕ ܗܘ
ܐܝܟܐ ܠܟܠܗܘܢ ܐܣܩܘ ܘܥܩܒܘ܆ ܕܗܕܐ ܢܓܠܝܢ ܗܘܐ ܗܘ ܦܛܪܝܪܟܐ
ܬܐܘܕܘܣܝܘܣ. ܒܕܕܐ ܕܥܦܪܐ ܠܐܠܗܐ ܡܠܠܘ܆ ܕܢܬܒܛܠܘܢ
ܪ̈ܘܚܐ ܕܫܪ̈ܪܐ܆ ܘܠܐ ܟܕ ܫܠܡܝܢ ܘܡܬܦܠܠܝܢ܆ ܢܬܚܙܘܢ ܒܡ̈ܪܚܐ
ܐܘܪ̈ܬܕܘܟܣܘ ܡܢ ܗܠܝܢ ܕܐܚܝܢ ܠܗܘܢ܆ ܘܡܣܡܟܝܢ [R 58] ܠܗܘܢ.
(§82) ܗܢܝܢ ܗܘ ܠܡܠܟܐ ܦܛܪܘܣ: ܟܕ ܥܠ ܠܐܦܣܩܘܦܘܣ: ܘܡܪܒܝܢܐ
ܕܐܠܗܐ ܠܡܕܝܢܬܐ ܕܐܠܟܣܢܕܪ̈ܝܐ ܐܬܐ: ܘܬܡܢ ܡܠܟ ܗܘܐ:
ܒܡ̈ܥܪܬܐ ܕܦܪܛܘܪܝܘܣ ܗܘ ܡܪܘܕܐ܆ ܫܡܥܢ ܘܒܥܐ ܐܢܐ ܠܟܠܗܘܢ
ܐܘܪ̈ܬܕܘܟܣܘ ܗܘ ܗܘܐ. ܘܟܕ ܐܝܟ ܠܐ ܡܬܒܪܝܢ ܗܘܐ ܕܢܬܒܢܐ.
ܠܐ ܡܠܟܘܬܐ ܘܠܐ ܕܝܢܐ ܡܢ ܗܘܢ ܕܐܚܝܕܝܢ ܥܕܪ̈ܐ. ܗܘ ܟܕ

[1] Throughout the *Vita Petri Iberi*, the notion of the "fear of God" is a characteristic element of anti-Chalcedonian spirituality. This also means that their opponents are seen as violating the necessary reverence and fear that God demands.

[2] I.e., Emperor Marcian. Born into modest circumstances around 392, Marcian joined the military and served in various parts of the empire, including North Africa and Lydia, eventually also in Constantinople. The imperial chief of staff, Aspar, and Theodius II's sister, Pulcheria, collaborated in bringing Marcian to the throne of the Eastern Empire in 450 via a marriage to Pulcheria that allowed her to stay faithful to her vow of virginity. In the face of ongoing theological dispute, Marcian summoned an ecumenical council on 23 May 451 that was scheduled to meet at Nicaea on 1 September but had to be postponed to October and relocated to Chalcedon. Thus Marcian's name was forever connected with the recognition of imperial support granted to the Fourth Ecumenical Council of Chalcedon in 451. Marcian died in 457.

[3] Under Theodosius's tenure of the See of Jerusalem, the Chalcedonian bishops of Jerusalem, Scythopolis, and Ashkelon were replaced with anti-Chalcedonian ones. Severianus of Scythopolis had been assassinated. See *Martyrologium Romanum*, 21 February (Cuthbert Johnson and Anthony Ward, eds., *Martyrologium Romanum: Reimpressio integra textus officialis cum*

God,[1] entered the emperor[2] who at that time was ruling and [who] readily listened to his commands. He made him [issue] an imperial decree to the holy and true high priests, [those] zealous for the fear of God who had been appointed by Theodosius,[3] the great and apostolic high priest, [that] they should be removed[4] from their thrones in all the cities of Palestine and if they were unwilling they would be expelled by force and be subject to punishment, whereas Theodosius, the head of the shepherds, where[ever] he be found, should suffer capital punishment,[5] since the emperor issued what is called a *forma*[6] against him.[7] At that time all [the bishops of the anti-Chalcedonians in Palestine] relented and left [their sees], this being what the Patriarch Theodosius advised in that he judged it more pleasing to God that the preachers of the truth should be preserved and not [that] when they would die and be slain the orthodox faithful would be deprived of those who had edified them and sustained **[R 58]** them.

(§82) At that time, when the blessed Peter[8] departed for Egypt and by the will of God came to the city of Alexandria and was hiding there in the days of Proterius, that rebel,[9] he became a support and consolation for all the orthodox. And while no one from those who were holding on to the truth and lay in hiding

emendationibus et variationibus usque ad Concilium Oecumenicum Vaticanum II convocatum effectis necnon nova introductione aucta [BELS 97, Instrumenta liturgica quarreriensia 7; Rome: C.L.V.-Edizioni Liturgiche, 1998], 44). On Leontius of Ashkelon, see *Pler.* 52. Theodosius selected several anti-Chalcedonian leaders of monasteries and bishoprics, including Abba Romanus (Monastery of Tekoa), Marcianus (a monastery near Bethlehem), Bishop Peter the Iberian (Maiuma, Gaza), Bishop Theodotus (Ioppe), and Bishop Timothy (see unknown; was abbot of the Monastery of Hypatios; see below, John Rufus, *Obit. Theod.* §2 [B 21]). See also Perrone, *La chiesa di Palestina*, 93–94.

4 Literally, "driven away."

5 Literally, "the condemnation of his head."

6 The Syriac transliterates the Latin *forma*. A *forma* is an authoritative, sealed, official document, named after the seal attached to it. See also William Smith and Samuel Cheetham, *A Dictionary of Christian Antiquities* (London: Murray, 1876), 682–83.

7 See also below, *Obit. Theod.* §2 (B 21).

8 See also John of Beth Aphthonia, *Vit. Sev.* (Kugener, 222–23).

9 In 451 Proterius replaced Dioscorus as bishop of Alexandria. In 457 Proterius was brutally murdered. See also below, *Vit. Pet.* §§93–95 (R 68).

ܒܦܘܪܫܢܐ ܐܝܬܘܗܝ ܗܘܐ: ܘܬܫܡܫܬܐ ܐܠܗܝܬܐ ܡܫܡܠܝܐ ܗܘܐ:
ܘܠܟܠܗܘܢ ܗܠܝܢ ܕܩܪܒܝܢ ܝܗܒ ܗܘܐ ܙܘܕܐ ܕܚܝܐ. ܠܐ ܫܒܩ
ܗܘܐ ܠܗܘܢ ܕܢܬܚܪܙ ܢܦܫܗܘܢ. ܘܠܐ ܕܢܬܕܒܪܘܢ ܡܢ ܛܠܝܐ ܘܡܢ
ܡܫܝܚܘܬܐ.

(§83) ܗܘ ܕܝܢ. ܘܫܘܐ ܕܣܓܝܐ ܕܐܝܟ ܗܢܐ ܐܫܬܘܝ، ܕܢܣܒܢܐ. ܟܕ
ܚܙܐ ܒܡܕܝܢܬܐ ܚܕܬܐ ܕܟܠܗ ܥܡܐ ܡܫܬܡܠܝܐ ܗܘܬ: ܒܕܘܒܪܐ
ܕܟܗܢܘܬܐ ܬܐܦܝܪܘܢ: ܟܕ ܙܒܢ ܟܠܢܫܐ ܗܘ ܥܡܐ ܡܗܝܡܢܐ. ܡܢ
ܫܠܝܐ ܟܕ ܐܬܬܘܟܠ ܡܢ ܚܝܠܐ ܐܠܗܝܐ. ܥܒܕ ܕܢܥܡܐ. ܕܢܣܩܘܪܘܦ
ܠܡܕܝܢܬܐ ܐܘܪܬܕܘܟܣܐ ܠܡܕܝܢܬܐ. ܡܕܝܢܬܐ ܠܬܪܘܢܘܣ ܕܠܗ.
ܘܢܗܕܘܢ ܚܕܬܐ ܕܦܪܩܘܣܘܢ. ܠܡܕܝܢܬܐ ܓܘܪ ܠܐܟܣܢܝܐ.
ܠܡܕܝܢܬܐ ܐܝܟܢܐ ܠܒܪ. ܘܟܕ ܟܠ ܩܠܐ ܐܫܬܡܥܬ ܟܕ ܡܕܟܪܝܢ
ܗܘܘ. ܠܕܝܘܣܩܘܪܘܣ ܡܢ ܡܕܒܪܐ ܕܕܣܝܛ ܐܠܗܐ: ܫܐܠܝܢ ܗܘܘ
ܕܢܬܒܥܐ ܡܢ ܐܒܘܣܩܘܦܐ ܒܥܠܬܐ: ܘܬܘܪܣܝܘܣ ܕܝܠܗ ܢܣܒ. ܕܐܝܟܐ ܕܝܢ
ܢܦܩܐ ܘܡܬܚܫܚ ܒܗ ܐܠܗܐ: ܦܩܕܐ ܣܓܝܐ ܕܢܬܒܥܐ. ܘܠܒܪ
ܡܬܒܝܢ ܡܢ ܟܢܘܫܬܐ ܩܕܝܫܬܐ. ܐܠܐ ܐܦ ܗܘ̈ܝ ܐܣܟܡܐ: ܟܕ ܚܝܘܢ
ܕܒܠܥܕܡ ܢܬܦܪܘܢ ܠܗܘܢ ܕܒܗܘ ܝܘܡܐ ܐܚܪ ܗܘܐ: ܘܠܡܘܬܪܘܢܗܘܢ
ܡܬܦܪܩܝܢ ܗܘܘ. [R 59] ܗܟܢܐ ܕܩܠܝܠܐ ܕܡܕܝܢܝܢ ܐܝܬܘܗܝ
ܘܐܒܕܘܗܝ ܠܬܐܦܝܪܘܢ. ܘܟܕ ܢܣܒܬܐ ܘܗܠܝܢ ܚܢܢܝܢ: ܟܠܗ ܗܢܐ
ܐܪܥܐ ܠܡܠܐ: ܐܢܚܢܐ ܕܟܕ ܠܒܪ ܚܙܝܢ: ܘܡܫܬܠܠܝܢ ܐܠܗܝܐ
ܕܬܐܦܝܪܘܢ ܡܫܬܡܫ ܠܫܪܪܐ: ܩܢܘܢܐ ܕܢܒܘܬܐ.

(§84) ܗܕܝܢ ܡܚܠ ܗܘ ܠܦܘܠܐ ܦܪܝܫܘ: ܟܕ ܒܦܘܪܫܢܐ ܐܝܬܘܗܝ،
ܗܘܐ ܐܝܟ ܕܐܡܪܬ. ܡܫܡܠܝܐ ܗܘܐ ܙܢܐ ܩܕܝܫܐ. ܘܟܕ ܒܬܫܡܫܬܐ
ܗܘܐ: ܢܣܒ ܢܦܫܬܐ ܩܘܪܒܢܐ ܕܗܕܝܢ ܡܢ ܟܠܗܝܢ ܘܡܬܚܠܠܝܢ

1 According to Payne Smith (112), the Syriac literally means "provision for a journey," "*viaticum,*" "victuals," "food," or "support." Here the word is used in reference to Holy Communion.

2 The author here shows how Peter the Iberian became a central figure in the anti-Chalcedonian community in Egypt. Note also the decisive role played by the eucharistic celebration.

3 In a note written along the right margin of the left column of MS A fol. 79v, is written in Karshuni ܐܠܡܩܐܡ, that is, the Arabic word المقام, "the place," in a different hand and even different pen.

dared to show himself, neither cleric nor monk, [Peter] was both celebrating the divine services [in hiding] and was giving to all those who desired the food[1] of life. He did not allow them to become faint-hearted or to diminish in zeal and faith.[2]

(§83) He was also esteemed worthy to see this dreadful vision. When a show for all the people was being performed in the city's so-called "theater,"[3] the believing people, fervent in zeal, suddenly began to shout, since they were moved by a divine power, "Dioscorus to the city! The orthodox one to the city! The confessor to his throne! May the bones of Proterius be burnt! Drive Judas into exile![4] Cast Judas out!" Other voices joined in, shouting "For Dioscorus, the helper of the fear of God!" demanding his return from his unjust exile and [that he] should take up his throne and that the wolf,[5] ravenous and contending against God, the new Caiaphas, should be cast out and utterly driven away from the holy churches.[6] The magistrates, anxious to be pleasing in every way to him who at that time was ruling,[7] and calculating in the interest of their own advantage, **[R 59]** commanded the greater part of the armed soldiers to come and surround the theater. Threatening to slay and kill, they alarmed all the people, so that as they were fleeing to the exit[s] they pushed one another down in the narrow entrances of the theater, [and] many died.[8]

(§84) During all this, the blessed Peter, being in hiding, as I have said, was celebrating the holy mysteries. Being in [a state of] amazement, he saw many souls being led by angels and taken

[4] The Syriac transliterates the Greek ἐξορία. Whereas above Juvenal was compared to Judas, here Proterius is cast in the role of the betrayer.

[5] Proterius is also compared to a wolf at *Vit. Pet.* §§90, 91 (R 63, 64) and at *Pler.* 66. Yet that identifier is not unique to Proterius. Calendion of Antioch is also compared to a wolf at *Vit. Pet.* §112 (R 81). For further anti-Chalcedonian polemic against Proterius, see *Pler.* 7, 34, 68–69, 76–77.

[6] For a discussion of the manner of Proterius's death in the context of the present riot, see Horn, *Asceticism and Christological Controversy*, 31–32 n. 104.

[7] I.e., Marcian.

[8] For another account of these events, see Zachariah Rhetor, *Chron.* 4.2 (Brooks, 1:171; Hamilton and Brooks, 66).

ܠܫܡܝܐ. ܟܕ ܐܬܘ ܕܝܢ ܐܢܫܝܢ ܡܢ ܡܕܝܢܬܐ: ܘܐܘܕܥܘ ܗ̇ܘ ܕܟܢܝܫܬ̇.
ܕܐܝܟ ܗܠܝܢ ܐܫܬܟܚܘ ܒܡܕܝܢܬܐ: ܗܠܝܢ ܕܒܡܠܦܢܐ ܒܗ̇ܘ ܦܘܣܩܐ
ܘܙܘܒܢܐ ܡܒܛܠܘ. ܐܝܟ ܒܒܝܬܐ ܢܩܫܬܐ. ܕܢܒܠܐ ܗ̇ܘ ܠܡܫܝܚܐ. ܟܕ
ܗ̇ܘܐ ܒܗ̇ܘ ܫܘܐ. ܘܒܕܡܒܥܬܗ ܕܗ̇ܘ ܚܢܢܐ ܕܐܬܝܗܒ ܠܗ ܠܡܫܝܚܐ.
ܒܗ ܒܕܒܪܐ ܘܗܠܝܢ. ܗ̇ܘ ܟܕ ܗ̇ܘ ܒܠܒܠܐ ܡܛܪܘ. ܒܝܕܐ ܫܒܬܐ ܟܕ
ܡܕܝܢܬܐ ܕܡܫܝܚܘܬܐ. ܕܐܝܟ ܗܢܐ ܟܕ ܐܬܪܐ ܢܛܪ: ܠܗܠܝܢ
ܕܐܬܟܬܫܘ ܘܫܬܬܐܠܬ ܚܕܝܢ ܐܟܘܬܐ: ܫܠܡ ܡܫܝܚܘܬܐ ܬܪܝܨܬ̈
ܫܒܩܝܐ. ܐܦ ܠܗܬ ܫܠܡܐ ܕܝܬܝܩܘܢ ܚܘܝܢ ܠܒܢܐ.

(§85) ܟܕ ܕܝܢ ܠܐ ܐܫܟܚܘ ܕܢܬܦܪܫܐ ܡܢ ܙܢܫܒܐ ܦܪܘܛܪܝܘܣ ܗ̇ܘ
ܠܡܫܝܐ ܦܛܪܘܣ: ܘܒܪܡܐ ܠܚܘܬܐ ܪܗܛ ܕܢܚܙܝܘܗܝ. ܘܫܪܝ ܒܠܠܝܐ
ܐܬܪܐ ܡܬܩ̈ܠܠܐ ܕܢܫܒܘܢܝܗܝ ܘܢܫܬܠܡܘܢܝܗܝ. ܐܬܐܡܪ ܕܢܬܪܘܡ. ܟܕ ܗܢ
ܗ̇ܘ ܕܫܘܒܚܗ ܘܡܝܬܪܘܬܗ: ܚܠܦ ܠܗ ܢܚܠܐ ܕܢܦܠܛ. ܟܕ ܗܢ ܡܪܗ
ܗܠܝܢ ܕܐܫܬܪܪܘ: ܠܛܪܐ ܠܐܒܝܐ ܕܢܦܠܛ ܗܘܐ ܠܗ ܒܡܕܝܢܬܐ
ܘܢܫܒܘ: [R 60] ܟܕ ܚܕܝܢ ܐܫܟܚܢܐ ܕܐܢܫܐ ܠܗ ܡܢ ܐܘܪܬܐܕܘܟܣܘ
ܐܢܬܬܗܘܢ ܘܒ̈ܢܝܐ: ܘܡܦܝܣܝܢ ܗܘܘ: ܕܗܢܐ ܠܓܠܝܘܢܐ ܠܗ
ܕܩ̈ܝܢܕܘܢܘܣܐ ܚܕܐ: ܢܚܒܪ ܡܕܡ ܕܢܓܒܘܬ. ܐܬܐܡܪ ܠܗ ܡܢ ܟܘܬ ܡܠܐ
ܡܕܝܫܬܐ: ܠܐ ܬܦܠܘܛ ܡ̈ܚܒܢܐ ܐܢܬܬܗܘܢ. ܗܢܝܢ ܐܡܪ ܠܐܢܫܐ
ܕܐܢܬ ܗܘܐ ܒܗܡ. ܠܐ ܐܝܬ ܢܦܠܘܛ ܛܪܘܕܐ. ܐܠܐ ܗ̇ܘ ܡܕܡ ܕܢܫܝܢ
ܐܢܬܘܢ ܠܝ ܕܚܒܪ. ܐܝܟ ܚܒܪܘ. ܘܟܕ ܗܦܟ ܒܡܪܟܐ ܠܡܒܝܐܬ
ܘܡܒܘ. ܡܢܐ ܒܡܠܐ ܙܒܢܐ ܗ̇ܘ ܘܐܢ̈ܫܐ ܕܒܡܗ. ܐܝܟ ܕܒܫܡܝܐ.

[1] See also *Obit. Theod.* §7 (B 24) and *Pler.* 54, where Peter recounts his vision of Theodosius of Jerusalem being raised up to heaven in white vestments.

[2] See Luke 23:43. The example of the good thief holds a prominent place in early Eastern Christian literature. See, e.g., John Chrysostom, *De cruce et latrone* (PG 49:399–408; "The Cross and the Good Thief," *Orate Fratres* 24.5 [1950]: 193–99).

[3] Literally, "they were insisting."

[4] Literally "dangers." The Syriac transliterates the Greek κίνδυνος.

[5] This comment reflects a concern on the part of fifth-century Christians in Alexandria that the baptism of young children was highly desirable. On infant baptism in the early church, see, e.g., Joachim Jeremias, *Infant Baptism in the First Four Centuries* (London: SCM, 1960); David F. Wright, "How Controversial Was the Development of Infant Baptism in the Early Church?" in *Church, Word and Spirit: Historical and Theological Essays in Honor of Geoffrey W. Bromiley* (ed. James E. Bradley and Richard A. Muller; Grand Rapids: Eerdmans, 1987), 45–63; idem, "Infant Dedication in the Early Church," in *Baptism,*

up to heaven.[1] When people from the city came and made known [to him] what had happened, those who had died in violence in this destruction and distress were found to be as many in number as the souls whom the blessed one had counted in that vision. In the likeness of that thief to whom the blessing was granted,[2] in that moment they also wove the same crown in one hour by [their] confession of the faith. For such a reward is kept for those who struggle and truly fight the fight for the orthodox faith, even if they show zeal [only] at the end of their life.

(§85) When the blessed Peter was no [longer] able to hide himself from the wicked Proterius, [who] hurried to inflict a mortal blow and had sent out some assassins at night to seize [Peter] and kill him, he was able to flee, since our Lord, his deliverer and his protector, revealed to him the secret plot. Those who were sent approached the door [of the place] where he was hidden inside the city and knocked, **[R 60]** pretending to be from the orthodox [faithful] and [claiming] to know [him]. They [were trying to] trick [him, saying],[3] "This little boy is [in] danger;[4] he should be baptized before he dies."[5] [However,] a holy voice said to him, "Do not open [the door]. They are malevolent." Then he said to the brethren who were with him, "No one shall open the door, but do what you see me do!" They had hastily bent the knee and got up [when] he and the brethren with him cried out with a loud voice, "Our Father [who art] in heaven![6] Behold, thieves![7] Help!" The

the New Testament and the Church: Historical and Contemporary Studies in Honour of R. E. O White (ed. Stanley E. Porter and Anthony R. Cross; JSNTSup 171; Sheffield: Sheffield Academic Press, 1999), 352–78; Kurt Aland, *Did the Early Church Baptize Infants?* (Philadelphia: Westminster, 1963); Everett Ferguson, "Inscriptions and the Origin of Infant Baptism," *JTS* NS 30 (1979): 37–46; David F. Wright, "The Origins of Infant Baptism—Child Believers' Baptism?" *SJT* 40 (1987): 1–23; and Cornelia B. Horn and John W. Martens, *"Let the Little Children Come to Me": Childhood and Children in the Early Christian Community* (Washington, D.C.: The Catholic University of America Press, forthcoming), ch. 7.

6 Matt 6:9. Peter and his friends had just begun to recite the "Our Father." For the full text of that prayer, see Matt 6:9–13 (cf. Luke 11:2–4). The frequent recitation of that prayer, at least three times a day, was recommended by *Didache* 8.3 (Willy Rordorf and André Tuilier, eds. and trans., *La Doctrine des Douze Apôtres: Didachè* [SC 248; Paris: Cerf, 1978], 174; Richardson, *Early Christian Fathers*, 174).

7 The Syriac transliterates the Greek ληστής.

ܗܐ ܠܦܚܬܐ ܓܒܪ. ܟܕ ܕܝܢ ܥܒܪܘ ܥܒ̈ܕܐ ܘܗܠܝܢ ܕܡܕܒܪܝܢ ܘܪܗܛܘ܆
ܚܪܒܘ ܗܠܝܢ ܡ̈ܕܒܪܐ. ܘܡܕܝܢܬܐ ܟܕ ܐܫܬܘܕܥܘ ܡܢ ܦ̈ܢܝܐ ܕܬܝ̈ܒܐ ܐܝܟ
ܕܟܬܝܒ܆ ܢܦܩܘ ܡܢ ܬܡܢ ܘܥܒܪܘ ܠܐܬܪܘܬܐ ܥ̈ܠܝܐ ܕܬܐܒܐܝܣ.

(§86) ܘܟܕ ܐܬܐ ܠܐܘܟܣܘܪܘܢܟܘܣ ܡܕܝܢܬܐ܆ ܬܡܢ ܟܬܪ܆ ܟܕ ܡܚܠܗ
ܐܚܕ ܡܢ ܪ̈ܫܢܐ ܕܡܕܝܢܬܐ. ܕܫܡܗ ܡܘܫܐ. ܒܒܪܐ ܪܫܗ ܡܫܝܚܐ܆
ܘܪܫܡ ܡ̈ܫܝܚܐ. ܘܠܒܫ ܢܘܬܪܐ ܒܡܫܝܚܘܬܐ ܘܡܢܟܝܢܐ. ܕܡܬܠܠܬܗ
ܡܫܬܠܛܐ ܗܘܐ ܗܘ ܠܗܠܝܢ܆ ܕܟܕ ܬ̈ܪܝܢ ܐܠܦܝܢ ܕܕܝ̈ܪܝܐ ܐܝܬ ܗܘܐ
ܠܗ ܒܓܠܠܬ ܒܥܝܬܐ܆ ܦܠܓܗܘܢ ܕܗܠܝܢ ܡܦܠܓ ܗܘܐ ܠܕܝ̈ܪܝܐ
ܘܠܡ̈ܣܟܢܐ ܘܠܐܟ̈ܣܢܝܐ. ܗܘ ܕܝܢ ܦܠܓܗܘܢ ܐܚܪܢܐ܆ ܠܣ̈ܢܝܩܬܐ
ܐܠ̈ܡܠܬܐ ܕܠܗ ܘܠܒܢ̈ܬܐ ܕܩܝ̈ܡܐ ܕܕܝܪܝܘܬܐ.

(§87) ܐܬܬܢܝ ܕܝܢ ܗܕܐ ܐܘܟܣܘܪܘܢܟܘܣ܆ ܡܕܝܢܬܐ ܪܒܬܐ ܘܡܗܝܡܢܬܐ
ܕܬܐܒܐܝܣ. ܕܟܠ ܗܘܢܐ ܟܠܗ ܐܚܝܕܐ ܠܡܘܬܗ ܕܡܫܝܚܐ܆ ܐܝܟܢܐ
ܕܟܕ ܟܠܗܘܢ ܗܘܘ [R 61] ܒܪ̈ܗܛܝܢܐ܆ ܠܐ ܟܪܝܢ ܡܢ ܒܣܪܐ
ܐܠܦܐ. ܒܝܫܐ ܕܕܝ̈ܪܐ ܕܒܗܝܢ ܒܕܝܪܬܐ ܚܕ̈ܪܝܗ. ܟܕ ܐܬܬܘܗܝ ܕܝܢ
ܬܡܢ܆ ܚܙܐ ܒܗ ܐܒܐ܆ ܕܗܘ ܪܫܢܐ ܘܡܬܚܫܒ ܥܡ ܐܠܗܐ
ܦܠܛܪܘܣ܆ ܚܙܝܐ ܠܗ ܒܚܠܡܐ ܢܛܪܝܢ ܘܪܘܚܐ ܠܡܬܠܒܫܘܬܐ
ܕܦܓܪܐ܆ ܘܢܚܙܐ ܒܗ ܢܒܥܐ ܘܡܠܐܟܬܐ܆ ܒܫܘܬ ܡܠܐܟ̈ܐ ܕܩܕܝܫܘܬܗ
ܕܠܘܬܗܘܢ܆ ܒܢܚܘܬ ܒܥܘܬܐ ܫܠܝܚܘܬܐ ܘܡܫܡܫܢܐ ܒܐܦ̈ܐ. ܟܕ
ܒܠܝܠ ܗܢܐ ܒܪܒܥܐ. ܟܕ ܕܝܢ ܗܘܐ ܐܬܪܐ ܘܩܡ ܟܠܗ ܥܡܐ܆ ܘܠܐ
ܐܬܚܙܝ ܕܠܐܚܕ ܡܢ ܗܠܝܢ ܡܫܬܐܠܐ ܢܚܬܐ܆ ܥܒܪ ܢܨܝܚܐ ܕܗܢܐ

[1] Ps 141:9.

[2] On the tripartite division of the Thebaid, see René-Georges Coquin, "Ṣaʿīd," *CE* 7:2080. According to this division, Oxyrhynchos is located at the edge of the Lower Thebaid and the Thebaid proper. The Upper Thebaid extends from Akhmīm to Aswan.

[3] Oxyrhynchos (al-Bahnasā) was about 300 km/180 miles south of Alexandria. No remains of monasteries have been attested. The sole witness to the monastic culture of Oxyrhynchos is the *Historia Monachorum in Aegypto*. This work recounts the visit of seven monks, one of whom was the author of the work, to Egypt during the winter of 395–396. Two recensions of the text exist: an anonymous Greek one and the Latin recension of Rufinus of Aquileia. The work was written for "the pious fraternity on the Mount of Olives," providing a connection with the monastic foundation of Rufinus and Melania. See Antoine Guillaumont, "Historia Monachorum in Aegypto," *CE* 4:1237–38. On Oxyrhynchos, see also Hugh MacLennan, *Oxyrhynchos: An Economic and So-*

neighbors and those who were near heard [them] and [came] running, [and] the malevolent ones fled. Thus they were delivered from the snares of the hunters, as it is written,[1] [and] left that place and departed to the upper regions of the Thebaid.[2]

(§86) He came to the city of Oxyrhynchos[3] [and] stayed there, while he was received by one of the magistrates of the city whose name was Moses, a Christ-loving man and a lover of the saints. He was clothed with profits in faith and [good]will, about whom the blessed one used to say that, having an income of two thousand dinars[4] a year, he used to distribute half of it to the saints, to the poor, and to foreigners. The other half [he used] for his own necessities and for the public[5] debt tax.[6]

(§87) This Oxyrhynchos was a great and prosperous city of the Thebaid, throughout which the grace of Christ reigned, such that all of the [inhabitants] were **[R 61]** Christians, [and] the company of monks who were dwelling in the monasteries surrounding it [was] not less than ten thousand. It happened while [Peter] was there that the wicked and God-fighting Proterius crafted and composed in writing an anathema for the deception of the simple. He deceitfully and covertly recounted in it the evil of the Council of Chalcedon with the slyness of great evil and with hypocrisy, mixing poison with honey.[7] However, when this was read in front of the whole people and it could not shake anyone of those [who were]

cial Study (Amsterdam: Hakkert, 1968). We are grateful to Sebastian Brock for this reference.

4 The value of the Roman silver denarius in the fifth century was between 7,200 denarii to one pound of gold (fourth century) and 6,6 to the pound (sixth century). See Alexander Mlasowski, "Denarius," *BNP* 4:301–2.

5 The Syriac transliterates the Greek δημόσιον.

6 The "debt tax" referred to might be identical with the *epikephalaion*, or "head-tax," which according to Roger S. Bagnall (*Egypt in Late Antiquity* [Princeton: Princeton University Press, 1993], 154) is attested in the papyri only for Oxyrhynchos for the years 297/298 to 319/320. For a helpful discussion of the taxation system in Egypt, see Bagnall, *Egypt in Late Antiquity*, 153–60. Bagnall also indicates that the taxation in Egypt, while a burden, was a bearable one.

7 See also Prov 5:2–4. The Muratorian Canon warns about Marcionite innovations to the Christian canon of accepted scriptural books, that "it will not do to mix gall with honey" (*NTApoc* 1:36).

ܠܐܦܝܣܩܘܦܐ ܕܐܬܚܛܦܬܗ، ܗ̇ܢܘܢ ܕܦܠܚܘ ܕܢܬܬܚܒܪܘܢ ܠܡܪܘܬܗ.
ܟܕ ܦܩܕ ܕܢܬܦܢܐ ܡܕܡ ܥܠ ܒܥܒܐ ܕܒܠ ܡܕܒܪܢܘܬܐ.
(§88) ܟܕ ܦܠܚ ܗܟܝܠ ܠܗܢܐ ܐܦܝܣܩܘܦܐ ܕܐܟܣܢܕܪܝܢܘܣ. ܘܡܪܝܗ،
ܡܕܡ ܥܠܗ ܒܥܡܗ: ܟܕ ܡܒܪܪ ܠܗ ܐܦ ܐܟܠܡܪ̈ܝܐ. ܣܓܝ ܗܘܐ
ܕܩ̈ܠܝܠܐܐ ܡܢ ܐܪܬܘܕܘܟܣܘ ܢܦܠܚܢܐ ܘܢܥܒܕ. ܘܟܕ ܩ̈ܠܝܠܐܐ
ܡ̈ܕܒܪܢܘܬܐ ܗܘܘ ܕܢܬܚܒܠܘ̇: ܐܝܟ ܗ̇ܝ ܕܦ̈ܬܓܡܐ ܐܬܚܙܝܘ̇
ܘܠܐ ܡ̈ܕܒܪܢܐ ܒܕܐܝܟ ܗܕܐ ܢܝܫܘܬܐ ܘܐܣܬܟܠܬܢܘܬܐ. ܐܬܦܠܣ
ܗ̣ܘ ܠܗܒܝܐ ܦܠܘܣ ܡܢ ܕ̈ܝܢܐ ܕܡܕܒܪܢܘܬܐ. ܘܒܗܢ ܕܗ̇ܘ ܕܦܠܚܗ
ܕܐܠܗܘܗ، ܙܒܢܐ: ܘܡܢ ܕ̈ܝܢܐ ܡ̈ܢܝܢܐ. ܕܢܩܪܘܢܗ، ܘܢܚܙܘܢ ܠܢܒܝܠܐ
ܘܠܒܝܬܕܐ. ܘܢܚܙܘܢ ܡܕܡ ܥܠܗ ܒܥܠܐ ܥܬܝܪܐ ܒܠܚܘܕ. ܘܟܕ ܦܓܥ
ܐܫܬܐܠ: ܐܝܟ ܗ̇ܝ ܕܠܐ ܡܕܒܪܢܐ ܐܢܬܘܢ، ܒܦ̈ܘܠܫܢܐ ܕܕܐܝܟ
ܗܠܝܢ ܘܒܦܐܪܗܣܝܐ ܕܡܕܡ ܒܥܠܐ. ܟܘܡ ܟܕ ܐܬܦܢܝ، ܢܣܒ ܢܦܫܗ
[R 62] ܠܡܣܕܘܬܐ. ܟܕ ܫܒܩܘܗܝ، ܗܟܝܠ ܐܦܣܩܘܦܗ، ܒܕܡܣܩܘܣ̇
ܒܕܘܒܠܐ ܕܪܕܝܐ ܥܠ ܒܣܝܣ ܕܐܣܛܘܠܐ. ܕܒܠܘܗܝ، ܘܥܒܕܐ ܣܛܠܐ
ܕܡܠܟܐ. ܘܟܕ ܛܒܥ ܒܐܝܕܘܗܝ، ܠܒܪܛܘܣܐ ܗ̇ܘ ܕܦܣܩܐ: ܡܬܚܙܐ
ܗܘܐ ܘܡܬܬܚܡܣ. ܕܐܡܒܘܠܐ ܢܣܒ ܠܡܟܐܒܐ ܕܩܛܠܝ ܒܗ. ܘܡܢ ܥܠܝܐ
ܒܪܐ ܠܛܘܒܢܐ ܬܐܘܕܘܣܝܘܣ ܐܦܝܣܩܘܦܐ ܕܐܘܪܫܠܡ: ܗ̇ܘ ܕܢܣܩܒ
ܒܕܬܐ: ܗ̇ܘ ܕܒܐܦܠܘܢܝܬܐ ܒܕܡܗ: ܗ̇ܘ ܕܗܘܐ ܡܢ ܒܪܗ ܘܐܬܩܛܠ.
ܒܡܕܒܪܢܘܬܐ ܘܒܫܡܘܕܘܬܐ ܒܡܕܢܚ ܡܠܟܘܬܐ: ܒܪܒܘܗܝ، ܕܡܪܩܝܢܘܣ
ܡܠܟܐ ܦܫܐ ܠܐܠܗܐ. ܘܐ ܕܝܢ ܕܡܬܚܙܐ: ܐܡܪܝܢ ܚܕ ܠܫܢܬܐ ܟܕ
ܐܠܗܐ ܡܣܩ. ܠܗܢܐ ܒܪܐ ܕܦܩܕ ܡܢ ܡܚܝܢܗ: ܘܡܢܒܥܐ ܡܫܩܕܒ
ܘܡܚܣܢܐ ܘܡܗܘܐ ܠܪܘܫܥܐ ܕܩܛܠܝ ܒܟܠ ܡܠܬܐ. ܘܗܠܝܢ ܕܥܒܕ ܗܘܐ

[1] This comment reflects a situation in which the ecclesiastical hierarchy seems to have sided with Chalcedon, while the secular leading class and the monks were anti-Chalcedonian.

[2] This comment, even though it also has a rhetorical edge to it, points to Peter's more withdrawn attitude while being bishop of Maiuma. Otherwise his exercise of public preaching in the community should have provided him with sufficient opportunity to display skills of public speaking.

[3] The Syriac transliterates the Greek βάσις.

[4] The Syriac renders the Greek στῦλος, which may have its origins in Persian.

[5] The Syriac ܣܛܠܐ, probably a further variant spelling for ܐܣܛܠܐ (see Payne Smith, 373) renders the Greek στήλη, which is to be translated as "post," "slab," "column," or "statue."

firmly established, he sent a copy of this to those bishops under him, who acceded to submit to his rebellion, while he ordered that it should be read before all the people of every city.

(§88) Now when the bishop of Oxyrhynchos received this and read it in front of all the people with the help of the devil, he was anxious to lead astray and to shake [the faith of] many of the orthodox. When [the words] threatened to scandalize many, since they were simple and not trained in such slyness and hypocrisy, the blessed Peter was persuaded by the magistrates of the city, by the zealous one who had received him, and by the holy monks to read it, confute the guile and the plot, and preach the truth openly in front of all the people.[1] Although he greatly demurred, claiming he was not trained in such confrontations and in [speaking with] freedom [of speech] in front of the people,[2] nevertheless, when he was compelled, he gave himself **[R 62]** to the testimony. When they lifted him up, they made him stand in a public place, which was high up on the base[3] of a column,[4] upon which stood the statue[5] of the emperor.[6] Bearing in his hands this snare of paper,[7] he was considering and debating [with himself] how he would rebuke the ambush hidden in it. Suddenly he saw the blessed Theodosius, bishop of Jerusalem, that new James,[8] the one who had ordained him,[9] the one who already had been perfected in confessorship and martyrdom in the royal city in the time of the God-hating emperor Marcian.[10] (The manner of his death we will tell at the end, when God permits.)[11] [Peter] saw this [man] standing on his right [hand, who] with his finger was pointing out and showing and rebuking the ungodliness that was hidden in every word. What he

[6] I.e., Emperor Leo I (457–471).

[7] The Syriac transliterates the Greek χάρτης.

[8] The reference is to James, the so-called "brother of the Lord," who, according to church tradition, was the first to hold the office of bishop of Jerusalem.

[9] See above, *Vit. Pet.* §78 (R 54).

[10] Marcian was emperor of the Eastern Roman Empire from 450 to 457.

[11] See below, *Obit. Theod.* §1 (B 21). The present comment is crucial in determining the identity between the author of the *Vita Petri Iberi* and the *De obitu Theodosii*. See also Horn, *Asceticism and Christological Controversy*, 29–30.

ܡܢܗ: ܡ̇ܢܝܚ ܡܡܠܠ ܗܘܐ ܠܡܠܟܐ. ܟܕ ܡ̇ܢ ܦܩܕ ܗܘܐ ܘܡܥܒܪ:
ܘܦܪܗܣܝܐ ܐܝܟ ܚܕܐ ܘܠܒܘܬܐ ܚ̇ܫܒܢ. ܘܟܕ ܗܟܢܐ ܗܘܝܢ ܐܦܣܩ
ܠܡܠܟܐ: ܘܠܟܠܗܘܢ ܥܕܪ: ܘܐܝܟ ܡܠܐܟܐ ܡܢ ܟܠܗܘܢ ܡܬܚܙܝܐ
ܘܡܬܪܘܡܡ: ܣܠܩ ܐܠܘܢ ܡܢ ܡܨܝ̈ܕܬܐ ܕܠܒܝܫܘܬܐ. ܟܕ ܐܟܒܫܬܗ
ܠܬܢܝܢܐ ܡܪܝܕܐ ܘܡܫܡ̈ܫܢܘܗܝ، ܘܡܫܝ̈ܚܘܗܝ،

(§89) ܒܗܿܘ ܙܒܢܐ: ܠܘܩܒܠ ܕܝܘܣܩܘܪܘܣ ܪܝܫܐ ܕܐܦܝܣܩܘ̈ܦܐ
ܟܕ ܐܘܟܠܘܣܐ ܥܦܪܐ ܕܡܕܝܢܬܐ ܐܬܬܚܕ: ܘܪܗܛܘ ܥܠܘܗܝ:
ܘܗܝܡܢܘܬܐ ܥܠܝܫܬܐ ܕܠܐ ܐܝܩܪܐ ܒܕܡܐ ܠܥܠܡܐ ܢ̇ܦܩ: ܟܕ
ܐܝܬܘܗܝ، ܒܐܒܗܘܬܐ ܐܫܬܟܠ ܒܝܠܕܝܢܐ ܡܕܝܢܬܐ: ܗܿ، ܕܐܝܬܝܗܿ
ܡܛܪܦܘܠܝܣ ܕܦܠܣܛܝܢܐ. [R 63] ܟܕ ܗܿܘ ܐܦܝܣܩܘܦܐ ܛܢ̈ܢܐ
ܥܒܕ ܘܬܠܬܐ ܢ̈ܝܫܐ. ܘܗܿܘ ܢܡܘܣܐ ܕܥܒܕ ܒܗ ܐܝܬܘܗܝ، ܗܘܐ:
ܥܡܐ ܒܐܠܘܠ. ܘܟܕ ܥܡܡܐ ܡܢܪܐ ܘܕܐܡܐ ܡܛܠܬܗ ܐܬܬܥܝܪ
ܠܡܕ̈ܝܢܬܐ ܕܐܠܟܣܢܕܪܝܐ: ܒܬܪ̈ܥܐ ܡܢ ܕܒܡ̈ܟܢܐ ܐܢܬܪܘܕܘܣܘܣ:
ܘܕܝ̈ܢܐ ܡܪ̈ܝܫܐ ܘܕܝܢܬܐ: ܐܬܬܟܪܘ ܒܩܦܝܐ ܡܢ ܚܝܐ ܐܝܟ ܡܥܝܐ
ܘܒܡܬܐ: ܟܕ ܦܣܩܘ ܗܕܪܐ ܡܟܠ ܕܦܘܪܣܝܘܢ.

(§90) ܗܿܘ ܕܝܢ ܕܐܒܐ ܡܥܝܐ ܘܡܬ̇ܪܐ ܕܡܟܐ ܦܪܘܛܪܝܘܣ: ܒܚܕܘܬܐ
ܪܒܬܐ ܘܒܦܪܗܣܝܐ ܡ̇ܕܝܢ ܗܘܐ ܘܡܫܬܥܝܐ. ܐܝܟ ܗܿ ܕܡܫܪܪܬܐ
ܡܛܠ ܐܝܬ ܠܗ ܪܥܝܘܬܐ ܘܕܠܐ ܥܓܠܘܬܐ. ܡܢ ܗܪܟܐ ܠܬ̈ܠܡܝܕܐ
ܘܠܕ̈ܝܪܝܐ ܗܠܝܢ ܕܠܐ ܢ̇ܟܦܝܢ ܗܘܘ ܕܢܫܬܐܠܘܢ ܠܗ: ܩ̈ܒܥܬܐ
ܡܫ̈ܠܬܐ ܚܫܘܟܐ ܗܘܐ. ܟܕ ܠܬܪ̈ܥܐ ܐܦ ܗܘܐ: ܘܡܐܢ̈ܝܗܘܢ ܟܠ
ܐܪ̈ܥܝܢ ܕܐ̈ܝܢܐ ܘܕܟܝܘܬܐ ܠܐ ܡܫܬܡܥܢܘܬܐ ܚܝܠܬܐ ܗ̣ܘ ܗܘܐ ܟܠ
ܐܘܪܬܕܘܟܣܘ. ܟܕ ܒܢ̈ܝܐ ܕܐܦܛܪܦܘܬܐ ܒܒ̈ܢܝܢܐ ܘܒܓ̈ܪܡܐ
ܐܟܠ ܠܡܕܝܢܬܐ. ܘܒܢ̈ܝܫܬܐ ܠܐ ܡܬܬܦܝܣܢܘܬܐ ܘܕܓ̈ܒܐ ܐܦ̈ܠܝܬܐ
ܬ̈ܠܝܢ. ܘܠܐ ܢܬܦ̈ܫܘܬܐ ܕܒܝܢܐ ܕܠܐ ܫܘܚܠܦܐ ܦܬ̇ܚ ܗܘܐ: ܟܕ ܒܕܡܐ
ܕܐܦ ܥܠ ܬ̈ܠܘܬܐ ܡܬܢܝܫܬܐ ܡܟܢܫ ܠܥܢܝܘܬܗ. ܐܠܐ ܠܐ ܥܠ ܟܠܬܐ.
ܗܘܐ ܗܿܘ ܕܢܝܐ ܒܟܐܒܐ ܘܚܠܬܝܐ ܘܡܚܣܪ ܪܘܚܐ: ܕܐܬܐ ܢ̇ܦܩ
ܪܘܚܐ ܥܠ ܒܢ̈ܝܫܬܐ ܕܕܐܝܟ ܗܠܝܢ: ܗܿܘ ܕܢܦܫܐ ܘܡܟܐܒܐ: ܘܕܪܐ

[1] One might contrast the present scene showing Peter accompanied by Theodosius of Jerusalem and Christ with Cyril of Scythopolis, *Vit. Sab.* 56 (Schwartz, 151,20–23; Price, 161), depicting Patriarch Elias of Jerusalem, flanked by Theodosius and Sabas, in defense of Chalcedon.

[2] See Pss 140:5; 141:9–10.

[3] See, e.g., Bel 23–27; Isa 27:1; Job 26:13. See also *Vit. Pet.* §81 (R 57).

heard from him, he recited to the people, while our Lord was near and helping [him] and bestowing at the same time freedom [of speech] and grace.[1] Having thus persuaded the people and confirmed them all, and being seen and lauded by all of them like an angel, he snatched them from the net of error,[2] putting to shame the rebellious dragon[3] and his servants and his attendants.

(§89) At that time, the blessed Archbishop Dioscorus, having fought the good fight[4] of confession and having completed his course, and having kept the apostolic faith without transgression unto the end, was perfected while in exile in the city of Gangra, which is the metropolis of Paphlagonia. **[R 63]** Having been bishop for seven years and three months, he fell asleep on the seventh of Elul.[5] When the bitter and painful report thereof was announced to the cities of the Alexandrians, multitudes of orthodox people and holy monks and nuns were broken in soul out of dire suffering and sorrow, because now the hope of their salvation was cut off.

(§90) Yet this hard and bloodthirsty wolf Proterius was exulting and raving with great joy and cheerfulness as one who now had firm and undisturbed governship.[6] Henceforth he exhibited evil and harsh treatment to those laypeople and monks who were not willing to be in communion with him. He bought the magistrates and through them brought all kinds of insults and intolerable sorrows upon the orthodox, bringing into the city multitudes of wild barbarian soldiers.[7] He inflicted without pity unrepeatable evils, both full of a myriad of lamentations and against the laws of nature, until he extended his madness even to the holy virgins. Yet the just, powerful, and longsuffering Judge[8] was no longer willing to continue suffering such evils. He, the Lord, who strikes and

[4] 1 Tim 6.12

[5] I.e., September.

[6] For another indication of the rivalry between Chalcedonian and anti-Chalcedonian bishops in Alexandria, see Zachariah Rhetor, *Chron.* 4.10 (Brooks, 1:182–83; Hamilton and Brooks, 78), who tells of attempts by Timothy Salophaciolus to reconcile with the mother of a newly baptized child who had received the sacrament from the hands of the anti-Chalcedonians.

[7] The Syriac transliterates the Greek στρατιῶται. Proterius found the support of the military of the Eastern Roman Empire.

[8] Note again the emphasis on God's judgment. See also *Vit. Pet.* §65 (R 46).

ܘܡܫܠܡ. ܐܠܐ ܐܬܬܥܝܪ ܡܪܝܐ ܐܝܟ ܗܘ ܕܕܡܟ܆ ܘܠܪܘܡܝܗ
ܐܟܪܙ܆ ܘܟܕ ܩܛܠ ܠܬܢܝܢܐ ܒܥܠܥܠܐ܆ ܠܡܪܩܝܢܘܣ ܐܡܪ ܐܢܐ
ܐܬܘܪܝܐ ܢܒܗܬܐ܆ ܟܕ ܡܚܝܗ܆ ܡܠܐܟܐ ܥܠ ܩܕܠܗ ܐܝܟ ܕܒܫܒܛܐ
ܡܚܘܬܐ ܠܐ ܡܬܐܣܝܢܝܬܐ܆ ܐܝܟܢܐ ܕܗ̇ܘܝܘܢ ܕܒ̈ܝܫܝܗܘܢ ܚܙܘ
ܘܐܬܚܪܪܘ ܐܣܝܪ̈ܐ.

(§91) ܗܝܕܝܢ [R 64] ܗܒܝܠ ܠܡܒܥܐ ܦܛܪܘܣ܆ ܟܕ ܫܡܥ ܗܘ̇
ܠܡܪܩܝܢܘܣ܆ ܦܢܐ ܠܐܠܟܣܢܕܪܝܐ. ܐܠܗܐ ܕܝܢ ܐܝܬܘܗܝ܇ ܗܘܐ
ܗܘ ܕܐܡܦܩܗ ܠܗܢ܆ ܡܛܠ ܡܕܒܪܢܘܬܐ ܐܠܗܝܬܐ ܕܒܬܪܐ ܗܘܬ
ܕܬܗܘܐ܆ ܠܒܢܝܐ ܕܥܕܬܐ ܡܗܝܡܢܐ܆ ܘܠܬܘܪܓܐ ܘܒܘܝܐܐ
ܕܡܗܝܡܢܘܬܐ ܬܪܝܨܬܐ ܫܘܒܚܐ. ܐܝܟܢܗ̇ ܕܝܢ ܗܕܐ. ܟܕ ܫ̇ܡܥ
ܠܡܕܝܢܬܐ ܕܐܠܟܣܢܕܪ̈ܝܐ ܫܒܝܥܐ ܕܡܘܬܗ ܕܡܪܩܝܢܘܣ܆ ܗܘ ܕܗܘ̣ܐ
ܪܥܝܐ ܘܚܠܬܐ ܘܩܘܡܐ ܕܒ̈ܢܝܬܐ ܕܕܐܝܟ ܗܠܝܢ܆ ܗܘܝܢ ܥܡ̈ܡܐ
ܡܗ̈ܝܡܢܐ ܕܡܢ ܟܕܘ ܡܫܪܝܢ ܗܘܘ ܘܡܚܝܡܝܢ: ܡܢ ܐܦܠܝܢܐ ܩ̈ܫܝܐ
ܘܪ̈ܕܘܦܝܐ ܕܐܬܘ ܥܠܝܗܘܢ ܐܝܟ ܕܐܡܪ: ܘܡܬܢ̈ܦܩܝܢ ܗܘ̈ܘ، ܐܢܫܝ̈ܗܘܢ:
ܟܕ ܗܟܢܐ ܕܢܦܫܬܐ ܐܫܟܚܘ. ܡܢ ܕܕܪ ܚܝܘ. ܘܬܫܒܚܘܬܐ ܕܩܘܒܠ
ܛܝܒܘܬܐ ܘܕܡܫܬܠܡܬ ܫܘܒܚܐ ܡܫܡܫ ܗܘܐ ܠܡܫܝܚܐ ܦܪܘܩܢ. ܗܘ
ܕܠܐ ܠܓܡܪ ܢܓܙ ܘܐܫܠܡ ܐܢܘܢ ܒܐܝ̈ܕܝܐ ܕܗ̇ܘ ܕܐܝܟܐ ܡܫܟܚܐ
ܘܥܬܐ ܕܥܠܐ. ܘܐܝܟ ܗ̇ ܕܟܬܒܐ ܕܐܠܗܐ ܘܫܒܩ ܠܗܘܢ ܚܝܘ. ܟܕ
ܐܬܟܢܫܘ ܟܢ̈ܫܐ ܕܕ̈ܝܪܐ ܡܗ̈ܝܡܢܐ: ܘܠܘ ܒܠܚܘܕ ܗ̇ܢܘܢ ܕܐܝܬ ܒܗ̇
ܒܡܕܝܢܬܐ: ܐܠܐ ܘܗ̇ܢܘܢ ܕܐܝܬ ܠܘܬܗ̇ ܒܗ̇ܘ ܕܡܨܪܝܢ ܐܝܠܝܢ:[1]
ܘܒܐܦܘܪܘܠܝܢ ܘܒܐܩܘܣܘܠܝܢ: ܘܒܫܪܟܐ ܕܕ̈ܝܪܬܐ ܡܨܪ̈ܝܬܐ: ܟܕ
ܟܠܗ ܥܡܐ ܡܗܝܡܢܐ ܘܦܪܝܫܐ ܕܐܠܟܣܢܕܪܝܐ ܡܕܝܢܬܐ: ܟܕ ܐܬܐ

[1] MS A has the following marginal note: ܕܘܟ̈ܝܬܐ ܐܝܬܝܗܝܢ ܗܠܝܢ ܕܒܡܨܪܝܢ ܒܗܝܢ ܕܝ̈ܪܐ. ܚܕܐ ܦܪܝܫܐ ܬܫܥܐ ܡ̈ܝܠܐ ܡܢ ܐܠܟܣܢܕܪܝܐ. ܘܚܕܐ ܬܡܢܬ ܥܣܪ. ܘܚܕܐ ܚܡܫܝܢ. ܘܡܬܩܪܝܢ ܥܠ ܡܢܝܢܐ ܕܡ̈ܝܠܐ ܕܦܪܝܫܝܢ ܡܢ ܡܕܝܢܬܐ.

[2] Deut 32:39.

[3] See Ps 78:65.

[4] Hab 3:11.

[5] See Isa 27:1.

[6] See Isa 10:24.

[7] Rufus portrays Marcian in the worst possible light. See also *Pler.* 2, 3, 7, 10, 12 (his death is predicted), 25, 27 (in hell), 29, 36, 61, 67 (reference to his death), 77, 91.

[8] Peter returned to Alexandria because the political climate for anti-Chalcedonians improved after Marcian's death.

heals and chastises and cures,[2] was aroused like one from sleep,[3] who flashed his spear[4] and with it killed the winding dragon,[5]—I am speaking of Marcian, the new Assyrian.[6] An angel struck him on his neck [with] an incurable blow as with a sword, as those who saw [it] with their eyes and were assured [of it] bore witness.[7]

(§91) At that time **[R 64]** the blessed Peter left Oxyrhynchos [and] returned to Alexandria,[8] or rather, it was God who led him there for [the act of] divine providence about to take place for the consolation of the believing people and for the reformation and establishment of the orthodox faith. It so happened that when report of the death of Marcian, that chief, cause, and director of such evils, reached the city of the Alexandrians, those believing people who already had fallen into despair from the many calamities and persecutions that had come upon them, as has been said, and [whose] strength was weak,[9] having been granted time to breathe, were revived. They sent up praise of thanksgiving and doxology to Christ, our Savior, who had not been completely angry and [had not] surrendered them into the hands of that rapacious and bloodthirsty wolf.[10] They saw that the time was fitting and opportune for them. Multitudes of holy monks assembled, not only those in the city but also those near it, in the [monastery] called Enaton,[11] and in the Oktokaidekaton,[12] and in the Eikoston,[13] and in the rest of the holy monasteries, with all the believing and zealous people of the city of Alexandria. They had [as] their

9 Literally, "[whose] hands were limp."

10 I.e., Proterius.

11 Literally, "the ninth." A marginal note, which is only in MS A, fol. 81r, col. 2, left margin, says, "These are places in which monks were dwelling: one nine miles remote from Alexandria, and one eighteen, and one twenty. And they are called on account of the number of miles that they are remote from the city." Raabe (64 n. 7) alerts the reader to the fact that Thomas of Harkel composed his translation of the Bible in the Enaton monastery. See also Jean Gascou, "Enaton," *CE* 3:954–58.

12 Literally, "the eighteenth." This was a monastery on the coastal strip separating the Mediterranean Sea from the western tip of Lake Mareotis, west of Alexandria. It is so named for its proximity to the eighteenth milestone from the city. See Jean Gascou, "Oktokaidekaton," *CE* 6:1826–27.

13 Literally, "the twentieth." A monastery located near the twentieth milestone west of Alexandria. See Jean Gascou, "Eikoston," *CE* 3:951.

ܠܗܘܢ ܪܥܝܐ ܘܡܕܒܪܢܐ ܕܠܗܘܢ: ܘܠܘܬ ܗܢܐ [R 65] ܡܟܝܠ ܪܗܛ ܘܡܩܝܡ
ܠܗܘܢ ܐܝܟ ܨܒܝܢܐ ܕܐܠܗܐ: ܠܦܘܠܚܢܐ ܒܗܘܢܐ ܘܒܝܢܐ ܪܒܐ
ܠܝܚܝܕܝܐ ܐܚܐ ܕܕܝܪ̈ܝܐ. ܟܕ ܓܒܐܝܬ ܐܬܢܨܒܘ ܥܠܝܗܘܢ. ܥܕܪܘ
ܐܢܫܝܢ ܕܠܗܕܐ ܠܣܘܥܪܢ. ܘܢܦܩܘ ܡܢ ܡܕܒܪܐ. ܟܕ ܠܐ ܦܪܩ ܐܠܦ
ܘܠܐ ܗܘ ܐܝܟ ܐܘܪܚܐ. ܠܡܪܕܝܐ ܠܡܬܐܠܨܘ. ܗܘ ܡܕܝܢܬܐ ܠܡܥܒܕ
ܘܗܕܐ ܥܒܪܐ. ܕܡܢ ܟܕ ܗܘ ܒܐܝܕܐ ܕܡܫܝܚܝܘܬܐ ܡܢ ܪܒܐ ܘܡܬܠܘܣ
ܪܥܝܐ ܕܐܦܝܣܩܘܦܐ ܐܬܡܢܝ ܗܘܐ. ܥܡ ܐܝܠܘܪܘܣ ܐܚܘܗܝ, ܫܠܝܚܐ
ܘܥܒܕܐ ܠܗ ܟܠܝܠܐ. ܟܪܙܐ ܕܡܫܟܚܬ ܒܟܠܗ ܗܝܡܢܘܬܐ ܘܠܒܝܒܘܬܐ
ܥܠܝܡܘܬܐ. ܘܬܪܐܝܬ ܒܫܬܩܘܬܐ ܘܟܠܝܠܐ ܫܡܫܐ ܕܡܫܝܚܝܘܬܐ
ܬܪܝܨܬ ܡܩܘܫܐ. ܘܒܕ ܐܬܚܙܝ, ܠܡܕܝܢܬܐ: ܠܡܕܝܢܬܐ ܕܡܬܩܪܝܐ
ܡܩܝܡܘ: ܟܕ ܟܠܗ ܡܕܝܢܬܐ ܐܝܟ ܚܕܐ ܐܝܟ ܕܠܡܐܡܪ: ܡܢ ܢܫ̈ܐ
ܘܓܒܪ̈ܐ ܐܬܟܢܫܬ: ܡܢ ܕܪ̈ܓܐ ܡܪ̈ܝܐ. ܗܘܡܒܐ ܕܦܪܘܛܘܠܦܝܣܐ
ܒܒܝܬܘܢܝܗܘܢ. ܘܢܦܫܗܘܢ, ܐܝܟ ܒܡܬܠܐ. ܒܦܘܪܐ ܘܡܬܟܬܫܢܐ ܕܫܠܦ
ܕܢܠܬ ܐܠܗܐ. ܐܠܐ ܟܕ ܚܙ ܠܡܘܕܘܗܝ, ܐܫܬܒܚ ܡܢ ܐܦܝܣܩܘܦܐ
ܐܪ̈ܬܕܘܟܣܘ: ܐܢܬܘܢ, ܗܘܐ ܗܢܐ ܕܝܢ ܐܘܣܒܝܘܣ ܕܦܠܘܣܝܢ:
ܡܛܠ ܗܝ, ܕܗܠܝܢ ܐܚܪ̈ܢܐ ܕܕܪ̈ܫܝܢ ܗܘܘ ܘܡܚܝܠܝܢ. ܘܠܐ ܡܚܪܝܢ
ܗܘܘ ܕܢܬܚܘܘܢ: ܟܕ ܐܬܒܕܪ ܠܗܕܐ ܡܪܥܝܬܐ ܕܐܠܗܐ: ܕܠܦܘܠܚܢܐ
ܦܝܪܘܣ ܗܘ ܕܠܝܬ ܗܘܐ ܐܢܬܘܢ, ܘܡܚܠܝܢ: ܕܪܕܦ ܒܟܠܗ ܘܐܬܐ
ܡܢ ܥܠܝܐ. ܠܕܘܟܬܐ ܗܝ, ܕܡܕܒܪ ܗܘܐ ܒܗ ܗܘ ܦܘܠܚܢܐ. [R 66]

[1] Longinus was an influential anti-Chalcedonian and abbot of the monastery of the Enaton. Information concerning Longinus rests primarily on the Coptic *Life of Longinus* (Orlandi, 46–92; Vivian, 10–30) and the *Sayings of Longinus*, five in number, that are included in the *Apophthegmata Patrum* (Ward, *Sayings of the Desert Fathers*, 122–23). See also Gascou, "Enaton."

[2] On "father of the monks," see also *Vit. Pet.* §77 (R 52).

[3] Literally, "stirred up."

[4] The reference is to Timothy Aelurus, also known as Timothy the Cat or Timothy the Weasel, the anti-Chalcedonian Patriarch of Alexandria 457–460 and 475–477. On him, see Donald B. Spanel, "Timothy II Aelurus," *CE* 7:2263–68; Rifaat T. Ebied and Lionel R. Wickham, "Timothy Aelurus: Against the Definition of the Council of Chalcedon," in *After Chalcedon: Studies in Theology and Church History Offered to Professor Albert Van Roey for His Seventieth Birthday* (ed. Carl Laga, Joseph A. Munitiz, and Lucas Van Rompay; OLA

head and chief the blessed ascetic and great prophet Longinus,[1] **[R 65]** the father of the monks,[2] [who was] inspired[3] and provided for them according to the will of God for this [purpose]. They all reached an agreement to send men who were suited for the task. By force [and] without his foreknowledge nor his being at all aware [of it] beforehand, they took from the desert the holy Timothy,[4] that famous confessor and true martyr,[5] who already had been honored with the dignity of the priesthood by the great Archbishop Cyril,[6] together with Anatolius,[7] his true brother and [one] equal to him in zeal, a man embellished with all effectiveness and apostolic grace, with special sincerity and fervent zeal for the orthodox faith. They brought him to the city, to the church called *Kaisarion*,[8] whe[re] the whole city was assembled as one, so to say, together with the women and the children. Together with the holy monks they made haste to perform his ordination and to raise him up as high priest, preacher, and fighter for the fear of God. Only one of the orthodox bishops was found, namely, Eusebius of Pelusium,[9] since others who had been persecuted and were hidden did not dare to let themselves be seen. When it was made known to the people by the will of God that our blessed Peter was there in hiding, the people ran and came at once to the place where the blessed one was dwelling. **[R 66]** Lifting him up by force and

18; Leuven: Departement Oriëntalistiek; Peeters, 1985), 115–66; and Rifaat T. Ebied and Lionel R. Wickham, "A Collection of Unpublished Syriac Letters of Timothy Aelurus," *JTS* NS 21 (1970): 321–69.

[5] Here Rufus lays stress on the significance of Timothy's contribution to the anti-Chalcedonian church by emphasizing his suffering for the faith.

[6] I.e., Cyril of Alexandria (412–444). On Cyril, see also *Vit. Pet.* §49 (R 33).

[7] He seems to be not known otherwise.

[8] The *Kaisarion* or temple of Augustus was located about halfway down the Great Harbor. See Peter M. Fraser, *Ptolemaic Alexandria* (Oxford: Clarendon, 1972), 24; Michael Whitby, *The Ecclesiastical History of Evagrius Scholasticus* (TTH 33; Liverpool: Liverpool University Press, 27), 85 n. 98.

[9] See also Evagrius Scholasticus, *Hist. eccl.* 2.8 (Bidez and Parmentier, 56,8–12; Whitby, 85). Eusebius of Pelusium is also known from the letters of Isidore of Pelusium. For further references, see Horn, *Asceticism and Christological Controversy*, 95–96.

ܘܟܕ ܫܘܠܡܗ ܒܡܦܩܢܐ܆ ܘܥܠ ܒܬܫܡܫܬܗܘܢ ܛܘܒܢܝ܇ ܐܘܒܠܘܗܝ
ܠܡܩܒܪܗ܆ ܐܝܟܢܐ ܕܐܬܝܬܘܗܝ ܗܘܘ ܒܢ̈ܝܫܐ ܕܒܡܕ̈ܒܪܐ܆ ܕܐܝܟ
ܢܩ̈ܘܫܐ ܬ̈ܠܡܝܕܐ ܘܟ̈ܬܒܐ ܒܟܬܒܐ ܕܕ̈ܘܩܝܐ ܡܫܡܫ ܗܘܘ ܢܒܟܘܢ.1
ܘܟܕ ܦܠܝܦܘܪܬܐ ܗܘܐ ܗ̇ܘ ܛܘܒܢܐ ܠܡܥܒܕ ܡܢ ܐܠܗܐ: ܕܢܝܚܒܢܗ
ܐܬܠܘܗܝ ܗܢܐ: ܐܝܟܢܐ ܕܐܬ̈ܝܢ ܩ̈ܠܝܠܐ ܒܫܐܠܬܐ ܓܠܝܐ ܠܬ̈ܠܡܝܕܘܗܝ
ܫ̈ܒܝܚܐ܇ ܗܟܢܐ ܕܝܢ ܗ̇ܘ ܐܦܝܣܩܘܦܐ ܐܚܪܢܐ ܠܒܪܛܘܒܢܐ
ܚܕ ܕܪܫܐ ܕܐܦ̈ܝܣܩܘܦܐ ܠܛܘܒܢܐ ܐܡܪܘ܇ ܟܕ ܠܛܘܒܢܐ ܐܝܬܘܬܐ ܕܐܠܗܐ
ܡܢܒܝܐ ܗܘܬ ܡܢܕܝܢ ܘܒܠܥܕܝܗ ܦܪܝܫܐ. ܟܕ ܕܝܢ ܒܠܥܘܗܝ ܚܒܝܫ
ܡܛܠ ܫܘܬܐ ܦܘܪܫܐ ܕܡܦܪܫܐ ܕܐܝܟ ܗܢܐ܇ ܐܡܪܝܢ ܕܢܬܠܒܐ ܗܘ
ܠܛܘܒܢܐ ܦܛܪܘܣ܇ ܟܕ ܚܙܐ ܒܝܬ ܚܕܐ ܘܐܬܐ ܐܬܬܠܝܛ. ܟܕ ܫܬܩ
ܡܪܝܐ ܗܘ ܕܓܠܐ ܠܗ܇ ܟܕ ܕܝܢ ܗܘܐ ܕܡܟܝܟ ܕܐܝܟ ܗܟ ܢܒܟܘ.
ܒܡܟܬ ܦܠܝܦܘ ܫܠܝܚܐ܇ ܕܟܕ ܐܚܝܕܗ ܠܗܘ ܡܗܝܡܢܐ ܕܡܢܗ.
ܡܣܪܐ ܠܗ ܐܬܝܢ܇ ܒܟܠܗܝܢ ܒܢ̈ܝ ܢܫܐ ܗܘܐ ܗܘ ܠܛܘܒܢܐ ܡܢ
ܐܡܪܐ ܘܫܡܥܐ ܕܒ̈ܝܫܐ܇ ܐܝܟ ܕܡܡܠܠܐ ܗܘܐ ܠܗ ܕܫܠܝܐ
ܕܠܐ ܢܬܦܐܪ ܗܘ ܕܢܚܡ ܠܗ܇ ܘܡܢܝܢܐ ܠܐ ܫܪܝܐ ܕܒܡ ܐܠܗܐ܇
ܐܦ ܒܝܘܡܐ ܠܦܘܠܚܢܐ ܢܦܩ ܢܫܡܗ ܐܝܟ ܕܚܙܐ ܠܗ ܐܫܬܡܥ. ܟܕ
ܒܪ ܒܛܠܘܢܝܐ ܕܝܢ ܒܡܘܬܐ ܕܪܒܐ ܠܛܘܒܢܐ ܐܬܐܡܪ: ܗܟܢܐ [R 67]
ܒܦܘܡܐ ܘܒܦܫܪܬܐ ܕܠܐܠܗܐ ܗܘܬ: ܒܛܝܒܘܬܐ ܘܒܚܘܒܬܐ
ܘܒܦܘܠܝܛܝܩܐ ܕܟܝܢܐ ܕܐܠܗܝܐ: ܘܒܝܘ̈ܚܢܐ ܘܡܣ̈ܬܠܐ ܢܒܚܐ

1 Marginal note, only in MS A (fol. 81 recto): ܒܡܫܬܥܝܢܘܬܐ ܐܚܪܬܐ ܕܡܫܬܥܝܐ ܥܠܘܗܝ ܕܛܘܒܢܐ ܦܛܪܘܣ. ܬܠܬܐ ܐܦܝܣܩܘܦܐ ܐܫܟܚܢ ܒܗ ܕܐܡܝܪ ܕܥܒܕܘܗܝ ܠܛܝܡܬܐܘܣ.

2 Literally, "persuaded."

3 A marginal note contained only in MS Sachau 321, fol. 81r, col. 2, right margin, says, "In another account composed about the blessed Peter, we found in it that it is said [that they were] three bishops who made Timothy [a bishop]." See also Raabe, 66.

4 An indication that certain stories circulated orally among an intimate group of anti-Chalcedonian insiders before Rufus put them into writing. In addition, it should also be noted that a mark of friendship in the ancient world was the sharing of secrets. See Cicero, *Amic.* 22; *Fin.* 2.85; Seneca, *Ep.* 3.2–3; Pliny the Younger, *Ep.* 5.1.12. On God as the friend of the saint, see Peter Brown, *The Making of Late Antiquity* (Cambridge: Harvard University Press, 1978), 54–80. Compare this to John 15:13ff., where Jesus' revelation of what he has "heard from the Father" prompts him to call the disciples his friends (see John T. Fitzgerald, "Christian Friendship: John, Paul, and the Philippians," *Int* 61

carrying him on their shoulders, they brought him to the *Kaisarion*, where a crowd of people was [assembled], being determined[2] to act according to the ancient laws and customs during times of persecution.[3] The blessed one had been assured by God beforehand that this was his will, as he has secretly revealed many times to his beloved friends.[4] Together with the other bishop he performed the ordination of Archbishop Timothy,[5] while the grace of God was near at that time and was effecting everything. While all were exuberant because of the joy and exultation of such hope, the blessed Peter managed to get out of sight,[6] passing through the midst of the people.[7] He went and hid himself, [or rather] the Lord who had revealed him now concealed him. All along he had feared to commit an act such as this one. Just as the apostle Philip,[8] who after baptizing the eunuch[9] of Candace immediately disappeared,[10] the blessed one fled each time from the honor and the glory of people because it prevented him from the undistracted quiet that was dear to him and [from] undisturbed converse with God, even though his goal was not permitted to come to fulfillment as [was] his desire.[11] For at the ordination of the great high priest Timothy **[R 67]** by the decree and good will of God, through the election, diligence, and vote[12] of the people of the Alexandri-

[2007]: 284–96, esp. 285). On the pious as friends of God, see Jas 2:23. We are grateful to John Fitzgerald for these observations.

[5] Timothy Aelurus was ordained in 457. This act was crucial in establishing an anti-Chalcedonian hierarchy in Egypt. Timothy Aelurus's first period of tenure as anti-Chalcedonian bishop of Alexandria lasted from 457 to 460.

[6] Again, Peter attempts to withdraw from the crowds, here successfully and with divine support.

[7] Luke 4:30.

[8] Being portrayed in parallel to the apostle Philip contributes to highlighting Peter's "apostolic" authority.

[9] Literally, "believer." For the translation "eunuch," see Payne Smith, 255.

[10] See Acts 8:26–40.

[11] See also *Vit. Pet.* §138 (R 103), where Rufus explains that Peter, burdened by the pastoral care for his flock, could not withdraw into a quiet life. Abba Isaiah as a monk, however, enjoyed that luxury.

[12] The Syriac transliterates the Greek ψήφισμα. Note the active role played by the people in electing a new bishop for the city.

ܕܝ̈ܢܐ: ܘܫܪܘܬܐ ܠܐ ܡܬܚܠܠܢܝܬܐ ܘܕܘܢܚܐ ܐܚܝܕ ܗܘܐ ܠܢ̈ܦܫܬܐ
ܕܟܠܗܘܢ: ܟܕ ܟܗ̈ܢܐ ܡܕܒܪܝܢ ܘܢܫ̈ܝܢ:

(§92) ܗܘ̇ ܪܫܝܥܐ ܘܛܠܘܡܐ ܒܟܠ ܦܪܘܛܪܝܘܣ: ܟܕ ܚܙܐ ܐܝܟ ܢܦܫܗ
ܕܟܡܝܪܘܬܗ ܐܬܬܘܗܝ، ܫܬܪܐ ܐܬܟܬܪ. ܘܟܕ ܐܦ ܠܓ̈ܝܣܐ ܕܪ̈ܗܘܡܝܐ
ܣܛܪܛܝܘܛܐ: ܘܫܪܝܪܐܝܬ ܠܗܘ̇ ܕܡܬܐܡܪ ܣܛܪܛܠܛܝܣ ܕܥܡܗ ܗܘܐ
ܕܝܘܢܘܣ: ܓܒܪܐ ܦܘܛܠܐ ܘܟܠܝܢ ܣܟܬܐ. ܠܥܘܡܬܐ ܕܐܝܟ
ܗܕܐ ܐܡܪ: ܐܡܝܢܐ ܕܟܕ ܣܘܟܠܐܐ ܕܩܠܝܠܐ ܬ̈ܘܕܝܐ ܒܡ̈ܪܢܝܐ
ܘܒ̈ܪܢܝܐ: ܢܗܘܐ ܠܒܪܬܐ ܡܕܝܢܬܐ ܕܐܠܗܐ: ܘܠܣܘܟܐܐ ܡܢ
ܟܠܡܢܐ ܘܕܝ̈ܢܝܬܐ ܕܠܐ ܣܘܦܢܐ ܢܦܠ. ܠܣܘܟܐܐ ܕܝܢ
ܒܡ̈ܣܘܬܐ ܢܦܫܗ. ܘܦܠܓܗ ܬ̈ܠܬܐ ܢܥܡܘܡ. ܘܠܣܬܪܬܐ ܠܐ ܐܡܟܝܢ؛
ܕܢܦܩ ܣܟܦܐ ܠܟܠ ܡܟܡܕܝܬܐ ܐܠܗܝܬܐ. ܡܟܝܢ ܕܝܘܕܪܝܢ ܡܕܝܢܐ
ܗ̇ܘ ܕܝܢ ܡܟܝܢ ܕܘܢܐ ܕܡܟܡܕܝܬܐ ܣܦܩܕܬܐ. ܢܣܛܦ ܡܪܘܕܐܝܬ
ܠܡܕܝܢܬܐ ܠܡܬܐܘܦ ܒܡ ܐܢܛܠܝܘܣ ܐܝܟܘܬܗ، ܘܒܟܠܘܢܝܗܝ،
ܠܦܘܣܝܢ ܣܘܦܪܐ ܦ̈ܪܟܝܬܐ. ܕܪܣܘܡܐ ܡܢ ܡܕܝܢܬܐ ܬܠܬܝܢ
ܬ̈ܠܐ. ܘܣܥܡܘܗ̇، ܬܡܢ ܒܪ ܡܬܒܪܝ ܡܢ ܐܣܛܪܛܝܘܛܐ. ܐܡܝܢܐ
ܕܩܒܠ ܟܕ ܐܢܫܝܢ ܘܒܢܝܐ ܕܐܒܗ ܠܥܘܡܬܗ ܗ̇ܘ ܪܫܝܥܐ ܦܪܘܛܪܝܘܣ.
ܒܢܝܬܐ ܣܒ̈ܝܟܬܐ ܛܘܒ ܣܘܐ ܠܗܘܒܠ ܕܝ̈ܢܐ ܘܟ̈ܠܡܝܢܐ: ܗܠܝܢ
ܕܠܐ ܢܟܢ ܕܢܬܬܦܩ ܠܪܘܫܥܗ. ܫܕܪܐܝܬ ܠܗܘܒܠ [R 68] ܗܠܝܢ
ܕܢܩܦ ܕܒܪܛܘܢܐ ܕܛܘܒܢܐ ܠܡܬܐܡܪܘܣ.

(§93) ܗܠܝܢ ܟܕ ܠܐ ܐܫܟܚܘ ܕܢܣܒܪܘܢ ܒܡ̈ܠܟܐ: ܘܦܩܘܣ ܣܒܪܐ:
ܘܡܟܠ ܡܛܠ ܢܦܫܗܘܢ ܘܣܒܟܘܢ ܡܢ ܒܡܬܐ: ܐܫܬܠܡܘ ܒܝܕܝܐ
ܣܗܕܐ. ܘܦܪܘ ܡܕܒܐ ܒܠܝܘܡ ܠܗܘܒܠ ܐܣܛܪܛܝܘܛܐ. ܘܡܕܒܐ
ܒܬܪܐ ܐܣܟܡܘ. ܒܡ ܩ̈ܛܠܐ ܘܐܫܬܕܘܬܐ ܕܕ̈ܡܐ.

(§94) ܟܕ ܕܒܠܗ ܡܟܠ ܦܘܗ ܝ̈ܫܢܐ ܕܡܕܝܢܬܐ. ܘܗܘ̇ ܕܡܬܐܡܪ
ܐܣܛܪܛܠܛܣ. ܕܠܐ ܬܐܡܪ ܡܕܝܢܬܐ ܕܐܝܟ ܗܕܐ ܕܫܠܡܐ: ܒܕܠܐ

[1] Note that Timothy Aelurus was ordained although Proterius was still alive and functioning as bishop. Thus, a parallel anti-Chalcedonian hierarchy had been established.

[2] It was not unheard off that the bishop of Alexandria would use monetary means to further his own political interests.

[3] The Syriac transliterates the Greek στρατηλάτης. Payne Smith (374) suggests "commander" or "general" as suitable translations.

ans and of the holy and cross-bearing monks, unspeakable joy and exultation took hold of the souls of all of them, while the people kept a feast and were merry.

(§92) [Meanwhile,] that wicked Proterius,[1] defiled in every way, seeing that he himself was in danger, grew more fierce. He had bought the magistrates with much gold,[2] especially the so-called *stratelates*,[3] Dionysius by name,[4] a man [who was] a murderer and of violent rage. [Dionysius] stirred up such madness: with a gang of armed, cruel, and barbarian soldiers he ran to the holy church of God and mercilessly slayed many of the laypeople as well as monks and nuns. Many [others] he wounded with blows and left them half-dead. Finally, he did not refrain from rushing in against the divine baptistry, and from the holy Jordan, that is, from the font of the worshipful baptism, like a rebel he took by force the holy Timothy along with Anatolius, his brother, and they led him to Taposiris,[5] a desert fortress[6] thirty miles distant from the city. There they imprisoned him under guard by soldiers,[7] so that from then on that impious Proterius, finding a time that was opportune for his madness, again manifested many evils against those monks and laypeople who were unwilling to take part in his wickedness, especially against **[R 68]** those responsible for the ordination of the blessed Timothy.[8]

(§93) Unable to endure such things and desperate, having become sated with grief in their souls, the people were inflamed by a martyr's zeal. Every day they drew up in a line of battle against the soldiers and stirred up a civil war with [acts of] killing and bloodshed.

(§94) The city magistrates and the so-called *stratelates* were afraid lest a city of the emperor's such as this should perish, al-

[4] Martindale, *Prosopography of the Later Roman Empire*, 2:364 ("Dionysius 7, comes Aegypti 457").

[5] Also known as Taposiris Magna, modern-day Abūṣīr, a city on Lake Mareotis, near Alexandria. See also Zachariah Rhetor, *Chron.* 4.1 (Brooks, 1:117,17; Hamilton and Brooks, 65); Peter Grossmann, "Abūṣīr," *CE* 1:34–36.

[6] The Syriac transliterates the Latin *castrum*. Taposiris was once a fortress and Roman military camp, built after 378.

[7] The Syriac transliterates the Greek στρατιῶται.

[8] Timothy Aelurus was in exile from 460 to 475.

ܕܒܚܝܠ ܢܦܩ ܘܠܐ ܐܬܒܕܒ ܠܗ ܡܢܗܘܢ ܡܠܝܢ ܕܗ̈ܘܝ، ܘܐܬܢܨܚܬ
ܟܠܝܠܗܘܢ: ܐܦ ܟܢ ܗܘܐ ܡܢ ܒܪܘ ܒܟܠܕܘܟ ܐܣܛܒܪܬ ܗܘܬ
ܩܛܣܛܣܝܣ ܘܡܣܪܚܘܬܐ ܕܡ̈ܠܟܐ ܚܕܬܐ[1] ܠܐܘܢ: ܐܬܢܨܒܘ
ܐܒܚܕܐ. ܕܐܦ ܠܗ ܠܦܪܘܛܪܝܘܣ ܢܦܩܘܢ ܠܒܪ ܡܢ ܡܕܝܢܬܐ.
ܘܡܟܠܝܢܘܗܝ، ܠܕܘܟܬܐ ܡܕܒܪ ܘܛܪܘܕܝܢܗܝ. ܒܕܡܘܬܐ ܕܒܪ ܡܠܘܦ ܠܡ̈ܠܟܐ.
ܢܦܩܘ. ܡܛܠ ܚܠܫ. ܡܢܗܘܢ ܗ̇ܝ، ܕܥܒܪܐ ܠܗ.

(§95) ܟܕ ܢܦܩ ܗܟܝܠ ܗ̇ܘ ܦܪܘܛܪܝܘܣ ܟܕ ܐܣܛܪܛܠܛܐ: ܠܢ
ܐܝܟ ܡܢܗܘܢ ܘܩܛܠܗ. ܒܐܪ̈ܒܥܐ ܒܢܝܣܢ. ܒܬܪ ܚܡܫ ܒܥ̈ܡܬܐ
ܕܒܢܛܘܪܝܢܐ ܕܛܘܒܢܐ ܛܝܡܬܐܘܣ. ܟܕ ܝܬܒ ܗܘܐ ܥܠ ܬܪܘܢܘܣ
ܫܢܝܢ ܚܡ̈ܫ ܘܫܬܐ ܝ̈ܪܚܝܢ. ܗ̇ܝ ܕܒܪ ܗܘܬ: ܘܒܬܪܗ ܟܠܗܘܢ ܐܒܝܫܐ
ܠܟܗ̈ܢܐ ܘܐܦܝܣܩܘ̈ܦܐ. ܐܫܬܟܚ ܟܕ ܓܒܪܐ ܒܫܘܡܠܐ ܒܕܡܘܬ
ܚܙܝܪܐ ܐܘ ܟܠܒܐ: ܗ̇ܢܘܢ ܕܒܡ̈ܦܩܢܘܗܝ، ܘܒܦܘܪܣܬܗ ܠܗܘܢ
ܐܬܕܒܪ. ܟܕ ܐܟܒܪܐ ܢܛܦ ܠܢܦܫܗ. ܗܠܝܢ ܕܝܢ ܗܟܝܠ ܕܒܗܠܝܢ ܕܟ̈ܕܒ
ܗ̈ܘܝ: ܕܠܟܠܗ̇ ܡܫܡܫܢܘܬܐ [R 69] ܕܕܚ̈ܠܝ ܐܠܗܐ ܒܢ̈ܝܢ. ܥܡܡܝܢ ܚܝ
ܠܐܚ̈ܪܢܐ ܕܢܫܬܒܩܘܢ ܘܢܟܬܒܘܢ. ܐܦ ܟܕ ܥܘܐ ܗܘܐ ܗ̇ܘ ܕܢܒܥ.
ܐܠܐ ܠܐ ܠܝ ܦܐܝܐ. ܘܠܐ ܕܢܒܚܪ ܗܠܝܢ ܕܐܝܟ ܗܢ ܘܠܐ ܕܢܬܠܐ.
ܟܕ ܐܝܟ ܕܟܬܒ ܢܒܝܐ ܚܝ ܕܐܫܬܒܠܬ ܟܠܗܝܢ، ܡܛܠ ܐܠܗܘܬܐ.
ܕܒܪܢܫܐ ܒܦܠܓܐ ܒܫܥܬܐ ܬܡܝܕܘܗܝ، ܠܐܒܕܢܐ. ܘܗ̇ܝ ܕܐܝܬ ܡܟܟܬ

[1] Inserted by a second hand in MS A fol. 82 recto. Also in MS B.

[2] The Syriac transliterates the Greek κατάστασις.

[3] I.e., Leo I (457–471).

[4] I.e., April.

[5] See the discussion of the evidence in Horn, *Asceticism and Christological Controversy*, 31–32 n. 104.

[6] Proterius was bishop of Alexandria from after 10 November 451 to 28 March 457.

[7] Because of their reputation as "dirty," both animals are used to illustrate despite in a polemical context.

though the emperor had not yet learned [of the events] and [the magistrates] had not yet reported to him these events, lest he be furious with them. In addition, the establishment[2] and the appointment of the new emperor Leo[3] already had been announced everywhere, so they immediately planned to cast Proterius out of the city and bring him somewhere and guard him until they had informed the emperor [and] he had issued command[s] concerning each of them as it pleased him.

(§95) When Proterius departed with the soldiers, one of them became moved by zeal and killed him on the fourth of Nisan,[4] twenty days after the ordination of the blessed Timothy.[5] [Proterius] had been sitting on the throne for five years and six months.[6] When this happened all the laypeople and soldiers immediately fled, [and] he was left cast down on the street, like a pig or a dog,[7] those [animals] like which he had become in his manners and in his mad passion, when he had drawn destruction upon himself. The [events], indeed, that then took place [and] that are thoroughly inappropriate **[R 69]** for an audience of the God-fearing, we leave to others to tell and to write.[8] For even if he deserved what he suffered,[9] it is not proper for us to hear things of this sort or to repeat [them]. Nevertheless, we see that the divine Word was fulfilled concerning him, as it is written, "Evil shall hunt the unjust man to [his] destruction,"[10] and this [word], "You

[8] For other accounts of these and related events, see *Pler.* 66; Zachariah Rhetor, *Chron.* 4.2 (Brooks, 1:171; Hamilton and Brooks, 66); Evagrius Scholasticus, *Hist. eccl.* 2.8 (Bidez and Parmentier, 56; Whitby, 85); *Life of Longinus* 29–37 (Orlandi, 78–88; Vivian, 24–29); Theodore Lector, *Hist. eccl.*, epitome 368 (Hansen, 103–4); Theophanes, *Chronographia* AM 5950 [457/458 C.E.] (de Boor, 1:110–11; Mango and Scott, 170). See also the discussion in Vivian, "Humility and Resistance," 6–9.

[9] Note Rufus's conflicting expression of satisfaction as well as his continued concern for purity of mind in this instance.

[10] Ps 140:11.

ܠܫܒܗ̈ܪܢܐ ܐܝܟ ܕܠܩܛܠܬܐ ܘܕܒܪܐ ܠܗܘܢ ܫܒܗ̈ܪܢܐ ܫܘܪ̈ܝ܂
ܘܕܠܘܬܐ ܕܒܗܬܬܗ ܡܛܠܬܐ ܪ̈ܫܝܥܐ܂

(§96) ܟܕ ܕܝܢ ܐܫܬܠܡ ܗܠܝܢ ܠܟܐܘ̱ ܡ̈ܠܒܐ܂ ܐܬܦܢܩ ܥܠ ܒܥܘܬܐ ܕܟܠܗ ܗܢܐ ܘܟܢܐ ܐܙܕܟܝ ܠܡܕܝܢܬܐ ܕܐܠܟܣܢܕܪ̈ܝܐ. ܘܟܕ ܫܡܥܘ ܟܠ ܗܠܝܢ ܕܐܬܒܝܫܘ܂ ܦܩܕ ܕܛܘܒܢܐ ܢܬܡܠܟܘܢ: ܗܘ ܕܦܩܕ ܗܢܘܢ ܐܢܐ ܡܢ ܐܠܗܐ܂ ܢܓܠ ܘܢܦܩ ܬܪܘܢܘܣ ܕܠܗܘܢ܂ ܘܡܟܝܠܐ ܗܝ ܡܕܝܢܬܐ ܬܫܬܠܡ ܘܬܬܦܨ ܒܫܝܢܐ܂ ܘܢܬܡܢ ܒܗܘܢܐ ܕܗܠܝܢ ܩ̈ܫܝܬܐ ܕܒܢ̈ܝ܂ ܗܘ ܕܐܦ ܗܘܬ ܠܗܘ̱ ܟܕ ܦܘܩܕܢܗ ܕܛܘܒܢܐ ܢܬܡܠܟܘܢ. ܒܥܠܕܒܒܘܗܝ ܟܕ ܐܝܬ ܗܘܐ ܠܡܕܝܢܬܐ܂ ܚܕܘܬܐ ܘܪܘܙܐ ܘܕܘܨܐ ܕܒܠܥܐ ܗܘܬ ܡܕܝܢܬܐ. ܟܕ ܒܢ̈ܝܐ ܩ̈ܘܫܬܐ ܕܠܐ ܡ̈ܗܝܡܢܐ ܪܗܛܝܢ ܗܘܘ ܘܡܟܕܝܢ. ܘܕܩ̈ܘܫܬܐ ܐܢܫ̈ܐ. ܫܡܥܐ ܐܬܬܗ ܡܕܝܢܬܐ ܕܐܠܟܣܢܕܪ̈ܝܐ ܒܗܠܝܢ ܒܝ̈ܘܡܬܐ.

(§97) ܟܕ ܗܘ̇ ܗܟܝܠ ܛܘܒܢܐ ܛܝܡܬܐܘܣ ܒܐܦܝܣܩܘܦܘܬܐ ܘܟܢܐ ܕܫܒܩ ܩ̈ܢܘܢܐ܂ ܬܘܒ ܫܐܕܐ ܢܫܡܬܐ ܟܕ ܠܐ ܡܫܡܠܝܐ ܕܢܦܫܐ ܦܘܪܢܐ ܕܩ̈ܢܘܢܐ܂ ܐܟܢܐ ܕܐܘܚܪܢܐ ܠܗ ܡܦܩܢܐ ܒܫܡܐ ܘܢܫܡܬܐ܂ ܠܐܦܝܣܩܘܦܐ [R 70] ܕܒܥܠܕܒܒܘܗܝ܂ ܘܐܬܬܪܝܬ ܠܗܘ ܕܟܘܢܣܛܢܛܝܢܘܦܘܠܝܣ. ܘܠܗܘ ܕܪܘܡܝ܂ ܐܦ ܟܕ ܐܬܬܗ ܗܘܬ ܠܗܘ̱ ܒܗܬܬܐ ܘܫܝܛܐ܂ ܘܛܠܡܘܣ ܘܥܘܡܝܢܐ ܘܕܘܒܪܐ ܘܦܐܪܫܝܐ ܕܒܠܗ ܕܛܘܒܢܐ܂ ܟܕ ܒܠܡܘܣ ܒܠܝܐܬ ܡܟܝܢ ܘܡܢ ܐܦܝ̈ܣܩܘܦܐ ܕܐܬܦܬܘܗܝ܆ ܘܩܠܝ̈ܪܝܘ ܘܕܝܪ̈ܝܐ ܘܫܠܒ̈ܐ. ܡܬܦܪܣܐ ܗܘܬ ܦܘܠܚܢܐ ܪܫܝܬܐ ܕܒܠܡܕܝܢܬܐ. ܘܟܕ ܒܙܘܓܐ ܩ̈ܢܘܢܐ ܕܟܠ ܓܒ̈ܝܢ ܐܬܦܢܝܘ ܘܒܫ̈ܡܗܬܐ: ܘܒܦܘ̈ܪܣܦܘܢܐ ܕܪ̈ܫܝܥܐ܂ ܟܕ ܐܫܟܚ ܕܝܢ ܪܫܝܬ ܒܗܦܟܐ ܓܕܝܢ ܗܠܝܢ ܕܒܗܘ ܘܟܢܐ ܐܚܝܕܝܢ ܗܘܘ܂ ܠܐ ܠܗܘܢܝܢ ܫܒܩ ܡܢ ܛܘܒܢܗܘ̱ ܘܒܫܘܥܬܗܘ̱܂ ܒܕܘܟܐ ܕܒܗ ܩ̈ܘܠܣܐ ܩ̈ܘܫܬܐ ܕܒܗܐ ܘܐܫܬܘܕܝܬܐ ܕܕܘܟܐ܂ ܒܕܝܘ ܕܢܫܒܪܐ ܠܐܟܣܢܕܪܝܐ ܛܘܒܢܐ

[1] See Ps 89:10; see also Job 40:11; Ps 119:21.
[2] See Prov 16:25.
[3] Job 21:30.
[4] Timothy Aelurus was patriarch of Alexandria from 457 to 460, was deposed, sent into exile, restored under Emperor Basiliscus in 475, and died in 477.
[5] This may include both pagans and Chalcedonian Christians. In either case, the outcome was that the number of anti-Chalcedonians in the city increased.

humbled the boastful ones like the ones who have been slain,"[1] and, "The Lord makes war against the boastful ones,"[2] and, "The wicked one is kept for the day of his slaughter."[3]

(§96) When [news of] these [events] reached Emperor Leo, he was moved with compassion at the adversities that all this time had beset the city of the Alexandrians. Sparing those who were left, he commanded that the blessed Timothy, who had received the laying on of hand[s] from God, should enter and take his throne, so that this city should find peace and that the people might take a respite from and find consolation for those evils that had occurred. Th[ese remedies] were accomplished through the return of the blessed Timothy.[4] For filling the city everywhere there was to be seen joy and exultation and leaping for joy. Many crowds of unbelievers[5] were running to be baptized. In short, the city of the Alexandrians became heaven in those days.

(§97) After the blessed Timothy had remained in the episcopate for seven years,[6] again an envious demon, not suffering to see the salvation of men, with anger stirred up bishops everywhere to evil and **[R 70]** envious zeal, especially the one in Constantinople[7] and the one in Rome.[8] The establishment and glory and way of life and freedom [of speech] of the blessed one were shame and reproach to them, since daily the wicked Council of Chalcedon was anathematized publicly[9] by him and by the bishops under him, by the clergy, by the monks, and by the laypeople. When they resorted in a great rush on all sides both to gifts and to the protection[10] of the wicked ones, since it happened that those who were ruling at that time were overcome by love of money, they did not cease any earlier from their machination[s] and their evildoing until, after many [incidents of] homicide and bloodshed, they had caused the blessed Timothy to be banished into exile and to [be

[6] Difficult to reconcile, because Timothy held the patriarchate twice, first for three and a half years and again for one and a half years.

[7] I.e., Gennadios, 458–471

[8] I.e., Leo, 440–461.

[9] I.e., in the context of the liturgy.

[10] The Syriac transliterates the Greek προστασία.

ܠܡܬܐܬܘܗ܂ ܘܢܚܘܬ ܠܐܠܟܣܢܕܪܝܐ ܡܕܝܢܬܐ܆ ܐܝܟܐ ܕܐܫܬܡܠܝ ܟܠܝܠܐ ܕܣܗܕܘܬܐ ܕܠܒܫ ܐܒܘܬܐ ܘܪ̈ܘܚܢܝܐ ܕܝܘܣܩܘܪܘܣ ܒܪ ܣܗܕܘܬܗ. (§98) ܗܕܐ ܐܬܬ ܟܠܗ ܗܝܕ ܠܬܘܟܠܢܐ ܦܪܘܣܗ ܕܠܐ ܐܬܒܛܠ܆ ܕܐܝܟ ܠܘܬܗ ܘܐܬܪܗ ܡܢ ܒܬܪ ܒ̈ܢܝܢܐ ܢܓܝܪܐ܆ ܘܐܬܦܢܝ ܒܫܠܡܐ ܗܘ ܕܪܚܡ ܠܗ. ܟܕ ܢܦܩ ܡܢ ܠܡܬܐܬܘܗ ܪܝܫܐ ܕܐܦ̈ܝܣܩܘܦܐ܆ ܘܐܫܬܠܡ ܠܐܟܣܘܪܝܐ ܒܦܘܡܐ ܘܒܫܘܠܛܢܐ ܡܠܟܝܐ܆ ܘܐܝܟ ܐܝܪܝܡ ܡܢ ܩ̈ܫܝܫܐ ܥܠ ܣܠܩܘܗܝ ܡܢ ܦܘܩܕܢܐ ܡܠܟܝܐ܆ ܕܐܫܟܚܗ ܟܕ ܠܡܬܐܬܘܗ܆ ܫܡܥܐ ܕܝܢ ܗܢܐ ܡܬܩܪܐ ܗܘܐ ܣܠܘܦܩܝܪܘܣ ܘܟܕ ܒܕܡܘܬܐ ܐܝܬ ܗܘܐ ܒܟܝܫܘܬ ܫܘܒܚܐ ܕܟܠܩܕܘܢܝܐ. ܟܕ ܚܙܐ ܦܛܪܘܣ ܗܘ ܡܚܣܢܐ ܕܐܠܗܐ ܘܒܪ ܠܒܝܐ [R 71] ܕܡܫܒܚܐ ܙܒܢܐ܆ ܫܡܥܐ ܕܐ̈ܚܐ ܡܗ̈ܝܡܢܐ܆ ܕܐܫܬܒܩܘ ܒܗ ܡܗܘܬܐ ܘܡܨܪܐ ܕܪ̈ܘܚܐ ܕܚ̈ܒܫܝܢ ܠܗܘܢ ܘܡܫܡ̈ܫܝܢ ܠܗܘܢ܆ ܘܡܣܬܘܕܥܝܢ ܒܢ̈ܝܢ ܕܢܬܕܒܪܘܢ ܡܢ ܫܪܪܐ ܕܗܝܡܢܘܬܐ܆ ܢܦܩ ܠܒܝܐ ܐܠܗܝܐ ܟܕ ܟܕܡܐ ܠܗܘܬܐ ܐܠܦ ܢܦܫܗ. ܟܕ ܗܠܝܢ ܡ̈ܠܐ ܠ̈ܚܒܪܘܗܝ ܒܟܠ ܕܥܠܝܡܐ ܡܬܪܒܐ ܘܡܬܗ̈ܘܢܐ܆ ܕܢܒܥ ܡܬܟܪܗ ܘܠܐ ܐܝܟ ܡܬܟܪܗ ܐܝܟ ܕܢܒܥ ܡܬܓܒܠ ܘܠܐ ܐܝܟ ܢܦܪ ܐܝܟ. ܘܟܕ ܠܥܠܘܬܐ ܕܠܗ ܙܪܡܒܐ܆ ܐܝܟ ܕܠܐ ܘܟܢܐ ܥܒܕ܆ ܐܙܠ ܗܘܐ ܠܡܕܝܢܬܐ ܕܐܠܟܣܢܕܪܝܐ ܘܠܡܘܬܪܐ ܩܕ̈ܝܫܐ ܕܣܪ̈ܝܢ. ܘܠܡܕܝܢܬܐ ܐܚܪܢܝܬܐ ܩܘܣܛܢܛܝܢܘܦܘܠܝܣ ܘܠܡ̈ܘܪܝܐ ܕܐܓܘܦܘܠܝܣ. ܟܕ ܩܛܝܢܐܝܬ ܟܠܕܘܟܝܢ ܡܬܟܪܝܢ. ܘܡܚܒܝܢܐ ܘܡܫܡܫܝܢ ܠܒܢ̈ܝܐ ܕܐܦܪܘܬܪܘܣܡܘ ܘܐܚܪܢܐ ܦܘܠܘܣ ܥܠܝܡܐ ܠܟܠܝܙ ܟܠ ܗܘܐ. ܟܕ ܒܟܠܗܝܢ ܘܒܟܬ̈ܒܐ ܕܗܟܢܐ ܘܢܚܘܬ܆ ܠܦܘܩܕܢܐ ܠܡܠܦܘܬܐ ܕܕܪ̈ܝܫܐ ܕܕܒܠܬ ܐܠܗܐ ܘܠܒܝܢܐ ܐܠܗܝܐ ܢܦܩ ܗܘܐ. ܕܐܬܠܝܢ ܥܠ ܗܝܟܠ ܬܕܡܘܪ̈ܬܐ ܘܐܬܘ̈ܬܐ ܙ̈ܘܥܬܐ܆ ܥܡܠ ܬܘܢ ܒܕ ܠܡܬܘܬܐ ܐܠܗܝܬܐ ܘܫܠܝܐ ܕܢܦܩ ܗܘܐ ܠܗ܆ ܘܒܟܝܐ ܐܣܝ̈ܘܬܐ ܘܒܟܝܐ ܫ̈ܠܝܐ܆ ܠܐ ܕܡܫܠܝܘܬܐ ܕܠܐ ܐܬܐܠܗ ܕܟܠܗܝܢ ܢܦܩܝ. ܟܕ ܡܬܟܡܕܝܢ ܚܝܢ ܕܝܢ

[1] Timothy was in exile once in Gangra, Colchis (modern-day southwestern Georgia/northeastern Turkey) between 460 and spring 475. He died in office in 477.

[2] I.e., where the martyrdom of Dioscorus had found its end.

[3] Σάλος σακιόλος "White Turban" or, more properly, "Wobble Cap," Chalcedonian patriarch of Alexandria from 460 to 482. Reference to Timothy Salophaciolus is also made at *Pler.* 74.

[4] Rufus depicts Peter the Iberian as closely in parallel with Moses. For

made to] go away to the city of Gangra,[1] where the crown of confession had been completed for the victory-clad and high priest Dioscorus, his fellow confessor.[2]

(§98) For this reason the blessed Peter could not, as was his prayer and his desire, depart from among the people and enjoy the quiet that was dear to him. After Archbishop Timothy left and was delivered up to exile by imperial command and authority, another man from the priests took his place by imperial command, whose name was [also] Timothy but [whose] name was rather called Salophaciolus[3] and [who] likewise held the evil opinion of the Chalcedonians. When Peter, the servant of God and fellow in zeal of the great **[R 71]** Moses,[4] saw the toil of the believing brothers, left between [the experience of] death and the desolation of those who were building them up and supporting them, and [as they were] running the risk of being shaken from the truth of the faith, he took on divine zeal, straining himself to the point of death, thinking about and meditating upon those most famous words of the Apostle, "Who is sick and I am not sick? Who is offended, and I do not burn?"[5] When he left [behind] the stillness beloved to him because it was in[appropriate] at the time, he went again to the city of the Alexandrians and to the holy monasteries surrounding it and to many other cities and villages of Egypt, secretly going around everywhere.[6] He was building up and supporting the crowds of the orthodox and, being another Apostle Paul, he was "all [things] to everyone,"[7] giving in word and in deed his way of life and his demeanor [as] an example for teaching the ways of life of the fear of God and divine zeal.[8] Now, all the wonders and great signs he accomplished there by divine grace and by the power adjoined to him, and how many healings and how many works of power, it is not within our weakness to de-

a fuller discussion of this *imitatio Mosis*, see Horn, *Asceticism and Christological Controversy*, 306–09.

[5] 2 Cor 11:29.

[6] This comment points to the underground activity in which Peter was engaged in Egypt to help build up and strengthen the anti-Chalcedonian community.

[7] 1 Cor 9:22.

[8] Note the emphasis on "fear of God" and "zeal" for God's work as two related key concerns of anti-Chalcedonian identity.

ܚܙܐ ܐܘ ܬܬܠܡ. ܗ̇ܠܝܢ ܕܐܡܪܬ: ܠܗ̇ܘܢ. ܕܒܝܫܘܬܐ ܘܒܗ̇ ܒܚܝܠܬܐ
ܐܪܪܒܐ: ܢܒܥܘܢ ܕܢܬܠܘܢ ܘܢܬܠܒܘܢ.

(§99) ܒܪܬܐ ܕܐܚܝ ܡܢ ܢܒ̈ܝܐ ܕܡܬܝܠܕܬܐ ܒܪܢܫܐ ܗܘܬ ܒܡܪܘܣܐ
ܡܥܝܢܐ. ܐܬܝܠܕܗ̇ ܗܘܬ ܕܝܢ ܚܢܝܢܬܗ̇: ܘܪܚܡܐ ܗܘܐ ܠܗ̇ ܐܝܟ
ܕܠܚܢܝܢܬܐ. ܕܗܘܐ ܐܡܪܐ ܡܢ ܪܚܡܬ ܠܡܥܒܕܐ [R 72] ܐܬܝܠܕܗ̇
ܗܘܬ ܘܡܫܡܫܢܝܬܐ. ܘܦܠܓܐ ܗܘܬ ܒܩܪ̈ܝܢܐ. ܐܒܐ ܕܝܢ.
ܒܦܘܠܝܛܐ ܗ̇ܝ. ܒܦܠܘܣܘܦܘܬܐ ܕܝܢ ܘܒܪܚܡܬܐ ܕܦ̈ܝܠܘܣܘܦܐ
ܡܠܦܢܐ ܦܠܓ ܐܚܪܝ ܗܘܐ. ܡܢ ܗ̇ܪܟܐ ܒܪ ܫܘ̈ܪܝܐ ܥܡܠ ܡܢ ܐܚܝ
ܪܥܝܢܘܗܝ ܕܢܩܝܦܐ: ܕܡܫܠܡ ܠܟܠܗܝܢ: ܐ ܗ̣ܘ ܕܢܩܝܦܗ̇ ܘܟܠܗܝܢ
ܘܒܠܒܗ̇ ܠܡܪܦܝܘ: ܘܐܬܚܙܝ ܢܥܒܕܐ ܒܠܒܗ̇ ܫܘ̈ܥܠܐ ܘܦܠܣܘܦܘܬܐ
ܕܐܘܩ̈ܝܢܘܬܐ ܕܢܬܥܒܕܐ: ܣܘܣܐܝܬ ܐܫܬܪܒ: ܘܡܦܠܓܢܐ ܗ̣ܘܐ
ܕܢܬܠܗ̇ ܠܦܠܓܐ. ܗ̇ܠܝܢ ܕܝܢ ܢܠܦܬ ܐܡܗ̇ ܡܢ ܓܒܪܐ ܐܚܝ ܕܐܡܪܬ:
ܕܐܬܝܗ̇ ܗܘܐ ܒܪܦܠܓܐ ܘܦܠܓ ܡܫܡܫܢܐ: ܒܪ ܫܢܬܗ̇ ܬܫܥ ܡܫܪܝܐ
ܠܘܬ ܦܠܓܐ ܦܝܪܘܣ: ܒܪ ܡܫܪܝܐ ܠܗ ܒܠ ܒܘܬܪܗ ܕܐܢܦܘܪܝܐ.
ܒܪ ܐܩܝܡܬ: ܕܠܐ ܢܡܚܐ ܒܗ̇ ܘܒܦܘܪܫܢܗ̇ ܘܒܦܠܓܘܬܐ: ܕܒܡܫܘܬܐ
ܥܕܪܐ ܡܣܝܘܥܢܐ ܚܪܫܐ ܕܢܦܠܘܢ. ܒܪ ܗ̇ܝ ܕܡܬܚܙܝܐ ܠܒܪܬܐ. ܒܪ
ܕܝܢ ܥܒܕ ܗܕܐ ܗ̣ܘ ܦܠܓܐ: ܘܐܫܠܡܗ̇ ܒܦܠܓܐ: ܐܘܒܕ ܒܡܠܬܐ
ܪܒܬܐ. ܡܪܢܐ ܐ ܢܐܢܫܐ ܗ̇ܘ ܪܥܝܢܐ. ܘܒܪ ܐܡܪ ܗܕܐ: ܡܚܙܐ
ܢܦܩ ܐܪܥܡ ܡܢ ܩܕ̈ܝܫܐ ܗ̇ܠܝܢ ܕܒܗܘܢ ܒܠܒܐ: ܘܐܘܠܦ ܠܗ̇ ܐܡܗ̇
ܕܦܠܓܐ. ܘܒܪ ܐܫܟܚܗ̇ ܕܢܬܠܒܐ ܝ̣ܬܝܪ ܒܪܬܗ̇: ܘܡܫܪܘܝܐ ܒܒܥܒܐ
ܘܒܐܩ̈ܠܬܐ: ܐܚܝܕܐ ܕܝܢ ܘܦܠܓܐ ܕܠܐ ܬܫܬܠܡ ܠܦܠܓܐ ܡܢ ܒܪܬܗ̇
ܠܗ̇ܘ ܪܥܝܢܐ: ܒܪ ܦܩܕ ܕܒܠܩܘܢ ܗܠܝܢ ܢܬܪܐ ܠܒܪ ܢܦܩܘܢ. ܥܡܠ

[1] Rufus is sufficiently familiar with the phraseology of rhetorical humility.

[2] Presumably, one could also substitute "daughter" for "child."

[3] The members of this family display the conflicting attraction, being drawn to the Christian religion, on the one hand, and to the traditional intellectual exercise of philosophical inquiry, accompanied by magical experiments, on the other. Thus they examplify well the ongoing struggle in the early Christian community of the fifth century between commitments to faith and to culture, still seen as opposing forces.

[4] The reference to activities of magical consecrations taking place at the Serapeum indicates that paganism had not been completely eradicated in Alexandria in the middle of the fifth century. For further comments, see Horn, *Asceticism and Christological Controversy*, 179.

scribe.[1] We mention one or two, leaving the rest for those who encountered [them] through [their own] experience and sight to recount.

(§99) The daughter of one of the city's notables was sick with a severe sickness. She was his only [child, moreover,] and he loved her like an only [child].[2] Her mother was a lover **[R 72]** of Christ and a believer, and she greatly rejoiced in the saints. The father was indeed a Christian, but he was very much seized by the error and friendship of pagan philosophers.[3] Hence, when he received promises from a certain leader of the magicians that, if [the magician] were to take the girl and bring her at night to the Serapeum[4] and there perform on her rites[5] and [other] abominations of the arts of magic, he could heal her, he gladly obeyed and prepared to give the girl over [to him]. When her mother learned these [things] from a slave who [had become] aware of [it], who was a Christian and a strong believer,[6] immediately she sent for the blessed Peter, informing him about the plan of the devil. She asked that he not disregard her and her husband and the girl, who were running the risk of falling into a real death through provoking the Lord to anger. The blessed one heard this and was inflamed with zeal, crying out with a loud voice, "Lord, shall the wicked live?"[7] Having said this, immediately he took some of those saints who were with him in the night, and they went to the girl's mother. He found her sitting with her daughter and tearing [herself] apart with weeping and lamentations and at the same time ensuring that the girl would not be delivered over by her husband to the wicked [magician]. Commanding that all those [who] were superfluous should

[5] The Syriac corresponds to the Greek τελευταί. Given that the setting is one of a sanctuary of a mystery religion, "rites" seems to be an appropriate translation, all the more so since τελέω is used in a context dealing with initiation into a mystery religion, and τελεῖν ἱερά means "to perform sacred rites." More literally, one might translate ܫܘܡܠܝܐ as "(a casting of) lots," "perfections," or "consecrations." See Payne Smith, 566. The Pešitta uses the word to render "Thummīm," part of the sacred lots "Urim and Thummim." See, e.g., Exod 28:30 (not at Ezra 2:63, which has in LXX [and Pešitta] "high priest").

[6] Note the precious example Rufus provides here of the interactions between an early Christian woman and a slave in her household.

[7] See Job 21:7.

ܓܚܟܐ ܘܡܚܟܝܢ ܠܛܠܝܬܐ. ܘܟܕ ܢܦܩ ܠܗ ܠܒܪ ܩܕܝܫܐ: ܘܠܐܡܗ
ܒܝܬܐ ܒܟܠܗ ܗܝܡܢܘܬܐ ܕܒܗܠܐ: ܘܠܒܒܗ ܕܕܠܐ ܦܘܪܫܐ ܟܠ
ܡܫܝܚܐ ܗܘ ܡܪܐ ܕܢܫܝܐ [R 73] ܬܬܟܠ. ܦܝܫܐ ܠܐܡܗܐ ܕܫܪܐ ܗܘܐ.
ܘܠܐܡܗܐ ܕܒܬܪܗ ܡܢܝܚܐ. ܗܝ ܕܝܢ ܠܛܠܝܬܐ. ܐܫܬܟܚܬ ܕܚܠܝܡܐ.
ܘܡܫܪܪܐ ܡܢ ܗܘ ܒܐܘܪܚܐ ܡܫܝܐ. ܗܘ ܕܝܢ ܦܠܣܛܘܦܐ ܚܕܐ ܡܢ
ܐܠܗܐ ܐܬܦܪܥ ܡܢܗ. ܟܕ ܓܝܪ ܕܒܝܬܐ ܕܗܘ ܡܕܝܢܬܐ ܣܘܦܐܝܬ
ܗܕܝܐ ܠܫܘܠܛܢܐ ܢܦܩ: ܗܘ ܕܟܕ ܐܬܩܪܒ ܐܘܟܝ ܟܕ ܐܡܪ: ܡܪܝܐ
ܐܠܐ ܢܚܝܐ ܗܘ ܪܚܡܐ. ܐܡܪܐ ܕܟܠܗ ܡܕܝܢܬܐ ܕܢܬܬܚܝܐ ܗܘܬܐ
ܗܝ ܬܕܡܘܪܬܐ. ܘܟܠܢ ܢܟܣܝܢ ܠܐܠܗܐ. ܥܠ ܛܝܒܘܬܗ ܕܐܬܚܙܝܬ
ܠܩܕܝܫܘܗܝ. ܘܠܘܬ ܛܘܒܢܐ ܢܗܝܪܐ ܘܐܬܢܝܚܘ. ܘܐܬܪܐܝܬ
ܐܬܢܣܒܘ ܒܡܫܡܫܢܘܬܐ ܬܪܝܨܬ ܫܘܒܚܐ.

(§100) ܐܦ ܓܝܪ ܘܗܕܐ ܐܬܪܐ ܓܕܫܬ ܕܬܗܘܐ ܗܘܕܝܢ. ܟܕ ܐܙܠ
ܗܘܐ ܒܠܠܝܐ ܥܡ ܗܢܘܢ ܕܢܦܩܝܢ ܠܗ: ܠܒܝܬܗ ܕܐܢܫ ܒܡܬܪܐ
ܕܢܥܒܪ ܠܒܪܝܬܐ: ܘܥܒܪ ܗܘܐ ܥܠ ܕܘܟܬܐ ܡܕܡ ܕܟܢ ܣܛܠܐ
ܕܨܝܪܐ ܕܝܘܠܝܢܘܣ ܡܠܟܐ ܩܝܡܐ ܗܘܬ. ܟܕ ܦܝܠܝܣܘܦܐ ܫܐܕܐ
ܡܗܝܢܐ. ܢܛܪܬ ܗܝ ܦܝܠܝܣܘܦܐ ܡܢ ܩܕܡܘܗܝ. ܘܪܗܛܐ ܗܘܬ ܒܬܪܗ.
ܘܟܕ ܐܬܚܙܝ ܗܘܐ ܗܠܝܢ ܕܡܬܗܠܟܝܢ ܒܒܝܬ ܒܗܘ ܢܚܠܐ ܘܡܫܬܥܝܐ:
ܘܢܐܘܗܝ ܠܗ ܦܝܠܝܣܘܦܐ. ܐܬܬܗܘܘ ܘܐܘܟܡܘ. ܟܕ ܩܪܝ ܠܛܘܒܢܐ
ܠܒܕܪܢܘܗܝ. ܗܘ ܕܝܢ ܟܕ ܐܫܬܡܥ ܕܠܐ ܐܙܠܝ: ܟܕ ܠܒ ܢܕܒ ܗܘܐ.
ܐܙܠ ܗܘܐ ܒܐܘܪܚܗ ܟܕ ܠܐ ܐܬܦܢܝ ܠܒܣܬܪܗ. ܟܕ ܕܢܚܠܝܢ ܕܝܢ
ܗܢܘܢ ܘܠܒܒܝܢ ܬܠܡܝܕܘܗܝ. ܐܬܦܢܝ ܗܘ ܛܘܒܢܐ ܘܦܩܕ ܥܡܗ ܕܝܪ
ܢܦܩ ܡܫܝܚܐ. ܘܢܦܠ ܒܗ ܒܦܝܠܝܣܘܦܐ. [R 74] ܘܡܫܝܚܐ ܟܕ ܐܢܫ
ܬܢܝܢܐ ܐܫܬܪܝܬ. ܠܐ ܡܬܚܙܝܢܝܬܐ ܗܘܬ. ܡܫܬܟܚܐ ܗܘܐ ܕܝܢ ܗܘ
ܠܛܘܒܢܐ.

(§101) ܘܗܕܐ ܕܗܘܬ ܒܥܠܡ ܩܫܝܬܐ ܒܐܠܟܣܢܕܪܝܐ. ܐܦܩܘ ܐܢܫ ܡܢ
ܟܢܘܫܝܐ ܠܐܚܪܢܝܢ ܡܢ ܩܕܝܫܐ. ܕܢܐܬܘܢ ܠܘܬܗ ܘܢܬܒܪܟܘܢ. ܘܒܬܪܗ

1 See Matt 9:24; Mark 5:40.

2 That Peter and his anti-Chalcedonian friends were able to connect with well-off residents might in part be due to Peter's own royal descent. Thus he provided for the anti-Chalcedonians' access to people of power and prestige.

3 The Syriac transliterates the Greek στήλη. Payne Smith (373), however, does not list the spelling given here.

4 I.e., Julian the Apostate (361–363). Having been reared as a Christian, Emperor Julian turned away from the Christian faith and made a conscious attempt to revive paganism in the Roman Empire. He is vilified by early Christian

go outside,[1] he took oil and anointed the girl. After he had given her the holy mysteries, had consoled her mother with many words of consolation, and had encouraged her to trust undoubtedly in Christ, the Lord **[R 73]** of life, he returned to where he was staying. The next day that girl was suddenly found healthy and free from her severe sickness. The philosopher, however, [who] had contended with God was laid to rest. In this way the judgment of the saint, which he cried out when he was enraged, saying, "Lord, shall this wicked one be alive?" proceeded swiftly to [its] fulfillment, so that in all the city this wonder would become known and everyone would praise God on account of his grace given to his saints, and they would run to the blessed one and cleave to [him], and they would be strengthened more and more in the orthodox faith.

(§100) This sign also took place at that time. With those who were joined to him he was going at night to the house of a rich man to visit someone who was ill.[2] As he passed by a place where a very large statue[3] of Julian the Rebel[4] was standing, a demon performed the following apparition: the statue came down from its height and ran after them.[5] Those who were walking with him became aware of the crashing and commotion and saw this apparition. They were alarmed and cried out, calling on the blessed one to help them. He, while he seemed not to be aware of [it], knew well [what was going on and] continued on his way, without turning his back. But they were afraid and were holding fast to his garments, so the blessed one turned and called the name of our Lord Jesus Christ. He breathed on that apparition, **[R 74]** and immediately it was dissolved like smoke [and] disappeared.[6]

(§101) The blessed one also used to recount an event that happened in those days in Alexandria. "A certain one of [our] friends

authors for that. See, e.g., Cyril of Alexandria, *Contra Julianum* 2.10 *et passim* (Burguière and Évieux, 224–27). See also above, p. 283, n. 4.

[5] This event visualizes at the hands of Rufus that under Julian the Apostate pagan idols came back to life.

[6] The act of breathing against what was perceived to be an evil spirit or a demon was a common feature of the early Christian baptismal ritual. See, e.g., Hippolytus, *Traditio Apostolica* 20 (Botte, 78–81). Also note the same gesture at *Pler.* 9 and 89.

ܢܣܬܡܟܘܢ ܒܦܬܘܪܐ. ܐܬܬܣܝܡܘܢ ܕܝܢ ܗܘܘܢ ܐܠܟܣܢܕܪ̈ܝܐ ܡܛܠܬܗ
ܕܗܕܐ ܦܩܕ ܣܓܝ̈ܐܐ ܘܩܪܝܘ ܒܟܠܐ. ܐܬܘܗܝ، ܗܘܐ ܕܝܢ ܡܢ ܒܢ̈ܝܕܐ
ܘܬܪ̈ܡܟܐ ܗܘ ܒܚܘܪܐ. ܐܦܝܣܘܢ ܕܝܢ ܕܐܦ ܠܗ ܠܒܪ ܢܫܟܚܘܢ
ܒܟܡܘܢ. ܗܢܘܢ ܕܝܢ ܐܟܡ̈ܐܬܐ ܟܕ ܢܚܡ ܠܡܟܣܘܬܐ ܕܝܠܗ:
ܕܟܣܝܐܝܬ ܐܝܬ ܠܗ ܠܘܬ ܦܬ̈ܘܪܐ ܕܕܐܝܟ ܗܠܝܢ: ܡܛܠ ܡܚܝܠܘܬܐ
ܡܣܟܢܐܝܬܐ: ܒܝܘܡ ܟܕ ܦܩܕ ܡܛܐ ܚܒܪܘܗܝ. ܟܕ ܐܡܪܝܢ: ܕܡܛܠ
ܕܐܬܘܗܝ، ܡܢ ܐܚ̈ܝܢܐ ܘܣܓܝ̈ܐܐ ܒܚܘܪܐ: ܠܐ ܙܕܩ ܕܢܥܠܘܢܗܝ، ܟܕ ܕܝܢ
ܐܬܒܥܝ ܐܫܬܡܟܘ ܥܠ ܦܬܘܪܐ. ܘܟܕ ܐܟܠܝܢ: ܫܪܝ ܕܢܬܡܘܗ ܠܒ̈ܝܬܐ
ܕܡܫܡܫܝܢ: ܘܒܟܐ ܒܟܡܘܢ ܒܡ̈ܠܐ ܕܐܠܐ ܦܣ̈ܩܝܢ: ܕܐܬܬܝܗܝܢ ܡܢ
ܒܪܐ ܒܒܝܬܐ ܕܟܠܗܐ. ܐܝܟ ܡܢ ܕܐܠܦܐ ܕܒܡ ܐܢܫ ܗܢܝܢ ܘܐܟܠ.
(§102) ܘܟܕ ܩܡܘ ܒܗܠܝܢ ܡ̈ܠܐ ܡܛܠ ܗܘܐ. ܗܘܐ ܗܘ ܡܠܐ ܠܘܬܗ، ܟܕ
ܐܡܪ: ܦܬܘܪܐ ܦܬܘܪܐ: ܥܕܡܐ ܡܬܗܦܟ. ܘܐܢܬ ܢܦܠ ܐܢܬ ܘܡܬܬܚܝܒ
ܐܢܬ: ܟܕ ܕܝܢ ܠܐ ܐܢܫ ܥܒܕ ܐܝܟ ܕܐܡܪ ܠܡܠܐ: ܐܠܐ ܐܢܐ
ܒܠܚܘܕ.. ܟܕ ܐܬܬܪܗܒ ܘܟܪܝܬ: ܡܣܟܢܐ ܗܘܬ ܕܫܬܐܝܬ ܐܬܥܕܪ.
ܘܟܕ ܬܠܬ ܙܒ̈ܢܝܢ ܗܘܐ ܗܘ ܡܠܐ: ܟܕ ܠܐ ܐܫܬܡܥܬ ܕܐܟܠܐ ܠܓܒ̈ܪܐ.
ܢܚܬܬ ܢܦܫ ܡܢ ܡܬܘܚܬܐ ܕܗܠܝܢ ܐܚܪ̈ܢܐ: ܐܝܟ ܗܘ ܕܐܡܪ ܐܢܐ
ܡܛܠ ܚܫܝܫܘܬܐ. ܘܗܟܢܐ ܢܦܩܬ ܘܪܗܛܬ ܠܡܠܬܐ. ܟܕ ܒܟܠܗ ܐܘܪܚܐ
ܡܬܬܢܚ [R 75] ܐܢܐ. ܘܐܒܠ ܐܢܐ. ܘܡܬܬܢܝܚ ܐܢܐ: ܕܐܝܟܢܐ ܠܐ
ܙܕܩܐ ܗܘܐ: ܐܦܠܐ ܡܢ ܗܠܝܢ ܕܡܫܬܒ̈ܚܝܢ ܕܐܬܬܝܗܒܘܢ ܠܒܪ̈ܝܬܐ
ܠܚܢܢܐ ܕܠܐ ܕܡܟܐ. ܠܐ ܫܡܥܢܐ ܘܠܐ ܡܠܬܐ. ܘܗܕܐ ܐܡܪ
ܐܬܐܡܗ: ܗܝ، ܕܐܡܪ ܣܘܟܠܐ ܫܠܝܛܘܢ. ܙܘܕܗ ܕܡܪܢܐ ܡܛܠ ܟܠܗ
ܬܟܠ. ܘܗܘ ܕܐܡܪ ܟܠ: ܢܟܠܬܐ ܐܝܬ ܠܗ ܕܠܟܠܗ. ܡܛܠ ܗܢܐ

[1] This description of an invitation to a dinner party evidences the existence of a tight network of social support of friends and friends of friends operative among anti-Chalcedonians in Egypt.

[2] One might read this as Peter's approving comment regarding the intensity of Egyptian hospitality. For a discussion of the relevance of the practice of hospitality for the survival and growth of the anti-Chalcedonian movement in Palestine, see Horn, *Asceticism and Christological Controversy*, 275–99.

[3] This could refer either to physical weakness or a difficulty on the part of Peter to interact properly in social settings that involve larger numbers of people. The rise such gatherings provided for occasions of temptations of a moral nature might also be in the background. The physical weakness might be the

convinced certain ones of the saints to come to his house and to bless him and take part with him at the table.[1] The Alexandrians are very diligent and lovers of labor for this cause [of hospitality].[2] This man, however, was one of the respected and notable people, and he also persuaded them to take me along. Although those fathers knew that my poverty has difficulty with such invitations because of great weakness,[3] nevertheless they stood [firm and] pressed me hard, saying that, since the man was one of the zealous and diligent ones, it was not right for us to offend him. When we came and reclined at table and were eating, he began to give orders to the slaves who were serving and to rebuke them with improper words, according to the evil custom of the world, like one who had forgotten with whom he was reclining and eating.[4]

(§102) "When he was carrying on with such words, a voice spoke to me, saying, 'Peter, Peter,[5] my name is being blasphemed, and you are sitting and keeping quiet!' Since no one else heard the voice," as he said, "except I alone, I was disquieted and wept copiously, waiting to be made certain. When that voice came three times, when I could not withhold [my] tears, I withdrew myself from the midst of those others as if I were in a hurry because of a need. Thus I went out and ran to [my] cell, moaning and mourning **[R 75]** all the way. I was thinking how nothing, not even of those [things] that are thought to be little, is disregarded by the eye that does not sleep,[6] neither deed nor word. This, then, is what the wise Solomon said: 'The Spirit of the Lord has filled the whole earth, and the one who possesses everything has knowledge

most likely reason in the light of Peter's later travel to the spring of Moses at Livias in search for healing. See *Vit. Pet.* §116 (R 83).

[4] Here one catches a glimpse of Peter's self-perception. He expected people to respect him as someone striving for moral and ascetic purity.

[5] Again, the name "Peter," spoken by the Lord when addressing him, is repeated. See above, *Vit. Pet.* §78 (R 54). Here it is stated explicitly that Peter heard the voice calling him three times. Note also that Peter breaks out in tears afterwards. It is possible that Rufus modeled this scene in parallel to John 21:15–17.

[6] See Ps 121:3–4.

ܠܝܬ ܐܢܫ ܕܡܟܠܠ ܚܘܠܐ ܘܡܬܓܪܢܐ. ܘܠܐ ܡܬܦܠܛ ܡܢ ܕܝܢܐ
ܕܡܟܣܢܘܬܐ. ܘܥܒܕܐ ܕܟܠܗܘܢ܆ ܐܝܬ ܠܗ ܡܪܝܐ ܠܡܟܣܢܘܬܐ
ܕܥܘܠܡܘܗܝ. ܡܛܠ ܕܐܕܢܐ[1] ܕܛܢܢܬܐ ܫܡܥܐ ܟܠܡܕܡ: ܘܗܘ ܕܝܢ ܡܪ̈ܛܢ
ܒܐܘܢܓܠܝܘܢ ܐܡܪ܆ ܕܟܠ ܡܠܬܐ ܒܛܠܬܐ. ܢܬܠ ܦܬܓܡܐ ܒܝܘܡܐ
ܕܕܝܢܐ. ܒܪܡ ܐܡܪ ܗܘܐ ܗܘ ܠܛܘܒܢܐ. ܕܡܢ ܗܕܐ ܗܘܬ ܥܠܬܐ
ܕܦܘܪܥܢܐ ܘܫܘܠܡܐ ܕܠܘܬ ܓܠܝܬܐ. ܠܗ̇ܘ ܕܫܪܐ ܐܝܟ. ܠܐ ܓܝܪ
ܢ̈ܟܐ ܡܪܝܐ ܒܡܘܬܗ ܕܫܠܝܐ܇ ܐܝܟ ܗ̇ܝ ܕܢܦܩܢܐ ܘܢܟܝܐ. ܘܗܕܐ
ܕܝܢ ܐܫܬܡܠܝܬ ܕܫܠܝܘܬܐ ܘܕܚܠܬܐ܀

(§103) ܐܝܠܝܢ ܕܠܐ ܢܚܘܡܘܢ܆ ܗ̇ܝ ܕܐܦ ܐܫܬܥܝ ܗ̇ܘ ܠܛܘܒܢܐ ܕܗܘܬ
ܒܗ̇ܘ ܙܒܢܐ. ܟܕ ܐܢܐ ܓܝܪ ܚܠܝܫ ܗܘܝܬ ܐܡܪ: ܕܐܦܪܟ ܡܘܪܒܢܐ
ܠܒܪ ܡܢ ܡܕܝܢܬܐ: ܒܚܕܐ ܡܢ ܕܝ̈ܪܬܐ ܩ̈ܕܝܫܬܐ. ܟܕ ܐܬܘ ܐܢ̈ܫܝܢ ܡܢ
ܛ̈ܥܝܢܐ ܡܕܡ ܘܩܕܝܫܐ. ܡܫܬܐܠܝܢ ܗܘܘ ܡܕܡ ܕܗܘܐ ܒܡܕܝܢܬܐ. ܕܠܝܬ
ܗܘܐ ܒܗ ܒܝܬܐ ܐܘ ܡܬܪܥܝܢܐ ܠܗܠܝܢ ܕܫܚܝܡܝܢ. ܐܢܐ ܕܝܢ ܫܬܩܬ
ܗ̇ܘܝܬ. ܟܕ ܠܐ ܫܡܥܬ ܐܢܐ ܠܗܠܝܢ ܕܡܬܐܡܪ̈ܢ. [R 76] ܘܠܐ ܫܐܠܬ
ܐܠܐ ܗܘܝܬ܆ ܥܠ ܕܠܐ ܐܫܟܚܬ ܐܝܟ. ܐܬܬܣܝܡܘ ܗܘܘ ܓܝܪ ܡܢ
ܢ̈ܟܝܐ ܕܡܕܝܢܬܐ. ܐܠܐ ܟܕ ܒܫܠܡܐ ܚܙܝܬ ܐܢܫ܆ ܚܠܦ ܕܐܦܪܟ
ܡܘܪܒܢܐ. ܘܟܕ ܫܡܥܬ ܡܕܡ ܡܕܒܚܐ ܡܕܝܢܐ܆ ܫܪܝܬ ܡܠܐܟܐ ܕܚܙܝܐ
ܒܚܘܒܗ ܘܪܚܠܬܐ܆ ܕܐܝܬܐ ܒܗ ܚܝܠܬܐ ܘܠܡܒܥܝ ܒܡܪܚܒܘܬܐ܆ ܘܢܟ̈ܐ
ܗܘܐ ܕܡܢ ܒܗܘܬܐ ܢܒܥܝܢ ܠܗܘܬ. ܘܟܕ ܐܢܐ ܚܟܐ ܐܢܐ ܘܡܟܠܠ
ܐܢܐ: ܘܡܫܐܠ ܐܢܐ ܕܚܙܐ ܗܘ̣ ܒܠܒܝ ܐܡܪ. ܡܛܠ ܡܢܐ ܟܕ ܚܠܝܫ
ܐܝܬ ܕܐܬܚܫܒ ܠܡܫܬܥܝܘܬܐ ܕܐܠܗܐ܆ ܘܬܘܩܦܘ ܡܕܡ ܡܕܒܚܐ ܡܕܝܢܐ܀
ܐܬܪܓܫܬ ܠܟܠܗ ܕܐܝܟ ܗܟܢ. ܘܟܕ ܐܢܐ ܐܡܪܬ: ܐܝܬ ܢܒܝ ܐܝܬ
ܡܪܝܐ. ܕܠܐ ܥܠܡܬ ܠܫܡܝ ܐܝܠܐ ܒܐܘܪܫܠܡ: ܘܠܐ ܓܠ ܗܘܝ
ܠܠܒܝ ܡܕܡ ܡܢ ܗܠܝܢ ܕܐܬܐܡܪ̈ܝ܆ ܐܡܪ. ܠܡܢܐ ܕܝܢ ܗܘܝ ܐܬܪܓܫܬ
ܕܕܐܝܟ ܗܠܝܢ ܟܠܗ ܩ̈ܠܠܬܐ ܐܫܬܡܥ. ܗܠܝܢ ܕܝܢ ܘܠܐ ܐܢܫ ܡܢ ܗܠܝܢ
ܕܡܪ̈ܒܝܢ ܗܘܘ ܫܡܥ ܗܘܐ. ܘܠܐ ܚܙܐ ܗܘܐ ܫܘܚܐ ܗ̇ܘ ܡܠܐܟܐ

[1] Marginal note in MS A: ܐܕܢܐ ܕܛܢܢܐ ܕܐܠܗܐ.

[2] The referent is either the earth or the Spirit, both of which are grammatically feminine here. The LXX of Wis 1:7 reads: καὶ τὸ πνεῦμα τοῦ κυρίου πεπλήρωκεν τὴν οἰκουμένην καὶ τὸ συνέχον τὰ πάντα γνῶσιν ἔχει φωνῆς: "The spirit of the Lord has filled the habitation, and, possessing all, has knowledge of voice." Some manuscripts read "voice of wisdom," while others read "voice of God." See Joseph Ziegler, ed., *Sapientia Salomonis* (Septuaginta Vetus Testamentum Graecum 12.1; Göttingen: Vandenhoeck & Ruprecht, 1962), 96.

of her[2] voice. Therefore there is no one who speaks iniquity and is hidden: he shall not escape from the judgment of reproof, and the hearing of his words shall come to the Lord for the reproof of his wicked deeds, because the ear of zeal[3] hears everything.'[4] In the Gospel our Lord said that 'for [every] vain word we shall give account on the day of judgment.'[5]" Nevertheless, the blessed one said that from this came the cause of salvation and change toward the good for the one who had invited them, for the Lord does not wish the death of the sinner[6] but rather that he may turn back and live.

(§103) We must not omit the fearful and frightening account that the blessed one also recounted [and] that occurred at this time. He said, "When I was about to offer the oblation outside the city in one of the holy monasteries, certain friends, having come before the liturgy,[7] were recounting something that happened in the city, in which there was no edification or profit for those who were listening. I, however, kept silent, not approving of those things that were being said, **[R 76]** and [yet] I did not stop [them], because I did not [want to] put them to shame, for they were from among the illustrious ones of the city.[8] Passing them over in silence, I entered to offer the oblation. When I stood in front of the holy altar, I saw an angel, fearful in his appearance and frightening, who came [toward me] with fury and grasped me at my waist,[9] wanting to throw me down out of the window. I, while weeping and wailing, asked what the reason for this was. He said, 'Before you were about to enter to the service of God and to stand in front of the holy altar, why did you give heed to such words?' I said, 'You know, Lord, that I did not consent to them, not even in appearance and nothing at all of those things that were said entered my heart.' He replied, 'But why did you give heed to hear such vain words at all?' Not

[3] A marginal note in MS A here says, "the ear of the zeal of God."
[4] See Wis 1:7–10.
[5] See Matt 12:36.
[6] See Ezek 33:11.
[7] More specifically and literally, "before the consecration."
[8] Here Peter showed regard for human rank.
[9] Literally, "at my middle part."

ܐܠܐ ܐܢܐ ܠܢܦܫܝ. ܟܕ ܐܠܐ ܕܫܪܝܢ ܗܘܘ ܠܝ܇ ܕܒܥܠܬܐ ܗܘܝܬ
ܘܒܫܢܝܬܐ. ܘܒܟܝܐ ܐܒܝܠ ܗܘܝܬ. ܘܠܫܪܬܐ ܐܡܪ ܗܘ ܡܠܐܟܐ.
ܗܐ ܐܫܬܟܚܬ ܠܟܝ ܗܕܐ ܚܕܐ ܙܒܢ. ܐܙܕܗܪܝ ܡܟܝܠ ܒܗ ܒܗܕܐ. ܐܢܬܝ
ܕܬܩܘܡܝ ܩܕܡ ܡܕܒܚܐ ܘܬܫܡܫܝ ܠܐܪ̈ܙܐ܇ ܐܚܪܢܐ ܕܫܦܝܪܐ ܘܕܟܝܐ
ܬܩܘܡ. ܟܕ ܢܛܪܝ ܐܢܬܝ ܢܦܫܟܝ ܡܢ ܟܠܗ ܚܛܗܐ ܘܣܪܝܩܘܬ ܡ̈ܠܐ. ܘܟܕ
ܗܕܐ ܐܡܪ ܡܠܐܟܐ ܠܐ ܡܬܚܙܝܢܐ ܗܘܐ. ܗܝ ܕܐܦ ܢܛܪܐ ܗܘܬ
ܚܦܝܛܐܝܬ ܗܘ ܦܘܩܕܢܐ. ܒܕܡܐ ܠܢܫܡܬܐ ܐܚܪܬܐ.

(§104) ܗܠܝܢ ܕܝܢ ܟܠܗܝܢ ܘܗܠܝܢ ܕܕܡ̈ܝܢ ܠܗܝܢ ܘܝܬܝܪ̈ܢ ܬܘܒ܆ ܟܕ
[R 77] ܡܬܚܙ̈ܝܢ ܗ̈ܘܝ ܠܐܒ̈ܗܬܐ ܕܒܦܠܣܛܝܢܐ܆ ܘܠܐܚ̈ܐ ܘܠܡܗ̈ܝܡܢܐ
ܐܘܪܬܕܘܟܣܘ܇ ܠܟܠܗܘܢ ܡܕܝܢ̈ܬܐ ܗ̈ܝ ܘܡܫ̈ܠܡܝܢ܇ ܠܘܬ ܙܘܥܬܐ
ܕܐܟܣܘܗܝ ܡܕܝܢܬܐ ܘܐܦܝܣܩܘܦܘܗܝ. ܘܟܕ ܐܬܐ ܠܘܬܗ ܡܕܝܢܬܐ
ܩܠܝܠܐ ܡܢ ܦܠܣܛܝܢܐ. ܡܬܟܫܦܝܢ ܗܘܘ ܠܗ ܕܢܗܦܘܟ ܘܠܡܕܝܢܬܗ
ܕܦܠܣܛܝܢܐ. ܡܛܠ ܕܡܕܝܢܬܐ ܐܝܬܝܗ̇ ܗܘܬ ܡܕܝܢܬܗ. ܘܠܐ
ܢܗܡܐ ܡܢܗ܇ ܕܟܠܗ ܗܢܐ ܙܒܢܐ ܡܕܒܪܢܐ ܗܘܬ ܡܢ ܡܣܡܟܬܗ ܘܡܢ
ܡܠܦܢܘܬܗ ܪܘܚܢܝܬܐ.

(§105) ܟܕ ܚܙܐ ܗܟܝܠ ܙܒܢܐ ܕܠܐ ܙܒܢ ܒܐܠܟܣܢܕܪܝܐ ܘܡܫܪܝܐ
ܕܐܓܘܦܛܘܣ܇ ܘܩܣܩܐܝܬ ܚܕ ܐܢܘܢ ܘܫܐܠ ܐܢܘܢ܇ ܟܕ ܐܬܬܦܝܣ
ܠܫܪܬܐ ܐܝܟ ܕܐܡܪܬ܆ ܡܠܘܢ ܕܝܢ ܘܡܢ ܐܠܗܐ ܐܬܦܩܕ ܠܗ܆ ܗܘ
ܕܡܢ ܟܠܒܘܗܝ، ܘܠܐ ܡܕܡ ܦܚܪ ܗܘܐ܇ ܦܢܐ ܠܐܬܪܘܬܐ ܕܦܠܣܛܝܢܐ.
ܘܟܕ ܐܬܐ ܠܐܣܩܠܘܢܐ ܡܕܝܢܬܐ܆ ܘܫܪܝܐ ܐܬܦܢܝ ܡܢ ܐܟܣܢܝܘܬܐ
ܘܐܚ̈ܐ ܕܬܡܢ. ܗܘ ܒܡܥܪܬܐ ܚܕܐ ܕܒܬܪܘܬܐ ܦܠܐܬܐ ܥܠ ܟܣܪܐ
ܐܣܛܪܘܬܐ ܡܢ ܡܕܝܢܬܐ. ܐܝܟ ܕܒܕ ܚܙܝ܆ ܘܩܛܠܐܐ ܡܢ ܟܠ
ܕܘܟ ܐܬܝܢ ܗܘܘ ܠܘܬܗ܇ ܠܗܠܝܢ ܬܢܢ ܡܫܬܠ ܗܘܐ. ܠܗܠܝܢ ܕܝܢ ܟܕ
ܡܟܝܪ ܚܘܣܦ ܗܘܐ ܠܟܕܬܐ ܬܪܒܝܬ ܥܡܘܕܝܐ. ܠܐܚܪ̈ܢܐ ܕܝܢ ܟܕ
ܡܫܡܠܝܐܝܬ ܕܢܒܩܘܢ ܒܝܘܬܪܢܗ ܕܥܠܡܐ ܠܗܪ ܗܘܐ܆ ܡܦܝܣ ܗܘܐ
ܕܒܬܪ ܡܫܡܠܝܘܬܐ ܢܪܗܛܘܢ܆ ܘܢܣܒܘܢ ܢܦܠܘܢ ܠܡ̈ܫܒܚܐ. ܘܟܕ

[1] The angel's words give expression to the demand for absolute purity expected of anyone involved in the celebration of the Eucharist. Rufus's work throughout witnesses to a strong concern for ritual purity on the part of anti-Chalcedonians. See also Horn, *Asceticism and Christological Controversy*, 107, 209 *et passim*.

[2] See Lamentations, in which Jerusalem is depicted as a widow (e.g., Lam 1:1). The church is frequently depicted as feminine in early Christian texts. When Rufus here speaks of the church as a widow, having lost her husband, he

one of those who were near heard these [words], and no [one] saw the vision of the angel but I alone; however, they did see that I was trembling and groaning and mourning in pain. Finally that angel said, 'Behold, it is forgiven you this one time. Henceforth, be careful when you are about to stand in front of the altar and celebrate the mysteries that you may stand pure and clean, guarding yourself from every captivity and vanity of words!'[1] Having said this, the angel disappeared." The blessed one kept this [admonition] diligently even to [his] last breath.

(§104) Now all these [things] and things like them and even greater [ones] **[R 77]** having been made known to the fathers in Palestine, to the brethren, and to the orthodox people, they stirred all of them up and inflamed [them] with love for their holy father and bishop. Many saints from Palestine came to him, [earnestly] entreating him also to visit his flock in Palestine, since it was rightfully his flock, and not to neglect it, which all this time was left widowed[2] of his superintendence and of his spiritual teaching.

(§105) When he had thus passed no little time in Alexandria and in the rest of Egypt and had sufficiently edified them and strengthened them, finally being persuaded, as I have said, or rather, [as] it was commanded to him by God, without whom he did nothing, he returned to the regions of Palestine.[3] He came to the city of Ashkelon[4] and was joyfully received by the fathers and brothers there. He stayed in a village called Palaea,[5] about ten stades from the city. While he dwelt there many were coming to him from every place; he strengthened some, and some he enlightened [and] added to the orthodox church. Others he incited to renounce the vanity of the world entirely, persuading [them] to run after perfection, to distribute their possessions to the poor,

at the same time expresses that the theology of the episcopacy sees the role of the bishop defined along gender lines and the office to be held by a male.

[3] Peter seems to have returned to Palestine around 475.

[4] For the location and references to relevant ancient literature on Ashkelon, see, e.g., Tsafrir, Di Segni, and Green, *Tabula Imperii Romani*, 68–70. See also Lawrence E. Stager, "Ashkelon," *NEAEHL* 1:103–12.

[5] Syriac ܦܐܠܐܐ in MS A and ܦܠܐܐ in MS B. On Palaea, see Charles Clermont-Ganneau, "Sur quelques localités de Palestine mentionnées dans la Vie de Pierre l'Ibère," in idem, *Etudes d'archéologie orientale* (2 vols.; BEHE 44, 113; Paris: Bouillon, 1895–97), 2:2–9; and Tsafrir, Di Segni, and Green, *Tabula Imperii Romani*, 200.

ܥܡܠܝ̈ ܨܠܘܬܗ ܕܩܕܝܫܐ܆ ܠܗ ܒܠܚܘܕ ܢܦܩܘ̣. ܕܟܡܐ̣ ܗܘܘ ܘܠܘܩܒܠܐ
ܦܪܘܦܘܣ܆ ܗܘ̇ ܕܢܓܦ ܒܟܠ ܘܕܒܫܪܪܐ ܒܪܢܫܐ ܕܐܠܗܐ ܓܪ܀
ܘܠܩܘܪܝܠܘܣ ܗܘ̇ ܓܪܒܐ [R 78] ܕܩܕܝܫܐ. ܠܬܪ̈ܝܗܘܢ̣ ܒܕ. ܡܢ ܚܠܡܐ
ܐܦܣ܆ ܠܐܬܪܐ ܕܡ̈ܠܐܟܐ ܐܘܟܠ. ܘܠܬܐܘܕܘܪܐ ܕܐܝܬܘܗܝ܆ ܗܘܐ
ܣܟܘܠܣܛܝܩܐ. ܗܘ̇ ܕܠܚܪܬܐ ܐܦ ܡܫܒܠܢܐ ܕܕܘܒܪܗ ܐܘܢܓܠܝܐ
ܘܕܛܒܝܗ ܘܕܪܝܫܢܘܬܐ ܕܒܡܕܝܢܬܗ ܗܘ̣ܐ܆ ܒܗ ܐܟܐ ܢܘܣܢ ܣܒܐ
ܡܫܡܪܐ܆ ܗܘ̇ ܙܟܝܐ ܘܫܒܝܚܐ ܘܕܒܟܠܗ̇ ܡܕܝܢܬܐ ܕܕܪ̈ܝܫܘܬܐ܀
ܘܬܪܐܝܬ ܒܡܫܡܫܢܘܬܐ ܡܫܒܚܬ ܗܘܐ. ܘܠܐܚܪ̈ܢܐ ܡܫܟܚܐ ܐܐ ܠܗ
ܒܠܚܘܕ ܒܚܪ̈ܐ܆ ܐܠܐ̣ ܘܫܝܐ ܢܝܚ. ܗܘܐ ܠܗ ܦܠܚܘܬܗ ܕܩܕܝܫܐ.
ܘܟܕ ܠܚܝܪܐ ܒܡܫܡܫܐ ܕܟܠܘܬܐ ܕܝܡܠܘ̣ ܡܫܦܠ ܗܘܐ܆ ܒܟܐ
ܡܛܪܬܐ ܘܡܠܝܐ ܕܚܒܪ̈ܐ ܡܠܐ ܠܡܪܐ ܡܠܟ ܗܘܐ. ܘܡܠܠܗ̇ ܕܐ
ܡܣܝܟܐܝܬ ܚܕ. ܗܘܐ ܥܘܢܝܐ ܡܢ ܕܗܒܬܐ ܠܕܘ̈ܟܝܬܐ ܐܚܪ̈ܢܝܬܐ.
ܒܗ ܡܢ܆ ܠܕܘ̈ܟܝܬܐ ܕܟܠ ܚܕ ܚܕܐ܆ ܘܗ̇ܝ ܕܡܬܩܪܝܐ ܡܫܡܫܬܐ
ܡܥ̇ܢܐ ܗܘܐ. ܒܗ̇ ܕܝܢ ܘܠܗܠܝܢ ܕܝܢ̈. ܡܨܪܝܐ ܘܐܘܪܫܠܡ܆ ܒܕܡܐ
ܠܐܬܪ̈ܘܬܐ ܕܐܪܥܢܐ. ܠܐܢܫܐ ܕܪܘܚܢܐ ܦܪܐ ܗܘܐ ܘܡܚܕܐ ܠܗ܆
ܒܟܠ ܕܘܟܐ ܘܛܒܘܬܐ ܡܥ̇ܒܕ ܠܗ. ܠܗ ܒܠܚܘܕ ܕܐܦ̈ܘܬܐ ܢܣܒܘܪ
ܘܪ̈ܘܚܐ ܢܪܕܘܦ܆ ܐܠܐ ܘܒܡܠܬܐ ܘܒܡܠܦܢܘܬܐ܆ ܘܒܝܕ ܐܬܘ̈ܬܐ
ܘܬܕܡܪ̈ܬܐ ܩ̈ܛܝܠܬܐ܆ ܐܝܟܢܐ ܕܒܠܕܘܟ ܡܬ̈ܚܫܒܬܐ ܕܡܗ̈ܝܡܢܐ
ܘܒܢ̈ܝܐ ܕܐܘܪܬܕܘܟܣܘ܆ ܘܕܪ̈ܬܐ ܘܡܕ̈ܬܐ ܢܦܩܘ ܒܗ. ܡܐܬܝܬܗ.

[1] The Syriac might render the Greek phrase ἐτύπωσεν ἄνθρωπον τοῦ θεοῦ. See 1 Tim 6:11.

[2] It is doubtful whether he is the same as Cyril the "orthodox innkeeper" of Ashkelon mentioned at *Pler.* 6.

[3] On this Theodore of Ashkelon, see also *Vit. Pet.* §§105, 112–113, 178, 191 (R 78, 81–82, 134, 144), and possibly "Abba Theodore the monk who later became bishop" of *Pler.* 33. Theodore of Ashkelon is also featured in Zachariah Scholasticus, *Vit. Sev.* 86 (Kugener, 86); and Zachariah Rhetor, *Chron.* 7.10 (Brooks, 2:51,10; Hamilton and Brooks, 180). Theodore is identical with Theodore the scholastic or Theodore the lawyer.

[4] Possibly John the Eunuch. See *Vit. Pet.* §73 (R 50) for the last reference to him.

[5] Miqa of Ashkelon, whose story Rufus tells at *Pler.* 43, is not presented as having been influenced by Peter the Iberian. Rufus does not provide names of female followers of Peter who originated from the Ashkelon area. Eugenia,

and taking up the cross of Christ to cleave to him alone. Among them [were] the blessed Procopius, who was chaste in everything and who in truth represented the man of God,[1] and Cyril,[2] that sheep **[R 78]** of Christ, [both of whom] he led out from the world and brought to the place of the angels, and Theodore,[3] a lawyer, who in the end was also the recipient of his evangelical way of life and of his zeal and of the governership of his monastery, together with Abba John,[4] the venerable old man, the one who was dear and beloved and who was adorned with every monastic virtue, especially with humility. He attracted to the army of Christ many others, not only men but also women.[5] He urged them to take up the sweet yoke of virginity, and he prepared for the Lord a people abundant and zealous for good works. For this end he frequently made trips from place to place. Sometimes, on the one hand, he headed off to the places that are at the shore of Gaza, called Maiuma,[6] sometimes, on the other hand, to those in the direction of Caesarea[7] and Jerusalem, as far as the regions of Arabia.[8] Wherever the Spirit[9] was calling and leading him, in every place he [the Spirit] also bestowed grace on him, not only to perform healings and to chase away evil spirits but also in word, in teaching, and by many signs and wonders, so that everywhere he might establish through his arrival flocks of believers, congregations of orthodox,

whose experience is discussed *Vit. Pet.* §§154 and 160 (R 115–116, 120) and who is the most prominent female recruit of Peter the Iberian, was a native of Tyre. Eventually she settled in a monastery south of Caesarea.

[6] Note that, when returning from Egypt, Peter did not immediately resettle in his former monastic headquarters in Maiuma, likely because the base of support for anti-Chalcedonians in that location was not strong enough at the time.

[7] I.e., Caesarea Maritima. See Tsafrir, Di Segni, and Green, *Tabula Imperii Romani*, 94–96.

[8] For a discussion of Peter's missionary activity, especially among the population east of the Jordan in the *provincia Arabia*, see Horn, "Chapter in the Pre-history of the Christological Controversies"; eadem, "Weaving the Pilgrim's Crown."

[9] Note that "Spirit" here is masculine, whereas earlier it is feminine.

ܘܠܘܬ ܟܢܘܫܬܐ ܟܠܗ̇ ܐܝܟ ܗܘܐ. ܕܠܐ ܡܫܡܥ ܗܘܐ ܒܗ̇ ܠܬܪܥܐ
ܦܘܪܩܢܐ ܕܢܨ̈ܚܬܐ ܗܝܡܢܘܬܐ. ܟܕ ܐܓܘܢܐ ܘܪܗܛܐ ܫܠܡܐ ܫܡܠܝ.
(§106) ܒܗܘ ܕܝܢ ܙܒܢܐ ܟܕ ܡܕܒܪ ܗܘܐ ܚܕ ܐܣܛܘܠܘܣܐ ܡܕܒܪܢܘܬܐ. ܗܘܬ
ܦܢܝܬܐ ܘܦܘܢܝܐ [R 79] ܕܡܢ ܐܟܣܘܪܝܐ. ܕܛܘܒܢܐ ܘܡܘܕܝܢܐ
ܪܫܐ ܕܐܦܝܣܩܘܦܐ ܛܝܡܬܐܘܣ ܡܢ ܓܠܘܬܐ ܕܐܠܗܐ. ܟܕ ܐܬܠܝܢ
ܒܡܠܟܘܬܗ. ܘܒܗܬܒܬܐ ܡܠܟܬܐ ܐܢܣܛܘܠܝ. ܟܠܗ̇ ܡܢ ܚܕܬܘܬ
ܦܢܩܐ ܕܐܬܬܟܪܢ ܒܟܠܡܕܘܢܐ ܠܘܩܒܠ ܡܗܝܡܢܘܬܐ ܬܪܝܨܬ ܫܘܒܚܐ.
ܡܢ ܐܦܝܣܩܘܦܐ ܢܩܦܘ ܒܟܦܐ ܡܬܦܪܣܐ ܗܘܬ: ܢܘܗܪܐ ܕܝܢ
ܕܡܗܝܡܢܘܬܐ ܬܪܝܨܬ ܫܘܒܚܐ. ܘܫܪܪܐ ܕܡܠ̈ܦܢܐ ܬܪ̈ܝܨܐ ܘܫ̈ܠܝܚܐ
ܬܘܒ ܡܚܘܝ ܗܘܐ ܘܡܫܬܪܪ. ܘܡܚ̈ܕܝܢܘܬܐ ܕܒܟܠܗܐ ܡܠܬܪ̈ܐ ܗܘ̈ܝ.
ܘܐܬܘܬܗ ܗܘܐ ܒܐܪܥܐ ܕܕܢܚܐ ܘܕܚܕܘܬܐ ܪܘܚܢܝܬܐ. ܕܐܝܟ ܗܘܐ
ܠܢܨܚܬܐ ܕܕܝ̈ܢܐ ܐܠܗܐ.
(§107) ܒܗ̇ܘ ܕܝܢ ܕܝܢ. ܗ̇ܘ ܠܐ ܫܒܩܐ ܕܒܠܒܗ: ܟܕ ܐܬܦܢܝ
ܠܒܗܘܬܐ. ܒܥܕܬܐ ܡܬܠܝܢ ܕܐܠܗܐ ܕܐܢܛܝܘܟܝܐ ܡܕܒܪܢܘܬܐ ܡܕܒܪ
ܗܘܐ. ܟܕ ܒܥܕܢ ܠܗ̇ܘ ܕܝܢܐ ܐܫܬܘ، ܕܢܛܘܪ ܠܐ ܡܬܗܦܟܐ
ܕܫܒ̈ܪܐ ܡܪ̈ܛܢܐ. ܟܕ ܗܘܐ ܡܢ ܐܟܡ̈ܬܐ ܫܡܠܝ.
(§108) ܐܠܐ ܟܕ ܬܘ̈ܒ ܩ̈ܢܝܢ ܒܬܪܗ ܗܕܐ ܘܐܛܠܛܠܘܣ ܫܦܝܪܬܐ:
ܘܐܢܝܕܘܬܐ ܕܡܗܝܡܢܘܬܐ ܬܪܝܨܬ ܫܘܒܚܐ. ܬܘܒ ܢܫܒܚܐ
ܕܐܟܠܘܪ̈ܝܐ ܘܒܫܘܬܗ ܠܡܐܬ ܒܟܠ. ܟܕ ܒܠܬܐ ܫܦܠܬ ܪ̈ܘܫܡܐ

[1] See 2 Tim 4:7.

[2] In 476 C.E.

[3] The usurpor Basiliscus occupied the imperial throne in Constantinople from 475 to 476.

[4] The term *encyclikon* more generally refers to a "circular letter" sent out by the emperor. See also Alexander P. Kazhdan, "Encyclical," *ODB* 1:696. The encyclical in question here was sent out by Emperor Basiliscus (475–476 C.E.), promoting Cyril and Dioscorus's theology and attacking both Nestorianism and the teachings of Eutyches. The receptive attitude with which the anti-Chalcedonian community in and associated with Palestine responded to the encyclical can be noted at *Pler.* 22, 44, 45, 46 ("divine encyclical"), 59, 82, 84, 86, and 89. The anti-Chalcedonians around Peter and John Rufus took great delight in this document. For the text of the encyclical, see Zachariah Rhetor, *Chron.* 5.2 (Brooks, 1:211–13; Hamilton and Brooks, 105–7), and Evagrius Scholasticus, *Hist. eccl.* 3.4 (Bidez and Parmentier, 101,6–104.19; Whitby, 134–37). See

monasteries, and churches. Since he had accepted the apostolic contest and race,[1] there was no place he went where he did not offer to the Lord the salvation of many souls.

(§106) At this time,[2] while he was dwelling near the city of Ashkelon, there occurred by the will of God **[R 79]** the recall and return from exile of the blessed confessor and archbishop Timothy, after Basiliscus[3] had come to the throne and by an imperial document [called] the *Encyclikon*[4] had anathematized all of the novelty of the decree that had been presumptuously confected at Chalcedon against the orthodox faith by the hypocritical bishops.[5] The light of the orthodox faith and the truth of the straight and apostolic teachings once again shone forth and became strong, and the professions [confirmed] in writing[6] were being proclaimed. It was a feast of exultation and of spiritual joy that took hold of the God-fearers' souls.

(§107) At this time the one [who is] useless to everyone,[7] having been called to the priesthood, was dwelling in the catholic church of God of the city of Antioch and hither to this time had been esteemed worthy to be guarded against being in communion with the heretical leaven,[8] whereas he had received [communion rather] from the fathers.

(§108) Yet after two years of adherence to the orthodox faith in this good state,[9] again the envy of the devil and his all-defiled evil called up wickedness, while taking as justification the many

also Frend, *Rise of the Monophysite Movement*, 170–71 with n. 1. On the encyclical, see E. Dovere, "L'*Ἐγκύκλιον Βασιλίσκου*: Un caso di normativa imperiale in Oriente su temi di dogmatica teologica," *Studia et documenta historiae et juris* 51 (1985): 153–88. In promulgating the encyclical, Basiliscus set a model for Zeno's *Henoticon*. On Basiliscus, see Timothy E. Gregory, "Basiliskos," *ODB* 1:267.

[5] Literally, "by bishops who openly accepted it."

[6] Literally, "the professions that are in writing," probably the creedal statements of Nicaea or the conciliar *horoi*. Note also the emphasis on "written documents" above, at *Vit. Pet.* §21 (R 14). See also §§176, 180 (R 132–133, 135).

[7] It is very likely that the author is referring to himself here. For a fuller discussion of the relevance of the following section for identifying the author of the *Vita Petri Iberi*, see Horn, *Asceticism and Christological Controversy*, 31–38.

[8] See Matt 16:6–12; Mark 8:15; Luke 12:1.

[9] The Syriac transliterates the Greek κατάστασις.

ܘܡܒܘܪ̈ܐ ܦܘܠ̈ܚܢܐ ܕܗܠܝܢ ܕܒܠܥܐ ܡܗܝܡܢܘܬܐ ܡܬܦܩܕܝܢ܆
ܡܢܗܪ̈ܝܢ ܦܢܝܬ ܠܙܒܢܐ. ܟܕ ܒܬܪܐ ܐܚܪܢܐ ܠܡܦܩ ܐܢܩܘܩܠܝܘܢ
ܒܠܚܘܕ ܕܢܗܘܐ܆ ܠܡܦܩܕܢܐ ܬܘܒ ܕܐܢܩܘܩܠܝܘܢ ܗ̇ܘ ܡܕܒܪܢܐ
ܕܬܪ̈ܬܝܢ ܐܝܬ ܗܘܐ ܒܗ܆ ܠܡܦܩܕܢܐ ܕܝܢ ܘܠܡܣܪܬܐ ܕܟܢܫܬ
ܗܝܡܢܘܬܐ ܕܟܠܩܕܘܢܐ.

(§109) ܗܢܝܢ ܡܟܝܠ ܗ̇ܘ ܠܛܘܒܢܐ ܦܛܪܘܣ ܒܝܘܒܢܐ ܕܥܢܝܐ܆ ܟܕ
ܐܬܢܦܫ ܡܢ [R 80] ܠܛܘܒܬܐܘܗܝ ܪܥܝܐ ܕܐܦܝ̈ܣܩܘܦܐ ܕܐܝܬܐ
ܠܘܬܗ ܠܐܠܟܣܢܕܪܝܐ܆ ܘܠܒܢܐ ܦܘܠܚܢܐ ܢܟܠܝܢ ܫܠܝܐ ܕܫ̈ܪܪܐ܆
ܗܕܐ ܕܝܢ ܟܕ ܒܢܝܢܐ ܕܢܝܚܘܬܗ ܘܕܡܟܝܟܘܬܗ ܡܬܚܫܚ ܠܐ ܢܪܓܐ
ܕܢܣܒ܆ ܒܟܬ̈ܝܒܬܐ ܕܝܢ ܕܐܫܬܕܪܬܐ ܘܒܐܝܠܝܢ ܕܬܘܪܬܐ ܕܦܘܠܚܢܐ
ܐܒ̈ܗܬܐ ܩܕ̈ܝܫܐ ܕܦܠܣܛܝܢܐ܆ ܟܕ ܦܢܐ ܐܡܪܐ ܕܡܬܬܣܝܒ
ܠܪܥܝܐ ܕܐܦܝ̈ܣܩܘܦܐ ܘܢܦܩ ܒܝܘܡܐ܆ ܗ̣ܘ ܡܕܝܢ ܗܘܐ ܒܐܬܪ̈ܘܬܐ
ܕܦܠܣܛܝܢܐ.

(§110) ܟܕ ܡܟܝܠ ܗ̇ܘ ܗܘܐ ܡܦܩܢܐ ܕܐܢܩܘܩܠܝܘܢ܆ ܘܒܬܪܐ ܕܠܘܩܒܠܗ
ܥܠ ܫܠܡܘܗܝ܆ ܘܬܘܒ ܐܝܟܢ ܢܦܩ ܡܠܟܘܬܐ܆ ܟܕ ܐܦ ܗܢܝܢ
ܠܡܠܟܘܬܗ܆ ܟܕ ܚܠܦ ܗܘܐ ܡܢ ܟܪܗ ܗ̇ܘ ܡܕܝܢܐ ܠܛܘܒܬܐܘܗܝ
ܕܬܘܒ ܠܐܟܣܢܕܪܝܐ ܕܬܬܐ ܢܗܕܪ ܒܫܘܠܛܢܐ ܡܠܟܝܐ. ܐܠܗܐ ܗ̇ܘ
ܗܟܢ ܐܓܘܢܐ ܠܩܕ̈ܝܫܐ܆ ܘܡܟܠܠܐ ܒܐܝܕܐ ܕܗ̇ܘܝܢ ܕܣܠܩ ܥܡܗ
ܡܬܟܬܫܝܢ܆ ܢܨܚܐ ܕܪܗ̇ܛܗ ܥܡܠ܆ ܘܐܓܘܢܐ ܫܦܝܪܐ ܐܬܟܬܫ܆

1 Anti-Chalcedonians greatly appreciated Basiliscus's efforts on their behalf. Thus, when addressing Basiliscus's promulgation of the *Anti-Encyclikon*, which promoted Chalcedonian teaching and thus was a blow to anti-Chalcedonian interests, Rufus does not mention by name Basiliscus as author of that document.

2 The discussion of the question of Peter the Iberian's potential authorship of the Pseudo-Dionysian corpus also needs to take into account to what extent writing activity on Peter's part is documented. At *Pler.* 22 Rufus inserts a short letter he claims was written by Peter to him. For a discussion of additional evidence that shows Peter the Iberian as the recipient and author of letters, see Horn, *Asceticism and Christological Controversy*, 238.

3 Zeno ruled the Eastern Roman Empire from 474 to 475 and again from 476 to 491. In an attempt to unify the opposing Christian parties and appease the anti-Chalcedonians, Zeno issued the *Henotikon* in 482. He was supported in his efforts by Acacius of Constantinople, who had entered into conversations with Peter Mongus, bishop of Alexandria. The resultant formula was intended to bring about union between the Chalcedonian orthodox and the anti-Chalcedonians. Although the formula condemned both Nestorius

wicked deeds and transgressions of those who were wantonly living in the world. It brought it to pass that there would be another writing, the *Anti-Encyclikon*,[1] on the one hand to overturn the first *Encyclikon*, which was according to the straight [path], and on the other hand to establish and renew the evil faith [proclaimed] at Chalcedon.

(§109) During that time of tranquility the blessed Peter was urged by **[R 80]** Archbishop Timothy to come to him to Alexandria, and after a long time they [again] corresponded concerning [their] mutual welfare. [Yet Peter] was unwilling to do this, on the one hand because he conducted himself according to his custom of quietness and humility, and on the other hand, by letters[2] of friendship and through an embassy of many holy fathers of Palestine, having shown forth due honor to the archbishop, he excused himself [and] remained dwelling in the regions of Palestine.

(§110) When therefore the repeal of the *Encyclikon* arrived and the *Anti-Encyclikon* was substituted for it, Zeno, having cast out Basiliscus, again assumed the reign.[3] When the holy Timothy was already about to be sent again into exile a second [time] by imperial authority, God, the one who decides the contest of the saints and justly bestows crown[s] to those who fight on account of his name, saw that the high priest Timothy had finished his course[4]

as representative of an extreme position with regard to a two-nature Christology and Eutyches as representative of the extreme position with respect to a one-nature Christology, the document never addressed the problem inherent in the choice of "nature" terminology. The basis of the proposed union between the opposing parties were the Nicene-Constantinopolitan Creed and Cyril of Alexandria's Twelve Anathemas. It should be noted, however, that there was probably no "Creed" promulgated at Constantinople in the manner that the Council of Nicaea had done. See Luise Abramowski, "Was hat das Nicaeno-Constantinopolitanum (C) mit dem Konzil von Konstantinopel (381) zu tun?" *Theologie und Philosophie* 67 (1992): 481–513. In any case, agreement with Chalcedon's decrees was not required. On the anti-Chalcedonian side, the *Henotikon* was received by many, but not by the more radical, strongly committed anti-Chalcedonians. Rufus presents Peter the Iberian as one of the latter group. The lack of mention of the *Tome of Leo* also caused suspicion in Rome. Instead of leading to union, a schism arose between Rome and Constantinople, the so-called Acacian Schism from 482 to 519.

[4] 2 Tim 4:7.

ܘܡܟܝܟܘܬܐ ܫܠܝܚܝܬܐ ܕܝܐܐ ܠܬܠܡܝܕܐ ܕܠܐ ܒܕܘܪܐ ܢܛܪ ܗܘ
ܓܝܪ ܚ̈ܡܝܐ ܠܓܒܬܐܘܣ: ܒܡܣܝܒܪܢܘܬܐ ܣܓܝܐܬܐ: ܒܐܘ̈ܠܨܢܐ:
ܒܐܢ̈ܢܩܐ: ܒܐܢ̈ܢܩܐܘܣ: ܒܐܟܣܘ̈ܪܘܣ: ܒܗ. ܒܕܘܟܐ ܠܡܘܬܐ ܚܙܝ.
ܥܒܕܗ ܠܐܬܪܐ ܕܫ̈ܡܝܐ ܕܢܛܪ ܠܗ: ܒܡܫܡܫܘܬܐ ܠܓܒܬܐ: ܒܫܘܒܚܐ
ܘܒܐܝܩܪܐ ܒܬܪܘܢܘܣ ܕܝܠܗ ܥܡ ܡܪܟܒܬܗ. ܒܗ ܬܪ̈ܬܝܢ ܫܢ̈ܝܐ ܒܠܚܘܕ.
ܚܝܐ ܡܢ ܒܬܪ ܐܟܣܘܪܝܐ. ܒܗ ܗܘܐ ܐܦܝܣܩܘܦܐ ܒܫܢܝܢ ܘܬܪ̈ܬܝܢ
ܫܢ̈ܝܢ. ܬܠܬ ܡܢ ܩܕܡ ܐܟܣܘܪܝܐ. ܘܥܣܪ̈ܐ ܒܐܟܣܘܪܝܐ. ܘܬܪ̈ܬܝܢ
ܡܢ ܒܬܪ ܐܟܣܘܪܝܐ. ܘܡܢܕܐ ܕܫܠܡ ܚܝܘ̈ܗܝ. ܒܗ ܒܙܒܢܐ ܒܗ. ܡܛܠ
ܦܘܩܕܢܐ ܕܢܦܩ ܒܐܟܣܘܪܝܐ: ܒܝܕ [R 81] ܩܘܐܣܛܘܪܘܣ ܘܐܦܪܛܘܪ.
ܠܟܠܗ̇ ܠܡܕܝܢܬܐ ܐܝܟ ܕܝ ܘܠܡܟܠܠܘܬ ܫܘܒܚܐ. ܕܐܟܚܕܐ ܡܬܟܬܫ ܥܠ
ܗܠܝܢ ܕܐܣܟܡ ܠܗ: ܘܡܫܟܚ ܠܗܠܝܢ ܕܡܫܟܚܝܢ ܠܗ: ܘܠܐ ܥܒܕ ܠܗܘܢ
ܕܢܬܪ ܡܢ ܡܕܡ ܕܥܒܝܕ ܢܦܫܗ.
(§111) ܒܗ ܗܒܠ ܠܚܡܘܬܐ ܕܡܪ̈ܝܢܘ ܕܐܬܪ̈ܝ ܚ̈ܝܢܐ: ܗܟܢܐ ܐܬܐ ܬܘܒ
ܚܠܬ ܠܒܪ̈ܬܐ ܩܕ̈ܝܫܬܐ ܕܐܠܗܐ: ܐܫܬܕܪܘ ܕܝܢ ܠܐܟܣܘܪܝܐ ܘܦܛܪܘܣ
ܓܝܪ ܐܦܝܣܩܘܦܐ ܕܐܢܛܝܘܟܝܐ ܘܦܘܠܐ ܕܐܦܣܘܣ. ܠܦܢܝܬܐ ܦܛܝܘܣ
ܒܗ ܡܕܝܪ ܗܘܐ ܒܦܠܛܝܢܐ: ܠܟܠܗ̇ ܗ̇ܘ ܗܘܐ ܡܦܩܚܢܐ.
ܒܗ ܒܙܒܢܐ ܢܗܘܪܐ ܕܡܫܝܚܐ ܠܢܦ̈ܫܬܐ ܕܒܥܝܢܐ ܐܘܪܬܕܘܟܣܘ
ܢܗܪ ܗܘܐ. ܠܐ ܒܠܚܘܕ ܠܗܠܝܢ ܕܒܦܠܛܝܢܐ: ܐܠܐ ܘܠܟܠܗ̇
ܕܩܘܣܛܢܛܝܢܘܦܘܠܝܣ ܘܕܚܕܪ̈ܝܗ̇. ܒܗ ܠܐ ܥܒܕ ܗܘܐ ܕܢܬܦܪܦܐ:
ܘܒܪܦܠܐ ܕܪܘܥܝܐ ܢܛܘܪܘ.
(§112) ܒܗ̇ ܗܘ ܙܒܢܐ. ܘܒܬܪܗ̇ ܕܐܟܣܘܪܝܐ ܒܗ. ܐܫܬܠܛ ܠܥܒܕܝ̈
ܥܒܕܐ ܘܠܡܢܘ. ܕܐܟܐ ܐܝܟ ܡܫܝܚܐ ܘܫܠܝܚܐ ܕܠܐ ܢܦܫܗ ܒܠ

[1] 1 Tim 6:12.

[2] The Syriac transliterates the Greek ἀνάγκη.

[3] 2 Cor 6:4–5.

[4] The Syriac transliterates the Latin *quaestor*. According to Payne Smith (511), in a Byzantine context the title refers to a secretary. Constantine I designated the *quaestor* to draft imperial laws and to respond to petitions to the emperor. After Justinian I (539), the *quaestor* had police and judicial powers in Constantinople. It is possible that the *quaestor* was assigned these powers already by the time the *Vita Petri Iberi* was composed. See Alexander Kazhdan, "Quaestor," *ODB* 3:1765.

and fought the good fight[1] and kept the apostolic faith to the end without transgression, in much patience, in calamities, in persecutions, in deprivations,[2] [and] in exiles,[3] persevering until death. He transferred him to the place of life reserved for him at a ripe old age, with glory and honor, on his throne with his flock, having lived only two years after [his] exile, having been bishop [for] twenty-two years, three before [his] exile and seventeen in exile and two after [his] exile. As soon as he had finished his life, at that [very] moment when through the *quaestor*[4] Martyrius[5] the command arrived **[R 81]** to go into exile, it brought everyone to amazement and glorification [of God], when they saw how [God] exerts great effort on account of those who love him, glorifying those who glorify him, and not allowing them to be tried more than what they are able to [bear].[6]

(§111) Now when thus the heretics' error of the two natures had yet again entered the holy churches of God and Peter, the archbishop of Antioch,[7] and Paul of Ephesus[8] were cast into exile, the blessed Peter, dwelling in Palestine, was a support for everyone. In the likeness of the light of the sun he was enlightening the souls of the orthodox, not only those in Palestine but also in Egypt and everywhere else, for he did not allow them to be weary and depressed by the dark fog of ungodliness.

(§112) [Meanwhile,] the church in Antioch had been delivered up to the foul name Calendion,[9] a man who was a hard and

[5] Martyrius was *quaestor* when Aelurus died. On him, see also Martindale, *Prosopography of the Later Roman Empire*, 2:732 ("Martyrius 3").

[6] See 1 Cor 10:13.

[7] Also known as Peter the Fuller. In 470 he emerged as leader of the anti-Chalcedonians in Antioch. He occupied the throne of the See of Antioch from 475 to 477. Having signed Zeno's *Henotikon*, Peter the Fuller was patriarch of Antioch from 484 to his death in 489.

[8] On Paul of Ephesus, see Ernest Honigmann, *Évêques et évêchés monophysites d'Asie antérieure au VIe siècle* (CSCO 127, Subsidia 2; Leuven: Durbecq, 1951), 3–4, 119.

[9] In 481, Acacius consecrated Calendion as pro-Chalcedonian patriarch of Antioch. Calendion held the throne of the church of Antioch until 484.

ܡܪܒܝܬܐ܆ ܘܛܢܢܐ ܕܐܪ̈ܣܝܣ ܕܟܠܩܕܘܢܐ܇ ܦܪܫ ܢܦܫܗ ܡܢ ܡܗܝܡܢܘܬܐ
ܘܫܘܬܦܘܬܐ ܕܗܢܐ ܥܒܕܐ ܠܐ ܚܫܝܫܐ ܗܘ ܕܦܪܘܩ ܐܬܐܡܪ܆ ܟܕ
ܐܝܬ ܠܗ ܡܢ ܙܒܢܐ ܣܓܝܐܐ ܚܘܒܐ ܐܚܝܢܐ ܘܡܚܒܪܐ܇ ܠܘܬ
ܬܐܘܕܘܪܐ ܐܣܟܘܠܣܛܝܩܘ ܗܘ ܕܐܡܪܢ܆ ܡܢ ܕܘܪܐ ܕܐܒܚܕܐ
ܕܒܒܪܘܛܘܣ. ܘܟܕ ܫܡܥ ܠܐܬܘ̈ܬܐ ܕܣܘܥܪܢܐ܇ ܪܗܛ ܠܘܬ ܐܪܒܐ
ܕܡܠܟܢܐ ܐܡܪ ܐܢܐ ܕܝܢ. ܠܦܠܣܛܝܢܐ܆ ܟܕ [R 82] ܬܐܕܘܪܐ ܪܗܛܐ
ܘܐܚܐ ܗܘ ܕܩܕܝܡ ܐܡܪܢ܆ ܘܟܒܝܫ ܩ̈ܛܝܠܐ ܟܕ ܒܬ̈ܟܝܬܐ ܠܘܬ ܗܕܐ
ܫܦܠܗ܆ ܕܢܐܬܐ ܘܢܫܡܥ ܘܢܐܬܪ ܡܢ ܦܪ̈ܝܫܐ ܕܦܠܣܛܝܢܐ.
ܘܢܬܪܐܐ ܡܢ ܪܒܐ ܦܛܪܘܣ ܗܘܕܐ ܚܙܐ.

(§113) ܟܕ ܐܬܐ ܗܟܝܠ ܠܦܠܣܛܝܢܐ܆ ܘܟܐܢ̈ܘܗܝ، ܐܫܬܘܝ، ܕܒܕܒܝܬܐ
ܘܟܢܝܫܐ ܕܗܘ ܡܕܝܢܐ ܢܗܘܐ. ܕܐܝܟ ܗܕܐ ܠܡܒܘܬܐ ܐܫܟܚ
ܡܕܝܡܘܗܝ، ܒܝܕ ܙ̈ܘܥܐ ܕܐܠܗܐ ܡܪܚܡܢܐ܆ ܗܘ ܕܐܬܐ ܕܢܦܪܐ
ܠܬ̈ܠܝܐ ܠܐܢܫܘܬܐ. ܐܝܟܢܐ ܕܐܡܝܪܐ ܪܒ ܫܘܬܦܘܬܐ ܘܐܦ ܪܒ
ܬܫܡܫܬܐ ܢܗܘܐ ܠܗ ܠܡܕܝܢܐ. ܘܗܟܢܐ ܐܫܟܚ ܠܘܬ ܡܗܝܡܢܘܬܐ
ܘܪܚܡܬܐ ܕܠܘܬܗ. ܐܝܟܢܐ ܕܢܒܥܐ܆ ܕܠܦܛܪܘܣ ܪܫܐ ܕܬ̈ܠܡܝܕܐ ܚܙܐ܆
ܘܠܗ ܡܢܬ ܘܟܡܐ ܡܠܦܢܐ܆ ܘܦܫ̈ܘܩܐ ܐܠܗ̈ܝܐ ܕܟܠ ܡܦܩ.
ܘܢܬܚܦܛ ܠܐܠܗܐ ܒܕܡܐ ܠܫܘܠܡܐ܆ ܕܢܦܩ ܢܗܘܐ ܠܫܬܪܐ ܕܕܐܝܟ
ܗܢܐ ܘܠܡܫܦܘܬܐ. ܗ̇ܝ ܕܐܦ ܥܒܕ ܐܠܗܐ ܪܚܡ ܐܢܫܐ܆ ܗܘ
ܕܡܠܒܒ ܕܢܫܘܩ ܘܗܘܢܐ ܡܦܬܟܐ. ܘܟܕ ܠܟܠܗ ܗܕܐ ܡܫܬܘܬܦ
ܚܝܐ ܘܣܘܟܠܐ܆ ܐܝܟ ܠܠܒܗ ܕܡܕܡ ܠܘܬ ܗܘ ܠܐ ܚܫܝܫܐ. ܐܝܟܢܐ
ܕܢܣܒܘܗܝ، ܘܟܕ ܟܡܪܐ ܢܟܪܝܗ، ܘܟܠܗܝܢ ܢܦܫܬܐ ܘܢܐܦ ܚܠܦ

[1] Calling Calendion "wolf," Rufus aggressively places Calendion in the same category of opponents into which he had placed Proterius of Alexandria.

[2] References to zeal, when applied to anti-Chalcedonians, carry an explicitly positive connotation in Rufus's works. Here, however, a Chalcedonian opponent is attacked with the word, used as a polemical slander.

[3] See above, *Vit. Pet.* §107 (R 79).

[4] In antiquity, Beirut was famous for its outstanding law school, which both Rufus and Theodore had attended together. For helpful discussions, see Paul Collinet, *Histoire de l'École de droit de Beyrouth* (Études historiques sur le droit de Justinien 3; Paris: Société anonyme du recueil Sirey, 1925); and Linda Jones Hall, "Berytus, 'Mother of Laws': Studies in the Social History of Beirut from the Third to the Sixth Centuries A.D" (Ph.D. diss., The Ohio State University, 1996). A revised version of this thesis appeared as Linda Jones Hall, *Roman Berytus: Beirut in Late Antiquity* (London: Routledge, 2004). See also

rapacious wolf,[1] who did not spare [his] flock, and [who was] a zealot[2] of the heresies that were [taught] in Chalcedon. At this time the useless servant who was mentioned before[3] separated himself from the harm[ful peril] and the fellowship of this [Calendion], who for a long time had had brotherly love and familiar acquaintance with Theodore, the ex-laywer who was mentioned [above], since [the days when they] dwelt together in Beirut.[4] [Theodore] had left the regions of Syria and hastened to the Promised Land,[5] I mean to Palestine, **[R 82]** [and this same] Theodore, [his] friend and brother, who was mentioned previously, many times urged him in letters to come and visit and benefit from the saints in Palestine, and especially from the great Peter [the Iberian], the living martyr.

(§113) So when he came to Palestine and through him [Theodore] was esteemed worthy to get to know and become acquainted with this saint, he found such grace with him by the mercies of the merciful God, who came to call the sinners to repentance,[6] that immediately he became for the saint a sharer in [his] communion and a companion of [his] ministry. He was so motivated toward faithfulness and love for him that he would think he was seeing Peter, the head of the apostles,[7] and [that he] was near him and conversing with him, enjoying the divine gifts that he possessed. He made supplication to God that he might be worthy of the protection of such [a man] and of adherence to [him] until the end, [something] that God, the friend of man,[8] who is ready to pardon and plentiful in mercies,[9] granted. He stirred the heart of the saint to such sympathy and love toward this useless

the contributions in Linda Jones Hall, ed., *Confrontation in Late Antiquity: Imperial Presentation and Regional Adaptation* (Cambridge: Orchard Academic Press, 2003).

[5] More literally, "the Land of Promise."

[6] Matt 9:13; Mark 2:17; Luke 5:32.

[7] Rufus takes considerable effort throughout his work to cast Peter the Iberian into clear parallel with the apostle Peter. For a discussion of the implications of that parallel for questions of leadership and church authority, see Horn, *Asceticism and Christological Controversy*, 180–181.

[8] See p. 138, note 4 for a discussion of God as friend.

[9] Ps 103:8.

ܦܘܪܢܣܗ ܐܝܟ ܐܒܐ ܡܪܚܡܢܐ. ܐܡܪܢܐ ܕܝܢ. ܡܢ ܐܘܣܘܪܐ ܕܬܝܒܘܬܐ
ܘܡܢ ܚܛ̈ܗܘܗܝ܆ ܩ̈ܒܠܐ ܢܦܫܗܘܢ܀ ܘܒܐܘܪܚܐ ܫܪܝܪܬܐ ܕܬܝܒܘܬܐ
ܢܦܫܬܗܘܢ܀ ܘܢܩܝܦ ܠܡܪܥܝܐ ܓܙܪܐ ܐܡܪܐ ܐܝܟ ܗܘ ܪܥܝܐ ܛܒܐ.
ܟܕ ܥܠ ܟܬܦܬܗ ܒܚܕܘܬܐ ܛܥܢ ܠܗ. ܘܦܪܥܐ ܐܚܝܕܐ ܠܡ̈ܫܡܫܢܘܗܝ܆
ܫ̈ܒܝܐ ܘܠܥ̈ܢܘܗܝ܀ ܠܚܕܘܬܐ ܓܘܫܬܐ ܕܡܫܝܚܘܬܗ ܕܗܢܐ.

(§114) ܡܛܠ ܗܕܐ ܘܕܚܠܬܐ ܐܚܝܕܐ [R 83] ܗܘܬ ܠܗ܃ ܘܡܐܡܪܐ
ܕܠܐ ܫܠܝܐ ܐܦ ܗܘܐ ܠܟܠܗ. ܕܠܟܠܐ ܣܘܒܠܐ ܬܪܬܐ ܢܗܘܐ ܠܗ.
ܐܘ ܒܠܬܐ ܡܫܠܬܐ ܕܡܫܡܫ ܒܪܫܐ܆ ܕܫܡܘܬܐ ܘܡܕܒܪܢܐ ܕܒܡ
ܡܕܝܢܐ ܕܐܝܟ ܗܢܐ܆ ܕܩܛܠܐܬܐ ܡܢ ܐܫܬܘ ܘܕܝܢܝܐ ܘܕܝܢܘܬܐ܆
ܗܠܝܢ ܕܡ̈ܫܡܫܝܢ ܕܐܦ ܠܠ̈ܚܡܘܬܐ ܕܒܢ̈ܝܫܐ ܠܡܪ̈ܥܝܬܐ ܢ̈ܫܝܢ
ܘܠܬܫܡܫܬܐ ܫܪܝܪܬܐ܆ ܟܕ ܢܛܪ ܕܝܢ ܒܫܡܫܘܬܗ ܘܡܫܡܫܢܘܬ ܠܟܠܗ.[1]
ܘܒܠܚܘܕ ܗܘܒܠܐ ܐܝܬ ܠܗ ܕܬܫܡܫܐ ܠܘ̈ܬܐ ܛܘܒ ܕܗܘ ܡܕܝܢܐ.
ܐܢܫ ܕܠܐ ܡܣܬܠܩܐܝܬ ܢܣܠܩܐ ܗܘܐ.܀

(§115) ܐܝܠܝܢ ܕܝܢ ܗܪܟܐ ܡܚܠ. ܗܠܝܢ ܕܡܘܗܒܬ ܐܫܬܝܘ ܕܢܝܚܐ܆
ܐܘ ܕܒܫܝܢܐ ܢܦܫ ܗܘ ܕܗܠܝܢ ܟܠܗ܆ ܐܘ ܐܦ ܡܢ ܦܘܡܗ ܕܝܠܗ
ܕܡܕܝܢܐ. ܗܘ ܪܫܡ ܫܪܪܐ ܘܠܐ ܕܟܠܐ ܫܒܩ. ܡܢ ܩܠܝܠܐܬܐ
ܘܒܗܪܬܐ ܐܫܟܚ ܢܝܚ ܐܦ ܕܫܠܝܢܐ ܡܠܬܐ ܘܠܐ ܦܘܫܐ ܠܗܘܬ
ܬܫܒܘܚܬܐ.

(§116) ܫܦܪ ܠܗ ܒܡܢ ܠܗܠܟܢܐ܆ ܕܐܦ ܠܐܬܪܘܬܐ ܕܐܪܒܥܐ ܢܦܠ.
ܒܠܬܐ ܕܡܣܝܠܘܬܗ ܠܢ. ܐܡܪܢܐ ܕܒܫܒܝܚܘܬܐ ܕܐܝܬ ܠܒܢܝܢܘܦ.
ܢܦܫܐ. ܗ̇ܝ ܕܡܬܦܪܢܣܐ ܕܡܕܝܢܝܐ ܡܦܫܐ. ܡܢ ܒܪܘ ܟܢܪ. ܟܕ ܡܢ

[1] In MS A one finds a lacuna of one folio from this point in the text until ܠܐ ܚܫܝܢ on *Vit. Pet.* §118 (R 86).

[2] Note Rufus's use of parental language, which by way of modification through the adjective "merciful" also suggests an intended link to the image of God as the merciful Father.

[3] For the centrality of repentance in Peter the Iberian's spirituality see *Vit. Pet.* §157 (R 119). The notion of repentance summarized the essence of the "rule of life" that Peter the Iberian laid down for his followers.

[4] Luke 15:5.

[5] The underlying Syriac word also carries connotations of "recovery" and "salvation."

[6] I.e., "the useless one," who should be understood as John Rufus.

[7] Rufus realized that contact with Peter the Iberian as a model leader and

one that he accepted him and made him [his] fellow-monk. He did everything to look after his salvation like a merciful father,[2] so that while removing him from the bonds of death and from his evil habits, he put him on the true way of repentance.[3] He presented to the Lord [this] lost sheep, like that Good Shepherd,[4] bearing him with joy on his shoulders and calling together his beloved friends and his neighbors to share [his] joy in finding him.[5]

(§114) On account of this, fear took **[R 83]** hold of him,[6] and unceasing grief was eating up his heart lest the knowledge of such a saint and dwelling with [someone like him] should become a greater condemnation or a severe cause for exacting punishment on him.[7] For, on the one hand, he was esteemed worthy to see and hear many things that can bring even hearts of stone to sensibility and to true repentance, while, on the other hand, he might persist in his blindness and his hardness of heart. His only hope for mercy is again the prayers of this saint, if he has not [already] been completely rejected.[8]

(§115) The kind[s] of things the writer was deemed worthy to see personally or to experience or that he heard from the mouth of that truth-loving and undeceitful saint I will put down carefully, [although but] a few out of many,[9] even if the word is full of fear and inadequate for the account.[10]

(§116) On one occasion it pleased the blessed one to go to the regions of Arabia to bathe in the hot spring[11] because of his infirmity. [This spring] is at Livias [and is] called "St. Moses'

exemplary Christian also demanded seriousness, responsibility, and accountability on the part of the people who interacted with him, including Rufus.

[8] This remark indicates that the author expected and intended to rely on the intercession of Peter the Iberian. It is likely that this comment was written after Peter's death, when his body was deposited under the altar of the church of the Maiuma Monastery. See also *Vit. Pet.* §§124, 128, 147, 148, 152, 162–163, 191, and especially 192 (R 92–93, 95, 110–11, 114, 121, 144, 145).

[9] For another instance of an author highlighting the selectivity of his account, see John 20:30–31; 21:24–25.

[10] Rufus knows well where to insert self-deprecatory rhetorical phrases.

[11] Lit., "heat."

ܘܡܟܠܬܗ ܡܕܡܝܬܐ ܢܦܝܚ ܗܘܐ ܦܓܪܗ. ܘܢܦܝܫܗ ܒܚܝ̈ܠܐ ܩܦ̈ܝܠܐ
ܘܡ̈ܦܬܚܐ ܕܚܘܣܬܐ. ܟܕ ܗ̣ܘ ܗ̇ܢ ܦܓܪܐ ܐܬܟܠܠ: ܠܚܘܕܪܘܗܝ ܕܝܢ
ܗ̣ܘ ܕܒܥܟܐ ܚܠ ܚܘ̈ܬܪܐ ܕܢ̈ܩܫܐ ܦܪܝܣ ܗܘܐ. ܘܗܠܟ ܦܚܡ ܙܘܥܐ.
ܒܡܥܒܕܘܬܗ ܡܚܝܠ ܠܕܐܝܟ ܗܕܐ ܡܣܝܒܠܬܐ ܐܝܬܐ: ܐܡܚܝܐ ܕܚܠ
ܢܦܩ: ܘܗ̇ܘ ܥܠܠ ܬܪܥܣܐ ܕܢܦܠ ܗܘܐ: ܡܣܕܐ ܒܬܚܬܐ ܒܡܡܬܐ
ܢܕܪܘܗܝ، ܒܝܡ ܕܚܕܐ ܘܫܘܕܘܝܐ. ܘܚܠܡܘ ܗܠܝܢ ܕܢܣܝܢ ܠܗ ܒܕ.
ܡܬܦܬܘܦܝܢ ܒܣܥܐ: ܡܚܝܠ ܢܦܫܗ ܘܗܒܪܐ ܕܘܡܢܚܐ ܕܢܦܠܗ.
ܒܓܘ ܘܐܚܝ ܡܢ [R 84] ܡܢܬ̈ܝܐ ܗܕܝܘܛܐ[1] ܒܡܠܬܐ: ܚܟܝܡܐ ܕܝܢ
ܒܝܕܥܬܐ. ܟܕ ܢܝܚܘ، ܕܝܢ ܕܗܡܢܐ ܡܬܚܫܒ ܡܢ ܬܒܥܬܐ: ܐܡܪ ܟܕ.
ܫܡܥ ܚܠܝܨ. ܕܐܚܝܢܐ ܕܢܦܫܗ ܕܗܢܐ ܡܕܝܢܬܐ: ܠܝܬ ܒܗ̇ ܡܕܡ ܡܢ
ܕܗܢܐ ܚܠܡܐ: ܗܡܢܐ ܘܠܐ ܒܗܘܢ ܡܦܩܝܢ ܕܡܕܡ ܡܢ ܕܗܢܐ ܚܠܡܐ
ܢܠܒܫܝܢ.

(§117) ܒܬܪ ܡܢ ܒܠܬ ܫܢܝܐ ܕܐܝܟ ܗܢܐ ܘܥܘܢܝܐ: ܟܕ ܚܠܛܝܕ ܗܘܐ
ܕܒܪܡܫܐ ܢܥܠܐ: ܟܕ ܫܡܠ ܗܘܐ ܬܘܪ̈ܝܢ ܐܘ ܬܠܬ ܒܬ̈ܚܐ ܐܘ ܥܠܠ
ܦܫ̈ܝܛܐ: ܒܐܚܘܬܐ ܕܐܠܗܐ ܕܠܒܝܢ ܗܘܐ. ܟܕ ܒܢܝܠܐ ܕܐܠܗܐ
ܠܒܝܢ ܗܘܐ. ܘܐܝܬ ܗܘܐ ܕܢܣܒܐ ܕܡܫܬܡܠܝܐ ܠܘܬܗ ܗ̇ܝ، ܕܫܠܝܚܐ.
ܕܢܝܘ ܐܢܐ ܕܝܢ. ܠܐ ܡܚܝܠ ܐ̱ܢܐ: ܢܝܘ ܒܝ ܕܝܢ ܡܚܝܠܐ.܀

(§118) ܘܒܓܘ ܠܡܬܡܐ ܕܒܬܪܗ: ܗܡܢܐ ܘܙ̈ܢܐ ܗܘܐ ܦܪ̈ܘܣܗ.
ܐܝܟ ܢܦܘܪܐ ܕܫܒܫܐ. ܟܕ ܩܪܘܒܐ ܒܗ ܠܒܥܘܬܐ ܐܠܗܝܬܐ.
ܡܠܠܗܕܐ ܚܠܬܐ ܠܡ ܫܦܪ ܠܗ ܕܠܠܡܚܝܕܘܣ ܢܐܠ. ܠܐܡܚܐ
ܕܡܚܡܚܐ ܕܢܣܡܚܬܐ ܐܝܬ ܗܘܐ. ܐܠܗܐ ܕܝܢ ܐܬܠܘܗܝ، ܗ̇ܘ ܕܐܦ
ܠܬܡܢ ܢܦܫܗ، ܠܚܢܕܪܗ ܠܝܕܥܐ ܘܦܘܪܫܢܐ ܕܢܦܫ̈ܬܐ ܩܕܝܫܬܐ.
ܡܠܠܗܕܐ ܟܕ ܐܝܟ ܠܠܡܚܝܕܘܣ: ܘܪܗܛܘ ܠܬܡܢ ܩܕܝܫܬܐ: ܡܢ

[1] Raabe misreads ܗܕܝܘܬܐ at MS B 12,174 fol. 65v, col. 1.

[2] Egeria, *Diary* 10.8 (Franceschini and Weber, 51; Gingras, 66–67) also reports about her visit to that site. For medicinal hot springs, see also Estée Dvorjetski, "Medicinal Hot Springs in Eretz-Israel and in the Decapolis during the Hellenistic, Roman, and Byzantine Periods," *ARAM* 4.1–2 (1992): 425–49; and Stefanie Hoss, *Baths and Bathing: The Culture of Bathing and the Baths and Thermae in Palestine from the Hasmoneans to the Moslem Conquest* (BAR International Series 1346; Oxford: Archaeopress, 2005). Our thanks to Sebastian Brock for providing these references.

[3] The Syriac ܗܕܝܘܛܐ transliterates the Greek ἰδιώτης. The phrase "uneducated in speech but wise in understanding" is an allusion to 2 Cor 11:6. See also 173 n. 7 below.

[Spring]."[2] For already since his earliest age he treated his body with insolence and inflicted it with severe pain from many toils and various [kinds of] asceticism. That body having vanished, only skin was spread out over the dried-up bones, and this [skin] was very thin. In his old age now, he became so infirm that every day even the little morsel of food that he took he would immediately throw up in obstinate vomiting with blood and lacerations. All those who saw him taking part in the suffering had given up hope for the [re]establishment of his strength. One of the saints, **[R 84]** uneducated[3] in speech but wise in understanding, seeing that he was thus wounded from vomiting, said while everyone was listening, "As the soul of this saint has nothing in it from [what is] of this world, so his flesh also refuses [to] retain anything from [what is] of this world."

(§117) Nevertheless, after such torment and torture, when he was ready to retire in the evening, having taken two or three eggs or a few morsels[4] [of bread], by the grace of God he slept, preserved by the power of God. [So that] we might see [the words] of the Apostle fulfilled in him: "I live, yet no longer I, but Christ lives in me,"[5] the next day his face[6] would be so shining like the light of the sun, with divine grace flashing in it.[7] So [then] he wanted to go to Livias, where there was a hot spring,[8] rather it was God who called his servant there to catch and save many souls.[9]

(§118) We came to Livias, and many ran there from the nearby region of Arabia, especially from among the first men and the magistrates of the city of Madeba[10] and from other places, for the news concerning him that had hurried ahead was summoning all of them, since they were anxious to be blessed and to enjoy his grace. When he had used the bath of that hot spring for one

[4] The Syriac seems to transliterate the Greek ψίχια, "crumb," "morsel," or "bit."

[5] Gal 2:20.

[6] The Syriac transliterates the Greek πρόσωπον.

[7] See Exod 34:30.

[8] Literally, "a source of heat."

[9] Thus the rationale behind Peter's missionary and proselytizing efforts was seen as being grounded in a divine commissioning.

[10] For references to Madeba and the Madeba Map, see lxxviii n. 197.

ܐܬܪܐ ܕܐܪܒܥܐ ܕܩܪܒ ܠܗܘܢ܆ ܘܬܢܐܪܬ ܡܢ ܩ̈ܕܡܝܐ ܘܪ̈ܒܝܥܐ
ܕܡܕܒܪܐ ܡܕܝܢܬܐ܆ ܘܡܢ ܕܘܟ̈ܝܬܐ ܐܣܛ̈ܢܝܬܐ܆ ܠܓܒܝܐ ܓܒܪ
ܕܡܛܠܠܗ ܦܘܡ ܢܓܪ܆ ܟܠܗܘܢ ܦܪܐ ܗܘܐ. ܟܕ ܢܣܩ ܕܢܬܒܪܟܘܢ
ܘܒܠܒܘܬܐ ܕܝܠܗ ܢܬܟܫܦܘܢ. ܟܕ ܚܙܐ ܢܘܗܪܐ ܒܠܚܘܕ ܐܬܢܝܚ
ܒܫܢܬܐ ܕܗ̇ܝ، ܫܡܥܬܐ ܕܠܗܘܢ܆ ܐܬܩܒܠ ܡܛܠ ܕܢܦܠ ܠܗ̇܆ ܟܕ
ܐܡܪ. ܕܐܦܠܐ ܚܕܐ ܡܢ ܥܢܘܬܐ ܦܬܠ ܕܡܬܘܪܢܐ ܕܡܢܗ̇. ܡܛܠܬܗ̇،
ܕܦܥܘܪ ܡܢܝܢܐ. ܟܕ ܕܝܢ ܗ̇ܢܘܢ ܕܐܬܘ ܡܢ ܐܪܒܥܐ ܐܡܪܝܢ ܗܘܘ.
[R 85] ܕܐܦ ܫܡܥܬܐ ܐܚܪܬܐ ܐܝܬ ܒܐܬܪܗܘܢ܆ ܕܦܥܘܪ ܫܡܥܬܐ
ܘܢܫܝܟܐ. ܒܗ̇ܘ ܕܡܬܩܪܐ ܢܒܘ. ܘܐܦܣܩܘܗ̇، ܟܕ ܚܙܝܢ ܠܗ ܕܒܗ̇
ܢܬܢܝܚ ܡܠܒܟܐܝܬ ܐܫܬܡܥ. ܒܙܒܢ ܕܡܛܠ ܐܢܫܐ ܥܠܬܐ ܡܢ
ܐܠܗܐ ܠܗܘܢ ܐܬܦܢܝ. ܠܡܘܫܐ ܡܟܝܠ ܕܒܬܪܗ܆ ܐܝܬ ܗܘܐ ܠܗ
ܐܘܪܚܐ ܠܡܕܒܪܐ. ܘܡܬܚܬܝܬܐ ܕܐܘܪܚܐ ܢܦܠ ܠܛܘܪܐ ܡܪܝܡܐ
ܕܡܘܫܐ. ܕܡܬܩܪܐ ܐܒܪܝܡ ܐܘܟܝܬ ܦܣܓܐ. ܐܝܟܢܐ ܕܐܡܪ ܠܗ
ܐܠܗܐ. ܣܩ ܘܚܙܝ. ܐܝܬ ܒܗ ܕܝܢ ܗܘܠܐ ܦܓܕܐ ܕܦܬܚ ܪܒ ܥܠ
ܥܡܗ ܕܢܗܪܐ. ܘܕܝ̈ܪܬܐ ܩ̈ܘܪܝܐܬܐ ܕܩ̈ܪܝܢ ܚܕ̈ܪܘܗܝ، ܟܕ ܡܬܚܙܝܢ.
ܘܟܕ ܒܚܙܘܬܐ ܗ̇ܘܝܢ ܒܦܓܪܗ̇ ܕܕܘܟܬܐ ܒܟܠܗ ܕܗܕܐ܆ ܓ̈ܢܘܬܐ
ܕܡܘܟܠ ܠܒܘܬܐ ܦܪ̈ܘܚܝܢ ܠܐܠܗܐ. ܗ̇ܘ ܕܐܫܩܝ، ܠܝ ܠܟܘܪܒܬܐ
ܘܠܣܓܕܬܐ ܕܕܐܝܟ ܡܘܫܐ ܢܒܝܐ. ܘܟܕ ܐܬܝܢ ܗܘܘ. ܡܢ ܒܬܪ
ܨܠܘܬܐ ܘܣܓܕܬܐ܆ ܐܚܕ ܠܝ ܗ̇ܘ ܣܒܐ ܠܥܠܝܬܐ ܡܕܡ ܘܡܘܪܬܐ܆
ܕܐܝܬ ܒܗ̇ ܐܝܟ ܫܒ̈ܥ ܐܡ̈ܝܢ ܦܬܝܐ ܘܐܘܪܟܐ. ܘܠܐ ܦܝܫ ܢܘܗܪܐ.
ܘܡܛܠܬܐ ܗܘܐ ܘܐܡܪ. ܕܒܗ̇ܘ ܐܝܟ ܟܕ ܐܢܫ، ܠܡܠܟܐ܆ ܘܣܝܡܬܐ
ܐܬܬ ܗܘܬ ܡܢ ܡܕܝܢܬܐ ܦܠܚܘܬܐ܆ ܕܐܬܬ ܠܡܚܐ ܠܛܘܪܐ ܐܝܟ

[1] For a discussion of the site, see Christa Clamer, "The Hot Springs of Kallirrhoe and Baarou," in Piccirillo and Alliata, *Madaba Map Centenary*, 221–25.

[2] Pisgah is a mountain identified in the Abarim mountain range, the southern extension of the Transjordan Range, east of the mouth of the Jordan River and northeast of the Dead Sea. See Arthur J. Ferch, "Abarim," *ABD* 1:6–7. Pisgah is also close to Mount Nebo. See Gerald L. Mattingly, "Pisgah," *ABD* 5:373–74.

[3] See Deut 31:4. Note, however, that the quotation does not occur in the Scriptures as words spoken by God.

[4] Literally, "encircling [it]." For several decades extensive excavations

day only, he excused himself thenceforth from entering it, saying that he had received not the slightest palpable benefit from it, because it was very cold. Some coming from Arabia were saying **[R 85]** that there is also another hot spring in their region that is very hot and beneficial, at the [place] called Baʾar,[1] and they strongly persuaded him to use it. He readily obeyed because he knew why he had been called there by God. On the next day the journey led us to Madeba. Halfway there we arrived at the holy mountain of Moses, called Abarim, that is, Pisgah,[2] where God had said to him, "Ascend and die!"[3] On it is a worshipful temple, very large, in the name of the prophet and many monasteries built around it in a circle.[4] We were joyous to come together at the place with the Old Man[5] and offered prayers of thanksgiving to God, who had esteemed us worthy of the blessing and the veneration of such a prophet. When we were there, after prayer and veneration, the Old Man led us into a small cell that was five cubits wide and long and not very bright. He told [us], "I remember when I was a boy, and I recently had come from the Royal City.[6] I came to this mountain [to see such] a sight and to pray. When I heard that one of the great Scetian[7] saints was dwelling here in quiet who had departed from Scetis with all the monks who were there when the band of robbers of the Maziks fell upon the monaster-

have been carried out on and around Mount Nebo. For reports, see Hilary Schneider, *Memorial of Moses on Mount Nebo* (Jerusalem: Franciscan Printing Press, 1950); Sylvester Saller and Bellarmino Bagatti, *The Town of Nebo (Khirbet el-Mekhayyat): With a Brief Survey of Other Ancient Christian Monuments in Transjordan* (Jerusalem: Franciscan Printing Press, 1949); Sylvester Saller, *The Memorial of Moses on Mount Nebo* (3 vols.; PSBF 1; Jerusalem: Franciscan Printing Press, 1941). For references to additional literature, see Horn, *Asceticism and Christological Controversy*, 181–184 *et passim*.

5 I.e., Peter the Iberian. "Old" also carries the connotation of "spiritual" and "wise" with it.

6 I.e., Constantinople.

7 Or "Scetiote," i.e., monks from the desert of Scetis in Egypt. "Scetiote" would normally be ܣܩܝܛܝܐ, not ܣܩܝܬܝܐ ("a Scythian"), yet the Syriac author or scribe at times replaces ܛ with ܬ in the transcription of Greek words. This could again be such an instance. See also 170 n. 3 above.

ܕܠܝܣܬܐ ܘܠܝܠܘܬܐ. ܘܟܕ ܫܡܥܘ ܕܐܬܝܢ ܗܘܘ ܡ̈ܙܝܩܐ ܙܒܪ̈ܢܝܐ ܣܩܛܝܣܐ
ܒܥܠܝܐ ܚܒܪ ܡܕܒܪܐ: ܕܢܦܠܘ ܗܘܐ ܗܘ ܣܩܛܝܣ ܒܗ ܒܠܗܘܢ ܕܝ̈ܪܐ
ܕܬܡܢ: ܟܕ ܢܦܠ ܗܘܐ ܚܫܫܐ ܕܡܪ̈ܢܝܬܐ ܥܠ ܕܝ̈ܪܬܐ ܕܬܡܢ: ܐܬܦܣܬ
ܠܦܪܘܣܝܐ ܕܠܗ ܕܐܠܘܪܐ: ܕܐܬܬܣܡܐ ܠܡܘܪܒܬܐ ܕܠܗ ܘܠܝܣܬܗ.
ܐܬܬܗ̇ ܕܝܢ ܗܕܐ ܡܠܬܐ ܕܢܘܢ ܐܬܘ. ܕܟܕ ܐܬܟܢܫ ܥ̈ܡܐ ܣܓܝ̈
ܘܗ̇ ܠܡܘܬܐ. ܟܕ ܠܐ ܢܦܩ ܠܒܪ ܡܢ ܬܪܥܐ ܘܠܐ ܣܓܝ ܐܣܩܘܦܘܬܐ.
ܓܒܪܐ ܚܘܒܐ ܘܢܟܝܐ: ܘܕܡܠܝܟ ܠܡܘܬܐ ܐܠܗܝܬܐ. ܐܬܬܝܡ ܗܘܐ
ܕܝܢ ܬܠܬܐ. ܐܝܟ ܘܡܘܬܝܢܐ ܢܘܣܝ ܕܠܟ: ܘܐܬܐ ܐܚܪܢܝܐ [R 86]
ܕܝܢܝܟ ܦܪܡܘܢܪܝܐ ܟܢܘܫܐ. ܕܢܘܡ ܗܘܐ ܒܗܘ. ܡܛܠ ܕܗ̇ܘ ܗܘܐ ܫܡܫܐ
ܒܐܬܪܗ. ܟܕ ܚܙܐ ܗܘ ܢܘܦܪܐ ܕܐܬܚܫܚܬ ܐܝܟ ܠܐܘܪܫܠܡ. ܘܚܙܐ
ܗܘ ܒܥܠܝܐ: ܠܐ ܕܝܢ ܢܕܥܝܢ ܗܘܘ ܠܕ̈ܝܪܐ ܘܠܐ ܠܗܠܝܢ ܕܬܡܢ:
ܕܢܦܠ ܐܬܘܢ ܗܘܘ ܗܘ ܐܚܐ. ܟܕ ܕܝܢ ܐܦܩ ܠܝ ܗ̇ܘ ܗܟܢܐ ܕܢܦܩ
ܠܗܬܗ: ܘܢܝܚܐ ܕܟܠܝ: ܡܚܘܝܐ ܐܢܐ. ܫܘܪ ܐܬܐܬ ܒܢܘܗܪܐ ܗܘ ܒܗ̇
ܕܡܫܡܫܢܘܬܐ ܒܝ ܡܫܡܫܢܘܬܐ. ܟܕ ܕܝܢ ܦܩܕ ܐܬܬܘܬܐ ܒܥܠܬܐ:
ܘܕܢܒܠܬܐ ܡܫܝܚܝܬܐ ܘܒܪܬܝܬܐ ܐܬܬܘܬܢܝܬ: ܬܘܒ ܐܡܪ ܠܝ ܗ̇ܘ
ܗܟܢܐ. ܒܝܕ ܛܠܘܬܐ. ܟܕ ܕܝܢ ܚܙܝܬ ܥܒܕܝܢ ܐܝܟ ܒܠܚܘܕܝܐ: ܚܙܬ ܟܕ
ܐܡܪ ܗ̇ܝ ܟܕ ܗ̇ܝ. ܟܕ ܐܬܚܙܝܬ ܗܘܬ ܐܢܬܐ ܦܪܨܘܦܐ ܐܬܝܐ. ܥܢܝܬ
ܠܝ ܡܪܝ: ܐܡܪܐ. ܬܠܬܐ ܐܢܬܝܢ ܘܡܠܟܝܐ. ܗ̇ܘ ܕܝܢ ܟܕ ܦܩܕ ܐܒܕܗ
ܠܗܬ ܗ̇ܘ ܦܪܡܘܢܪܐ ܐܡܪ. ܫܡܥܝܬ ܒܝܕ ܛܠܘܬܐ. ܠܐ ܬܫܬܥܐ
ܠܡܘܬܐ. ܟܕ ܕܝܢ ܗܘܬ ܛܠܘܬܐ. ܐܡܝܢܐ ܒܪ ܠܐ ܒܥܝܢ. ܗܘܐ
ܘܗ̇ ܕܢܟܝܢ: ܟܕ ܡܙܝܩܐ ܕܕܐܝܟ ܗܢܐ ܦܩܕ: ܐܦܩ ܠܝ ܕܢܦܩ. ܘܟܕ
ܦ̈ܠܚܐ ܟ̈ܠܗ ܐܠܗܝܬܐ ܘܦܪܘܣܝܐ ܘܬܫܡܫܬܐ ܘܒܘ̈ܟܐ ܢܦܩ

[1] The Maziks invaded Scetis in 407–408, and Scetis was destroyed a second time in 434. Hugh Gerard Evelyn-White discusses the Maziks' invasion of Scetis in the first half of the fifth century in *The History of the Monasteries of Nitria and Scetis* (ed. Walter Hauser; vol. 2 of *The Monasteries of the Wâdi ʿn Natrûn*; 3 vols.; New York: Metropolitan Museum of Art, Egyptian Expedition, 1932), 150–67.

[2] The Syriac transliterates the Greek παραμονάριος, a variant of *prosmonarios*. The *prosmonarios* or *paramonarios* was a resident of the church or monastery, responsible for maintaining the grounds and locking the church and storage rooms when not in use. This was a cleric whose position was assigned

ies there,[1] I persuaded the sacristan[2] of the mountain to allow me the blessing and sight of him. It was in this cell that you are seeing where that blessed one dwelt for forty years, not going outside of the door nor crossing the threshold, an ascetic man, a prophet, and one full of divine grace. We were three: I, my blessed John,[3] and some other **[R 86]** monk, a Cappadocian by race, who was traveling with us.[4] Because he was a deacon[5] in his country, fleeing from the burden of the ministry, he came to Jerusalem and dwelt there in quiet. But we did not know each other and were unknown to those who were here. [They did not know] who we were and from where [we came]. But when the old man gave us permission to enter to him and saw that we had entered, he immediately said, 'You are welcome, Nabarnugios son of Bosmarios son of Bosmarios.'[6] I was very amazed at [his] utterance and was seized by much fear and trembling. The old man spoke again, saying to us, 'Recite the prayer!' We, being laymen, kept silence, but he continued saying the same. Since I was daring then [and] headstrong, I said, 'Forgive us, lord Abba, we are sinners and laymen.' He stretched out his hand toward the Cappadocian [and] said 'Deacon, recite the prayer! Do not hide the grace!' Once the prayer was [finished], for how could he not be willing to do [it] when such a saint commanded [him], he bade us to sit. After having given us by his

by appointment, not by ordination, but ordained clergy also held this position. See Paul Magdalino, "Prosmonarios," *ODB* 3:1739.

3 I.e., John the Eunuch.

4 That a Cappadocian monk was accompanying Peter and John on their short pilgrimage to Mount Nebo might indicate that Peter and John's long pilgrimage journey from Constantinople to Jerusalem also led them through Cappadocia. While possible, this is certainly not necessary. Their contact with that deacon, however, establishes a significant link to Cappadocian theology. Especially the ideas of Basil of Caesarea can be detected at several instances in the *Vita Petri Iberi*, most explicitly at §§150, 179 (R 113, 135). See also Horn, *Asceticism and Christological Controversy*, 157, 200 *et passim*.

5 *Pace* Raabe, 83, who reads "slave." Schwartz (*Johannes Rufus*, 27) suggests "deacon," which we have accepted.

6 For Peter's genealogy, see *Vit. Pet.* §6 (R 5).

ܠܝ ܕܐܬܒܥܬܗ܇ ܠܣܓܝܐܬܐ ܡܢ ܟܠܗ̇ ܦܬܘܪܐ ܕܢܦܫܐ܇ ܐܡܪ ܠܐܠܝܨܘ.
ܗܒ ܠܐܚ̈ܐ ܘܐܟܝܠ ܐܢܘܢ. ܡܢ ܥܠܡܐ[1] ܓܝܪ ܐܬܠܐܝܘ.

(§119) ܠܡܚܪܐ ܕܝܢ ܕܒܬܪܗ ܟܕ ܥܠܝܢ ܠܘܬܗ: ܕܬܠܬܝܗܘܢ ܘܥܡ ܨܠܘܬܐ ܢܛܪܬܐ܇ ܫܪܝܐܝܬ ܦܬܠ. ܘܬܘܒ ܟܕ ܡܡܠܠ ܠܝ ܡ̈ܠܐ ܕܡܘܬܪ̈ܬܐ ܐܝܟ ܕܠܡܘܬܪܬܐ܇ ܟܕ ܢܦܠ ܒܪܐ ܠܝ. ܟܕ ܢܦܩܢ ܚܢܢ ܕܝܢ܇ ܫܩܠ ܣܠܬܐ ܕܠܝ ܘܠܚܡܐ. ܟܕ ܐܬܦܢܝܬ ܕܝܢ ܐܢܐ ܠܘܬܗ܇ ܪܡܙ ܠܝ ܒܐܝܕܗ ܕܐܬܦܪܩ. ܟܕ ܠܗܠܝܢ [R 87] ܐܣܝ̈ܢܐ ܥܒܕ ܕܢܦܩܘܢ. ܘܟܕ ܦܢܝܬ ܦܩܕ ܠܝ ܕܐܬܠܒ ܥܠ ܒܘܪܟܐ ܡܕܡ ܕܟܘܪܐ ܕܚܒܝܫ ܗܘܐ ܬܡܢ. ܘܐܡܪ. ܢܘܪܐ ܕܡܫܚܐ ܗ̇ܝ ܕܝܗܒ ܠܟ ܐܠܗܐ܇ ܠܐ ܒܟܝܠ ܐܫܬܘ ܐܝܟ ܕܢܗܘܐ ܐܝܬ ܠܗ ܒܡܝܐ ܕܪܐ. ܚܙܝ ܡܫܚܐ ܠܐ ܬܬܒܥܝܘܗܝ. ܐܠܐ ܠܓܪܘܗ̇ ܘܪܐܝܬ. ܘܠܐ ܬܬܡܪ ܡܢ ܐܝܟ ܐܚܪܢ܇ ܐܠܐ ܡܢ ܗܢܐ ܐܝܟܐ ܕܐܬܝܐ ܒܟܝ. ܟܕ ܠܛܘܒܢܐ ܢܘܚܝ ܐܘܢܘܡܣܐ ܡܫܘܕܥ ܗܘܐ. ܟܠܗ ܕܝܢ ܐܠܗܐ ܢܬܠ ܡܢܟܝ ܦܠܚܘܬܐ. ܐܘܨܦܘ ܕܐܬܐ ܐܝܟ ܠܘܬܟܝ. ܐܘ ܐܦܝܣܩܘܦܐ ܐܘ ܩܫܝܫܐ ܐܘ ܕܝܪܝܐ ܐܘ ܥܠܡܝܐ. ܐ̱ ܬܫܬܘܘܢ ܘܠܐ ܬܠܦܘܢܗ̇ ܕܢܝ̈ܘܗܝ ܘܦܘ̈ܩܕܢܘܗܝ ܕܐܠܗܐ. ܗܠܝܢ ܕܝܢ ܐܡܪ. ܟܕ ܦܩܕ ܫܠܐ ܒܪܘܚܐ. ܘܡܘܕܐ ܫܘܒܚܐ ܕܒܡܘܬܐ. ܗ̇ܝ ܕܒܬܪ ܡܦܩܬ ܕܐܬܚܙܝܘ ܠܗ ܐܢܐ. ܗܘ ܕܗܘܐ ܠܐ ܫܦܝܪ ܡܦܩܬ. ܐܢܐ ܕܝܢ ܟܕ ܐܫܬܟܚܬ ܒܟܠܬܐ. ܘܡܬܪܐܝܬ ܒܟܡܠ: ܕܐܝܢ ܐܝܬܝ ܐܢܐ ܕܗܠܝܢ ܡܦܩܕܐ ܠܝ ܡܕܥܬܘܢ: ܗܘ ܕܠܐ ܒܟܟܠ ܐܦ ܠܐ ܕܐܗܘܐ ܬܠܡܝܕܐ ܫܪܝܪܬ. ܐܡܪ ܠܝ. ܗܘ ܡܕܡ ܕܫܒܩܬ ܥܒܕܬ. ܘܗܘܝܐ ܟܕ ܠܟܝ ܠܐܚܪ ܘܢܦܩܗ: ܘܫܩܠ ܨܠܘܬܟ ܒܪܟ.

(§120) ܬܡܢ ܗܟܝܠ ܡܢ ܗܘܢ ܕܒܗܬܢ ܒܗܘ ܛܘܪܐ ܕܢܓܒ܇ ܕܐܒܗܐ ܦܠܣܛܝܢܝ̈ܐ ܗܘܘ ܗܠܝܢ ܕܟܠܗ ܗܘ ܡܕܒܪܐ܇ ܕܦܩܕܗ ܕܡܕܝܢܬܐ ܡܘܫܐ ܬܡܢ ܚܒܫ. ܘܠܟܠ ܡܢܗ ܗܘ ܡܕܒܪܐ ܐܬܢܓܕ. ܘܦܬܪܐ ܘܡܕܒܚܐ ܦܐܝܢ. ܘܠܬܚܬ ܡܢ ܡܕܒܚܐ ܘܒܗܘܪܐ ܕܓܫܝܐ ܘܣܒܟܐ. ܟܕ ܝܠܕ ܒܠܚܘܕ ܐܠܗܐ ܡܗܝܡܢܐ ܐܡܪ ܠܒܢܝܐܝܬ: ܕܒܝܬ ܡܘܫܐ ܚܙܝܗ ܕܡܪܝܐ ܒܛܘܪܐ ܕܡܘܐܒ ܒܡܠܬܗ ܕܡܪܝܐ. [R 88]

[1] So MS B. MS A has ܥܡܠܐ ("labor" or "work").

[2] Reading with MS A, one could perhaps translate "for they are [tired] from the labor."

[3] On the significance of this encounter between Peter the Iberian and the Scetian monk, see Horn, *Asceticism and Christological Controversy*, 181–82, 309.

[4] This vessel of oil and mercy may have had a function similar to that of sarcophagi of martyrs that exuded oil, which was mixed with dust, water, and

grace many divine and saving words and stories and consolations, finally after the table for the soul he said to [his] cell-mate, 'Take the brethren and refresh them, for they are from the world!'[2]

(§119) "The next day, however, when we entered to him to receive a blessing and to be dismissed with a prayer, he received [us] joyfully. Having again spoken to us a few words for [our] benefit, he prayed [and] dismissed us. As we were going out, he took [hold of] my coat and kept me [back]. Yet when I turned to him, he made signs to me with his hand that I should remain [behind]. He let **[R 87]** those others go out, while I remained. He commanded me to sit down on some small chair that was set there, and he said, 'This fire of his love that God has given you, hardly anyone was esteemed worthy to have it in this generation. Take heed, then, that you do not quench it but keep it securely! Do not dwell with any other man except with this brother who came with you!' indicating the blessed John the Eunuch. 'God is going to demand an answer from you if anyone should come to you, either bishop or clergyman or monk or layman, [and] you remain silent and do not teach him the judgments and the commandments of God.' He said those things because he foresaw in the Spirit and announced the gift of the priesthood of which I, one who was not at all worthy of it, was going to be esteemed worthy. I was troubled at [his] word and wept bitterly, saying, 'Who am I that your holiness is commanding these things to me, who have not yet not even begun to be a disciple?' He said to me, 'What you have heard, you have heard.' In this way, having held my head and kissed it, he finished the prayer and dismissed me."[3]

(§120) There at that time we learned from those who were dwelling on the mountain how those who built the temple had been fully assured that the body of the holy Moses was laid there, above which the temple was built, the table and the altar set up, and under the altar the vessel of oil and mercy,[4] even though the divine Scripture clearly says thus, "Moses, the servant of the

the relics of saints or at times with earth taken from the holy places to anoint the sick or impart blessings at other occasions. See Payne Smith, 149; Wilhelm Gessel, "Das Öl der Märtyrer: Zur Funktion und Interpretation der Ölsarkophage von Apamea in Syrien," *OrChr* 72 (1988): 183–202. Sebastian Brock kindly provided clarification of this point.

ܘܩܒܪܘܗܝ܆ ܒܐܪܥܐ ܥܠ ܓܒܝ ܒܝܬܗ ܕܦܥܘܪ܂ ܘܠܐ ܐܢܫ ܝܕܥ
ܠܩܒܪܗ ܥܕܡܐ ܠܝܘܡܢܐ. ܡܫܬܥܝܢ ܗܘܘ ܠܝ܂ ܕܐܢܫ ܪܥܝܐ
ܕܡܢ ܢܒܘ ܛܘܪܬܐ ܗ̇ܝ܆ ܕܣܡܝܟܐ ܥܠ ܓܒܗ ܬܚܘܡܐ ܕܦܓܘܪܐ. ܟܕ
ܪܥܝܐ܂ ܐܝܬܝ܆ ܠܟܘܢ ܥܕܡܐ ܠܗܕܐ ܕܡܥܪܬܐ܂ ܘܟܕ ܐܬܐ ܠܗ܂ ܚܙܐ
ܐܝܟ ܕܒܚܙܘܐ ܡܥܪܬܐ ܕܢܦܩ ܪܒܐ. ܕܡܠܝܐ ܢܘܗܪܐ ܣܓܝܐܐ
ܘܪܝܚܐ ܒܣܝܡܐ ܘܢܝܚܘܬܐ. ܘܟܕ ܐܬܒܗ܃ ܘܠܐ ܡܚܘܬܗܘܢ ܠܒܪ
ܡܕܡ ܕܐܝܟ ܗܟܢܐ ܐܬܝܕܥ܆ ܒܗ̇ ܕܡܥܪܬܐ܂ ܟܕ ܐܬܚܫܒ ܒܚܝܠܐ
ܐܠܗܝܐ܂ ܐܬܕܟܪ ܕܢܒܝܘܬ ܠܗ܆ ܡܥܪܬܐ. ܘܚܙܐ ܠܐܢܫ ܗܢܐ ܡܩܦܪܐ܂
ܕܢܘܪܐ ܦܪܨܘܦܗ ܘܡܠܟܐ ܒܠܗ̇ ܠܒܝܬܐ. ܕܢܦܩ ܐܝܟ ܕܒܪܘܚܐ
ܢܗܝܪܬܐ܂ ܘܡܛܪܘܬܐ ܒܫܘܒܚܐ ܘܟܠܝܠܘܬܐ. ܘܟܕ ܐܬܩܪܒ ܕܢܗܘ
ܐܝܬܘܗܝ܆ ܩܕܝܫܐ ܡܫܝܚܐ܂ ܡܢ ܕܢܚܬܐ ܘܚܙܘܬܐ ܪܒܬܐ܂ ܡܚܘܝܐ
ܪܗܛ ܠܡܢܬܐ܂ ܟܕ ܡܣܬܒܪ ܕܢܘܕܥ ܚܘܝܐ ܠܗܠܝܢ ܕܐܬܝܢ. ܘܟܕ ܡܢ
ܐܠܗܐ ܐܬܢܚܡ܂ ܚܙܝ ܒܟܐܦܐ ܕܥܕܡܬܐ܂ ܘܐܩܝܡ ܦܓܪܐ ܩܕܝܫܐ
ܒܗ̇ ܕܡܥܪܬܐ܂ ܐܝܟܢܐ ܕܚܙܐ ܗ̇ܘ ܚܙܘܐ. ܟܕ ܐܬܢܫܒ܂ ܕܕܠܩܐ ܗܘܐ
ܕܐܘܠ. ܬܘܒ ܗ̇ܘ ܕܡܥܪܬܐ ܠܐ ܢܚܬܐ ܬܚܘܡܐ܂ ܗ̇ܝ ܕܐܝܟ ܗܘܬ.
(§121) ܟܕ ܓܝܪ ܥܒܕ ܗܠܝܢ ܕܗ̇܆ ܩܪܝܬܐ܂ ܒܠܚܘܕ ܒܫܝܢܘܬ ܪܘܚܗ
ܠܘܬ ܗ̇ܘ ܚܘܒ ܘܟܦܝܢ ܗܘܘ ܠܗ܆ ܡܥܪܬܐ. ܘܐܡܪ ܗ̇ܘ ܪܥܝܐ ܟܕ
ܦܪܐ ܗܘܕܐ ܠܐܠܗܐ܂ ܕܒܗܕܐ ܕܡܥܪܬܐ ܐܝܟܢܐ ܕܗܒܝܚܝܢ ܗܠܝܢ
ܓܡܐ ܫܪܝܬ ܗ̇ܘ ܚܘܒܐ. ܘܢܚܬܬ ܠܗ܆ ܡܥܪܬܐ܂ ܘܫܪܝܬܗ ܠܢܒܥܐ
ܡܝܫܐ. ܘܡܬܠܗܕܐ ܐܦܢܝܬ ܠܗܠܝܢ ܓܡܐ܂ ܐܝܟܢܐ ܕܐܦ ܫܬܝܬܐ
ܬܘܒ ܗ̇ܘ ܢܒܥܐ ܒܦܘܪܥܢܐ ܕܐܠܗܐ܂ ܟܕ ܠܕܘܟܬܐ ܗ̇ܝ ܓܡܐ
ܢܕܒܘܢ. ܘܗܟܢܐ ܟܕ ܐܬܦܢܝܘ܆ [R 89] ܘܩܛܝܢܐܐ ܡܕܝܫܐ
ܐܚܪ̈ܢܐ܂ ܕܪܥܘܬܐ ܐܝܬܘܗܝ܆ ܢܘܚܐ. ܒܠܚܘܕ ܩܢܝ ܐܬܪܐ ܟܕ ܐܚܝܕܐ
ܪܗܛ: ܘܐܝܬܘܗܝ ܗܠܝܢ ܕܫ̈ܒܝܚ ܠܒܝܬܐ܂ ܡܒܠܐ ܗܘܐ ܐܬܝܢ܂ ܟܠ
ܫܢܐ ܕܢܒܥܐ ܪܒܐ ܘܦܐܝܩ ܢܒܘܣܐ. ܟܕ ܓܠܝܐܬ ܘܕܠܐ ܦܘܫܒܐ
ܠܒܠܝܢ ܟܦܪܐ ܓܒܘܬܗ ܘܫܠܡܗ܂ ܟܕ ܐܬܦܬܚܐ ܘܬܕܡܘܪ̈ܬܐ ܘܐܣܘܬܐ܂
ܕܐܡܝܢܐܝܬ ܡܢ ܗܕܝܢ ܡܬ̈ܬܚܠܝܢ ܒܗܕܐ ܕܡܥܪܬܐ. ܒܗ ܐܣܘܬܐ
ܓܝܪ ܓܘܢܐ ܐܝܬܘܗܝ܆ ܕܢܦ̈ܫܬܐ ܘܦܓܪ̈ܐ܂ ܘܟܠ ܓܘܫܐ ܕܒܠܚܘܕ
ܗܠܝܢ ܕܡܢ ܒܠܒܗܝܢ ܐܝܬܝܢ ܠܗܪܟܐ ܘܡܬܐܡܢܝܢ ܒܢܦܫܐ܂ ܘܐܣܝܪܝܢ
ܒܚ̈ܫܐ ܡ̈ܫܬܚܠܦܐ.
(§122) ܟܕ ܢܓܠܝܢ ܗܟܝܠ ܬܘܒ܆ ܘܐܙܕܕܩ ܢ̈ܓܠܘܗ̇ ܕܢܒܥܐ ܪܒܐ ܫܟܝܚܝܢ

[1] Deut 34:5–6.
[2] See Num 32:3, 38; Isa 15:2.

Lord, died in the land of Moab according to the word of the Lord, **[R 88]** and they buried him in the land on the side of Beth Peʾor, and no one knows of his end until this day."[1] They told us that a certain shepherd from the village of Nebo,[2] which is situated at the southern side[3] of the mountain, brought his flock up to this place while shepherding it. Coming toward it, he saw as in a vision a very great cave, full of much light and sweet odor and splendor. Being amazed—for nothing like this had ever been seen in this place—he was strengthened by divine strength [and] dared to go down [in]to this cave. He saw a venerable old man whose face was shining[4] and full of all grace, reclining as it were on a bed, bright and flashing with glory and grace. When he understood that this was the holy Moses, he immediately ran to the village with fear and great joy, hastening to make known the vision to those who were there. Since he had been made wise by God, he gathered small stones and raised up many cairns in the place where he had seen the vision, thinking that perhaps after he went away this place would again become unknown, and this is what happened.

(§121) When the [inhabitants] of the village heard [about it], all of them ran in a throng to the vision and were looking for this cave. The shepherd said, calling God as a witness, "In that place where these cairns are set I saw the vision, and I went down to this cave and saw the holy prophet. I therefore raised up these cairns so that even if the prophet would again be hidden at the command of God, nevertheless these cairns would make the place known." When thus they and many **[R 89]** other saints were convinced that the vision was true, all the inhabitants ran together and brought those things needed for a building. This temple was built in the name of the great prophet and law-giver, publicly and indubitably proclaiming to everyone his grace and his power through signs, wonders, and healings, which from that time have continually been performed in this place. For it is a house of healing of souls and of bodies for all people, and a place of refuge for all those who arrive here from every place and who are in sorrow within [their] soul and are seized by various sufferings.

(§122) After we prayed there and had been graced with the

[3] Accepting the reading of MS B.

[4] See Exod 34:30, 35.

ܠܡܕܝܢܬܐ ܕܐܡܒܪܐ[1]܆ ܟܕ ܡܗܘܕܐ ܠܝ ܘܡܦܩܕ ܡܪܢܐ܆ ܘܡܥܡܕ ܠܥܡܗ
ܘܠܥܒܕܗ܆ ܟܕ ܐܬܬܘܐ ܘܐܬܟܫܦܬܐ ܕܥܒܪ܆ ܡܛܠ ܕܐܦ ܗܕܝܢ ܥܒܕ.
ܟܕ ܚܙܐ ܗܘ ܐܬܪܐ ܒܫܘܢܝܘܬ ܡܠܝܐ ܫܠܝܐܬܐ ܐܠܝܨ ܗܘܐ:
ܐܚܪܢܐ ܕܠܘ ܒܠܚܘܕ ܢܬܒܠܐ ܘܬ̈ܪܥܐ ܡܢܕܘܢܣܐ ܢܚܒܫܘܢ܆. ܐܠܐ
ܘܗܘܝܢ ܒܡܕܒܪܐ ܟܕ ܚܝܘܬܐ ܫܠܝܐܬܐ ܡܫܬܝܢ: ܘܒܡܐܐ ܘܠܐ
ܚܕ ܐܝܬ ܠܗܘܢ ܕܢܗܘܐ: ܘܠܐ ܠܗܘܢ ܘܠܐ ܠܒܥܝܪܝܗܘܢ: ܐܦ ܚܙܐ
ܡܛܠܠܬܗ ܕܗܕܐ ܚܠܬܐ ܢܬܐܪܐܬ ܢܦܩܝܢ ܗܘܘ ܡܛܠ ܕܐܬܘ: ܕܗܘ
ܡܕܝܢܐ ܠܗܘ ܐܬܪܐ ܢܐܙܠ: ܠܐ ܦܪܘ ܡܢ ܡܛܪܬܗܘܢ. ܟܕ ܚܙܐ ܕܪܕܝܢ
ܒܐܘܪܚܐ: ܘܟܠ ܚܕ ܛܘܥܢܐ ܡܩܒܠ ܕܠܗ ܕܡܕܝܢܬܐ: ܡܫܠܡ ܗܘ܇
ܥܡܐ ܡܩܒܠ ܚ̈ܒܪܐ. ܘܬ̈ܪܥܐ ܡܠܠܗ. ܘܟܪܘܐ ܢܦܩܘ. ܘܟܠܗ ܗܕܐ
ܥܘܡܘܬܐ ܕܡܠܝܐ: [R 90] ܡܠܘ ܕܝܢ ܒܡܘܪܟܬܐ ܕܐܠܗܐ: ܢܚܬܬ
ܘܐܫܦܥܬ ܠܟܠܗ ܗܘ ܐܬܪܐ: ܐܚܪܢܐ ܕܡܢܕܘܢܣܐ ܡ̈ܢ ܢܚܒܫ. ܚܝ ܟܕ.
ܡܬܦܪܢܣܝܢ ܒܡܘܪܟܬܐ. ܟܠܗܘܢ ܕܝܢ ܡܩ̈ܒܠܢܐ ܕܒ̈ܢܝܐ: ܡܛܠ ܕܟܠܝܢ
ܘܗܠܝܢ ܕܕܡܘܫܐ ܢܬܡܠܘܢ ܡܢ ܒܡܘܪܟܬܐ: ܘܦܐܪܐ ܐܪܥܐ ܢܐܣܘܢ ܟܢܝ.
ܟܕܢܐ ܘܟܡܪܐ. ܘܟܕ ܟܠܗܘܢ ܢܬܕܟܪܘܢ܆. ܐܟܚܕܐ ܢܦܩܘܢ ܠܐܘܪܚܗ
ܕܡܕܝܢܬܐ܆ ܥܡ ܕܢܒܠܬ ܐܪܬܬܐ ܘܚܕܘܬܐ ܘܩܘ̈ܠܣܐ. ܟܕ ܡܢܥܡܝܢ ܠܗ
ܘܡܫܒܚܝܢ܆ ܘܐܠܦܐ ܕܐܬ̈ܪܡ ܘܡܫܥܐ ܦܪܝܢ ܗܘܘ ܠܗ. ܗܘ ܕܝܢ ܐܝܟ
ܕܝ ܕܦܠܝܛ ܥܡܘܡܐ ܟܠܗ ܬܠܬ ܫ̈ܢܝܐ ܒܚܕܢܐ ܕܫܘܢܝܘܬ ܡܠܝܐ: ܗܢܐ
ܕܝܢ ܐܝܟ ܕܝܢ ܕܡܢ ܒܟܐܦܐ ܫܪܝܪܬܐ ܐܚܕ ܡ̈ܝܐ ܠܗܠܝܢ ܕܡܢܕܘܢܣܐ
ܒܚܕܝܢ ܗܘܘ ܡܢ ܣܘܪܚܢܐ. ܐܝܬܘܗܝ܇ ܗܘܐ ܕܝܢ ܗܘ ܘܒܢܐ ܕܡܕܒܪ
ܠܗ ܠܡܕܒܪܬܐ. ܡܕܡ ܡܠܠ ܚܙܐ ܢܒܥܬܐ ܕܦܠܣܛܝܢ ܐܝܬܘܗܝ܇
ܗܘܐ. ܟܪ̈ܝܗ ܡܕܒܪܐ ܥܡ ܝܘܣܬܐ ܘܡܕܒܪܢܘܬܐ ܪܒܘܬܐ ܗܘܘ
ܠܘܬܗ: ܘܡܫܟܚܝܢ ܗܘܘ ܫ̈ܠܘܦܘܬܗ ܢܩܒܫܬ ܡܢ ܐܠܗܐ: ܐܚܪܢܐ
ܕܫ̈ܠܝܐܬܐ ܡܗܝܡܢܘܗܝ܆. ܫܘܐܠܬ ܢܬܡܠܘܢ ܠܬܪܘܬܐ ܕܡܗܝܡܢܘܬܐ[2]
ܬܪܝܨܬ ܥܡܘܡܝܐ܆ ܥܡ ܒ̈ܢܝܗܘܢ܆ ܘܢܫ̈ܝܗܘܢ܆. ܘܡܫܬܘ̈ܬܦܐ ܕܠܝ
ܢܗܘܘܢ܆. ܘܐܢܫ̈ܐ ܫܦܝܪ ܒܡܗܝܡܢܘܬܐ ܘܬܪܝܨܘܬܐ ܠܡܫܠܡܢܐ ܕܒܬܪ.
(§123) ܘܡܢ ܒܬܪ ܗܠܝܢ܆ ܢܦܠܬ ܠܗ܇ ܕܬܠܡܝܕܐ ܟܒܪ. ܐܚܪܢܐ ܕܐܝܬ
ܣܚܒܬܐ. ܘܢܦܠܬ ܒܗ ܠܐܡܗ ܘܠܢܣܘܗ ܕܡܕܝܢܬܐ: ܘܪ̈ܝܫܢܐ

[1] I.e., Madeba. See *Vit. Pet.* §§118, 122 (R 84, 89–90).

[2] For more detail on cisterns and underground water supplies for desert monasteries and caves, see Patrich, *Sabas*, 78–81 *et passim*.

prayers of the great prophet, we arrived at the aforementioned town,[1] while the Lord was leading and protecting us and was glorifying his name and his servant through signs and wonders that he performs [now] and also performed then. That region was afflicted by a great lack of rain, so that not only the plants and seeds were in danger but also the inhabitants themselves, since they were being tormented by a great drought. There was not one comfort for them from the drought, neither for them nor for their animals. Especially for this reason those who came were anxious that the saint should go to this region. Their hope did not fail them. As we journeyed on the way and were approaching the boundaries of the town, the sky itself suddenly covered over [with] clouds and thunder sounded and [flashes of] lightning went forth. Such an abundance of rain, **[R 90]** or rather, a blessing of God, came down and watered that whole region so that we, indeed, were in danger of being drowned on the way. All the water reservoirs,[2] those of each [individual] and those of the public, were filled from the blessing. They restored the crops to life in one short moment. All of them being amazed, they went out together to meet with the saint with fear and trembling and joy and eulogies, kissing and embracing him. And they were calling him a second Elijah and Moses, the former, on the one hand, as one who at the time of lack of rain opened the heaven[s] after three years,[3] the latter, on the other hand, as one who brought forth water from solid rock for those who were in danger from thirst.[4] It was also the season that magnified the wonder, for it was a few days before Pentecost. Therefore they ran to him in this way with love and faith and were listening to his God-inspired teachings, so that many from among them would cheerfully obey the preaching of the orthodox faith with their children and their wives and would become our associates and fellow brethren in the faith and zealous for the perfection of the church.

(§123) After these [things] we went down to that [place] called Baʾar,[5] where the hot spring is. There went down together with

[3] See 1 Kgs 18.

[4] See Exod 17; Egeria, *Diary* 11.2 (Franceschini and Weber, 51; Gingras, 67).

[5] See Clamer, "The Hot Springs," 222–23, 224–25.

ܕܬܠܡܘܗܝ ܘܕܒܝܫܐ ܗ̈ܕܡܝܐ. ܠܐ ܡܢ ܡܕܒܪܢܘܬܐ ܒܠܚܘܕ: ܐܠܐ ܘܡܢ
ܐܣܛܪܛܝܘܛܐ ܗܠܝܢ ܕܬܡܢ ܗܦܟܝܢ ܘܐܣܝܪܝܢ ܗ̈ܕܡܝܐ. ܟܕ ܗܕܐ
ܕܝܢ ܣܢܝܩܝܢ ܗܘܘ [R 91] ܕܐܦ ܒܓܠܝܘܬܗ: ܦܬܓܡܐ ܢܬܢܝܫܘܢ
ܗܘܘ ܒܡܫܘܡܬܐ ܕܠܗܘܢ. ܡܛܠ ܕܒܪ ܝܕܥܐ ܕܗ̇ܝ، ܕܗܘܬܐ ܘܕܫܠܝܬܐ.
ܕܠܠܐܬ ܐܝܟܐ ܗܘܐ ܐܝܟ ܠܗܘܢ ܡܢ ܩܕܡ ܗܢ. ܘܟܕ ܐܬܝܢ ܠܗܘܢ.
ܒܝܡ ܟܠ ܬܕܡܘܪܬܐ. ܟܕ ܒܪ ܢܚܠܐ ܒܥܘܡܩܐ ܐܬܚܙܝ ܗ̇ܘ، ܕܗܘܬܐ:
ܘܡܢ ܟܠ ܓܒܝܢ ܒܠܘ̈ܥܐ ܙ̈ܥܘܪܐ ܣܓܝܐܐ: ܪ̈ܕܝܐ ܕܡ̈ܝܐ ܫ̈ܚܝܢܐ
ܕܡܫܬܠܗܒܝܢ: ܠܐ ܒܠܚܘܕ ܡܢ ܠܬܚܬ ܡܢ ܐܪܥܐ: ܐܠܐ ܐܦ ܟܕ ܡܢ
ܠܥܠ ܡܢ ܛܘܪܐ ܡܬܢܫܒܝܢ. ܡܝܐ ܡܪܬܚܝܢ ܠܟܠܗ ܗ̇ܘ ܢܚܠܐ.
ܐܝܟܢܐ ܕܗܠܝܢ ܛܘܪܐ ܕܒܪܝܟܝܢ ܠܗ. ܒܛܝ̈ܢܐ ܫ̈ܚܝܡܐ ܕܐܡܝܢܝܢ
ܒܗܘܢ ܢܒܥܝܢ. ܐܝܟ ܦܘܡܐ ܕܡܦܚܠܐ ܬܢܘܪܐ. ܘܡܬܠܗܒܐ ܡܢ
ܬܚܘܡܬܐ ܕܐܐܪ ܘܣܘܡܟܐ. ܠܡܚܫ ܒܒܝܢܐ ܕܫܘܬܐ ܒܠܚܘܕ: ܗܠܝܢ
ܕܟܒܝܢ ܡܢ ܒܡܕܒܪܢܘܬܗ، ܕܐܬܪܐ ܕܢܒܥܘܢ ܘܒܡܫܡܫܢܘܬܐ ܬܬܬܢܫܘܢ.
ܟܕ ܗܦܟܝܐ ܡܬܦܢܝܢ ܗܕܐ ܒܟܕܝܢ. ܘܡܚܕܐ ܡܬܝܢ ܠܕܘ̈ܟܝܬܗܘܢ.
ܟܕ ܠܐ ܡܫܟܚܝܢ ܗܦܟܐܘܬܗ ܕܡܣܟܢܘܬܐ. ܒܩܕ ܟܠܗܘܢ ܗܠܝܢ
ܒ̈ܥܠܬܐ ܕܠܗܘܢ ܗ̇ܘܐ ܗ̣ܘ ܠܦܘܢܐ: ܕܐܝܟ ܗܕܐ ܦܘܪܢܘܬ ܡܘܕܝܐ
ܕܐܐܪܘܦ ܗܘ̣ܬ ܘܦܩܥܐ. ܕܟܕ ܙܘܥܐ ܚ̇ܫܡܐ ܢܓܕ ܗܘܐ: ܢܗܬܪ
ܕܙܘܥܐ ܕܛܠܠܐ ܢܓܕ. ܐܝܟܢܐ ܕܠܗܠܝܢ ܬܠܬܐ ܛܠ̈ܠܐ ܗ̇ܘ ܐܬܘܢܐ
ܕܟܠܕܝܐ ܗ̣ܘܐ. ܘܗ̇ܢܘܢ ܕܢܦܠܘ ܒܗܝܢ ܟܕ ܡܬܕܟܝܢ ܒܐܬܪܐ.
ܠܐ ܡܬܚܘܝܢ ܒܝܡ ܬܕܡܘܪܬܐ ܕܐܝܟ ܗܠܝܢ. ܗܘܬ ܕܝܢ ܘܐܚܪܬܐ
ܬܕܡܘܪܬܐ: ܡܛܠ ܗ̇ܝ، ܕܐܬܪ ܢܗܝܪܘ̈ܢ ܘܫܬܪ̈ܘ.

(§124) ܐܚܝܢܗ̇ ܕܝܢ ܗܕܐ. ܗ̇ܢܘܢ ܕܒܗܘܬܐ ܢܚܬܝܢ ܗܘܘ ܠܗܘܢ:
ܐܝܟܢܐ ܕܦܪܝܩܝܢ ܐܡܪܝܢ. [R 92] ܡܛܠ ܕܠܝܬ ܗܘܐ ܬܡܢ ܡ̈ܝܐ: ܘܠܐ
ܡܛܝܐ ܕܢܬܚܒܫܐ ܒܗ̇ܘ ܢܚܠܐ ܒܗ ܡܥܪܬܐ ܡܛܠ ܫܚܝܡܘܬܗ
ܕܐܐܪ: ܟܕ ܚܙܘ ܩܫܝܐ ܡܢ ܪ̈ܓܠܬܐ: ܕܕ̈ܕܐ ܒܡܥܒܪܬܗ ܕܢܚܠܐ ܗ̇ܘ
ܕܡܬܐܡܪ ܕܐܪܢܘܢ. ܒܥܕܘ ܠܗܘܢ. ܬܠ̈ܠܐ ܗ̈ܦܟܐܝܬ ܟܕ ܐܫܬ̈ܝ
ܩ̈ܫܕܕܐ. ܟܕ ܥܢܘ ܡܚܠ ܘܟܝܢܐ ܕܡܦܠܐ ܚܒܪ: ܘܐܝܟ ܠܗܘܢ ܠܐ
ܐܬܐ: ܬ̇ܡܢ ܗܠܝܢ ܬ̈ܠܠܐ ܟܕ ܦܩܪ ܥܪܘܬܐ ܘܕܪ̈ܓܝܢ. ܠܟܦ̈ܐ ܡܢ

[1] On Ba'ar (Hammamat Main), see also Eusebius, *Onom.* (Klostermann, 112,14–17; Freeman-Grenville, Chapman, and Taylor, 32; our translation): Καριαθαείμ. πόλις ἣν ᾠκοδόμησαν "οἱ υἱοὶ ʽΡουβίν." καὶ νῦν ἔστιν ὅλη Χριστιανῶν κώμη, παρὰ Μηδαβὰν πόλιν τῆς 'Αραβίας, λεγομένη Καραιάθα, ἀπὸ ι′ σημείων τῆς Μηδαβῶν πρὸς δυσμᾶς ἐπὶ τὸν Βάρην (listed under "Beelmeon"): "Kariathaeim. A city that the 'sons of Reuben' settled, but now it is an en-

us, for the honor and pleasure of the saint, both their magistrates and a great multitude, not only from the city but also from those soldiers stationed there,[1] and many others. With this they were anxious **[R 91]** that also on his account they would use the bath there [so] easily. Because of the desolation of that place and fear, rarely was anyone coming there before this. When we came there, we all saw wonders. For this place is a deep valley and enclosed on all sides by high mountains. Boiling streams of hot water are poured out not only from below the ground but also from above from the mountains, thus making that whole valley so hot that those surrounding mountains turn black with the dense smoke [cloud]s that are continually in them like a chimney receiving smoke. On account of the sweltering heat of the air, in the wintertime [and] only under difficulty do inhabitants from the region who seek to go down and refresh themselves in the hot spring assemble in a crowd to do this, and immediately return to their homes, since they cannot endure the severity of the heat. Nevertheless, all those days the blessed one was there the temperature of the air and breathing space [were] so pleasant that when a gentle wind blew it would seem that a dewy wind blew, as was the furnace of the Chaldaeans for those three children.[2] Those who had gone down with us, being amazed, would say, "Never have we seen wonders as these!"

(§124) There was another wonder on account of which they would believe more and would become strengthened. It is this: Those who used to go down there in the winter, as we said before, **[R 92]** because there were no houses there and it is not possible that a hostelry be built in that valley because of the heat of the air, when they gathered reeds from the torrent that flowed in the middle of the valley, which is called Arnon,[3] they made for themselves many booths, fastened to each other. When they departed

tirely Christian village, around the city of Madeba of Arabia [which is also] called Karaiatha; from the tenth marker of the Madebean area to the west along Bara." A Roman-period legion was stationed at "Castra Arnonensia," primarily to guard the road from Elath to Bozrah, where it crossed the Arnon Valley. See "Arnon," *EncJud* 3:487; Kaswalder, *Onomastica Biblica*, 49, 277.

[2] See Dan 3:50 (LXX), πνεῦμα δρόσου.

[3] River in Transjordan, second largest river after the Jordan in the Dead Sea drainage basin (see "Arnon," *EncJud* 3:486–87).

ܚܘܡܐ ܘܒܨ̈ܥܪ. ܗܠܝܢ ܡܟܝܠ ܕܢܦܠܬܘ ܒܗܝܢ. ܟܕ ܐܫܬܟܚܘ ܐܢ̈ܫܝܢ
ܕܛ̈ܠܝܢ: ܫܪܘ ܒܗܘܢ. ܐܬܬܗܝܢ ܗ̈ܘܘ, ܕܝܢ ܦ̈ܠܚܬܐ ܘܕܪ̈ܝܫܝܢ ܗ̈ܘܘ,
ܒܫ̈ܕܪܐ. ܘܟܕ ܐܚܕ ܡܢܗܘܢ ܐܕܠܩ ܢܘܪܐ: ܐܝܟ ܡܐ ܕܢܒܫܠ ܠܗ
ܩܘܢܝܘܢ. ܥܒܪܬ ܦܢܛܩܘܣܛܐ: ܘܐܬܒܕܪܬ ܒܩܝܛܐ. ܫܪܘܢ ܕܝܢ ܩ̈ܝܛܐ. ܟܕ
ܐܝܟ ܣܘܪܬܐ ܕܡܬܪܝܚܐ ܒܗ̇ ܢܘܪܐ ܡܚܕܐ ܕܠܗܘ: ܢܓ̇ܠܘ ܘܠܗܠܝܢ
ܛ̈ܠܠܐ ܕܬ̈ܡܢ. ܘܡܟܝܠ ܠܟܠܗܝܢ ܒܪܦܦܐ ܕܥܝܢܐ ܐܬܦܩ̈ܕܘ ܐܬܚܪܒ
ܩ̈ܘܡܘ, ܡܠܟܐ. ܘܒܠܗܘ ܗܢܐ ܠܬܘܡܟܐ ܗܠܟܬ ܢܘܪܐ ܐܡܪܢܐ ܕܛ̈ܠܠܬܐ
ܢܩ̈ܘܡ ܘܐܩ̈ܠܝܬܐ ܘܬܚܢ̈ܝܬܐ. ܐܝܟ ܡܐ ܕܐܬܒܪܘ ܠܗܘܢ ܟܠܗܘܢ
ܗܠܝܢ ܕܒܛ̈ܠܠܐ ܐܫܬܟܚܘ. ܗܝܕܝܢ ܡܟܝܠ ܗܘ ܛܘܒܢܐ: ܟܕ ܒܒܟܝܐ
ܗܘ̣ܐ ܘܒܕܚܠܬܐ: ܐܝܟ ܡܐ ܕܒܟܠܬܗ ܟܠܗܘܢ ܢܦܠܘ. ܩܡ ܩܕܡ
ܟܠܗܘܢ ܘܦܫܛ ܐܝܕ̈ܘܗܝ ܠܫܡܝܐ. ܘܟܕ ܫܠܡ ܦܘܡܗ: ܟܠܝܘܗܝ
ܟܠܗ ܒܕܡܘܬ ܡܘܫܐ ܢܒܝܐ ܗܘܐ ܠܘܬ ܐܠܗܐ. ܐܘ ܠܚܝܠܐ ܠܐ
ܡܬܟܠܠܐ ܘܡܣܒܪܐ ܐܒܗܘܬܐ ܕܐܠܗܐ. ܗܘ ܕܐܡܪ ܠܗܠܝܢ ܕܩ̈ܪܝܢ
ܠܗ. ܕܥܕ ܥܕܟܝܠ ܡܡܠܠ ܐܢܬ: ܐܡܪ ܕܗܐ ܩܪܝܒ ܐܢܐ. ܟܕ ܐܚܕ
ܓܝܪ ܠܐ ܡܟܝܠ ܗܘܐ ܘܠܐ [R 93] ܫܥܬܐ ܚܕܐ ܗܘܐ: ܕܥܢ̈ܢܐ ܢܕܥܟܝܢ
ܠܗ̇, ܟܕܘܠܬܐ ܕܟܠܗܘܢ ܗܠܝܢ ܛ̈ܠܠܬܐ ܡܚܕܐ ܟܠܗܝܢ ܫܠܡܐ ܘܡܠܟܐ
ܗܘ̈ܝ, ܩ̈ܝܡܐ ܓܝܪ ܗܘܘ. ܘܩܝ̈ܡܐ ܒܫܝܢܐ. ܘܒܬܪ ܘܠܐ ܐܢܫ ܡܢ
ܒܢܝ̈ܢܫܐ ܘܠܐ ܒܥܝܪܐ ܘܠܐ ܡܐܢܐ ܘܠܐ ܢܦܠܬܐ ܐܫܬܟܚ ܕܢܒܕ.
ܘܐܟܢ: ܐܠܐ ܐܢ ܚܠܘܕ ܐܘܟܡܐ ܕܪܝܫ ܣܥܪܐ. ܐܝܟܢܐ ܕܠܚܠܝܢ
ܢ̈ܒܥܐ ܬܘܗܐ: ܕܟܠܗܘܢ ܢܘܕܥܬܗ ܘܡܟܡܘܬܗ ܕܡܕܝܢܬܐ ܟܠܗ ܠܫܐܦܘ
ܕܢܘܪܐ. ܘܦܘܪܩܢܐ ܕܐܝܟ ܗܢܐ ܫܒܪܬ܀

(§125) ܗܕܐ ܕܝܢ ܘܬܕܡܘܪܬܐ ܐܚܪܬܐ ܬܘܒ: ܟܕ ܓܝܪ ܐܘܕܥܘ ܠܝ
ܗ̇ܢܘܢ ܕܫܒܩܝܢ ܢܝܫܢ̈ܐ ܕܝ, ܕܡܚܬܐ: ܕܠܗ̇ܘܢ ܕܐܬܝܢ ܠܬܡܢ.
ܕܐܝܟ ܗܠܝܢ ܛܦܐ ܕܕ̈ܒܒܐ ܫܠܝܢ ܘܩܕܫܝܢ. ܟܕ ܡܢܩܦ ܠܗ ܒܠܚܘܕ
ܠܐܪܥܐ ܘܠܐܐܪ: ܐܠܐ ܘܠܦܪ̈ܨܘܦܝܗܘܢ ܡܢܟܬܝܢ. ܐܝܟܢܐ ܕܢܓܙܪܘܢ
ܒܫܝܢܗܘܢ. ܒܪܡ ܒܗܠܝܢ ܥܠܠ ܥ̈ܡܠܬܐ ܕܗܘܐ ܗܘ ܛܘܒܢܐ ܬܡܢ:
ܠܐ ܐܬܚܙܝ, ܠܘܬ ܠܘܬ ܕܕܒܒܐ ܒܗܠܝܢ ܕܕ̈ܒܒܬܐ.

(§126) ܐܬܬ ܕܝܢ ܘܚܙܬܐ ܕܥܘܠܐ ܠܬܕܡܘܪܬܐ ܒܗ̇, ܕܡܚܬܐ. ܐܬܬ
ܬܒܥ ܡܚܪܬܐ. ܘܡܢ ܚܕܐ ܐܬܬܐ ܕܠܗ̇ ܕܡܚܪܬܐ: ܬܪ̈ܝܢ ܢܩܒ̈ܐ

1 Exod 17:11–12.
2 See also Exod 17:1–7.
3 The same phrase from Isa 58:9 was already used; see *Vit. Pet.* §53 (R 36).

then and the time of the summer arrived and no one came there, those very booths, truly worn out and deserted, became dried up by the heat and parched. Those who went down with us, when they found them prepared, lodged in them. [The booths] were many, and they were joined to each other. When someone kindled a fire as one does for one's need, a spark leapt out and laid hold of the reeds. When these reeds blazed up immediately like stubble into which fire is blown, they transmitted [the fire] also to the adjoining booths. Therefore in a short instant all of them were crumbled together and turned into ashes. The fire rose up to such a height that there were wailings and laments and groans as if they had lost all those [things] that were found in the booths. At that time the blessed one, while he was weeping and in fear as the one for whose sake they all had gone down, stood in front of all of them and stretched out his hands to heaven.[1] And while his mouth was silent, in his heart only he was crying out to God like Moses.[2] O the ineffable power and compassion for humanity of God, who said to those who are worthy of him, "While you are still speaking, I say, 'Behold, I am near!' "[3] For while no one was able or **[R 93]** dared to quench with water the conflagration of all those booths, all of them immediately became dust and ashes, for they were reeds, and [moreover] dried reeds. Nevertheless, not one of the men, nor an animal, nor a vessel, nor an [outer] garment was found burnt and perished, except for only a pack-saddle of one donkey, so that it would become known to everyone that the prayer and the intercession[4] of the saint alone stopped the violence of the fire and provided such a deliverance.

(§125) There happened there another wonder. For although those who had experience of that place made known to us that such swarms of flies pestered and tormented those who would go down there, not only covering earth and air but also biting their bodies so that they would [want to] give up their life, nevertheless on those few days the blessed one was there, hardly any fly was seen in those places.[5]

(§126) There is in that place another sight worthy of wonder. There is a cave there, and from one wall of the cave two holes about

4 See also above, *Vit. Pet.* §115 (R 83).

5 Exod 8:31.

ܕܢܣܒܘܢ ܡܢ ܫܪܝܪܐ ܐܝܟ ܡܫܘܚܬܐ ܕܐܡܬܐ ܡܪܕܝܢ ܡܝ̈ܐ. ܗ̇ܘ ܕܝܢ
ܕܦܠܓ ܡ̈ܝܐ܆ ܗ̇ܘ ܕܝܢ ܕܦܠܓ ܣܓܝܐܝܢ. ܘܗܘܐ ܟܠܗ܆ ܒܗܢܐ ܕܠܐ
ܢܟܝܢ ܐܝܟ ܕܢܬܡܦ ܒܗܘܢ. ܗܢܝ ܕܝܢ ܡ̇ܢ ܒܠܬܗ ܕܡܕܝܢܬܐ܆ ܒܟܝܢܐ
ܠܦܬܐ ܘܠܢܘܪܐ ܘܠܡܡܡܐ ܐܝܟ ܡܫܘܚܬܐ ܕܙܘܓܐ. ܘܠܬܠܬܝܢ ܒܪ
ܗܠܝܢ ܣܓܝ̈ܐܐ ܒܗ ܗܠܝܢ ܡ̈ܝܐ܆ ܕܪܝܢ ܘܢܦܩܝܢ ܡܢ ܬܪ̈ܝܗܘܢ ܢܦܩܐ܆
ܡܫܘܚܬܐ ܥܒܝܪܬ [R 94] ܡܘܠܟܐ ܘܕܡܝܢ ܢܦܫܗ ܡܫܟܠܝܢ. ܕܒܗܘܢ
ܒܪ. ܡܬܢܦܫܝܢ ܗܠܝܢ ܕܢܦܠܝܢ ܠܗܘܢ܆ ܒܡܘܬܪܐ ܕܒܝܢܬܗܘܢ ܡܬܟܫܦܝܢ.

(§127) ܟܕ ܫ̇ܠܡܝܢ ܚܝܢ ܗܟܝܠ ܬܡܢ ܒܐܬܪܐ ܡܕܒܪܐ ܕܣܘܠܩܗ ܕܡܪܢ܆
ܬܘܒ ܠܡܐܪܒܐ ܦܢܝܢ. ܟܕ ܠܘ ܒܠܚܘܕ ܒܗܢܐ ܕܡܕܝܢܬܐ܆ ܐܠܐ
ܘܕܒܘܪ̈ܝܐ ܘܕܐܓܘܪ̈ܣܐ ܒܐܘܪܚܐ܆ ܒܗ ܚܕܘܬܐ ܘܡܗܝܡܢܘܬܐ
ܠܐܘܪܚܐ ܢܦܩܝܢ ܗܘܘ܆ ܘܪ̈ܗܛܝܢ ܠܘܬܗ ܘܡܬܒܪ̈ܟܝܢ. ܘܬܪܐܝܬ܆
ܡܛܠ ܕܢܦܝܫܘ ܗܠܝܢ ܬܘܕ̈ܝܬܐ ܕܗܘ̈ܝ ܒܝܘܡܐ. ܟܕ ܒܐܠܝܢ ܚܝܢ ܕܝܢ
ܠܡܕܝܢܬܐ܆ ܐܝܟ ܒܐܘܪܚܐ ܕܩܠܝܠܐ ܕܢܦܫܗ ܡܘܡܬܐ܆ ܕܐܢܬܘܬܗ܆ ܗܘܐ
ܒܦܪܐ܆ ܐܘ ܐܢܬܬܐ ܒܡܘܪܬܐ ܐܢܬ ܗܘܐ ܠܗ܆ ܡܛܠ ܗܕܐ ܗܘܐ ܕܠܐ
ܒܢ̈ܝܐ ܐܢܬܘܬܗ܆ ܗܘܐ܆ ܟܕ ܦܪܥ ܠܗܘܢ܆ ܡܦܝܣ ܗܘܐ ܠܗ ܐܝܟ
ܕܬܬܦܩܕ ܠܨܠܘܬܐ܆ ܕܬܠܐ ܒܠܝܗܘܢ ܕܢܗܘܘܢ ܠܗܘܢ ܒܢ̈ܝܐ. ܟܕ
ܚܕ ܕܝܢ ܐܡܪܝܢ ܠܗ܆ ܕܚܕ ܠܟ ܡܢܝܢ ܚܕ ܕܗܕܐ ܢܦܫ܆ ܐܠܐ ܕܠܝܢ
ܐܢܬܬܗ ܕܬܦܘܩ ܠܡܫܟܐ ܙܒܢܐ܆ ܦܪܝܐ ܡܗܡܢܐ ܘܐܬܪܘܕܘܡܣܐ
ܣܓܝܐܐ܆ ܗ̇ܘ ܕܐܦ ܦܩܠ ܠܝ ܕܢܦܪܘܩ ܐܕܘܗܝ܆ ܘܢܦܠ ܡܕܡܘܗܝ
ܕܡܕܝܢܐ ܘܒܟܠܐ ܡܢܗ܆ ܚܝܢ ܟܪܐ ܠܗ ܡܟܪܝܣܝܢ ܕܕܐܝܟ ܗܕܐ

[1] For dimensions of ancient cisterns, see Patrich, *Sabas*, 81 fig. 25, 83 fig. 26.

[2] See Clamer, "The Hot Springs," 222–23; Horn, *Asceticism and Christological Controversy*, 241–43, 252–53.

[3] Peter, his followers, and people from the local area thus stayed at the hot spring of Baʾar only for a few days, probably only for the celebrations of the Feast of the Ascension, right before Pentecost. Note the reference to Pentecost earlier, at §122 (R 90). A number of reasons may have motivated Peter and his followers to celebrate such a significant feast in the relative seclusion and wilderness of a small site east of the Dead Sea. One might have been Peter's desire to withdraw from the crowds, albeit unsuccessfully here. The spirituality of the feast that commemorates Christ's final withdrawal from this world into the heavenly realm also lent itself to being celebrated in a more remote

the measure of a cubit apart from each other issue forth water, one very cold, the other very hot, and to such an extent that no one can touch it. There is, however, in the middle of the cave [a depth that is] in breadth and height and depth like the measure of a cistern.[1] The hot [water] together with the cold [water] flows and comes down from both holes, perfecting a well-tempered, **[R 94]** natural bath that those going down to [the water] use, enjoying profit from [the water].[2]

(§127) After we had thus celebrated there the holy Feast of the Ascension of our Lord,[3] we returned again to Madeba. Not only the people of the town but also [those] of the villages and of the farms on the way were going out with joy and faith to meet [the saint] and were running to him and were receiving a blessing, especially because they had heard [of] those wonders that had happened in the valley. While we were entering the town, however, someone of note among the soldiers whose name was Qaiuma,[4] who was sterile or had a barren wife,[5] because of which he did not have children, approached us, asking us [earnestly] to entreat the blessed[6] one to pray for them[7] that they might have children. We said to him, "We cannot do this, but it is for you to take Moses, the magistrate"—a believing and orthodox man, a wise [man], who also received us to lodge with him[8]—"and he will fall down in front of the saint and beseech him, for we do not dare

space, withdrawn from the world. Another reason may have been that, as an anti-Chalcedonian, Peter felt he could not or did not want to celebrate such a significant feast in a larger city that was not in anti-Chalcedonian hands. That Peter did not celebrate Pentecost in Madeba but in the little village of Batmin (see *Vit. Pet.* §130 [R 96]) might also point in that direction. Since Rufus, however, does not specify a reason, no final clarity can be reached.

[4] The name is of Aramaic origin.

[5] Rufus's comment here helpfully reflects a way of thinking that did not lay blame for barrenness exclusively on the shoulders of the wife. For contemporary knowledge concerning women's health and fertility, see Clark, *Women in Late Antiquity*, 63–93.

[6] One catches here another glimpse at the practice of obtaining favors through a go-between intercessor.

[7] Literally, "to pray over them." The prayer may have included the laying of hands on the one who received the prayerful blessing.

[8] A further glimpse at the anti-Chalcedonian support network. Again support is provided by members of the local establishment.

ܦܪܗܣܝܐ ܗܘܬ ܠܝ ܠܘܬܗ܇ ܒܕ̈ܢܚܝܢ ܠܡܫܡܫܘܬܗ ܘܠܐ ܙܒܢܬ
ܥܘܡܪܢܐ ܕܝܠܝ ܐܬܬܦܝܣ܂ ܘܟܕ ܩܪܒ ܠܘܬܗ ܘܫܐܠܗ܆ ܡܕܡ ܕܢܫܐܠ
ܡܕܡ܂ ܡܕܡ ܗܘ ܡܕܝܢܐ ܘܐܡܪ ܠܗ܂ ܡܪܝ ܢܥܘܠ ܡܥܡܪܢܐ ܢܗܘܐ
ܒܗ ܘܙܟܝ܂ ܗܘ ܕܝܢ ܟܕ ܐܬܕܟܪ ܒܗ ܗܘ ܙܒܢܐ܇ ܘܒܡܫܡܫܢܘܬܐ
ܡܠܗ ܠܟܠܬܐ܂ ܡܢܐ ܟܠܗ ܦܐܪܐ ܢܦܩ ܕܟܘܪܟܬܐ܂ ܐܝܟܢܐ
ܕܠܣܢܬܝ ܐܟܐ ܕܒ̈ܢܝܐ ܦܓܥܬܐ ܢܗܘܐ܂ ܘܗܕܐ ܠܗ ܠܗ ܒܠܚܘܕ܆
ܐܠܐ ܘܠܐܣ̈ܝܢܐ ܒܗܠܝܢ ܐܬܪ̈ܘܬܐ [R 95] ܘܒܪ̈ܘܚܢܝܬܐ ܦܓܥܬܐ܂
ܟܕ ܡܦܩܣ ܐܬܝܗܒ ܗܢܐ ܥܘܗܕܢܐ܂ ܒܝܕ ܨ̈ܠܘܬܗ ܕܩܕܝܫܐ܂

(§128) ܐܦ ܓܒܪ ܐܚܕ ܐܣܝܪܐ ܡܛܠܬܗ ܕܟܠܬܐ܇ ܦܢܝܐ ܗܘܐ
ܠܐܢܬܬܗ ܘܛܪܕ ܗܘܐ ܠܗ܇ ܘܦܩܕ ܕܠܐ ܡܚܒܠ ܚܙܐ ܠܗ܂ ܐܒܘܗ̇
ܕܗܕܐ ܟܕ ܩܪܒ ܠܘܬ ܩܕܝܫܐ܂ ܒܥܐ ܗܘܒܢܐ܂ ܘܡܦܝܣ ܗܘܐ ܕܟܕ
ܡܬ̈ܬܝܢܘܬܗ܂ ܢܦܩ ܠܒܪܐ ܕܢܬܪܟܐ ܠܐܢܬܬܗ܂ ܟܕ ܐܫܬܟܚ ܘܓܠܬܐ
ܕܗܢܝܬܐ ܘܕܡܗܦܟܢܘܬ ܐ̈ܦܐ܂ ܗܘ ܕܝܢ ܟܕ ܚܙܝܗ̇ ܠܛܠܝܐ܂ ܡܪܬܐ
ܗܘܐ ܠܗ ܐܟܡܐܝܬ܂ ܘܡܦܝܣ ܗܘܐ܂ ܟܕ ܒܟܝܐ ܕܝܢ ܗܘ ܘܐܡܪ܇
ܕܠܐ ܡܥܒܕ ܗܕܐ ܠܡܥܒܕ܆ ܐܡܪ ܠܘܬܗ ܗܘ ܛܘܒܢܐ܂ ܐܢ ܡܛܠ
ܕܪܚܡ ܐܢܬ ܒ̈ܢܝܐ ܗܒܢܐ ܦܝܣܢܬ܂ ܐܬܬܦܝܣ ܠܝ ܒܪܝ܆ ܘܐܬܟܢܫ ܡܢ
ܫܘܪ̈ܬܝ܆ ܘܩܒܠ ܦܝܣܬܝ ܘܗܒ ܐܢܬܬܟ܂ ܘܡܗܝܡܢ ܐܢܐ ܒܡܪܝܐ܂
ܕܡܫܡܠܐ ܪ̈ܚܡܝܟ ܠܗܒܢܐ܂ ܗܘ ܕܝܢ ܟܕ ܐܬܬܦܝܣ ܠܡܕܝܢܐ ܘܗܦܟ܂
ܐܬܪ̈ܥܝ ܠܐܢܬܬܗ܂ ܘܒܬܪ ܒܗ ܕܐܝܟ ܗܕܐ ܦܓܥܬܐ ܒ̈ܢܝܐ ܗܘܬ
ܠܗ܂ ܐܝܟܢܐ ܕܢܗܘܐ ܐܒܐ ܕܬܫܥܐ ܒ̈ܢܝܐ܂ ܕܒܪ̈ܐ ܥܒܕܝ ܘܬܪ̈ܬܝܢ
ܢܩܒ̈ܬܐ܂

(§129) ܘܬܘܒ ܟܕ ܐܝܬܝܗ̇ ܒܡܐܕܒܪܐ܇ ܚܙܐ ܡܢ ܩ̈ܘܡܬܐ ܡܢ ܒܬܪ
ܕܐܟܠܝܢ܇ ܟܕ ܢܦܩ ܡܢ ܦܘܪܬܐ܂ ܓ̇ܒܝܢ ܕܢܐܡܪ ܬܫܡܫܬܐ ܕܣܘܟܠ
ܛܒܘܬܐ܂ ܘܡܢܝܠ ܐܬܚܙܝ ܗܘ ܛܘܒܢܐ ܘܗܘܐ ܒܬܡܗܐ܂ ܘܒܬܪ
ܐܝܟ ܚܕܐ ܫܥܬܐ ܘܦܠܛܗ̇܂ ܟܕ ܒ̈ܢܝܗܘܢ ܕܠܐ ܥܠܝܐ ܚܙ̈ܝ ܗܘ̈ܘ

[1] The Syriac transliterates the Greek παρρησία.

[2] Peter is presented as participating in quasi-divine foreknowledge, knowing what is needed before the request has been made.

[3] There is less evidence for divorce in the fourth and fifth centuries than in earlier periods, due to the overall decline in records. Constantine introduced restrictions on unilateral divorce, which were repealed by Emperor Julian (361–363) and later reintroduced by Theodosius II, albeit in a more lax form than Constantine's measures. Women seeking divorce were treated more harshly

to have such freedom [of speech][1] toward him, because we know his humility and his dislike [of] praise." He consented, and when he approached him and bowed himself, before he would ask anything, the saint preempted [him] and said to him, "Our Lord Jesus Christ be with your seed."[2] The [soldier] was amazed, together with the magistrate, and received the word in faith. He received such fruit from the blessing that eventually he became the father of many children. And this [happened] not only to him but also to others in those regions **[R 95]** and in many places. [For] what[ever] they asked, the gift was granted through the prayers of the saint.

(§128) Another man, for the same reason hated his wife and had chased her away, having decided that from that time [on] he would not see her [again]. The father of this [woman],[3] when he approached the saint, informed him [of] the deed and urged [him] that through his admonitions he should persuade the man to be reconciled to his wife, while he also related the reason of the hatred and of the rejection of [her] presence. [The saint] called the young man [and] admonished him like a father and persuaded [him]. When he wept and said that he could not do this, the blessed one said to him, "If you decided thus because you desire children, obey me, my son, and reverence my white hair! Accept instruction and take your wife! I trust in the Lord that he will fulfill your desire to the full[est]." Obeying the saint and believing, he was reconciled to his wife. Afterwards he had such a multitude of children that he became the father of nine children, seven male and two female.[4]

(§129) Again, while we were in Madeba, one day after we had eaten, when we had arisen from the table, we began to say the doxology of thanksgiving. Suddenly the blessed one was carried off and was in amazement. He persisted [in it] for about an hour and a half, while his eyes were ceaselessly gazing [at something] in

than men. By the fifth century, it is likely that public and Christian ecclesiastical opinion and canons were more of a deterrent than the civil law, as evidenced in this story. See also Judith Evans Grubbs, "Divorce," in Bowersock, Brown, and Grabar, *Late Antiquity*, 414.

[4] The survival of aged parents depended in many cases on their having produced offspring who would care for them in their old age. For a discussion of miracles related to barrenness and childbirth in Rufus's work, see Horn, "Chapter in the Pre-history of the Christological Controversies."

ܒܡܕܒܪܐ. ܚܙܐ ܕܝܢ ܟܕ ܒܫܠܝܐ ܡܨܠܐ ܚܙܐ: ܘܒܬܪܥܐ ܩܪܝܒܝܢ ܚܙܐ.
ܠܣܪܝܬܐ ܟܕ ܠܘܬ ܢܦܫܗ ܗܘܐ. ܡܛܠ ܒܡܠܟܐ [R 96] ܕܪܟܐ ܟܕ ܚܒܝܐ.
ܘܟܕ ܠܐܢܫ ܡܕܡ ܠܐ ܐܡܪ: ܘܠܐ ܨܠܘܬܐ ܚܒܪ. ܢܓܕ ܟܠ ܠܥܠܬܐ
ܐܝܟܐ ܕܐܝܬܝܗ̇ ܗܘܬ ܬܫܘܝܬܗ. ܘܟܕ ܐܝܟ ܬܪܥܐ: ܗܘ ܟܕ ܐܚܝܠ
ܘܡܬܬܝܩ ܒܕܡܘܬܐ ܠܪܡܫܐ. ܕܐܝܠܝܢ ܕܝܢ ܐܬܝܗܘܢ ܗܠܝܢ ܕܚܙܐ: ܠܐ
ܐܝܟ ܡܢ ܐܡܪܝܢ ܕܢܫܬܠ ܒܬܪ ܗܕܐ. ܘܠܐ ܕܝܢ ܗ̣ܘ ܐܡܪ: ܡܢ ܗܠܝܢ
ܕܝܢ ܒܩܠܬܐ ܕܗܘܝܐ ܒܠܗܘܢ ܒܢ̈ܝ ܡܕܡܝܢ. ܕܗܠܝܢ ܒܢ̈ܫܬܐ ܕܟܬܒ̈ܝ
ܗ̈ܘ ܕܢܕܪܘܢ ܠܬܒܠ ܐܬܦܠܬ ܠܡܪܢܫܐ ܒܫܘ ܚܘܝܐ. ܐܝܟ ܢܒܝܘܬܐ
ܕܟܡܘܣ ܢܒܝܐ ܕܐܡܪ: ܡܛܠ ܕܠܐ ܢܒܕ ܡܪܝܐ ܦܘܪܫܢܐ: ܕܠܐ
ܢܓܠܐ ܡܪܕܘܬܗ ܠܥܒܕ̈ܘܗܝ ܢܒ̈ܝܐ. ܘܬܘܒ ܦܓܪܐ ܗܢ ܗܠܝܢ ܦܓܠ
ܗ̣ܘ ܠܡܟܢܐ. ܘܡܛܠ ܗܕܐ ܗܘܝܢ: ܟܕ ܒܚܐܦܐ ܕܢܫܐ ܡܬܠܒܢܐ
ܐܬܬܚܕ: ܠܐ ܐܫܟܚ ܕܠܐܢܫ ܡܢ ܒܢ̈ܝ ܡܕܝܢܬܐ. ܟܕ ܐܬܐ ܐܝܟ
ܚܕܐ ܠܐܦܘܗܝ ܘܦܓܕܬܗ ܢܦܠ ܒܒܝܬܐ: ܒܕܡܐ ܠܗܘܡܐ ܕܟܬܪܗ.
(§130) ܟܕ ܗܘ ܡܚܝܠ ܒܡܕܝܢܬܐ ܗ̇ܝ ܥܠܠ ܢܩܠܬܐ: ܘܒܬܪ ܐܝܟ
ܘܫܪܪ ܐܝܟ. ܡܫܪܟ ܗܘܐ ܕܢܦܩܐ. ܘܟܕ ܢܦܩ ܡܢ ܬܡܢ
ܘܐܬܦܫܛ: ܐܬܐ ܠܩܪܝܬܐ ܚܕܐ ܕܡܬܩܪܝܐ ܒܠܚܝܡ. ܘܟܕ ܚܒܪ.
ܬܡܢ ܒܐܬܪܐ ܕܦܠܣܛܝܢ ܡܕܝܢܬܐ: ܘܫܟܠ ܒܝܫܐ: ܘܟܪܗ ܠܕܘܟܬܐ

[1] Rufus occasionally reports visions that Peter received. See, e.g., also *Vit. Pet.* §§28, 53, 57–58, 59, 60, 62, 69, 83–84, 103, 129, 147, 150, 169, 185–187 (R 19, 36–37, 38–41, 40–41, 41–42, 44, 47, 58–59, 76, 95–96, 110, 113, 125–26, 139–41), and, e.g., *Pler.* 6, 37. These visions form an important element also in claiming special, divinely sanctioned authority for Peter. All in all, however, he does not paint Peter's portrait as that of a constant visionary lost in the *visio beatifica*. Rather, Rufus uses the few instances of visionary events he describes as teaching moments for his audience, warning them that Peter already had foreseen what Rufus interprets as the gloomy aftermath of the decisions of Chalcedon.

[2] The Syriac transliterates the Greek λεκτίς, "litter." See also LSJ, 1037.

[3] Literally, "where his bed was."

[4] This is likely a reference to the turbulences caused by the monk

heaven.[1] But while we were standing in silence and were wet with tears, when he finally [came back] to himself, he cried out with a loud **[R 96]** voice, weeping. Speaking to no one and without reciting the prayer, he leapt upon the couch[2] where he had made his bed.[3] After he had shut the door, he remained [there] mourning and sighing until evening. But of what kind those [things] he had seen were, no one from among us dared afterwards to ask nor did he speak [about them]. However, from those adversities, which at present occur daily,[4] we surmise that these evils that were about to come upon the habitable earth were revealed to the saint in this vision, as it says in the prophecy of Amos the prophet, "Because the Lord will not perform a deed without revealing his [plan of] chastisement to his servants, the prophets."[5] The blessed one endured many more [things] than those; wherefore, being held captive in the vehemence of pain,[6] before the next day he could not receive anyone from among the citizens for conversation when they came as was [their] custom to honor and reverence him.[7]

(§130) After remaining thus in the town for a few days and having edified them and strengthened them, he hastened to return. When he departed from there he was persuaded to come to a village called Batmin.[8] When he had spent the Feast of Holy Pen-

Nephalius. See Zachariah Rhetor, *Chron.* 6.1 (Brooks, 2:4,5–7; Hamilton and Brooks, 134). See also Frend, *Rise of the Monophysite Movement*, 201; Honigmann, *Évêques et Évêchés Monophysites*, 8.

[5] Amos 3:7 [LXX, against Pešitta].

[6] This comment seems to point toward a certain level of pain and suffering that Peter's visionary insights caused for him.

[7] Peter is shown as receiving honor and recognition from people who were not from the lowest classes of society.

[8] See Eusebius, *Onom.* 151 (Klostermann, 48,11–12; Freeman-Grenville, Chapman, and Taylor, 33): Βοτνία ἡ καί Ποτεέιν. πέραν τοῦ Ἰορδάνου, πόλις φυλῆς Γάδ. καὶ εἰς ἔτι νῦν ὁμοίως ἐν τοῖς τόποις χρηματίζει (listed under "Botnia/Bothnim"): "Botnia or Poteein, along the bank of the Jordan, a city of the tribe of Gad, that even up to the present also lends its name to the surrounding area."

ܘܠܡܣܬܪ̈ܗܒܘ ܦܝܫ ܠܐܘܪܫܠܡ. ܟܕ ܚܝܦ ܕܢܐܬܐ ܠܘܬ ܐܒܗ̈ܘܗܝ، ܘܠܒܝܬ ܫܠܝܗ.

(§131) ܒܬܪܐ ܕܝܢ ܐܝܟ ܙܢܐ ܡܫܟܢܐ ܘܙܢܐ ܡܕ̈ܝܢܐ: ܘܙܢܐ ܡܫ̈ܒܚܐ ܘܙܢܐ ܐܟܣ̈ܢܝܐ: ܣܓܝܐܐ ܒܡܣܟܢܘܬܐ ܘܐܫܬܪܕܘܬܐ ܙܢ̈ܝܐ ܕܥܒܕܗ ܐܠܗܐ: ܕܐܬܐܘܗܝ، ܗܘܐ ܒܥܠܠܬܗ ܠܐܘܪܫܠܡ: ܕܒܬܪ ܗܘܐ [R 97] ܒܐܘܪܫܠܡ ܘܐܬܐܘܗܝ، ܗܘܐ ܫܠܝܐ ܘܒܬܪ ܟܠܗ ܐܬܐ ܕܡܫܡܫܢܘܬܐ ܘܬܪܬܝܢ ܫܒܝܢܐ ܐܘܪܚܘܬܐ ܡܠܟܬܐ: ܕܡܢ ܟܕ ܘܕ ܐܝܬ ܗܘܐ ܠܗ ܕܒܥܠܬܐ ܠܘܬ ܩܕܝܫܐ ܘܢܒܝܐ ܕܦܠܒܝܬܗ: ܟܕ ܟܕ ܒܢܝ ܗܘܐ ܒܐܪ̈ܥܘܗܝ؛ ܒܐܝܕ̈ܘܗܝ، ܠܐܘܪܫܠܡ ܐܫܝܐ؛ ܦܩܕ ܐܬܟܬܒ ܘܐܦܩܘܗܝ. ܕܡܛܠ ܕܡܝܬܐ ܐܬܐܘܗܝ، ܘܫܡܥܐ ܩܕܝܫܐ ܐܝܬ ܒܡܣܟܢܘܬܐ: ܘܟܠܐ ܟܕ ܐܬܐܘܗܝ، ܗܘܐ ܗܘ ܕܒܬܪ ܦܠܣܛܝܢܐ؛ ܕܒܬܪ ܟܠܗܘܢ ܒܐܝܕܐ ܕܒܬܪ ܫܢܝܐ. ܘܠܐ ܕܝܢ ܗܘ ܕܟܗ ܐܬܒܠܡ ܐܕ̈ܢܘܗܝ؛

(§132) ܗܘ ܦܠܣܛܝܢܐ ܐܫܬܟܚ ܠܝ ܟܕ ܐܡܪ. ܕܟܕ ܡܕܝܢ ܗܘܐ ܗܘ ܦܘܠܝܢܐ ܒܐܬܪܐ ܕܐܬܠܘܬܐ: ܗܘܝܢܐ ܗܘܐ ܠܝ ܕܐܬܐ ܠܗ ܠܡܕܝܢܬܐ. ܘܟܕ ܚܙܝܬ ܕܡܘܬܪܐ ܐܬܐܘܗܝ، ܗܘܐ ܦܘܠܝܢܐ؛ ܟܕ ܠܐ ܒܕܟܠ ܐܝܬ ܗܘܐ ܠܝ ܦܐܪܘܬܐ ܘܡܚܝܢܐ ܠܘܬܗ؛ ܐܬܦܪܢܣܬ ܕܠܡܦܪܥܬܐ ܕܡܢܗ ܐܫܬܘܐ. ܐܝܟ، ܗܘܝܬ ܕܝܢ ܕܒܥܐ ܗܘܝܬ ܒܐܘ̈ܪܚ ܡܢ ܘܟܕܐ ܫܟܢܐܐ. ܘܟܕ ܐܬܐܡܪ ܠܗ ܡܛܠܬܝ، ܣܓܝܐܬ ܦܠܝܠ. ܘܟܕ ܟܠܬܐ ܐܢܐ ܕܐܦܠ ܥܠ ܪ̈ܓܠܘܗܝ، ܘܐܦܩܒܕ ܠܗ؛ ܠܟܒܪ ܒܢܫܝ ܘܐܡܟܝ. ܘܟܕ ܬܬܒܡܝ ܐܕ̈ܢܘܗܝ، ܫܡܥ ܟܠ ܐܕ̈ܢܝ: ܐܡܪ ܠܝ ܕܟܠܐ ܠܝ ܕܐܦܠ ܡܕܡܘܗܝ؛ ܢܫܡܥ ܒܢܫܝ. ܘܡܚܝܕܐ ܒܗ ܒܫܡܠܐ ܐܬܦܝܣܬ ܡܫܡܠܝܬ، ܘܡܛܠ ܗܕܐ ܡܢ ܡܕܡ؛ ܕܐܝܟ ܗܕܐ ܗܘܝܘܬܐ

[1] See *Vit. Pet.* §§122, 131, 141, 146, 162 (R 90, 97, 106, 109, 121).

[2] The Syriac renders the Greek σύναξις, "meeting," "assembly," but specifically refers to the eucharistic celebration.

[3] This comment taken together with the rest of the sentence could mean that Peter stayed again at the monastery he had built in Jerusalem. However, one does not have to read the sentence in this way. It also could mean that he returned to Jerusalem and while there nourished a desire to return further west to his monastery in Gaza.

[4] The "house of quiet" describes either the monastic cell or the monastery as a whole. See also *Vit. Pet.* §138 (R 102).

[5] The *tribunus* was the lowest-ranked plebeian magisterium in the *cursus honorum* of the Roman state. Only plebeians could hold this post, since among

tecost there,[1] had completed the [service of the] gathering,[2] and blessed the place and its inhabitants, he returned to Jerusalem,[3] being anxious to come to his brethren and to his house of quiet.[4]

(§131) Now a certain man, a lover of Christ and a lover of the saints, a lover of the poor and a lover of strangers, fervent in faith and a zealous orthodox, whose name was Elijah, [earnestly] entreated and urged him very much to stay in the mountain[s] until the heat had passed, because it was summer **[R 97]** and the heat was great in the plain, for this was the time after Pentecost. He was in his rank a tribune[5] who was dwelling in Jerusalem and had a position of authority in the household of the believing and orthodox Empress Eudocia,[6] who already had had become acquainted with the saint and experienced his grace, for though he had been deaf in his ears, he was esteemed worthy of healing at his hands.

(§132) This tribune told us the manner in which his ears had been healed,[7] saying, "When the blessed one was staying in the region of Ashkelon, I had business [for] which I [had to] come to the city. And when I heard that the blessed one was in the neighborhood, while I did not yet have freedom of converse[8] and familiarity with him, I earnestly desired to be esteemed worthy of a blessing from him. Yet I had been deaf in my ears for a long time. When he was told about me, he received me gladly. I was about to fall down at his feet and reverence him when he took me by my head and raised me up. He placed both of his hands on my ears, so as to prevent me from falling down before him, [and] he kissed me on my head. Immediately in that very moment my hear-

its powers was veto over the Senate's legislation, in order to provide a check against the patrician class. After Constantine, this position became restricted to the maintenance of roads, buildings, and monuments in the city of Constantinople.

[6] Literally, "was taskmaster and steward of the believing and orthodox Empress Eudocia." See Horn, "Empress Eudocia and the Monk Peter the Iberian."

[7] The following episode happened at a previous point in time. Thus Elijah had been aware of and in contact with Peter and his friends for a while. That he invited Peter to spend the summer months in a mountain resort ought to be read as an attempt on Elijah's part to demonstrate his gratitude to Peter.

[8] The Syriac renders the Greek παρρησία (Raabe, 93 n. 1).

ܘܦܠܪܘܦܘܪܝܐ ܗܘܬ ܠܗ ܒܛܘܒܢܐ܆ ܐܝܟ ܕܟܬܝܒ ܡܢ ܥ̈ܠܝܡܐ.
ܟܕ ܐܬܡܠܟܬ ܐܬܐ ܗܘܐ ܠܘܬܗ܆ ܘܡܫܐܠܬ ܐܝܬ ܗܘܐ ܠܗ
ܕܢܦܘܩ ܡܢ ܚܢܝܢܗ. ܐܝܟܢܐ ܕܢܫܬܐܠ܆ ܕܐܦ ܒܚܕܝܢܐ ܕܫܐܠܬܗ
ܕܛܘܒܢܐ ܢܬܚܣܝ܆ [R 98] ܘܒܒܘܪܟܬܐ ܕܡܢܗ ܢܫܬܘܬܦ. ܐܠܐ ܠܘܬ
ܗ̇ܝ ܕܦܪܝܫܐ ܚܒܝܒܐ ܢܒܝܐ.

(§133) ܟܕ ܥܠܒܗ ܗܟܝܠ ܠܛܘܒܢܐ ܠܡܪܬܐ ܕܝܠܗ ܕܡܬܩܪܝܐ ܒܝܬ
ܛܦܫܐ܆ ܟܠ ܣܓܝܐܐ ܬ̈ܠܡܐ ܡܢ ܡܕܝܢܬܐ ܩܕܝܫܬܐ ܐܝܟ ܕܠܡܪܘܒܐ܆
ܬܚܘܬ ܡܦܩܐ ܕܛܘܪܐ܆ ܕܢܦܫܪ ܐܐܪ ܕܝܠܗ ܦܠܓ ܘܠܟ ܡܥܒܪ܆ ܐܬܐ
ܠܟܪܡ ܒܠܗ ܡܝܛܐ. ܐܝܟܢܐ ܕܐܝܬ ܡܒܝܢܐ ܒܡܫܘܬܐ܆ ܕܗ̇ܝ ܟܕ ܗ̇ܝ
ܐܝܬܝܗ̇ ܘܦܫܩܝܢ܆ ܕܡܪܢܝܐ ܡܠܠ ܢ̈ܩܝܐ ܘܒܘܕ̈ܐ. ܘܟܕ ܐܙܠ ܗܘܐ
ܐܚ ܡܢ ܐܚ̈ܐ ܕܝܠܝ܆ ܕܢܕܒ ܗܘܐ ܕܢܩܘܕ܆ ܡ̈ܐܙ ܗܘܐ ܬܘ̈ܒ ܒܠܝܘܕ.
ܒܥܡܡܐ܆ ܐܝܟ ܕܠܒܘܝܐܐ ܕܡܫܠܡܘܬܗ ܕܫܡܐ. ܘܡܕܡ ܡܬܢܝܬ
ܠܐ. ܐܝܟܢܐ ܕܡܬܕܟܪ ܒܠܒܝ. ܐܦ ܓܒܪ ܟܕ ܒܪܢܫ ܗܘܐ ܐܚܕ ܡܢ
ܥ̈ܝܢܝܐ ܒܡܕܝܢܬܐ܆ ܘܠܘܬ ܗܠܝܢ ܡܫ̈ܒܠܬܐ ܐܝ̈ܟܢܝܬܐ ܠܝܬ ܗܘܐ
ܠܗ ܡܢܝܐܬ܆ ܟܕ ܒܠܦ ܗ̇ܘ ܡܕܝܢܬܐ܆ ܦܩܕ ܕܢܬܐܬܝܕ ܠܗ ܡܢ ܡܚܝܢܐ
ܡܠܠ ܢ̈ܩܘܫܐ ܘܢܬܒܪܘ ܠܗ. ܟܕ ܒܓܠ ܗܟܝܠ ܗ̇ܘ ܕ̈ܝܐܪ. ܬܠܬܐ
ܢ̈ܩܘܫܬܐ ܡܢ ܓ̈ܦܪܐ ܘܒܕܡܐ ܠܡܫܚܐ܆ ܡܬܪ ܡܢ ܗܠܝܢ ܬܘ̈ܒ ܠܐ
ܐܫܟܚ ܕܢܩܘܕ. ܘܐܠܐ ܐܝܟ ܕܦܣܝܕܐ ܗܘܬ ܗ̇ܝ ܡܚܝܢܐ܆ ܕܗܠܝܢ
ܬܘ̈ܒ ܬܬܠ ܠܡܫܝܚܘܬܗ ܕܫܡܐ܆ ܠܐ ܡܕܡ ܡܬܢܝܐ ܓ̈ܒܝܐ ܗܘܬ ܕܬܬܠ.
ܐܝܟܢܐ ܕܐܬܓܠܝ ܗ̇ܘ ܠܛܘܒܢܐ܆ ܕܗ̇ܘܝܘ ܗܠܝܢ ܬܘ̈ܒ ܕܫܘܝܘܗܝ ܢܓܕ
ܠܗ̇ܘ ܒܪܝܫܐ.

(§134) ܒܬܪ ܗܠܝܢ܆ ܟܕ ܙܒܢܐ ܕܒܬܪ ܡܢܛܐ ܚ̈ܒܪ܆ ܦܝܫܐ ܗ̇ܘ ܛܘܒܢܐ
ܠܘܬ ܐܚ̈ܐ ܠܦܩܕܬܐ. ܘܟܕ ܐܙܠ܆ ܛܠܒ ܐܚ̈ܪܢ ܒܦܫܪܗܘܢ ܘܐܡܪܘ.
ܕܐܝܟܢܐ ܟܕ ܒܠܗܘܢ ܗܠܝܢ ܢ̈ܩܘܫܬܐ ܗܘ̇ ܟܠ ܓܒܪ ܐܬܪܥܝܘ܆ ܠܐ
ܐܬܓܒܪ ܗ̇ܘ ܛܘܒܢܐ ܕܢܒܠ ܠܡܕܝܢܬܐ ܡܢܝܬܐ ܐܦ ܒܠܠܝܐ܆
ܘܢܚܙܐ ܠܕ̈ܘܟܬܐ [R 99] ܩ̈ܕܝܫܬܐ ܘܢܬܪܐܬ ܠܓ̈ܘܠܓܘܠܬܐ ܡܕܝܢܬܐ
ܘܠܡܕܝܢܬܐ ܡ̈ܫܚܐ ܫ̈ܢܝܐ. ܘܒܬܪ ܚܕ ܝܘܡܐ ܕܝܘܡܣܘܗ܆ ܐܦܠܐ ܐܚܕ
ܡܢ ܐܚ̈ܐ ܕܦܫܦܫ ܦܓܪ ܘܐܬܚܡ. ܘܐܡܪ ܠܗܘܢ܆ ܚܘܐ ܕܢܠܐ
ܫܢܬ ܒܗܢܐ ܠܠܝܐ. ܡܣܬܒܪ ܗܘܐ ܠܝ ܓܒܪ܆ ܕܠܐܝܟܐ ܦܠܚܘ

1 Peter is shown as foreknowing what Elijah's need for healing was.

2 This reflects the high level of authority that Peter enjoyed among his followers and supporters.

ing was opened."[1] Because of this he had henceforth such faith and full trust in the blessed one as if in one of the apostles[2] and was constantly coming to him. It was [only] with difficulty that he would abstain from converse with him, so that he would be esteemed worthy also to be found [present] at the time of the death of the blessed one **[R 98]** and to share in the blessing from it. Yet we shall return to what was set down first.

(§133) When he had thus taken the blessed one to his village called Beth Tafsha,[3] about five miles to the north of the Holy City, on the slope of the mountain, the air of which is very pleasing and well-tempered, he held him there all summer: there is a deep spring that at the same [time] is also a fish pond[4] that breeds a few small fish. When one of our brethren who knew [how] to fish went there, he was catching only two a day, as [if enough] for the comfort of the old man's weakness, and nothing more, to everyone's amazement. [It happened that] one among the friends in the city became sick and did not take pleasure in other foods.[5] When the saint learned [about it], he ordered a few little fish to be caught for him from the spring and to be sent to him. When the one who was fishing had labored thus for three days from early morning until evening, he could not catch more than these [usual] two. As if that spring had been ordered to give these two for the use of the old man, it was not willing to give any more, so that the blessed one was compelled to send to the sick one those two that were for his supply.

(§134) After these [things], when the time after summer arrived, the blessed one returned to the brethren in the plain. When he went, some were indignant in their soul and said, "How, when he abode all these days beside Jerusalem, did the blessed one not desire greatly to enter the Holy City, even if by night, and venerate the worshipful **[R 99]** places, and especially the holy Golgotha and the life-giving tomb?" The day after his departure, one of the brethren who was very simple and innocent came and said to them, "I saw a fearful vision this night. For it seemed to me that I was seeing Abba Peter the bishop, who was saying to me, 'Can

[3] See Tsafrir, Di Segni, and Green, *Tabula Imperii Romani*, 86.

[4] See L. Delekat, "Ein frühbyzantinischer Fischteich bei Jerusalem," *ZDPV* 84 (1968): 185–86.

[5] Literally, "did not have those other foods gladly."

ܐܦܝܣܩܘܦܐ ܚܙܐ ܗܘܬ ܕܐܡܪ ܠܝ: ܡܫܡܫ ܐܢܬ ܐܢܫܐ ܕܐܬܬܠ ܠܝ
ܐܚܕܐ. ܗ̇ܘ ܕܝܢ ܒܗ̇ ܒܠܚܘܕܘܗܝ، ܫܩܠܗ ܒܗ̇ܘ ܚܘܐ ܠܡܕܝܢܬܐ
ܩܕܝܫܬܐ: ܒܗ̇ ܒܠܠܝܐ ܕܒܗ̇ ܒܬܪ ܗܘܐ ܕܢܚܘܡ. ܥܠ ܡܪܟܒܬ ܠܒܝܬ
ܣܗ̈ܕܐ ܕܡܕܝܢܐ ܣܛܐܦܢܘܣ. ܗ̇ܘ ܕܡܪܟܒܬ ܣܓܕ ܒܗ̇. ܘܟܕ ܢܚܬ
ܠܡܥܪܬܐ ܣܓܕ ܠܓܘܪܢܗ. ܘܟܕ ܢܦܩ ܡܢ ܬܡܢ ܪܗܛ ܠܓܓܘܠܬܐ
ܩܕܝܫܬܐ ܘܠܩܒܪܐ ܩܕܝܫܐ. ܘܡܢ ܬܡܢ ܢܚܬ ܠܒܝܬܐ ܗ̇ܝ ܕܡܬܐܡܪܐ
ܕܦܝܠܛܘܣ. ܘܡܢ ܬܡܢ ܠܗ̇ܝ ܕܗ̇ܘ ܡܫܪܝܐ. ܘܡܢ ܒܬܪ ܗ̇ܝ ܠܒܝܬ ܚܣܕܐ.
ܘܟܕ ܐܬܩܪܒ ܐܦ ܒܪ̈ܘܟܠܬܐ ܩ̈ܕܝܫܬܐ ܕܨܗܝܘܢ: ܣܠܩ ܡܚܠ ܠܥܠܝܬܐ
ܕܬܠܡ̈ܝܕܐ. ܘܒܬܪܟܢ ܠܣܘܠܩܐ ܩܕܝܫܐ. ܘܡܢ ܬܡܢ ܠܒܝܬ ܠܥܙܪ. ܘܡܢ
ܒܬܪ ܗ̇ܘ ܐܬܐ ܒܐܘܪܚܐ ܕܡܬܝܐ ܡܢ ܬܡܢ: ܒܕܡܟܐ ܕܠܗ̇ ܠܒܝܬ
ܠܚܡ ܩܕܝܫܬܐ ܣܓܕ: ܘܟܕ ܢܦܩ ܬܡܢ ܦܢܐ ܥܠ ܩܒܪܗ̇ ܕܪܚܝܠ. ܘܟܕ
ܢܦܩ ܬܡܢ: ܘܒܡܫ̈ܒܠܐ ܘܟܕ ܢܦܠ̈ܬܐ ܕܫܪܟܐ ܕܒܐܘܪܚܐ: ܢܚܬ ܠܘܬ
ܫܠܘܚܐ. ܘܡܢ ܬܡܢ ܟܕ ܣܠܩ ܠܨܗܝܘܢ ܩܕܝܫܬܐ: ܘܫܩܠ ܪܗܛܐ
ܩܕܝܫܐ: ܘܟܠ ܕܘܟܐ ܣܓܕ ܠܡܪܢܐ: ܠܚܪܬܐ ܦܝܫܐ ܠܒܝܬ ܓܦܫܐ
ܩܢܬܐ: ܟܕ ܐܢܐ ܠܝ ܒܟܠ ܕܘܟܐ ܡܣܦܩܝܢ ܗܘܬ ܠܗ. ܘܠܡܣܡܟܐ
ܕܒܬܪܗ: ܡܣܕܪܐ ܕܫܢܬܐ ܗ̇ܘ ܚܘܝܐ: ܦܝܫܐ ܗ̣ܘ ܐܒܢܐ ܠܐܘܪܚܗ.
ܗܪܐ ܕܝܢ ܗ̣ܘܬ: ܕܬܬܦܫܩ ܗܠܝܢ ܕܐܬܒܗ ܗܘܘ. ܕܗ̇ܘ ܓܘܪܢܐ ܒܟܠ
ܕܘܟܬܐ ܩܕܝܫܬܐ ܒܠܚܘܕ [R 100] ܒܬܪ ܕܝܢ ܘܠܫܒ ܡܦܪܫ ܗܘܐ

[1] St. Stephen, whose bloody witness for his faith is recounted at Acts 7:54–60, is venerated as the first martyr, the protomartyr, of the church. His *martyrion*, the church built to commemorate his martyrdom and house his relics, is located slightly north of the Old City of Jerusalem. The remains of the Byzantine church found there go back to the building erected by Empress Eudocia.

[2] The Syriac transliterates the Greek γοῦρνα. See Payne Smith, 66, "vessel," "stone bath," or "urn." Hassan Bar-Bahlul, *Lexicon Syriacum* (Rubens Duval, ed., *Lexion Syriacum auctore Hassano bar Bahlule voces syriacas graecasque cum glossis syriacis et arabicis complectens ex multis operas scientificis biblicis et philosophicis compilatum saeculo X* [Paris: E Reipublicae typographaeo, 1888–1901], 1:475), indicates that the word may also describe a sarcophagus. For further occurrences of the word, see *Vit. Pet.* §188 (R 141 and R 142) below, where John Rufus reports that Peter the Iberian had ordered the construction

you give me a hand, brother?' When he alone took me in this vision to the Holy City, in the same night in which he was about to depart, he first entered the *martyrion* of the holy Stephen,[1] upon which he happened [to come] first. And when he went down to the cave, he venerated his sarcophagus.[2] And when he went out from there, he ran to the holy Golgotha and the holy Tomb. And from there he went down to the church that is called [that] of Pilate and from there to that of the Paralytic.[3] And after this, to Gethsemane. When he had gone around also in the holy places that [are in] its surroundings, after this he went up to the Upper Room of the disciples, and afterwards to the holy Ascension, and from there to the house of Lazarus. Next he came onto the road bringing [him] from there until he arrived at the holy Bethlehem. When he had prayed there, he turned [back] toward Rachel's Tomb.[4] And when he had prayed there and in the rest of the temples and houses of prayer on the road, he went down to [the Church of] Shiloah. From there, after he had gone up to holy Zion and had completed a holy course[5] and had worshiped the Lord in every place, finally he returned to the village of Beth Tafsha, while I, indeed, in every place was supporting him. On the very next day, [after the one on] which I had seen that vision, the Abba returned to his journey." This, however, was [done] so that those who were indignant might be instructed that the blessed one was offering in every holy place

of three connected sarcophagi for his own burial and that of two of his ascetic companions.

[3] The Church of the Paralytic is also known as the Church of the Probatike. For extensive references to ancient and modern literature, see Horn, *Asceticism and Christological Controversy*, 250, n. 111.

[4] This marks a site holy to both Jews and Christians. The location of Rachel's Tomb in Benjamin is rejected by many modern scholars, who prefer a location in Bethlehem. See Lamontte M. Luker, "Rachel's Tomb," *ABD* 5:608–9.

[5] Peter's visit to the different holy places constitutes a typical pilgrimage route. For detailed references to the individual sites, see Horn, *Asceticism and Christological Controversy*, 245–54.

ܒܪܘܚ ܡܬܕܒܪܬܐ ܠܒܪܝܬܐ. ܟܠܗܝܢ ܓܝܪ: ܕܪܘܚܢܐ ܠܟܠܡܕܡ ܕܐ̄ܢ. ܗ̇ܘ ܕܝܢ ܡܢ ܐܢܫ ܠܐ ܡܬܬܕܝܢ.

(§135) ܗܠܝܢ ܕܝܢ ܐܫܬܥܝ ܗ̇ܘ ܐܢܫܐ ܢܟܦܐ ܗ̇ܢܘܢ ܥܠ ܐܩ̈ܝܡܘܗܝ ܘܣܓܕܘ ܠܒܪܝܬܐ. ܘܡܫܒܚܝܢ ܗܘܘ ܠܪܒܘܬ ܐܢܫܘܬܗ ܠܐ ܡܬܡܠܠܢܘܬܐ ܘܠܡܫܘܚܘܬܗ: ܕܐܝܟܢܐ ܠܦܘܫܩܐ ܕܗܘ̇ܐ ܒܗܘܢ ܠܐ ܫܒܩܗ ܕܠܐ ܦܫܩܐ: ܐܦܠܐ ܒܕܝܢܐ ܕܒܪܐ. ܘܐܝܟܢܐ ܗ̇ܢܘܢ ܩ̈ܕܝܫܐ: ܟܕ ܠܗ ܠܡܫܝܚܐ ܠܒܝܫܝܢ ܘܒܗ ܚܝܝܢ: ܒܟܠ ܕܘܟ ܡܩܪܒܝܢ ܒܪܘܚ: ܘܬܫܡܫܬܐ ܡܠܝܠܬܐ ܘܣܓܕܬܐ ܒܟܠܕܘܟܐ ܡܩܪܒܝܢ ܠܗ: ܘܐܦ ܡܬܕܒܪܝܢ ܕܪܘܚܢܝܢ ܒܦܓܪ. ܘܠܗܕܐ ܟܕ ܚ̇ܙܐ ܦܘܠܘܦ ܐܒ̣ܐ. ܐܢܐ ܗ̇ܢ ܓܝܪ ܟܕ ܪܚܝܩ ܐܢܐ ܒܦܓܪ ܩܪܝܒ ܐܢܐ ܕܝܢ ܒܪܘܚ. ܡܢ ܟܕܘ ܕܢܚܬ ܐܝܟ ܡܩܒܠܐ: ܟܕ ܡܬܚܫܒܝܢ ܐܢܘܢ ܘܪܘܚܢܐ ܕܝܠܗ: ܟܡ ܚܠܝܐ ܕܡܢ ܢܦܫ ܡܫܝܚܐ. ܘܬܘܒ. ܐܦ ܓܝܪ ܒܟܘܢ ܪܚܝܩ ܐܢܐ: ܐܠܐ ܒܪܘܚܝ ܥܡܟܘܢ ܐܢܐ. ܟܕ ܚ̇ܕܐ ܘܐܚܕܪܐ ܚܕܐ ܐܢܐ: ܕܚܙܐ ܐܢܐ ܛܘܟܣܟܘܢ.

(§136) ܟܕ ܕܝܢ ܡ̇ܛܐ ܠܦܘܡܒܬܐ: ܘܐܩܒܠ ܠܐ̈ܚܐ ܗ̇ܘ ܦܠܘܢܝܐ ܕܥܠܡܐ: ܟܕ ܥܒܪ ܡܢ ܬܡܢ ܐܬܐ ܠܕܘܟܬܐ ܐܚܪܬܐ. ܘܡܢ ܬܡܢ ܠܗܘܬ ܐܚܪܬܐ: ܠܐܝܢܐ ܕܪܘܚܢܐ ܗ̇ܘ ܕܡܬܩܪܐ ܦ̇ܪܐ ܗܘܐ ܠܗ: ܠܦܘܪܥܢܐ ܕܢܦܫܬܐ ܩ̈ܕܝܫܬܐ: ܘܠܚܘܕܪܢܐ ܕܪ̈ܚܡܘܗܝ ܕܐܚܝܢ.

(§137) ܟܕ ܐܬܐ ܕܝܢ ܡܕܝܢܬܐ ܐܝܬ ܗܘܐ ܐܣܟܘܠܣܛܝܩܐ ܚܕ ܐܚܝ ܐܦܝܛܪܘܦܘܣܐ ܕܫܡܗ̇ ܕܝܘܣܩܘܪܘܣ. ܘܐܝܬ ܗܘܐ ܠܗ ܐܢܬܬܐ ܘܡܫܡܫܬܐ ܘܐܢ̈ܫܐ [R 101] ܐܦܝܛܪܘܦܘܣܘܬܐ. ܒܫܡܐ ܒܪܝܟܐ ܘܡܫܪܝܬܐ. ܘܪܬܚ ܗܘܐ ܒܡܗܝܡܢܘܬܐ ܘܒܫܘܒܚܐ ܕܠܗ ܕܡܪܝܐ. ܘܟܕ ܐܬ̈ܬܐ ܩ̈ܒܠܬܐ ܘܚܫ̈ܠܐ ܘܐܘܩ̈ܬܐ ܐܫܬܘ, ܕܢܣܒܐ ܕܗܘ̈ܝ, ܒܐܝ̈ܕܘܗܝ; ܟܕ ܢܦܩ ܕܢܐܙܠ ܒܘܪܟܬܐ ܕܒܝܢ. ܐܦܝܣܗ ܕܒܪܬܗ ܢܟܬ ܕܡܬܩܪܝܐ

[1] The scene illustrates some of the tension and difference of opinion in regard to what positions anti-Chalcedonians ought to take toward the holy places. While they had intrinsic value, at least among some anti-Chalcedonians an awareness grew that, since many of them were in the hands of Chalcedonians, a visit to those holy places was no longer an option. In the *Plerophoriae*, that growing awareness is further and more strongly detailed. For a fuller discussion, see Horn, *Asceticism and Christological Controversy*, 322–28.

[2] 1 Cor 2:15.

[3] See Rom 12:1.

[R 100] every day, undoubtedly also at every hour, worship to the Lord in [his] spirit.[1] For it is written, "The spiritual one judges everything. He himself, however, is not judged by anyone."[2]

(§135) When that brother had told these [things], those [brethren] fell down upon their faces and worshiped the Lord. They glorified his unspeakable compassion for humanity and his grace, how he did not leave the doubt that was in them without instruction, not even for a short time, and how those saints, being clad with Christ and living with him and in him, in every place are near [to him] in spirit and are offering to him everywhere rational service[3] and worship, even if they seem to be far away in body. Making this known, Paul said, "For I, being yet far away in body, but being near in spirit, have already pronounced judgment as [though] I were near, while you and my spirit are gathered together in the power of our Lord, Jesus Christ."[4] And again, "For even if I am far away in the flesh, yet I am with you in the Spirit, rejoicing and rejoicing together [with you] because I am seeing your [good] order."[5]

(§136) The blessed one, having come to the plain and greeted the brethren, departed from there. He came to another place and from there to another, to where[ver] the Spirit, who was guiding [him], was calling him for the salvation of many souls and for the aid of those dwelling [there].

(§137) In the city of Gaza was a lawyer,[6] an orthodox man whose name [was] Dionysius. He had an orthodox mother and grandmother and **[R 101]** brothers, a chosen and blessed family.[7] He was fervent in faith and in the love for the saint. When he was esteemed worthy to see many signs, mighty deeds, and healings that happened at his hands, since he was anxious to inherit a blessing from him, he persuaded him to stay in his village, which is

[4] 1 Cor 5:3–4.

[5] Col 2:5. See also Phil 2:17 for the expression of joy.

[6] Members of the legal profession constituted a significant number of Peter the Iberian's recruits. See also *Vit. Pet.* §§150–151 (R 113–14).

[7] This is one of the few instances of evidence in Rufus's works that whole families joined the anti-Chalcedonian cause. In some cases, e.g., *Pler.* 38, the conflict over Chalcedon even led to divisions between married couples.

ܡܓܕܠ ܬܘܬܐ. ܡܢ ܬܫܒܘܚܐ ܠܓܒܪܐ. ܥܠ ܒܝܬ ܡܚܠܐ ܕܩܕܝܫܐ
ܐܝܠܪܝܘܢ܆ ܚܘܝܐ ܪܒܐ ܘܢܒܝܐ ܘܐܒܐ ܕܕ̈ܝܪܝܐ. ܘܟܕ ܚܙܐ ܩ̈ܠܝܬܐ
ܕܠܢ̇ܫܡ ܐܝܟ ܕܠܢ̇ܝܫܗ ܕܛܘܒܢܐ ܒܢܦܫܬܐ ܥܦܝܦܬܐ܆ ܗܝܕܝܢ ܐܚܕ.
ܗܘܐ ܠܗ ܠܩܕܝܫܐ ܬܡܢ ܬܠܬ ܫ̈ܢܝܢ. ܘܟܕ ܟܠܗ ܢܝܚܐ ܡܦܪܥ ܠܗ.
ܘܠܦܘܪܥܢܬܐ ܕܥܒܕܗ ܐܒ̣ܘܗܝ، ܘܠܦܘܪܢܣܐ. ܡܫܬܐܠܐ ܗܘܐ ܠܝ ܡܚܝܠ
ܗ̇ܘ ܓܒܪܐ ܪ̇ܚܡ ܠܡܫܝܚܐ. ܟܕ ܬܠܬ ܡܐܐ ܕܕܪ̈ܝܟܘܢܐ ܐܦܩܬ ܥܠ
ܒܢܝܢܐ ܘܬܘܩܢܐ ܕܝܠܗ̇ ܕܥܕܬܐ܆ ܟܕ ܗ̣ܘ ܠܝܠ ܡ̈ܫܟܢܬܐ܆ ܗ̇ܘ ܕܝܢ ܡܠܝܢ
ܬܠܬ ܡܐܐ ܕܕܪ̈ܝܟܘܢܐ ܐܚܠܬ܆ ܡܢ ܐܝܟܐ ܕܠܐ ܡܬܘܡ ܦܩܚܬ ܐܘ
ܗܠܦܬ ܥܠ ܠܒܝ. ܘܒܚ̈ܡܪܐ ܗܠܝܢ ܕܐܝܬ ܗܘܐ ܚܕ̈ܪܘܗܝ ܕܝܠܗ ܡܕܒܪܬܐ܆
ܕܚܕܪ̈ܝܢ ܗܘܘ ܚܡܪܐ ܥܒܝܐ ܘܡܫܝܚܐ. ܐܦ ܓܒܪ ܚܠܝܬܐ ܘܪܥܘܬܐ
ܐܝܬܝܗ̇ ܗܘܬ ܐܪܥܐ܆ ܟܕ ܢܗܘܐ ܠܩܕܝܫܐ ܘܐܟܠܗ ܠܟܠ ܚܕ ܡܢ
ܚ̈ܡܪܐ܆ ܡܦܝܣ ܗܘܐ ܠܗ ܕܢܒܢܐ ܠܟܘܬܐ ܘܢܥܒܕܝܗ̇ ܠܓܦܬܐ.
ܘܡܢ ܗܕܝܢ܆ ܗ̇ܘ ܡܕܡ ܕܠܐ ܡܬܚܙܐ ܒܗ܆ ܐܝܟ ܡܢ ܦܠܚܘܬܗ ܕܝܠܗ̇
ܐܪܥܐ܆ ܥܒ̇ܪ ܕܢܒܢܐ ܚܡܪܐ ܒܟܪ̈ܡܐ ܦܪ̈ܝܫܬܐ ܘܫܦ̈ܝܪܐ. ܘܗܕܐ
ܠܚܘܒܬ ܦܐܪܐ ܐܡܝܢܐܝܬ ܢܗ̇ܘܐ ܗܘܘ ܗܠܝܢ ܚ̈ܡܪܐ܆ ܟܠܗ ܡܟܝܠ
ܕܢܦܫܗ ܕܛܘܒܢܐ.
(§138) ܒܗ̇ܘ ܘܢܒܝܐ ܕܝܢ܆ ܘܛܘܒܢܐ ܐܡܝܢܐ ܗ̇ܘ ܐܒܘܦܠܝܐ܆ ܗ̇ܘ
ܚܘܝܐ ܪܒܐ ܘܢܒܝܐ܆ [R 102] ܘܕܐܡܝܢܐ ܬܪܝܢܐ ܡܫܬܡܗ ܗܘܐ
ܡܢ ܟܠܢ܆ ܐܝܟ ܕ̣ܡܢ ܕܝܠܗ ܠܛܘܒܬܐ ܐܝܬ ܗܘܐ ܠܗ ܘܡܚܘܬܐ ܘܚܝܠܐ
ܕܗ̇ܘ ܢܒܝܐ ܪܒܐ܆ ܕܒܚ̈ܪܢ ܗܘܐ ܒܥܠܝܐ ܒܗܠܝܢ ܕܩ̈ܒܠܬܐ܆ ܒܡܪܬܐ

[1] Or "Magdal Thavatha," literally, "tower of the sycamore tree," for Greek πύργος συκαμίνου. See Raabe, 96 n. 1. For further references to literature on Magdal Tutha or Migdal Tutha, see also Tsafrir, Di Segni, and Green, *Tabula Imperii Romani*, 246.

[2] For the account of the life of Hilarion, see Jerome, *Vita Hilarionis* (PL 23:29–54; Hurter, 42–59; Ewald, 245–80). Hilarion was born in Migdal Tutha in 291. Having visited Egypt, he was baptized and settled in the Maiuma region as a solitary ascetic. For a discussion of the relevance of Hilarion in establishing a claim of primacy of ascetic life in the Gaza area that was intended to benefit the anti-Chalcedonian community, see Horn, "Peter the Iberian and Palestinian Anti-Chalcedonian Monasticism," 113–15.

[3] The daric is a Persian gold coin. Its name derives from Darius Hystaspes. See also Payne Smith, 97.

[4] An ancient Christian reader of this text might have been reminded of Jesus' miracle of turning water into wine at the wedding feast of Cana (John 2:1–11). In the miracle recounted here, good wine is produced in a place where

called Magdal Tutha,[1] south of Gaza, by the side of the temple of the holy Hilarion,[2] the great ascetic and prophet and father of the monks. He built houses that were fitting, so to say, for the rest of the blessed one, at abundant expense, and thus kept the saint there for three years. While he was offering him every comfort, he also was esteemed worthy of the blessing that was [going out] from him and [of] salvation. That Christ-loving man then was telling us, "When I had spent three hundred darics[3] on the building and the preparation of that place, after a few days I recovered these three hundred darics from where I never would have expected nor [from where] it would have come to my mind." Surrounding that village are vineyards that used to produce low-quality wine in meager quantities because the soil was sandy and shallow. When he took the saint and brought him to each one of the vineyards, he asked him to make a prayer and to bless the place. Thereafter [each vineyard] began to produce wine many times double [the quantity] and [wine that] stored well, something that no one from among the workers of that soil [could] remember ever happening. These vineyards continued to give such a yield of fruit throughout the lifetime of the blessed one.[4]

(§138) Also at that time the blessed Isaiah the Egyptian,[5] the great ascetic and prophet, **[R 102]** who was called a second Isaiah by everyone because he had the grace and the wisdom and the power of that great prophet, was dwelling in quiet in the sur-

previously only humble wine in low quantity could be harvested. Gaza and Ashkelon were famous throughout the Mediterranean for the wine produced and traded there. On ancient wine production in the Gaza area and references to relevant early Christian and monastic literature, see the articles by Philip Mayerson in *Monks, Martyrs, Soldiers and Saracens: Papers on the Near East in Late Antiquity (1962–1993)* (Jerusalem: Israel Exploration Society in association with New York University, 1994), particularly "The Wine and Vineyards of Gaza in the Byzantine Period," originally published in *BASOR* 257 (1985): 75–80.

[5] Ancient sources that provide information about Abba Isaiah include the *Vita Isaiae* (202 n. 4 below) and the *Sayings* ascribed to him in the *Apophthegmata Patrum*. For the latter, see Ward, *Sayings of the Desert Fathers*, 69–70. On Abba Isaiah, see Derwas Chitty, "Abba Isaiah," *JTS* 22 (1971): 47–72. On the relationship between Abba Isaiah and Peter the Iberian, see Horn, *Asceticism and Christological Controversy*, 152–70.

ܕܡܬܩܪܝܐ ܒܝܬ ܕܠܬܐ܆ ܥܠ ܐܬܪܘܬܐ ܬ̈ܠܬܐ ܡܢ ܐܒܐ ܦܝܪܘܣ. ܗܘ
ܕܕܒܪܗ ܐܘܪܚܐ ܘܡܘܬܪܐ ܕܫܘ̈ܒܚܘܗܝ، ܕܡܢ ܓܠܝܘܬܗ ܘܡܕܒܪܐ
ܠܫܡܥܘܬܗ܆ ܠܘ ܕܡܣܬܠܩܬ ܐܢܬܝܢ ܕܢܬܡܠܠ. ܥܠ ܟ̈ܠܬܐ ܓܝܪ
ܩ̈ܠܝܠܐ ܫܘܝܐ ܗܕܐ. ܐܢܫܐ ܕܡܦܩܝܢ ܗܠܝܢ ܕܥܒܠܘ ܢܦܫܐ
ܕܫ̈ܘܒܚܘܗܝ، ܘܡܫܕܪܝܢ ܡܐܡܪ̈ܐ ܕܥܠܬܗ ܘܬܫ̈ܡܫܬܐ. ܐܦ ܓܝܪ
ܟܠܗ ܗܢܐ ܥܒܕ ܦܓܪܗ ܒܢܝܘܬܐ܆ ܐܝܟܢܐ ܕܒܗ. ܐܝܟ ܒܐܦܐ ܗܘܬ
ܒܪܫܗ܆ ܢܓܡܘܢ ܠܫܪܪܐ ܡܢ ܒܡܥܢܝܐ܆ ܘܬܢܦܩܘܢ ܓܠܝܠܗ ܠܒܪܗ.
ܒܫܡܘܬܗ ܕܝܢ ܐܟܠ ܗܘܐ ܒܠܚܘܕܘܗܝ܀ ܒܪ ܫܒܪܬܐ ܘܡܪܬܐ ܥܡܠ
ܗܘܐ ܒܠܚܘܕ. ܒܬܪ ܘܠܐ ܠܗܕܐ ܒܠܠܠܬܐ ܥܡܠ ܗܘܐ܆ ܐܠܐ ܐ
ܠܡܕܪܝ ܬܠܬ ܐܡ̈ܗܬܐ ܕܡܬܝܕܥܬܐ ܦܪܫ ܗܘܐ ܦܠܚܢܐ ܕܐܝ̈ܕܘܗܝ܆ ܒܪ
ܣܓܝ ܕܝܢ ܢܦܫܗ ܒܝܬ ܥܠܡܘܬܗ܆ ܐܦܘܪܢܣܐ ܢܗܪ ܗܘܐ ܠܗܠܝܢ
ܕܐܬܝܢ ܗܘܘ ܠܘܬܗ. ܒܝܕ ܐܒܐ ܦܝܪܘܣ ܡܫܡܫܢܐ ܬܠܡܝܕܗ. ܒܬܪܐ
ܕܠܡܘܬܐ ܕܫܘܝܐ ܠܕܠܗ ܐܝܬ ܗܘܐ ܠܗ. ܘܢܝܚܘܬܐ ܘܡܟܝܟܘܬܐ
ܘܫܠܝܐ. ܐܠܗܐ ܕܝܢ ܐܝܬܘܗܝ ܗܘܐ܆ ܗܘ ܕܠܡܟܟܘܬܐ ܗܕܐ ܦܪܫܗ.
ܘܕܗܠܝܢ ܬܪ̈ܝܢ ܢܗܪ̈ܐ܆ ܐܚܪ̈ܢܐ ܕܝܢ ܕܐܒܐ ܦܝܪܘܣ ܐܦܣܩܘܦܐ
ܘܕܐܒܐ ܐܫܥܝܐ. ܡܛܠ ܗܘ ܕܗܘܐ ܕܐܬܝܢ ܡܛܠ ܘܬܘܪܐ ܓܝܪ
ܫܪ܆ ܢܗܘܐ ܥܠܝܗ ܠܗܘܢ܆ ܕܡܢ ܡܘܪܟܐ ܢܬܬܪܘܢ. ܐܦ ܡܢ ܗܘ
ܐܚܪܢܐ. ܘܗܟܢܐ ܒܪ ܡܬܒܥܝܢ ܒܬܪ̈ܥܝܬܗܘܢ [R 103] ܘܡܫܬܪܪܝܢ
ܢܦܫܗܘܢ ܠܬܠܡܝܕܘܗܝ. ܒܬܪ ܡܢ ܚܝܝܐ ܕܠܘܬ ܢܬ̈ܐ: ܫܒܚܐ ܗܘܬ ܠܗ
ܢܦܫܗ ܠܗ ܠܬܘܒܢܐ ܐܫܥܝܐ ܒܪܡܐ ܠܫܘܠܡܐ. ܒܪ ܠܗܢܐ ܦܫܘܛܐ
ܢܓܪ ܕܠܐ ܒܡܘܪܢܐ ܐܝܟ ܒܚܘܒܐ܆ ܘܕܠܝܬ ܗܘܐ ܠܗ ܕܐܝܟ ܗܕܐ
ܐܚܝܕ܆ ܗܘ ܕܐܝܬ ܗܘܐ ܠܗ ܠܛܘܒܢܐ ܦܝܪܘܣ܆ ܕܐܝܬܘܗܝ ܗܘܐ

[1] The Syriac may render the Greek τόποι (Raabe, 96 n. 7).

[2] See Tsafrir, Di Segni, and Green, *Tabula Imperii Romani*, 81.

[3] Note Rufus's use of rhetorical phrases of deprecation.

[4] Abba Isaiah's discourses have been edited in Augoustinos, Τοῦ ὁσίου πατρὸς ἡμῶν ἀββᾶ Ἡσαΐα λόγοι κθ' (2nd ed.; Volos: Schoinas, 1962). A new critical edition by Ekkehard Mühlenberg is in progress. See also Hervé de Broc, trans., *Abbé Isaïe—Recueil Ascétique* (2nd ed.; Spiritualité Orientale 7; Abbaye de Bellefontaine: Maine & Loire, 1976); and Chryssavgis and Penkett, *Isaiah of Scetis*. See also n. 139 in the introduction.

[5] A *Life of Isaiah* attributed to Zachariah Rhetor is preserved (see Brooks; see also p. lix, n. 151 in the introduction).

[6] On that rather specific form of asceticism, see Horn, *Asceticism and Christological Controversy*, 188–90 *et passim*.

roundings[1] of the village called Beth Daltha,[2] about four miles from Abba Peter. His evangelical way of life and the wealth of his gifts, which were from childhood until his old age, are not for our weakness to tell,[3] for this would require many books, just as the conviction of those who received the experience of his gifts and [as] the discourses[4] and accounts concerning him[5] bear witness. He too was torturing his body in Naziriteship[6] so much that, his belly having become like a stone, his spleen [and] his liver adhered to each other from the swelling and cleaved to [each other]. In his old age he used to eat alone, taking a little food every day. He did not take this idly, however, but [only] if first he had repaid three cubits of netting, the work of his hands.[7] Although he had shut himself up [in] his house of quiet,[8] he would respond[9] to those who came to him by means of Abba Peter,[10] the priest, his cell-mate, a man who had grace that was equal to his own, and serenity and humility and power. It was God who arranged this proximity of these two luminous ones—I am speaking, however, of Abba Peter the bishop and of Abba Isaiah—for the sake of those who were coming to be benefited by one [of them], so that it was possible for them also to gain from the proximity of the other. Thus edified and strengthened **[R 103]** in their minds, they would return to their houses. However, the blessed Isaiah [kept] himself abstinent from converse with women up to the end and kept this precept without transgression,[11] as an ascetic and [as one] who did not have the

[7] Note the emphasis laid here on the need for physical labor also for the ascetic.

[8] The Syriac may render the Greek ἡσυχαστήριον (Raabe, 97 n. 4). For the same expression, see also *Vit. Pet.* §130 (R 96).

[9] The Syriac transliterates the Greek ἀπόκρισις.

[10] Abba Peter, the disciple of Abba Isaiah, was the immediate recipient of one instruction of his teacher. See Isaiah of Gaza, *Asceticon*, discourse 25 (Chryssavgis and Penkett, 183–209). Discourse 26 (Chryssavgis and Penkett, 211–18) was taken down by Abba Peter, who likely wrote down several if not all of the other discourses of Abba Isaiah. See also W. Enßlin, "Petrus (95)," PW 19.2:1330.

[11] See also the comments in Abba Isaiah, *Asceticon*, discourses 3, 9, and 16 (Chryssavgis and Penkett, 52, 95, and 126). For a fuller discussion of this passage, see Horn, *Asceticism and Christological Controversy*, 164–65.

ܐܦܝܣܩܘܦܐ ܘܐܟܢܐ ܕܟܠܢܝ. ܘܠܟܠ ܚܢܐ ܘܩܘܡܬܐ ܦܩܕ ܗܘܐ ܡܢ
ܐܠܗܐ ܕܕܘܩܐ ܢܗܘܐ ܘܢܛܪܐ.

(§139) ܕܬܘܕܝܬ ܕܝܢ ܫܘܐ: ܒܗܝܡܢܘܬܐ ܘܒܫܘܒܚܐ: ܗܘ ܕܡܫܢܘܗܝ
ܗܘܘ ܠܘܬ ܫܕܪܐ ܗܘܢ ܡܠܟ ܩܕܝܫܐ. ܐܦ ܓܒܪ ܚܠܝܡ ܡܕܝܪ ܗܘܐ
ܗܘ ܠܡܢܝܢܐ ܦܠܓܘܣ ܠܐܟܢܐ ܐܫܥܝܐ ܗܟܢܬܐ: ܐܝܟ ܕܠܗܟܢܐ
ܘܟܢܘܫܐ ܘܡܫܠܚܐ ܒܦܓܪܐ. ܗܕܐ ܕܝܢ ܐܬܬܗܝ ܗܘܬ: ܠܫܡܥܐ ܚܕ.
ܕܡܫܪܐ ܡܢ ܓܒܪܐ ܡܢ ܡܠܟ ܕܐܟܠ ܗܘܐ: ܘܡܟܐܣܬܐ ܕܒܪܘܩܐ
ܘܕܒܪܬܐ ܕܡܕܝܢܬ ܘܡܫܒܚܐ ܘܐܬܪܝ ܢܘܩܫܐ ܕܟܘܪܐ. ܘܗܘ ܗܦܟ
ܗܘܐ ܡܕܝܪ ܬܠܬܐ ܒܩܘܢܐ. ܟܕ ܒܠܥܕ ܒܝܘܡ ܒܡ ܫܕܪܐ ܐܬܬܗܘܢ
ܗܘܘ: ܘܐܟܫܪܐ ܟܡܪܝܢ ܗܘܘ ܒܗܦܟܐ ܐܘܪܚܐ ܘܥܡܠܐ.

(§140) ܟܕ ܒܗܠܝܢ ܐܬܬܗܘܢ ܗܘܘ: ܐܬܚܙܝ ܠܐܢܘܢ ܟܠܒܐ ܗܠܠ
ܠܓܒܘܬܐ ܘܫܠܡܐ ܕܗܢܘܢ ܩܕܝܫܐ. ܘܟܕ ܠܓܠܬܐ ܐܬܝܐ ܕܢܫܝܬܐ
ܠܒܘܪܟܬܐ ܕܟܗܢܘܢ. ܫܕܪ ܠܡܩܕܫܐ ܐܘܢܒܫܐ: ܕܐܬܬܗܝ ܗܘܐ
ܚܕ ܡܢ ܡܒܘܠܪܐ ܩܕܡܝܐ ܘܫܒܝܚܐ ܕܠܗ ܒܡ ܩܬܒܬܐ: ܐܝܟ
ܗܿ ܕܢܦܫ ܐܢܘܢ ܕܡܢ ܒܠܦܪܘܣ: ܢܬܬܝܣܘܢ ܒܕܡܟܐ ܠܘܬܗ. ܟܕ
ܡܢܦܩ ܘܡܥܬܕܪܐ ܕܓܢܪܐ ܠܗܘܢ ܒܓܠ: ܘܠܟܠܗܘܢ ܗܠܝܢ ܕܒܠܒܝܢ
[R 104] ܠܗ ܐܝܟ ܕܠܗܬܪܝܗ ܡܬܬܦܝܣ. ܟܕ ܗܕܐ ܫܡܥ ܗܘ ܠܒܢܝܐ
ܦܠܓܘܣ: ܐܬܬܟܝܡ ܦܠܓ ܘܟܕ ܒܟܐ: ܒܐܟܠܐ ܕܠܐ ܥܝܟܐ ܐܬܘܗܝ,
ܗܘܐ ܘܒܫܓܬܐ. ܘܡܕܡܘܗܝ, ܕܡܕܒܚܢܐ ܡܕܝܐ ܢܦܠ ܒܠ ܐܩܘܗܝ,
ܡܕܡ ܡܢܐܒ ܟܕ ܐܡܪ. ܡܢܐܒ ܦܓܥ ܡܢ ܒܥܘܡܐ ܕܒܢܝܫܐ. ܡܢܐ
ܚܒܝܢ ܡܢ ܒܢܝܫܐ. ܡܢܐ ܚܒܝܢ ܡܢ ܒܥܘܡܐ: ܟܕ ܐܡܪܝܢ ܕܐܝܬ ܠܝ
ܗܘ ܡܕܡ ܕܠܝܬ ܠܝ: ܘܐܡܪܕ ܗܘ ܡܕܡ ܕܠܐ ܡܢܟ ܐܢܐ. ܗܕܐ
ܕܝܢ ܐܡܪ: ܡܛܠ ܕܗܠܝܢ ܕܐܘܪܒܘ ܡܛܠܬܗܘܢ ܠܟܠܒܐ ܐܡܪܘ:
ܕܬܪܝܗܘܢ ܐܬܬܗܘܢ ܢܟܝܠܐ: ܘܒܒܕܝܢ ܐܬܓܐܬܐ ܘܬܕܡܪܬܐ. ܟܕ
ܐܬܢܨܒ ܗܒܠ ܠܡܫܠܘܬܗ ܗܓܡܘܢܘܬܐ: ܘܐܝܟ ܗܿ ܕܫܪܐ ܒܡ
ܐܫܬܕܪ, ܠܐܠܗܐ: ܕܠܐ ܬܘܒ ܢܦܘܩ ܠܒܪܝܢ ܡܢ ܐܒܒܐ ܕܢܦܩ.

1 The Syriac transliterates the Greek ἀνάγκη.

2 This could also be celery or some other field green.

3 For a parallel account of the following scene, see Zachariah Rhetor, *Chron.* 6.3 (Brooks, 2:6–7; Hamilton and Brooks, 137), who also describes Isaiah's reaction.

4 See also the account on Cosmas's mission to Alexandria in Zachariah Rhetor, *Chron.* 6.2 (Brooks, 2:4–6; Hamilton and Brooks, 134–36). See also Martindale, *Prosopography of the Later Roman Empire*, 2:326–327 ("Cosmas").

same duty[1] that the blessed Peter had, being a bishop and father of everyone and [who] beyond nature and age was commanded by God to be a watchman and a benefactor.

(§139) The faith and love that these same saints were showing to each other is worth our wonder. For every day the blessed Peter used to send food to Abba Isaiah appropriate for an old man and ascetic and one who was weak in body: one loaf of bread of the finest wheat flour from Gaza, from those that he [himself] was eating, and a bunch of parsley[2] and of leeks, cleaned and washed, and two little fish. And that one [Abba Isaiah] used to send in return three round cakes, while all the time they were together with each other in the spirit, enjoying together an evangelical and heavenly banquet.

(§140) While they were [engaged] in these [things], Emperor Zeno became informed about the grace and power of those saints.[3] When he had conceived a desire to become worthy of a blessing from them, he sent Cosmas the Eunuch,[4] who was one of his chief and favorite chamberlains, with letters so as to persuade them by all means to take the trouble upon themselves [to come to him], urging [them] and promising that he would let them go [back] quickly and would consent to all those things **[R 104]** that they might advise him for his benefit. When the blessed Peter came to know this, he was very distressed.[5] Weeping and with unceasing mourning and groaning before the holy altar, he fell upon his face before the Lord, saying, "Lord, deliver me from the slander of men! What do men want from me? What are the slanderers seeking from me, when they are saying that I have something that I do not have and [that] I should do that which I cannot?" He was saying this because those who had informed the emperor about them had said that both of them were prophets and were working signs and wonders.[6] Considering thus his great weakness and that he had once promised to God not again to return to Egypt

[5] It is most likely that Peter's weariness is to be explained as him fearing that Emperor Zeno intended to force him to sign the *Henotikon*.

[6] With the signatures of such famous holy men, Zeno's attempt at reconciliation via the *Henotikon* would have gained greater publicity and acceptance among the anti-Chalcedonians.

ܡܫܟܚܐ ܐܚܝܕܐ ܘܠܐ ܡܬܚܪܝܢܐ ܕܝܢ ܕܐܬܐܡܘܗܝ، ܣܘܦܩܐ ܕܐܦܢ
ܗܘܐ. ܘܡܬܠܗܕܐ ܟܕ ܡܬܥܕܪܐ ܡܢ ܪܘܚܐ ܩܕܝܫܐ ܕܐܡܪ ܠܗ܆
ܐܬܦܢܝ ܕܢܦܫܐ ܠܘܬ ܐܬܪܐ ܠܐܬܪܘܬܐ ܕܦܘܢܝܩܐ ܕܬܬܠܡ ܢܬܠܐ܆
ܒܪܡܫܐ ܕܒܝܬ ܡܫܒܚܘܗܝ܆ ܦܘܢܝܩܐ ܕܝܢ ܐܬܐܡܘܗܝ ܗܘܘ ܗܘܘ ܗܠܝܢ
ܒܡܘܢܦܣܝܛܝܣܘܬܗ܆ ܟܕ ܒܥܘܬܐ ܘܐܠܦ ܠܬܠܡܝܕܐ ܡܫܝܚܘܬܗ
ܦܘܢܝܩܐܝܬ ܙܒܢܐ܆ ܘܐܬܦܢܝ، ܟܕ ܡܢ ܕܢܦܫܗ܆ ܕܢܥܒܕ ܠܗ ܚܒܠܐ
ܕܐܦܢ ܗܘܐ. ܗܘ ܕܐܦ ܗܘܐ܆ ܟܕ ܡܢ ܚܙܐ ܠܒܥܘܬܗ ܕܩܕܝܫܐ.
(§141) ܒܗ ܕܝܢ ܒܥܕܢܐ ܟܕ ܥܒܪ ܠܦܘܢܝܩܐ܆ ܚܙܐ ܠܡܕܝܢܬܐ ܕܡܬܩܪܝܐ
ܐܪܩܐ. ܥܠ ܬܪܥܘܗܝ ܩܒܠܘܢ ܡܢ ܡܕܡ܆ ܡܢ ܐܦܝܣܩܘܦܐ ܕܝܢ ܥܠ
ܫܘܬܦܘܬܐ. ܐܝܟ ܕܝܢ ܕܫܡܥܘ ܡܫܡܫܢܐ܆ ܪܫܝܐ ܕܗܘ ܡܕܝܢܬܐ܆
ܚܒܪܐ ܢܦܩܐ ܘܢܒܚܐ [R 105] ܘܡܬܪܐ܆ ܦܠܛ ܠܗ ܒܦܪܘܣܛܝܘܢ
ܕܝܠܗ܆ ܡܢ ܚܠܝܐ ܕܡܕܝܢܬܐ ܐܢܕܪܐܘܣ ܫܠܝܚܐ ܕܬܡܢ ܩܒܝܪ܆ ܘܩܦܠ
ܡܬܝܩܪ ܡܢ ܟܠܗ܆ ܘܐܬܪܐܝܬ ܡܢ ܒܥܘܬܗ، ܕܗܘ ܐܬܪܐ܆ ܡܟܠ
ܫܠܐ ܦܘܢܝܩܐ܆ ܘܐܦܩܘܬܐ ܕܩܘܡ ܡܢܗ. ܩܕܡ ܚܕ ܕܝܢ ܢܐܬܐ
ܠܗܠܝܢ ܕܩܕܝܫܬܐ܆ ܒܠܠܝܐ ܬܠܬ ܙܒܢܝܢ ܟܕ ܐܬܚܙܝ، ܗܘ ܫܠܝܚܐ
ܠܦܪܘܡܘܛܪܐ ܕܗܘ܆ ܕܒܥܠܬܐ ܐܡܪ ܠܗ. ܘܠܐ ܝܕܥ܆ ܡܫܡܫܢܐ ܪܫܝܐ
ܘܐܡܪ ܠܗ. ܗܐ ܡܥܕܪ ܠܝ ܐܠܗܐ ܩܘܡܐ ܙܟܝܐ܆ ܗܘ ܕܠܐ ܡܬܘܡ
ܗܟܝܠ. ܘܟܠܗ، ܗܟܝܠ ܚܕ ܟܠܗ ܣܘܟܠܐ ܘܠܓܪܦܘܣܐ ܘܢܘܗܪܐ ܠܝ
ܒܠܒܝ ܩܘܡܐ ܘܡܫܬܪܝܢܐ ܡܢ ܟܠܗܘܢ ܢܫܘܢܐ. ܟܕ ܐܬܦܟܠܝ
ܗܟܝܠ ܡܢܗ ܫܡܥܬܗ܆ ܘܟܠܗ ܢܝܫܐ ܐܫܬܘܝ ܫܢ ܡܢܗ. ܗܘ

[1] It is not quite obvious why Peter would have made that promise. What is clear is that it was not a promise not to flee.

[2] Peter's motivation to leave for Phoenicia is not a strategic missionary expansion plan but his felt need to have to flee imperial powers.

[3] In addition to having established networks of support among influential members of society throughout Egypt and also having managed to connect with some in Palestine, Peter the Iberian could still rely on a network of highly placed friends in the Eastern capital.

[4] Also known as Arca Caesarea and Caesarea Libani. See Ernest Honigmann, "Libanos," PW 13.1:5–6 (map of northern Lebanon). For further information on the bishopric of Arca, see also Honigmann, *Évêques et Évêchés Monophysites*, 41–42.

[5] Here one notices that also in Phoenicia Peter gained easy access to people of power and influence.

[6] The Syriac transliterates the Greek προάστειον.

[7] On Andrew, see Jean-Marc Prieur, *Acta Andreae* (CCSA 5–6; Turnhout: Brepols, 1989); V. Calzolari, "La Versione Armena del *Martirio di Andrea*

from where he had left,[1] he judged that such a journey was [both] difficult and at the same time impossible. Because of this, guided by the Holy Spirit dwelling in him, he thought to depart rather to the regions of Phoenicia to hide himself there[2] until through his friends, who were many in Constantinople,[3] he had written a petition and informed the emperor of his manifold infirmity and was enabled by the hand of our Lord to persuade him to spare him such a toil. This also came to pass, since our Lord was supportive of the saint's petition.

(§141) As he was departing for Phoenicia, he came to a town called Arca,[4] about twelve miles away from the sea and about fifteen from Tripoli. A man whose name was Maximus,[5] a magistrate of this town, a chaste, quiet, **[R 105]** and rich man, received us on his suburban estate[6] on account of a revelation of the holy apostle Andrew,[7] who is laid there and is greatly honored by everyone, and especially by the inhabitants of that region because of the many mighty deeds and the healings that happen through him.[8] Before we reached those places, this apostle appeared at night three times to the *paramonarius*[9] of this place [and] said to him, "Go to Maximus the magistrate and say to him, 'Behold, God is sending to you a great support,[10] one whom you have never expected. Receive him, then, with all love and assurance,[11] and he will be for you at all time[s] a support and a protector against

e il suo rapporto con la tradizione manoscritta dell'originale Greco," *Mus* 111 (1998): 139–56.

[8] The claim that Andrew was especially highly venerated in that region seems to depend on the present witness. The particular function of the apostle Andrew in this context at least to some extent might have resulted from a relatively strong emphasis that Georgian Christians placed on him, believing that Andrew was the one who preached Christianity to them and converted them to the faith. Peter the Iberian, as a native Georgian, could also have held and expressed a special veneration for Andrew. For attempts to locate Andrew also archaeologically in Georgia, see, e.g., Vakhtang Licheli, "St Andrew in Samtskhe—Archaeological Proof?" in *Ancient Christianity in the Caucasus* (ed. Tamila Mgaloblishvili; Iberica Caucasica 1; Surrey, U.K.: Curzon, 1998), 25–37.

[9] I.e., the sacristan of the church. The Syriac transliterates the Latin *paramonarius* and the Greek παραμονάριος.

[10] This could also be translated by "manager," "superintendent," "patron," or "protector."

[11] MS B substitutes "and faith."

ܕܡܬܐܡܪ ܐܦܝܣܩܘܦܐ ܕܗ̇ܝ ܡܕܝܢܬܐ: ܕܐܬܬܘܗܝ ܗܘܐ ܐܝܟ ܕܘܠܐ
ܘܟܘܡܪܐ ܘܛܢܦܐ ܒܟܠ. ܟܕ ܠܐ ܡܫܝܪ ܠܥܒܕܘܬܗ ܕܡܪܝܐ:
ܕܗܘܝܐ ܗܘܬ ܠܡܫܡܫܘܬܗ ܘܠܫܘܕܪܗ: ܟܕ ܐܝܬ ܠܗ ܕܢܬܠܝܟ ܠܗ
ܘܐܒܘܗܝ̈ ܐܚܠܦܝ̈ܐ. ܥܠܝܗ ܠܛܘܒܢܐ ܟܕ ܐܡܪ. ܐܘ ܐܫܬܘܬܦ ܚܒܝ
ܐܘ ܚܢܢܐ. ܠܐ ܓܝܪ ܡܟܫܪܐ ܡܕܝܢܬܐ ܕܬ̈ܪܝܢ ܐܦܝܣܩܘ̈ܦܐ ܢܗܘܐ
ܐܝܬ ܠܗ̇. ܟܕ ܗܠܝܢ ܥܒܕ ܗ̱ܘ ܛܘܒܢܐ. ܡܚܕܐ ܥܪܩ ܘܢܦܩ ܡܢ ܗ̇ܝ
ܡܕܝܢܬܐ. ܟܕ ܐܦܠܐ ܗ̣ܘ ܗܘ̇ ܢܗܘܐ ܓܒܐ ܕܒܥܠܬ: ܒܗ̇ ܕܒܥܠܬܐ
ܕܡܫܡܫܐ ܡܦܠܓܢܐ ܕܠܝ ܓܒܐ. ܘܫܦܝܪ ܐܫܬܘܫ ܡܛܠܠܘܢ
ܕܪܘܦܝܐ ܕܗܘܐ. ܟܕ ܠܡܘܟܟܗ ܡܠܬܐ ܕܒ. ܟܕ ܐܡܪܝܢ ܠܝ ܓܒܪ.
ܡܚܕܐ ܕܘܒ ܠܐܪܬܘܕܘܟܣܐ [R 106] ܡܕܝܢܬܐ ܕܟܠ ܗܦܟ ܢܚܬ:
ܘܟܕ ܐܦܩܗ ܠܐܦܝܣܩܘܦܐ ܕܠܗ̇ ܟܪܣܐ ܕܢܘܣܝܗ: ܕܗܓܡܘܢܘܣ
ܐܟܣܢܝܬܐ ܘܫܘܟܢܐ ܐܝܬ ܗܘܐ ܠܗ: ܗܬܪ ܡܢ ܗܠܝܢ ܐܚܪ̈ܢܐ
ܕܐܫܕܝܢ ܒ̈ܙܬܐ. ܚܕܐ ܠܝ ܕܒܗܘܢܐ ܕܬܠܝܬܐ ܕܗܘܝܐ ܠܗܘܢ
ܢܟܪ̈ ܗܘܬܐ. ܐܦ ܓܝܪ ܠܝܬ ܗܘܐ ܕܒܗܬܐ ܐܚܪܬܐ ܕܠܝܬܐ
ܒܡܕܝܢܬܐ: ܡܛܠ ܕܒܥܘܬܐ ܐܬܬܘܗܝ. ܘܒܥܘܬܐ ܒܗܘܝܢܐ. ܘܒܬܪ
ܟܕ ܒܥܬ ܐܫܬܡܗ ܐܝܟ ܕܠܡܐܡܪ ܕܕܐܝܟ ܗܢܐ ܒܥܘܬܐ ܗܘܘ.
ܐܝܟ ܗ̇ܘ ܕܒܠܒܠܝܢ ܡܕܝܢܝܢ ܗܘܘ: ܘܐܝܬ ܗܘܐ ܠܝ ܟܠܗ ܢܝܫܐ.
ܗܒܝܐ ܫܒܠܝܢ ܚܕ ܬܚܬ ܠܗܘܢܐ ܕܒܥܠ ܕܒܝܬܐ ܡܕܝܢܐ ܘܕܦܝܣܐ

[1] The Syriac may render the Greek παμμίαρος (Raabe, 99 n. 4).

[2] See John 8:44.

[3] Early Christian literature explicitly requesting that there be only one bishop in any given town or city (monepiscopacy) begins with Ignatius of Antioch, *Phld.* 4.1 (Camelot, 142–44; Richardson, *Early Christian Fathers*, 108–9); see also his *Magn.* 6.1 (Camelot, 98; Richardson, *Early Christian Fathers*, 95). For helpful discussions of the development of this aspect of the episcopate, see Ernst Dassmann, "Zur Entstehung des Monepiskopats," *JAC* 17 (1974): 74–90; idem, "Entstehung und theologische Begründung der kirchlichen Ämter in der Alten Kirche," *IKZ* 22 (1993): 350–62; Reinhard M. Hübner, "Die Anfänge von Diakonat, Presbyterat und Episkopat in der frühen Kirche," in *Das Priestertum in der Einen Kirche: Diakonat, Presbyterat und Episkopat* (ed. Albert Rauch and Paul Imhof; Aschaffenburg: Kaffke-Verlag, 1987), 45–89; Hermann Wolfgang Beyer and Heinrich Karpp, "Bischof," *RAC* 2:394–407, esp. 404–6; Hermann J. Pottmeyer, "Bischof. II Historisch-Theologisch," *LTK* 2:482–86; E. Kirsten, "Chorbischof," *RAC* 2:1105–14; and Johannes Neumann, "Bischof I," *TRE* 6:653–82.

[4] Peter's behavior might indicate quite a range of possible motivations: (1) he may have tried to avoid causing the establishment of an independent

all tribulations.' " When thus we had been lovingly received by him and were esteemed worthy of every comfort, he who is called bishop of that town, who was a wretched, daring, and totally defiled[1] man, not enduring the proximity of the saint, which was to his reproof and reproach because he had the devil [as] the one advising him and [as] his father,[2] sent to the blessed one, saying, "Either be in communion with us or depart, for a town cannot have two bishops."[3] When the blessed one heard these [things], he immediately departed and left this town,[4] not willing to stay for even that day in the place of Maximus, our good host. Although he was very distressed about this persecution that had taken place, he increased his love [all the] more. For when he had reached us, he immediately ran to Orthosias,[5] **[R 106]** a town on the seashore. He asked its bishop, a man [who was] his friend,[6] who had a hospitable character[7] and more love than these others who were occupying the churches, to arrange for us to pass the winter[8] in a salt depot[9] near there, for there was no other suitable place in the town, because it was small and [had only] a few people. Although we were dwelling in such a prison, so to speak, we were dwelling as if in a palace, having every comfort. In this way we celebrated there the

church; (2) it might simply have been a reaction that attempted to avoid conflict and controversy; (3) it might have grown out of a dislike of having to deal with Chalcedonian official personnel, unless they had become personal friends of his.

[5] This town was located south of the mouth of the Eleutheros River, about twelve miles away from Tripoli. For further comments on the bishopric of Orthosias, see Honigmann, *Évêques et Évêchés Monophysites*, 43.

[6] The local bishop of Orthosias was a Chalcedonian. Nevertheless, despite their religious disagreements, Peter the Iberian was able and willing to entertain a friendly converse, even a friendship with him.

[7] The Syriac transliterates the Greek κατάστασις.

[8] The Syriac may render the Greek διαχειμάζειν (Raabe, 100 n. 3).

[9] The Syriac transliterates the Greek ὥριον or ὡρεῖον ("depot," "magazine") (Raabe, 100 n. 2). See also Anthony Rich, *Dictionnaire des Antiquités Romaines et Grecques* (Paris: Firmin-Didot, 1873; repr., Paris: Payot & Rivages, 1995), 322. Rev. Dr. Abdo Badwi (Director of the School of Sacred Art, Holy Spirit University, Kaslik, Lebanon) kindly discussed this question of the physical circumstances that allow for this identification between the Greek and Syriac terms.

ܡܕܝܢܬܐ. ܒܕܡܘܬܐ ܠܦܝܠܝܣܛܘܦܘܠ ܡܕܝܢܬܐ. ܟܕ ܐܦܝܣܩܘܦܐ ܕܗܘ̇ܝ
ܡܕܝܢܬܐ. ܫܦܝܪܘܬ ܟܝܢܐ ܗܘܠܐܬܐ ܗ̇ܘ. ܘܐܡܝܪܐ ܘܫܘܝܕܬܐ
ܠܛܘܒܢܐ ܦܛܪܘܣ. ܟܕ ܠܐ ܐܫܟܚ ܕܢܦܫܘܩܝܗܝ. ܕܠܘܬ ܒܢܝܢܐ
ܕܒܦܪ̈ܘܣܦܐ ܢܐܬܐ. ܡܛܠ ܕܡܫܘܬܦܐ ܐܝܬܘܗܝ ܗܘܐ ܕܗܠܝܢ
ܐܩܣܢܘܣܦܐ ܐܣܝܐ. ܐܠܗܐ ܕܝܢ ܐܝܬܘܗܝ ܗܘܐ. ܗ̇ܘ ܕܠܐܪܚܐ
ܘܠܐܪܬܘܣܩܣܐܕ݂ ܠܡܕܝܢܬܐ ܕܠܗ ܦ̇ܐܪܐ ܘܡܥܒܕܢ. ܡܛܠ ܦܘܪܢܣܐ
ܕܗ̇ܘܢ ܕܒܬܪܝܢ ܗܘܘ ܕܐܦ ܒܗܠܝܢ ܕܒ̈ܥܬܐ ܠܦܩܘܗ̇. ܐܦ ܟܕ
ܡܢ ܐܘܪܚܐ ܡܕܝܢܬܐ ܘܡܢ ܐܪܬܘܣܩܣܐܕ݂: ܟܕ ܥܒܕܐ ܥܒܕܬܐ ܦܪܒ
ܠܡܪܝܐ. ܒܕܡܘܬܐ ܕܐܦ ܠܗ ܠܡܘܪܝܐ ܘܠܐܚܘܗܝ. ܐܦܢ ܠܡܫܡܫܘܬܐ
ܬܪ̈ܝܢ ܫܡܫܐ ܘܠܕܘܟܪܢܐ ܡܠܬܪܐ.

(§142) ܗ̣ܘܬ݂ ܕܝܢ ܐܦ ܡܬܚܠܦܢܘܬܐ ܕܙܒ̈ܢܐ ܕܗ̇ܕܐ̈ ܡܕܝܢܬܐ ܕܐܬܚܙܝ
ܫܠܡܝܢ ܗܘܘ. ܕܠܘܩܒܠ ܘܕܦܘܩܕܢܐ ܘܕܪܘܚܐ ܘܕܟܢ̈ܝ ܠܐܬܪܘܗܝ. ܗܘ̣ܬ݂
ܕܝܢ ܡܕܒܪܐ. ܚܕܐ ܐܝܬ ܐܝܬܐ ܗܘܐ ܕܡܪܝܒܐ ܗܘܬ [R 107] ܢܦܩ ܕܝܢ ܗ̇ܘ
ܗܘܪܢܐ. ܕܚܒܝܒܗ ܩܘܣܛܢܛܝܢ ܗܘܐ ܟܠܗܘܢ. ܐܝܬܝܗ̇ ܕܝܢ ܗ̇ܝ
ܡܕܝܢܬܐ ܕܒܗ ܣܝܡܐ. ܘܕܟܘܟܐ ܩܕܝܫܐ ܐܦܘܟܐ. ܕܢܝܬܝܢ ܡܢ ܠܟܠ
ܡܢ ܛܘܪܐ ܕܠܒܢ. ܗ̇ܘ ܡܟܝܠ ܚܢܢܐ ܕܠܗ ܕܕܘܟܬܐ: ܟܕ ܐܝܟ ܢܒܝܐ
ܐܝܬܘܗܝ ܘܗܦܟ ܦܓܪܗ: ܘܢܟܦܐ ܘܕܠܐ ܐܢܬܬܐ: ܢܒܝܐ ܟܠܠܐ.
ܕܐܬܟܠܝ ܠܗ ܗܕܪܐ ܡܕܝܢܬܐ ܘܐܡܪܝܢ ܠܗ: ܢܕܥ ܐܢܬ ܡܢܘ ܐܝܬܝܟ.
ܟܕ ܕܝܢ ܐܡܪ ܗ̇ܘ ܕܠܐ ܝܕܥ: ܐܡܪܝܢ ܠܗ. ܚܢ ܐܝܬܝܢ ܥܒ̈ܕܝܟ.
ܗ̇ܢܘܢ ܕܠܘܬܟ ܫܕܪܝܢ ܚܢ ܘܡܚܒܝܢ ܡܕܝܢܬܐ ܚܢ: ܘܢܛܪܝܢ ܚܢ ܠܟ
ܘܠܡܩܛܠܟ. ܗ̇ܘ ܕܝܢ ܐܡܪ. ܘܡܢܘ ܐܝܬܘܗܝ. ܗ̇ܘ ܕܝܢ ܗܘܕܐ
ܐܡܪܘ ܠܗ. ܠܦܘܩܐ ܦܘܩܐ ܘܪܘܡܢܐ: ܘܡܠܝܢ ܐܢܫܐ ܕܠܡ. ܐܬܒܝܬܘ

[1] Peter and his friends stayed in the city for about half a year at the least.

[2] The Syriac may render the Greek καλοθέλεια (Raabe, 100 n. 4), εὐδοκία (suggested by Sebastian Brock), or εὔνοια, (suggested by John T. Fitzgerald, given the reference to friendship in this context).

[3] The choice of the word "captives," not to be taken literally here, connects this passage with previous sections that emphasized the word field "to catch." The Syriac may render the Greek expression αἰχμαλωσίαν αἰχμαλωτεύσας (Raabe, 100 n. 5).

[4] The Syriac transliterates the Greek ὡρειάριος (Raabe, 100 n. 6).

[5] See Horn, "Transgressing Claims to Sacred Space."

[6] The most likely candidate for identification is Phocas, the gardener from Sinope, who was denounced as a Christian, offered hospitality to the soldiers who had come to kill him, dug his own grave, and was then decapitated.

day[s] of holy Epiphany and of holy Pascha, until holy Pentecost,[1] while the bishop of this city showed great goodwill[2] and honor and reverence to the blessed Peter. Nevertheless, he could not persuade him to come to converse in person [with him], because he was in communion with these other bishops. Yet it was God who was calling his saint to Arca and to Orthosias and [who] was glorifying [him] on account of the salvation of those who were to be saved in these places also. For from the town of Arca and from Orthosias he led away captives,[3] offering [them] to the Lord until he had turned even the keeper of the salt depot[4] and his brother to the orthodox faith and to a virtuous way of life.

(§142) Yet there also happened a revelation of the bones of holy martyrs that were laid there,[5] of Lucas, Phocas,[6] Romanus,[7] and their companions. It happened this way. There was a garden near **[R 107]** the [salt] depot from which we obtained our daily supply. Now, this town is well-irrigated and is flooded by much water, which comes down from above, from Mount Lebanon.[8] Now the gardener of the place, since he was a quiet man and very simple and pure and unmarried, saw at night that the holy martyrs revealed themselves to him and were saying to him, "Do you know who we are?" But when he said that he did not know, they were saying to him, "We are your neighbors, those who are dwelling with you and are lodging with you. We are guarding you and your garden." He again said, "And who are you?" Those martyrs

His cult is attested by Asterius of Amaseia, *Homily* 9 (PG 40:299–314; Datema, 114–27). His feastday is 22 September or 22 July. Phocas, the martyred bishop of Sinope, is probably identical with the gardener. See *BHG* 2:206–7, entries 1535y-1540b. See also Charles van de Vorst and Paulus Peeters, "Saint Phocas," *AnBoll* 30 (1911): 252–95; Alexander Kazhdan and Nancy Patterson Ševčenko, "Phokas," *ODB* 3:1666–67. For further discussion and references, see Horn, *Asceticism and Christological Controversy*, 266, 269.

7 Romanus might be identifiable with the martyr Romanus of Caesarea, who suffered in Antioch. See Eusebius of Caesarea, *Mart. Pal.* 2 (Cureton, ܛ-ܝ [Syriac], 6–8 [English]; see also the Greek witness, Schwartz, 909). For further references, see Horn, *Asceticism and Christological Controversy*, 266.

8 Mount Lebanon is part of the mountain chain that runs parallel to the Mediterranean on the west of the Orontes River. The name "Lebanon" is derived from *lbn*, "white," possibly referring to the snow covering its peak year-round.

ܒܬܪ ܣܓܝܐܬܐ. ܘܙܕܩ ܠܝ ܕܐܚܙܐ ܢܛܓܠܐ. ܘܟܕ ܬܫܟܚ
ܠܝ. ܟܕ ܦܢܐ ܐܢܬ ܠܐܒܐ ܦܛܪܘܣ ܐܦܝܣܩܘܦܐ: ܗܘ ܕܗܪܟܐ
ܐܬܘܗܝ ܒܐܟܣܢܝܘܬܐ. ܠܗ ܐܫܠܡ ܠܝ.

(§143) ܟܕ ܐܬܬܥܝܪ ܡܟܝܠ. ܡܚܕܐ ܪܗܛ ܠܘܬ ܐܢܫܐ ܕܝܠܢ ܦܘܠܘܣ
ܪܟܝܢܬܐ. ܟܕ ܡܫܘܕܥ ܠܗ ܚܙܘܐ. ܗܘ ܕܝܢ ܟܕ ܕܒܪܗ. ܐܝܬܝܗ ܠܘܬ
ܛܘܒܢܐ ܦܛܪܘܣ. ܗܘ ܕܒܥܪܪܐ ܪܫܝܡ ܗܘ̈ܕܪܐ. ܘܟܕ ܐܫܬܥܝ ܠܗ
ܡܠܝܢ ܕܚܙܘܐ. ܐܡܪ ܠܘܬܗ ܗܘ ܛܘܒܢܐ. ܘܠܐ ܐܦܝܣ ܐܢܘܢ ܕܢܬܘܒ
ܢܬܒܝܘܢ ܠܝ. ܘܢܣܒܘܢ ܠܝ ܕܘܟܬܐ ܕܒܗ ܫܒܩܝܢ ܓܪ̈ܡܝܗܘܢ.
ܘܥܒܕ ܡܚܕܐ.

(§144) ܒܬܪ ܡܢ ܝܘ̈ܡܝܢ ܡܟܝܠ ܟܕ ܦܠܚ ܗܘܐ ܒܓܢܬܐ. ܢܟܪܐ ܗܘܐ
ܒܠܐܒܬ. ܟܕ ܠܟܠ ܡܢ ܫܒܝܚܐ ܘܚܘ̈ܒܐ ܦܪܝܫ. ܕܟܠܗ ܘܡܘܬܐ ܠܘܬܗ.
ܘܟܕ ܒܬܪܝܗܐ ܗܘܐ. ܢܦܠ ܥܠ ܐܦ̈ܘܗܝ ܘܫܟܒ. ܟܕ ܢܦܫ ܕܡܢܘ
ܐܬܝܘܗܝ ܗܢܘܢ ܕܒܝܬܗ [R 108] ܚܘܐ ܢܝܚܐ ܗܘܐ. ܘܐܡܪܝܢ ܠܗ.
ܡܛܠ ܕܝܢ ܕܗܕܐ ܚܙܐ ܐܢܬ ܕܬܐܠܦ: ܕܐܝܟܢܐ ܫܒܩܝܢ ܓܪ̈ܡܐ
ܕܝܠܝ. ܗܐ ܒܗܕܐ ܕܘܟܬܐ ܫܟܝܚܝܢ. ܐܠܐ ܗܒ ܠܐܒܐ ܦܛܪܘܣ
ܐܦܝܣܩܘܦܐ ܘܐܬܝܗ، ܠܗܪܟܐ. ܘܟܕ ܢܥܒܕ ܨܠܘܬܐ. ܡܚܕܐ ܟܕ
ܢܦܩ ܐܢܬ ܘܡܫܟܚ ܐܢܬ ܠܝ ܐܫܠܡ ܠܝ ܠܗ. ܟܕ ܗܠܝܢ ܢܩܦ ܗܘ
ܛܘܒܢܐ. ܥܒܪ ܕܢܒܥܐ. ܘܟܢܫܬܐ ܢܦܠܐ ܘܢܐܡܪܝ. ܡܢܗ ܐܢܬܝ.
ܐܢܐ ܗܘ ܕܠܐ ܥܘܐ ܘܡܕܡܐ ܕܫܠܝܐ. ܕܚܘܒܐ ܕܐܝܟ ܗܢܐ
ܢܣܘܢ ܠܗܝ، ܩܪ̈ܝܒܐ. ܐܘ ܐܝܟܢܐ ܡܫܟܚ ܐܢܐ ܕܐܦܠܘܬ ܐܢܘܢ
ܘܐܡܪܝܢ ܐܢܘܢ ܟܡܐ. ܟܕ ܐܢܬ ܐܟܚܕܐ ܘܬܘܒܬܐ. ܘܠܝܬ ܠܝ ܘܠܐ
ܫܕܐ ܕܚܘܒܐ. ܕܟܕ ܐܦܝܣ ܐܢܘܢ ܘܐܝܟܢ ܕܢܓܡܘܢ ܐܡܪ ܐܢܘܢ.
ܟܕ ܦܠܝܪܘܦܘܪܝܐ ܡܟܝܠ ܗܘܐ ܡܢ ܡܪܢ. ܐܡܪ ܠܚܒܝܒܐ. ܠܐ
ܬܕܚܠ. ܡܕܡ ܕܐܡܪ ܐܢܐ ܠܟ ܥܒܕ. ܒܠܚܘܕ ܒܬܪ ܚܕܐ. ܐܢܐ ܡܛܠ
ܐܡܪܐ ܕܡܕܝܐ. ܐܢܐ ܟܕ ܒܪܢܫܐ ܐܢܬ، ܐܟܚܕܐ ܐܝܟ ܕܒܢܝܐ
ܐܢܬ: ܘܡܬܟܪܝܢ ܐܢܐ ܡܢ ܕܘܟܬܐ ܠܕܘܟܬܐ. ܠܐ ܡܫܟܚ ܐܢܐ

[1] The Syriac renders the Greek ξενιτεία. The word also carries the notion of "pilgrimage."

[2] See also *Vit. Pet.* §147 (R 110) ("our agent").

[3] The Syriac may render the Greek τὰ τοῦ ὁράματος (Raabe, 101 n. 2).

said to him, "Lucas, Phocas, and Romanus; and these [are] our brethren"—for a great company had appeared—"and we ought to be uncovered immediately. When you find us, call Abba Peter the bishop, who is here on travels[1] [and] hand us over to him."

(§143) Thus when he woke up, he immediately ran to our brother Paul the steward,[2] making the vision known to him. [Paul], however, led him to the blessed Peter, who in truth [is] a lover of the martyrs. When he had told him these[3] [words] of the vision, the blessed one said to him. "Go, ask them to appear to you again and to show you the place where their bones are laid." And so he did.

(§144) One day, then, when he was working in the garden, he saw them clearly, flying above the hedges and thorns, [and they] entered and stood near him. Since he was in amazement, he fell on his face and reverenced [them], knowing that they were those whom **[R 108]** he had seen in the vision. They said to him, "Since you are seeking to learn where our bones are laid, behold, they are laid in this place. Take Abba Peter the bishop and bring him here. When he makes the prayer and when you dig and find us, hand us over to him." When the blessed one learned these [things], he began to weep and to cry out with groaning and to say, "Who am I, I the unworthy and the first of sinners that the saints should show such love to me? Or how can I receive them and carry them around with me, when I am a stranger and a foreigner and do not have a single place in which I could lay them and honor them as they deserve?"[4] When he then was fully assured[5] by our Lord, he said to the gardener, "Do not be afraid! Do what I tell you, for I am doing all these [things] for the honor of the saints. Since I am a stranger, as you see, and am moving about from place to place, I

[4] For a discussion of the conflict between the need to worship relics of saints in a fixed space and the anti-Chalcedonian experience of constantly having to be on the move either on flight or on self-imposed wandering, see Horn, "Transgressing Claims to Sacred Space."

[5] The underlying verb is derived directly from the word πληροφορία.

ܕܐܛܥܢ ܐܢܘܢ ܘܐܚܕܪ ܐܢܘܢ ܠܩܕܝܫܐ. ܐܠܐ ܙܠ ܐܘܕܥ ܗܠܝܢ
ܠܐܦܝܣܩܘܦܐ ܕܡܕܝܢܬܐ. ܢܦܩܐ ܕܝܢ ܐܝܬܘܗܝ. ܘܗܘ ܝܕܥ ܕܐܝܟܢܐ
ܐܝܟ ܕܫܦܝܪ ܢܥܒܕ ܐܢܘܢ. ܘܫܕܪܗܘܢ ܠܒܝܬܗ.

(§145) ܗ̇ܝ ܕܐܦ ܗ̇ܕܐ. ܟܕ ܫܡܥ ܒܪܝ ܐܦܝܣܩܘܦܐ: ܘܦܩܕ
ܒܚܕܘܬܐ ܗ̇ܕܐ. ܫܒܩ ܠܗܠܝܢ ܕܢܦܩܘܢ ܡܢ ܩܠܝܬܗܘܢ. ܘܐܬܐ ܠܗ̇،
ܕܥܕܬܐ. ܘܟܕ ܗ̇ܘ ܒܒܝܬܐ ܫܢܝ ܠܗܘܢ. ܣܓܕܘ ܐܝܟ ܡܥܠܬܐ
ܕܒܪܐ. ܘܐܫܟܚܘ ܡܠܬܐ ܕܐܟܪܐ. ܘܟܕ ܦܬܚܘܗ̇. ܒܗ̇ ܫܘܠܡܐ
ܕܓܪ̈ܡܐ ܕܩܕܝܫܐ. ܘܫܩܠܘ ܒܗ̇. ܘܗܟܢܐ ܟܕ ܐܫܬܘ ܐܢܘܢ
ܒܫܡܫܬܐ. ܐܘܒܠܘ ܘܣܡܘ ܐܢܘܢ ܒܒܝܬ [R 109] ܕܝܩܘܢܝܩܘܢ
ܕܥܕܬܐ. ܢܦܩ ܕܝܢ ܛܒܐ ܕܒܛܠܬܗܘܢ ܒܟܠܗ̇ ܗ̇ܝ ܐܬܪܐ. ܘܡܢ ܟܠܗ̇
ܕܢܦܩ ܒܐܬܪܐ ܫܓܝܐܐ ܕܦܪܝܫܐ ܩܕܝܫܐ: ܟܕ ܐܬܟܢܫܘ ܐܟܚܕܐ
ܥܡ̈ܡܐ ܣ̈ܓܝܐܐ ܡܢ ܡܕ̈ܝܢܬܐ ܘܩܘܪ̈ܝܐ ܕܚܕܪܝܗ̇: ܒܬܠܬܐ ܒܐܕܪ
ܢܛܝܪܐ ܗܘܐ ܥܐܕܗܘܢ. ܒܒܘܣܡܐ ܣܓܝܐܐ. ܐܬܬܫܒܚܘ ܕܝܢ ܒܝܕ
ܐܣ̈ܘܬܗܘܢ ܒܚܝܠܐ ܗ̇ܕܐ ܐܬܪ ܐܢܫܐ. ܕܩܕܝܫܐ ܫܪܝܢ ܘܟܐܒܐ.
ܗܠܝܢ ܕܐܬܝܢ ܡܫܬܒܪܝܢ ܘܡܬܬܣܝܢ. ܟܕ ܗܘܘ ܫܬܕܪܐ ܩܕܝܫܐ.
ܗܕܐ ܟܕ ܓܠܝܐ ܫܒܩܘ. ܕܒܗ̇ ܕܥܕܬܐ ܢܬܬܫܒܚܘܢ ܐܟܚܕܐ
ܥܡ ܟܬܪ ܫܘܕܥܬܗܘܢ. ܐܫܬܘܝ ܕܝܢ ܘܗܢܝ ܒܝܕ̈ܝܐ: ܕܟܕ ܩܕܝܫܐ
ܐܟܘܢ ܢܬܒܪܟ. ܘܡܢ ܡܟܐ ܩܕܝܫܐ ܗ̇ܘ ܕܗܘܝܢ ܗܘܘ ܒܗ. ܘܡܢ
ܒܦܪ̈ܐ ܩܕܝܫܐ ܕܐܡܪܐ ܕܐܬܬܫܒܚܘ ܒܬܕ̈ܡܪܬܗܘܢ. ܕܐܝܟ ܗܕܐ
ܕܝܢ ܡܫܒܚܘܬܐ ܘܦܠܝܪܘܦܘܪܝܐ ܐܝܬ ܗܘܐ ܠܗ ܒܗܘܢ ܠܛܘܒܢܐ
ܦܛܪܘܣ. ܐܝܟܢܐ ܕܒܕܟܝܐ ܠܫܘܠܛܢܐ ܕܫ̈ܝܢܘܗܝ. ܐܚܝܢܐܝܬ ܐܝܬ

[1] This passage can also be understood as saying, "I cannot carry the saints and make them go around" or "I cannot bear them and carry them around the saints." The way we have translated it allows one to interpret it with regard to the concern of anti-Chalcedonians, who seem to have attempted to replace given, physically fixed holy places by movable relics. That this still posed its own difficulties is acknowledged here by Peter the Iberian himself. See Horn, *Asceticism and Christological Controversy*, 260–70.

[2] The virtue of purity is so highly esteemed that it is recognized and acknowledged even by Chalcedonians.

[3] The Syriac may render the Greek σώφρονες (Raabe, 102 n. 1).

[4] The Syriac transliterates the Greek διακονικόν. See *PGL*, 351. The term διακονικόν refers to either a sacristy, vestiary, sanctuary, or a chapel containing an altar. This term appears in texts from the fourth century C.E. onwards. It designates a special room or building used by deacons in which the sacred

cannot bear them and carry them around to the saints.[1] But go, make these [things] known to the bishop of the town! For he is a pure [man],[2] and he knows how to honor them as they deserve and [how to] perform their deposition."

(§145) This is what happened. The bishop heard [this] and in great joy took those from among the clergymen who were pure[3] and came to this place. The gardener showed them [the spot, and] they dug about a man's height and found an urn of lead. And when they opened it, they saw a multitude of burnt bones laid in it. And so, when they raised them up with a [ritual] service, they brought [them] and laid them [in] the **[R 109]** *diakonikon*[4] of the church. The news about them went out into all the region. After the worshipful feast of holy Pascha had passed, when many people from the surrounding towns and villages gathered together on the third of the month of Iyor,[5] their deposition took place with a great [and] solemn procession. They were laid with their brethren in the *martyrion*, I mean [that] of Saints Sergius and Bacchus,[6] who are venerated and honored there, since those holy martyrs asked through a revelation that they would be laid in this place together with the companions of their martyrdom. We unworthy ones were esteemed worthy, together with the saint, our father, to be blessed both from that holy vessel in which they were laid and from the holy soil [of the place] where their bones were found. The blessed Peter had such faith and full assurance in them that until the end of

vessels were kept. It was the place where the prosphora and chalice were prepared for the eucharistic liturgy. The deacons carried these elements from the διακονικόν to the adjacent church and brought them to the celebrating priest. This is remembered in the Great Entrance of the eastern liturgies and has been introduced into the Roman Catholic Novus Ordo, with volunteers from the laity walking with the bread and wine from the back of the church to the priest awaiting them in front of the sanctuary. Related terms are σκευοφυλάκιον and παστοφορία. See Robert F. Taft, William Loerke, and Mark J. Johnson, "Pastophoria," *ODB* 3:1594, with further literature.

[5] I.e., May.

[6] Sergius and Bacchus were imperial *notarii* who are said to have suffered martyrdom under Maximian in Rasapha (Augusta Euphratesia) in 290 C.E. See Raabe, 102 n. 3. See also Horn, *Asceticism and Christological Controversy*, 268; Alexander Kazhdan and Nancy Ševčenko, "Sergius and Bakchos," *ODB* 3:1879; and Elizabeth Key Fowden, *The Barbarian Plain: Saint Sergius between Rome and Iran* (The Transformation of the Classical Heritage 28; Berkeley and Los Angeles: University of California Press, 1999).

ܗܘܐ ܠܗ ܡܗܘܕܢܐ ܕܡܬܛܠܠܘܗܝ܆ ܒܡܗܘܕܢܐ ܕܕ̈ܐܪܐ ܘܪ̈ܫܢܐ
ܘܒܢ̈ܝܠܘܬܗ. ܗܘ̈ ܕܝܢ ܘܒܗܠܝܢ ܕܒܝ̈ܬܐ ܟܕ ܠܒܝܬܗ ܕܐܠܗܐ܆
ܐܬܘ̈ܬܐ ܦܪ̈ܝܫܬܐ ܘܚ̈ܝܠܐ ܘܐܣܘ̈ܬܐ܆ ܟܕ ܛܝ̈ܒܘܬܐ ܕܡܫܝܚܐ.
ܡܛܠ ܗܠܝܢ ܕܠܐ ܐܬܝܗ̇ ܗܫܐ ܕܢܐܡܪ ܒܐܝܕܐ ܐܝܕܐ.

(§146) ܘܡܢ ܒܬܪ ܝܘܡܐ ܕܝܢ ܕܦܛܘܠܡܝܣ ܡܕܝܢܬܐ܆ ܐܬܐ ܠܐܬܪܐ
ܕܛܪܝܦܘܠܝܣ. ܕܢܦܠܗ ܗܘܐ ܐܪܣܛܘܒܘܠܘܣ ܐܝܟ ܩܘܡܝܣ ܡܢ ܪ̈ܫܢܐ
ܕܡܕܝܢܬܐ. ܘܟܕ ܦܝܫ ܗܘܐ ܒܦܪܘܐܣܛܝܘܢ ܚܕ ܕܝܠܗ ܕܡܬܩܪܐ
ܒܥܪܐ܆ ܥܠ ܬܘ̈ܡ ܩ̈ܠܝܠܐ ܡܢ ܡܕܝܢܬܐ܆ ܡܛܠ ܐܦܘܪܣܘܣ ܕܚܘܬܐ
ܘܕܠܒܢܬܐ ܡܢ ܡܕܝܢܬܐ [R 110] ܡܠܒܘܬܐ. ܕܟܕ ܐܬܬܦܣܘ ܡ̈ܠܒܐ܆
ܥܒܕ ܕܠܐ ܢܬܬܣܝܡܘܢ ܗܠܝܢ ܡ̈ܫܝܢܐ ܘܢܦܩܘܢ ܠܘܬܗ.

(§147) ܟܕ ܕܝܢ ܐܢܘܢ ܬܡܢ܆ ܣܒܘܪܐ ܕܠܝ ܟܕ ܓܠ ܠܡܕܝܢܬܐ ܕܢܝܚ
ܠ ܣܬܘ̈ܝܬܐ܆ ܐܫܬܘܕܥ ܕܐܢܬܬܐ. ܘܟܕ ܢܬܟܢܫ ܠܘܬܗ ܕܩܪܒܐ ܘܦܢܝ
ܥܡ ܟ̈ܬܒܐ܆ ܗܢܐ ܕܝܢ ܐܢܬܘܢ، ܗܘܐ ܒܝܘܡ܆ ܕܒܢܝܬ ܟ̈ܢܘܫܐ ܕܬܬܠ
ܩ̈ܪܝܢ ܘܕܢܚ ܘܕܬܐܒ ܒܟܪܝ ܡܠ̈ܝܐ܆ ܥܕ، ܕܢܐܡܪ ܗܘ ܗܘ ܫܠܝܐ ܒܡ
ܫܘܬܐ ܘܕ̈ܟܝܐ. ܘܒܗ ܡܟܝܢ ܕܢܬܕܪ ܒܠܒܘܬܐ ܘܒܚܝܠܐ ܕܡܕܝܢܐ
ܠܐܘܛܝܣ ܗܘܕܐ. ܚܝܗ، ܒܪ ܐܝܟ ܒܗܘܢܐ ܠܠܒܐ ܕܐܡܪ ܠܗ܆ ܒܪ
ܐܟܣܢܝܘܬܐ܆ ܟܕ ܠܘܬܐ ܚܠܦ ܗܘܢܐ ܠܠܒܐ ܕܬܠܬܠܡ. ܘܗܘ ܐܡܪ
ܠܗܘܬܗ. ܚܕܐ ܐܢܐ ܡܢܝ ܗܘܕܗ ܕܡܪܢܐ܆ ܕܠܝ ܐܢܬܘܢ، ܗܢܐ

[1] One might count this again as a reference to the originally oral setting in which Rufus seems to have delivered earlier forms of the *Vita Petri Iberi.*

[2] A port city in Phoenicia, modern-day Ṭarābulus, Lebanon. According to tradition, the apostle Peter founded a church in Tripoli. Pilgrimage to Leontius's shrine made Tripoli the most important pilgrimage destination in Phoenicia. See Alexander Kazhdan, "Tripolis," *ODB* 3:2119–20.

[3] See Martindale, *Prosopography of the Later Roman Empire*, 2:123.

[4] The Syriac transliterates κόμης, Latin *comes*. See Payne Smith, 496. A *comes* was an official of the Byzantine court, chief officer, prefect, or commander.

[5] Also in Tripoli, Peter and his friends found the support of members of the local elite.

[6] The Syriac may render the Greek προάστειον (Raabe, 103 n. 3).

[7] Although Peter had been "hiding" in Phoenicia, he appears to have stayed in constant contact via messengers and potentially written notices and letters with the outside world, specifically Constantinople.

[8] Literally, "make readings" or "perform readings." It is noteworthy

his life he continually made mention of them in the celebration of the holy mysteries and in his prayers. But there also happened in these places through the grace of God many signs, mighty deeds, and healings through the prayers of the saints, about which it is not [possible for us] at this hour to speak one by one.[1]

(§146) After the day of the holy Pentecost we came to the region of Tripoli,[2] to which Apringius,[3] a *comes*[4] from among the magistrates of the city,[5] had urged him [to come]. While we were abiding there on one suburban estate[6] of his, which is called Gišra [the "Bridge"], about two miles from the city, we received an answer[7] of joy and good [news] from the imperial **[R 110]** city that, since the emperor had been persuaded, he allowed that these saints should not take the trouble to go up to him.

(§147) While staying there, when our agent entered the city in order to buy for us what we needed, he delayed coming [back]. While we were sitting with the old man and were reading the Scriptures—for this was his custom that between the times of the third hour and of the sixth and of the ninth he would hold readings[8]—the old man began to say with joy and tears, "Who can be amazed at the goodness and power of the holy martyr Leontius?[9] For this night someone[10] saw him, [and Leontius] said to him, 'My fellow-traveler, make a prayer for this child that he may be healed!' And he said to him, 'I am beseeching you, martyr of the

that Rufus takes care to indicate that Peter was not neglecting the hours of the daily office.

9 Leontius was a general in the army who converted two soldiers, Hypatios and Theodoulos. These two suffered martyrdom, and, shortly thereafter, Leontius did also. Greek tradition places this martyrdom under Emperor Vespasian (*BHG*, 986–87); for sources on his martyrdom in Oriental Christian traditions see the Syriac witnesses (*BHO* 563). Leontius's feast day is observed on 18 June. See F. Halkin, "Passions et miracle posthume de St. Léonce martyr à Tripoli en Phénicie," *AnBoll* 82 (1964): 319–40; G. Garitte, "Textes hagiographiques orientaux relatifs à Saint Léonce de Tripoli," *Mus* 78 (1965): 313–48; 79 (1966): 335–86; and 81 (1968): 415–40.

10 Here Peter the Iberian is referring to himself in the third-person singular. See *Vit. Pet.* §148 (R 111).

ܬܘܪܓܐ܆ ܕܐܝܬ ܠܝ ܦܐܪܗܣܝܐ ܠܘܬ ܝܫܘܥ. ܐܝܟ ܠܒܪ ܢܦܠܐ ܐܬܐ܂ ܘܟܕ ܗܕܐ ܐܡ̣ܪ ܫܬܩ.

(§148) ܚܕ ܕܝܢ ܡܢ ܡܬܦܫܩܝܢ ܚܕ ܒܢܦܫ: ܕܟܗܢܐ ܗܘ ܓ̈ܒܐ ܚܘܪܐ ܕܩܕܝܫܐ: ܘܠܐ ܡܡܪܚܝܢ ܕܢܫܐܠܘܢܗܝ܁ ܗ̣ܘ ܣܒܘܪܐ ܕܒܠܝ ܟܕ܂ ܐܘܚܪ ܒܡܕܝܢܬܐ ܠܒܪ ܡܢ ܒܝܬܐ܂ ܠܡܚܣܢ ܦܝܐ ܠܐܩܪ ܥܕܒ ܬ̈ܚܡܝ. ܟܕ ܐܬܦܪܫ ܕܝܢ܆ ܦܓܥܐ ܢܦܫܗ ܘܚܒܪ ܡܟܠܝܢܐ܆ ܘܡܫܬܟܚܐ ܗܘܐ ܐܬܪܐ ܕܗܦܟܬ ܒܡܚܠܐ ܕܩܕܝܫܐ ܠܐܘܢܛܝܘܣ܆ ܠܐܣܛܪܛܝܠܛܐ ܒܪ ܐܚܐ ܐܡܪ: ܡܢ ܗܠܝܢ ܕܒܟܬܪܝܢ ܒܐܠܟܣܢܕܪܝܐ: ܕܐܝܬ ܗܘܐ ܠܗ ܒܪܐ ܕܡܫܬܥܒܕ ܡܢ ܫܐܕܐ ܐܬܟܠ ܠܗ܆ ܕܐܬܚܢܢܬ ܠܐ ܡܬܒܠܡ ܛܠܝܐ܆ ܐܝܟ ܗ̇ܘ ܕܠܐ ܢܦܩ ܐܝܬ ܠܗ ܘܡܚܒܠ ܐܝܬ ܠܗ ܠܛܪܦܘܠܝܣ. ܠܘܬ ܩܕܝܫܐ ܣܗܕܐ ܠܐܘܢܛܝܘܣ ܘܗ̣ܘ ܫܠܚܘܗܝ، ܟܕ ܫܡܥܬܗ ܡܚܠ ܟܕ ܫܠܡ ܠܛܠܝܐ [R 111] ܐܝ̇ܟ ܠܛܪܦܘܠܝܣ. ܘܟܕ ܡܛܐ ܠܒܝܬ ܣܗ̈ܕܐ ܕܩܕܝܫܐ ܠܐܘܢܛܝܘܣ܆ ܟܕ ܡܚܢܩ ܠܗ ܫܐܕܐ ܠܗ̇ܘ ܛܠܝܐ ܟܠܗ ܢܦܫܗ ܘܟܠܗ ܠܛܠܝܐ܆ ܟܠܗ ܗܘܢܐ ܥܦܠܗ. ܐܝܟܢܐ ܕܟܪܝ ܟܠܠ ܚܫܒܘܗܝ ܘܢܚܡܘܗܝ، ܡܬܠܐ. ܘܠܐܩ̈ܠ ܓܦܪܐ ܟܕ ܐܬܒܪ، ܗ̣ܘ ܩܕܝܫܐ ܘܣܗܕܐ܆ ܒܥܝܐ ܒܗ̇، ܙܘܥܐ ܠܦܠܓܬܐ ܘܚܪܪܗ ܠܛܠܝܐ. ܘܗܫܐ ܗ̣ܘ ܛܠܝܐ ܟܕ ܗܘܐ ܚܠܝܡܐ܆ ܘܐܬܐ ܗܘܐ ܒܒܝܬ ܣܗ̈ܕܐ ܥܡ ܐܒܘܗܝ، ܟܕ ܡܫܒܚ ܠܬܕܡܘܪ̈ܬܗ ܕܐܠܗܐ. ܟܕ ܪܗܛܬ ܕܝܢ ܐܚܒܪܐ ܟܠܗ̇ ܡܕܝܢܬܐ ܠܫܘܬܗ ܕܬܕܡܘܪܬܐ܆ ܘܐܝܟܢܐ ܐܡܪ ܗ̣ܘ ܣܒܘܪܐ ܕܝܠܝ܆ ܪܗܛܬ ܕܐܚܝܢܐ ܠܗ̇، ܕܗܦܟܬ. ܘܫܠܚܬ ܠܗ̇ܘ ܛܠܝܐ ܕܐܬܚܪܪ. ܟܕ ܚܙܝ ܒܐ̈ܒܘܗܝ، ܠܗ̇ܘ ܒܝܬ ܣܗ̈ܕܐ ܩܕܝܫܐ. ܟܕ ܒܠܝܢ ܚܒܐ ܗܘܐ ܘܡܫܒܚ ܠܐܠܗܐ ܘܠܣܗܕܗ ܩܕܝܫܐ܆ ܟܠ ܐܬܪܐ ܕܗܦܟܬ. ܗ̇ܝ ܕܝܢ ܡܚܠ ܐܫܬܟܠܠ ܕܗܕܐ ܗܦܟܬ܆ ܗ̇ܝ ܕܐܫܬܟܚ ܗܘܐ ܒܡܐܢܬ ܗ̇ܘ ܠܡܚܠܐ ܦܛܪܘܣ ܟܕ ܙܟܝ ܕܐܬܘܗܝ، ܗܘܐ ܥܡ ܣܗܕܐ ܩܕܝܫܐ܆ ܟܕ ܦܩܕ ܐܣܘܬܐ ܕܗ̇ܘ ܕܡܫܬܥܒܕ ܗܘܐ.

(§149) ܒܬܪ ܗܠܝܢ ܬܫ̈ܥܝܬܐ ܕܝܢ ܡܢ ܒܬܪ ܕܩܒܠܝ ܗ̇ܝ، ܐܦܘܪܘܣ ܡܢ

[1] Hausherr (*The Name of Jesus*, 100) notes that it was the traditional point of view that only martyrs and their equals had the necessary familiarity, i.e., *parrhēsia*, with Jesus to address the Son of God in prayer merely by "Jesus" and have their prayers answered.

[2] That is, around 1:00 in the early afternoon.

[3] The Syriac renders the Greek μετάνοια (Raabe, 103 n. 7).

Lord, yours is this righteous action, because you have boldness [of speech] with Jesus,[1] for I am a sinner.' " When he had said this, he was silent.

(§148) While we were doubting in ourselves what the vision of the saint wanted [to indicate] and did not dare to ask him, our agent, having delayed in the city beyond what was usual, returned only just before the seventh hour.[2] But when he was reprimanded, he cast himself down and made a prostration[3] and was relating the sign that had happened in the temple of the holy Leontius.[4] "To a certain soldier,"[5] he was saying, "[one] from among these who are staying in Alexandria, who had a son who was possessed by a demon, it was revealed that 'The child will otherwise not be healed except that you take him and bring him to Tripoli to the holy martyr Leontius, and he will heal him.' Taking up the child, that same hour **[R 111]** he arrived in Tripoli. When he arrived at the *martyrion* of the holy Leontius, the demon was tearing [at] that child all day and all night, throwing him down to such an extent that he almost choked him and left him for dead. Toward dawn, when this saint and martyr appeared, he rebuked the impure spirit and set the child free. At present the child, being healthy, is standing in the *martyrion* with his father, [both] proclaiming the wonders of God. But when the whole city ran together to see the miracle, also I," our agent was saying, "ran to see what had happened. I saw the child who had been set free sweeping with his own hands that holy *martyrion*,[6] while everyone was weeping and glorifying God and his holy martyr because of the sign that had happened." Thus we understood that it was this that the blessed Peter had related in a veiled manner, hinting [at the fact] that he had been with the holy martyr, who was effecting the healing of the one who had been possessed.

(§149) After these days, after we had received the reply from

[4] The *martyrion* of Leontius was located in Tripoli. For a discussion of the location of the sanctuary, see Jean Maurice Fiey, "Un grand sanctuaire perdu? Le martyrion de St. Léonce à Tripoli," *Mus* 95 (1982): 77–78; see also Horn, *Asceticism and Christological Controversy*, 269–70.

[5] The Syriac renders the Greek στρατιώτης.

[6] Compare *Vit. Pet.* §11 (R 7), where Bakurios is presented as regularly sweeping the local church as a sign of his humility.

ܡܕܝܢܬ ܡܠܟܘܬܐ܂ ܡܩܒܠܝܢ ܗܘܘ ܠܗ ܠܡܕܒܪܢܐ܂ ܕܢܦܩܐ ܡܩܒܠ
ܠܒܘܪܟܬܗ܂ ܗܘ ܕܐܦ ܗܘ ܣܪܩ ܗܘܐ܂ ܟܕ ܡܢ ܟܕܘ ܦܩܕ ܗܘܐ ܫܪܝܐ܂
ܕܢܬܠ ܫܠܡܗ ܘܫܘܡܫܗ ܕܠܘܬ ܡܪܢ܂ ܟܕ ܦܩܕ ܗܘܐ ܫܕܪ ܚܕ ܡܢ
ܐܚ̈ܐ ܕܒܗܢ ܠܐܪܣܛܘܦܘܠܘܣ: ܟܕ ܐܡܪܐ ܕܢܕܟܪܢ ܠܝ܂ ܚܒܪ ܕܬܬܦܠܛ
ܐܠܦܐ ܕܠܣܩܐ ܕܢܦܩ ܒܗ܂ ܟܕ ܥܒܪ ܕܝܢ ܗܘ ܡܢ ܡܚܘܪܐ ܘܪܗܛ
ܐܚ̈ܘܗܝ: [R 112] ܡܡܠܠܢܐ ܕܝܠܗ ܕܢܝܚܐ ܡܡܫܡܫܢܐ܂ ܢܦܩ ܠܐܘܪܚܬܗ
ܘܠܒܘܗܝ܂ ܘܐܬܐ ܡܢ ܐܘܪܚܐ ܠܐܪܣܛܘܦܘܠܘܣ܂ ܕܢܦܩ ܠܡܕܒܪܢܐ ܘܢܚܬܘܢܐ
ܠܡܘܪܟܠܐ ܕܒܢܘܗ܂ ܟܕ ܢܛܠܒ ܕܝܢ ܒܡܕܝܢܬܐ܂ ܥܒܪ ܚܕ ܟܢܫ ܗܘܪܘܢ
ܚܠ ܚܘܪ ܡܢܐ܂ ܘܟܕ ܐܚܠܝܢ ܫ̈ܐܝܠܝܢ ܘܥܒܕܘܢ ܠܐܠܦܐ܂ ܡܫܩܠܝܢ
ܗܘܝܢ ܕܟܠܗ ܠܠܝܐ ܢܦܩ ܠܗ ܠܡܕܒܪܢܐ ܘܢܦܩ܂ ܘܟܕ ܢܦܩ ܐܡܪ ܕܠܢܝܚ܂
ܡܢܗܝܢ ܗܘܘ ܠܝ ܐܠܦ̈ܐ ܕܢܦܠ ܠܐܠܦܐ܂ ܗܘ ܕܝܢ ܠܡܘܟܢܐ ܟܕ
ܐܠܗܐ ܥܠܠ ܠܨܒܝܢܗ ܐܡܪ܂ ܐܝܟܐ ܐܬܠܘܦ ܠܐ ܡܫܟܚ ܐܢܐ܂
ܡܠܝܢ ܕܨܒܝܢ ܕܢܬܠܘܦܘܢ ܢܚܬܘܢ ܠܐܠܦܐ܂ ܠܝ ܓܝܪ ܙܕܩ ܠܝ܂ ܕܟܕ
ܡܫܠܡ ܐܢܐ܂ ܚܠ ܒܝܘܠܦܣ ܐܚܕܪ ܡܕܝܢܬܐ܂ ܟܕ ܡܬܕܡܪܝܢ ܕܝܢ
ܐܚ̈ܐ ܘܐܡܪܝܢ܂ ܠܡܢܐ ܡܚܒܠ ܠܐ ܦܩܕ ܐܒܐ ܗܕܐ܂ ܘܡܬܠܒܟܐ
ܗܘܬ ܠܗ ܒܟܢܪܐ܂ ܘܡܠܝܢ ܕܠܘܬ ܣܘܥܪܢܐ܂ ܘܐܠܦ̈ܐ܂ ܒܥܠܠܝܢ
ܘܥܣܩܝܢ ܘܡܢܗܝܢ ܠܝ܂ ܦܪ ܡܡܫܡܫܢܐ ܕܢܝܚ ܟܕ ܐܡܪ܂ ܠܐ ܐܢܫ
ܢܥܣܩܘܢܝ ܠܗܟܢܐ܂ ܗܠܝܢ ܕܨܒܝܢ ܢܬܠܘܦܘܢ܂ ܐܝܟܐ ܓܝܪ
ܘܠܡܬܠܡ ܚܝܠܐ ܐܝܬ ܠܗܟܢ ܘܡܠܝܢ ܕܠܘܬ ܣܘܥܪܢܗ ܡܬܠܒ ܐܢܐ܂
(§150) ܘܟܕ ܗܕܐ ܐܡܪ܂ ܚܕ ܡܢ ܗܠܝܢ ܠܐܠܦܐ܂ ܘܟܕ ܬܪܒܝܐܝܬ
ܪܕܝܢ܂ ܡܢܚܝܢ ܠܡܕܝܢܬܐ ܐܪܒܠܐ܂ ܡܢ ܐܟܚܕܐ ܕܐܬܝܬܘܗܝ ܗܘܐ ܚܕ
ܡܢ ܐܚ̈ܐ ܕܝܠܗ ܕܥܡܗ ܒܫܠܕܗ܂ ܗܘ ܕܐܟܚܕܐ ܒܗܢ ܠܐܦ
ܗܘܐ܂ ܘܟܕ ܠܘܬܗ ܢܦܠ܂ ܒܠܝܠ ܐܢ̈ܫܘܗܝ ܪܕܝܢ܂ ܟܕ ܡܩܒܠܝܢ ܚܕ
ܠܟܐܬܬܐ ܕܐܟܘܢ܂ ܐܝܟ ܕܝܢ ܕܠܫܪܬܐ ܐܫܬܪܪܝ܂ ܟܕ ܫܘܐ ܒܢܐ
ܗܘܐ ܗܘ ܗܟܢܐ܂ ܡܚܒܢܐ ܐܫܬܠܦ ܗܘܐ ܒܬܪܟܝܬܗ ܕܠܐ ܡܚܒܠ
ܢܛܘܦ܂ ܐܠܐ ܚܠ ܒܘܪܛܘܣ ܢܚܒܪ: ܐܟܒܢܐ ܕܐܦ ܬܘܡ ܠܡܦܩܕܐ
ܕܐܘܪܬܘܕܘܟܣܝܐ ܢܛܠܡ܂ ܘܟܕ ܢܩܫܬܐ [R 113] ܩ̈ܠܝܬܐ ܒܐܪ ܢܦܩܒ

[1] See *Vit. Pet.* §141 (R 104–5).

[2] Literally, "to greet," "to give his 'shalom.'"

[3] The Syriac renders the Greek ὡρεῖον (Raabe, 105 n. 2).

[4] The author creates the impression that Peter had become completely conformed to the will of God, even to the extent that God now guided his will.

[5] Geographers and archaeologists of Phoenicia have not been able to identify the location of that site. See also *Vit. Pet.* §151 (R 114).

the imperial city, we persuaded the saint that we should return now to our place, something about which he also was anxious, since he already was foreseeing that his end and his departure to our Lord were near. Therefore he sent one of the brethren who were with us ahead to Tripoli together with people who knew us [and] arranged that a ship should be made ready, one suitable for us [on which] to embark. When that honorable one and friend of strangers, our **[R 112]** host, the magistrate Maximus[1] heard [of this], he took his wife and his children and came from Arca to Tripoli to say goodbye[2] to the saint and to be esteemed worthy of a blessing from him. We went down [to the sea] in the evening and were lodging in a spot in a depot[3] on the seashore. We had brought our luggage and the things we needed into the ship, expecting that we would take the saint [on board] that night and embark. Since a fitting breeze blew, the sailors were hurrying us to go on board the ship. But the blessed one, since God had changed his will,[4] said, "I cannot sail. Those who are wishing to sail may go on board the ship! For me it is right that, when I move forward, I should make a journey to Beirut." The brethren were amazed and were saying, "Why, then, did he not say this before? An animal would have been made ready for him, and these [things that are necessary] for the journey!" and the sailors were offended and vexed and were hurrying us. Maximus the magistrate replied, saying, "May no one vex the old man! Those who are wishing to sail shall sail, for I shall bring a litter for the old man and prepare what [is necessary] for his journey."

(§150) When this was settled, we indeed went on board the ship. We traveled straight on and arrived at Long Village.[5] One of our brethren whose name was Basilides, who was sailing together with us, was from [this village]. We disembarked there and lodged at the house of his family[6] while awaiting the arrival of our father. But as we were assured subsequently, when the old man had seen a vision, he had changed his mind that he would not sail then but pass by to Beirut so that there too he could light the lamp of orthodoxy. He caught **[R 113]** many souls and offered

[6] While on travel, Peter and his friends appear to have enjoyed repeatedly the support of a network of relatives and close friends.

ܠܐܠܗܐ. ܗ̇ܘ ܕܝܢ ܚܙܘܐ ܐܬܚܙܝ، ܗܘ̣ܐ ܕܐܝܟ ܗܢܐ. ܦ̇ܩܕ ܗܘܐ
ܕܫܢܐ ܢܦܫܗ ܕܟܠܚܕ. ܕܩܘܪܒܢܐ ܩܕܝܫܐ ܢܩܪܒ. ܘܠܫ̈ܡܫܐ ܦܩܕ
ܗܘ̣ܐ ܗܠܝܢ ܕܐܝܬ ܗܘܐ ܠܗ ܒܝܕܐ. ܠܐ ܓܒܪ ܡܢ ܥܡܘܕܐ ܐܝܟ
ܕܐܬܐܐ ܩܛܠܬܐ ܗܘܐ ܡܦܩܕ ܗܘܐ: ܐܠܐ ܒܪ ܡܥܕܪ ܗܘܐ ܐܢܫ
ܕܠܝܫ ܠܐܝܒܐ ܕܢܒܕܝܢ ܠܣܒܥܐ: ܬܡܢ ܠܠܫ̈ܡܫܐ ܡܟܬܒ ܗܘܐ:
ܕܢܦܩܘܢ ܡ̇ܢ ܘܢܘܪܝܢ. ܘܕܢܩܘܡ ܠܩܘܪܒܢܐ ܕܐܠܗܐ. ܕܒܗܘܪܝܢ ܕܝܢ ܦܠܓ
ܒܡܥܡܘܕܝܬܐ. ܘܟܕ ܩ̈ܠܝܠܐ ܕܐܝܟ ܗܠܝܢ ܚܙܐ ܗܘܐ ܘܡܚܕܪ:
ܘܒܡܐܢܐ ܕܒܢܐ ܢܛܪ ܗܘܐ ܠܐܝܒܐ ܕܗܘ̣ ܕܐܙܠ ܗܘܐ: ܘܩܘܪܒܢܐ
ܩܕܝܫܐ ܡܢ ܗܠܝܢ ܡܬܩܠܐ ܗܘܐ. ܫ̇ܕܝܢ ܗܘܐ ܒܚܘܪܐ ܗ̣ܘܐ ܟܠܐ
ܠܘܬܗ ܕܐܝܪ: ܢܓܒܐ ܐܢܐ ܕܠܫ̈ܡܫܐ ܕܥܡܘܕܐ ܬܦܩܕ ܠܝ: ܘܡܚܘܣܢ
ܠܐܘܪܬܘܕܘܟܣܘ ܬܫܡܫܬܐ. ܒܗܠܝܢ ܓܒܪ ܡܬܬܚܡܣ ܐܢܐ. ܘܟܕ ܐܬܥܢܝ
ܘܐܬܢܚܡ ܡܢ ܐܠܗܐ: ܐܫܬܐܠ ܠܦܘܡܗ ܕܚܘܝܐ: ܕܢܓܒܐ ܐܠܗܐ
ܕܬܦܩܕ ܠܗ ܡܢ ܐܘܪܬܘܕܘܟܣܘܬܐ: ܕܩ̈ܢܘܢܐ ܩ̈ܠܝܠܐ ܘܩ̈ܕܝܫܐ ܩ̈ܠܝܠܐ:
ܕܓܝܪ ܕܢܫܠܡܘܢ ܝܠܕܗ ܘܢܐܙܠܘܢ ܒܬܪܗ. ܕܒܡܫ̇ܠܡܬܐ ܕܒܣܝܠܝܘܣ
ܘܓܪܝܓܘܪܝܘܣ ܘܝܘܚܢܢ ܘܐܪܣܢܝܘܣ ܘܕܢ̇ܚܝܢ ܕܡܝܢ ܠܗܘܢ ܒܠܒܐ.
ܠܝܘܢ ܓܒܪ ܕܐܝܟ ܗܠܝܢ: ܩ̈ܘܡܐ ܐܦ ܗ̣ܘ ܒܝܕܐ ܡܢ ܕܢܦܪܐ:
ܐܚܝܢܐ ܕܐܦ ܒܠܒܐ ܕܦܪܘܡܘܣ ܡܬܠܒܐ ܒܪ ܐܡܪ ܗܘܐ ܡܚܝܢܐ. ܐ
ܗܟܝܠ ܕܡܢܝܢܘܣ ܘܐܘܪ̈ܝܢܐ ܕܒܗܘܢ ܐܝܬ ܠܗܘܢ ܡܠܬܐ ܠܘܬ ܐܢܫ.
ܩ̈ܘܡܐ ܢܬܘܢ ܘܐܘܪܬܘܕܘܟܣܘ ܐܬܬܝܗܘܢ ܢ̣ܦܩܘ ܠܫ̈ܒܪܐ.

(§151) ܒܕ [R 114] ܫܠܡܗ ܗܟܝܠ ܒܦܪܘܦܝܠܝܣ ܠܡܩܒܠ ܐܦܝܣܩܘܦܐ
ܦܠܓܐ ܡܚܣܢܢܐ ܕܢܫܝܐ ܕܐܪܡܝܐ: ܘܚܪܗ ܘܠܗ̈ܘܢܘܗܝ، ܘܐܦܠܓܗ
ܠܦܪܢܐ: ܘܫܒܩ ܠܗ ܡܩܡܘܬܐ ܘ[ܐ]ܦ̈ܝܕܐ ܦ̈ܪܢܝܐ ܠܒ̈ܢܬܗ ܩ̈ܕܝܫܬܐ:
ܒܪ ܦܠܓ ܗ̇ܘ ܠܡܦܠܡ ܘܟܠܗܘܢ ܗܠܝܢ ܕܫܡܥܐ ܕܠܘܬ ܢܘܡܐ: ܗܟܢܐ

1 The comments in the last two sentences provide valuable information on how the eucharistic gifts were prepared, selected, and stored, at least in one setting in a fifth-century, Syro-Palestinian context.

2 The Syriac may render the Greek λογικός (Raabe, 106 n. 2). See also Rom 12:1.

3 The Syriac may render the Greek ὁλοκαυτώματα (Raabe, 106 n. 3).

4 I.e., Basil of Caesarea (330–379 C.E.).

5 It is not clear whether this refers to Gregory of Nyssa (331/40-ca. 395 C.E.) or Gregory Nazianzen (ca. 329–390 C.E.).

6 I.e., John Chrysostom (ca. 347–407 C.E.).

7 Arsenius (ca. 360–449 C.E.) was a native of Rome, of senatorial rank, whom Emperor Theodosius I appointed as educator of his sons, Arcadius and

[them] to God. This vision, however, was such: He was thinking that he was seeing himself about to offer the holy oblation and was placing the bread [upon the altar], as was his custom. For he was not used to having [breads] brought like [those that were] coming from the market and offer [them], but he would send someone suitable to where they were making bread and have [loaves of] bread prepared there, which were beautiful, white, and worthy for the oblation of God [and] yet very small in size. He [had] many like these made and dried [them] up and kept [them] in a clean vessel, [so that] where[ver] he went, he offered the holy oblation from these.[1] But then, in this vision, a voice came to him, saying, "I want you to offer to me market [loaves of] bread and to celebrate the Eucharist from them. For with these I am pleased." Since he was strengthened and made wise by God, he understood the interpretation of the vision, that God wanted that there should be offered to him also from [among] the lawyers rational[2] sacrifices and whole burnt offerings,[3] able to carry his cross and follow him, like Basil[4] and Gregory[5] and John[6] and Arsenius,[7] and those who are like them in zeal. For those who [are lawyers] by custom are called market men,[8] as also the book of Acts relates, saying thus: "If, then, Demetrius and the craftsmen who are with him have a complaint[9] against anyone, they should bring market men; as for the proconsuls—may they accuse each other!"[10]

(§151) After **[R 114]** having said goodbye then in Tripoli to the good host of strangers, Maximus, the magistrate of Arca, and having blessed him and his children and having entrusted him to the Lord and having left him [in] the protection and great provision of his holy prayers, after that one [Maximus] had prepared

Honorius. Yet in 394 Arsenius left the palace for the life of an anchorite in the desert of Egypt. He gained a reputation for his learning, austerity, and strict practice of silence. For forty-four sayings preserved by him in the *Apophthegmata Patrum* collection, see Ward, *Sayings of the Desert Fathers*, 9–19.

8 The Syriac might render the Greek ἀγοραίοι, lit. "those who frequent the market [ἀγορά]," "public speakers, orators, lawyers." Raabe (106 n. 5) also refers to Dio Cassius, frag. 114: ἀνὴρ ἀγοραῖος καὶ ἐκ δικαστηρίων τὸν βίον ποιούμενος: "An orator, or one who makes his livelihood from the law courts."

9 Literally, "word."

10 See Acts 19:38.

ܘܡܣܟܢܘܬܐ ܐܝܟ ܗܘܐ ܒܐܘܪܚܐ. ܟܕ ܡܪܢܐ ܙܪܥ ܗܘܐ ܒܠܒܗ̈
ܘܬܪܥܝ̱ ܐܘܪܚܗ.

(§152) ܘܟܕ ܐܬܐ ܠܒܝܪܘܬܘܣ܆ ܡܚܕܐ ܐܬܝܕܥ ܠܛ̈ܠܝܐ
ܐܣܟܘܠܣܛܝܩܐ܆ ܕ̈ܘܒܪܐ ܕܝܠܗ ܡܢ ܦܠܣܛܝܢܐ ܘܡܢ ܐܠܟܣܢܕܪܝܐ.
ܗ̇ܢܘܢ ܕܐܦ ܠܗܠܝܢ ܕܫܪܟܐ܆ ܟܕ ܛܒܒܐ ܒܝܕܗ ܠܡܕܝܢܬܐ܆
ܠܟܠܗܘܢ ܢܓܕܘ ܠܘܬܗ. ܟܕ ܚܙܝܢ ܕܢܗܘܘܢ ܒܢܝܢܗ ܘܡܬܬܥܝܪܝܢ
ܒܗ܆ ܘܒܟܠܘܩܝܬܗ ܦܪܘܫܬܐ ܢܬܠܡܕܘܢ. ܘܟܕ ܡܪܢܐ ܓܒܐ
ܠܒܝܬܗ܆ ܗܢܐ ܟܠܗ ܐܒܝܕܬ ܡܠܬܗ܆ ܐܝܟܢܐ ܕܢܩܫܬܐ ܩ̈ܠܝܬܐ
ܐܦ ܡܢ ܬܡܢ ܢܦܘܩ ܘܢܦܪܘܩ ܠܡܪܢܐ. ܘܐܢ̈ܫܝܢ ܡ̣ܢ ܡܢܗܘܢ܆ ܟܕ
ܒܕܒܠ ܣܘ܆ ܐܢ̈ܫܝܢ ܕܝܢ܆ ܘܡܢ ܒܬܪ ܒܘܠܝܢܗ܆ ܢܓܕܘ ܫܪܝܘܬܗ
ܕܟܠܒܐ ܘܠܘܬܗ ܢܬܩܠܘܢ. ܘܡܢ ܒܬܪܗ ܠܗ ܬܠܡ̈ܝܕܘܗܝ ܘܬܪ̈ܝܗܘܢ܆
ܕܡܪܢܐ ܕܝܚܝܕܝܘܬܐ[1] ܢܓܕܘܢ܆ ܘܡܢܗܘܢ ܢܬܒܥܘܢ ܠܒܪܗ ܒܫܡܝܐ
ܕܡܪܢܐ. ܕܡܕܒܪܐ ܕܗܠܝܢ ܐܠܝܨܐ ܗܘܐ܆ ܗܘ ܕܒܝܕܗܘܢ ܡ̣ܢ ܠܗܡܢܐ.
ܗܘ ܢܒܝܐ ܘܡܕܒܪܢܐ. ܘܡܛܠ ܗܠܝܢ ܡܢ ܟܠܗܘܢ ܡܫܬܡܥ ܫܡܗ ܗܘܐ
ܓܘܢܐ ܕܡܪܢܐ.

(§153) ܒܬܪ ܗܠܝܢ ܟܕ ܚܒܪ ܡܢ ܬܡܢ܆ ܐܙܠ ܠܗ ܒܗ̇܆ ܕܒܬܘܪܐ
ܡܕܝܢܬܐ ܐܪܒܝܐ. ܘܬܡܢ ܐܝܬ ܥ̈ܒܕܐ ܕܒܝܘܬܐ ܐܠܗܝܬܐ. ܘܡܢ
ܒܬܪ ܗ̇ܘ܆ ܚܙܐ ܡܬܦܠܣܡ܆ ܕܐܝܟ ܗܢܐ ܠܡܦܩܕܐ [R 115]
ܐܠܗܝܐ ܐܬܠܗ ܒܦܘܩܕܢܐ ܕܗܠܝܢ ܕܫܡܥܘܢ܆ ܐܝܟܢܐ ܕܢܗܘܐ ܪܒܐ

[1] So MS B. MS A and Raabe have ܕܝܚܝܕܘܬܐ.

[2] See Ps 5:8; Isa 40:3.

[3] Presumably by way of mouth, Peter's fame had spread like wild-fire among the young law-school students. See also Horn, "Peter the Iberian and Palestinian Anti-Chalcedonian Monasticism," 117–20.

[4] One could also translate, "drew all the rest to his love."

[5] The Syriac may render the Greek ἐπιλαμβάνεσθαι (Raabe, 107 n. 2).

[6] Literally, "after him."

[7] Severus of Antioch was one of the latter.

[8] The Syriac here uses the term ܝܚܝܕܝܘܬܐ[,] , which literally means "singleness," a concept central to the definition of asceticism in the Syro-Palestinian realm. See AbouZayd, *Iḥidayutha*; Sidney H. Griffith, "Asceticism in the Church of Syria: The Hermeneutics of Early Syrian Monasticism," in *Asceticism* (ed. Vincent L. Wimbush and Richard Valantasis; New York: Oxford University Press, 1995), 220–45.

[9] See Matt 11:29–30.

[10] See also Zachariah Rhetor, *Vit. Sev.* 55, fol. 120a (Kugener, 55,6–8).

the litter and all the rest of these [things that are necessary] for the journey, he [Peter] then cheerfully went on his way, while the Lord was traveling with him and was making his way straight.[2]

(§152) When he came to Beirut, he was recognized immediately by the young lawyers, his acquaintances from Palestine and from Alexandria, who had made the saint famous to the rest[3] and drew all of them to love him[4] and who were anxious to be in converse with him and be captivated by him[5] and enjoy his saving teaching. Since the Lord granted his grace, his word worked to such a degree that he caught many souls from there and offered [them] to the Lord. Some of them while he was still alive and some after his departure would reject the vanity of the world and run to him and after his death[6] to his disciples and his heirs.[7] They would choose the way of life of solitude,[8] and with them they would carry the sweet yoke[9] of the Lord. The first of these was Elisha,[10] who by his race indeed [was] a Lycian,[11] quiet and humble; because of these [characteristics], he was named by all of them "the Lord's sheep."[12]

(§153) After this he departed from there [and] caught up with us in what is called Long Village,[13] where he [had] sown seeds of divine grace.[14] After this, in the metropolis of Tyre,[15] he lit such a divine **[R 115]** lamp[16] in the souls of those who were listening that

[11] I.e., from the southern coast of Asia Minor, southwest of Pamphylia.

[12] Anti-Chalcedonian sources related to the circle of Peter's followers and subsequent generations contain several instances where expressive cognomina for individual members are preserved; see, e.g., *Vit. Pet.* §105 (R 77–78; Cyril, that sheep of Christ); Zachariah Rhetor, *Vit. Sev.* 87, fol. 128a (Kugener, 87,2–3; John called Lazarus, Theodore the Just). One might interpret this phenomenon as an indicator of the rather tightly knit structure and the close, brotherly relationship in which members of the community found themselves.

[13] See *Vit. Pet.* §150 (R 112).

[14] I.e., he preached the gospel and instructed the people. See also Matt 13:18–30; Mark 4:3–20; Luke 8:4–15.

[15] A port city in southern Lebanon. Josephus, *C. Ap.* 1.70 (Thackeray, 190–91), witnesses to the existence of a Jewish community at Tyre, yet the inhabitants of Tyre were bitter enemies of the Jews. Eventually Tyre developed into the wealthiest town of the eastern provinces. See Eliyahu Ashtor, "Tyre," *EncJud* 15:1488–90.

[16] See also Mark 4:21–23; Luke 8:16–18.

ܘܡܢ ܡܪܝܐ ܢܣܒ܀ ܘܠܘܬ ܢܦܫܬܐ ܕܟܠܗ ܘܠܘܬ ܟܘܡܪܐ ܕܒܟܡ
ܬܠܡ̈ܝܕܘܗܝ، ܢܗܦܟܘܢ. ܘܠܐ ܟܠܝܘܡ ܠܘܬ ܬܠܡ̈ܝܕܘܗܝ، ܢܬܦܩܘܢ
ܗܠܝܢ ܐܣܟܝܡܐ܆ ܐܠܐ ܘܐܚܪܢܐ ܒܕܝ̈ܪܬܐ ܐܚܪܢܝܬܐ ܕܐܒ̈ܗܬܐ
ܐܘܪܬܕܘܟܣܘ܆ ܠܟ̈ܢܫܐ ܥܠܡܐ ܐܚܪܢܐ ܘܪ̈ܗܒܐ ܕܐܠܗܐ ܘܟ̈ܢܫܬܐ
ܟܒܪ܆ ܠܐ ܟܠܝܘܡ ܒܪ̈ܢܫܐ ܐܠܐ ܐܦ ܢܫ̈ܐ.

(§154) ܕܒܡܠܝ ܘܛܠܝܬܐ ܚܕܐ ܒܬܘܠܬܐ ܡܢ ܛܠܗܘܡܐ ܕܒܟܐ ܝܕ܀
ܡܢ ܚܒܫܐ ܙܒܢܐ ܕܨܘܪ ܡܝܛܪܦܘܠܝܣ ܕܐܬܝܠܕܬ ܗܘܬ ܡܢ ܫܬܡܥܬܐ
ܡܢ ܐܒܐ܆ ܐܝܬ ܗܘܐ ܠܗ̇ ܕܝܢ ܐܡܐ ܢܘܟܪܝܬܐ. ܟܕ ܗܘܬ ܒܪܬ
ܟܒܢܝܢ܆ ܟܕ ܣܦܩܬܐ ܕܐܝܟܐ ܢܟܦܐ ܘܩܕܝܫܐ ܘܪܚܡܬ ܐܠܗܐ܆ ܟܕ
ܐܬܬܝܗ̇ ܘܐܒܘܗ̇ ܬܪܒܝܬܗ̇܆ ܢܦܩܬ ܡܢ ܡܢ ܦܠܚܘܬܐ ܣܓܝܬܐ ܕܒܗ̇
ܡܬܡܨܝܐ ܐܚܪܝܐ ܗܘܬ܆ ܡܪܝܡܬ ܕܝܢ ܠܗܘܪܝܐ ܕܕܝܠܗ ܐܠܗܐ. ܟܕ
ܡܟܪܝܗ̇ ܠܡܟܝܢܐ ܟܠܬܐ ܕܒܠܝܬܐ. ܘܗܟܢܐ ܟܕ ܐܬܬܝ ܠܠܒܗ̇
ܒܝܘܡܐ ܐܠܗܝܐ܆ ܐܝܟܢܐ ܕܟܕ ܐܚܝܕܐ ܡܗܝܡܢܘܬܐ ܬܗܘܐ
ܘܬܪܝܨܬ ܥܡܘܕܝܐ܆ ܘܟܠܗ̇ ܙܗܝܘܬܐ ܘܡܘܕܝܢܘܬܐ ܘܥܡܘܕܝܐ ܘܢܝܚܘܬܐ
ܕܚܒܫܐ܆ ܘܥܘܦܪܐ ܕܦܓܪܐ ܕܝܠܗ̇܆ ܘܐܝܟ ܢܠܐ ܢܦܪܬ܆ ܟܠܗ̇ ܗ̇ܝ ܠܗ̇
ܒܥܘܕܪܢܐ ܘܒܦܓܪܐ ܬܟܠ ܠܡܥܢܝܐ܆ ܟܠܬܐ ܕܠܐ ܠܐ ܛܠܝܥܐ܆ ܛܒܝܢܬ
ܓܠܝܐ ܘܡܗܝܡܢܬܐ܆ ܘܟܕ ܡܫܝܢܐ ܕܗܠܝܢ ܣܓܝ ܦ̈ܘܠܚܢܐ ܣܒ̈ܝܚܬܐ.
ܡܢ ܡܪܝܐ ܘܦܠܚܘܬܐ ܐܠܗܝܬܐ ܟܕ ܒܬܪܐܝܬ ܒܥܕܬ ܟܡ܆ ܐܡܪܐ

[1] This imagery is related to the one found at *Vit. Pet.* §141 (R 106), where the author speaks of Peter taking many captives with his teachings. Fishing imagery is quite prominent throughout the text. See also §§133, 170, 171 (R 98, 127–28). The obvious context for this is twofold: (1) Jesus' Gospel command inviting his followers to fish for people (Mark 1:17); (2) Peter and his friends' travels along the seashore, down the eastern Mediterranean coast from Tripoli to Gaza.

[2] For studies of the prominent role of women in the anti-Chalcedonian milieu of fifth-century Palestine, see Cornelia Horn, "Fighting with the Devil: The Central Function of Women in John Rufus's Anti-Chalcedonian Polemics" (paper presented at the Annual Meeting of the North American Patristics Society, Chicago, 2002); and eadem, "Towards a Feminist Ecumenical Reconstruction of the Social History of Anti-Chalcedonian Monasticism in Syria-Palestine in the Fifth and Sixth Centuries" (paper delivered at the American Academy of Religion/Society of Biblical Literature Annual Meeting, Toronto, 2002).

[3] For studies of that girl's story, see Baruch Rosen, "משומרת מצור בארץ־ישראל בתחילת המאת השישית לספירה [A Convert from Tyre in the Land of Israel at the Beginning of the Sixth Century AD]," *Cathedra* 16

he caught a great catch[1] from there also, and they ran both to adhere to him and to dwell with his disciples. Not only did these take the habit with his disciples, but also others in other monasteries of the orthodox fathers he made at the same time bearers of the cross and friends of God and members of [his] household, not only men but also women.[2]

(§154) Among these he caught one girl,[3] a virgin from a well-known family [and] from a great lineage of the metropolis of Tyre, who, on the one hand, was orphaned of [her] father and, on the other hand, had a Jewish mother.[4] When she was in converse with him through the care of chaste and holy and God-loving brethren, he instructed her and enlightened her mind. He dragged her away from heathen error[5] in which she formerly had been held [and] brought her near to the light of the fear of God,[6] betrothing her to Christ [as] a pure virgin.[7] Having inflamed her heart with divine love, so that at the same time she became a believer and an orthodox,[8] she also trod underfoot all high-standing, opulence, glory, splendor of race, and the beauty of [her] body,[9] shaking them off like dust. She committed herself entirely, in soul and body, to Christ, a spotless bride,[10] a bearer of the cross and an ascetic, and one of the number of those five wise virgins.[11] Henceforth di-

(1991): 54–66; Cornelia Horn, "Anti-Jewish Polemic and Conversion of Jews to Anti-Chalcedonian Asceticism in the Holy Land: The Case of Eugenia of Tyre," *ARAM* 18 (2006): 33–48; and eadem, "Eugenia, a Fifth-Century Jewish Convert to Anti-Chalcedonian Asceticism in Palestine" (paper presented at the Upper Midwest Regional Meeting of the American Academy of Religion/Society of Biblical Literature, St. Paul, Minnesota, 2002).

[4] The girl's religious affiliation as a Jew was defined by her birth from a Jewish mother.

[5] The author of this text identifies the Jewish faith as a form of heathenism.

[6] By which the author refers to anti-Chalcedonianism.

[7] An allusion to 2 Cor 12:2.

[8] For an exploration of the significance of that double-conversion, see Horn, "Anti-Jewish Polemic and Conversion of Jews."

[9] For the image of treading upon the enemy, see also Luke 10:19. Note also the related expression in *Vit. Pet.* §50 (R 34), where Peter is described as despising the beauty of his body.

[10] See also Eph 5:29.

[11] See Matt 25:1–13.

ܘܡܕܒܪܢܘܬܐ ܘܪܕܝܬ ܕܪܓܐ ܕܬܫܘܠܡܬܐ ܩ̈ܕܝܫܬܐ ܫܡܠܝܬܗ̇. ܘܗܢܐ
ܥܠܗ̇ ܒܡܬܪܐ ܕܡܫܡܫܬܐ ܐܠܗܝܬܐ: ܘܪܘܫܡܐ ܘܪܘܪܒܘܬܐ [R 116]
ܓܒܝܬ ܠܗ̇. ܐܝܟܢܐ ܕܒܢܝܐ ܕܩܪܝܒܐܝܬ ܟܠܗܘܢ ܠܡܫܝܚܐ ܬܟܢܫ.
ܐܝܟ ܗܠܝܢ ܕܡܬܠܠܗܘܢ ܟܬܒ. ܢܬܝܒܠܢ ܠܡܠܟܐ ܒ̈ܬܘܠܬܐ ܒܬܪܗ̇.
ܗܠܝܢ ܕܠܘܬܗ̇ ܢܝܬܘܢ ܠܟ. ܢܬܝܒܠܢ ܒܚܕܘܬܐ ܘܒܪܘܙܐ. ܬܬܘܣܦ ܕܝܢ.
ܘܒܡܕܝܢܘܬܐ ܘܒܢܟܦܘܬܐ. ܘܡܛܠ ܕܒܗ̇ ܒܢܝܐ ܬܬܚܝܐ ܕܢܚܠܐ
ܚܒܠܬ ܘܐܦܠܝܬ: ܢܨܝܪܘܬ ܠܦܓܪܐ ܕܡܫܝܚܐ ܐܢܫܝܬ. ܘܕܐܠܗܝܬ
ܐܘܓܢܝܐ ܐܬܬܨܝܦ ܠܗ̇ ܫܡܐ. ܒܠ ܕܒܢܝܐ ܘܒܕܘܒܪܐ ܘܒܠܒܢܐ
ܘܒܢܝܘܬܐ ܐܡܝܢܐ. ܘܒܐܣܟܡܐ ܠܒܬ ܘܐܬܕܒܪܬ. ܕܐܘܓܢܝܐ
ܣܗܕܬܐ ܢܨܝܚܬ ܘܒܬܘܠܬܐ.

(§155) ܐܦܘ ܕܝܢ ܘܐܩܝܡ ܡܢ ܬ̈ܪܥܝܐ ܠܗܠܝܢ ܡܕ̈ܝܢܬܐ ܠܘܬܗ ܕܪܗܘܡܐ.
ܒܪ ܠ̈ܐܚܝܢ ܕܢܬܚܪܘܢ ܘܡܬܠܬܠܘܬܗ ܢܬܚܫܒܘܢ. ܘܒܪ ܐܡ̈ܪܝܢ ܥܠ
ܢܦܫܗܘܢ ܕܬ̈ܠܝܬܐ ܐܚܬܗܘܢ ܘܗܢܝܢ ܕܒܬܘܠܬܐ ܒܠܚܘܕ. ܐܡܪ.
ܐܝܬ ܠܝ ܒܗ ܐܘܣܝܬܐ ܡܬܝܒܪܬܐ ܕܐܠܗܐ: ܕܐܡܝܢܐܝܬ ܦܠܚܬ
ܠܡܫܝܚܐ. ܒܝܬܐ ܗܟܝܠ ܡܢ ܚ̈ܕܪܐ ܕܝܠܝ ܘܕ̈ܚܕܪܐ ܘܕ̈ܪܐ ܦ̈ܠܐ
ܢܐܪܦ. ܘܐܝܟ ܕܐܝܟ ܢܬܟܢܫ ܠܗܘܢ ܫܦܝܪܬܐ: ܘܡܬܝܒܪܬܐ ܐܢܬܬܗܘܢ
ܡܪܢܐ: ܗܘ̣ ܕܐܦܐ ܕܢܘܪܐ ܠܬ̈ܠܝܬܐ ܠܡܫܝܚܘܬܐ: ܠܘܬ ܗ̇ܝ ܕܢܩܪܘܢ
ܘܢܬܪܘܡ ܘܠܡܠܟܘܬܗ ܢܒܘܐ ܠܝ. ܒܠܚܘܕ ܐ̈ ܗ̣ܘ ܕܒܪܢܫܐ ܠܝܬܪܐ

1 Evidence for the existence of female monasteries in the anti-Chalcedonian tradition is also provided, e.g., at *Pler.* 82.

2 Note how Rufus depicts the young woman in a leadership position.

3 See Ps 45:13–15.

4 1 Tim 2:15.

5 The Syriac may render the Greek διαφθορεύς (Raabe, 109 n. 2).

6 The Syriac may render εὐγένεια (Raabe, 109 n. 3).

7 From early on Christians had a predilection to employ the language of family relationships when referring to one another. See, e.g., Matt 5:47; Gal 6:10; Heb 2:11; 1 Pet 4:17. The accounts of the apologists, e.g., preserve evidence that this usage of calling one another brother and sister even led to pagan suspicions and accusations of incestuous behavior against the Christians. See, e.g., Athenagoras, *Leg.* 3, 32–34 (Pouderon, 80–83, 192–201; Richardson, *Early Christian Fathers*, 303, 336–38).

8 The Syriac may render the Greek καλλίνικος (Raabe, 109 n. 5). Eugenia, according to hagiography the daughter of Philip, prefect of Egypt in the third century, converted to Christianity. She dressed as a man (displaying the

vine grace, since it dwelt in her abundantly, appointed her mother, nurse, and head of a monastery of holy virgins.[1] It bestowed upon her such wealth of divine wisdom and of understanding **[R 116]** and of holiness that she would gather daily a congregation of many for Christ,[2] like those about whom it is written, "Virgins shall follow her to the king; these with her shall go to you. They will go with joy and with exultation,"[3] and it should be added, "and with holiness and with chastity."[4] Since she hated and abhorred the evil whispers of the corrupter[5] [and] she loved the beauty of the family[6] of Christ,[7] her name was rightly changed [to] Eugenia. Both in manner and in way of life and in zeal she emulated and conducted herself at the same time both in the asceticism and in the pilgrimage of Eugenia, the martyr [of] fair victory.[8]

(§155) Some from among the magistrates of these cities[9] came also to the saint,[10] desiring to receive a blessing and to enjoy his teaching. And when they were saying about themselves that they were sinners and needed him to pray on their behalf, he said, "We have a house of healing[11] prepared by God that is continuously open for repentance. Let us therefore cease from our ancient customs and take pains [to do] good deeds, and let us fight against sin as it is right; and the Lord, who came to call sinners to repentance,[12] is ready to save and justify [us] and make us worthy of

typical behavior of transvestite saints) and entered a monastery, of which she eventually became abbot, named Eugenios. Accused of fathering a child, her true identity as a woman was revealed in front of the judgment seat of her own father, who converted to Christianity and suffered martyrdom. Eugenia herself traveled to Rome, where also she suffered martyrdom, possibly under Emperor Valerian in 258. She was known to Avitus of Vienne and Venantius Fortunatus. See *BHL*, 2666–70; *BHG*, 607w-608b; and *BHO*, 281–84. See also Agnes Lewis Smith, *Select Narratives of Holy Women from the Syro-Antiochene or Sinai Palimpsest, as Written above the Old Syriac Gospels by John the Stylite, of Beth-Mari-Qanun in A.D. 778* (Studia Sinaitica 9–10; London: Clay, 1900), ܐ-ܠܗ (Syriac), 1–35 (English).

[9] I.e., of Tyre and Beirut.

[10] Note again how highly placed citizens paid Peter a visit.

[11] The unusual expression "house of healing" highlights the salvific function of repentance.

[12] Matt 9:13; Mark 2:17; and Luke 5:32.

ܢܥܒܕ ܠܢ ܕܐܚܝܕܝܢ ܚܢܢ ܗܟܢܐ ܦܘܠܚܢܐ ܛܒܐ. ܗ̈ܠܝܢ ܓܝܪ ܐܬܦܩܕܢ
ܐܘܪ̈ܚܬܐ ܕܙܕܝܩܘܬܐ ܠܘܬ ܐܠܗܐ. ܐܝܟ ܒܢ̈ܝܐ ܕܗܝܡܢܐ ܫܠܝܚܐܝܬ
ܘܕܠܐ ܥܠܒܐ ܡܬܚܫܒ ܠܘܩܒܠ ܢ̈ܫܐ: ܐܝܟܢܐ ܕܡܫܬܡܠܝܐܝܬ ܢܫܬܘܐ
ܕܢܗܘܐ ܘܢܬܥܬܪ ܡܢ ܥܒܕܘܬܗܘܢ ܡܕܡ ܫܘܠܡܗ. ܘܐܝܬ ܐܚܪܢܐ:
ܕܡܬܒܥܐ ܡܢܗ ܡܢ ܟܠܗ ܫܠܡܗ: ܘܦܩܕܐ ܠܢ̈ܫܐ: ܘܟܠܡܕܡ ܚܪܝܦ
ܘܚܟܡ: [R 117] ܐܝܟܢܐ ܕܠܗ̇ ܟܕ ܠܗ̇ ܠܚܐܪܘܬܐ ܢܫܬܘܐ. ܘܟܕ
ܠܐ ܒܕܒܠ ܗ̇ܝ ܡܫܬܡܠܝܐܝܬ ܗܕܪ ܥܒܕ. ܟܕ ܐܡܪ ܠܗ̇ ܟܕ ܠܗ̇
ܠܫܘܝܘܬܐ: ܠܗܢܐ ܟܡ ܗ̇ܘ ܕܢܗܘܐ ܒܐܢܫܐ: ܟܡ ܟܕ ܟܡ
ܒܠܚܘܕ ܡܩܝܡ ܒܗܘܢܐ ܕܕܢܝܐ: ܘܠܦܘܪ̈ܥܢܐ ܫ̈ܘܝܐ ܡܫܘܐ.

(§156) ܬܘܒ ܘܗܕܐ ܒܦܐܪܗܣܝܐ ܦܪܫ ܠܟܠܗܘܢ ܗ̇ܘ ܠܓܒܝܐ ܟܡ
ܡܬܚܘܝܢܘܬܐ: ܠܘܬ ܫܘܠܝܐ ܕܡܟܪܙ ܘܕܬܘܒܠܐ ܕܟܠ ܐܠܗܐ. ܟܕ
ܗܟܢܐ ܐܡܪ. ܟܠܗܘܢ ܓܝܪ ܦܘܩ̈ܕܢܘܗܝ ܕܡܪܝܐ ܠܟܠܗܘܢ ܒܢ̈ܝܢܫܐ
ܐܬܝܗܒܘ. ܠܣ̈ܒܐ ܘܠܛ̈ܠܝܐ. ܠܓܒܪ̈ܐ ܘܠܢ̈ܫܐ. ܠܥܒ̈ܕܐ ܘܠܒ̈ܢܝ
ܚܐܪ̈ܐ. ܠܕܝܪ̈ܝܐ ܘܠܥܠܡ̈ܝܐ. ܘܠܗܕܐ ܐܘܕܥ ܗ̇ܘ ܡܪܢ. ܟܕ ܫܕܪ
ܠܬܠܡܝ̈ܕܐ ܠܟܪܘܙܘܬܐ: ܟܕ ܡܦܩܕ ܘܐܡܪ ܠܗܘܢ: ܙܠܘ ܬܠܡܕܘ
ܠܟܠܗܘܢ ܥܡ̈ܡܐ. ܟܕ ܡܥܡܕܝܢ ܐܢܬܘܢ ܠܗܘܢ: ܒܫܡܐ ܕܐܒܐ
ܘܕܒܪܐ ܘܕܪܘܚܐ ܩܕܝܫܐ: ܘܡܠܦܝܢ ܐܢܬܘܢ ܠܗܘܢ ܕܢܛܪܘܢ: ܟܠܡ
ܡܐ ܕܦܩܕܬܟܘܢ. ܘܠܐ ܕܡܠܡ ܡܢ ܢܛܪܘܢ: ܗܠܝܢ ܕܝܢ ܠܐ. ܐܠܐ
ܟܠܡ ܗܠܝܢ ܕܦܩܕܬܟܘܢ. ܗܢܐ ܓܝܪ ܫܘܠܡܐ ܟܠܢܫ ܕܕܝܪ̈ܝܐ
ܘܕܥܠܡ̈ܝܐ: ܫܘܕܥܐ ܕܫܘܠܡܬܐ ܘܕܡܫܡܫܢܘܬܐ. ܒܪܡ ܡܛܠ
ܘܠܡܫܠܡܘܬܐ ܕܡܟܢܫܘܬܐ ܘܠܡܬܡܣܟܢܘܬܐ ܐܫܬܪܓܠ ܗܢܐ ܕܕܪܐ
ܕܝܠܢ: ܡܬܚܙܐ ܗܢܐ ܒܡܪܝܐ: ܕܟܠ ܒܪܫܠܝܐ ܐ ܗ̇ܘ ܕܐܝܟ:
ܕܗܠܝܢ ܬܠܬܐ ܦܘܩ̈ܕܢܝܢ ܢܛܪ ܘܬܪܝ ܒܫܘܝܘܬܐ: ܠܐ ܢܗܘܐ
ܡܦܠܐ ܡܢ ܪ̈ܚܡܘܗܝ ܕܡܪܢ. ܘܠܐ ܡܢ ܡܬܠ̈ܬܐ ܕܠܟܠܢ. ܗ̇ܘ ܕܝܢ

[1] Tit 3:8.

[2] For evidence that the view of God as judge is rather prominent throughout this work, see *Vit. Pet.* §§61, 65, 90, 119 (R 43, 46, 63, 87).

[3] See also Matt 20:1–16 for an example of how God rewards all equally, according to his own measure.

[4] See also Gal 3:28.

[5] See Matt 28:20.

[6] This comment reflects a position that requires a radical commitment with ascetic dimensions of all Christians.

his kingdom, only if he finds us until the end holding on to this good work.[1] For there are two ways of righteousness toward God. There is the man who is fighting so mightily and without ceasing against the passions that he is esteemed wholly worthy to escape and be set free from their slavery before his end. Then there is another one who, on the one hand, is working courageously with all his strength and hates the passions and is anxiously laboring in everything **[R 117]** to be esteemed worthy of the same freedom. Although he has not yet completely corrected [his ways], he falls asleep, holding [on] to the same cheerfulness. On the day of judgment the just Judge[2] will hold this one in the same rank with the first and will esteem [him] worthy of equal rewards."[3]

(§156) Again, the blessed one explained also the following to each of them with freedom [of speech], with condescension for the advance of hope and of trust in God, while saying, "All the commandments of the Lord were given to every person, to pagans and to barbarians, to men and to women, to slaves and to the freeborn, to monks and to laypeople.[4] Our Lord made this known when he sent out the disciples for preaching, commanding and saying to them, 'Go, make disciples [of] all peoples, baptizing them in the name of the Father and of the Son and of the Holy Spirit, and teaching them to keep all these [things] that I have commanded you,'[5] not that they should keep some and not others, but 'all these [things] that I have commanded you.' For the only difference between monks and laypeople is the promise of virginity and of self-control.[6] Nevertheless, because our generation has slid into great weakness and negligence,[7] I have faith in the Lord that every Christian, if he is careful to keep these three commandments and does [them] rightly in cheerfulness, will not be rejected from the mercies of our Lord nor from eternal good [things].[8] Those

[7] The following paragraph and a half is also found in a slightly modified form in nineteenth-century manuscripts. See MS Mingana 4, fols. 107v-108r (A. Mingana, *Syriac and Garshūni Manuscripts* [vol. 1 of *Catalogue of the Mingana Collection of Manuscripts*; Cambridge: Heffer & Sons, 1933], 14) and MS Harvard Syriac 99, fols. 154r-155r.

[8] Despite a seemingly radical outlook and judgment of the situation in which he found himself, Peter ultimately proposed a moderate view, one of trust in God's mercy, at this instance.

ܬܠܬܐ ܦܪ̈ܨܘܦܐ ܗܠܝܢ ܐܝܬܝܗܘܢ. ܘܡܛܠܗܢܐ: ܕܢܗܘܐ ܐܢܫ ܠܗ
ܗܝܡܢܘܬܐ ܬܪܝܨܬ ܫܘܒܚܐ. ܗܕܐ ܓܝܪ ܐܝܬܝܗ̇ ܫܬܐܣܬܐ ܕܝ̈ܠܢ
ܘܦܘܪܩܢ. ܟܠܗ̇ ܗܝܡܢܘܬܐ ܓܝܪ ܠܐ ܡܫܟܚܐ ܕܢܫܦܪ ܠܐܠܗܐ ܐܝܟ
ܕܟܬܝܒ. [R 118] ܕܬܪ̈ܬܝܢ: ܕܢܡܠܠ ܫܪܪܐ ܡܢ ܠܒܐ ܘܡܢ ܠܫܢܐ. ܟܬܝܒ
ܓܝܪ: ܕܬܘܒܕ ܠܟܠܗܘܢ ܗܠܝܢ ܕܡܡܠܠܝܢ ܕܓܠܘܬܐ. ܘܕܓܠܘܬܐ ܡܢ
ܐܟܠܩܪܨܐ ܐܝܬܝܗ̇ ܘܬܘܒ. ܡܠܠܘ ܫܪܪܐ ܟܠ ܐܢܫ ܠܘܬ ܩܪܝܒܗ. ܗ̇ܘ
ܕܝܢ ܕܬܠܬܐ ܐܝܬܘܗܝ: ܕܡܫܡܠܝܐ ܘܕܟܝܐ ܢܛܪ ܦܓܪܐ: ܡܢ ܓܐܬܐ
ܕܙܢܝܘܬܐ ܘܕܫܪܝܚܘܬܐ. ܟܬܝܒ ܓܝܪ ܒܕܝܐܬܝܩܝ ܗ̇ ܥܬܝܩܬܐ: ܗ̣ܘܘ
ܩܕܝܫܐ: ܡܛܠ ܕܐܢܐ ܩܕܝܫܐ ܐܢܐ. ܒܫܪܒܬܐ ܕܝܢ ܗ̇ܝ ܕܟܬܒ̈ܝ ܫ̈ܠܝܚܐ:
ܪܕܘ ܒܬܪ ܫܠܡܐ ܥܡ ܟܠܢܫ. ܘܒܬܪ ܩܕܝܫܘܬܐ ܗ̇ܝ ܕܒܠܥܕܝܗ̇ ܠܐ
ܐܢܫ ܚܙܐ ܠܐܠܗܐ. ܘܬܘܒ. ܗܢܐ ܓܝܪ ܐܝܬܘܗܝ ܨܒܝܢܐ ܕܐܠܗܐ
ܩܕܝܫܘܬܐ ܕܝܠܟܘܢ. ܐܪܚܩܘ ܡܢ ܙܢܝܘܬܐ ܘܢܕܥ ܟܠܢܫ ܡܢܟܘܢ:
ܕܠܡܐܢܐ ܕܝܠܗ ܢܩܢܐ ܒܩܕܝܫܘܬܐ ܘܒܐܝܩܪܐ. ܘܠܐ ܒܚܫ̈ܐ ܕܪ̈ܓܬܐ:
ܐܝܟ ܥܡ̈ܡܐ ܗܠܝܢ ܕܠܐ ܝܕܥܝܢ ܠܐܠܗܐ. ܘܗܠܝܢ ܐܡܪ ܐܢܐ: ܠܐ
ܕܡܢ ܟܠܦܪܘܣ ܕܝܐܐ ܢܗܘܐ ܟܠ ܒܪܢܫܝܐ. ܠܘ ܓܝܪ ܟܠܢܫ ܚܙܐ ܠܗ̇
ܠܡܠܬܐ ܗܕܐ. ܐܝܟܢܐ ܕܐܦ ܗ̣ܘ ܡܪܢ ܐܡܪ. ܐܠܐ ܗ̇ܘ ܕܠܐ
ܡܫܟܚ ܕܢܣܒܗ̇: ܢܣܒ ܐܝܬܝܗ̇ ܐܝܟ ܡܘܗܒܬܐ ܕܐܠܗܐ. ܡܝܩܪ ܗ̣ܘ
ܓܝܪ ܙܘܘܓܐ ܒܟܠ. ܘܥܪܣܐ ܕܟܝܐ. ܘܬܘܒ. ܡܛܠ ܙܢܝܘܬܐ: ܟܠ ܐܢܫ
ܠܐܢܬܬܗ ܢܐܚܘܕ. ܘܟܠܚܕܐ ܠܓܒܪܐ ܕܝܠܗ̇ ܬܐܚܘܕ. ܟܕ ܢܛܪܝܢ
ܐܢܘܢ ܢܡܘܣܐ: ܡܢ ܟܠ ܣܘܛܢܝܐ ܐܚܪܢܐ ܠܐ ܢܬܗܦܟܐ. ܠܒ̈ܢܝܐ
ܕܝܢ ܘܠܒ̈ܢܬܐ ܕܝܗܒ ܐܠܗܐ.

(§157) ܗܠܝܢ ܐܝܬܝܗܘܢ ܬܠܬܐ ܦܪ̈ܨܘܦܐ: ܕܠܗܘܢ ܡܦܣ ܐܢܐ ܕܟܠ
ܒܪܢܫܝܐ ܢܛܪ ܒܝܚܝܕܘܬܐ. ܘܗ̇ܘ ܕܢܛܪ ܗܠܝܢ ܐܢܐ [R 119] ܡܩܒܠ
ܐܢܐ ܦܪܨܘܦܗ: ܟܕ ܣܗܕ ܐܢܐ ܒܬܘܗܡܐ ܕܠܐ ܚܘܣ ܕܒ̈ܝܬܗܘܢ
ܕܐܠܗܐ. ܐܠܐ ܐܡܪ ܐܢܐ: ܘܡܚܝܢܐ ܐܚܪܢ ܕܐܫܬܪܪܬ ܒܟܠܗܘܢ:
ܘܐܬܚܪܬܠܗ ܒܚܝܠܐ ܕܡܠܟܘܬܐ. ܡܢ ܗܫܐ ܢܚܕܐ ܫܦܝܪܐ: ܘܠܐ

1 See Heb 11:6.

2 Ps 5:7.

3 John 8:44.

4 Eph 4:25.

5 Lev 19:2.

6 By referring to "apostles" in the plural, Rufus here indicates that he counted Paul among the apostles.

7 Heb 12:14.

three commandments are these: First, that he has the orthodox faith, for this is the foundation of our life and of our salvation. For, 'Without faith it is not possible that we should please God,'[1] as it is written. **[R 118]** Second, that he should speak the truth from [his] heart and from [his] tongue, for it is written, 'You will destroy all these who are speaking a lie,'[2] and, 'The lie is from the devil,'[3] and again, 'Speak the truth, every one to his neighbor.'[4] The third, however, is that he should keep the body spotless and pure from the filth of fornication and lasciviousness. For it is written, on the one hand, in the Old Testament, 'Be holy, because I am holy,'[5] [and], on the other hand, in the New [Testament] [is written] by the hand of the apostles,[6] 'Pursue peace with everyone and holiness, without which no one is seeing God,'[7] and again, 'For this is the will of God, your holiness. Separate from fornication, and let everyone among you know [how] to possess his vessel in holiness and in honor, and not in shameful passions, like these peoples who do not know God.'[8] I am saying these [things] not that every Christian by all means should become a monk. For not everyone comprehends this word, as also our Lord himself said.[9] But let the one who cannot restrain himself[10] take a wife according to the law of God, for 'marriage is honorable in everything, and the [marriage] bed is pure,'[11] and again, 'Because of fornication, every man shall hold to his [own] wife, and every [woman] shall hold to her husband,'[12] while you keep yourselves from all other unlawful intercourse. But 'fornicators and adulterers, God will judge.'[13]

(§157) "These are the three commandments that I instruct every Christian to keep diligently. The one who keeps them, I **[R 119]** guarantee his salvation, taking into account the boundless depth of the mercies of God. If someone should say, 'And what shall I do, [I] who fell [into sin] in my youth and wallowed in the

[8] 1 Thess 4:3–5. "Holiness (Syriac ܩܕܝܫܘܬܐ)" is here employed in its technical, ascetic sense of marital continence.

[9] Matt 19:11.

[10] 1 Cor 7:9.

[11] Heb 13:4.

[12] 1 Cor 7:2.

[13] Heb 13:4.

ܡܛܠ ܒܗܢ ܕܝܢ ܒܗܝܢ ܢܬܬܟܠ. ܘܐܝܟܐ ܗ̇ܘܐ ܐܝܟ ܫ̇ܡܥܘܢܐ
ܕܦܘܪܩܢܗ ܕܗܢܐ: ܐܦ ܗ̣ܘ ܕܒܕܡܐ ܠܫܪܬܐ ܗܢܐ ܦܘܠܚܢܐ ܠܟܠܐ
ܢܫܘܐ. ܟܠܝܒ ܓܒܪ ܕܗ̇ܘ ܕܡܫܟܚܪ ܒܕܡܐ ܠܫܪܬܐ ܗܢܐ ܢܬܦܪܩ.
ܘܐܝܟ ܕܐܡܝܢܬܐ ܗܪ̈ܡܝܢܝܢ ܕ̈ܡܒܪܢܐ ܠܡܗܝܡܢܘܬܐ ܘܠܟܘܠܗܐ:
ܠܘܬ ܗ̇ܝ ܕܬܟܘܠܢ. ܗܕܝܢܐ ܗܘܫܐ ܐܡܝܢܐ ܗܪ̈ܡܝܢܝܢ ܕ̈ܒܪܐ
ܠܟܐܢܘܬܐ: ܠܘܬ ܩܕܝܫܘܬܐ. ܗܐ ܗܕܐ ܐܝܬܝܗ̇ ܬܝܒܘܬܐ: ܘܗܝ
ܒܢ̈ܝܐ ܕܬܝܒܘܬܐ.

(§158) ܟܕ ܗܠܝܢ ܘܕܐܝܟ ܗܠܝܢ ܡܠܠ ܠܐܚ̈ܐ: ܘܒܝܢܐ ܐܝܟ ܐܝܟܢܐ ܘܐܡܪ
ܐܝܟ ܠܘܬ ܦܘܠܚܢܐ ܕܬܝܒܘܬܐ: ܘܠܘܬ ܐܘܪܚܐ ܕܫ̈ܢܝܐ ܕܠܒܠܗ
ܢܦܩ ܐܝܟ. ܟܕ ܒܥܐ ܡܢ ܬܡܢ. ܐܬܐ ܠܦܛܠܡܐܝܕܐ. ܘܟܕ
ܐܬܦܢܝ ܬܡܢ ܡܢ ܗܪܘܢ[1] ܟܦܪܐ ܡܗܝܡܢܬܐ: ܘܐܘܪܬܕܘܟܣܐ
ܘܢܚܡ ܩܕܝܫܐ: ܗ̇ܘ ܕܟܠ ܡ̇ܠܝܚܘܬܐ ܕܬܡܢ ܡܢܗ ܗܘܐ: ܘܡܢܟܘܗ
ܘܠܒܝܬܗ: ܘܐܪܬܚ ܠܠܒܗ ܒܪܚܡܬܐ ܐܠܗܝܬܐ. ܟܕ ܥܒܪ ܠܨܘܪܐ.
ܘܗܘܢܐ ܐܬܕܒܩ ܒܗܘܟܐ ܕܡܫܝܚܐ ܗ̇ܘ ܡܗܝܡܢܐ ܗܪܘܢ. ܐܝܟܢܐ
ܕܬܪ ܘܒܢܐ: ܢܛܪܐ ܘܬܪ̈ܝܢܐ ܘܬܐܓܘܪܬܐ ܕܗܢܐ ܥܠܡܐ: ܘܢܫܒܘܩ
ܒܢ̈ܝܐ ܘܡܩܒܪܢܐ ܘܟܠ ܕܐܝܬ ܠܗ. ܘܢܩܒܠ ܨܠܝܒܗ ܕܡܫܝܚܐ: ܘܢܪܗܛ
ܠܗܘܪܢܐ ܕܐܪ̈ܚܡ ܟܪܒܪܐ ܩܕܝܫܐ. ܘܠܐܣܟܝܡܗ ܢܫܬܘܐ.
ܘܡܫܝܚܐ ܒܐܘܪܚܐ ܦܣܝܩܬܐ ܢܪܕܐ: ܗ̇ܝ ܕܡܫܠܡܐ ܠܫܡܝܐ.

(§159) ܟܕ ܗܟܝܠ ܐܬܐ ܠܨܘܪܐ. [R 120] ܐܫܬܘܕܥ ܠܟܠܗܘܢ ܐܢܫܐ
ܒܢ̈ܝ ܡܕܝܢܬܐ ܕܫܡܥܝܢ ܠܟܐܢܘܬܗ. ܗܠܝܢ ܕܝܢ ܡܟܠ ܠܝ. ܒܗ ܒܠܚܘܕ
ܚܕܘܬܐ ܘܪܘܙܐ ܒܐܪܥܐ ܙܟܐ ܫܟܠܘ ܒܡܐܬܝܬܗ ܕܩܕܝܫܐ ܟܕ.

[1] MS B reads ܐܗܪܘܢ.

[2] Literally, "hour."

[3] See also *Vit. Pet.* §§83–84 (R 59), where Peter sees the souls of those slaughtered at the hands of the Roman soldiers and the comment is made that even those who come to confess only at the very end of their life will be able to enter heaven.

[4] See Mark 13:13; Matt 24:13.

[5] See Rom 6:19.

[6] I.e., Akko. See Tsafrir, Di Segni, and Green, *Tabula Imperii Romani*, 204–5.

[7] The Syriac may render the Greek ἐδήχθη, for which Raabe (112 n. 1) refers to Plato, *Symp.* 218a: πληγεὶς τε καὶ δηχθεὶς ὑπὸ τῶν ἐν φιλοσοφίᾳ

mud of defilement?' From this moment[2] he shall make a [new] beginning and no longer wallow in these same [things]. I stand as a guarantee for that one's salvation, if he shows this good work until the end. For it is written, 'He who endures until the end[3] will be saved,'[4] and 'As you presented your limbs [as] servants to defilement and to iniquity to work iniquity, so at this hour present your limbs [as] servants of righteousness for holiness.'[5] Behold, this is repentance, and this is the work of repentance."

(§158) When he had spoken these and [words] like these to the brethren and had consoled them and aroused them to the work of repentance and had exhorted them to the way of eternal life, he passed from there and came to Ptolemaïs.[6] When he was received there by Aaron, a believing orthodox man and a lover of the saints who was the superintendent of the salt-pan there, he blessed him and his house. [Having] inflamed his heart with divine love, he passed on to Caesarea. This believing Aaron was so pricked by the love of Christ[7] that after a while he cast [off] the possessions and the business of this world and left [his] children and [his] dwelling [place] and everything he had,[8] and taking up the cross of Christ he ran to a monastery of some holy men and was found worthy of their habit. He journeyed with them on the blessed way that leads to heaven.

(§159) When we came to Caesarea, **[R 120]** we found all the brethren, our fellow-believers, expecting our arrival. When these had received us full of joy and exultation, they celebrated a great feast at the coming of the saint, rising early every day and coming

λόγων: "struck and bitten by philosophical discourses." However, the underlying Greek verb, δάκνω, is typically used to refer to snake bites, as the passage cited from the *Symposium* illustrates. Figuratively it has a negative connotation, as in Gal 5:15. A more likely term for "prick" underlying the Syriac might be κατανύσσομαι. This verb renders the "pricked heart" of Ps 108:16 and Acts 2:37; note also the use of the word "heart" in the preceding line. We gratefully acknowledge this contribution from John Fitzgerald.

8 Rabbula of Edessa displays the same behavior. See *Life of Rabbula* (Overbeck, 166).

ܡܦܪ̈ܕܝܢ ܒܟܠܗܘܢ ܘܡܬܟܢܫܝܢ ܠܘܬܗ܂ ܘܡ̈ܠܘܗܝ، ܡܬܠܡܕܢܘܬܐ ܥ̈ܒܕܝܢ
ܘܡܫܬ̈ܪܪܝܢ܂ ܘܠܡܘܗܒܬܐ ܕܐܝܕܗ̇ ܘܠܫܘܬܦܘܬܐ ܡܫܬܘܬܦܝܢ.

(§160) ܐܝܬ ܕܝܢ ܩܘܪܝܐ ܕܡܬܩܪܝܐ ܐܦܬܘܪܝܐ: ܡܢ ܬܚܘܡܐ ܠܡܕܝܢܬܐ ܒܠ ܬܪ̈ܥܣܪ ܡ̈ܝܠܝܢ܂ ܘܒܗ̇ ܐܝܬ ܬܪ̈ܝܢ ܒܥܘܡܪ̈ܐ ܕܐܘܪܬܕܘܟܣܘ. ܚܕ ܡܢ ܕܓܒܪ̈ܐ܂ ܐܚܪܢܐ ܕܝܢ ܕܢ̈ܫܐ. ܠܗܢ ܕܝܢ ܕܝܪܐ ܡܢ [ܕ]ܗܘ̇ ܕܓܒܪ̈ܐ ܫܡܗ ܗ̇ܘܐ ܒܪܘܦܝܢܘܣ. ܗܢܐ ܩܕܝܫܐ ܘܒܗܘܢ ܡܬܒܥܒܥܐ. ܘܕܡܢ ܠܠܡܘܬܗ̇ ܒܬܠܘܬܐ ܐܝܟ. ܘܠܕܝܪܐ ܕܡܫܝܚܘܬܐ ܡܢ ܕܝܠܗ ܩܪ̈ܝܒܐ ܐܝܬܘ، ܘܦܫܟ ܐܝܬܘܗܝ، ܗܘܐ ܪ̈ܚܡܐ ܫܬܝܬܐ ܕܐܝܟܐ ܦܠܓܘܣ ܐܦܣܩܘܦܐ ܘܣܗܕܐ. ܕܗ̇ܘ ܕܝܢ ܕܢ̈ܫܐ ܐܝܬܝܗ̇ ܗܘܬ ܪܝܫܐ ܠܒܢ̈ܝܬܐ ܗܕܝܢܐ. ܕܐܝܬܝܗ̇ ܗܘܬ ܒܪܬ ܚܬܗ ܕܓܪܓܘܪܝܘܣ ܪܝܫ ܕܝܪܐ ܕܗܘ̇ ܒܥܘܡܪܐ ܕܓܒܪ̈ܐ. ܕܠܘܬܗ̇ ܗܘ̣ܝ، ܐܘܓܝܢܐ ܕܡܢ ܨܘܪ: ܗܿ، ܕܡܕܝܢܬܐ ܐܡܝܪܬܐ ܒܪ ܐܬܓܠܣܬ ܘܐܬܦܟܠܬ: ܘܬܘܒ ܐܣܬܪܬ ܘܥܒܠܬ ܐܣܟܡܐ ܩܕܝܫܐ. ܒܬܪ ܒܥܘܕܪܗ ܕܦܠܓܝܘܣ ܩܕܝܫܐ. ܐܫܬܘܕܝܬ ܠܐܒܘܢ ܘܠܬܠܡܝܕܘܬܐ.

(§161) ܟܕ ܗܟܝܠ ܒܗܠܝܢ ܐܬܝܢ ܗܘܘ ܒܦܠܣܛܝܢܐ: ܘܒܠܟ ܐܒܐ ܒܪܘܦܝܢܘܣ ܕܒܠܟ ܗܘ̣ ܠܡܕܝܢܬܐ: ܘܠܘܬܗ ܐܬܐ ܘܩܒܠܗ. ܒܬܪ ܡܛܠ ܟܕ ܢܦܩ ܠܝ܂ ܒܪܡܫܐ ܕܐܬܝܢ ܠܡܕܝܢܬܐ. ܘܟܕ ܦܓܥܬܗ ܐܬܟܫܦ ܠܗ ܘܐܦܝܣܗ܂ ܫܐܠܗ ܠܗ ܠܩܕܝܫܐ ܘܐܝܬܝܗ ܠܒܝܬܗ ܟܕ ܢܓܗ ܐܚܕܐ ܘܬܪܘ. ܘܗܟܢܐ [R 121] ܐܬܬܢܝܚܘ ܒܒܝܬܐ ܕܢ̈ܕܪܐ. ܐܚܝܢܐ ܕܢܠܒܘܟ ܠܝ ܬܘܒ ܐܪܒܥܐ ܝ̈ܘܡܝܢ.

(§162) ܟܕ ܫܠܡܝܢ ܕܝܢ ܗܟܝܠ ܠܘܬܗ: ܠܥܐܕܐ ܪܒܐ ܘܦܘܪܩܢܐ ܕܦܨܚܐ ܩܕܝܫܐ ܘܕܦܢܛܩܘܣܛܐ ܩܕܝܫܬܐ܂ ܢܦܩ ܘܐܬܐ ܠܐܘܪܫܠܡ ܕܥܠ ܗܦܟ ܢܟܐ. ܟܕ ܙܘܥܐ ܡܗܕܝܢܐ ܐܦ ܠܗܠܝܢ ܦܪܐ ܗܘܐ ܠܗ ܠܩܕܝܫܐ: ܠܘܬ ܫܘܒܚܐ ܘܦܘܪܩܢܐ ܕܢܩ̈ܫܬܐ܂ ܘܠܟܘܕܪ̈ܐ ܕܗ̇ܘܢ ܕܒܚ̈ܝܢ ܒܗ̇، ܡܕܝܢܬܐ. ܐܝܟܢܐ ܕܟܕ ܐܬܬܦܝܣ ܗ̇ܘ ܗܟܢܐ ܡܢ

[1] One gets the impression that anti-Chalcedonians in Caesarea did not live together in one single house but rather spread out throughout the city.

[2] The reference here might be both to social exchange with Peter and to the reception of the Eucharist from Peter's hand. In the latter case, one has here a further example of how anti-Chalcedonians throughout Syria-Palestine restricted their eucharistic participation to insiders within the movement. See, e.g., *Pler.* 58, 70, 71, 78, and 86.

[3] See Clermont-Ganneau, "Sur quelques localités de Palestine," 18–20.

together in his [presence],[1] listening and being strengthened by his burning words, [and] being esteemed worthy of a blessing from him and of communion [with him].[2]

(§160) There is a village called Aphthoria,[3] about twelve miles south of the city. In it are two monasteries of the orthodox, one of men, the other of women. The abbot [of] the men's [monastery] had the name Gregory, a holy, ascetic, and humble old man and one who from his boyhood loved virginity. He had been esteemed worthy of the rank of the priesthood from early on and was a very faithful friend of Abba Peter the bishop and beloved [by him]. The head of the women's [monastery] was the blessed Sabina, who was the daughter of the sister of Gregory,[4] the abbot of the men's monastery, at whose [place][5] also the aforementioned Eugenia from Tyre, when she had taken refuge and had been received [there], was tonsured and received the holy habit. After the departure [from this world] of the blessed Sabina, she was esteemed worthy of the honor and the leadership [of the monastery].

(§161) While we were still in Ptolemaïs, Abba Gregory learned that the blessed one had returned, so he came there and received him. He then remained attached to us until we came to Caesarea. When he had earnestly entreated him with many [supplications] and had persuaded him, he took the saint and brought him to his monastery, being both glad and exulting. They were **[R 121]** so pleased with each other's converse that he kept us there for four months.

(§162) When we had thus celebrated at his [place] the great and saving feast of holy Pascha and of holy Pentecost,[6] we went out and came to Ashdod[7] at the seashore, because the guiding Spirit was also calling the saint there for the deliverance and salvation of souls and for the benefit of those who were dwelling in this

[4] For other instances of promotion of anti-Chalcedonian structures and life via family connections, see *Vit. Pet.* §137 (R 100–101).

[5] The referent is Sabina and her monastery.

[6] Note how both Pascha and Pentecost are recurring themes in the *Vita*, functioning as markers of time.

[7] See Tsafrir, Di Segni, and Green, *Tabula Imperii Romani*, 72. For a fortress located immediately at the seashore, see Jacob Kaplan, "Ashdod-Yam," *NEAEHL* 1:102–3.

ܦܓܥܬܐ: ܕܟܠܗ ܡܕܝܢܬܐ ܢܚܙܐ. ܟܕ ܠܐ ܐܬܬܦܝܣ. ܒܡܘܪܝܘܢ
ܕܩܝܡ ܥܠ ܣܦܪ ܝܡܐ ܪܒܐ. ܕܒܗܬܐ ܐܠܝܨܬܐ ܘܒܚܣܝܪܘܬܐ: ܘܕܠܐ ܫܕ.
ܢܣܟܐ ܦܘܪܢܣܐ ܐܝܬ ܒܗ. ܒܒܝܬ ܡܥܪ̈ܬܐ ܓܒܪ ܕܕܐܝܟ ܗܠܝܢ ܫܕܐ
ܗܘܐ ܗ̇ܘ ܠܦܘܢܐ: ܐܝܟ ܐܟܣܢܝܐ ܘܬܘܬܒܐ.

(§163) ܟܕ ܫܠܡܘ ܗܟܝܠ ܟܠܗܘܢ ܝܘ̈ܡܘܗܝ: ܗ̇ܢܘܢ ܕܒܐܣܩܠܘܢܝܐ
ܘܒܓܐܙܐ ܘܒܡܝܘܡܐ: ܘܕܐܬܪ̈ܘܬܐ ܕܣܕܪ̈ܝܗܘܢ: ܐܬܬܟܢܫܘ ܘܐܬܘ
ܠܘܬܗ ܕܩܕܝܫܐ: ܟܕ ܡܣܬܪܗܒܝܢ ܕܢܩܒܠܘܢ ܠܒܘܪܟܐ ܕܝܠܗ. ܘܢܚܙܘܢܝܗ
ܘܢܬܒܣܡܘܢ ܕܕܝܢܐ ܐܠܗܝܐ. ܘܕܠܒܝܒܐ ܡܫܟܚܐ ܡܢ ܡܠܦܢܘܬܗ
ܘܡܘܕܥܬܗ ܘܡܬܦܣܬܗ ܢܦܩܘܢ ܘܡܬܒܠܝܢ. ܘܟܕ ܒܟܠܗ ܕܐܝܟ
ܗܢ ܕܚܠܬܐ ܐܟܚܕܐ ܘܐܬܟܢܫܘ: ܠܕܐܝܟ ܗܕܐ ܕܒܗܬܐ ܐܠܝܨܬܐ
ܘܒܚܣܝܪܘܬܐ ܐܝܟ ܗ̇ܘ ܕܒܥܠ ܡܠܟܘܬܐ ܟܚܢ̈ܝܢ ܗܘܝܢ: ܡܚܝܠܐ
ܦܓܥܬܐ ܘܣܓܝܐܬ ܠܟܠܗܘܢ ܡܦܩܢܝܢ ܗܘܝܢ: ܟܕ ܒܟܝܢ ܠܐ
ܡܬܐܠܨܝܢ ܗܘܘ. ܟܕ ܡܠܬܐ ܐܠܗܝܬܐ ܡܬܡܠܠܐ ܗܘܬ ܐܦ
ܠܗܝܢ. ܟܕ ܡ̈ܠܬܗ ܕܩܕܝܫܐ: ܕܒܐܘܠܨܢܐ ܐܪܘܝܬ ܠܝ.

(§164) ܟܕ ܟܠܗܘܢ ܡܢܦܩܝܢ ܘܡܦܝܣܝܢ: ܕܠܐܬܪܐ ܕܓܐܙܐ ܢܐܬܐ ܢܠܘܦ:
ܘܠܕܒ̈ܝܬܐ ܗܠܝܢ [R 122] ܕܒܗܝܢ ܡܟܝܢ ܗܘܐ ܡܕܡܐܢܬ ܕܢܚܙܐ
ܟܥܠܝܐ. ܦܣܩ ܘܠܚܕܐ ܐܫܠܝ. ܕܠܐ ܡܚܝܠ ܡܛܠ ܗܕܐ ܢܣܩܘܢܗ̇.
ܕܡܢ ܟܕܘ ܦܩܕ ܗܘܐ ܢܬܐ ܟܐܘܣ: ܕܒܙܒ ܢܡܟܐ ܕܟܘܕܝܢܗ. ܘܟܠܗܘܢ
ܚܒܪ ܗܘܐ ܘܢܦܩ. ܕܟܐܟܣܢܝܐ ܢܬܡܠܐ. ܘܟܠܟܠ ܕܐܟܣܢܝܘܬܐ
ܛܥܬܐ ܘܒܗ ܟܫܘܠܛܐ ܢܛܘܪ. ܘܫܡܛܘܬܐ ܟܕܡܐ ܠܗܕܐ ܢܚܝ. ܟܕ
ܡܬܕܡܐ ܟܡܠܟ. ܘܡܫܠܐ ܠܫܡܫܢܐ ܘܐܝܣܪܐ ܕܡܢ ܟܝܢܫܐ.

(§165) ܡܢ ܗܪܟܐ ܡܚܝܠ ܬܘܒ ܦܬܪܐ ܠܝ: ܕܠܘܬ ܫܘܠܡܐ ܠܦܘܬܝܐ
ܘܫܟܝܢܬܐ ܕܡܛܠܬܗ ܢܦܩܝܢܢ ܠܚܠܬܐ. ܐܝܟܢܐ ܕܐܦ ܒܗܕܐ
ܢܐܠܦ: ܕܐܝܟܢܐ ܘܒܡܢܐ ܫܘܠܡܐ ܡܫܒܚ ܐܠܗܐ ܠܗܠܝܢ ܕܡܫܒܚܝܢ
ܠܗ. ܟܕ ܛܒ ܡܠܠ ܥܒ̈ܕܘܗܝ ܡܢ ܗܠܝܢ ܕܠܗ. ܒܗܠܝܢ ܕܩ̈ܕܝܫܝܢ
ܐܡܪ̈ܝܢ ܐܬܒܣܡܘ. ܗ̇ܝ ܓܝܪ ܕܢܗܘܐ ܕܟܠܗܝܢ ܢܬܟܬܒ: ܕܕܡܝܐ

[1] Peter defined his ascetic existence as that of a permanent foreigner to the world. For a discussion, see Horn, *Asceticism and Christological Controversy*, 230 *et passim*.

[2] See Job 36:16; Ps 4:2.

[3] Other possible translations include "in exile" or "on travel."

[4] This expression captures into one the two notions of martyrdom and pilgrimage, allowing Rufus to present Peter the permanent pilgrim and traveler as one equal to the martyrs. For a discussion of this motif, see Horn, "Weaving

city. There the old man, although he was asked by many to dwell inside the city, since he was not [so] persuaded lodged in a depot set up at the seashore, a narrow and despicable place and without any bodily comfort. For in lodgings like these the blessed one rejoiced, as [one who is] a stranger and a foreigner.[1]

(§163) Now when all his acquaintances, those in Ashkelon and in Gaza and in Maiuma and [those] of the surrounding regions, learned [about this], they gathered together and came to the saint, hastening to receive their father, both the light and the lamp of the fear of God, and to be saturated and filled for a long time from his teaching and his blessing and his communion. When so many people ran together and were assembled, we were dwelling in such a narrow and despicable place as if it were a royal palace, so joyfully and gladly were we receiving all of them, not finding ourselves constricted in any way, because the divine word was fulfilled also with us through the prayers of the saint, "In narrow places you gave space to me."[2]

(§164) When they were all urging and persuading [him] to return to the region of Gaza and to the places **[R 122]** in which he was formerly accustomed to dwell in peace, he cut [them] off and entirely rejected that we should importune him any longer about this that he already had foreseen in the Spirit: that the day of his departure [from this world] was near. He painstakingly did all these [things] so that he would be perfected in a foreign land[3] and also at the end [of his life] weave the crown of a good pilgrimage,[4] loving contempt so much as to become like our Lord[5] and despising glory and honor from men.

(§165) Now from here on, time calls us to turn the discourse to [his] blessed demise and its narration, so that in this we may learn how even at the end God glorifies those who glorify him, although we mentioned very briefly [only] a few matters[6] concerning his demise in what has been already said. For that we would

the Pilgrim's Crown"; eadem, *Asceticism and Christological Controversy*, 271–73.

[5] Here the author employs the motif of the imitation of Christ as a driving force for the saint's behavior.

[6] The Syriac may render the Greek ὀλίγα καὶ μικρά (Raabe, 114 n. 1).

ܐܬܬܢܝܗ̇܂ ܠܗ̇ܝ ܕܐܝܟ ܚܝܒܐ ܕܒܬܫܡܫܬܐ ܘܪ̈ܘܪܒܐ ܕܢܫܐ ܒܗ. ܡܗ̇ܝܡܢ
ܢܒ̣ܙܐ܂ ܐܘ ܕܠܛ̈ܠܠܐ ܢܦܠܐ܂ ܐܝܟ ܕܐܦ ܒܥܘܪܐ ܐܪܥܐ ܐܡܪܝܢ܂

(§166) ܒܗ ܐܬܝܡ ܡܚܠ ܒܡܘܪܝܐ ܗ̇ܘ ܕܐܡܪܬ ܕܐܘܦܠܘܣ ܡܒܝܬܐ
ܕܚܠ ܢ. ܒܫܢܐ܂ ܓܒܪ ܕܝܢ ܗ̇ܢܐ ܠܗܒܢܐ ܒܟܘܪ̈ܗܢܐ ܦܓܪܢܐ ܢܦܠ
ܐܡܝܢܐ ܕܐܦ ܕܢܬܬܢܝܚ ܢܒܥܐ. ܒܗ ܗܘܐ ܢܟܒ ܐܠܝܐ ܟܘܪ̈ܗܢܐ ܗ̇ܘ
ܕܐܡܪܝܢ: ܗ̇ܘ ܕܐܬܘܬܗ̇ܝ ܗܘܐ ܡܗܝܡܢܐ ܕܐܘܕܘܩܝܐ ܡܠܟܬܐ ܘܪܒ
ܒܝܬܐ. ܗܘܐ ܙܒܢ ܒܐܘܪܫܠܡ܂ ܚܝܦ ܕܢܦܩ ܠܘܬܗ. ܕܒܥܐ ܗܘܐ ܙܒܢ
ܗܘܐ ܓܝܪ ܗܘ ܡܕܝܢ ܡܫܒܚܐ ܗܘܐ ܠܦܘܠܚܢܗ. ܘܒܗ ܐܫܟܚܗ
ܕܢܦܩ ܡܢ ܒܘܪ̈ܗܢܐ܂ ܒܗ ܦܓܥ ܐܬܟܫܦ ܠܗ ܐܦܝܣܗ܂ ܕܢܬܠܦ ܗ̇ܘ
ܒܝܬ ܡܫܪܝܐ. ܡܛܠ ܕܠܐ ܠܢܦܫܐ [R 123] ܐܬܘܗܝ ܗܘܐ ܠܓܒܪ
ܘܒܗܝܠܐ. ܘܟܠܐ ܡܠܦܢܘܬܐ ܘܒܐܠܝܨܘܬܐ܂ ܘܟܠܐ ܡܫܝܢܘܬܐ
ܕܐܐܪ̈ܘܦ ܒܫܡ ܠܫܘܬܐ. ܡܢ ܒܗ ܓܒܪ ܐܬܘܗܝ ܗܘܐ ܡܚܒܠ ܘܒܢܐ
ܕܬܫ̈ܪܝܬܐ. ܡܢ ܟܠܗ̇ ܕܒܟܢ ܒܐܕܐ ܕܐܢܘܫܐ ܕܝ̈ܠܕܐ ܫܓܝܐܐ. ܘܒܗ
ܫܠܡܦ ܐܚܒܪܗ ܠܗ̇ܘ ܕܡܬܐܡܪ ܡܫܘܪܐ ܕܢܒܝܢ ܡܒܢܬܐ܂ ܕܚܠ ܢ.
ܒܟܢܐ ܐܬܘܗܝ، ܘܒܕܘܒܬܐ ܡܫܝܢܬܐ܂ ܘܦܩܕ ܠܢܫܡ ܠܡܫܠܡܘܬܗ
ܕܡܕܝܢܐ. ܘܗܘܐ ܟܒܪ܂ ܐܝܟ ܡ̇ܢ ܕܐܝܬ ܠܗ ܦܐܪܗܣܝܐ ܘܒܥܘܬܬܐ
ܠܘܬ ܐܦܛܪܘܦܐ ܡܠܟܬ̈ܐ܂ ܘܫܠܝܛܢܐ ܕܗ̇ܘ ܒܝܬ ܡܫܪܝܐ. ܡܛܠ
ܕܕܡܠܟܘܬܐ ܗܘܐ܂ ܘܒܝܬ ܡܚܕܪܐ ܗܘܐ ܒܝܕ ܕܐܘܕܘܩܝܐ ܡܠܟܬܐ.
ܗ̇ܢܐ ܓܒܪ ܒܗ ܡܢ ܒܘܪ̈ܗܢܐ ܦܓܪ̈ܢܐ ܡܫܚܐܢܬ ܡܬܬܟܒܐ
ܗܘܬ: ܡܠܒܫܗ ܐܣܘ̈ܬܐ ܕܕܒܘܬܐ ܕܕܐܝܟ ܗܕܐ ܬܒܥܐ܂ ܕܒܗ̇ ܒܗ

1 See above, *Vit. Pet.* §21 (R 13).

2 The Syriac transliterates the Greek διαθήκη (Raabe, 114 n. 2). Most people did not think about drafting a will before they fell seriously ill, were in or had overcome a life-threatening danger, or knew they were lying on their deathbeed. For a discussion of deathbed testation, see John T. Fitzgerald, "Last Wills and Testaments in Graeco-Roman Perspective," in *Early Christianity and Classical Culture* (ed. John T. Fitzgerald, Thomas H. Olbricht, and L. Michael White; NovTSup 110; Leiden: Brill, 2003; repr., Atlanta: Society of Biblical Literature: 2005), 637–72, esp. 654–58.

3 See above, *Vit. Pet.* §131 (R 96).

4 One may also render "who was a eunuch and the steward of Empress Eudocia."

5 Literally, "the Teshrins," which are the months of October and November. In Syriac, both months share the same name.

dare to write down all of them would be like someone wanting to proceed to walk on the great depths of the sea or to count the waves, as we said at the beginning.[1]

(§166) While we were then in that [afore]mentioned depot of the city of Ashdod beside the sea, it happened that the blessed one fell into a bodily sickness, so that he made [out] a will.[2] When Elijah, the tribune whom we mentioned,[3] who was dwelling in Jerusalem and who was a trusted member of the household of Empress Eudocia,[4] [came to] know this, he was anxious to go down to [visit] him. For he had previously been eagerly awaiting his return. Finding him recovered from sickness, he entreated him very earnestly and persuaded him to change this lodging because it was **[R 123]** utterly unfitting and despicable, disordered and confining, and [given] the harshness of the weather it was rough during the winter. For it was already the time of the autumn months,[5] after the feast of the Encaenia[6] of the worshipful cross had passed by.[7] When he took him, he transferred him to what is called the fortress[8] of the city of Jamnia,[9] which is near the sea and in a peaceful place and very fitting for the saint's infirmity. This he did as one who had freedom [of speech][10] and a relationship to the imperial procurators,[11] and authority over this lodging [place], because it was [part] of the imperial property and once had been a dwelling place of Empress Eudocia. For since she was frequently weighed down by bodily diseases, the physicians advised her to seek such a place in which, with the change of air,

[6] The Syriac transliterates the Greek ἐγκαίνια (Raabe, 114 n. 4). The term is used for a festival of dedication or of consecration.

[7] Egeria's account of her pilgrimage to Jerusalem furnishes us with the earliest extant description of the Feast of the Cross, celebrated on 14 September. While the emphasis of the feast first focused on the *inventio*, i.e., the finding of the cross, in the course of the sixth century a shift to a rite of elevation and exaltation of the cross occurred.

[8] The Syriac word ܚܣܢܘܢܐ is used to describe a little, fortified town. It may render the Greek πολίχνιον (Raabe, 114 n. 5).

[9] See Tsafrir, Di Segni, and Green, *Tabula Imperii Romani*, 149–50.

[10] The Syriac transliterates the Greek παρρησία.

[11] The Syriac transliterates the Greek ἐπίτροποι. Again one gains a glance at the strong network of high-placed officials and nobility to which Peter and his followers had access.

ܡܣܠܩܐ ܐܐܪ܆ ܘܡܬܒܣܡܐ ܒܡܢܝܬܐ ܛܒܐ. ܡܬܬܠܗܢܐ ܠܗܕܪܐ
ܕܥܒܕܐ ܒܗܿ. ܘܡܛܠ ܕܒܠܚܘܕ ܒܡܚܙܝܬܗ ܕܗܿ، ܡܬܝܠܐ ܥܩܪܐ
ܐܬܐܣܝܘ܆ ܒܗ ܒܗܿ ܡܫܟܚܐ ܕܪܐ܆ ܟܠ ܥܒܕܐ ܠܐ ܘܡܛܠ ܗܢܟܐ܆
ܕܐܬܦܠܣܦܘ ܪܫܐ ܕܗܪ̈ܣܐ ܘܕܬܘܬܐ ܫܠܝܚܐ. ܘܕܗܦܟܐܐ
ܗܪ̈ܣܐ ܦܢ̈ܝܐ. ܘܐܣܝܪܬ ܒܗ ܗܠܝܢ ܕܒܗ ܙܕܩ ܢܦܩܘ ܠܐܠܗܐ܆
ܘܒܠܠܬܐ ܕܗܘܦܐ ܗܒܬ ܘܬܘܒܬܗ ܠܗܿ ܢܚܫܬܗ ܒܗ ܡܪܬܐ ܢܒܦܐ.
ܕܠܗ ܒܪ ܠܛܘܒܢܐ ܐܘܟܠ ܗܘ ܪܢܫ ܠܡܚܫܒܐ ܐܠܗܐ ܠܦܪܘܢܐ܆
ܘܒܒܗ ܡܚܠ ܐܝܟ ܕܒܣܘܓܐܐ ܡܢܝܢ ܗܘܐ ܬܡܢ܆ ܒܪ ܡܠܠ ܡܢܗ
ܡܢܝܢ ܗܘܐ܆ ܐܝܟ ܕܢܣܒܘܪ ܠܬ̈ܪܝܢ ܒܥܬܗ܆ ܬܡܢ ܗܦܟ ܗܘܐ ܠܘܬܗ
ܠܬܡܢ܆ ܘܒܒܗ ܗܘܐ ܗܘܐ. ܐܢܒܝܐ ܕܢܥܬܘܬܐ [R 124] ܕܐܦ ܒܗ
ܒܡܘܢܝܗ ܕܦܪ̈ܫܐ ܢܬܠܒܫ܆ ܘܒܡܪܬܬܐ ܕܒܝܬܗ ܢܗܒ.

(§167) ܒܪ ܐܬܬܝܡ ܡܚܠ ܬܡܢ܆ ܐܣܬܟܢܝ ܒܡܘܢܝܐ ܐܘܟܠܬ ܥܪܝܐ܆
ܕܗܘ ܕܒܗܬ ܦܪ̈ܫܐ ܐܝܟ ܕܕܢܝܐ ܐܝܟܐ ܐܫܟܚܢܐ܆ ܒܗܘܢܐ ܪܒܐ
ܘܢܒܠܐ܆ ܕܐܬܬܝܣ ܒܣܪܗܦ ܒܐܒ ܢܘܢܐ. ܓܒܪ ܕܝܢ ܕܗܘ ܕܠܗܕܐ
ܗܒܪܬܐ ܐܝܟ܆ ܒܗ ܒܒܕܢܐ ܬܒܝܒ. ܒܗܘ ܕܒܗ ܡܬܒܝܢ ܗܘܘ ܟܠ
ܦܬܘܪܐ ܘܐܬܠܡ ܣܝܡ. ܒܪ ܗܘ ܗܒܠܐ ܠܦܘܠܢܐ ܒܠܝܫܘܕܗܘܢ، ܟܠ
ܚܒܝ ܡܠܟ ܗܘܐ܆ ܘܬܘܪܣܝܐ ܘܬܘܪܐ ܥܩܠ ܗܘܐ. ܘܡܛܠ ܕܠܐ
ܢܗܒܘ ܘܠܗ ܘܠܗܠܝܢ ܕܐܟܠܝܢ܆ ܗܘܝ ܐܢ̈ܫܐ ܪ̈ܥܝܢܐ ܡ̈ܫܡܫܢܘܗܝ،
ܕܗܒܐ܆ ܕܢܦܘ ܦܪܫܐ ܦܠܠܗܘܢ، ܠܒܡܒܐ܆ ܐܬܬܗܘܘ ܕܥܒܕܬܐ
ܕܢܪܒܘܢܗܝ، ܒܡܘܢܝܗ ܕܛܘܒܢܐ ܐܫܟܚܢܐ܆ ܒܪܒܐ ܕܡܐܒܘܠܬܐ

[1] A visit of Eudocia at baths of Hammat Gader is evidenced by inscriptions. See Judith Green and Yoram Tsafrir, "Greek Inscriptions fom Hammat Gader: A Poem by the Empress Eudocia and Two Building Inscriptions," *IEJ* 32 (1982): 77–96; Alexander Scheiber, "Parallels to a Topos in Eudocia's Poem," *IEJ* 34 (1984): 180–81; Ephrat Habas (Rubin), "A Poem by the Empress Eudocia: A Note on the Patriarch," *IEJ* 46 (1996): 108–19; and John T. Fitzgerald, "Gadara: Philodemus' Native City," in *Philodemus and the New Testament World* (ed. John T. Fitzgerald, Dirk Obbink, and Glenn S. Holland; NovTSup 111; Leiden: Brill, 2004), 343–97, esp. 387–93.

[2] Samaritans formed a well-established group that was part of the larger Jewish spectrum. They rejected Jerusalemite hegemony, temple service, and the Jerusalemite priesthood and claimed that Mount Gerizim, Nablus/Shechem, their ancestral site, was the place where the true worship of God was to be conducted. For Samaritans, only the Torah counted as holy scripture. A parallel between anti-Chalcedonians and Samaritans may be seen in the latter's punctiliousness in observing the requirements of ritual cleanliness. See Jacob Neusner

she would receive a condition of regained strength,[1] [and] for this reason she built this place. Since all the inhabitants of this village were Samaritans,[2] she built in it a large temple in the name of and because of the deposition [of the relics] of Stephen, the head of the martyrs and of the apostle Thomas and of many [other] holy martyrs.[3] She appointed to it those who would rightly serve God therein, and she stipulated sufficient income [for them]. For her [own] use she had constructed it [as] a modest lodging [place], to which the Christ-loving tribune Elijah brought the blessed one. Thenceforth he [Elijah] dwelt there together with him for the most part, while he separated [himself] from him [only] a little so as to visit his household. [Elijah] would return again to him there and [stay] with him so that he would be esteemed worthy **[R 124]** to be found [present] at the departure [from this world] of the saint and to receive his blessing.

(§167) While we were there [the news] was announced to us of the departure, that is to say, the release[4] of him who belonged to the saints,[5] the father of the monks, Abba Isaiah, the great ascetic and prophet,[6] who took [his] rest on the eleventh of the month of Ab.[7] It happened, however, that the one who brought these tidings arrived at the moment at which we were sitting at table and were eating, while the blessed Old Man[8] was seated alone near us and was taking [only] a little nourishment. In order to alarm neither him nor these who were eating, those chief brethren, the attendants of the Old Man who were the first to receive the report, delayed for the moment announcing the departure [from this

and William Scott Green, eds., *Dictionary of Judaism in the Biblical Period 450 B.C.E. to 600 C.E.* (Peabody, Mass.: Hendrickson, 1999), 546–48; and Robert T. Anderson, "Samaritans," *ABD* 5:940–47.

[3] Empress Eudocia here displays major efforts at trying to convert the Samaritan population to the Christian faith by introducing different holy sites as competing sanctuaries. See also *Vit. Pet.* §43 (R 30), referring to Poemenia's efforts at Christianizing the Samaritans.

[4] See Luke 2:29. Also note below, *Vit. Pet.* §173 (R 131).

[5] See also Zachariah Rhetor, *Vit. Sev.* 107, fol. 133a (Kugener, 107,1).

[6] The author compares Abba Isaiah with the Old Testament prophet Isaiah.

[7] I.e., August. Isaiah died on 11 August 491.

[8] I.e., Peter the Iberian.

ܫܘܠܡܐ ܛܒ. ܟܕ ܣܟܐ ܗܘܐ ܕܢܬܒܥܐ ܠܗ ܠܫܡܝܐ. ܘܠܐ ܦܪܝܩ ܝܕܥ ܒܪܘܚ: ܠܡܢܝܚܗ ܕܛܘܒܢܐ ܐܫܥܝܐ.

(§168) ܘܟܕ ܫܡܠܝܢ ܗܘܝܢ ܘܬܠܬܝܢ ܕܝܘܡܝܢ. ܐܡܪ ܠܗ ܐܚܕ ܡܢ ܐܚ̈ܐ ܕܫܡܫ ܠܒܪܢܫܐ. ܡܪܝ ܐܒܐ: ܐܝܟܢܐ ܙܟܐ ܐܚܪܢ ܠܐܘܪܬܘܕܘܟܣܘ. ܐܒܐ ܐܫܥܝܐ ܫܒܩ. ܗܘ ܕܝܢ ܐܝܟ ܗܘ ܕܠܐ ܡܕܡ ܐܚܪܢܐ ܫܒܩ. ܐܠܐ ܕܗܘܐ ܡܢ ܟܕܘ ܩܕܝܡ ܗܘܐ ܝܕܥ ܠܗ. ܢܝܫܐܝܬ ܐܚܝܕܐ ܘܕܠܐ ܫܘܫܛܬܐ ܦܪ. ܘܡܛܠܐ ܗܕܐ ܕܡܚܝܬ ܐܫܥܝܐ. ܪ̈ܥܝ ܐܟܣܘܬܐ ܘܬܟܒܐ ܘܟܠܗܘܢ ܩܪ̈ܝܫܐ: ܠܐ ܡܬܒܠܘ. ܘܡܛܠܐ ܪ̈ܒܐ ܐ̱ ܗܘ ܕܐܟܦ ܐܫܥܝܐ. ܗܝ، ܟܕ ܗܝ، ܐܘܪܚܐ ܐܙܠ. ܐܝܟܢܐ ܕܟܠ ܢܬܕܡܪ ܒܗܠܝܢ. ܒܬܪ ܟܕ ܗܕܐ ܐܡܪ: ܡܚܝܐ ܗܡ ܘܟܠ ܠܡܠܬܐ ܐܝܟܢܐ ܕܡܬܐܡܪ [R 125] ܗܘܐ. ܘܟܒܪ ܦܠܓ ܟܢܬ ܠܗ ܠܢܦܫܗ. ܘܗܕܐ ܟܠܝܘܡ. ܐܡܪ ܟܕ ܥܡܝܡ ܚܙܝ ܠܗ: ܕܡܟܝܠ ܕܝܠܝ ܐܢܬܘܢ.

(§169) ܒܬܪ ܕܝܢ ܩܠܝܠ ܝܘܡ̈ܬܐ. ܐܬܐ ܠܘܬܗ ܕܢܠ ܠܐܠܗܐ ܡܫܝܚܐ ܐܒܐ ܦܛܪܘܣ. ܗܘ ܒܪ ܥܘܡܪܗ ܘܡܫܡܫܢܗ ܘܝܪܬܗ ܕܐܒܐ ܐܫܥܝܐ. ܕܗܕܐ ܐܬܦܩܕ ܡܢܗ ܕܛܘܒܢܐ ܐܫܥܝܐ: ܕܢܐܬܐ ܡܢ ܒܬܪ ܡܢܝܚܗ ܠܘܬ ܐܒܐ ܦܛܪܘܣ ܐܦܝܣܩܘܦܐ. ܘܢܫܩ ܪ̈ܓܠܘܗܝ ܘܒܟܐ. ܘܢܘܚܐ ܗܘܐ ܟܕ ܡܘܪܒܐ ܡܪܫܐ ܠܐܚ̈ܐ. ܡܛܠ ܕܟܕ ܚܝ ܗܘܐ: ܠܐ ܡܬܚܘܡ ܨܒܐ ܗܘܐ ܕܢܦܪܘܫ ܡܘܪܒܐ ܡܢ ܦܛܪܘܣ. ܗܘ ܕܟܕ ܐܬܐ: ܡܫܬܐܠܐ ܗܘܐ ܠܝ ܬܕܡܘܪܬܐ ܕܫܘܠܡܗ ܕܛܘܒܢܐ. ܟܕ ܓܪ ܐܡܪ ܐܬܟܢܫܠ: ܘܦܩܕ ܡܢ ܟܕܘ ܕܢܬܬܘܬܗ. ܟܕ ܚܠܬ ܐܝܟ ܕܠܡܬܘܪܬܗ ܘܠܢܝܚܗ. ܐܫܟܚܬܗ: ܐܝܟ ܗܘ ܕܠܐܝܫ ܡܬܠܠ. ܟܡ ܟܠܗ ܫܪܘܬܐ ܘܦܘܫܩܬܐ. ܘܟܕ ܐܬܘܣܬ ܩܠܝܠ: ܘܫܠܝ ܡܢ ܡܡܠܠܐ ܘܡܢ ܗܘ ܫܒܩ ܟܠܗ. ܘܟܕ ܢܦܩ ܐܒܐ ܪܘܫܐ ܫܠܦ ܬܘܣܪܬܐ ܐܡܪ ܗܘܝܬ. ܕܡܢ ܟܕܘ ܡܢ ܩܕܝܡ ܟܪܝܐ ܗܘܟܝܐ ܐܬܬ ܗܘܬ. ܐܠܐ ܟܕ ܐܫܟܚܬ ܠܡܪܫܘܬܟ ܕܡܡܠܠܐ ܥܡ ܐܚܝ. ܐܬܟܠܬ ܕܠܐ ܐܬܟܠ. ܘܟܕ ܢܦܠܬ ܥܠ ܐ̈ܦܝ. ܡܦܩܣ ܗܘܬ ܠܗ. ܕܢܐܡܪ ܕܡܢܐ ܐܬܬܘܗܝ. ܗܘ ܕܠܘܬܗ ܡܡܠܠ ܗܘܐ. ܘܐܝܠܝܢ ܐܢܬܘܢ ܗܠܝܢ ܕܡܡܠܠ ܗܘܐ ܥܡܗ. ܘܦܩܕ ܟܕ ܐܡܪ: ܕܢܘܚܝ ܡܡܠܠܢܐ ܐܢܬܘܢ، ܗܘܐ. ܕܐܬܐ

[1] The Syriac may render the Greek ξένον (Raabe, 115 n. 3).

[2] This comment reflects the high rank that Peter assigned to his friend Abba Isaiah.

world] of the blessed Isaiah until the meal came to an end, thinking that his passing had escaped the notice of the Old Man and he had not known it beforehand in the spirit.

(§168) When we had satisfied our need and were about to get up, one of the brethren, whose name was Zachariah, said to him, "My lord Abba, great sorrow has come upon the orthodox. Abba Isaiah has fallen asleep." He, however, as if he heard nothing strange[1] but [rather something] that was then already known to him beforehand, answered quietly and at the same time without commotion, "So what if Isaiah died? Did not the patriarchs and the prophets and all the saints die?[2] What great [thing is it] if also Isaiah has gone the same road, so that all of us should be amazed about these [things]?" Nevertheless, when he had said this, he immediately got up and entered [his] cell, where he remained. **[R 125]** He wept much by himself and said only this, when we were hearing him, "Now it is my [turn]."[3]

(§169) After a few days there came to him the God-fearing priest, Abba Peter, the cell-companion and attendant and heir of Abba Isaiah, to whom it was commanded by the blessed Isaiah that he should come after his departure [from this world] to Abba Peter the bishop and receive the prayer from him as well and conduct the holy oblation for the brethren. For while he was alive this Peter never wanted to offer the oblation. When he came, he recounted to us the wonder of the blessed one's end. "When he became weak," he said, "and the moment of his death was already near, when I entered to visit him and to comfort him, I found him as if he were talking to someone with all joy and cheerfulness.[4] When I had moved off a little and he ceased from talking and from this vision, I entered. Excusing myself for being tardy, I said, 'I had come already a long time before, but when I found your holiness talking with someone, I refrained from entering.' Falling upon my face, I asked him to say to whom he was talking and what these [things] were [about] which he was talking with him. He an-

[3] I.e., Peter is presented as having foreknowledge of the approach of his own death.

[4] Zachariah Rhetor's *Life of Isaiah* does not recount this episode and only presents a relatively brief reference to the end of Isaiah's life. It does refer to his disciple Peter, however.

ܕܢܫܡܫܘܢܗܝ. ܗܟܢܐ ܓܝܪ ܐܝܬ ܚܒܝܒܐ ܠܐܠܗܐ. ܕܠܩܕ̈ܝܫܘܗܝ، ܟܕ
ܗ̇ܢܘܢ ܕܓ̇ܘܒܝܢ ܘܐܬܝܗܘܢ ܩ̈ܘܫܝ ܒܡܕܒܪܐ ܘܩ̈ܘܫܝ [R 126] ܒܒܪܝܐ
ܢܗܒ. ܐܝܟ ܕܐܦ ܠܛܘܒܢܐ ܐܒܐ ܕܝܠܢ ܘܐܦܝܣܩܘܦܐ ܦܛܪܘܣ:
ܐܚܒܢܐ ܕܒܕܒܢܗ ܬܘܕܒܢܝ. ܡܫܐܠ ܗܘܐ ܕܝܢ ܐܡܪ ܗ̣ܘ ܐܒܐ
ܐܫܟܚܐ ܠܗ ܠܡܕܒܪܢܐ: ܕܗܟܢܐ ܐܝܬܝܗܘܢ ܗܘܘ ܡܩ̈ܪܝܐ ܗܠܝܢ
ܕܒܡܕܒܪܐ ܐܟܠ ܗܘܐ. ܘܦܩܕ ܕܗܠܝܢ ܐܝܬܝܗܘܢ ܗܘܘ: ܥܫ̈ܒ ܚܘܪܐ
ܕܒܪܐ. ܘܟܕ ܐܫܬܥܝܬ ܬܫ̈ܥܝܬܐ ܐܡܪ ܗܘܐ ܦܛܪܘܣ: ܡܟܦܫ ܗܘܬ
ܠܗܕܐ ܐܒܐ ܐܫܟܚܐ ܕܢܦܫ ܠܐܠܗܐ: ܕܢܫܡܫܘܢܗܝ، ܕܢܗܘܐ ܒܟܠ
ܙܒܢܐ: ܡܛܠ ܕܢܦܩ ܗܒܝܢ ܟܠܗܘܢ، ܫܪܒܐ ܕܐܘܪ̈ܬܘܕܘܟܣܐ. ܗ̣ܘ ܕܝܢ
ܟܕ ܐܬܚܙܝ ܐܡܪ ܠܗܘܢ. ܐܠܐ ܢܕܥ ܗܘܐ ܒܫ̈ܢܬܐ ܕܬܠܬܝܢ ܕܕܝܪ̈ܝܢ:
ܟܕ ܡܨܠܐ ܗܘܐ ܠܐܠܗܐ ܘܢܦܩ ܗܘܐ: ܕܗܘ ܡܕܡ ܬܒܥ. ܘܬܘܒ
ܟܕ ܐܢܫ ܡܫܡܫ ܗܘܐ ܕܬܬܝܗܒ ܠܝ ܡܢܗ: ܕܗܢܘ ܡܬܒܥܐ ܠܗ ܕܗܘ
ܒܬܪ ܒܘܢܝܗ ܢܐܟܘܠ ܕܝܠܢ: ܘܕܡܫܡܫ ܕܢܫܡܠܐ ܡܘܪܒܢܐ ܡܕܫܢܐ
ܠܐܢ̈ܫܐ: ܡܛܠ ܗ̇ܝ، ܕܠܐ ܡܫܡܫܢܐ ܐܢܬ؛ ܘܠܐ ܥ̇ܘܐ ܠܡܫܡܫܘܬܐ
ܕܐܝܟ ܗܕܐ: ܐܡܪ ܠܗܘܢ. ܠܐ ܡܫܡܫ ܐܢܬ ܐܢܐ ܐܝܟ ܕܐܒܐ ܐܢܬ.
ܐܠܐ ܐܢ ܠܗܘ ܢܫܝܐ ܐܦܝܣܩܘܦܐ ܐܒܐ ܕܝܠܢ ܐܒܐ ܦܛܪܘܣ:
ܘܦܩܕ ܡܢܗ ܨܠܘܬܐ ܘܡܘܕܪܢܐ ܘܡܫܠܐ ܒܥܕܐ ܕܐܠܗܐ. ܒܕܡܐ
ܟܪ ܠܗܘ، ܘܠܘܬܟ: ܐܝܬܝܗܘܢ ܗܠܝܢ ܕܗܕܐ ܕܟܠܬܐ.

(§170) ܟܕ ܦܓܥ ܗܘܐ ܠܛܘܒܢܐ ܦܛܪܘܣ ܡܫܝܚܐ ܠܕܢܚܗ: ܚܕ ܐܝܬܝܗ
ܗܘܐ ܒܗ̇ܘ ܡܫܘܐ ܕܡܟܝܢ ܡܕܝܢܬܐ: ܟܕ ܡܕܫܢܐ ܐܒܘܢ
ܐܦܝܣܩܘܦܐ. ܩ̈ܪܝܐܬܐ ܕܝܢ ܐܦ ܬܡܢ: ܬܕܡܪ̈ܬܐ ܘܐܣܘ̈ܬܐ
ܘܦܘܪ̈ܩܢܐ ܕܫ̈ܐܕܐ: ܥܒܕ ܒܐܬܪ̈ܘܗܝ، ܐܠܗܐ. ܠܐ ܡܬܡ̈ܢܝܢܐ ܒܠܚܘܕ
ܘܒܪ̈ܢܫܐ: ܐܠܐ [R 127] ܘܒܒܥܝ̈ܪܐ ܘܒܡܫܪ̈ܝܢܐ. ܘܬܘܪܐܬ

[1] The Syriac may render the Greek ὁμόζηλοι and ὁμοήθεις (see Raabe, 116 n. 1).

[2] See below, *Vit. Pet.* §174 (R 131).

[3] This curious question regarding the identity of John the Baptist's locusts reflects early Christian ascetic concerns about food, specifically whether an ascetic like John the Baptist would have eaten meat. It also functions as an identification of John's asceticism as a Nazirite. For a fuller discussion and for references to relevant literature, see Raabe, 116–17 n. 2; Horn, *Asceticism and Christological Controversy*, 169–70; see also most recently the survey article by James A. Kelhoffer, "'Locusts and Wild Honey' (Mk 1.6c and Mt. 3.4c): The *Status Quaestionis* concerning the Diet of John the Baptist," *CurBR* 2.1 (2003):

swered, saying that it was John the Baptist who had come to take him [away]." For so it is the custom with God to take [away] his saints by those who are like-minded and equal in zeal and **[R 126]** in way of life,[1] as also [happened] to our blessed father and bishop Peter, as we shall make known in its time.[2] "Yet Abba Isaiah," he was saying, "was asking the Baptist what these locusts were that he used to eat in the desert.[3] He answered that these had been the heads of roots from the desert. Since I found mercy," Peter was saying, "I asked the old man Abba Isaiah to ask God to let him be with us for a time, because the rest of the orthodox were in much need of him.[4] He, however, while he was strongly moved, said to me, 'If you knew the evils that are about to come,[5] doubtless you would be praying to God and be anxious to be taken away before me!' Again, when I asked that he inform me who he thought should take care of me after his departure and would be able to perform the holy oblation for the brethren, because I was unexperienced and not worthy of such a service, he said to me, 'You shall not find anyone such as you are seeking, but go to the reverend bishop, our father Abba Peter, and receive from him prayer and help, and perform the work of God. For unto me and unto you are the [affairs] of this place.' "[6]

(§170) When the blessed Peter the priest now returned to his monastery, we were in the fortress of the city of Jamnia with our holy father the bishop. But there also God worked many wonders and healings and [acts of] casting out demons by his hands, not only on believers and Christians but **[R 127]** also on Jews and

104–27; and idem, *The Diet of John the Baptist: "Locusts and Wild Honey" in Synoptic and Patristic Interpretation* (WUNT 176; Tübingen: Mohr Siebeck, 2005).

[4] For a similar argument formulated in reference to Peter the Iberian see *Vit. Pet.* §173 (R 131).

[5] This comment does not specify any adversities that afflicted anti-Chalcedonians in Palestine. It is possible that it refers more generally to Sabas's efforts and growing influence on behalf of Chalcedon in Palestine and the events after Justin I's accession in 518, which definitively turned the tables against the anti-Chalcedonians in Palestine.

[6] The author seems to stress a sense of responsibility for the affairs of his monastery, which Isaiah passed on to his disciple Peter.

ܒܗܘ ܕܝܢ ܒܒܗܘܪ̈ܐ ܕܡܘܪܬܐ ܘܕܢܚܡܢ ܘܡܕܢܚܬܐ ܘܕܒܢܝܢܗ̇.
ܕܡܬܩܠܣܝܢ ܐܦ ܢܝܩܐ ܕܒܐܝܕܐ ܒܐܝܕܐ ܢܬܠܒܐ: ܟܠ ܡ̈ܠܐ
ܡܣܒܪ̈ܬܐ ܦܫܝܩܢ ܚܢ ܘܡܬܚܒܠܘܬܐ. ܒܬܪ ܟܕ ܫܡܥ ܗܘܘ ܗ̇ܢܘܢ
ܡ̈ܗܝܡܢܐ ܗܠܝܢ ܬܕܡܪ̈ܬܐ: ܘܡܬܦ̈ܣܩܝܢ ܗܘܘ ܒܒܘܕܪ̈ܐ ܕܡܠܝܢ.
ܡܘܫܐ ܕܬܪ̈ܝܢ ܩܪܝܢ ܗܘܘ ܠܗ. ܐܝܟ ܕܝܢ ܢܡܘܣܐ ܢܩܕܐ ܕܢܩ̈ܝܐ: ܒܕ
ܒܒܘܪܗܢܐ ܢܦܠ ܕܟܢܫ ܡ̈ܕܝܢܬܐ. ܠܒܢܝ̈ܗ, ܟ̈ܕ ܚܙܘ ܘܐܬܘ̈ܗܝ, ܠܘܬ
ܛܘܒܢܐ. ܗ̇ܘ ܕܝܢ ܟܕ ܣܡܟ, ܒܨܒܐ ܘܐܡܪ ܠܘܬܗ. ܐܦ ܡܬܚܡܠ
ܐܢܬ ܒܡܥܝܢܝ ܡܫܒܚ ܕܐܠܗܢ. ܐܝܟ ܠܢ ܫܩܠܐ ܐܢܬ, ܗ̇ܘ ܕܝܢ
ܒܨܐ. ܘܒܨܒܐ ܐܦ ܗܘܝܐ ܒܚܡܗ. ܘܒܕ ܘܡܢܐ ܐܡܪ ܫܠܡܗ̇ ܠܒܪܘܗ.
ܘܐܡܪ ܠܗܠܝܢ ܕܐܬܘ̈ܗܝ, ܘܠܘ ܒܨܒܘ ܒܝܬܐ ܙܩܦܝ ܘܚܘܒܐ ܠܗ
ܥܠ ܒܪܘܗ. ܘܡܢ ܒܬܪ ܬܠܬܐ ܝܘ̈ܡܝܢ. ܐܬܐ ܟܕ ܚܠܝܡ. ܘܡܫܒܚ
ܠܐܠܗܐ. ܘܐܝܟܢ, ܠܐ ܣܡܟܬܐ ܕܢܩܝܐ ܡܢ ܗܠܝܢ ܕܡܝܐ..

(§171) ܡ̈ܢܝܢ ܕܝܢ ܗܢܝܢ ܐܝܟ ܒܕܩܐ: ܕܡܠܘܐܐ ܕܐܪ̈ܥܐ ܢܘܚ ܡܫܥܐ
ܐܘܢܒܣܐ. ܕܐܬܘ̈ܗܝ, ܗܘܐ ܒܪ ܦܠܛܐ ܕܐܪ̈ܥܐ ܦܠܝܛܘܣ. ܡܛܠ ܗ̇ܘ
ܕܐܦ ܡܢ ܠܒܠ ܒܡܗܕܝܢ ܒܨܕܝܢ. ܗ̇ܘ ܕܡܫܬܡܠܐ ܒܐܪ̈ܒܥܐ ܒܬܫܪ̈ܝܢ
ܩܕܝܡ. ܘܒܕ ܐܝܟ ܒܝܕܗ ܠܩ̈ܛܡܬܐ ܩܪܐ ܗ̇ܘ ܛܘܒܢܐ: ܘܬܪ̈ܬܐ
ܠܗ̇ܘܢ ܕܦܠܓ̈ܘܬܐ ܕܩܪܒܝܢ. ܟܕ ܚܙܐ ܗܘܐ ܕܒܣܐܐ ܢܟܦ ܠܗܘܢ.
ܦܩܕ ܕܢܩ̈ܝܐ ܩ̈ܛܡܬܐ ܢܟܦܘܢ ܡܢ ܡܟܐ ܕܩܪܒ ܗܘܐ. ܘܒܨܒܐ
ܡܢܗ ܕܟܠܗ ܗ̇ܢܐ ܢܗܘܐ ܫܘܠܐ ܡܢܥܠ. ܘܫܘܬ ܡܛܠܐ ܩܛܡܬܐ.
[R 128] ܐܝܟܢܐ ܕܠܒܪ ܢܦܘܩ ܘܠܐ ܢܬܚܙܐ. ܢܩܕܐ ܡܢ ܡܟܐ. ܚܢ
ܡܟܝܠ ܒܕ ܡܢܘܢ. ܡܛܠ ܗ̇ܝ ܕܠܐ ܡܬܚܙܐ ܚܢ. ܕܐܝܟ ܦܘܩܕܢܗ
ܕܡܘܫܐ ܢܒܝܐ ܠܐܟ̈ܗܢܘܬܐ. ܗܘܬ ܫܦܝܪܘܬܐ ܠܡܫܪܝܘܬܐ. ܒܕ ܢܒܝܬ

[1] Peter the Iberian seems to have shared Eudocia's and Poemenia's concern for and efforts directed toward the conversion to Christianity of Jews and Samaritans. See *Vit. Pet.* §166 (R 123).

[2] It is possible that the author here explicitly called Peter a "second Moses" to portray Peter as one who was trying to reach out to Samaritans, who expected "a prophet like Moses." For discussion and reference to relevant literature, see Horn, *Asceticism and Christological Controversy*, 366–69. Horn has benefited from conversations with Stacy Dopson on this issue.

[3] Literally, "the sickness that gathers water."

[4] See also Matt 9:1–8; Mark 2:1–12.

[5] Syriac ܪܫܡ, with ܨܠܝܒܐ expressed or understood, means "to make the sign of the cross," "to sign with the cross," "to cross s.o." (Payne Smith, 163).

[6] The numerous references to the imagery of fishing and catching fish raise the question of the theological significance of why the author identifies the

Samaritans,[1] and especially on the inhabitants of the village and of the city of Jamnia and its surroundings. If we should want to narrate these one by one, we should need many words and writings. Nevertheless, when those believers had seen these wonders and were enjoying his help, they called him a second Moses.[2] A certain Jew, however, a fisherman, when he fell into the sickness of dropsy,[3] his kindred carried him and brought him to the blessed one.[4] Seeing him, he wept and said to him, "If you believe in Christ, he can heal you, for I am a sinner." That one, however, wept, and the old man also wept together with him. Having also said this, he made the sign [of the cross][5] [on] his belly. And he said to these who had brought him, "Go, prepare some bandage, and put it on his belly." After three days he came, being healthy and praising God, and brought us a multitude of fish from those he had caught.[6]

(§171) There came, however, at this time as usual, the commemoration of the priest Abba John the Eunuch, who had been the cell-mate of Abba Peter, about whom we have also made mention above,[7] who was perfected on the fourth of First Teshrin.[8] When the blessed one, as was his custom, invited many and especially those who were in the nearby mountains, since he was anxious to provide comfort for them, he commanded [us] to buy many fish from the sea that was nearby. It so happened that suddenly there was so great a winter [storm] and [so] much rain came down **[R 128]** that fishing from the sea ceased completely, and there was no catch. When therefore we were sad because we could not refresh the fathers, as had been the saint's command, want turned

Jewish man as a fisherman in this section. While the passage could be read in a straightforward historical sense, it also allowed Rufus to signal to his anti-Chalcedonian audience how Peter not only turned Chalcedonians, who were understood to hold the same faith as the Jews, into true believers but also how he managed to transform them into effective workers for the anti-Chalcedonian cause. For a fuller treatment of this issue, see Horn, "Eugenia."

[7] For the last few references to John the Eunuch, see *Vit. Pet.* §§73, 105, 118–119 (R 50, 78, 85–87),.

[8] The First Teshrin is the month of October. See also Schwartz, *Johannes Rufus*, 20, correcting Raabe's translation of "December" for "October" here.

ܚܢܢ ܡܬܪ̈ܐ ܩܘܪܩܝܢܐ ܒܗܘ ܠܠܝܐ܆ ܢܗܘܪܐ ܗܘ̇ ܕܐܬܘܬܗ̇، ܗܘܐ
ܒܥܒܕܢܘܬܗ܆ ܗܢܐ ܟܠܗ ܟܕ ܡܢ ܛܘܪܐ ܡܛܠ ܡܠܠܬܗ ܙܕ̈ܩܐ܆
ܐܝܟܢܐ ܕܢܫܒܚ܆ ܘܠܬܘܕܝܬܐ ܕܢܕܪ̈ܘܗܝ، ܘܠܚܡ̈ܝܐ ܒܚܒܝܒ. ܘܠܡܘܡܐ
ܕܬܠܬܗ ܟܕ ܬܠܬܐ ܢܣܒܘ. ܐܫܟܚܘ ܩܘܪܩܝܢܐ ܕܢܘ̈ܢܐ܆ ܘܡܢܗܘܢ ܗܠܝܢ
ܡܬܪ̈ܣܩܝܢ. ܐܝܟܢܐ ܕܢܐܡܪܘܢ ܒܥܒܪ̈ܐ ܕܐܬܪܐ. ܕܠܐ ܡܬܚܫܒܝܢ
ܒܡܕܝܢ ܕܝܡܐ ܬܕܡܘܪܬܐ ܕܐܝܟ ܗܕܐ ܒܥܘ̈ܡܩܬܗܘܢ. ܐܝܟ ܕܡܬܠ
ܠܐ ܢܣܦܩ ܚܢܢ܆ ܠܣܘܓܐܐ ܕܢܘ̈ܢܐ ܕܐܬܝܢ ܗܘܘ ܠܕܘܟܪܢܗ ܕܗܘ̇
ܩܕܝܫܐ. ܐܝܟܢܐ ܕܬܫܬܡܠܐ ܐܦ ܥܠܘܗܝ܆ ܗ̇ܝ ܕܐܡܝܪܐ ܕܕܘܟܪܢܟ
ܒܒܘܪ̈ܟܬܐ.

(§172) ܟܕ ܒܗܠܝܢ ܐܝܬܝܢ ܗܘܝܢ܆ ܡܪܥܬ ܦܘܪܥܬܐ ܘܚܫܝܫܘܬܐ ܕܝܠܗ
ܕܦܓܪܐ܆ ܕܢܦܩܐ ܠܗ̇ ܢܦܫܗ ܗܘ̇ ܕܢܣܝܡ ܠܗ. ܘܠܐ ܕܝܢ ܟܕ ܠܐ
ܢܟܝܐ ܗܘܬ ܘܠܐ ܡܫܬܚܠܦܐ ܗܘܬ. ܠܗ ܕܝܢ ܦܪܥܬ ܐܬܬܥܝܪܬ
ܘܦܪܥܬܗ ܐܣܬܥܪܬ ܡܢ ܘܟܐܒܐ ܩܫܝܐ. ܘܠܐ ܕܝܢ ܕܟܐܒܐ
ܕܪܘܚܩܐ. ܠܗ ܕܝܢ ܪܣܡܬܐ ܘܡܫܬܚܠܦܘܬܐ. ܕܠܘܬܗ ܐܦ ܪܘܡ
ܗܘܐ ܒܟܠܝܘܡ. ܟܕ ܠܡܣܒܠ ܢܟܝܐ ܪܕܦ ܗܘܐ܆ ܠܘܬ ܟܠܝܠܐ ܕܦܪܥܬܐ
ܕܠܥܠ ܕܐܠܗܐ. ܘܟܕ ܐܝܬ ܗܘܐ ܠܗ ܒܝܕܐ ܕܠܘܬ ܢܒܝܐ ܢܐܙܠ
ܥܡ ܐܚ̈ܐ ܘܢܬܠܝܢ ܘܢܒܥܐ ܕܘܪܫܐ ܬܡܢ܆ [R 129] ܘܫܐܠܬܐ ܡܢ
ܟܠܗܘܢ ܢܦܩܘܢ܆ ܘܢܦܩܐ ܠܗ ܟܠܗ ܡܢܗܘܢ܆ ܗ̇ܝ ܕܡܒܕܪܐ ܘܐܬܝܬܗ̇
ܕܦܘܪܩܢܐ܆ ܟܕ ܡܢ ܫܘܚܬܐ ܟܕ ܚܠܝܦ ܠܗ ܒܗ ܡܪܥܐ: ܐܝܟܢܐ
ܕܗܘ̇ ܕܡܫܬܐܠܝܢ ܗܘܐ ܟܠܗܘܢ، ܐܫܬܐܠ ܠܝ ܒܬܪ ܒܘܢܝܗ: ܕܐܬܘܬܗ̇،
ܗܘܐ ܐܝܟ ܦܫܝܛܐ ܘܠܐ ܡܙܝܢܐ ܘܡܬܚܫܚܢܐ. ܟܕ ܡܛܠܐ ܬܪܥܐ ܦܡ
ܗ̇ܘ ܗܟܢܐ. ܘܟܕ ܒܗܘܢܐ ܐܬܚܫܒ ܐܡܪ ܠܗ ܢܦܫܗ܆ ܟܕ ܚܙܐ ܐܢܐ
ܬܘܒ ܒܗܘܢܐ ܬܪܥܐ܆ ܘܐܡܪ ܠܗ ܢܦܫܗ. ܠܐ ܦܬܚ ܐܢܐ. ܘܟܕ ܫܠܡ
ܒܫܠܡܬܐ܆ ܬܘܒ ܗ̇ܝ، ܟܕ ܗ̇ܝ، ܐܡܪ. ܟܕ ܩܠܝܠ ܐܢܐ ܬܘܒ ܒܗܘܢܐ
ܫܠܡܬܐ. ܐܡܪ ܠܗ. ܘܟܕ ܒܬܪܥܐ ܟܠܗ ܚܙܐ܆ ܬܘܒ ܠܗ ܢܦܫܗ
ܗ̇ܝ، ܟܕ ܗ̇ܝ، ܐܡܪ. ܟܕ ܚܙܐ ܐܢܐ ܬܘܒ ܒܗܘܢܐ ܬܪܥܐ܆ ܘܦܩ ܟܕ

[1] The Syriac seems to transliterate the Greek κορακῖνοι or κόρακες, a kind of fish most likely named with reference to its raven-like black color. See LSJ, 980; Raabe, 118 n. 2.

[2] Rufus may have intended the "fish" to refer both to the fish caught in the water and the many women and men who came to the commemoration of the saint.

[3] Literally, "your commemoration is in blessings." Ps 10:7 says, "The memory of the just is blessed." See also Sir 45:1.

into abundance. For because much rain came down that night, the river that was in our neighborhood, being so greatly replenished from the mountains, came down [so] swiftly that it overflowed and flooded the surrounding areas and the vineyards. The next day, after the waters had receded, they found a multitude of fish. Those [fish] were *coraces*,[1] so that the inhabitants of the region would say that they did not remember that there ever was a miracle like this in their days. Consequently, we were not enough for the multitude of fish that were coming to the saint's commemoration,[2] so that also concerning him would be fulfilled what is said, "Your commemoration is blessed!"[3]

(§172) While we were [involved] in these [things], the calling and the repose of the blessed one came near, that he should depart to Jesus, whom he loved. While for us it was unknown and unexpected, for him it had been foreknown and foretold for a long time,[4] and for us [it was an event] of pain and of loss, but for him, longed for and awaited, [an event] toward which he was always running, "rushing toward the goal, for the crown of the higher calling of God."[5] Since he had the habit of going to the sea with the brethren and walking and making [spiritual] disputation there[6] **[R 129]** and accepting questions from all of them, and replying to each one of them as was helpful and unto salvation, one day, when he returned to the lodging [place]—the one on whom he was leaning,[7] who was a simple and guileless and innocent man, told us [this] after his departure—when he reached the door, the old man stood and, while he considered in [his] mind, said to himself, "Now, shall I be entering again by this door?" He replied to himself, "I do not think [so]." He went up the staircase [and] again said the same, "Now, shall I again be going up this staircase?" He said, "No." He entered by the upper door [and] again said the same to himself, "Now, shall I be entering again by this door?" He

[4] See *Vit. Pet.* §§168–169 (R 125).

[5] See Phil 3:14.

[6] See *Pler.* 2.

[7] By now Peter seems to have been old and weak, so that when walking he needed to rely on the help and stabilizing support of another person's physical assistance.

ܐܡܪ. ܠܐ ܫܦܪ ܐܢܐ. ܘܟܕ ܐܡܪ ܗܠܝܢ ܒܟܠܠ ܡܠܠ ܡܬܒܠܒܠ ܗܘܐ.
ܘܕܡܟܐܬ ܒܪ̈ܓܠܘܗܝ. ܘܟܠܗܝܢ ܒܥܕܢܐ ܕܦܓܪܗ. ܟܕ ܒܗ ܚܝܐ ܗܘܐ
ܢܦܫܗ: ܗ̇ܘ ܒܐܝ̈ܕܘܗܝ ܡܫܠܡܐ ܗܘܐ ܬܫܡܫܬܐ ܕܒܪܐ ܘܪܘܚܢܝܐ.
ܘܟܠܗܘܢ ܐܡܝܢܐܝܬ: ܗ̇ܝ ܕܥܕܪ ܢܦܫܗ ܘܦܓܪܗ ܘܒܚܝܐ ܘܚܝ ܐܡܪ
ܗܘܐ. ܘܟܕ ܡܛܝ ܫܠܡܗ ܕܪܘܚܗ..

(§173) ܐܬܐܢܣܝܘܣ ܕܝܢ ܐܒܐ ܡܫܒܚܐ ܐܣܟܘܦܠܝܐ ܕܕܝܪܐ ܘܒܚܦܐ:
ܗ̇ܘ ܕܐܝܬܘܗܝ ܗ̇ܘܐ ܬܠܡܝܕܐ ܕܣܒܐ ܠܦܘܬܢܐ ܢܣܝܒܐ ܕܡܬܩܪܐ
ܗܘܐ ܐܒܐ ܫܢܐ: ܒܬܪ ܡܘܬܗ ܕܫܢܐ ܗܢ. ܐܬܐ ܠܘܬ ܠܦܘܬܢܐ
ܐܒܐ ܦܛܪܘܣ ܐܦܝܣܩܘܦܐ: ܘܚܙܐ ܠܫܘܬܦܘܬܐ ܕܕܘܒܪܗ
ܐܘܢܓܠܝܐ: ܐܬܪܓܪܓ ܕܢܚܙܐ ܒܥܝܢܗ ܕܣܒܐ. ܘܟܕ ܫܡܥ ܐܦܝܣ.
ܗ̇ܘܐ ܠܗ ܐܝܟ ܪܚܝܡܘܗܝ ܕܢܚܙܐ ܒܗ. ܒܐܣܟܝܡܐ ܥܦܪܐ ܫܦܝܪ
ܘܒܢܦܩܘܬܐ. [R 130] ܒܒܪܐ ܕܝܢ ܐܬܐ ܗܘܐ ܠܝ ܠܬ̈ܡܢ. ܠܝ ܘܠܗ.
ܕܟܠ ܚܕ ܫܪ̈ܪܐ ܢܩܘܡ ܒܬܫܡܫܬܐ ܕܠܠܝܐ ܘܕܐܝܡܡܐ. ܗܢܐ
ܗܟܝܠ ܟܕ ܐܬܩܒܠ ܗ̇ܘ ܣܒܐ ܠܦܘܬܢܐ: ܐܝܟ ܡܕܡ ܒܣܪܐ ܢ̈ܩܝܡ
ܕܒܘܢܝܗ: ܒܣܕ ܡܢ ܠܠܘ̈ܬܐ ܟܕ ܡܐܟܡ ܘܐܬܐ ܥܠ ܠܒܝܬܗ: ܒܒܥܐ ܫܦܝܪ
ܡܬܢܐܝܬ ܘܕܠܐ ܥܠܝܠܐ ܡܬܬܢܝܚ ܗܘܐ. ܐܡܝܢܐ ܕܐܬܕܡܪ ܐܢܐ.
ܒܬܪ ܡܠܠ ܕܫܘܠܡܐ ܕܬܫܡܫܬܐ ܕܠܠܝܐ ܟܕ ܢܦܩܬܗ: ܡܦܝܣ ܗܘܝܬ
ܠܗ: ܕܢܐܡܪ ܠܝ ܟܠܬܐ ܕܡܠܝܡ ܬܐܢܝ̈ܚܬܐ ܘܪܘܚܗ̇ ܒܟܝܢܐ ܦܫܝܩܐܝܬ.
ܗ̇ܘ ܕܝܢ ܟܕ ܣܓܝ ܗܘܐ ܕܢܦܫܐ ܐܝܟ ܕܐܬܐ ܒܒܪܐ ܠܩ̈ܕܝܫܐ ܟܠܬܐ
ܐܣ̈ܝܢܬܐ ܐܡܪܘ. ܟܕ ܫܡܥܢܬ ܕܝܢ ܐܢܐ ܘܡܦܝܣ ܐܢܐ ܠܗ: ܐܡܪ.
ܡܬܠܗܕܐ ܚܒܠܐ ܐܢܐ ܘܐܟܠ ܐܢܐ. ܥܠ ܕܝܬܝܪܐܝܬ ܐܟܠܐ ܕܝܠܝ
ܥܒܕ ܠܝ ܘܣܝܡ ܠܘܬ ܡܪܢܐ. ܟܕ ܐܢܐ ܓܝܪ ܐܡܪ ܒܟܘܬܐ ܫܒܝܠܬܐ
ܐܚܕ. ܐܢܐ: ܘܒܟܒܝܪܘܬܐ ܡܛܠ ܡܣܝܒܠܘܬܗ. ܐܡܪܝܢܐ ܕܐܦܠܐ
ܐ̇ܕܡܝ ܡܥܒܕ ܐܢܐ: ܡܢ ܥܠܝܐ ܫܢܬ ܠܐܟܠܐ ܕܠܝ ܦܬܐ ܕܡܐܟܡ
ܘܐܡܪ ܠܘܬܝ. ܠܡܢܐ ܐܟܠ ܐܢܬ ܘܫܒܩ ܐܢܬ ܗܒܢܐ ܡܬܢܐܝܬ
ܘܫܒܩ ܐܢܬ ܢܦܫܟ ܒܫܢܝܩܘܬܐ. ܐܢܐ ܕܝܢ ܐܡܪܬ ܠܗܘܢ. ܘܐܡܪܢܐ
ܠܐ ܙܕܩ ܠܝ ܕܐܬܐܟܠ ܘܐܬܬܢܝܚ. ܕܗܐ ܒܬܪ ܒܡܢܝܢܐ ܕܡܫܝܚܘܬܟ.

1 Ps 43:3.

2 See Ps 119:76–77.

3 This Abba Sana is not featured in the *Apophthegmata Patrum*.

4 This concern for perfection is telling of what appears to have been a driving force among many of the anti-Chalcedonians. Throughout the text one notices phrases and expressions that bespeak a desire and strong striving for the

replied, saying, "I do not think [so]." After this, little by little, he became weak, first in his feet and afterwards in the rest of his body. Nevertheless, he forced himself to celebrate the usual services and [the service] of the oblation with his own hands. Every day he was saying this unceasingly, even when lying down on his bed: "Send out your light and your truth,[1] and it shall comfort [me] and [I shall] live."[2]

(§173) Athanasius, a certain Egyptian priest, a monk and a chaste [man] who had been the disciple of the famous old man [and] hermit called Abba Sana,[3] when he came after Sana's death to the blessed Abba Peter the bishop and saw the strictness of his evangelical way of life,[4] he earnestly yearned to dwell with the old man. After he had asked much, he had it according to his wish that he would dwell with us in a very beautiful manner[5] and in chastity. **[R 130]** We two, he and I, had the habit of standing beside each other during the service of the night and of the day. When the blessed old man had become weak about ten days before his departure, during one of the nights, while he and I were standing side by side, he wept very bitterly and was groaning without ceasing, so that I was amazed. Shortly after the end of the night service, I followed him and asked him to tell me the reason for these groans and for such great weeping. Being anxious to hide [it], as the saints have the custom [to do], he offered other reasons. When I persisted and asked him, he said, "On this account especially[6] am I weeping and mourning, because our father is leaving us and is going away to the Lord. For," he was saying, "while I was seized with great sadness and in mournfulness because of his weakness, so that I could not even sleep, suddenly I saw my Abba Sana, standing [there] and saying to me, 'Why are you mourning and weeping so bitterly and torturing yourself with sighs?' Yet I said to him, 'Why is it not right for me to mourn and groan, that after the departure of your holiness, God bestowed on me that I would be esteemed

preservation of purity and the precise fulfillment of liturgical and other requirements. Underlying such a concern may be a sense that exact compliance with God's laws assists one on the way toward righteousness.

[5] The Syriac may render the Greek εὐσχημοσύνη (Raabe, 120 n. 2).

[6] The Syriac may render a phrase ὅτι μάλιστα καταλείπει (see Raabe, 120 n. 3).

ܫܒܩ ܠܝ ܐܠܗܐ ܕܐܫܬܘܐ ܕܐܚܙܐ ܗܕܐ ܕܐܝܟ ܗܢܐ ܐܚܪܢ܆ ܘܗܐ
ܚܙܝܬ. ܐܢܐ ܕܐܦ ܡܢܗ ܐܬܚܒܠ ܡܛܠ ܚܛܗ̈ܝ. ܗܘ ܕܝܢ ܐܡܪ ܐܡܝܢ.
ܐܠܐ ܠܐ ܬܬܟܪܝ. ܡܢ ܐܠܗܐ ܓܝܪ ܐܬܬܘܗܝ ܦܩܘܕܐ ܘܦܪܬܐ.
ܒܘܫܠܐ ܓܝܪ ܗܢܐ ܒܫܡܝܐ ܡܫܬܠܡܐ [R 131] ܐܬܚܙܝ܆ ܟܕ ܡܕܝܢ
ܚܙܝܬ ܡܪܢܐ ܘܟܠܗܘܢ ܩܕܝܫܘ̈ܗܝ. ܘܡܠܐܟ̈ܐ ܘܪ̈ܘܚܐ ܡ̈ܠܐܟܐ܆ ܡܢ
ܡܢܝܢ ܘܡܢ ܗܟܠܐ ܡܢܗܘܢ. ܘܫܘܒܚܐ ܣܓܝܐܐ ܡܛܠ ܡܫܠܡܘܬܗ
ܕܗܟܢܐ ܐܟܢܐ ܦܠܚܘܗܝ ܗܘܐ܆ ܘܟܠܗ ܡܢ ܫܠܝܘܗܝ. ܡܦܩܘܢ ܗܘܘ
ܘܐܡܪܝܢ. ܕܗܟܢ ܟ̈ܠܗܝܢ ܩܕܝܫܐ ܘܡܫܬܠܐ ܐܢܬ ܠܗ܆ ܘܫܒܚܐ
ܐܬܘܬܗ܆ ܦܬܚ ܘܡܬܚܠܬܐ. ܘܟܕܢܐ ܗܘ ܡܟܝܠ ܕܢܬܬܪܐ ܘܢܫܬܒܚ
ܢܦܫܐ. ܕܕܐܝܟ ܗܕܐ ܒܫܘܒܬܐ ܘܐܘ̈ܠܝܢܐ ܘܦܘܪ̈ܫܢܐ܆ ܗܠܝܢ ܕܢܠܦ
ܫܘܒܚܐ ܕܫܒܩܝܢ ܡܕܝܢܐ. ܗܠܝܢ ܕܝܢ ܐܡܪܝܢ ܗܘܘ܆ ܕܗܟܢܐ ܟܠܗܘܢ
ܒܕܬܝܢ ܡܢ܆ ܘܒܫܟܐ ܕܐܘܪܬܐ ܕܒܫܝܐ. ܡܛܠ ܕܟܠܗܘܢ. ܟܕ ܬܠܝܢ.
ܘܗܘ ܐܢܬ ܠܗܘܢ ܗܟܢܐ ܘܒܫܢܐ. ܘܠܓܝܢ ܡܠܘܢ ܫܘܒܚܐ
ܕܗ̇ܘ ܕܢܫܬܪܐ. ܘܐܫܬܕܪ ܡܛܠ ܗܕܐ ܦܠܚܘܗܝ ܗܫܕܐ܆ ܘܪܫܝܐ
ܕܐܦܝܣܩܘܦܐ ܕܐܠܟܣܢܕܪܝܐ ܕܗܘ ܢܡܘܣܗܘܢ. ܚܙܝܬ. ܗܘܐ ܕܝܢ
ܕܡܟܪܝܗ ܕܢܗܘܐ ܓܝܪ ܡܢ ܟܬܪ ܫܒܥܐ ܝܘܡܝܢ. ܗܐ ܗܕܐ ܐܬܬܘܗܝ܆
ܕܡܢ ܠܟܠ ܦܘܩܕܢܝ ܐܡܪܬ. ܕܟܕܐ ܐܢܬ ܠܗ ܠܐܠܗܐ ܕܠܩܕܝܫܘܗܝ܆ ܟܕ.
ܗܠܝܢ ܕܫܒܩܝܢ ܠܗܘܢ܆ ܘܕܫܒܩܝܢ ܠܗܘܢ ܒܢܝܐ ܘܟܬܒܐ ܢܦܫ.

(§174) ܟܕ ܕܝܢ ܗܕܐ ܫܡܥܬ ܐܬܬܒܪ ܠܒܝ. ܐܦ ܐܢܐ ܓܝܪ ܒܗ̇
ܟܕ ܒܗ̇ ܒܫܢܬܐ ܘܒܡܟܪܝܘܬܐ ܐܚܝܕ. ܗܘܝܬ ܘܬܘܢܐ. ܒܝܘܡ ܟܕ.
ܐܡܪܝܢ ܕܝܬܒܝܢ ܕܐܠܗܐ ܢܗܘܐ܆ ܡܫܟܚܝܢ ܗܘܝܢ ܕܡܦܩܝܢ ܕܢܦܘܩ
ܢܦܫܐ. ܘܐܬܬܕܟܪܬ ܗܕܐ ܐܦ ܠܗ ܠܬܘܟܠܢܐ. ܘܐܡܝܢܐܝܬ ܐܡܪ
ܗܘܐ ܟܕ ܡܛܐ. ܡܕܝܢܐ ܦܠܚܘܗܝ ܠܐ ܬܫܬܘܕܪ. ܕܐܝܟ ܗܕܐ ܓܝܪ
ܙܒܢܬܐ ܘܗܝܡܢܘܬܐ ܘܫܘܒܚܐ ܕܠܗ ܕܕܝܢ ܒܪܘܚܐ ܘܩܫܕܐ ܐܬܐ
[R 132] ܗܘܐ ܠܗ ܒܟܠܗܝܢ܆ ܐܝܟܢܐ ܕܟܠ ܚܕܐ ܟܕ ܡܫܬܡܠܐ
ܗܘܐ ܕܡܟܪܝܗ܆ ܗܘ ܒܫܘܒܚܗ ܠܡܫܝܚܐ ܕܗܘܕܘܬܗ ܦܪܐ ܗܘܐ.

[1] See Rev 7:11. Although this passage offers no detailed description of an explicit hierarchical ordering of the heavenly hosts, an argument connecting Peter the Iberian with Pseudo-Dionysius should pay attention to this vision and its details. For a vision John the Eunuch had of the heavenly realm, see *Vit. Pet.* §61 (R 42–43).

[2] See Luke 2:29.

[3] For a similar argument for Abba Isaiah, see *Vit. Pet.* §169 (R 126).

worthy to dwell with an old man like this, and now I am about to be deprived also of him because of my sins?' He said, 'Yes, but do not lose heart, for the sentence and the call is from God. At this hour an assembly has come together in heaven **[R 131]** on account of this, the Lord seated first and all his saints and angels and archangels standing on [his] right and on [his] left.[1] There was much deliberation about the weakness of the old man, Abba Peter. Some, on the one hand, were making petition for him and [were] saying, "My Lord, he has [endured] many struggles and labors, and he is very old and weak. It is time now that he should be released[2] and find rest from such asceticism and afflictions and persecutions, which [he endures] for the glory of your holy name." Others were saying, "Your church, my Lord, and the people of the orthodox are in need of him, because all of them depend on him, and he is for them a support and consolation."[3] He rather adopted the counsel that he should be released. Because of this, Peter the martyr and archbishop of Alexandria[4] was sent that he himself would take him away.' " His memorial was to take place in seven days.[5] Behold, this is what we said above earlier, that God has the custom of taking away his saints through those who are like-minded to them and who are equal to them in way of life and in zeal.[6]

(§174) When I heard this, my heart was broken. For I was seized with the same sadness and mournfulness, and [even] greater. Nevertheless, when we said, "God's will be done,"[7] we were waiting to see the outcome of the vision. This was also known to the blessed one. He was saying continually, while lying down, "Saint Peter,[8] do not delay!" For he always had such affection and faith and his love for the high priest **[R 132]** and martyr that every year when his memorial was being celebrated he recited in person

[4] Succeeding Bishop Theonas, Peter of Alexandria (300–311) was the seventeenth bishop of the See of St. Mark. Venerated as the last and "seal" of the martyrs by Christians in Egypt, Peter was a man of moderation marked by a spirit of reconciliation and charity. See Donald B. Spanel and Tim Vivian, "Peter I," *CE* 6:1943–47; Tim Vivian, *St. Peter of Alexandria, Bishop and Martyr* (Philadelphia: Fortress, 1988).

[5] Given that Peter of Alexandria's martyrdom took place on 25 November 311, the present event appears to have taken place around 18 November 491.

[6] See *Vit. Pet.* §169 (R 125–26).

[7] See Acts 21:14.

[8] I.e., Peter of Alexandria.

ܘܡܘܪܒܢܐ ܡܩܕܫܐ ܗܘܐ ܡܩܪܒ ܒܣܦܣܛܠܛܐ݂ ܒܗ ܒܟܠܗ ܙܒܢܐ.
ܐܝܟܢܐ ܕܢܣܒܘܗܝ ܕܦܐܝܢ ܘܡܟܝܟܝܢ ܒܗ.

(§175) ܒܙܒܢ ܚܕ ܟܕ ܒܥܐ ܚܠܦ. ܗܘܐ ܕܢܫܡܠܐ ܫܘܡܠܝܐ ܕܐܪ̈ܙܐ ܒܕܘܒܪܗ. ܥܠ ܗܘ ܛܘܒܢܐ ܕܢܛܪ ܡܕܒܚܐ. ܐܝܟ ܒܥܕܐ ܕܐܝܬ ܗܘܐ ܠܗ. ܕܒܠܒܝܗ ܗܘ ܒܐܝܕܘܗܝ. ܗܕܐ ܥܒܕ ܗܘܐ. ܘܠܐ ܫܒܩ ܗܘܐ ܠܐܢܫ ܐܚܪܝܢ. ܘܟܕ ܐܦܩ ܡܢ ܦܬܘܪܐ ܕܩܘܕܫܐ ܚܕ. ܙܒܢܐ ܕܗܢܐ ܥܠ ܡܕܒܚܐ ܩܕܝܫܐ ܢܦܪܘܣ. ܟܕ ܩܐܡ ܗܘܐ ܕܝܢ ܥܠ ܓܒܗ ܐܚܕ ܡܢ ܗܠܝܢ ܕܓܒܗ ܡܫܡܫܝܢ. ܡܬܚܙܐ ܗܘܐ ܒܢܦܫܗ ܟܕ ܐܡܪ. ܠܒܢܐ ܟܝ ܠܗ ܗܢܐ ܦܬܘܪܐ ܟܠܗ. ܦܪܘܣ ܗܘ ܐܒܐ ܐܠܐ ܐܢܬ. ܗܘ ܗܘ. ܕܝܢ ܟܕ ܚܙܐ ܗܠܝܢ ܕܒܠܒܗ ܐܡܪ ܠܗܘܢ. ܫܬܘܩ. ܗܘ ܕܐܝܬܘܗܝ ܕܒܪܝܫܗ. ܗܘ ܡܢ ܠܗܘܢ ܘܐܡܪ ܠܝ ܕܗܢܐ ܐܦܪܘܣ. ܘܟܕ ܕܚܠ. ܫܬܩ. ܐܝܟܢܐ ܕܗܢ ܗܕܝܢ ܘܒܕܘܟܬܐ ܠܗܢܐ ܢܠܒܘܫ ܚܙܐ. ܕܒܕܘܒܪܢܐ ܕܗܘܕܐ ܡܫܡܫܢܐ ܘܪܫܐ ܕܐܦܝܣܩܘܦܐ ܦܛܪܘܣ. ܗܘ ܗܘ ܦܬܘܪܐ ܢܦܫܗ ܘܟܕ ܢܠܒܫܘܢ ܘܢܣܒܘܢ ܦܬܘܪܐ ܩܕܝܫܐ.

(§176) ܟܕ ܗܟܝܠ ܢܚܬ ܕܡܢ ܒܝܬܐ ܕܦܛܪܝܬܗ ܕܡܢ ܠܥܠ. ܚܙܐ ܕܢܬܐܡܪ. ܟܕ ܐܩܝܡ ܐܪܒܥܐ ܬܪ̈ܬܐ. ܩܕܡܝܐ ܐܚܪܐ ܢܣܝܒ ܡܫܡܫܢܐ. ܗܘ ܕܦܩܕ ܢܚܬ ܗܘܐ ܠܗ ܕܢܛܪܐ ܗܘܐ ܒܐܘܦܠܛܘܣ ܡܛܠ ܕܡܢ ܒܐܘܦܣܝܣ ܩܪܝܬܐ. ܕܡܢ ܬܚܒܢܐ ܠܓܘܐܪܐ ܐܝܟ ܬܪ̈ܝܢ ܬܠܬܐ ܫܒ̈ܚܐ ܐܝܬܘܗܝ ܗܘܐ. ܕܢܬܐ ܡܢ ܓܠܝܘܬܗ ܘܬܠܡܝܕܐ ܗܘܐ ܕܓܒܝܢܐ [R 133] ܐܦܠܐܦܝܘܣ ܗܘ ܕܐܝܬܘܗܝ ܗܘܐ ܪܫܐ ܕܡ̈ܫܡܫܢܐ ܕܟܕܢܬܐ ܩܕܝܫܬܐ. ܘܡܛܠ ܓܒܝܢܐ ܕܡܫܡܫܢܘܬܐ ܬܪܝܨܬ ܫܘܒܚܐ ܥܠ ܕܠܐ ܢܬܬܦܫ ܠܟܘܪܝܐ ܕܗܘܢܘܣ ܕܟܠܝܪܝܘܣ. ܟܕ ܫܟܒ ܠܡܠܝܘܣ ܕܐܘܪܫܠܡ. ܢܦܩ ܒܐܟܣܢܝܘܬܐ. ܘܒܐܟܣܢܝܘܬܐ ܐܫܬܡܠܝ. ܕܡܛܠ ܕܒܪܘܗ ܫܠܝܚܐ ܘܣܝ̈ܒܘܗܝ. ܡܢܚܐ ܐܪ̈ܬܐ. ܥܠ ܡܬܠܒܢܘܬܐ ܕܒܥܬܐ ܚܒܝܫ ܗܘ ܕܡܫܬܥܐ ܡܛܠܬܗ. ܡܛܠ ܗܕܐ ܟܕ

[1] This reference provides a clue to the kind of setting for which also the *Vita Petri Iberi* was composed. Raabe (121 n. 5) also refers to a parallel expression in Eusebius of Caesarea, *Hist. eccl.* 7.32.

[2] On Rufus's intentional use of the apostle Peter and Peter of Alexandria as foils against which to interpret the figure of Peter the Iberian, see Horn, *Asceticism and Christological Controversy*, 184–88.

[3] I.e., Peter of Alexandria.

[4] I.e., Peter the Iberian.

[5] This comment points to the precision with which liturgical customs

the account of his martyrdom[1] and was offering the holy oblation diligently with all his exultation, so that he would see him standing and serving as a priest with him.[2]

(§175) Therefore, at the time when the consecration of the mysteries on his[3] memorial was about to take place, the blessed one[4] entered to arrange the altar; it was his custom to do this always with his own hands and to allow no one else [to do it]. As he was bringing out one of the coverings that are placed, he wanted to spread it out on the holy altar. But while there was standing beside him one of those who were serving with him, he thought to himself, "Now why did the father not rather spread out this covering, but that?" He, however, since he saw these things that were in his heart, said to him, "Be silent! He whose memorial it is, he stood by me and said to me that I should spread out this one." Since he was afraid, he was silent, so that from then on and until this hour we retain the custom that, on the memorial of the glorious martyr and archbishop Peter, we take out exactly this cover and deck and adorn with it the holy table.[5]

(§176) Knowing that the time of his calling from above was near, he made a will, appointing four heirs.[6] The first was Abba John the deacon, whom he loved much,[7] the one called the Canopite because he was from the village of Canopis,[8] situated about two miles south of Gaza. He was a monk from his childhood and a disciple of the blessed **[R 133]** Stephen[9] who was archdeacon of the Holy City. Because of [his] zeal for the orthodox faith, in order not to be in communion with the transgression of the Council of Chalcedon, when he left the clergy of Jerusalem he went out wandering in exile and was perfected on the road. On account of his apostolic and excellent way of life, a special written narration

were observed in the anti-Chalcedonian community surrounding Peter the Iberian. For some discussion of this concern for strict observance, see Horn, *Asceticism and Christological Controversy*, 208.

[6] See also Zachariah Rhetor, *Vit. Sev.* 86 (Kugener, 86).

[7] Or, "who loved him much."

[8] See Clermont-Ganneau, "Sur quelques localités de Palestine," 14–15; see also Zachariah Rhetor, *Vit. Sev.* 86, fol. 127b (Kugener, 86,9).

[9] See also *Pler.* 8 and 79. It might be that the priest Stephen, referenced at *Pler.* 58, is also identical with the present blessed Stephen.

ܒܠܗܝܢ ܗܠܝܢ ܐܣܛܝܢܬܐ ܓܒܝܠܝܢ ܚܕ: ܗܕܐ ܒܠܚܘܕ. ܐܟܘܬ ܚܕ.
ܠܬܫܘܒܘܚܬܐ ܕܝܠܗ̇، ܕܗܟܢܐ ܫܦܪ ܠܐܠܗܐ.

(§177) ܟܕ ܒܠܠܝܐ ܗܘܐ ܒܪ ܕܝܢܐ. ܘܢܚܬܘ ܠܘܬ ܢܦܫܗ: ܘܫܩܠ ܗܘܐ ܒܡܫܠܝܘܬܐ ܡܬܐܟܠܐ ܘܠܐ ܡܬܬܪܥܝܢܘܬܐ: ܚܙܐ ܗܘܐ ܚܘܙܐ. ܟܕ ܐܬܘ ܕܝܢ ܐ̈ܢܫܝܢ ܡܢ ܩ̈ܕܝܫܐ ܕܢܨܚܢܘܬܗܘܢ، ܘܐܫܬܘܕܥܘܗ، ܒܚܙܘܐ: ܡܚܝܢ ܗܘܘ ܟܕ ܡܩܒܠܝܢ ܕܫܘܠܡܐ ܚܙܘ̈ܐ. ܟܕ ܦܩܕ ܗܟܝܠ ܡܢ ܚܙܘܐ: ܐܡܪ ܠܘܬܗ ܐܪ̈ܚܝܢܘ ܕܒܗܘܢܐ: ܕܡܒܥܐ ܗܘܐ ܢܬܠܒܘܢ ܒܪܬܐ ܕܝܢܐ ܒܪܘܚܐ ܐܠܗܐ ܘܣܥܪܐ. ܐܡܪܐ ܐܬܐܝܢ ܗܘܝܬ ܐܡܪܐ: ܕܒܥܝܬ ܡܬܒܐܝܐ ܐܢܬ ܠܝ ܗܘܐ ܕܐܚܙܝܢ ܚܕ ܠܝ. ܗܘ ܕܝܢ ܐܡܪ. ܐܡܪܐ ܕܡ̈ܠܐ ܠܐ ܡ̈ܬܡܠܠܢܘܬܐ: ܗܠܝܢ ܕܠܐ ܫܠܝܛ ܠܒܪܢܫܐ ܕܢܡܠܠ. ܘܟܕ ܦܬܚܬ ܫܥܬܐ ܕܒܘܝܐܐ ܕܠܗ ܕܠܦܘܬܝܐ ܡܬܦܐܝܐ. ܟܕ ܠܐ ܡܬܬܪܥܝܢܐ ܐܢܬܘܢ، ܗܘܐ ܒܗܠܝܢ ܬ̈ܫܒܚܬܐ ܕܡܕܡ ܗܟܢ. ܡܢ ܥܠ ܓܘܪ ܡܢ ܚܘܪܒ ܘܡܪ̈ܝ ܢܦܫܗ: ܟܕ ܒܥܐ ܠܩ̈ܕܝܫܐ ܗ̈ܢܘܢ ܕܐܝܟ ܕܢܨܚܢܘܬܗܘܢ، ܘܟܡܐ ܡܢܗܘܢ ܠܒܪܢܫܐ. ܘܟܕ ܫܪܟ ܠܗ̇ ܒܡ ܣܘܬܐ ܘܦܫܝܩܘܬܐ: ܬܘܒ ܐܝܟ: ܘܡܚܘܝܢ ܥܡܗ ܙܘܥܐ. ܕܐܒܪܗܡ ܕܝܢ ܡܬܬܠܡܕ ܒܐܪܒܥܐ ܒܒܪܘܢ ܘܡܢܐ ܒܬܪ [R 134] ܬܠܬܐ ܫ̈ܢܝܐ ܕܕܘܒܪܐ ܕܐܒܐ ܦܛܪܘܣ ܐܦܝܣܩܘܦܐ ܕܝܠܗ.

(§178) ܬܠܡܝܕܐ ܫܡܥܘܢ ܕܗܢܐ. ܐܝܬܘܗܝ، ܗܘܐ ܗܘ ܐܒܐ ܢܘܚ. ܗܘ ܕܐܩܝܡ ܢܬܐ. ܘܡܚܡܠ ܗܒܝܒܐ: ܘܐܬܕܪܘܢ ܦܝܠܝܩܘܣ ܕܝܠܗ. ܘܟܡܐ ܡܢܗܘܢ ܬܐܘܕܘܣܝܘܣ ܗܘ ܐܦܝܣܩܘܦܐ ܕܐܦܣܩܘܦܘܬܗܘܢ: ܕܠܘܬܗ ܒ̈ܢܝ ܠܚܪܬܐ ܒܡ ܗܠܟܐ ܢܘܚ. [ܠܗܠܝܢ ܐܘܪܬܐ][1] ܒܠܗ ܒܐܦܪܝܐ ܗܢܐ: ܘܦܠܦܠܘܣ ܘܪܫܝܡܘܬܐ ܕܟܠ ܐܢ̈ܫܐ. ܐܝܟ ܗ̇ܘ ܕܒܠܚܘܕܝܗܘܢ ܗܦܟܝܢ ܗܘܘ ܘܡܚܝܢ: ܕܢܝܚܘܬܐ ܗܕܐ ܢܦܫܗܘܢ ܘܡܕܒܪܢܘܬܐ ܕܒܐܠܗܐ.

(§179) ܟܕ ܦܢܐ ܕܝܢ ܠܦܘܠܚܢܐ ܠܒܠܗܘܢ ܐܢ̈ܫܐ ܐܚܪ̈ܢܐ: ܡܬܪܢܝܢܘܬܐ ܐܪܬܝܬܐ ܐܪܬܝ، ܐܝܟܢ. ܟܕ ܡܫܐܠ ܠܗܘܢ ܗܠܝܢ ܕܠܘܬ ܦܘܪܫܢܐ. ܘܡܕܒܪܢܘܬ ܗ̇ܘ ܕܡܫܝܚܘܬܐ ܬܪܝܨܬ ܫܘܒܚܐ ܫܬܐܝܬ ܘܕܠܐ

[1] The words ܠܗܠܝܢ ܐܘܪܬܐ are neither in MS Sachau 321 nor in BM Add. 12,174. Raabe inserted them in order to make sense of the text.

[2] The present comment evidences that also local clergy were involved with the anti-Chalcedonian cause.

[3] An allusion to 2 Cor 12:4. We owe this reference to John T. Fitzgerald.

telling about him is needed. Therefore, leaving all other [things aside], we recount only this [anecdote] to demonstrate how much he pleased God.

(§177) Just before he departed to go on the journey to Jesus and was lying in great weakness and immobility, he saw a vision. Meanwhile, some of the saints came to visit him, and, finding him in a vision, they stood [there], waiting to see the end. When he returned from the vision, the archdeacon of Maiuma,[2] whose name was Nestabus, a man well-known for fear of God and wise, said to him, "Where have you been, father? We waited a long time for you." He, however, said, "Where there are words unutterable, which it is not lawful for a man to speak."[3] When the hour of the departure of the blessed Stephen drew near, having been immobile for the days prior in this manner, suddenly he leapt from [his] bed and straightened himself, when he saw the saints, those who had come to take him, and with them the Lord. Having adored him with joy and cheerfulness, he reclined again and immediately gave up his spirit. His memorial is celebrated on the fourth of First Kanon [December],[4] three **[R 134]** days after the memorial of Abba Peter, our bishop.

(§178) His beloved disciple was Abba John, whom he [Peter] appointed [his] heir,[5] and with him Zachariah and Andrew, his cell-mates,[6] and with them Theodore of Ashkelon the ex-lawyer,[7] who remained with him at the end, together with the old man John. [To these he bequeathed] his whole monastery and the administration[8] and leadership of the brethren, those who alone were sufficient and able to take up this guardianship and guidance that is from God.

(§179) When the blessed one had called all the brethren together, he admonished them [with his] last exhortation, witnessing to them these [things] that [are essential] for salvation. First,

[4] December is named "First Kanon," while January is commonly called "Other Kanon" or "Second Kanon." See Payne Smith, 218.

[5] After the digression about Stephen, the author now finishes his account of Peter the Iberian's will (see Raabe, 123 n. 1).

[6] The Syriac transliterates the Greek σύγκελλοι (Raabe, 123 n. 2).

[7] The Syriac transliterates the Greek ἀποσχολαστικός (Raabe, 123 n. 3).

[8] The Syriac transliterates the Greek κατάστασις.

ܡܫܠܡܢܐ ܢܛܪܘܢ܆ ܥܕܡܐ ܠܡܘܬܐ. ܘܠܟܠ ܗܪ̈ܣܝܣ ܢܚܪܡܘܢ
ܘܢܣܠܘܢ. ܢܕܟܐܝܬ ܠܗܝܡܢܘܬܗ ܕܟܠܗܕܘܪܐ܆ ܘܠܬܠܝܬܝܘܬܐ ܣܓܝܕܬܐ
ܘܐܠܗܘܢ ܢܛܪܘܢ. ܘܢܣܠܘܢ. ܐܝܟܢܐ ܕܙ̈ܒܢܬܐ ܩܘܠܣܐܬܐ ܐܡܪ
ܦܩܕܬ ܠܟܘܢ. ܘܟܠܗܘܢ ܩ̈ܢܘܢܐ. ܗܢ ܐܡܪ ܐܢܐ܆ ܕܐܢ ܡܢ ܗܘ ܕܠܐ
ܗ̇ܘ ܕܐܝܟ ܕܐܡܪܬ ܐܢܬܘܢ ܐܢܬ ܠܟܘܢ ܡܕܡ܆ ܚܢܢ ܐܢܬܘܢ ܠܝ
ܡܬܘܡ ܕܡܫܬܐܠ ܐܢܐ ܘܐܡܪ ܐܢܐ ܠܟܘܢ܇ ܕܠܐ ܡܕܡ ܕܟܝܢ ܐܢܬ
ܒܗ̇ ܒܗܝܡܢܘܬܐ ܕܟܠܗܕܘܪܐ܆ ܬܗܘܘܢ ܡܣܝܪܝܢ ܐܢܬܘܢ ܡܢ ܐܒܐ
ܘܡܢ ܒܪܐ ܘܡܢ ܪܘܚܐ ܩܕܝܫܐ܆ ܐ̄ ܗ̇ܘ ܕܠܐ ܒܐܝ̈ܕܝ ܡܣܝܪܝܢ
ܐܢܬܘܢ ܠܝ܆ ܘܚܪܡܝܢ ܐܢܬܘܢ ܡܢܝ ܐܝܟ [R 135] ܕܡܢ ܒܡܘܪܐ܆
ܘܕܟܡ ܢܘܗܪܐ ܡܫܠܡܢܐ ܐܢܬ ܠܝ ܡܢܝܬܐ. ܒܠܚܘܕ ܕܝܢ ܗܡܝܢܘܬܐ܆
ܡܕܡܝܘܬܐ ܕܢܦܫܐ ܘܕܦܓܪܐ ܚܝܒܘ ܕܬܛܝܒܘܢ. ܘܫܬܐܬܝܬ ܬܛܪܘܢ.
ܗܝ ܕܟܠܒܝܢܝ ܠܐ ܐܝܬ ܚܝܐ ܠܒܪܢܫܐ. ܘܫܡܥܐ ܕܠܒܬ ܫܪܪܐ.
ܘܫܘܬܦ ܢܦܫܐ ܡܢ ܠܒܐ ܘܡܢ ܬܐܪܬܐ ܛܒܬܐ. ܘܡܢ ܗܝܡܢܘܬܐ
ܕܠܐ ܡܣܒ ܒܐ̈ܦܐ ܐܝܟ ܕܟܬܝܒ. ܘܛܪܘ ܕܠܐ ܬܛܥܘܢ ܦܐܪܗܣܝܐ.
ܠܘ ܒܠܚܘܕ ܠܘܬ ܟ̈ܢܫܐ܆ ܐܠܐ ܘܠܘܬ ܫܪܪܐ. ܦܐܪܗܣܝܐ ܓܝܪ
ܡܫܠܡܢܘܬܐ ܐܝܬܝܗ̇ ܘܡܫܠܕܢܘܬܐ ܕܒܠܗܘܢ ܫ̈ܪܟܐ. ܐܬܡܠܟܘ
ܕܝܢ ܘܩܒܪܘ ܒܠܒܟܘܢ܆ ܒܡܠܬܐ ܕܢܒܝܘܬܐ ܗ̇ܘ ܕܡ̈ܠܐܟܐ ܕܐܡܪ.
ܕܛܒܐ ܒܠܫܢܗܘܢ ܐܦܣܩܘܦܐ. ܘܐܝܟ ܬܠܡܝܕܘܬܗ ܩܕܝܫܬܐ

[1] Or "reject and anathematize." This restatement of Peter's instructions from *Vit. Pet.* §§155–157 (R 116–19) is presented with greater intensity and advises the followers to take to more radical measures when expressing their orthodoxy.

[2] Also here an earlier warning not to neglect Peter's instructions is turned into an explicitly Trinitarian curse. It is quite possible that one sees here more clearly the hand of the author of the *Vita Petri Iberi* and less the actual words of Peter.

[3] See *Vit. Pet.* §§47, 76, 83 (R 32, 52, 58).

[4] See Rom 2:11.

[5] See 1 Tim 1:5.

[6] The Syriac transliterates the Greek παρρησία. All throughout Rufus emphasized that Peter spoke with παρρησία. That restrictions are being imposed here may reflect the notion that only the saint is allowed to speek with freedom, while it is more advisable for his followers to control their tongues constantly and rather practice silence. The ancient world placed remarkable value on the exercise of παρρησία in communal settings, at least in theory. That this

indeed, they should keep the orthodox faith accurately and without change until death and reject and curse all heresies,[1] expressly the Council of Chalcedon, and reject and curse the wicked *Tome of Leo*, "as many times," he said, "I have witnessed to you and to all men, when I was saying that if you ever see me, the same who, as you are saying, is a saint for you, having changed and saying to you that there is nothing evil in the Council of Chalcedon, may you be under a curse[2] from the Father and from the Son and from the Holy Spirit, if you do not curse me to my face and flee from me as **[R 135]** from a heathen and [as from one] who has part with Judas the betrayer.[3] After faith, however, be anxious to gain and to keep accurately the sanctity of the soul and of the body, without which no one sees the Lord, as well as love toward each other and equanimity [that comes] from the heart and from a good conscience and from a faith that is not hypocritical,[4] as it is written.[5] Be on your guard not to obtain freedom [of speech],[6] not only toward foreigners but also toward each other. For freedom [of speech] is the kindler and begetter of all the passions. Meditate, however, and read always in the book on asceticism, the *Questions of the Brethren* of the blessed Basil the bishop.[7] Straighten out your ways of life

could lead to numerous problems in actual practice is illustrated, for example, in a treatise on the topic from the pen of the Epicurean philosopher Philodemus of Gadara. See, e.g., Philodemus of Gadara, *On Frank Criticism* frgs 52–73. See also Clarence E. Glad, "Frank Speech, Flattery, and Friendship in Philodemus," in *Friendship, Flattery, and Frankness of Speech: Studies on Friendship in the New Testament World* (ed. John T. Fitzgerald; NovTSup 82; Leiden: Brill, 1996), 21–59; and L. Michael White, "A Measure of Frank Speech: The State of the Manuscript of PHerc. 1471," in *Philodemus and the New Testament World* (ed. John T. Fitzgerald, Dirk Obbink, and Glenn S. Holland; NovTSup 111; Leiden: Brill, 2004), 103–30. Abraham J. Malherbe (*Paul and the Thessalonians: The Philosophic Tradition of Pastoral Care* [Philadelphia: Fortress, 1987], 84–86) offers a helpful discussion of the treatise in the light of pastoral concerns. We are grateful to John Fitzgerald for bringing Philodemus's treatise to our attention.

[7] Basil's works were read and appreciated in the sixth-century Palestinian monastic milieu. Zosimus, Barsanuphius, and Dorotheus of Gaza all refer to his *Rules*. Lucien Regnault ("Les Apophthegmes des Pères en Palestine aux ve-vi^e^ siècles," *Irén* 54 [1981]: 328) comments that Dorotheus is the only ancient witness who guarantees the antiquity of the *apophthegma* attributed to Basil in the *Alphabeticon*. See Dorotheus of Gaza, *Instructions* 24 (Regnault and Préville, 182–85).

ܘܦܩܕ ܒܦܢ̈ܩܝܣܘܗܝ܆ ܛܘܦ̈ܣܐ ܕܟܬ̈ܒܐ ܘܢܒ̈ܝܐ܂ ܐܟܘܬܐ ܕܒܪ
ܕܟ̈ܬܒܐ ܢܩܝܦܝܢ ܗܘ ܐܠܗܐ ܪܘܚܐ ܩܕܝܫܐ ܐܬܬܙܝܥܘ܆ ܗܟܢܐ
ܘܗܕܐ ܡܬܟܬܒܢܘܬܐ܆ ܟܠܗܘܢܬܐ ܐܠܗܝܬܐ ܘܟܪܘܒܐ ܩܕܝܫܐ ܦܩܘܕܬ:
ܡܛܠ ܕܗܕܐ ܫܠܝܛܐ ܘܬܘܪ̈ܐ ܘܦܘܩܕܢܐ ܕܟܬܒܐ ܕܟܠܗܘܢ.

(§180) ܘܟܕ ܐܫܬܢܝܬܐ ܩܠܝܠܐܬܐ ܒܗ ܡܠܟ ܦܬܪ ܘܐܡܪ ܠܝ: ܗܠܟ ܕܐܬܩ ܠܘܬ ܢܘܪܐ ܘܡܗܝܪܘܬܐ ܘܦܘܪܩܢܐ܆ ܠܫܘܐܬܐ ܟܕ ܠܟܠ ܟܢܫܝܢ ܘܐܬܟܫܦ ܠܝ ܠܡܟܪܐ܆ ܗܟܢܐ ܕܢܐ ܠܝ. ܟܕ ܕܝܢ ܚܙܝ. ܗܘܐ ܕܟܗ ܒܗܘ ܠܠܝܐ ܢܦܠ ܙܘܥܐ܆ ܐܬܟܢܫܘ ܐܦܝܣܩܘܦܐ ܩܕܝܫܐ: ܗܘ ܕܡܢ ܠܟܠ ܐܬܟܢܫܘ܆ ܫܘܐ ܕܐܢܝܢ ܗܢܐ ܒܢܝܐ. ܒܬܪܐ ܪܟܒܬܐ ܕܟܠܢܐ ܢܘܗܪܐ ܘܩܘܠܣܐ ܩܠܝܠܐ. ܘܟܘܢܫܐ ܕܩܕܝܫܐ ܩܠܝܠܐ. ܘܦܩܕܗ ܕܢܦܫܗ ܒܝܬ ܡܘܬܒܐ. ܠܗܘܢܐ ܕܝܢ ܦܩܘܕ [R 136] ܪܫܐ ܕܐܦܝܣܩܘܦܐ ܕܐܠܟܣܢܕܪܝܐ. ܟܕ ܩܐܡ ܥܠ ܒܐܡܐ ܪܟܝܒܬܐ: ܘܟܬܒܦ ܐܣܛܠܐ ܡܢ ܒܝܬ ܫܘܪܬܐ ܘܕܝܢܚܐܝܬ ܡܕܝܢܬܐ܆ ܘܐܡܪ ܡܐܡܪܐ ܕܩܘܠܣܐ ܒܡܠܐ ܪܒܐ܆ ܥܠ ܦܘܠܚܢܐ ܦܩܘܕܘܗܝ. ܟܕ ܒܠܚܘܕ ܡܢܗ ܩܕܝܫܐ ܐܟܚܕܐ ܥܡܟܝܢ܆ ܘܐܟܚܕܐ ܡܬܒܥܝܢ ܠܗ ܒܚܕܘܬܐ ܪܒܬܐ ܘܒܕܡܝܐ. ܘܡܢ ܗܕܐ ܐܬܥܠܠ܆ ܕܟܕ ܒܗܘ ܢܡܟܐ ܟܠܢܫ. ܕܢܗܘܐ ܥܡܠܝܢ ܕܦܘܠܚܢܐ. ܒܗܘ ܕܐܦ ܡܟܝܠ ܗܘܐ ܢܡܟܐ ܬܠܬܐ ܕܕܪܝܢܐ ܕܠܗ ܕܢܪܫܐ ܐܦܝܣܩܘܦܐ ܘܗܕܐ ܦܩܘܕܘܗܝ. ܐܝܟ ܒܕܐ ܕܠܒܝ ܟܐܠܟܣܢܕܪܝܐ܆ ܕܬܠܬܐ ܢܩܪ̈ܬܐ ܗܘ̇ܐ ܕܗܘܝܗ.

(§181) ܟܕ ܢܦܩ ܗܟܝܠ ܒܠܗ ܗܘ ܢܡܟܐ܆ ܒܟܢܫܘܬܐ ܘܒܡܬܐ ܡܕܝܬܐ ܘܒܥܕܐ ܒܠܝܐ ܒܕܡܐ ܠܢܦܫܐ. ܟܕ ܗܘ ܦܘܠܚܢܐ ܡܟܝܠ ܒܡܦܘܩܗ ܒܢܦܫܐ ܗܘܐ܆ ܘܒܗ ܡܢ ܡܟܝܠ ܗܘܐ. ܩܪܒ ܗܘܐ ܕܝܢ ܗܢܝܢ܆ ܘܐܟܢܐ ܒܪܢܫܘܗܝ ܕܡܢ ܐܦܘܪܢܐ ܗܘ ܕܐܣܒܪܢ. ܟܕ ܒܕܡܐ ܠܢܦܫܬܐ ܐܣܢܬܐ ܢܦܩ ܕܒܢܐܝܬ ܘܢܟܐ ܘܐܬܪܐܬܐ

[1] The Syriac may render the Greek γραφαὶ θεόπνευστοι (Raabe, 124 n. 4). See also 2 Tim 3:16.

[2] Scripture and Basil's *Rules* are considered as being of equal authority, given that both ultimately come from the same author.

[3] See above, *Vit. Pet.* §§173 (R 129–131).

[4] The Syriac transliterates the Greek βῆμα, which designates the elevated podium within the church building from which the bishop often delivered his sermon. Newly baptized Christians were also made to stand on the βῆμα while being presented to the congregation. See, e.g., Gregory Nazianzen, *Orat.*

and your manners according to his holy ordinances and his legislation. For as the God-inspired Scriptures[1] were written down by the Holy Spirit, so also was this writing [written] by divine grace and the Holy Spirit for an accurate way of life, right action, and the salvation of monasteries everywhere."[2]

(§180) When he had commanded and instructed us [in] many other things along with these that are fitting for benefit, [for] admonition, and [for] salvation, he blessed all of us one last time and entrusted us to the Lord [and] likewise dismissed us. Since he was about to surrender his spirit in this very night, Athanasius, the Egyptian priest of whom we made mention above,[3] saw a vision like this: a great church, full of light and much glory; and an assembly of many saints; and the body of the blessed one laid out in [its] midst; the martyr Peter, **[R 136]** archbishop of Alexandria standing on a high *bema*[4] and wearing, indeed, some white and splendidly shining vestment[5] and in a loud voice delivering a homily of eulogies about the blessed Peter, while all those saints together were listening and were praising him together in great joy and in exultation. From this we understood that the end of the blessed one would be taking place on that same day, which occurred on the third day of the memorial of the archbishop and martyr Peter,[6] according to the custom that one adopted in Alexandria, that his memorial was [to be celebrated] for three days.

(§181) Therefore we fasted the whole day, remaining until the evening in mournfulness and grave sadness and in suffering, while the blessed one henceforth prepared for his departure, speaking with our Lord. At that time Abba Gregory from Aphthoria, whom we have mentioned,[7] was near, since until his last breath he

40.46 (Moreschini and Gallay, 308,2–4 [Greek] and 309 [French]). See A. M. Schneider, "Bema," *RAC* 2:129–30; Mark J. Johnson, "Bema," *ODB* 1:281.

[5] The Syriac renders the Greek στολή. For a reference to the white vestment of the bishop of Jerusalem, see also below, *Obit. Theod.* §7 (B 24). For a discussion, see Paul Devos, "Cyrille de Scythopolis: Influences littéraires—Vêtement de l'évêque de Jérusalem—Passarion et Pierre l'Ibère," *AnBoll* 98 (1980): 25–38.

[6] Peter of Alexandria was martyred on 25 November 311, but his three-day memorial is observed 8–10 December. See 264 n. 2 below.

[7] See above, *Vit. Pet.* §160 (R 120).

ܠܘܬܗ ܕܛܘܒܢܐ. ܟܕ ܕܝܢ ܚܙܝ ܙܒܢܐ: ܘܫܩܠܗ ܘܐܝܬܝܗ ܠܐܒܘܢܐ: ܗܘ ܐܒܐ ܐܘܦܪܘܣܝܘܣ ܘܥܠܝ ܩܕܡ ܐܒܘܢܐ: ܘܐܚܕ ܒܛܝܒܘܬܗ ܒܟܠ ܦܬܘܪܐ ܕܢܨܒ ܫܒܥܬܐ. ܘܒܦܠܓܗ ܕܒܕܢܐ ܕܡܐܟܘܠܬܐ: ܐܡܪ ܐܘܦܪܘܣܝܘܣ ܗܘ ܕܐܚܝܕ ܗܘܐ ܡܕܒܪܢܘܬܗ ܕܡܕܝܢܬܐ ܘܡܫܡܫ ܠܗ: ܕܒܝܬܐ ܒܟܦܐ ܘܕܦܠܓ ܐܢܫ ܗܘܐ ܡܢܗ ܕܡܕܝܢܬܐ: ܐܒܐ ܢܦܩ ܠܗ: ܬܘ ܐܬܟܪܟ. ܘܟܕ ܥܒܪܢ ܘܩܡܢ ܡܢ ܦܬܘܪܐ: ܟܡ ܕܩܕܡܐ ܘܬܫܒܘܚܬܐ ܘܨܠܘܬܐ: ܪܗܛܝܢ ܠܘܬ ܒܝܬܗ. [R 137] ܘܡܛܠ ܕܠܐ ܢܬܚܫܒܘܢ، ܠܗ ܠܛܘܒܢܐ: ܕܐܝܬܘܗܝ ܗܘܐ ܒܩܘܒܠܐ ܐܘܪܚܐ: ܗܘ ܐܘܦܪܘܣܝܘܣ ܗܘ ܕܐܬܚܙܝ ܟܕ ܐܬܐ ܠܚܢܝܢܗ ܕܡܕܝܢܬܐ: ܚܘܫܒ ܗܘܐ ܠܟܠܗ ܕܢܬܝܗܒ ܘܢܬܒܪܟ. ܘܠܦܓܥܬܐ ܢܦܩ ܗܘܐ ܗܘ ܠܛܘܒܢܐ ܘܒܗ، ܫܒܚܬܐ: ܡܢ ܓܢܒܘܬܐ ܕܡܫܝܚܘܬܐ ܘܕܘܒܪܐ ܕܐܝܬ ܗܘܐ ܠܗ ܠܘܬܗܘܢ. ܟܕ ܕܝܢ ܐܫܠܡ ܪܘܚܗ ܗܘ ܛܘܒܢܐ: ܒܦܪܝܫܘܬܐ ܦܓܥܬܐ ܘܫܠܡܘܬ ܟܐܢܘܬܗ، ܕܐܠܗܐ: ܗܘ ܕܡܪܒܐ ܗܘܐ ܠܗ ܐܦ ܗܢܝܢ ܘܢܨܒܗ: ܐܒܐ ܐܘܦܪܘܣܝܘܣ ܡܫܡܫܢܐ ܐܫܬܘ، ܕܢܨܒܗ ܐܒܘܗܝ، ܘܡܪܒܝܢܗ،.

(§182) ܐܝܬܘܗܝ، ܕܝܢ ܡܟܝܠ ܙܒܢܐ ܒܥܘܡܪܐ. ܘܢܦܩܗ ܗܘܐ ܗܘܬ ܒܥܘܬܐ. ܟܕ ܐܬܩܪܒ ܕܝܢ ܠܦܓܪܗ ܩܕܝܫܐ: ܘܒܠܒܫܝܗ، ܐܣܛܠܐ ܩܕܝܫܬܐ ܟܕ ܕܘܟ ܗܘܐ: ܒܗ، ܕܟܕ ܗܘܐ ܕܢܦܩ ܬܐܘܪܐ ܩܕܝܫܐ. ܗܟܢܢܝܗ، ܒܟܦܐܝܟ ܘܡܦܢܝܐܝܬ. ܘܟܕ ܢܣܝܒܐ ܦܓܪܐ ܘܡܪܘܝܐ ܐܕܠܡܐ. ܟܠܗ ܠܠܝܐ ܥܒܠܝܢ: ܟܕ ܥܡܪܝܢ ܒܡܙܡܘܪܐ ܘܬܫܒܘܚܬܐ ܘܒܡܕܚܬܐ ܪܘܚܢܝܬܐ. ܟܕ ܢܓܗܐ ܕܝܪܝܢ ܗܘܘ ܠܗ ܘܟܡܐ ܡܩܕܫܝܢ ܗܘܘ ܕܒܪܝܢ ܕܡܕܝܢܬܐ: ܐܝܟ ܚܘܝܐ ܕܡܫܝܚܐ ܐܬܟܢܫܘ ܟܠܗܘܢ ܡܕܝܢܬܐ. ܘܗܘ ܗܘܕܐ ܡܕܝܢܐ ܘܪܒܝܐ ܕܐܦܝܣܩܘܦܐ ܦܠܪܘܣ. ܐܝܬ ܗܘܐ ܕܝܢ ܠܓܒܝܐ ܘܠܓܒܥܘܬ: ܒܟܠܬܐ ܘܠܠܬܐ ܗܦܟܬܐ ܕܡܩܕܫܝܢ ܕܝ، ܦܓܪܬܐ. ܟܕ ܟܠܗܘܢ ܚܙܝܢ ܠܓܠܝܘܬܗܘܢ ܕܟܘܢܗ: ܡܛܠ ܗ، ܕܡܗܕܝܢ ܗܘܘ ܬܫܒܘܚܬܐ ܦܓܥܬܐ: ܘܐܬܦܬܬܐ ܘܐܦܣܬܐ ܡܠܝ ܕܟܐܒܘܗܝ، ܣܘ، ܠܗܘܢ ܐܠܗܐ. ܘܡܬܢܐܬ ܒܡܕܝܢܐ ܙܘܪܒܐ ܘܙܒܢܬܐ: ܡܠܝ ܕܐܚܕ ܗܘܐ ܠܗܘܢ ܗܘ ܛܘܒܢܐ. [R 138] ܟܕ ܗܘ ܗܘܐ

[1] Rufus does not mention Euphrosius outside of the *Vita Petri Iberi*.

[2] This was the third day of the commemoration of Peter of Alexandria, whose memorial begins on the 29th of Hator (8 December). The present event therefore should have taken place on 10 December.

[3] See Eph 5:19.

kept pure [his] love and conscience toward the blessed one. When the evening drew near and Abba Gregory and these other old men urged and compelled the brethren, we sat down with them at table to take food. Halfway through the time of the meal, Euphrosius,[1] who was standing in front of the saint and was serving him, a pure monk and much beloved by the saint, cried out, "The father is departing! Come, receive a blessing!" Leaping up and getting up from the table, with tears and groans and wailings we ran to his bed. **[R 137]** In order not to importune the blessed one who was in his last breathings, Euphrosius, of whom we have made mention, holding the saint's right hand, was stretching [it] out for everyone to kiss it and receive a blessing. And to many the blessed one gave also in this hour a sense of the faith and of the love he had toward them. When the blessed one had surrendered his spirit in great cheerfulness and quietly into the hands of God who was near to him even at that hour and received him, Abba Gregory, the priest, was esteemed worthy to lay his hands [on his eyes] and close them.

(§182) It was then late evening, [near] dawn on Friday.[2] When we had washed his holy body and had wrapped around it the holy vestment in which he used to offer the holy mysteries, in the correct manner, we laid him out purely and honorably. We lit many lights and candles [and] spent the whole night, keeping vigil in [singing] psalms and hymns and spiritual songs,[3] while it was known that all of the saints and the holy martyr and archbishop Peter were near us and glorifying with us the saint's memorial according to the vision of the priest Athanasius.[4] There was to be seen and heard much weeping and wailing of the inhabitants of the village,[5] all of them weeping at their being deprived of him, because they were remembering the many wonders and signs and healings that God showed them through him, and especially the great acts of relief and almsgiving that the blessed one performed

[4] See above, *Vit. Pet.* §§173 (R 130–31).

[5] While Peter and his friends as anti-Chalcedonians may have had a broad basis of support among the villagers, it is also possible, and likely, that the inhabitants, independent of their taking a stance with regard to Chalcedon, were at that moment in grief and sadness over having lost a holy man and benefactor. See also *Vit. Pet.* §184 (R 138).

ܕܝܢ ܢܦܩܬ܂ ܟܕ ܒܪܟܝܗ̇، ܘܢܫܩܝܗ̇، ܠܦܓܪܗ ܕܩܕܝܫܐ ܐܝܟ ܥܝܕܐ܂
ܫܡܝܢܗ̇، ܩܕܡ ܡܕܒܚܐ ܩܕܝܫܐ. ܐܝܟܢܐ ܕܟܕ ܫܒܩ܂ ܢܬܦܪܫ ܘܩܘܪܒܢܐ
ܩܕܝܫܐ ܢܣܒܘܗ̇. ܡܛܠ ܕܐܝܬ ܗܘܐ ܐܢܫܝܢ ܡܢ ܐܢ̈ܫܐ܆ ܕܠܐ ܒܕܒܠ
ܫܡܠܝܢ ܗܘܘ ܐܫܬܡܫܐ ܩܕܝܫܐ܂ ܟܕ ܐܬܘ ܠܗܘܢ ܩ̈ܫܝܫܐ܆ ܘܡܢ
ܐܢ̈ܫܐ ܕܗ̇ܘ ܦܓܪܐ ܩܕܝܫܐ ܠܗܠܝܢ ܚ̇ܙܘ܂ ܡܢܗܘܢ ܐܠܒܫܘ ܐܢܘܢ
ܒܚܕܘܬܐ.

(§183) ܟܕ ܐܬܦܪܥ ܗܟܝܠ ܘܐܫܬܡܠܝܘ ܣܘܦܗ̇، ܕ̈ܐܪܐ ܩ̈ܕܝܫܐ܂
ܢܘܦܬܐ ܡܫܟܚܬܐ ܒܒܪܘ ܗܘܘ ܬ̈ܘܬܗ̇، ܘܡܪܗܒܘ ܕܢܫܒܘܢ
ܠܦܓܪܗ܂ ܘܢܫܡܫܘܢܗ̇، ܒܕܝܢܐ ܕܝܠܗ ܗ̇ܝ، ܒܠܘܠܬܐ܂ ܕܫܒܩܐ
ܒܡܘܫܚܐ ܕܟܠ ܚܕ ܡܫܘܡܢܐ ܕܒܐܪܐ܂ ܩܕܡ ܕܬܫܡܫ ܫܒܬܐ
ܕܡܘܬܗ ܠܒ̈ܢܝ ܡ̈ܕܝܢܬܐ܂ ܒܐܪܐ ܘܡܫܘܡܢܐ. ܐܦ ܓܝܪ ܕܢܦܩ ܗܘܐ܂
ܕܠܐ ܟܕ ܢܦܪܫܘܢ ܢܫܡܫܘܢ܂ ܢܗܦܟܘܢ ܢܐܬܘܢ ܒ̈ܢܝ ܡ̈ܕܝܢܬܐ܂
ܘܢܫܩܠܘܢ ܦܓܪܗ ܩܕܝܫܐ܂ ܘܟܕ ܡܢ ܗܝܟܠܐ ܕܒܗܠܝܢ ܡ̈ܕܝܢܬܐ
ܢܫܡܫܘܢܗ̇܆ ܡܛܠ ܗܝܡܢܘܬܐ ܦܫܝܛܬܐ ܘܫܘܒܚܐ ܕܐܝܬ ܗܘܐ
ܠܗܘܢ ܠܘܬܗ. ܐܦ ܓܝܪ ܒܠܗܘܢ ܗܠܝܢ ܕܠܐ ܡܫܬܘܕܥܝܢ ܗܘܘ ܠܝ܂
ܐܝܟ ܡܠܐܟܐ ܘܐܝܟ ܢܒܝܐ.

(§184) ܐܣܝܪ ܗܘܐ ܠܗ. ܟܕ ܡܠܠܐܝܬ ܗܟܝܠ ܥܠ ܥܠ̈ܬܐ ܠܓܒܝ
ܠܟܠܗܘܢ ܩ̈ܕܝܫܐ ܐܝܠܝܢ ܗܘܘ ܒܐܘܪܚܐ. ܟܕ ܚܠܦ ܠܗ̇ ܠܗ
ܗܠܝܢ ܕܠܗ ܒܠܚܘܕ܆ ܐܠܐ ܘܦܫܘ ܒܒܘܪܐ ܕܗ̇ܝ، ܕܒܗܠܝܢ ܛܘܪܐ

1 For references to later practices of νεκροχειροτονία, consecration or ordination at the hands of a dead person, see Honigmann, *Évêques et Évêchés Monophysites*, 34–35 with 35 n. 1.

2 The veneration of saints and their relics in antiquity as much as today in the Middle East can function as an effective form of ecumenical rapprochement between different Christian groups or even different religions. For a discussion of such dimensions of a sacred site, e.g. Mamre, sacred to Jews, Christians, and Muslims, see Aryeh Kofsky, "Mamre: A Case of a Regional Cult?"

for them. **[R 138]** When it was early morning, having wrapped and bound the saint's body according to custom, we laid it in front of the holy altar so that, while it was set [there], the holy oblation would be offered on his behalf. There were some of the brethren who had not yet taken the holy habit. They brought garments for them, and by the hands of the holy body these were blessed, and thus they clothed them with joy.[1]

(§183) When the holy mysteries were offered and completed on his behalf, his heirs applied much care and hastened to take his body and lay it in his old monastery, located in the congregation beside Maiuma of Gaza, before the news of his death was heard by the inhabitants of the city of Gaza and Maiuma. For they were afraid that, if the inhabitants of the city would hear [about it] ahead of time, they would come at a run and take his holy body by force and lay it in one of the temples in these cities because of the great faith and love they had for him. For even all those who were not in communion with us[2] esteemed him like an angel and like a prophet.

(§184) Now, hastily taking up his holy coffin[3] upon [our] shoulders, we set out on the road, while not only his own [people] were accompanying him but also those inhabitants of this place for

in *Sharing the Sacred: Religious Contacts and Conflicts in the Holy Land: First-Fifteenth Centuries CE* (ed. Arieh Kofsky and Guy G. Stroumsa; Jerusalem: Yad Izhak Ben Zvi, 1998), 19–30.

[3] The Syriac transliterates the Greek γλωσσόκομον. See also *Vit. Pet.* §34 (R 23). When describing the container into which Peter's body was laid, the author chooses the same term previously used for the golden reliquary box in which the bones of the Persian martyrs were transported. Thus the connection between Peter and the martyrs is again highlighted.

ܣܓܝܐܐ. ܘܩܠܝܠ ܒܬܪ ܫܒܬܐ ܐܬܬܢܝܚܘ̱. ܗ̇ܘ ܕܐܦ ܬܕܡܘܪܬܐ
ܐܬܬܢܝܗ̇ ܗ̣ܘܬ.

(§185) ܒܪ ܢܦܩ ܗܟܝܠ ܗ̇ܘ ܚܝܘ̱ ܘܪ̈ܕܝܢ [R 139] ܗܘܘ ܒܐܘܪܚܐ. ܣܝܡ
ܘܗܠܝܢ ܗܟ̈ܢܐ ܒܬܪ̈ܝܢ ܒܗܘ ܡܟܘܪܐ ܒܡ ܐܣ̈ܢܐ ܕܫܪܒܐ. ܒܪ ܗܪܟܐ
ܡܬܦܪܫܝܢ ܗܘܘ ܡ̣ܢܗ̱ ܬܠܬܐ ܕܐܠܗ ܕܦܠܚ̈ܐ: ܘܡܛܠ ܢܦܘܪܬܐ
ܕܟܐܒܐ: ܘܡܛܠ ܕܠܐ ܡܫܟܚܝܢ ܢܗܘܐ ܠܡܬܕܒܪܘ ܗ̇ܘ ܒܢܝܫܐ
ܣܓܝܐܐ. ܒܪ ܟܠܗ ܡܫܠ ܗ̇ܘ ܢܘܗܪܐ ܝܬܒ ܒܚܙܘܬܐ: ܒܪ ܐܪܪ̈ܝܢ
ܕܓܝܫܐ: ܒܬܕ̈ܝܢ ܗܘܝܢ ܕܢܦܩ ܡܫܪܬܐ. ܐܬܬܢܝܚܘ̱ ܗܘܐ ܗܘܘ ܕܝܢ ܒܡܢ
ܘܡܬܬܪ̈ܝܢ ܘܬܪ̈ܝܢ ܗܦ̈ܟܐ ܡ̈ܫܝܚܐ. ܐܒ̈ܐ ܐܬܐܡܝܢܘܣ ܐܓܘܦܝܠܐ
ܗ̇ܘ ܕܐܡܪܝ: ܘܐܒ̈ܐ ܡܟܝܢܘܣ. ܢܒܪܐ ܦܣܝܠܐ ܘܒܫܪ̈ܪ̈ܝ
ܠܐ ܡܬܢܝܚܐ. ܕܡܢ ܢܠܟܘܬܗ ܒܕܡܟܐ ܠܫܟܢܘܬܗ: ܒܡܕܝܫܘܬܐ
ܘܒܟܝܢܘܬܐ ܘܒܟܠܠܬܐ ܠܕܟܪܐ ܕܒܢܝܢܘܬܐ ܒܢܦܪ. ܢܒܝܐ
ܘܡܟܝܢܟܐ ܘܪܘܫܠܐ ܦܠܟܘܬܐ ܪܘܚܢܝܬܐ. ܗ̇ܘ ܕܗ̣ܘ ܦܠܒܢܐ ܡܟܪ
ܗܘܐ ܕܒܟܡܗ ܢܡܟܢܘܗ̇. ܚܠ ܡܕܒܪܐ ܩܕܝܫܐ: ܒܪ ܦܠܚܝܢ ܡ̈ܦܣܬܐ
ܩ̈ܕܝܫܬܐ: ܡܛܠ ܦܠܛܪܘܢܐ ܕܐܝܬ ܗܘܐ ܠܗ ܒܗ. ܗܢܐ ܗܟܝܠ ܩܕܡ
ܕܢܚ ܢܗܪ ܠܡܐܟܠ: ܡܢ ܫܠܝ ܝܘܡܐ ܒܪ ܐܡ̈ܪ. ܫܡܥܘܢܝ ܫܘܡܥܘܢܝ.
ܒܗ̇ܘ ܕܢܦܩ ܢܦܫܗ: ܘܫܟܒ ܠܩܕܝܫܐ ܕܠܗ ܒܗܢܐ ܒܠܒܟܐ: ܘܒܬܪ
ܕܬܢܝܐ ܢܥܒܘܗܝ, ܒܫܢ̈ܬܐ ܕܠܚܡ. ܒܡ ܟܠܗ ܫܪܪܐ ܫܟܝܒܘ ܗܟܝܠ
ܕܟܒܪ ܡܬܐܡܪ̈ܝܢ. ܘܒܪܡܟܐ ܠܡܫܬܐ ܡ̈ܬܠܫܝܢ ܗ̇ܘ̈, ܡܛܠ ܦܘܩܕܢܗ.
ܒܡܕܝܢ ܐܬܘ̱ ܒܪ ܕܒܪ ܠܐ ܓܘܐ ܝܗܒ ܐܢܐ: ܒܒܡܗ ܓܦܠ ܗܘܐ
ܠܗ ܐܬܝܢ ܩ̈ܠܝܠܐ. ܘܡܐܟܠ ܗܘܬ ܒܒܡܗ ܕܐܫܟܚ ܠܡܕܒܪܐ ܩܕܝܫܐ:
ܒܪ ܠܐ̈ܬܘܪܐ ܩ̈ܕܝܫܐ ܡܫܟܠܬܐ ܗܘܐ. ܒܪ ܡܐܟܠ ܐܢܐ ܗܟܝܠ ܒܒܡܗ:
ܒܫܪ ܡܢ ܩܘܕܫܐ ܗܠܝܢ ܐܚܪ̈ܢܐ ܕܠܗ: ܫܪܝܬ ܐܝܟ ܒܝܢܐ ܕܪ̈ܕܝܢ
ܠܐܪ̈ܓܘܢܐ. [R 140] ܘܡܒܝܬ ܦܣܬܐ ܕܐܒܪܝ ܕܦܫܝܛܐ ܠܒܠ ܡܢ
ܡܕܒܪܐ. ܘܒܪ ܕܢܦܠ ܘܒܬܡܗܐ ܗ̇ܘܬ: ܒܪܡܠܬܐ ܫܠܡܐܬܐ ܐܡܪ.

[1] Throughout the text, Samaritans are featured as a significant minority group and quite as prominently as the Jews. Writing about his own, relatively small minority community, the anti-Chalcedonian author may have found it helpful to provide his audience with models of other oppressed minority groups.

[2] See also *Pler.* 10.

[3] The fans are liturgical devices used at the entrances during the liturgy. Another form is used during the anaphora, originally to keep flies off, later theologized to represent the Holy Spirit fluttering over Christ at his baptism. In Latin the fans are called *flabella*; Greek refers to them as *rhipidia* or *hexapteryga*;

a long distance, and these although they were Samaritans,[1] which was also a miracle.

(§185) When they had gone out and were **[R 139]** moving along on the road, we and these old men remained in the fortress with the rest of the brethren, since those heirs of the blessed one had [devised] this plan. [We stayed behind], both to guard the vessels and because the numerous company should not be a hinderance to the journey. While we had thus fasted the whole day in sadness, when evening came we were about to take food. Two senior priests were staying with us, Abba Athanasius the Egyptian, who was mentioned, and Abba Maxos,[2] a simple man and truly without guile, who from his childhood until his old age kept the way of life of asceticism in holiness, humility, and virginity, being gentle and humble and full of spiritual grace, whom the blessed one used to have stand with him at the holy altar, carrying the holy fans,[3] because of the full assurance he had in him. Before we would sit down to eat, this one suddenly cried out, saying, "Listen to me! Listen to me! By him [God] who took his soul and glorified his saint in this world and is about to glorify him more in the eternal life! With all truth [I am telling you], hear these things that are being said by me and [that] until this hour were hidden because of his command. For you recall that, although I am not worthy, he brought me with him many times, and I used to stand with him to serve at the holy altar while he was celebrating the holy mysteries. While I was standing then with him, during one of these last holy [services] of his, I saw as it were a cloud that was like a purple[4] [robe] **[R 140]** and from it the palm of a hand[5] stretched out over the altar. Since I was afraid and in amazement,

the latter, meaning "six-winged," is also the customary epithet for the seraphim. See also Marlia M. Mango, "Rhipidion," *ODB* 3:1790–91; and H. Leclercq, "Flabellum," *DACL* 5:1610–25.

4 Syriac ܐܪܓܘܢܐ. "[T]he violet or hyacinthine hue obtained from the Tyrian murex, purple" (Payne Smith, 27).

5 The presence of God the Father, more difficult to depict than that of Christ, was often represented in the form of a hand in early Christian visual art. See also a few lines below, where the arm of God, up to the elbow, is spoken of as becoming visible.

ܗ̇ܘܝܬ܀ ܘܫܠܡ ܗܘܝܬ ܟܕ ܙܠܝܢܬ ܐܝܬܝ. ܟܕ ܚܙܐ ܗܘܐ ܕܟܢ ܗ̣ܘ
ܡܪܝܫܝܬ ܘܡܬܠܟܬܐ. ܠܐ ܕܝܢ ܐܡܪ ܗܘܐ ܡܕܡ ܡܛܠ ܕܪܕܐ ܗܘܐ ܠܗ̇
ܠܟܠܗܝܢ. ܘܟܕ ܐܫܬܡܠܝܬ ܬܫܡܫܬܐ ܡܪܝܫܬܐ܆ ܐܬܬܢܝܚܬ ܒܦܓܪ
ܘܪܘܚܬ܀ ܕܠܐ ܡܟܝܠ ܐܡܪܝܢ ܕܐܢܘܢ ܒܢ̈ܝܐ ܕܬܒܠܐ ܕܐܝܟ ܗܠܝܢ.
(§186) ܘܠܦܘܪܫܢܐ ܐܚܪܢܐ ܕܒܬܪ ܢܘܟܐ܆ ܗ̇ܘ ܕܐܚܪܢܐ ܒܟܪܗ ܗ̣ܘ
ܠܦܟܝܢܐ܆ ܬܘܒ ܦܩܕ ܠܝ ܕܐܡܘܬ ܒܟܪܗ. ܘܟܕ ܠܐ ܡܫܟܚ ܐܢܐ ܘܠܐ
ܡܟܪܝܢ ܐܢܐ ܕܐܗܦܟ ܒܠܗܘܢ܀ ܟܠܒܬ ܘܫܡܫܬ ܒܟܪܗ. ܘܬܘܒ ܢܫܝܬ܆
ܠܐ ܡܟܝܠ ܒܠܚܘܕ ܦܫܛܬ ܕܐܝܕܐ܆ ܐܠܐ ܒܠܗ̇ ܐܝܕܐ ܒܪܡܐ
ܠܐܘܡܢܐ܆ ܕܦܫܝܛܐ ܡܢ ܗ̇ܝ ܒܝܢܐ ܠܟܠ ܡܢ ܡܪܒܝܢܐ܆ ܐܝܟܢܐ
ܕܡܟܝܠ ܐܢܐ ܒܪܢܫ ܡܠܠ ܐܡܘܬ ܡܢ ܕܫܠܝܬܐ. ܟܕ ܐܫܬܟܠܠ ܗܟܝܠ
ܡܦܪܫܢܐ܆ ܟܕ ܠܐ ܡܟܝܠ ܡܫܟܚ ܐܢܐ ܕܐܡܘܬ: ܘܟܠܗ ܠܡܠܬܗ
ܕܠܦܟܝܢܐ܆ ܐܝܟܢܐ ܕܐܡܪܬ ܘܩܡ ܐܦܠܐ ܡܪܝܫܬܐ܆ ܥܪܩܬ ܢܦܫܝ ܟܠ
ܐܝܟܢܐ. ܘܡܦܩܫ ܗܘܬ ܠܗ ܟܕ ܐܡܪ ܐܢܐ ܥܒܕܬ ܠܝ. ܗ̇ܘ ܕܝܢ ܟܕ
ܢܒܥ܆ ܘܦܩܕ ܕܢܦܩܘܢ ܠܒܪ ܟܠܗܘܢ ܕܡܫܡܫܝܢ ܠܗ ܐܡܪ ܠܗܘܢ܆ ܡܢܐ
ܠܝ ܗܫܐ܆ ܠܒܢܐ ܥܒܕܝ ܐܢܬ. ܘܟܕ ܢܦܩ ܠܝ ܐܝܟܢܐ ܐܡܝܢܝ. ܟܕ
ܙܒܢ ܐܝܟ ܘܡܬܠܐ ܐܝܬܐ. ܟܕ ܕܝܢ ܚܙܝܬ ܗܘܝܬ ܕܐܬܟܠܠ ܘܐܬܦܬܚܬܐ
ܚܘܐ܆ ܟܕ ܦܩܕ ܡܠܬܝ ܐܡܪ ܠܝ ܫܠܘܡ. ܦܬܓܡܐ ܐܝܬ ܠܝ ܕܐܬܠ
ܠܒܪܗ ܕܐܠܗܐ ܒܡܘܡܬܐ ܕܕܝܢܐ܆ ܐ ܬܦܘܩ ܗܪܐ ܡܠܬܐ ܡܢ
ܦܘܡܟ ܒܫܝܢ. ܟܕ ܢܦܩܬ ܡܟܝܠ ܦܘܩܕܢܗ [R 141] ܒܪܡܫܐ ܠܡܫܐ܆
ܡܫܐ ܟܕ ܗ̣ܘܐ ܘܒܢܐ܆ ܡܐ ܚܠܦܬ ܠܒܘ܆ ܘܡܚܪܐ ܐܝܟܐ ܠܟܠܢܫ.
ܕܒܡ ܕܐܝܟ ܐܢܐ ܡܪܝܫܐ ܐܫܬܘܝ ܥܡ ܕܒܪܝܢ܆ ܘܡܢ ܕܐܝܟ
ܐܢܐ ܐܡܪܐ ܘܪܥܝܐ ܘܐܦܣܩܘܦܐ ܘܡܫܝܚܐ ܕܐܠܗܐ ܘܩܘܡܐ
ܕܢܦܫܬ܆ ܦܬܓܡܐ ܐܬܦܪܥܝ.
(§187) ܗܠܝܢ ܕܟܕ ܗ̣ܘ ܗܫܐ ܡܬܟܬܒܐ ܗܘܐ܆ ܒܡ ܕܩܪ̈ܒܐ ܦܓܪ̈ܝܐܬܐ
ܘܬܐܒܝܬܐ܆ ܒܠܝ ܟܕ ܒܬܡܗܐ ܘܒܡܬܬܒܝܘܬܐ ܗܘܝܢ ܥܒ̈ܕܝܢܐ
ܕܪ̈ܒܟܐ ܐܫܪܝܢ܆ ܘܬܐܒܝܬܐ ܠܐ ܡܬܐܒܝܬܐ ܡܢ ܒܡܡܠܐ
ܕܠܒܐ [ܐܫܬܝܢ]. ܘܐܝܟܢܐ ܕܦܪܫ ܘܢܦܩܘ: ܗ̇ܘܢ ܕܗܦܟܝܢ ܕܒܙܘ

1 This comment can be read as a sign of Peter's humility, expressive of the saint not wanting to be drawn into the center of everyone's attention. The last comment especially, however, also is a fine rhetorical device starting off the development of an oral hagiographical tradition immediately following the saint's death, a tradition in which Rufus participated with his work.

2 Creating a framework for the whole work, the author here resumes a

I was seized by great fear, and I stood [there] trembling, whereas the saint was looking and observing [it] but said nothing, because he knew the cause. When the holy service was finished, I thought it over and decided that henceforth I would not dare to stand before such dreadful mysteries."

(§186) "During another holy [service] the day after that last one that the blessed one performed, again he commanded me to stand with him. Being unable and not daring to object, I entered and served with him. Again I saw, no longer only the palm of the hand, but all of the hand up to the elbow stretched out from the cloud over the altar, so that now I almost died from fear. When the holy [service] was finished, since I could no longer stand [with him], I also entered the cell of the blessed one, where he took off and laid down his holy vestment. I threw myself upon the earth and was asking him, saying, 'Forgive me!' But he, since it was well known [to him] and [when] he had commanded those who were attending him to go outside, said to me, 'What do you have, old man? Why are you troubled?' While he gave me [his] hand, he made me stand up, while I was quivering and weeping. But when I was about to speak and tell the vision, as he cut off my word, he said to me, 'Keep silence! You will have to give answer to the Son of God on the day of judgment if you let this word go out from your mouth during my life[time].'[1] While I have kept his command **[R 141]** until now, since now the time has come, I have revealed to you and I proclaim to everyone with what kind of a saint we were esteemed worthy to dwell together and from what kind of a father and shepherd and bishop and servant of God and firm supporter of our souls[2] we have become bodily[3] separated."

(§187) When the old man was telling these [things] with many tears [and] groans, we all, while we were in amazement and in compunction, shed streams of tears.[4] [We brought up] unspeakable groans[5] from the depth of the heart, as those who are capable

description of Peter the Iberian that he has presented in similar terms and by listing titles and appellations for Peter already at the beginning. See *Vit. Pet.* §§2, 189 (R 3,143).

3 Implied is, "but not spiritually."

4 Literally, "springs of tears."

5 An allusion to Rom 8:23, 26. We owe this reference to John Fitzgerald.

ܘܦܪ̈ܫܘܢ ܗܠܝܢ ܕܕܐܟܢ ܗܟܢ܇ ܦܪ̈ܫܬܗ ܕܗܢ ܠܟܠ ܡܘܒܕ ܗܘܐ
ܚܘܐ ܕܗ̇ܘ܆ ܐܓܪܐ. ܐܝܟ ܕܝܢ ܕܐܠܗܐ ܐܘܣܦ ܗܘܐ ܠܗ ܐܓܪܐ
ܘܦܪܥܐ ܠܗ ܠܘܬܗ ܐܝܟ ܕܟܬܝܒ܇ ܕܝܡܝܢܗ ܕܡܪܝܐ ܥܒܕܬ ܚܝܠܐ.
ܝܡܝܢܗ ܕܡܪܝܐ ܪܡܪܡܬܢܝ܇ ܘܠܐ ܐܡܘܬ ܐܠܐ ܐܚܐ. ܘܐܫܬܥܐ
ܥܒ̈ܕܘܗܝ ܕܡܪܝܐ. ܘܬܘܒ. ܐܚܕܬ ܐܝܕܝ ܕܝܡܝܢܐ. ܘܒܡܠܟܟ ܕܒܪܬܢܝ.
ܘܥܡ ܫܘܒܚܐ ܢܣܒܬܢܝ ܠܘܬܟ. ܘܗܠܝܢ ܕܝܢ ܗܟܢ.

(§188) ܗ̇ܘܘ ܕܝܢ ܫ̈ܢܝܐ ܕܟܠܗ: ܒܗ ܥܡܠܗ ܦܓܪܗ ܕܛܘܒܢܐ: ܘܪ̈ܕܐ ܗܘܐ ܒܟܘܡܗܘܢ ܘܐܟܠܐ ܠܦܓܪܗ ܦܫܝܫܐ. ܠܐܦ̈ܝ ܪܓܫܐ ܒܗ. ܡܢܗ ܠܐܫܩܠܘܢܐ܆ ܒܪܘ ܗܢܘܢ ܠܒܪ ܡܢ ܫܘܪܐ ܒܡܫܟܢܐ ܚܕ. ܕܐܘܪ̈ܬܕܘܟܣܘ. ܘܒܗ ܡܢܗ ܒܪܡܫܟܢܘܬܐ܆ ܒܠܗ ܠܠܝܐ ܘܠܐܠܐܬ ܒܝܘܡ. ܘܩܕܡ ܢܦܩܪܐ ܡ̇ܢܗ ܠܕܢܚܗ ܚܠܘܦܬܐ ܕܩܕܝܫܐ܆ ܩܕܡ ܕܢܬܒܥ ܫܒܥܐ ܠܩܪ̈ܝ ܒܐܘܪܐ ܘܡܫܘܡܥܐ. ܘܡܛܠ ܕܗܘ ܒܥܒܠ ܚܪ ܗܘܐ: ܘܡܟܪ ܗܘܐ ܬܡܢ ܒܥܠܬܐ ܗ̇ܘ ܛܘܒܢܐ: ܛܠܠ ܒܡ̈ܐܪܐ ܕܢܩܦܘ ܠܣ̈ܪܕܐ ܛܒ ܗܘܐ: [R 142] ܒܗ̇ܝ ܡܚܝܠܘܬܐ ܗܘܒ ܠܦܓܪܗ ܩܕܝܫܐ. ܒܗ ܐܦ ܗܠܝܢ ܬܪ̈ܬܝܢ ܐܬܐ ܗܘܐ ܒܗܝܢ ܒܪ̈ܡܫܐ ܕܩܕ̈ܝܫܐ. ܒܗ̇ܝ ܕܝܢ ܕܗܢ ܡܚܝܠܐ܆ ܦܓܪܐ ܩܕܝܫܐ ܕܐܒܐ ܢܘܚܝ ܐܘܢܘܒܣܐ. ܒܗ̇ܝ ܕܝܢ ܕܗܢ ܗܠܝܢ ܕܐܡܪܐ ܐܒܪܗܡ ܗ̇ܢܐ ܐܚ ܩܕܝܫܐ ܘܟܗܢܐ ܐܬܪ̈ܟܝܐ: ܗ̇ܘ ܕܒܐܬܪ̈ܘܬܐ ܗܠܝܢ: ܒܗ ܠܕܘܟܪܐ ܕܫܝܕܘܬܐ ܒܥܡ ܒܠܗ ܫܬܬܘܬܐ ܘܡܕܝܢܬܐ ܐ̈ܚܪܢ: ܠܫܪܬܐ ܕܝܢ ܒܠܝܢܐ ܕܐܝܟ ܗܢܐ ܐܬܝܗ̇، ܠܗ ܕܦܩܕ ܠܗ܆ ܕܡܛܠ ܕܦܪܘܥ ܫܘܠܛܢܗ܆ ܢܐܙܠ ܠܐܬܪ̈ܘܬܐ ܕܦܠܣܛܝܢܐ ܠܘܬ ܐܦܣܩܘܦܐ ܦܛܪܘܣ ܐܝܒܪܝܐ. ܐܝܟܢܐ ܕܗ̇ܘ ܒܗ ܗ̇ܟܢ ܐܒ̈ܗܘܗܝ، ܟܠ ܟ̈ܢܫܘܗܝ، ܢܣܪܘܗܝ، ܠܘܬ ܡܪܝܐ. ܘܒܗ ܥܒܕ ܕܒܪܗ ܠܘܬܗ ܕܛܘܒܢܐ. ܘܒܗ ܟܬܒ ܠܗ ܗܠܝܢ ܕܗܢ ܒܠܝܢܐ: ܒܗ ܬܠܬܝܢ ܫ̈ܢܝܐ ܒܠܝܫܐ ܐܬܦܟܠ ܠܘܬܗ. ܡܚܝܠܐ ܐܫܬܡܠܝ ܐܝܟ ܚܘܝܐ

[1] The Syriac may render a form of the Greek φωτίζειν (Raabe, 128 n. 4).

[2] See Ps 118:16–17.

[3] Ps 73:23–24 [LXX, against Pešitta].

[4] The Syriac may render the Greek καὶ οὗτοι μὲν οὕτως (Raabe, 129 n. 3).

[5] Anti-Chalcedonians appear to have been strong enough in the Ashkelon area to be in charge of a separate church building.

[6] See also above, *Vit. Pet.* §134 (R 99) and 196 n. 2.

[7] This place is located thirty miles north of Cairo. See Randall Stew-

of expounding and explaining such things have explained and elucidated,[1] making known the vision of the hand [as] his calling from above, as if God stretched out [his] hand to him and called him to himself, as it is written, "The right hand of the Lord worked a mighty deed; the right hand of the Lord lifted me up. And I shall not die, but live, and recount the works of the Lord."[2] And again, "You have seized my right hand, and according to your will you have guided me. And you have taken me to you with glory."[3]

(§188) So it happened.[4] His heirs, while they carried the body of the blessed one and Abba Gregory the priest was traveling with them, toward evening, when they arrived at Ashkelon, they lodged there outside of the [city] wall in a temple belonging to the orthodox.[5] And when they got up in haste, they journeyed swiftly the whole night. And before [day]light they arrived at the saint's old monastery, before the report was made known to the people of Gaza and Maiuma. The blessed one, when he was still alive and was dwelling there in quiet, had constructed three sarcophagi,[6] which were joined to each other. **[R 142]** They laid his holy body in the middle one, while these [other] two also had in them the bones of saints: in the one on the right, the holy body of Abba John the Eunuch; and in the one on the left, [the body] of Abba Abraham, a holy and ascetic old man of Athrīb[7] to whom, after he had straightforwardly led the way of life of solitude in these regions with all sincerity and holiness, finally appeared such a revelation that commanded him, because his end was near, to go the regions of Palestine to Bishop Peter the Iberian, so that he, laying his hands on his eyes,[8] would send him to the Lord. On hearing [this], he ran to the blessed one. When he revealed to him these [things] from the revelation, after he was only acquainted with him for thirty days, he was perfected according to the manner of the vi-

art, "Atrīb," *CE* 1:307. The reference to Abraham of Athrīb establishes a further clear connection between Egyptian and Palestinian anti-Chalcedonians. See also the discussion in Horn, *Asceticism and Christological Controversy*, 209, where further references are provided. The connection between Egyptian and Palestinian asceticism is featured prominently in Rubenson, "Egyptian Relations"; see also Steppa, *John Rufus and the World Vision*, ch. 1.

[8] In order to close his eyes permanently.

ܕܐܬܝܕܥ ܠܗ. ܟܕ ܗܘ ܠܛܘܒܢܐ ܦܛܪܘܣ ܒܥܝܢܗ ܘܫܟܠܗ܇ ܘܫܡܥܗ ܗܘ
ܒܐܝܕܘܗܝ، ܒܡܘܬܐ ܗܘ، ܕܢܦܩܐ ܡܢ ܥܠܡܐ.

(§189) ܟܕ ܗܘܐ ܕܝܢ ܨܦܪܐ܇ ܘܐܫܬܡܥ ܠܒܡܘܪܐ ܕܒܝܘܡܬܐ
ܘܕܒܐܪܐ ܒܡܢܝܢܗ ܕܛܘܒܢܐ ܘܡܘܬܪܬܐ ܕܦܓܪܗ܇ ܟܠܗܘܢ ܐܟܚܕܐ
ܡܢ ܢܫ̈ܝܢ ܘܓܒܪ̈ܝܢ܇ ܪܗܛܘ ܠܗ، ܕܢܚܐ܇ ܟܕ ܚܝܒܝܢ ܕܢܣܬܦܩܘܢ،
ܠܦܓܪܗ ܩܕܝܫܐ. ܘܐܦ ܗܘ ܕܠܐ ܢܬܟܣܘܢ ܕܗܕܐ ܢܟܪܘܢ܆ ܐܦ
ܚܝܠܐ ܕܗܘܝܢ ܒܠܗܘܢ ܢܫܒܩܘܢ ܘܢܦܠܓܘܢ܆ ܘܗܘܐ ܢܗܘܐ ܠܗܘܢ
ܠܛܘܪܬܐ ܕܢܩܫܬܐ ܘܕܦܓܪܐ܆ ܠܒܘܪܟܬܐ ܙܒܢܬܐ. ܟܕ ܕܝܢ ܐܫܟܚܘ
ܕܐܬܬܚܝܡ ܠܗ܇ ܢܦܠܘ ܘܣܓܕܘ ܠܦܓܪܗ ܩܕܝܫܐ. ܘܡܢ ܬܠܝܬܐ
[R 143] ܡܢܥܝܢ ܗܘܘ ܘܡܬܢܟܦܝܢ ܟܕ ܡܬܦܪܫܝܢ. ܟܕ ܩܥܝܢ ܒܫ̈ܒܚܬܐ
ܘܒܟܒܬܐ ܘܒܬ̈ܟܫܦܬܐ܆ ܐܝܟ ܒ̈ܢܝܐ ܝ̈ܬܡܐ ܕܗܘܘ ܝ̈ܬܡܐ ܡܢ
ܐܒܐ ܕܐܝܟ ܗܢܐ. ܘܠܐ ܒܠܚܘܕ ܐܒܐ܇ ܐܠܐ ܘܡܕܒܪܢܐ ܘܪܥܝܐ
ܘܐܦܝܣܩܘܦܐ.

(§190) ܘܡܟܝܠ ܗܠܝܢ ܥܒܕܐ ܡ̈ܬܠܐ ܕܒܬܪܟܢ܆ ܟܕ ܡܬܟܢܫܝܢ ܗܘܘ
ܟܠܗܘܢ ܐܟܚܕܐ܆ ܡܢ ܟܠܗ ܚܕܘܬܐ ܘܡܫܠܡܢܘܬܐ܆ ܒ̈ܢܝܐ ܘܫܘܪܐ
ܡܫܡܠܝܢ ܗܘܘ ܠܟܠ ܡܕܡ܇ ܡܢ ܬܫܒ̈ܚܬܐ ܘܬܫ̈ܡܫܬܐ ܘܡܢܪ̈ܬܐ
ܕܩܘܝܬܐ. ܟܕ ܡܫܒܚܝܢ ܘܡܒܪܟܝܢ܆ ܠܐܠܗܐ ܕܝܗܒ ܘܠܐܒܘܗ
ܕܛܘܒܢܐ. ܘܐܬܪܐܬ ܠܒܘܢܐ ܕܒܗܬܗܘܢ ܘܕܒܟܪܝܘܬܗܘܢ܆ ܗܘ،
ܕܐܬܐ ܗܘܐ ܠܟܠܗܘܢ ܡܛܠ ܥܘܕܪܢܐ ܦܓܪܢܐ ܕܛܘܒܢܐ ܦܛܪܘܣ
ܐܒܘܗܘܢ܆ ܪܚܡܐ ܠܐܠܗܐ ܘܐܦܝܣܩܘܦܐ. ܡܢ ܩܕܡ ܢܘܡܐ ܕܝܢ
ܕܐܪܒܥܝܢ܆ ܥܒܕܘ ܡܩܒܠܢܐ ܘܢܘܪ̈ܬܐ ܕܠܝܠܗ܆ ܘܦܢܘ ܠܐܬܪܐ ܘܠܝ ܡܢ ܗܘ
ܡܫܘܪܐ ܕܡܥܝܢ܆ ܘܚܙܝܘ ܠܝ ܠܗܘܢ ܠܗ، ܕܢܐ ܒܬܘܬܐ ܕܒܗ
ܐܬܬܚܝܡ ܦܓܪܗ ܕܛܘܒܢܐ. ܐܝܟܢܐ ܕܢܬܬܚܝܡ ܐܦ ܗܘ ܕܡܬܦܣܘܢ
ܢܦܫܐ ܕܡܪܝܐ ܕܝܘܡܐ ܕܐܪܒܥܝܢ ܕܩܕܝܫܐ܆ ܡܢ ܟܠܗ ܚܝܣܘܬܐ
ܘܒܢܫܐ ܕܟܠܗ ܥܡܐ.

(§191) ܟܕ ܢܝܚܘ ܕܝܢ ܗܢܘܢ ܒ̈ܬܪܘܗܝ ܕܛܘܒܢܐ܆ ܕܕܘܟܬܐ ܕܒܘܪܬܐ
ܐܢܬܘܢ܆ ܘܠܐ ܫܦܝܪܐ ܠܡܘܬܪܐ ܕܐܝܢܐ ܩܛܝܢܐ܆ ܡܛܠ ܕܢܝܪ
ܐܢܬܘܢ ܗܘ̈ܐ، ܩ̈ܠܝܬܐ. ܘܩ̈ܢܝܢ ܗܠܝܢ ܕܡܢܟܘܢ ܗܘܐ ܩ̈ܕܝܢ.

[1] I.e., the garment would have been used as a substitute relic, given that bones of the saints were not accessible any longer.

[2] The Syriac may render the Greek ὀρφανοὶ ἐγένοντο τοιούτου πατρός (Raabe, 130 n. 1).

sion that had been shown to him, and the blessed Peter closed his [eyes] and wrapped him up and laid him with his own hands in this sarcophagus that was joined on the left.

(§189) When it was morning and [the news of] the departure of the blessed one and the burial of his body was heard by the inhabitants of Maiuma and of Gaza, all of them together with their wives and their children ran to the monastery, anxious to take his holy body by force, and if they were not allowed to do this, at least to tear asunder and distribute the long outer garment that was lying upon him, [so that] this should be for them a guardian of [their] souls and bodies and a great blessing.[1] But when they found they had buried him, they fell down and [performed acts of] veneration at his holy sarcophagus. With lamentations **[R 143]** they kissed and embraced [it], prostrating themselves, while weeping with sighs and with shouts and with supplications, like beloved children who were orphaned of such a father,[2] and not only a father but also a foster-father and a shepherd and a bishop.[3]

(§190) The next seven days, while they were all assembled together with great joy and eulogies, they performed over him gatherings and vigils, with praises and services and spiritual songs, while they kept and celebrated [feasts] to the glory of God and to the honor of the blessed one, and especially for the consolation of their sadness and their sorrow, which they all had because of the bodily departure of the blessed Peter, their father, the good shepherd and bishop. Before the fortieth day, however, his hosts and heirs sent and called the brethren and us from that fortress of Jamnia. They gathered us with themselves in that old monastery in which the body of the blessed one was laid, so that we also would be esteemed worthy to celebrate with them the memorial of the fortieth day of the saint, with all splendor and the assembly of all the people.[4]

(§191) But when those heirs of the blessed one saw that the place was small and not sufficient for a dwelling place of many brethren, for the cells were few and [such] that they had been ne-

[3] See also *Vit. Pet.* §2 (R 3) and §186 (R 141) with 270–71 n. 2.

[4] It was, and continues to be, the practice in Eastern Christian churches to celebrate the memorial of a recently deceased person on the fortieth day after the person's death. This service also is known as the Trisagion for the Dead.

ܐܬܦܠܓܘ ܕܢܘܡܘܣܘܗ̇ ܠܕܘܟܬܐ. ܘܟܕ ܚܘܡܫܬܐ ܐܝܬ ܗܘܐ ܕܢܦܩܬܐ
ܩܠ̈ܝܠܬܐ: ܘܗ̇ܘ ܠܡܒܢܐ ܡܠܠ ܡܕܡ ܥܒܕ: ܕܠܡܣܟܢܐ [R 144]
ܦܩܕ ܗܘܐ ܠܟܠ ܫܩ̈ܠܬܐ ܠܦܘܪܫܢܐ ܕܐܚ̈ܐ: ܕܢܦܩܘܢ ܗܘܘ ܐܝܟ
ܬܠܬܝܢ ܒܡܣܟܢܐ: ܒܗܢܝܢ ܓܝܪ ܘܐܘܪܚܝܐ ܕܐܬ̈ܝܢ ܟܠܝܘܡ. ܥܒܕ
ܘܗ̇ܘ ܠܡܒܢܐ ܠܢܦܩܬܐ: ܡܛܠ ܗ̇ܝ ܕܠܡ̈ܣܟܢܐ ܗܘܝܢܐ ܗܘܐ ܡܦܠܓ
ܗܘܐ: ܘܠܝܬ ܗܘܐ ܘܠܐ ܣܝ ܦܘܪܫܐ: ܠܐ ܡܢ ܥܠܠܬܐ ܕܐܪܥܐ
ܘܠܐ ܡܢ ܦܘܠܚܢ ܐܝ̈ܕܝܐ ܕܐܚ̈ܐ: ܡܛܠ ܕܡܫܟܠܐ ܘܡܣܟܢܐ ܚܒܝܫ
ܗܘܘ ܟܠܗܘܢ.. ܕܩ̈ܕܝܫܐ ܘܐܟ̈ܣܢܝܐ ܗܠܝܢ ܕܐܡܣܝܢܝܐ ܐܝܬܝܗܘܢ ܗܘܘ
ܠܗܝܢ ܒܫ̈ܢܘܗܝ ܕܠܡܒܢܐ: ܐ̈ ܕܝܢ ܡܦܢܝ ܗܘܐ ܐܢܫ ܡܕܡ:
ܗܘܝܢܐ ܐܝܟ ܕܐܡܪܬ ܡܢܕܐ ܠܡ̈ܣܟܢܐ ܡܦܠܓ ܗܘܐ:. ܟܕܡ ܟܕ.
ܥܠ ܒܡܘܬܪܐ ܕܗܝܡܢܘܬܗ ܕܐܠܗܐ ܐܬܬܟܠ: ܘܡܫ̈ܠܡܢܘܬܗ ܕܡܕܒܪܢܐ
ܐܬܥܠܠ ܒܗ̇ܘ ܝܘܡ̈ܬܐ: ܥܢܘ ܒܡܕܢܚܐ ܕܡܒܝܢܐ. ܐܬܐܪܬܐ ܕܝܢ
ܚܘܦܐܝܢܐ ܕܐܘܪܕܘܢܐ ܘܗ̇ ܐܦܘܡܠܦܛܘܢ.: ܒܣܘܢܝܘܣܬܐ
ܦܠܝܐܬܐ ܘܡܘܫܚܘܬܐ ܘܡܟܝܪܐ: ܕ̈ ܠܒܢ̈ܝܐ ܢܦܠ ܥܠܝ ܟܡܣܢܐ. ܘܟܕ
ܐܠܗܐ ܢܕܪ: ܘܠܐ ܡܬܚܫܒܢܝܬ ܢܡܟ ܚܠܐ ܘܣܘܡܚܬܐ ܘܢܦܩܬܐ:
ܒܟܠܠ ܫ̈ܡܬܐ ܐܝܟ ܕܒܝܐ ܠܡܕܝܢ̈ܬܐ ܘܠܕܝܪ̈ܬܐ ܕܟܘܗܝ. ܘܟܕ ܢܦܠ ܚܕܐ ܕܡ̈ ܗ̇ܘ ܟܕ
ܟܕܪ̈ܬܐ. ܘܠܩܘܪܝܐ ܕܕܝܪܐ ܒܒܝ̇ ܘܐܡܪܝܢ. ܘܩܠܝܬܐ ܦܩ̈ܠܬܐ ܘܬܦ
ܘܬܫ̈ܬܬܐ ܘܬܠܝܬܐ. ܘܠܐܦ̈ܣܩܝܢܐ ܘܠܐܦܣܩܝܢܐ ܘܠܕܝܪ̈ܬܐ ܐܡܪܝܢ
ܥܦܪܐ ܘܡܐܪܒ ܣܘܢ. ܘܟ̈ܠܝܐ ܐܬܬܡ: ܘܕܥܪ̈ܒܝܐ ܕܝܫܘܥܬܐ ܘܕܝܡܝܢܐ
ܕܕܝܪܐ. ܘܕܦܠܣܛܝܢܐ ܕܐܝ̈ܕܝܐ ܕܐܚ̈ܐ ܣܓܝ ܗܘܐ. ܟܕ ܬܒܥ ܗܘܐ
ܟܠܗܘܢ.: ܥܠ ܠܡܒܢܬܐ ܘܢܦܩܬܐ ܘܡܕܝܕܝܢܐ ܕܡܕܝܢܐ. ܘܟܕ ܥܒܕ
ܚܕܐ ܕܡܒܢܐ ܘܟܕ [R 145] ܠܡܬܐ ܡܫܘ: ܣܓܝ ܕܝܢ ܕܡܬܐ ܢܦܩܬܐ

[1] The Syriac may render the Greek ἐν αἷς ἠμελημένον ἦν (Raabe, 131 n. 1).

[2] For the following, see further Horn, *Asceticism and Christological Controversy*, 210–11; eadem, "Peter the Iberian and Palestinian Anti-Chalcedonian Monasticism," 120–28.

[3] For comments on Peter's recruitment of disciples, see Horn, "Peter the Iberian and Palestinian Anti-Chalcedonian Monasticism," 117–20.

[4] Given that Dionysius had spent three hundred darics (gold coins) on entertaining Peter for three years (*Vit. Pet.* §137 [R 101]), twenty-four dinars (sometimes silver, sometimes gold coins) would not have lasted very long.

[5] See also *Vit. Pet.* §§66–67 (R 46–47), when Peter spent his money on the poor and the pilgrims to Jerusalem.

glected,[1] they prepared to renovate the place.[2] There was want of many supplies, and the blessed one had left [behind] little, hardly **[R 144]** sufficient for a few days' nourishment of the brethren, who were about thirty in number.[3] For the blessed one had left only twenty-four dinars[4] for expenses, because he used to distribute the greater part [of his money] to the poor;[5] moreover, there was also not one [source] of income,[6] neither from the produce of the soil nor from the work of the hands of the brethren, because they had been occupied only with the reception and refreshment of these saints and strangers who were continually coming there during the life[time] of the blessed one.[7] If anyone offered anything, most of it, as I have said, he immediately distributed to the poor. Nevertheless, while those heirs relied upon the wealth of God's kindness and were strengthened by the prayers of the saint, they began the construction of the building. Theodore the ex-lawyer [was] especially diligent;[8] accepting the work, he began building with much cheerfulness and faith and hope. Since God was helping and invisibly gave strength and cheerfulness and supplies, in a few days he built the tower and the church in it and a house of prayer in the church.[9] He built also the wall of the monastery and made [it] surround [it]. He constructed many cells, both lower and upper [chambers]. He led a wall around the porticos,[10] the pillars,[11] and the courtyard and dug a well. He arranged gardens and took care of the rest of what was necessary for the building of the monastery and for the work of the hands of the brethren, relying only on the grace and care and help of the Lord. When he had finished the construction of the building and they had decorated **[R 145]**

6 The Syriac transliterates the Greek τόπος, "means," "way," and "resource."

7 For crowds of visitors to Peter, see also, e.g., *Vit. Pet.* §163 (R 121).

8 On Theodore, who took on a central position of leadership within the community, see also *Vit. Pet.* §§105, 112–113, §178 (R 78, 81–82, 134); possibly *Pler.* 38; Zachariah Scholasticus, *Vita Isaiae* 3–4 (Brooks, 1:3–4 [Syriac], 2:3 [Latin]), and *Vit. Sev.* 78, 86–87, 100, 107, 109, 111 (Kugener, 78,10–11, 86,11–87,3, 100,8, 107,1, 109,1–13, 111,9–10).

9 I.e., a chapel or the sanctuary.

10 The Syriac renders the Greek στοά.

11 Again, the Syriac renders the Greek στῦλος, which in turn may be of Persian origin.

ܠܬܚܬ ܡܢ ܡܕܝܢܬܐ. ܘܐܥܒܪܘܗ، ܠܗܘܢ ܠܦܓܪܗ ܕܩܕܝܫܐ ܠܓܘܬܐ
ܕܒܬܪܗ܆ ܩܕܡ ܚܕ ܝܘܡܐ ܕܫܘܢܝܗ.

(§192) ܐܚܐ ܕܝܢ ܐܝܬ ܠܗ ܦܓܪܐ ܕܚܒܝܒ ܠܛܘܒܢܐ ܒܐܘ̈ܢܐ
ܫ̈ܒܝܢܐ ܐܝܬ ܗܘܐ ܠܗ ܕܘܪܐ. ܟܕ ܒܪܘܫ ܩܐܡ ܩܕܡ ܡܢܪܐ
ܘܡܫܡܫ ܠܗ ܒܟܠܗܘܢ ܩ̈ܕܝܫܐ. ܘܗܘܐ ܡܩܪܒ ܒ̈ܥܘܬܐ ܘܨ̈ܠܘܬܐ
ܘܬܟ̈ܫܦܬܐ ܕܚܠܦܝܢ. ܒܗ ܦܐܪܫܐ ܡܫܝܚܝܬܐ. ܟܕ ܠܐܢܫܘܬܐ
ܡܫܡܫܐ ܗܘܐ. ܘܡܦܩܕ ܘܡܟܢܫ ܘܡܗܕܪ. ܘܐܝܟ ܕܒܣܘܟܠܐ
ܐܚܝܕܐ ܗܘܐ. ܠܐܢ̈ܫܝܢ ܕܝܢ ܦܪܘܫܐܝܬ ܡܬܚܙܐ. ܘܠܒ̈ܢܝܗ
ܡܐܟܐ. ܘܡܬܒܝܐ ܘܡܥܕܪ ܠܟܠܗܝܢ ܕܒܣܢܝܩܘܬܐ ܕܡܣܟܢܘܬܐ
ܘܕܒܝܬܐ ܕܕܘܒܪ̈ܐ ܬܪ̈ܝܢ܆ ܘܐܫܬܘܝܘ ܕܢܚܙܘܢ ܒܚܙܘܐ ܕܐܝܟ
ܗܢܐ ܕܩܕܝܫܐ.

(§193) ܐܫܬܡܥ ܕܝܢ ܗܘ ܠܛܘܒܢܐ܆ ܐܚܐ ܕܝܠܢ ܘܐܦܝܣܩܘܦܐ
ܦܘܠܘܣ܆ ܟܕ ܒܬܒܘܢ ܦܫܛ ܟܕ ܢܦܩ ܚܕ ܒܫܒܐ. ܒܝܘܡܐ
ܕܬܠܬܐ ܕܕܘܒܪܗ ܕܦܘܠܘܣ ܗܘܕܐ ܕܒܐ ܘܪܝܫܐ ܕܐܦܝ̈ܣܩܘܦܐ
ܕܐܠܟܣܢܕܪܝܐ ܡܕܝܢܬܐ. ܐܝܟ ܚܙܘܐ ܕܐܬܚܙܝ ܠܐܬܢܣܝܘܣ ܩܕܝܫܐ.
ܘܡܢ ܟܠܗ ܣܓܝܐܐ ܕ̈ܚܝܢ ܕܒܫܘܢܝܗ ܕܩܕܝܫܐ ܐܒܘܢ ܐܒܐ ܐܫܟܚܐ
ܒܘܠܐ. ܐܡܪܢܐ ܕܩܕܡ ܗܘܐ ܐܡܪ ܠܝ ܗܘ ܛܘܒܢܐ܆ ܟܕ ܐܬܐܡܪ ܠܝ
ܒܫܘܢܝܗ ܕܗܘܐ. ܘܒܫܬܐ ܕܬܪ̈ܬܝܢ ܩܕܡ ܚܕ ܝܘܡܐ ܕܕܘܒܪܗ ܕܐܒܐ
ܦܘܠܘܣ. ܐܡܪܢܐ ܘܫܒܩ ܒܪ̈ܟܬܗ، ܠܗ. ܒܒܬܐ ܕܨܠܘܬܐ ܠܬܚܬ
ܡܢ ܡܕܝܢܬܐ. ܟܠܗ ܕܝܢ ܘܟܢܫܐ ܕܥܡܗ، ܕܟܠ ܐܢܫܐ ܗܘܐ ܐܝܟ
ܡܬܒܐܝܢ ܣ̈ܓܝܐܝܢ. [R 146] ܡܢ ܕܝܢ ܗܘ ܠܗ ܒܫܘܢܝܗ ܕܐܒܐ ܕܝܠܢ ܗܘܐ.
ܚܕ ܒܫܒܐ ܩܕܡ. ܫܢܝܬܗ ܕܝܢ ܩܕܡܝܐ ܕܐܪܒܥܐ܆ ܒܬܪ̈ܝܢ ܒܗ
ܒܢܝܣܢ. ܥܡܝܕܘ ܕܝܢ ܘܫܢܝܬܗ ܕܠܬܚܬ ܡܕܝܢܬܐ܆ ܒܬܠܬܝܢ ܒܬܫܪܝ
ܐܚܪܝ. ܘܒܫܢܬܐ ܕܝܢ ܕܫܢ̈ܝܗ، ܐܝܟ ܡܬܒܐܝܢ ܣ̈ܓܝܐܝܢ. ܡܛܠ ܗܕܐ ܐܬܬܐ
ܫ̈ܢܝܐ ܡܫܟܠܝܢ ܚܕ ܕܒܪܝܢ. ܒܫܢܬܐ ܡܩܦܐ ܕܐܒܘܢ ܕܠܬܚܬ ܡܢ

[1] I.e., 492 C.E.

[2] Rufus presents Peter here as the ideal intercessor who has found unlimited access to God but who at the same time stayed intimately close to and involved in the community and its affairs.

[3] This appears to be the only instance in Rufus's works that speaks of visions anti-Chalcedonians had of Peter the Iberian.

[4] Ps 143:10. See also Ps 5:8; Isa 40:3; Matt 3:3; Mark 1:3; Luke 3:4; John 1:23; Heb 12:13

the house of prayer, they dug a place of reverence under the altar and transferred to there the body of the saint during the following year,[1] one day before [the anniversary] of his departure.

(§192) Although the blessed one had his body laid here, he had [a] dwelling in the heavenly mansions, standing in the spirit before the Lord and serving him with all the saints. There he was offering petitions and prayers and supplications for us with much freedom [of speech], frequently visiting the brotherhood and protecting and inspiring and guiding [them] and for the most part was singing together with them.[2] To some he appeared personally,[3] both healing the sick and comforting and strengthening those who in sincerity of faith and in purity of [their] ways of life went on the straight [path][4] and were esteemed worthy to be in such converse with the saints.

(§193) The blessed one, our father and bishop Peter, was perfected on the first [day] in the First Kanon,[5] when Sunday was dawning, on the third day of the memorial of Peter, the great martyr and archbishop of the city of Alexandria,[6] according to the vision that appeared to Athanasius the priest, and five months after the departure of our holy father Abba Isaiah the ascetic, as the blessed one foretold to us, when the departure of the old man [Isaiah] was announced to us. In the second year, one day before the memorial of Abba Peter, we transferred and laid down his bones inside the house of prayer, under the altar. The whole time of his life on earth was about eighty years.[7] **[R 146]** Now, the departure of our father was on the first of First Kanon. His first deposition in the ground in the earth was on the second of the same month. His *translatio*, however, and his deposition under the altar [was] on the thirtieth of Second Teshrin.[8] The time of his life, however, [was] about eighty years; because of this we celebrate his memorial [on] three [separate] days. On the first day, we keep the feast of his *translatio*, which was to [the place] under the altar; on the

5 I.e., December.

6 This description conflicts with the dating of the commemoration of Peter of Alexandria indicated above at *Vit. Pet.* §182 (R 137).

7 Thus, if Peter died in 491, his year of birth is to be dated to around 410.

8 I.e., November.

ܡܕܒܚܐ. ܒܫܢܬ ܕܬܠܬܐ. ܟܕ ܐܬܐ ܗܘܐ ܥܠܘܗܝ ܥܕܢܐ. ܒܫܢܬ ܕܬܫܪܝ.
ܕܫܘܢܝܗ ܕܒܐܪܥܐ ܒܡܕܒܪܐ: ܒܡܫܝܚܐ ܝܫܘܥ ܡܪܢ ܐܠܗܐ ܕܥܠ
ܟܠ: ܕܠܗ ܫܘܒܚܐ ܘܐܝܩܪܐ ܘܣܓܕܬܐ ܠܥܠܡ ܥܠܡܝܢ ܐܡܝܢ.

[1] On the day of his death, which also was acknowledged publicly through people's reverencing him.

second [day], [we keep the commemoration of the event] when all the people were coming [together];[1] on the third [day, the feast] of his deposition in the earth.[2] In Christ Jesus, our Lord, God, who [is] over all, to whom be glory and honor and power unto the ages of ages! Amen.

2 I.e., his original burial.

ܡܛܠ ܥܘܗܕܢܐ ܕܐܝܟܢܐ ܫܢܝ ܠܘܬ ܡܪܗ ܠܛܘܒܢܐ ܬܐܘܕܘܣܝܘܣ ܐܦܝܣܩܘܦܐ ܕܐܘܪܫܠܡ܀

(§1) ܡܛܠ ܕܝܢ ܕܒܥܐ ܐܢܐ: ܕܒܗܠܝܢ ܕܡܢ ܠܥܠ ܐܫܬܘܕܝܬ: ܕܡܫܬܒܚܬܐ
ܐܢܐ ܠܢܐ ܕܒܢܝܚܗ ܕܠܛܘܒܢܐ ܬܐܘܕܘܣܝܘܣ ܐܦܝܣܩܘܦܐ ܕܐܘܪܫܠܡ
ܘܡܕܒܪܢܐ ܘܗܕܝܐ. ܐܝܟ ܕܗܘܪܒܐ ܠܫܘܠܡܐ ܐܦܪܘܫ ܒܡܟܬܒܢܘܬܐ.
(§2) ܟܕ ܐܬܪܕܦ ܕܝܢ ܐܝܟ ܦܘܩܕܢܗ ܕܡܪܩܝܢܘܣ: ܘܫܢܝ ܡܢ ܐܘܪܫܠܡ.
ܒܐܓܝܦܛܘܣ ܡܥܪܩ ܗܘܐ. ܟܕ ܫܠܝܚ ܘܠܐ ܝܕܝܥ. ܒܗ ܕܝܢ ܒܗܘ ܙܒܢܐ.
ܘܐܒܐ ܪܗܘܡܢܐ ܐܒܐ ܕܕܝܪܝܐ ܡܢ ܡܕܝܢܬܐ ܘܡܠܬܐ ܕܬܩܘܥ ܐܒܐ ܕܒܡܠܟܘܣ
ܟܦܘܪܐ. ܟܕ ܐܬܠܒܟ. ܐܬܦܣܩ ܕܒܐܢܛܝܘܟܝܐ ܢܗܘܐ ܘܢܬܢܝܚ. ܘܒܗܘ
ܐܬܠܒܟ. ܘܠܡܬܐܬܘܣ ܕܐܬܘܗܝ ܗܘܐ ܪܫܝܥܐ ܕܕܝܢܐ ܕܗܦܟ. ܗܘ̇
ܕܥܠ ܫܡܟܐ ܬܠܐ ܡܢ ܡܕܝܢܬܐ ܘܡܕܝܢܬܐ. ܟܕ ܗܘ̇ ܕܝܢ ܗܘܐ ܐܦܝܣܩܘܦܐ ܡܢ
ܠܛܘܒܢܐ ܬܐܘܕܘܣܝܘܣ̇ ܒܝܕ ܐܢܫܐ ܡܢ ܡ̈ܗܝܡܢܐ ܕܐܬܚܙܝܘܗܝ: ܟܕ ܐܬܚܙܝܘ
ܒܐܢܛܝܘܟܝܐ: ܗܘ̇ܬ ܠܒܪܘܬ ܢܦܫܐ ܡܕܡ ܘܒܥܠܬܐ ܒܝܬܘܢܘܗܝ: ܡܛܠ
ܫܘܠܡܐ ܬܪ̈ܝܨܐ ܘܡܛܠ ܗܝܡܢܘܬܐ. ܡܬܐܢܚ ܗܘܐ ܠܒܝܫ ܗܘ̇

[1] See above, *Vit. Pet.* §88 (R 62).

[2] I.e., Emperor Marcian. See above, comments on *Vit. Pet.* §81 (R 57), 121 n. 9, and §90 (R 63). See also Theophanes, *Chronographia* AM 5945 [452/3 C.E.] (de Boor, 1:106–7; Mango and Scott, 164–65).

[3] On Abba Romanus, see *Vit. Pet.* §77 (R 52) and 111 n. 11 with references there to sections of the *Plerophoriae* that feature him and comments on the occurrence of the title "father of the monks" throughout Rufus's works.

[4] The Syriac ܟܦܘܪܐ has a range of meanings from "infidel," "unbeliever" to "heathen" and "pagan" or also "apostate" (Payne Smith, 222). Rufus's choice of the epithet "the Apostate" for Juvenal immediately would have reminded the early Christian audience of Emperor Julian (361–363), who had been raised a Christian but who through his attempts at oppressing Christianity and reviving

On the Memory of How the Blessed Theodosius, Bishop of Jerusalem, Departed to Our Lord

(§1) Remembering that I promised in the previous matters[1] to relate the manner of the death of the blessed Theodosius, bishop of Jerusalem, confessor, and martyr, it is necessary that I repay back the debt here in a few [words].

(§2) When according to the command of Marcian[2] [Theodosius] was driven away and had departed from Jerusalem, he dwelt in Egypt, hiding himself and remaining unknown. At that time also Abba Romanus, the father of the monks,[3] having been captured according to Juvenal the Apostate's[4] malice and plan, was ordered to remain under guard in Antioch.[5] Together with him, Timothy was seized,[6] who was archimandrite[7] of the monastery of Hypatios, about seven miles from the Holy City,[8] because he was a bishop, [having been appointed] by the blessed Theodosius in one of the cities under his [jurisdiction].[9] During their exile,[10] there were uncertainty and disputes between them concerning the

pagan cults infuriated early Christians so much that they would commonly speak of him as "Julian the Apostate." See also comments above, *Vit. Pet.* §47 (R 32), 64 n. 2; below, *Obit. Theod.* §8 (B 25).

5 See below, *Obit. Theod.* §9 (B 25).

6 This Timothy and the Timothy who was a monk in the monastery of Abba Romanus (see *Pler.* 87) do not seem to be the same.

7 An archimandrite is a term equivalent to the Syriac ܪܝܫ ܕܝܪܐ or "head of the monastery," "abbot," often of an important monastery of a city or diocese. See George Nedungatt, "Archimandrit," *LTK* 1:948.

8 Attempts at further identifying the monastery of Hypatios have not been successful.

9 See above, *Vit. Pet.* §81 (R 57).

10 The Syriac renders the Greek ἐξορία.

ܠܚܒܪܬܗܘܢ܆ ܐܝܟ ܗܿܝ ܕܡܫܬܘܬܦ ܗܘܐ ܒܗܪܣܝܣ ܕܐܘܛܘܟܝܢܘܬܐ܆
ܘܫܕܪ ܕܢܐܡܪ ܗܿܝ ܕܒܪ ܚܢܢ.

(§3) ܟܕ ܗܠܟ ܕܢܬܟܬܫܘܢ ܥܒܕ ܗܿܘ ܕܝܢ ܐܦܝ̈ܣܩܘܦܐ ܬܐܘܕܘܣܝܘܣ
ܟܕ ܡܕܒܪ ܗܘܐ ܒܐܠܟܣܦܘܠܘܣ܆ ܘܕܒܝܠ ܗܿܝ ܒܚܝܠܐ ܕܡܫܝ̈ܚܐ܆ ܒܗ̇܆
ܕܪ̈ܥܝܐ ܐܬܬܣܝܡܘܢ ܗܘܘ [B 22] ܕܐܪ̈ܬܕܘܟܣܘ܆ ܟܕ ܐܠܝܨ ܢܦܫܗ܆ ܣܓܝ
ܗܿܘ ܕܢܐܬܐ ܡܬܥܝܩܐܝܬ ܠܦܘܪܫܐ ܠܐܢܛܝܘܟܝܐ ܡܕܝܢܬܐ܆ ܘܪ̈ܢܬܐ
ܐܝܟ ܠܐܘܟܠܬܐ ܘܠܥܫܝܢܐ. ܐܬܥܫܢ ܕܝܢ ܐܡܪܝܢ܆ ܕܝܬܝܪܐܝܬ ܡܬܠܠܗܕܐ
ܐܦܛܪܗܘܢ ܕܢܐܬܐ ܒܐܘܪܚܐ ܗܕܐ ܗܿܘ ܪܥܝܐ ܛܒܐ. ܟܕ ܝܿܕܥܐ ܕܢܚܬ
ܘܢܐܬܐ ܠܘܬ ܡܕܝܢܐ ܫܡܥܘܢ܆ ܗܿܘ ܕܗܘܐ ܗܘܐ ܥܠ ܐܦܣܩܘܦܘܬܐ ܕܗܠܝܢ
ܐܬܪܘܬܐ܆ ܘܡܫܬܥܒܕ ܗܘܐ ܒܢܦܩܘܬܐ ܡܢ ܗܝ̈ܡܢܐ. ܘܠܐ ܢܩܒܠܘܢܝܗܝ
ܕܢܦܠܓܐ ܡܢ ܬܐܘܕܘܪܝܛܘܣ ܘܡܢ ܡܪ̈ܛܝܩܐ ܐܚܪ̈ܢܐ܆ ܘܢܦܠܓܘܢ ܠܦܘܪܫܘܬܗܘܢ܆
ܐܝܟ ܗܿܝ ܕܦܠܓܘܬܐ ܐܝܬܘܗܝ ܗܘܐ ܘܒܪܢܫܐ ܘܠܐ ܠܡܥܦ ܠܟܣܪ: ܘܠܐ
ܡܕܝܢܐ ܒܫܘܬܦܘܬܐ ܕܡܠܦ̈ܢܐ ܬܪ̈ܝܢ ܕܟܕܐ܆ ܘܬܗܘܐ ܗܕܐ ܬܘܩܠܬܐ
ܠܣ̈ܓܝܐܐ.

[1] The followers of Eutyches were thought to hold that Christ was consubstantial only with the Father, and thus in no way human as we are, that there is no obvious resemblance between Christ's nature and human nature. The author here seems to refer to disputes that arose among the anti-Chalcedonians and that split them into at least two parties: more moderate anti-Chalcedonians whose main concern was the nonacceptance of Chalcedon; and those who theologically followed Eutyches. Eutyches was regularly anathematized by the followers of Severus of Antioch. By referring to Eutyches' teachings as "heresy," Rufus indicates that his position was not a "Monophysite" position in the strict theological sense of the word. From comments throughout his work, especially those on Peter the Iberian and himself at *Pler.* 22, one sees him supporting a more explicitly "anti-Chalcedonian" position, directed against any efforts that promoted the Council of Chalcedon and the novelties it seemed to introduce. For examples of and comments on probably related disputes among ascetics in Egypt, see *Pler.* 50.

[2] This comment witnesses to the fact that anti-Chalcedonians in Egypt and in Syria were able to communicate with one another.

[3] Square brackets include page references to E. W. Brooks's edition of the *De obitu Theodosii*.

[4] Traveling up to Antioch, Theodosius appears to have expected conflict with some of the leaders of the anti-Chalcedonians there.

[5] See John 10:1–18, 10:14 as a reference to the "Good Shepherd." Note

orthodox doctrines and concerning the faith. For it was said that Timothy was in communion with the heresy of the Eutychians and avoided saying the [words] "consubstantial with us."[1]

(§3) When Archbishop Theodosius heard [of] their conflicts,[2] although he was residing in Egypt, fearing that many would be scandalized because [the two] had been rulers **[B 22]**[3] of the orthodox,[4] he forced himself and was anxious to come secretly to Syria, to the city of Antioch, and to bring them concord and peace. Yet some claim that the good shepherd[5] made haste to come this way especially because he desired to visit the holy Simeon, who in those regions was standing on a pillar and was praised by many for [his] temperance.[6] [His purpose] was not to allow [Symeon] to be led down the wrong path by Theodoret[7] and by other heretics and to follow their apostasy, as though he were someone simple, ignorant, entirely unlearned, and untrained in the accuracy of the orthodox doctrines of the church, because this would be a stumbling-block for many.

also that immediately afterwards at 10:19–21, a scene of division and dispute is recounted. See also *Pler.* 25, where Theodosius is called "shepherd."

[6] The reference here is to St. Simeon Stylites the Elder (ca. 390–459). For convenient access to the literary treatment of Simeon's adventures, see the English translation of the hagio-biographical tradition in Robert Doran, trans, *The Lives of Simeon Stylites* (CSS 112; Kalamazoo, Mich.: Cistercian, 1992). Both parties, Chalcedonians and anti-Chalcedonians, in their respective literatures enlisted Simeon's support for their causes. Note the anti-Chalcedonian attempt in the present instance. For Chalcedonian claims on Simeon, see, e.g., *The Syriac Life of Saint Simeon Stylites* 128 (Doran, *Lives of Simeon*, 194), and Cyril of Scythopolis, *Vit. Euth.* 30 (Schwartz, 47,21–48,6; Price, 44). On Simeon Stylites, see also André Jean Festugière, *Antioche païenne et chrétienne: Libanius, Chrysostome et les moines de Syrie* (BEFAR 194; Paris: de Boccard, 1959), 388–401; and Susan A. Harvey, "The Sense of a Stylite: Perspectives on Simeon the Elder," *VC* 42 (1988): 376–94.

[7] I.e., Theodoret of Cyrrhus (born ca. 393, d. 466). Early on, Theodoret was a supporter of Nestorius and refuted Cyril of Alexandria's Twelve Anathemas in writing. Having been deposed from his episcopal see by the Robber Council in 449, Theodoret was reinstated as bishop of Cyrrhus two years later. For the rest of his life he led a rather quiet and withdrawn existence. Theodosius's visit with Simeon Stylites appears to have taken place before Theodoret's death.

(§4) ܐܠܐ ܒܬܪ ܠܫܘܢܩܘܬܗ܂ ܫܠܝܚܐ ܗܘ ܥܡܗ ܕܐܝܣܪܐܝܠ܂ ܕܟܕܡ ܠܗ ܡܢ ܡܕܡ ܕܢܗܘܐ ܒܚܝܘܗܝ ܕܫܡܥܐ܂ ܘܟܕ ܡܬܬܚܝܕܘܬܗ ܚܒܫ܃ ܟܕ ܐܣܪ ܫܡܠܝ ܘܡܕܡ ܦܪܟܘܢ ܐܣܘܪܗ܂ ܟܕ ܒܬܪ ܡܢ ܟܕܘ ܐܘܪܚܐ ܟܠܗ ܒܣܝܦܘܬܐ ܙܪܐ܃ ܡܢ ܐܦܝܣܩܘܦܘ ܒܕܡܟܐ ܠܩܘܪܝܐ܂ ܟܕ ܡܕܡ ܬܪܒܐ ܕܐܝܠܘܢܒܐ ܡܕܝܢܬܐ ܗܘܐ܂ ܦܓܥ ܒܓܐܝܢܘܣ ܟܘܪ ܐܦܝܣܩܘܦܐ ܕܒܕܬܐ ܕܬܡܢ܂ ܟܕ ܡܢ ܣܓܝܐܐ ܡܕܒܪ ܗܘܐ܂ ܘܟܕ ܢܕܥܗ ܐܝܟ ܡܢ ܫܡܗ ܕܐܝܠܝܢ ܗܘܘ ܡܕܥܝܗ܃ ܐܝܟ ܗܘ ܕܒܥܠܡ ܐܬܘܪܬܐ ܒܟܒܪ ܗܘܐ ܠܗ܃ ܟܕ ܕܬܠܡܝܕܐ ܕܢܒܐ ܕܟܗܬ ܡܪ، ܟܪ܃ ܘܠܗ ܠܒܪ ܐܦܝܣܩܘܦܐ ܐܘܪܚ܃ ܡܫܕܐ ܐܬܠܒܝ ܐܝܟ ܝܕܥܐ ܪܒܐ܂ ܘܕܡܐ ܡܕܡ ܒܚܕܘܬܟ ܡܬܒܥܐ ܗܘܐ܂

(§5) ܘܟܕ ܠܬܫܥܝܐ ܕܡܕܝܢܬܐ ܐܫܬܠܡ܂ ܒܝܠܘܬܪܬܐ ܐܬܚܫܒ ܡܢܗܘܢ܂ ܘܡܫܕܐ ܐܘܪܚܗ ܠܓܠܝܐ܂ ܟܕ ܕܝܢ ܡܪܘܣܘܣ ܒܠܚ ܡܢܗܘܢ ܠܒܝܬܗ ܕܪܫ ܐܦܝܣܩܘܦܐ܂ ܦܓܥ [B 23] ܕܢܬܪܕܪ ܘܢܦܩ ܠܩܘܣܛܢܛܝܢܘܦܘܠܝܣ܂ ܟܕ ܡܬܒܥܠ ܡܢ ܡܕܝܢܬܐ ܠܡܕܝܢܬܐ ܒܝܕ ܦܠܣܛܝܢܐ܂ ܘܟܕ ܫܠܡ܂ ܡܕܡܐܬ ܡܢ ܣܓܝ

[1] See also 2 Cor 12:7, where Paul says that "there was given to me a thorn in the flesh, a messenger of Satan to torment me." Note that MS BM Add. 12,174 substitutes "[human] race" for "Israel."

[2] I.e., Simeon Stylites.

[3] Literally, "while he was being bound."

[4] Functioning for the reader as a reminder of the exodus and the pharaoh who made life miserable for the Israelites during their years in exile in Egypt, "pharaoh" is here used as a polemical code-word for the emperor or the emperor's representative, negative forces that oppose Theodosius.

[5] References to Gaianos in early Christian literature outside the present instance could not be identified.

[6] "Chorbishop" from the Greek χώρας ἐπίσκοπος, "overseer of the countryside," was an ordained cleric with administrative oversight for churches and at least in Syria probably also monasteries and hermits. The chorbishop was subordinate to the bishop of the diocese. A chorbishop could ordain to lower orders only with the permission of the diocesan bishop. The power of the chorbishop to ordain was gradually weakened until he could only tonsure readers. According to Canon Ten of the Council of Antioch (341), chorbishops may ordain lower ranks of clergy (to the rank of subdeacon), but deacons and priests only with the agreement of the bishop of the diocese; see Franz Gillmann, *Das Institut der Chorbischöfe im Orient* (Munich: Lentner, 1903), 90. In principle, a chorbishop was also able to consecrate an abbot or abbess (Gillman, *Das Insitut der Chorbischöfe,* 94), a duty consistent with a supervisory position over monks and nuns outside of the city. On the canonical subordination of the chorbishop to the urban bishop, see also Onorato Bucci, *Il corespiscopato nella storia della chiesa* (Rome: Editrice universitaria di Roma-la Goliardica, 1993), 90–91. Following the Decian persecution, the *periodeutai* or "traveling priests"

(§4) But Satan, that thorn of Israel[1] who was lying in ambush for him before he could converse with the old man,[2] obstructed his cheerfulness, effecting his capture in chains,[3] carrying him off and making him stand before Pharaoh.[4] For after having already journeyed the whole way in anxiety from Egypt to Syria, when he was in front of the gates of the city of Antioch, he met upon Gaianos,[5] the chorbishop[6] of the church there, while he was borne [about] by many [people]. One of those walking in front of [Gaianos] recognized him[7] to be an inhabitant of the area,[8] [who was dwelling] in what is called the monastery of Bēth Mār Bazai,[9] and made [this] known to the chorbishop. [Theodosius] was seized immediately as a great catch, who previously had been tracked down everywhere.

(§5) After he was delivered up to the magistrates of the city, he was placed by them under guard, [and] they immediately informed the emperor. When Marcian learned from them [about] the capture of the archbishop,[10] he commanded **[B 23]** that he should be taken up[11] to Constantinople under escort from city

gradually replaced the chorbishop in both East and West. In the West following the Carolingian reforms, the chorbishop enjoyed a brief revival in the course of the eleventh to twelfth centuries. See Theodor Gottlob, *Der abendländische Chorepiskopat* (Bonn: Schroeder, 1928; repr., Amsterdam: Schippers, 1968), 136–40; Vinzenz Fuchs, *Der Ordinationstitel von seiner Entstehung bis auf Innozenz III. Eine Untersuchung zur kirchlichen Rechtsgeschichte, mit besonderer Berücksichtigung auf Anschauungen Rudolph Sohms* (Bonn: Schroeder, 1930; repr., Amsterdam: Schippers, 1963), 211–36.

7 I.e., Theodosius.

8 Literally, "in those regions."

9 Literally, "the house of my lord Baz(ai)." According to Zachariah Rhetor, *Chronicle* 3.9 (Brooks, 1:162,5; Hamilton and Brooks, 55), Theodosius was arrested at Sidon. Honigmann (*Évêques et Évêchés Monophysites*, 179 and n. 1) locates a monastery of Bēth Mār Bizī in Seleucia I and identifies a certain Bishop George Ourṭāyā as possibly having been a resident at, and Zenobius as archimandrite of, the monastery in the sixth century (235–36 and n. 8).

10 Note that the author continues to refer to Theodosius as archbishop, understood of Jerusalem. However, in the meantime Juvenal of Jerusalem had already returned and repossessed the See of the Holy City. This passage may also be considered a pointer to a growing awareness among anti-Chalcedonians of being members of a church of their own. See also the comments in Horn, *Asceticism and Christological Controversy*, 86–88.

11 Literally, "be sent and go up."

ܗܘܐ܂ ܕܟܕ ܛܩܣܝܘ̈ܛܐ ܢܦܩܘܗܝ، ܠܓܠܘܬܗ܂ ܘܦܩܣܘܗܝ، ܕܢܒܠܘܢ ܠܥܘܕܪܘܗܝ
ܪ̈ܗܝܒܬܐ ܕܟܠܡܕܡ̈ܐ܂ ܟܕ ܡܫܬܘܕܐ ܠܗ ܪܚܡܘܬܐ ܕܠܘܬܗ܂ ܘܫܒܝܚܘܬܐ
ܘܡܘܗ̈ܒܬܐ ܩܘܠܣ̈ܐ܂ ܟܕ ܕܝܢ ܠܐ ܡܬܬܦܝܣܢܐ ܘܠܐ ܡܬܚܠܠܢܐ ܘܠܐ
ܡܬܦܠܓܢܐ ܚܙܘܗܝ܆ ܘܕܡܠܟ ܠܟܠ ܐܘܠܨܢܐ ܘܡܫܥܒܕܢܘܬܐ܂ ܐܫܠܡܗ
ܠܢܛܘܪ̈ܐ ܕܕܝܪܐ ܕܡܬܩܪܐ ܕܕܝܘܣ܆ ܒܒܪܐ ܟܦܢܝܐ ܕܟܒܝܫܘܬ ܬܪܥܘܬܗ
ܕܢܣܬܪܩܘܗܝ܂ ܘܡܬܟܬܫܢܐ ܕܢܫܦ ܗܘܝܘܗܝ ܕܟܠܡܕܡ̈ܐ܂ ܟܕ ܡܫܬܘܕܐ
ܠܡܠܟܐ ܕܢܚܪ ܠܗ ܕܢܒܠܘܢ ܠܦܘܩܕܢܐ܂ ܐܘ ܕܝܢ ܗܘ ܕܠܐ ܢܟܐ܆ ܒܟܠܗ
ܪ̈ܢܐ ܘܡܫܬܠܛܬܐ ܘܐܘܠܨܢܐ ܢܛܠܠ ܠܗ܂ ܘܟܕ ܫܠܡ ܟܠܗ܆ ܒܟܘܪܗܢܐ ܡܢ
ܒܐܘܪܚܐ ܘܒܚܫܐ ܦܓ̈ܥܐ ܐܝܟ ܗܘܐ ܠܗ܂ ܟܕ ܢܟܝܪ ܠܗ ܕܢܒܥܐ
ܠܡܠܟܐ ܘܢܫܬܘܦ ܠܥܘܢܝܘܗܝ ܪ̈ܫܝܬܐ܂ ܟܕ ܦܓܥܬ̈ܐ ܡܢ ܢܟܝܪ
ܗܘܐ ܘܡܫܬܘܪܐ܂ ܦܓܥܬܐ ܕܝܢ ܚܘܪ ܗܘܐ܂ ܟܕ ܕܝܢ ܦܫ ܡܢ ܣܒܪܗ܆
ܘܗܘ ܠܦܘܠܚܢܐ ܬܐܘܕܘܣܝܘܣ܆ ܡܪܗܒܬ ܐܝܟ ܗܘܐ ܠܩܒܠܐ ܐܠܗܐ

[1] The Syriac transliterates the Greek ταξιῶται. See also E. W. Brooks, *Vitae virorum apud Monophysitas celeberrimorum* (2 vols.; CSCO 7–8; CSCO Scriptores Syri 3/25; Paris: E Typographeo Reipublicae; Leipzig: Harrassowitz, 1907), 2:16 n. 2. Rufus may also intend to portray Theodosius's imprisonment as being parallel to the triumphal march in which Timothy Aelurus was dragged from city to city into exile.

[2] Literally, "had gone up."

[3] Literally, "him friendship with him."

[4] Compare to Zachariah Rhetor's description of Marcian's dealings with Juvenal of Jerusalem in *Chronicle* 3.3 (Brooks, 1:155–57; Hamilton and Brooks, 49–50). See also *Vit. Pet.* §76 (R 52).

[5] An anti-Chalcedonian audience may well have noticed that, in contrast to Juvenal, Theodosius did not give in to the emperor's enticements.

[6] That Constantinopolitan monastery was founded by the monk Dios, a native of Antioch and a contemporary of Bishop Atticus of Constantinople (406–425 C.E.). On Saint Dios, see the entry in the *Synaxarion of Constantinople* (Hippolyte Delehaye, ed., *Synaxarium ecclesiae Constantinopolitanae: Propylaeum ad Acta Sanctorum Novembris* [Brussels: Socios Bollandianos, 1902], 830). See also Nicholas P. Constas, "Four Christological Homilies of Proclus of Constantinople: Introduction, Critical Edition, Translation, and Commentary"

to city by officials of the magistrate.[1] Once [Theodosius] had arrived,[2] indeed, [the emperor] was first of all anxious to weaken his zeal through allurements and to persuade him to adhere to the wicked council of Chalcedon, promising Theodosius his friendship,[3] favor, and many benefits.[4] But when he saw that he was not to be persuaded, inflexible, and unchangeable and that he was prepared for every hardship and endurance,[5] he handed him over to the archimandrite of the monastery that is called "that of Dios,"[6] a man [who was] a zealot[7] of the evil doctrine[8] of Nestorius and a combatant on account of the Council of Chalcedon. He promised the emperor to make [Theodosius] agree to the impious opinion.[9] Or, if he was unwilling [to do this], by every shame and perversity he would get rid of him through torture. In the beginning, when he received him, indeed he held him in honor and with much luxury, [trying to] coax him to obey the emperor and be in communion with the wicked council, soothing [him] and promising many [things],[10] but [also] threatening [him] much. Yet when he

(Ph.D. diss., Washington, D.C., The Catholic University of America, 1994), 24 n. 71, as well as idem, ed. and trans., *Proclus of Constantinople and the Cult of the Virgin in Late Antiquity: Homilies 1–5, Texts and Translations* (VCSup 66; Leiden: Brill, 2003), 27 n. 71. On the monastery of Dios, see Theophanes, *Chronographia* AM 5980 [AD 487/8 C.E.] (de Boor, 1:132,27–30; Mango and Scott, 204); and Honigmann, *Évêques et Évêchés Monophysites*, 81 and n. 2. Eliseus of Sardis, who participated in the struggle against the tritheists, was imprisoned in the Monastery of Dios in 571 (Honigmann, *Évêques et Évêchés Monophysites*, 230 with n. 2).

7 Note that, whereas "zealous" is often used in a very positive meaning in describing activities of anti-Chalcedonians throughout Rufus's work, it may also, as in the present case, be used as a negative characterization of Chalcedonians.

8 Literally, "of the evil of the doctrine."

9 I.e., of Nestorius and of the Council of Chalcedon, understood to have promoted the continuation of Nestorius's ideas.

10 The archimandrite thus displayed the same behavior that already characterized Emperor Marcian above. The author may have wished to imply that too close of an association with the secular powers can and will lead to corruption of ascetics.

ܘܠܣܗܕܘܬܐ ܬܪܝܨܘܬ ܫܘܒܚܐ. ܢܟܝܫܗ ܒܡܠܬܐ ܗܕܡ ܐܠܝܨܘܬܐ ܕܡܠܟܐ
ܗܘܬ ܟܠܗ ܒܙܒܢܐ ܕܣܬܘܐ. ܘܒܠܗ ܗܢܐ ܢܦܫܗ ܒܐܘܠܨܢܐ ܘܒܥܘܩܢܐ.
ܐܝܟܢܐ ܕܟܠܗ ܦܓܪܗ ܘܪ̈ܓܠܘܗܝ، ܘܒܐܣܛܘܡܟܗ ܠܥܒܪܗ. ܘܡ̈ܟܐܒܐ
ܡܪ̈ܝܪܐ ܠܡܚܪ. ܟܕ ܒܟܘܒܐ ܘܒܚܫܐ ܘܒܩܘܪܫܐ ܐܬܬܢܝܚ.. ܟܕ ܠܐ ܐܝܟ
ܡܢ ܢܩ̈ܒܘܗܝ، ܡܫܬܠܡ ܗܘܐ ܕܢܫܡܪܢܘܗܝ.

(§6) ܒܬܪ ܗܢܐ. ܬܘܒ ܕܬܐܘܕܘܣܝܘܣ ܢܚܬ. ܟܕ ܡܛܝܐ [B 24] ܚܒܫܗ، ܘܟܕ
ܝܕܥ ܗܘܐ ܕܐܬܝܗܒ ܗܘܐ ܠܗ: ܕܒܩܘܒܠܐ ܐܚܪܢܐ ܐܢܬܘܢ، ܗܘܐ ܗܘܐ ܗܘ
ܡܕܝܢܬܐ ܐܩܣܘܣܬܘܪܘܣ ܐܪܕܘܬܐ: ܘܒܬܪ ܕܢܨܒܬ. ܐܘܪܚܐ ܥܡܪܘܗܝ
ܠܐܠܗܐ. ܗܘ ܕܗܘܝܘ ܐܦܠܐ. ܘܟܕ ܐܦܣ. ܫܡܥ ܕܢܫܟܢܘܗܝ، ܗܠܝܢ
ܕܠܗ. ܗܘܐ ܕܝܢ ܫܠܡܘܗܝ، ܘܐܘܒܠܗܘܢ، ܠܩܘܡܐ. ܘܟܕ ܡܠܟ ܢܦܩܬܐ
ܒܝܐ: ܘܐܚܪܬܗ ܡܫܠܡܘܬܐ ܥܠܝܡܬܐ. ܡܟܢܐ ܐܫܬܡܠܝ. ܟܕ ܒܠܒܐ
ܕܡܕܝܢܬܐ ܘܕܡܕܝܢܬܐ ܩܝܡ.

(§7) ܟܕ ܐܫܬܡܠܝ ܕܝܢ. ܗܘ ܛܘܒܢܐ ܦܛܪܘܣ ܐܒܐ ܕܝܠܢ ܐܬܘܗܝ، ܗܘܐ
ܒܩܠܩܘܕܪܐ. ܘܟܕ ܒܗܘ ܠܠܐ ܚܙܝܗ، ܒܚܙܘܐ: ܟܕ ܡܢ ܩܘܡܐ
ܕܩܠܝܒܐ ܡܕܝܢ: ܘܡܚܙܝܐ ܐܘܣܛܐ ܚܘܪܬܐ: ܗܿ، ܕܐܝܟ ܐܝܬ ܗܘܐ ܟܕܪܐ

[1] Rufus readily casts the description of one's struggle for orthodoxy into the language of martyrdom. See also, e.g., his characterization of Peter the Iberian as a "living martyr" at *Vit. Pet.* §112 (R 82). The motive of "martyrdom" on behalf of one's conviction by accepting the fate of living as a permanent pilgrim, traveler, and in exile is constitutive of Rufus's thought world. See Horn, "Weaving the Pilgrim's Crown."

[2] Literally, "during the time of the winter."

[3] Quicklime, i.e., calcium oxide (CaO), is a strong base that when dissolved in water can have as corrosive an effect as acid. When brought in contact with skin, it irritates the skin; in larger quantities or under prolonged exposure, it will cause painful burns and eat away at the human body.

[4] The Syriac transliterates the Greek στόμαχος.

[5] The Syriac noun and adjective are in the plural.

[6] This comment indicates that anti-Chalcedonians entertained a certain representation in Constantinople.

[7] According to Zachariah Rhetor, *Chronicle* 3.9 (Brooks, 1:161–63; Hamilton and Brooks, 55–56), Theodosius entertained many conversations and disputes with people while being imprisoned in a cell filled with lime.

[8] On the death of Marcian, see also the comments at *Vit. Pet.* §91 (R 64) and at *Pler.* 12, 27 (depicting Marcian's torments in hell), and 67. Note that at *Pler.* 67 it is the horse representing Marcian that is being confined to a cell.

had fallen short of his hope and the blessed Theodosius held on to the divine zeal and the orthodox faith like a martyr,[1] he imprisoned him during the winter[2] in a narrow cell that was full of [quick]lime.[3] He beat him so much with affliction and torture that he fell sick [in] his whole body, [in] his feet, and in his stomach.[4] Oppressed by bitter pain,[5] he was seized by hunger, thirst, and frost, while no one from among his acquaintances[6] was allowed to visit him.[7]

(§6) At this time it happened that Marcian died, since the Lord **[B 24]** struck him.[8] When those[9] who kept him [imprisoned] saw that the confessor,[10] Bishop Theodosius, was at [his] last breath and was about to die, they made his condition known to Leo, who at that time had come to the throne.[11] Granting permission, [Leo] allowed those who were his own to take him away, [and] they took him and brought him to Sykai.[12] After he had lived for [only] a few [more] days, a grave illness laid hold of him. In this way he was perfected,[13] weaving the crown of confessorship and of martyrdom.[14]

(§7) [At the time] when [Theodosius] was perfected, the blessed Peter, our father, was in Alexandria. In that night he saw him in a vision,[15] being borne by a multitude of angels and clothed

[9] Literally, "these."

[10] Rufus uses the full range of martyr-related language, here the title "confessor" for Theodosius.

[11] When ascending the throne of the Eastern Roman Empire, Leo I (457–474 C.E.) was immediately confronted with having to decide whether Timothy Aelurus rightfully held the patriarchal throne of Alexandria. Agreeing with the poll he had taken among the bishops (the so-called *Codex Encyclicus* preserves the documents), Leo I banned Timothy from his see in 460. Leo I also was instrumental in getting the anti-Chalcedonian Peter the Fuller removed from the See of Antioch. From the comments immediately following, however, one gets the impression that Leo I may at least initially have had some sympathies for individual anti-Chalcedonians.

[12] Also known as Galata and Pera in later times, the settlement of Sykai was located to the north of the Golden Horn, facing Constantinople. See Cyril Mango, "Galata," *ODB* 2:815–16.

[13] I.e., he passed away.

[14] For a study of the central importance of these motives in Rufus's works, see Horn, "Weaving the Pilgrim's Crown."

[15] For an additional account of that vision, see *Pler.* 54.

ܠܚܢܢܐ ܕܐܦܝܣܩܘܦܘܬܐ ܕܐܘܪܫܠܡ ܕܒܪ ܚܘܪܐ. ܣܛܘܠܐ. ܡܚܝܠܐ
ܡܬܟܠܠܐ ܗܘܐ ܠܥܡܡܐ. ܟܕ ܕܝܢ ܠܐܚܪ̈ܢܐ ܗ̇ܢܘܢ ܕܒܚܡܐ ܐܬܢܣܘܢ
ܗܘܐ ܐܫܬܡܥܬ: ܕܡܬܬܢܝܚܝܢ ܗ̇ܢܘܢ ܬܪ̈ܝܢ ܒܢ̈ܝܐ: ܕܢܣܬܦܘܢ ܠܦܓܪܗ
ܘܢܫܒܚܘܢܝܗܝ. ܟܕ ܡܢ ܗܘܠܟܐ ܕܝܠܗܘܢ: ܘܢܦܩܘܢ ܠܓܒܐ ܐܚܪܝܢ ܕܗܘܐ ܡܢ
ܒܪܘ ܚܠܦ ܠܗܘܢ ܘܐܫܬܬܦܘ ܠܘܬܒܗܘܢ. ܒܟܠܗ̇ ܣ̈ܦܝܢܬܐ ܐܬܦܪܣܘ.
ܘܟܕ ܡܠܠܐܝܬ ܠܦܓܪܗ ܘܐܢܫܐ ܥܡܗ ܘܐܪܓܝܘ ܒܐܠܦܐ. ܡܛܝܐ ܐܢܫܐ ܠܓܒ.
ܘܟܕ ܐܬܐ ܠܩܘܦܪܘܣ. ܗܟܢܐ, ܠܚܢܢ ܒܢܗܪܐ ܘܡܕܝܢܬܐ ܘܩܘܕܡܐ. ܒܬܪܐ
ܕܟܠܗ̇ ܐܝܠܢܐ. ܕܬܪ̈ܝܢ ܐܦܝܣܩܘܦܘܬܐ ܐܚܪܝܢ ܗܘܘ ܠܗ̇ ܘܒܟܢܫܝܢ ܒܗ̇.
ܗ̇ܘܐ ܕܝܢ ܕܩܕܝܫܘ. ܒܬܠܬܝܢ ܒܟܢܘܢ ܩܕܡ. ܡܛܝܐ ܒܬܪ ܝܘܡܐ ܕܕܘܟܪܢܐ
ܕܝܥܩܘܒ ܗ̇ܘ ܕܡܬܩܪܐ ܐܚܘܗ̇ ܕܡܪܢ ܘܫܠܝܚܐ, ܘܒܬܪ. ܗ̇ܘ ܕܐܦ ܩܕܡܝܐ ܗܘܐ

[1] The Syriac transliterates the Greek στολήν. For a discussion of that garment, see Devos, "Cyrille de Scythopolis," 33–36, 38. See also the reference to the white vestment of the bishop of Alexandria at *Vit. Pet.* §180 (R 136), which at that instance is a sign of the victorious martyr.

[2] I.e., the Chalcedonians.

[3] Obviously in order to weaken anti-Chalcedonian resistance and to gain as converts from among the anti-Chalcedonians those who had followed Theodosius.

[4] More literally, "threw."

[5] For the presence of anti-Chalcedonians on Cyprus, see also *Pler.* 28.

[6] I.e., December.

[7] In the Byzantine tradition, James the brother of the Lord (Gal 1:19) or James of Jerusalem (Acts 12:17; 15:13; 21:18; Gal 2:9, 12; 1 Cor 15:7) is commemorated on 23 October. James son of Alphaeus (Matt 10:3; Mark 3:18; Luke 6:15; Acts 1:13), whom ancient tradition as documented since Jerome identifies with James the Less(er) (Mark 15:40; 16:1; Matt 27:56; Luke 24:10), is commemorated on 9 October. The Roman rite, identifying James of Jerusalem and James of Alphaeus, celebrates his feast on 1 May (J. A. Lefrançois, "James [Son of Alphaeus], St.," *NCE* 7:700–701). Neither of these dates corresponds with the date suggested here. However, the Byzantine tradition knows of a second feast that commemorates James the brother of the Lord, celebrated on the Sunday after the Nativity as the Commemoration of the Holy Righteous Ones: Joseph the Betrothed, David the King, and James the Brother of the Lord. While the precise date of that feast varies from year to year, it falls within the last week of December and thus is probably the feast alluded to in this passage. A feast of the apostle James and John the Evangelist was celebrated on 29 December. See Gérard Garitte, *Le Calendrier Palestino-Géorgien du Sinaiticus 34 (xe siècle)* (Subsidia hagiographica 30; Brussels: Société des Bollandistes, 1958),

in a white vestment,[1] the one that the archbishop of Jerusalem used to wear when he baptized; in this manner, he was carried up to heaven. Yet when those brothers who had been with him heard that those [of] the two natures[2] intended to take his body by force, deposit it in one of their temples, and spread a rumor that he had joined them already and was in communion with their wickedness, they devised [a plan] with all diligence.[3] They quickly took his holy body, stowed[4] [it] on a ship, and immediately set sail. When they came to Cyprus, they buried the high priest, confessor, and martyr in a monastery that orthodox monks held at that time and in which they dwelt.[5] His commemoration is on the thirtieth of First Kanon,[6] immediately after the day of the commemoration of James,[7] who is called the "just one"[8] and the brother of our Lord,[9] the one who also was the first[10] of the bishops of

420–21. There was also a feast of David and James the brother of the Lord on 26 December (Garitte, *Le Calendrier Palestino-Géorgien*, 418).

[8] See Eusebius of Caesarea, *Hist. eccl.* 2.1.2; 2.23.4; 4.22.4 (the latter two based on Hegesippus) (Schwartz and Mommsen, 1:104,1, 166,10, 370,9; Williamson, 36, 59, 129). James is also referred to as the "just one" or "righteous one" in apocryphal texts such as the *Gos. Heb.* 7, which was known to Jerome, *Vir. ill.* 2.13 (Richardson, 8; Halton, 8).

[9] James is called the brother of the Lord at Gal 1:19. He is mentioned first in the list of Jesus's brothers at Mark 6:3; Matt 13:55. See also Eusebius of Caesarea, *Hist. eccl.* 2.23.22 (Schwartz and Mommsen, 6.1:172,22; Williamson, 61). On James the brother of the Lord, see also Henri Leclercq, "Jacques le Mineur," *DACL* 7.2:2109–2116; Wilhelm Pratscher, "Jakobus (Herrenbruder)," *RAC* 16:1227–43; Eugen Ruckstuhl, "Jakobus," *TRE* 16:485–88; Florence Morgan Gillman, "James, Brother of the Lord," *ABD* 3:620–21; Lorenz Oberlinner, "Jakobus der Jüngere, Apostel," *LTK* 5:719–20; Hannes Möhle, "Jakobus, Bruder Jesu," *LTK* 5:720–21; R. B. Ward, "James of Jerusalem in the First Two Centuries," *ANRW* 2.26.1:779–812; Bruce Chilton and Jacob Neusner, eds., *The Brother of Jesus: James the Just and His Mission* (Louisville: Westminster John Knox, 2001); Patrick J. Hartin, *James of Jerusalem: Heir to Jesus of Nazareth* (Collegeville, Minn.: Liturgical Press, 2004); Bruce Chilton and Craig A. Evans, eds., *James the Just and Christian Origins* (NovTSup 98; Leiden: Brill, 1999); John Painter, *Just James: The Brother of Jesus in History and Tradition* (Columbia: University of South Carolina Press, 2004).

[10] Literally, "head."

ܪܫܐ ܕܐܦܝܣܩܘܦܐ ܕܐܘܪܫܠܡ. ܘܫܡܥܘܢ ܕܐܬܡܢܝ ܕܐܚܪܢܐ ܫܡܠܝܬ
ܕܡܕܝܢܬܐ ܕܝܠܗ ܒܗ̈ܢܐ ܩܕܝܫܐ ܕܐܘܪܫܠܡ. ܘܕܡܕܝܢܬܐ ܕܬܐܘܕܘܣܝܘܣ
ܐܦܝܣܩܘܦܐ [B 25] ܐܪܬܕܘܕܘܟܣܐ ܐܟܚܕܐ ܪܗܛܐ.

(§8) ܠܪܘܡܢܐ ܕܝܢ ܪܫܝܥܐ ܐܝܟ ܕܕ̈ܝܢܐ ܘܪܫܐ ܐܢܛܝܘܟܝܐ. ܒܗ ܚܒܫ ܗ̈ܘܘ
ܥܡܠ ܒܐܦܘܠܘܢܝܐ ܒܐܟܣܘܪܝܐ: ܘܠܩܘܛܝܢܐ ܐܡܝܪ ܒܡܪܘܬܐ
ܐܪܬܕܘܕܘܟܣܘܬܐ: ܘܡܢ ܠܚܝܫܘܬܐ ܠܘܬ ܥܕܪܐ ܐܝܟ ܐܦܢ. ܗܘ ܕܝܢ ܠܗܢ
ܡܬܚܫܛ ܥܡ ܐܠܗܐ ܡܢܘܣܐ: ܒܢܫܐ ܐܚܪܢܐ ܘܒܡܣܘܬܐ ܢܦܫܗ
ܠܦܘܠܚܢܐ ܗܢܘܢ. ܡܛܠ ܕܕܘܢܦܠܘܢܝܐ ܐܬܬܘܚ ܗܘܬ ܗܘ; ܡܕܝܢܬܐ ܒܗܘ
ܘܒܗܢܐ: ܐܝܟ ܗ̇ܝ ܕܗ̇ܘܬ ܐܟܐ ܕܦܘܠܐ ܫܘܦܠܐ ܘܕܢܫܦܘܪܘܗ ܪ̈ܫܝܥܐ.
ܘܟܡܐ ܘܒܗܢܐ ܪ̈ܫܥ ܚ̈ܫܢܐ ܕܐܝܟ ܗܠܝܢ ܘܡܠܬ̈ܝܗ ܘܡܫܟܚܐ ܕܬ̈ܠܡܝܕܐ
ܡܬ̈ܠܠܝܢ ܗܘܘ ܒܗ̇. ܫܡܥܐ ܗܘܐ. ܕܦܠܝܓܐ ܫܠܝܛܐ ܕܡܫܝܚܐ ܠܪܘܡܢܐ
ܪܘܡܢܐ: ܐܘ ܡܬܬܦܝܣ ܘܡܬܬܠܚܦ ܡܢ ܡ̈ܦܠܝܢܘ: ܐܘ ܡܣܬܒܪܢܘܬܐ
ܒܟܪ ܘܐܟܪ. ܐܠܐ ܗܘ ܕܐܝܟ ܕܠܬܓ̈ܝܪܐ ܟܪ̈ܝܟܬܗ: ܗܘ ܕܡܬܚܫܛ
ܫܠܦ ܟܠܗ ܠܗܘܢ ܕܡܟܪܙ ܒܗ: ܠܗ; ܕܠܦܘܠܢܐ ܐܘܦܟܗ ܠܗܘܢܗ.
ܒܗ ܠܒܪܢ ܒܠܗ ܗܢܐ ܠܚܘܫܬܐ ܘܒܛܠܬܐ ܘܫܠܝܐ ܢܦܫ. ܐܚܪܢܐ
ܕܠܩܘܛܝܢܐ ܡܢ ܒܢܝ ܥܡܡܐ ܒܗ ܐܦܝܢ ܘܐܡܝܪ ܡܢ ܪܘܫܥܐ. ܐܟܢ

[1] James is here presented as the leader of all the apostles. Thus Theodosius, who is understood to be the rightful successor of James, could lay claim to absolute leadership within the church and by implication would not be subject to any other bishops, neither Juvenal, nor the bishop of Old or New Rome, nor anyone else. For a discussion of the model character James of Jerusalem exercised for anti-Chalcedonian ascetics, see Horn, *Asceticism and Christological Controversy*, 188–96.

[2] Thus, "coincide." This comment strongly restates Theodosius's claim as James's rightful successor to the See of Jerusalem.

[3] For comments on Romanus's exile to Antioch, see also *Pler.* 25 and *Obit. Theod.* §2 (B 21).

[4] Despite being imprisoned, as the following comments state, Romanus seems to have been able to be in touch with others, certainly Chalcedonians

Jerusalem.[1] It is worthy that we should be amazed that the commemoration of the first high priest of Jerusalem and the commemoration of the orthodox bishop Theodosius **[B 25]** occurred at the same time and in the same fashion.[2]

(§8) The blessed Romanus, the father of the monks and the head of the fathers, completed five years in Antioch in exile,[3] enlightened many through [his] orthodox preaching, and turned [them] from error to the truth.[4] For Marcian, indeed fighting against God,[5] imprisoned the blessed one there for another purpose and end, since the city was at the time [a city] of the Nestorians,[6] in that it had been the mother of the wicked Paul of Samosata[7] and Nestorius, and at that time similar[-minded] high priests, clergymen, and the greater part of the laypeople were in power. [Marcian] expected that the mighty soldier of Christ,[8] the blessed Romanus, would either be persuaded and perverted by the heretics or be in danger and perish. But the one who frustrates the clever plans of the wise,[9] the one who fights on behalf of all those who hope in him, turned [Marcian's] assault to the contrary. He gave his servant such grace, wisdom, and strength that he caused many of the heterodox, changing and arousing [them] from [their] ungodliness, to return to the fear of God and made [them] zealous

who were "turned ... from error to the truth" and most likely also anti-Chalcedonians.

[5] Rufus characterizes Marcian as "God-hating" at *Vit. Pet.* §88 (R 62).

[6] Anti-Chalcedonians tended to refer to Chalcedonians polemically as "Nestorians." See, e.g., *Pler.* 14, 62, and 88, where "Nestorians" are either followers of Nestorius or Chalcedonians.

[7] Paul was bishop of Samosata ca. 260–268. His modalistic or monarchical Trinitarian teachings as well as his emphasis on Jesus' ordinary manhood of body and soul and rejection of Jesus' preexistence led to his condemnation by two synods held in Antioch in 264 and 268.

[8] Note the military image. See also *Vit. Pet.* §50 (R 33), which speaks of John the Eunuch as Peter's "fellow-soldier," and the reference to further examples in other early Christian literature.

[9] See 1 Cor 3:19.

ܠܕܚܠܬ ܐܠܗܐ܂ ܘܛܢܢܐ܂ ܚܒܪ ܕܗܝܡܢܘܬܐ ܬܪ̈ܝܨܬܐ ܫܒܘܩܐ܂ ܟܕ ܡܬܟܬܫܢܐ
ܠܘܬܗ̇ ܡܠܬܐ ܢܨܝܚܬܐ ܕܐܪ̈ܥܐ܂ ܘܢܣܘܢ ܩ̈ܛܝܠܐ ܗ̇ܘܢ ܕܒܘܟܘܗܝ܂
(§9) ܒܗܠܝܢ ܕܝܢ ܙܒܢܐ ܗ̇ܘ ܕܗ̣ܘܐ ܗܘ ܠܗܒܢܐ ܘܪܥܒܐ ܒܐܬܪ̈ܘܬܐ܂
ܕܐܝܟ ܗܢܐ ܟܦܢܐ ܘܡܘܬܢܐ ܡܬܝܪܐ ܐܕܪܟ ܠܟܠܗ̇ ܦܠܣܛܝܢܐ܂ ܐܝܟܢܐ
ܕܬܐܟܘܠ ܐܪܥܐ܂ ܘܡܫܬܘܕܝܐ ܢܚܪܒܘܢ ܠܟܠܗܘܢ ܕܬܫܒܠܘܢ ܡܢ ܟܦܢܐ܂
ܘܟܕ ܡܟܠܐ ܗܦܟܬܐ ܗܘܬ ܠܗܘܟܠ ܟܦܢܐ ܘܡܘܬܢܐ ܡܢ ܟܠܡܕܡ ܥܠܡܐ
ܕܗ̇ܘ ܐܬܪܐ܂ ܐܝܟ ܡܢ ܕܗ̣ܘܐ [B 26] ܗ̣ܘܐ ܟܠܗ̇ ܐܬܪܐ ܕܐܟܣܘܪܝܐ ܕܗ̇ܘ
ܡܪܝܐ܂ ܘܡܛܠܗܕܐ ܐܡܪܝܢ ܗܘܘ ܕܫܒܩ ܟܠܗܘܢ ܡܢ ܐܠܗܐ ܘܥܛܪܐ
ܒܐܢܫܐ ܕܐܝܟ ܗܢܐ܂ ܟܕ ܕܥܠ ܗ̇ܘ ܕܗܘܐ ܕܠܐ ܢܬܒܥܘܢܝܗ̇܂ ܒܒܝ̈ܫܬܐ܂
ܐܘ ܕܐܣܬܪܩܬ ܢܘܟܪ̈ܝܘܬܗ܂ ܕܠܐ ܡܬܚܫܒܢ ܡܣܬܟܠܐ ܗܘ̣ܐ ܗܘܐ ܠܘܬ
ܡܣܪ̈ܢܘܗܝ܂ ܟܕ ܐܦܝܣ ܐܦ ܠܐܘܪܫܠܡ ܕܡܠܟܬܐ ܕܒܝܬ ܐܦܣܩܘܦܝܗ܂ ܡܛܠ
ܦܘܠܚܐ ܕܐܒܘ̈ܗܝ ܪܘܡܢܐ܂ ܘܟܕ ܗ̇ܘ ܐܦܣ[1] ܠܘ ܠܗ ܠܗ ܒܠܚܘܕ܂ ܐܠܐ
ܘܒܟܠܗ̇ ܦܢܕ ܕܟܠܗܘܢ ܩ̈ܕܝܫܐ ܕܐܟܣܘܪܝܐ ܐܬܬܣܝܡܘ܂ ܟܠ ܚܕ
ܒܕܝܗ ܢܦܩܐ ܠܐܘܟܠܣܗ܂ ܘܗܒܢܐ ܦܢܐ ܗ̣ܘ ܠܗܒܢܐ ܠܐܬܪܗ ܒܐܘܣܬܐ܂ ܗ̇ܝ
ܕܐܬܐܘܒ ܡܟܢܐ܂ ܕܥܕ ܗܘܐ ܡܢ ܬܡܢ܂ ܘܡܛܠ ܕܒܩܠܝܠܘܬܗ ܕܐܘܟܠܣܘܣ
ܡܟܢܐ ܗܘܬ܂ ܘܡܛܠ ܕܬܚܦܝܦܐ ܗܘܬ ܩܛܝܬܐ ܕܦܪܕܟܐ ܗܘܬ ܠܗܘܢ ܡܢ

[1] Here Brooks (26, 7) misreads ܗܦܐ.

[2] Note the combination of two of the central characteristics of anti-Chalcedonians as portrayed by Rufus: fear of God and zeal for the right faith.

[3] See Jer 30:16.

[4] Dionysios Ch. Stathakopoulos, *Famine and Pestilence in the Late Roman and Early Byzantine Empire: A Systematic Survey of Subsistence Crises and Epidemics* (Birmingham Byzantine and Ottoman Monographs 9; Aldershot, U.K.: Ashgate, 2004), 238, catalogue entry 64 (based on Evagrius, *Hist. eccl.* 2.6) lists a famine and epidemic affecting Phrygia, Galatia, Cappadocia, Cilicia, and Palestine from 451 to 454, which may be related to the one referred to here. Stathakopoulos does not include the *De obitu Theodosii* in his sources. Brian Croke, "Famine," *ODB* 2:777-78 does not list this famine.

[5] Literally, "as [against] the one who."

[6] See *Obit. Theod.* §2 (B 21). *Pler.* 25 states that Abba Romanus was sent into exile upon the command of Emperor Marcian.

[7] I.e., Juvenal of Jerusalem.

[8] *Pler.* 25 connects Abba Romanus very closely with Empress Eudocia, almost, but not necessarily, suggesting that the two were in Antioch at the same time. On Eudocia's support for the anti-Chalcedonians, see Horn, "Empress Eudocia and the Monk Peter the Iberian."

[9] I.e., Marcian.

[10] The Syriac renders the Greek ἐξορία. See Brooks (26,7), *Vitae viro-*

for the orthodox faith,[2] so that the prophetic word of Jeremiah was fulfilled with regards to him, "And those who led you into captivity will become captives."[3]

(§9) During the whole time [when] the blessed Romanus was in Antioch, such hunger and lack of rain came upon all of Palestine that the earth dried up and all of them were in danger of being destroyed by hunger.[4] There arose a great outcry from the inhabitants of the region against Juvenal the Apostate because[5] he was **[B 26]** the cause of that saint's exile,[6] and they said that such justified wrath had been laid upon them by God. That wretched one[7] was so afraid they would stone him with rocks or bring him to naught in another way that against his will he came to be [Romanus's] advocate before Marcian. He also asked Empress Eudocia to petition [Marcian] with him for the return of our father Romanus.[8] When that one[9] not only gave permission to him but also ordered on account of him that every one of the saints who were in exile[10] should return to his place,[11] the blessed one likewise returned to his old monastery that is located in Tekoa,[12] from where he had departed. [However,] because [the monastery] was located in the diocese[13] of Juvenal and because the village that was near them had been stirred up by evil people,[14] he came [instead] to the re-

rum, 18 n. 1 (Latin). Literally, "that all the saints who were in exile, [that] every one of them."

11 The amnesty granted to anti-Chalcedonians in Syria allowing their return to Palestine does not seem to have affected anti-Chalcedonians in Egypt. Peter the Iberian, who had joined his fellow-believers in Egypt, stayed in the country for almost two decades.

12 According to *Pler.* 25, Abba Romanus headed a monastery of about six hundred monks in Tekoa, a village fifteen miles south of Jerusalem. See also Cyril of Scythopolis, *Vit. Euth.* 30, 45 (Schwartz, 49,10–13, 67.16–17; Price, 46, 64). Tekoa was also home to the prophet Amos. Eventually, after Romanus's death and during the days of St. Saba, the monastery became known as the site of the "New Laura." See, e.g., Cyril of Scythopolis, *Vit. Sab.* 36 (Schwartz, 123,4–8; Price, 132). For further reference to the site, see also Tsafrir, Di Segni, and Green, *Tabula Imperii Romani*, 248; and Claudine Dauphin, *La Palestine byzantine: Peuplement et Populations* (3 vols.; BAR International Series 726; Oxford: Archaeopress, 1998), 3:928.

13 The Syriac word more literally describes a place, region, or sphere over which authority is exercised.

14 An indicator that the local population had joined the Chalcedonian side.

ܐܬܪܐ ܒܝܬܝܐ. ܘܐܬܐ ܗܘܐ ܠܐܬܪܐ ܕܐܠܘܬܪܘܦܘܠܝܣ ܡܕܝܢܬܐ. ܘܟܕ
ܫܡܥ ܣܓܝܐܐܝܬ ܐܬܦܨܚ ܡܢܗܘܢ܂ ܗܘ̇ ܒܗ̇ ܒܡܕܝܢܬܐ. ܩܕܡ ܡܕܝܢܬܐ ܐܬܬܣܝܡ
ܡܕܝܢܬܗ܆ ܘܐܫܟܚ ܕܘܟܐ ܚܕ ܕܠܝܬ ܠܒܪܐ ܘܠܥܡܪܐ ܕܡܕܝܢܬܐ܆ ܟܠ
ܬܪܝܢ ܡ̈ܝܠܐ ܡܢ ܗܝܟܠܐ ܕܢܒܝܐ ܙܟܪܝܐ ܘܐܬܪܐ. ܒܬܚܘܡܐ ܕܡܕܝܢܬܐ
ܕܡܬܩܪܝܐ ܟܦܪܙܟܪܝܐ. ܕܐܬܬܣܝܡ ܕܐܘܕܘܩܝܐ ܡܠܟܬܐ. ܘܡܩܒܠܝܢ ܠܗ ܕܝܢ
ܗ̇ ܐܘܕܘܩܝܐ ܡܠܟܬܐ܆ ܘܒܢܬ ܬܡܢ ܕܢܒܝܐ ܙܟܪܝܐ ܘܦܐܝܬܐ. ܟܕ ܗ̇ܘ
ܐܠܗܐ ܓ̇ܒܪ ܘܫܠ. ܘܡܠܟܘܬܗ ܢܗܘܐ ܘܥܕܪ. ܕܟ̈ܠܬܐ ܢܒܪܟ. ܟܕ ܚ̇ܙܐ ܒܗ̇
ܗܝܟܠ ܘܫܒܝܐ ܘܕܟܐ ܫܦܝܪܐ. ܘܢܦ̈ܩܬܐ ܫ̈ܦܝܪܬܐ ܠܗ̇ ܒܟܠܗ̇ ܡܕܝܢܬܐ
ܘܕܘܟܪܐ ܐܘܢܓܠܝܐ. ܘܐܡܝܢ. ܠܐܠܗܐ ܓ̈ܒܪܐ ܬ̈ܠܝܠܐ܆ ܕܒܝܬܐ ܫܢܝܐ
ܕܫܦܪ ܠܡܕܝܢܬܐ. ܘܟܕ ܗܠܝܢ ܟܕ ܐܝܟܢܐ ܫܦܝܪܐ ܐܬܚܙܝ܆ ܘܐܝܟܢܗ̇ ܚ̈ܕܬܐ:
ܘܡܫܡܫܢܘܬܐ ܬܪܝܨܬ ܫܘܒܚܐ ܒܕܘܟܐ ܠܫܘܠܡܐ ܢܛܪ܆ ܒܡܫܡܫܢܘܬܐ ܓ̇ܠܝܬܐ
ܟܕ [B 27] ܡܠܟܐ ܢܩ̈ܦܬܐ܆ ܒܝܘܡ ܠܘܬ ܢܥܘܠ ܗܘ ܕܢܣܩ ܠܗ. ܘܦܠܚܘܗ̇
ܡܕܝܢܬܐ ܬܡܢ ܐܬܬܩܝܡ܆ ܬܘܒ ܡܕܒܪܢܐ ܡܕܝܢܬܐ.
(§10) ܬܕܡܘܪܬܐ ܕܝܢ ܪܒܬܐ ܘܒܡܕܐ ܗ̇ܘܬ. ܗ̇ܝ ܕܠܐ ܪܚܩ ܕܢܬܚܫܒ. ܟܕ
ܕܝܢ ܡܬܚܫܒܢܐ ܗܘܬ ܕܒܬܪ ܕܡܠܟܐ: ܘܐܝܟܢ ܗܘܘ ܐܢܫܐ ܕܢܩܦܘܢ܂
ܘܢܬܩܢܘܢ ܕܒܬܪ ܬܘܒ ܦܬܓܡܐ ܡܕܝܢܬܐ. ܕܢܬܬܣܝܡ ܒܗ̇ ܗܘ ܠܗ̇ܘܢܐ.
ܐܫܬܐܠ ܗܘ. ܘܠܐ ܢܪܓܐ ܗܘܐ ܕܬܬܗܘܐ. ܗܘܢ ܕܝܢ ܟܕ ܠܐ ܡܬܪܥܝܢ
ܗܘܘ ܕܕܠܘܡܠܐ ܢܗܘܘܢ܂ ܢܦܩܘ ܗܘܘ ܒܠܚܘܕ ܕܢܩܘܡܘܢ ܠܐܪܥܗ

[1] Also known as Beth Guvrin. See Amos Kloner, "Beth Guvrin," *NEAEHL* 1:195–201; and Jerome Murphy-O'Connor, *The Holy Land: An Oxford Archaeological Guide from Earliest Times to 1700* (Oxford: Oxford University Press, 1998), 183–88.

[2] I.e., the local population welcomed anti-Chalcedonians and presumably sympathized with them. The comments on the differences in attitude between the local populations of Tekoa and Eleutheropolis also point toward the existential dependence in which anti-Chalcedonians found themselves with regard to finding support among the laity.

[3] The ruins of that monastery have not yet been identified.

[4] The relics of the prophet Zachariah and of the protomartyr Stephen were found at the same time in 415, the former about four to five miles north of Eleutheropolis, the latter at Kefar Gamala. For further references, see the entry "Caphar Zachria, Beth Zacharia" in Tsafrir, Di Segni, and Green, *Tabula Imperii Romani*, 99–100. One may wish to add the reference to Theophanes, *Chronographia* AM 5919 [426/7 C.E.] (de Boor, 1:86; Mango and Scott, 135).

gion of the town of Eleutheropolis.[1] Since he was received by them very affectionately,[2] he remained in this place. The Lord had prepared [it] before his [arrival], [and so] he also found a height that was fitting for a monastery and the establishment of a residence[3] about two miles from the temple of the holy prophet Zachariah,[4] within the boundary of the village called Kefar Turban,[5] which belongs to Empress Eudocia. At the request of Empress Eudocia he built a large and comely monastery there,[6] while God assisted and strengthened [him]. He gave [him] everything and sent [him] out to go around [to] the houses [of the neighborhood].[7] Thus dwelling in it, he lived [there] for a long time. He prepared many souls in all holiness and [in] the way of life of the gospel. He raised up for God sheep endowed with reason, a living sacrifice[8] pleasing to the Lord. When with these [deeds] he had fought the good fight, finished his race, and kept the orthodox faith until the end,[9] at a good old age **[B 27]**, full of days, he departed to Jesus, whom he loved.[10] His holy body was buried there under the holy altar.[11]

(§10) A great wonder, however, also happened at this [occasion], which we ought not to hide. When, namely, the site of the temple was under construction and the brothers had wanted to dig and construct a place under the holy table in which the blessed one would be buried, he refused and did not want [this] to be done. Since they did not dare to oppose [him], they were con-

5 See the entries "Beththerabis" and "Caphar Tob, Torban" in Tsafrir, Di Segni, and Green, *Tabula Imperii Romani*, 87 and 99.

6 Rufus's account witnesses again to Eudocia's support of anti-Chalcedonians. See Horn, "Empress Eudocia and the Monk Peter the Iberian."

7 Romanus appears to have visited with the locals, both to request their material support and to provide them with instruction in the faith, as the following comments make even clearer.

8 For this combination of imagery, compare also *Vit. Pet.* §150 (R 113) on Peter's recruiting efforts among the law-school students of Beirut.

9 See 2 Tim 4:7.

10 Romanus is portrayed as entertaining a relationship with Jesus on a very personal and intimate level, similar to Peter's as described at *Vit. Pet.* §§38, 53, 69, 99, 127, 147 (R 27, 36, 47, 73, 94, 110).

11 See the same practice followed in the case of Peter the Iberian and referred to at *Vit. Pet.* §§192–193 (R 145–46). See also §120 (R 87) in reference to the site of the prophet Moses.

ܕܡܚܠܐ. ܐܬܬܢܝܚ ܗܘܬ ܕܝܢ ܫܢܬܐ ܡܫܢܐ. ܘܒܝ. ܬܪܝܢ ܘܚܡܫܝܢ܆ ܡܚܕܐ
ܐܬܦܬܚܬ ܡܥܪܬܐ ܡܢ ܢܦܫܗ ܘܩܒܠܬ ܠܐܠܗܐ. ܘܐܦܣܩܐ ܕܐܬܦܪܐ
ܒܠܫܘܢ ܠܦܘܪܗ ܕܡܕܒܪܐ. ܘܒܝ. ܒܗܘ ܙܒܢܐ ܐܝܟ ܕܐܡܪܝܢ ܡܢܗ܆ ܒܗ̇
ܐܬܬܣܝܡ ܬܚܝܬ ܡܩܒܪܐ ܕܝܪܐ. ܒܡܥܪܬܐ ܫܝܢܝܬܐ ܘܒܐܣܝܪܐ.

(§11) ܗܘܐ ܕܝܢ ܕܡܕܒܪܗ ܕܡܕܒܪܐ ܐܒܘܢ ܪܘܚܢܝܐ ܡܫܝܚܐ ܘܪܫܝܕܪܐ܆
ܒܚܙܝܢ ܘܫܡܥܐ ܒܬܫܪܝܢ ܐܚܪ܆ ܡܢܟ ܫܬܐ ܫܢܝܬܐ ܕܕܘܒܪܗ ܕܐܒܘܢ
ܦܠܝܘܣ ܐܦܣܩܘܦܐ. ܘܙܟ ܗܘܐ ܠܗܘܢ ܚܒܪ. ܒܝ. ܐܘܪܚܬܐ ܘܡܫܝܚܬ
ܒܐܝܣܪܐ ܡܢܗ ܡܬܠܬܪܬܐ. ܐܚܪܢܐ ܘܡܚܒܒܐ ܢܦܫܐ ܐܝܬ ܠܗܘܢ܆ ܐܦ
ܕܘܒܪܐ.

(§12) ܗܢ ܗܢ ܒܝ. ܒܡܘܗܒܐ ܗܘܐ܆ ܕܘܒܪܐ ܕܠܘܩܒܠܐ ܦܣܪܘܢ ܡܫܝܚܐ.
ܗܘ ܡܬܬܪܡܐ ܡܩܒܠܢܐ ܘܡܕܒܪܢܐ ܢܬܬܠܐ. ܗܘ ܕܐܦ ܗܘܐ ܪܫܝܕܪܐ
ܕܡܕܒܪܐ ܐܒܘܢ ܪܘܚܢܝܐ. ܗܘ ܕܐܦ ܒܗ ܡܩܒܠܢܐ ܠܒܝܬܐ ܒܢܐ. ܘܗܘ
ܕܡܢܗ ܬܘܒܐ ܕܡܕܒܪܬܐ ܡܫܝܚܬܐ ܡܢ ܡܕܒܪܐ. ܕܒܗܘܢ ܐܦ ܠܝ ܢܗܘܐ
ܡܫܝܚܐ ܦܘܠܚ ܠܒܠܚܘܕܝܬܐ ܕܫܡܝܐ. ܠܥܠܡ ܐܡܝܢ܀

(§13) ܫܠܡܬ ܬܫܥܝܬܐ ܕܥܠ ܡܘܬܗ ܕܬܐܘܕܘܣܝܘܣ. ܐܦܝܣܩܘܦܐ ܡܕܝܢܬܐ
ܕܐܘܪܫܠܡ܀ ܘܠܐܠܗܐ ܫܘܒܚܐ܀

¹ For a description of a cave in which the body of the prophet Moses was laid to rest, see *Vit. Pet.* §120 (R 88).

² I.e., November.

³ See *Vit. Pet.* §§192–193 (R 145–46).

⁴ On Passarion, see *Vit. Pet.* §52 (R 35), with references in 72 n. 2. See also Cyril of Scythopolis, *Vit. Euth.* 16 (2x), 27 (Schwartz, 26,18–19, 27,2–4, 42,12–14; Price, 22 [2x], 38), and *Vit. Sab.* 30 (Schwartz, 114,27–115,4; Price, 124); Theophanes, *Chronographia* AM 5920 [AD 427/8 C.E.] (de Boor, 1:86–87;

cerned only to level the ground of the temple. Now, the ground was hard rock. While they were hewing and leveling, suddenly a natural cave opened up, [one] built by God, that was just large enough to contain the body of the saint.[1] After some time when he had died, as was said, he was buried in it under the holy altar with much praise and honor.

(§11) The commemoration of our holy Abba Romanus, the priest and archimandrite, is on the twenty-fifth of Second Teshrin,[2] six days before the commemoration of our Abba Peter, the bishop.[3] Since they gained brotherly and in honor equal virtues, it is fitting for them also to have commemorations [that] would be brothers and neighbors to each other.

(§12) On the very same day is the commemoration of the blessed Passarion, the priest[4] who nourished the poor and raised orphans, who was archimandrite [of the monastery] of our holy Abba Romanus, [and] who built the famous house for the poor, the one outside the gates of the Holy City, to the east. [May] Christ our Savior also deem us with them worthy of the kingdom of heaven unto the ages. Amen.

(§13) The account concerning the death of Theodosius, the holy bishop of Jerusalem has come to an end.[5]

Mango and Scott, 135–36); and F. Delmas, "St. Passarion," *EO* 3 (1899): 162–63.

[5] This last sentence may well be an addition by the scribe, likely the monk Joseph, who copied MS BM Add. 12,174 in the twelfth century while he was residing at the Monastery of Abū Ghālib. See William Wright, *Catalogue of the Syriac Manuscripts in the British Museum* (3 vols.; London: British Museum, 1870–72), 1137–38. MS BM Add. 12,174 adds at the very end: "May his prayer be with us."

Bibliography

PRIMARY SOURCES: EDITIONS AND TRANSLATIONS

Amélineau, Emile. *Monuments pour servir à l'histoire de l'Égypte chrétienne aux IVe, Ve, VIe et VIIe siècles*. 2 vols. MMAF 4.1–2. Paris: Leroux, 1888–95.

Antoninus Placentinus. *Itinerarium*. Paul Geyer, ed. Pages 129–53 in *Itineraria et Alia Geographica*. CCSL 175. Turnholt: Brepols, 1965.

Antony of Choziba. *Vita Sancti Georgii Chozebitae*. C. Houze, ed. "Sancti Georgii Chozebitae confessoris et monachi vita auctore Antonio eius discipulo." *AnBoll* 7 (1888): 97–144 (chs. 1–9) and 336–59 (chs. 10–11).

———. *Vita Sancti Georgii Chozebitae*. Tim Vivian, trans. Pages 53–105 in *Journeying into God: Seven Early Monastic Lives*. Minneapolis: Fortress, 1996.

Asterius of Amasea. *Homilies*. Cornelis Datema, ed. *Asterius of Amasea: Homilies I–XIV: Text, Introduction and Notes*. Leiden: Brill, 1970.

Athanasius of Alexandria. *Vita Antonii*. G. J. M. Bartelink, ed. and trans. *Athanase d'Alexandrie: Vie d'Antoine*. SC 400. Paris: Cerf, 1994.

———. *Vita Antonii*. Robert C. Gregg, trans. Pages 29–99 in *Athanasius: The Life of Antony and the Letter to Marcellinus*. CWS. Mahwah, N.J.: Paulist, 1980.

Athenagoras. *Legatio pro Christianis*. Bernard Pouderon, ed. and trans. *Athénagore, Supplique sujet des Chrétiens et Sur la Résurrection des Morts*. SC 379. Paris: Cerf, 1992.

Augustine. *De opere monachorum*. Mary Muldowney, trans. Pages 323–94 in *St. Augustine: Treatises on Various Subjects*. FC 16. New York: Fathers of the Church, 1952.

———. *De opere monachorum*. Joseph Zycha, ed. Pages 529–96 in *Sancti Aureli Augustini De fide et symbolo, De fide et operibus, De agone christiano, De continentia, De bono coniugali, De sancta virginitate, De bono viduitatis, De adulterinis coniugiis lib. II, De mendacio, Contra mendacium, De opere monachorum, De divinatione daemonum, De cura pro mortuis gerenda, De patientia*. CSEL 41. Vienna: Tempsky, 1900.

Balestri, Giuseppe, and Henri Hyvernat, eds. *Acta Martyrum*. 4 vols. CSCO 43–44, 86, 125. CSCO/Copt 3–4, 6, 13. Leuven: Durbecq, 1951–55.

Basil of Caesarea. *Letters*. Roy Joseph Deferrari, ed. and trans. *Saint Basil: The Letters*. 4 vols. LCL. Cambridge: Harvard University Press, 1961.

———. *Letters*. Agnes Clare Way, trans. *Letters*. 2 vols. FC 13, 28. New York: Fathers of the Church, 1951.

Besa. *Vita Sinuthii Archimandritae*. David N. Bell, trans. *The Life of Shenoute*. CSS 73. Kalamazoo, Mich.: Cistercian, 1983.

———. *Vita Sinuthii Archimandritae*. Johannes Leipoldt and Walter E. Crum, eds. *Sinuthii Archimandritae Vita et Opera Omnia*. CSCO 41. CSCO/Copt 2/2. Paris: E Typographeo Reipublicae; Leipzig: Harrassowitz, 1906.

Brock, Sebastian P., and Susan Ashbrook Harvey. *Holy Women of the Syrian Orient*. Transformation of the Classical Heritage 13. Berkeley and Los Angeles: University of California Press, 1998.

Cicero. *De amicitia*. William Armistead Falconer, ed. *De senectute, de amicitia, de divinatione*. LCL 154. Cambridge: Harvard University Press; London: Heinemann, 1964.

———. *De finibus*. L. D. Reynolds, ed. *M. Tully Ciceronis: De finibus bonorum et malorum*. Oxford: Clarendon, 1998.

Clement of Alexandria. *Stromata*. John Ferguson, trans. *Stromateis: Books One to Three*. FC 85. Washington, D.C.: Catholic University of America Press, 1991.

———. *Stromata*. Otto Stählin, ed. *Clemens Alexandrinus*. 4 vols. GCS 12, 15, 17, 39. Leipzig: Hinrichs, 1905–36.

Constitutiones apostolicae. Marcel Metzger, ed. and trans. *Les Constitutions Apostoliques*. 3 vols. SC 320, 329, 336. Paris: Cerf, 1985–86.

———. James Donaldson, trans. "The Constitutions of the Holy Apostles." *ANF* 7:385–508.

Cyril of Alexandria. *Contra Julianum*. Paul Burguière and Pierre Évieux, eds. and trans. *Cyrille d'Alexandrie: Contre Julien*. SC 322. Paris: Cerf, 1985.

Cyril of Scythopolis. *Lives of the Monks of Palestine*. R. M. Price, trans. *Cyril of Scythopolis: The Lives of the Monks of Palestine*. CSS 114. Kalamazoo, Mich.: Cistercian, 1991.

———. *Lives of the Monks of Palestine*. Eduard Schwartz, ed. *Kyrillos von Skythopolis*. TU 49.2. Leipzig: Hinrichs, 1939.

Delehaye, Hippolyte, ed. *Synaxarium ecclesiae Constantinopolitanae: Propylaeum ad Acta Sanctorum Novembris*. Brussels: Socios Bollandianos, 1902.

Doran, Robert, trans. *The Lives of Simeon Stylites*. CSS 112. Kalamazoo, Mich.: Cistercian, 1992.

Dorotheus of Gaza. *Instructions*. Dom L. Regnault and Dom J. de Préville, eds. *Dorothée de Gaza: Œuvres Spirituelles*. SC 92. Paris: Cerf, 1963.

Drijvers, Han J. W., and Jan Willem Drijvers, eds. and trans. *The Finding of the True Cross: The Judas Kyriakos Legend in Syriac*. CSCO 565. Subsidia 93. Leuven: Peeters, 1997.

Egeria. *Diary*. "Itinerarium Egeriae." Ezio Franceschini and Robert Weber, eds. Pages 37–90 in *Itineraria et alia geographica*. CCSL 175. Turnholt: Brepols, 1965.

———. George E. Gingras, trans. *Egeria: Diary of a Pilgrimage*. ACW 38. New York: Newman, 1970.

Elias. *Life of Bishop John of Tella*. E. W. Brooks, ed. and trans. Pages 29–95 in vol.–1 (Syriac) and 21–60 in vol.–2 (Latin) of *Vitae virorum apud Monophysitas celeberrimorum*. 2 vols. CSCO 7–8. Scriptores Syri 3/25. Paris: E Typographeo Reipublicae. Repr., Leuven: Durbecq, 1955.

Ephraem the Syrian. *Hymns against Julian*. Edmund Beck, ed. and trans. Pages 71–91 in vol.–1 (Syriac) and 64–86 in vol.–2 (German) in *Des Heiligen Ephraem des Syrers* Hymnen de Paradiso *und* Contra Julianum. 2 vols. CSCO 174–75. Scriptores Syri 78–79. Leuven: Secrétariat du CorpusSCO, 1957.

———. *Hymns against Julian*. Judith M. Lieu, trans. "From Ctesiphon to Nisibis: Ephraem the Syrian. Hymns against Julian, the King, Who Apostasised and against the False Teachers and against the Jews (*Hymni contra Julianum*)." Pages 89–128 in *The Emperor Julian: Panegyric and Polemic: Claudius Mamertinus, John Chrysostom, Ephrem the Syrian*. Edited by Samuel N. C. Lieu. 2nd ed. TTH 2. Liverpool: Liverpool University Press, 1989.

———. *Hymns against Julian*. Kathleen E. McVey, trans. Pages 226–57 in *Ephrem the Syrian: Hymns*. CWS. Mahwah, N.J.: Paulist, 1989.

Eusebius of Caesarea. *De martyribus Palestinae*. William Cureton, ed. and trans. *History of the Martyrs in Palestine, by Eusebius, Bishop of Caesarea: Discovered in a Very Ancient Syriac Manuscript*. London: Williams & Norgate; Paris: Borrani, 1861.

———. *De martyribus Palestinae*. Eduard Schwartz, ed. "Paralipomena: Eusebius über die Märtyrer in Palaestina." Pages 907–50 in vol.–2 of *Die Kirchengeschichte*. Vol. 2.2 of *Eusebius Werke*. Edited by Eduard Schwartz and Theodor Mommsen. 2nd ed. edited by Friedhelm Winkelmann. GCS NS 6.2. Berlin: Akademie, 1999.

———. *Historia ecclesiastica*. Eduard Schwartz and Theodor Mommsen, eds. *Die Kirchengeschichte*. 3 vols. Vols. 2.1–3 of *Eusebius Werke*. 2nd ed. edited by Friedhelm Winkelmann. GCS NS 6.1–3. Berlin: Akademie, 1999.

———. *Historia ecclesiastica*. G. A. Williamson, trans. *Eusebius: The History of the Church from Christ to Constantine*. Revised by Andrew Louth. Baltimore: Penguin, 1989.

———. *Onomasticon*. Erich Klostermann, ed. *Das Onomastikon der biblischen Ortsnamen*. Vol. 3.1 of *Eusebius Werke*. GCS 11.1. Leipzig: Hinrichs, 1904. Repr., Hildesheim: Olms, 1966.

———. *Onomasticon*. Stewart Parker Freeman-Grenville, Rupert L. Chapman, and Joan E. Taylor, trans. *The Onomasticon: Palestine in the Fourth Century A.D.* Jerusalem: Carta, 2003.

———. *Vita Constantini*. Ernest Cushing Richardson, trans. "The Life of Constantine." *NPNF* 2/1:481–559.

———. *Vita Constantini*. Friedhelm Winkelmann, ed. *Über das Leben des Kaisers Konstantin*. Vol. 1.1 of *Eusebius Werke*. GCS NS 7. Berlin: Akademie, 1975.

Evagrius of Pontus. *Praktikos*. John Eudes Bamberger, trans. *Evagrius Ponticus: The Praktikos and Chapters on Prayer*. CSS 4. Kalamazoo, Mich.: Cistercian, 1981.

———. *Praktikos*. Antoine Guillaumont and Claire Guillaumont, eds. *Évagre le Pontique: Traité Pratique ou Le Moine*. SC 171. Paris: Cerf, 1971.

———. *Praktikos*. Robert E. Sinkewicz, trans. *Evagrius of Pontus: The Greek Ascetic Corpus*. Oxford Early Christian Studies. Oxford: Oxford University Press, 2003.

Evagrius Scholasticus. *Historia ecclesiastica*. Joseph Bidez and Léon Parmentier, eds. *The Ecclesiastical History of Evagrius with Scholia*. London: Methuen, 1898.

———. *Historia ecclesiastica*. Michael Whitby, trans. *The Ecclesiastical History of Evagrius Scholasticus*. TTH 33. Liverpool: Liverpool University Press, 2000.

Flemming, Johannes Paul Gotthilf, ed. *Akten der ephesinischen Synode vom Jahre 449*. Abhandlungen der Königlichen Gesellschaft der Wissenschaften zu Göttingen, Philologisch-historische Klasse NS 15. Göttingen: Weidmann, 1917.

Georgian Chronicle. S. Qauxč'išvili, ed. ქართლის ცხოვრება ანნა დედოფლისეული ნუსხა [*K'art'lis C'xovreba anna dedop'liseuli nusxa*]. Tbilisi: n.p., 1942.

Gerontius. *Vita S. Melaniae Junioris*. Elizabeth A. Clark, trans. *The Life of Melania the Younger: Introduction, Translation, and Commentary*. New York: Mellen, 1984.

———. *Vita S. Melaniae Junioris*. Denys Gorce, ed. *Vie de Sainte Mélanie*. SC 90. Paris: Cerf, 1962.

Gregory Nazianzen. *Orationes*. Claudio Moreschini and Paul Gallay, eds. and trans. *Grégoire de Nazianze: Discours 38–41*. SC 358. Paris: Cerf, 1990.

Gregory of Nyssa. *De pauperibus amandis*. Adrianus van Heck, ed. *Gregorii Nysseni De pauperibus amandis orationes II*. Leiden: Brill, 1964.

———. *Encomium in xl martyres* 1 and 2. Otto Lendle, ed. Pages 137–42, 145–56, and 159–69 in vol.–2 of *Gregorii Nysseni Sermones*. Edited by Günter Heil, Johannes P. Cavarnos, and Otto Lendle. GNO 10.1. Leiden: Brill, 1990.

Hardy, Edward Rochie, ed. *Christology of the Later Fathers*. LCC 3. Philadelphia: Westminster, 1954.

Hennecke, Edgar, and Wilhelm Schneemelcher, eds. *New Testament Apocrypha*. 2nd ed. Translated by R. McL. Wilson. 2 vols. Louisville: Westminster John Knox, 1991.

Hippolytus. *Traditio apostolica*. Bernard Botte, ed. *Hippolyte de Rome: La Tradition Apostolique d'après les anciennes versions*. 2nd ed. SC 11bis. Paris: Cerf, 1984.

History of the Kings of K'art'li. Robert W. Thomson, trans. Pages 2–84 in *Rewriting Caucasian History*. Oxford Oriental Monographs. Oxford: Clarendon, 1996.

Ignatius of Antioch. *Letters*. P. Th. Camelot, ed. *Ignace d'Antioche, Polycarpe de Smyrne, Lettres; Martyre de Polycarpe*. SC 10. Paris: Cerf, 1969.

Isaiah of Gaza/Scetis. *Asceticon*. Augoustinos, ed. *Τοῦ ὁσίου πατρὸς ἡμῶν ἀββᾶ Ἡσαΐα λόγοι κθ'*. 2nd ed. Volos: Schoinas, 1962.

———. *Asceticon*. Hervé de Broc, trans. *Abbé Isaïe—Recueil ascétique*. 2nd ed. Spiritualité Orientale 7. Abbaye de Bellefontaine: Maine & Loire, 1976.

———. *Asceticon*. John Chryssavgis and Pachomios (Robert) Penkett, trans. *Isaiah of Scetis: Ascetic Discourses*. CSS 150. Kalamazoo, Mich.: Cistercian, 2002.

Jerome. *De viris illustribus*. Thomas P. Halton, trans. *Saint Jerome: On Illustrious Men*. FC 100. Washington, D.C.: Catholic University of America Press, 1999.

———. *De viris illustribus*. Ernest Cushing Richardson, ed. *Hieronymus liber De viris inlustribus; Gennadius liber De viris inlustribus*. TUGAL 14. Leipzig: Hinrichs, 1896.

——. *Vita Hilarionis*. Marie Liguori Ewald, trans. "Life of St. Hilarion by St. Jerome." Pages 245–80 in *Early Christian Biographies*. Edited by Roy J. Deferrari. FC 15. New York: Fathers of the Church, 1952.

——. *Vita Hilarionis*. H. Hurter, ed. Pages 42–59 in *Studies in the Text Tradition of St. Jerome's* Vitae Patrum. Edited by William Abbott Oldfather. Urbana: University of Illinois Press, 1943.

John Chrysostom. *De cruce et latrone*. Translated as "The Cross and the Good Thief." *Orate Fratres* 24.5 (1950): 193–99.

John of Beth Aphthonia. *Vita Severi*. Marc-Antoine Kugener, ed. and trans. Pages 207–64 in *Vie de Sévère par Jean de Beith-Aphthonia*. PO 2.3. Paris: Firmin-Didot, 1907.

John of Ephesus. *Lives of the Eastern Saints*. E. W. Brooks, ed. and trans. 3 vols. PO 17.1, 18.4, 19.2. Paris: Firmin-Didot, 1923–25.

John Rufus. *De obitu Theodosii*. E. W. Brooks, ed. and trans. Pages 21–27 in vol.–1 (Syriac) and 15–19 in vol.–2 (Latin) of *Vitae virorum apud Monophysitas celeberrimorum*. 2 vols. CSCO 7–8. Scriptores Syri 3/25. Paris: E Typographeo Reipublicae. Repr., Leuven: Durbecq, 1955.

——. *Plerophoriae*. François Nau, ed. M. Brière, trans. *Jean Rufus, évêque de Maïouma: Plérophories, c.-à-d. témoignages et révélations*. PO 8.1. Paris: Firmin-Didot; Fribourg en Brisgau: Herder, 1912.

——. *Vita Petri Iberi*. Derwas J. Chitty, trans. "Peter the Iberian." Draft of English translation of the Syriac *Life of Peter the Iberian*. Unpublished manuscript kept at the Library of the House of St. Gregory and St. Macrina, Oxford, 1967.

——. *Vita Petri Iberi*. Richard Raabe, ed. and trans. *Petrus der Iberer: Ein Charakterbild zur Kirchen- und Sittengeschichte des 5. Jahrhunderts: Syrische Übersetzung einer um das Jahr 500 verfassten griechischen Biographie*. Leipzig: Hinrichs, 1895.

Johnson, Cuthbert, and Anthony Ward, eds. *Martyrologium Romanum: Reimpressio integra textus officialis cum emendationibus et variationibus usque ad Concilium Oecumenicum Vaticanum II convocatum effectis necnon nova introductione aucta*. BELS 97. Instrumenta liturgica quarreriensia 7. Rome: C.L.V.-Edizioni Liturgiche, 1998.

Josephus. *Jewish Antiquities*. Henry St. James Thackeray and Ralph Marcus, eds. and trans. Vols. 4–9 in *Josephus*. 9 vols. LCL. Cambridge: Harvard University Press; London: Heinemann, 1958–65.

——. *Contra Apionem*. Henry St. James Thackeray, ed. and trans. Pages 162–411 in *Josephus: The Life, Against Apion*. LCL. Cambridge: Harvard University Press; London: Heinemann, 1961.

——. *De bello Judaico*. Henry St. James Thackeray, ed. and trans. *Josephus: The Jewish War, Books IV–VII*. LCL. Cambridge, Mass.: Harvard University Press; London: Heinemann, 1961.

Juansheri. *Life of Vaxt'ang Gorgasali*. Robert W. Thomson, trans. Pages 153–251 in *Rewriting Caucasian History*. Oxford Oriental Monographs. Oxford: Clarendon, 1996.

Justin Martyr. *1 Apologia*. André Wartelle, ed. *Saint Justin, Apologies*. Paris: Études Augustiniennes, 1987.

Lang, David Marshall. *Lives and Legends of the Georgian Saints*. London: Allen & Unwin; New York: Macmillan, 1956.

Lake, Kirsopp, ed. and trans. *The Apostolic Fathers*. 2 vols. LCL. Cambridge Harvard University Press, 1970.

Leo the Great. *Epistula* 28. Eduard Schwartz, ed. Pages 24–33 in *Collectio Novariensis de re Eutychis* 5. Vol. 2.1 of *Acta Conciliorum Oecumenicorum*. Berlin: de Gruyter, 1932.

——. *Letters*. Peter and Jerome Ballerini, eds. PL 54. Pages 593–1262. Paris, 1865.

Lieu, Samuel N. C., ed. *The Emperor Julian: Panegyric and Polemic: Claudius Mamertinus, John Chrysostom, Ephrem the Syrian*. 2nd ed. TTH 2. Liverpool: Liverpool University Press, 1989.

Life of John of Lycopolis. E. Amélineau, ed. and trans. Pages 650–65 in *Monuments pour servir à l'histoire de l'Égypte Chrétienne aux* IVe, V[e], VIe *et* VIIe *siècles*. Vol. 4.2 of *Mémoires publiés par les membres de la mission archéologique française au Caire*. Paris: Leroux, 1895.

Life of Longinus. Tito Orlandi, ed. Pages 46–92 in *Vite dei Monaci Phif et Longino*. Milan: Cisalpino-Golliardica, 1975.

——. Tim Vivian, trans. "Humility and Resistance in Late Antique Egypt: The Life of Longinus." *CCR* 20 (1999): 2–30.

Lolashvili, Ivane. *არეოპაგიტული კრებული: დიონისე არეოპაგელი და პეტრე იბერიელი ძველქართულ მწერლობაში* [*Areopagite Chronicle: Dionysius the Areopagite and Peter the Iberian in Classical Georgian Hagiography*]. Tbilisi: Mecniereba, 1983.

Mark the Deacon. *Vita Porphyrii Gazensis*. Henri Grégoire and Marc-Antoine Kugener, eds. and trans. *Marc le diacre: Vie de Porphyre, évèque de Gaza*. Paris: Belles Lettres, 1930.

——. *Vita Porphyrii Gazensis*. George Francis Hill, trans. *Marcus Diaconus: The Life of Porphyry, Bishop of Gaza*. Oxford: Clarendon, 1913. Repr., Willits, Calif.: Eastern Orthodox Books, 1975.

———. *Vita Porphyrii Gazensis*. Claudia Rapp, trans. Pages 53–75 in *Medieval Hagiography: An Anthology*. Edited by Thomas Head. New York: Garland, 2000.

Marr, Nicola(i) Y., ed. and trans. "ცხოვრება პეტრე იბერისა [*Life of Peter the Iberian*]." *Pravoslavnyy Palestinskiy Sbornik* 47 = 16.2 (1896): 1–78 (Georgian text) and 81–115 (Russian translation).

Martyrdom of Shushanik. David Marshall Lang, trans. Pages 44–56 in *Lives and Legends of the Georgian Saints*. London: Allen & Unwin; New York: Macmillan, 1956.

Mikhail, Maged S., and Tim Vivian. "Zacharias of Sakhâ: An *Encomium* on the Life of John the Little." *CCR* 18 (1997): 1–64.

Moses of Khoren. *History of the Armenians*. Robert W. Thomson, trans. *Moses Khorenats'i: History of the Armenians*. Cambridge: Harvard University Press, 1978.

Musurillo, Herbert, ed. and trans. *The Acts of the Christian Martyrs*. Oxford: Clarendon, 1972.

Nau, François, ed. and trans. *Documents pour servir à l'histoire de l'église nestorienne: Textes syriaques*. PO 13.2. Paris: Firmin-Didot, 1919.

Overbeck, J. Josephus, ed. *S. Ephraemi Syri, Rabulae episcopi Edesseni, Balaei aliorumque opera selecta*. Oxford: Clarendon, 1865.

Palladius. *Historia Lausiaca*. Dom Cuthbert Butler, ed. *The Lausiac History of Palladius*. 2 vols. TS 6.1–2. Cambridge: Cambridge University Press, 1898–1904.

———. *Historia Lausiaca*. Robert T. Meyer, trans. *Palladius: The Lausiac History*. ACW 34. Westminster, Md.: Newman; London: Longmans, Green, 1965.

Percival, Henry R., trans. *The Seven Ecumenical Councils of the Undivided Church: Their Canons and Dogmatic Decrees*. *NPNF* 2/14:1–587.

Philodemus. *On Frank Criticism*. David Konstan, Diskin Clay, Clarence E. Glad, Johan C. Thom, and James Ware, eds. and trans. *Philodemus: On Frank Criticism*. Society of Biblical Literature Texts and Translations 43; Graeco-Roman Series 13. Atlanta: Scholars Press, 1998.

Pliny the Younger. *Epistulae*. Betty Radice, ed. *Letters and Panegyricus*. 2 vols. LCL 55 and 59. Cambridge: Harvard University Press; London: Heinemann, 1972.

Prieur, Jean-Marc, ed. *Acta Andreae*. CCSA 5–6. Turnhout: Brepols, 1989.

Proclus of Cyzicus/Constantinople. Nicholas Constas, ed. and trans. "On the Holy Virgin Theotokos Delivered While Nestorius Was Seated in the Great Church of Constantinople." Pages 136–47 in *Proclus of Constantinople and the Cult of the Virgin in Late Antiquity: Homilies 1–5, Texts and Translations*. VCSup 66. Leiden: Brill, 2003.

Richardson, Cyril R., ed. and trans. *Early Christian Fathers*. LCC 1. New York: Westminster, 1953. Repr., New York: Simon & Schuster, 1996.

Rordorf, Willy, and André Tuilier, eds. and trans. *La Doctrine des Douze Apôtres: Didachè*. SC 248. Paris: Cerf, 1978.

Rufinus of Aquileia. *Historia ecclesiastica*. Philip R. Amidon, trans. *The Church History of Rufinus of Aquileia, Books 10 and 11*. New York: Oxford University Press, 1997.

———. *Historia ecclesiastica*. Eduard Schwartz and Theodor Mommsen, eds. Vol. 2 of *Die Kirchengeschichte*. Vol. 2.2 of *Eusebius Werke*. 2nd ed. edited by Friedhelm Winkelmann. GCS NS 6.2. Berlin: Akademie, 1999.

Sanda, A., ed. *Severi Antiiulianistica*. Beirut: Typographia Catholica, 1931.

Sardzveladze, Alexandre, Zurab Sardzveladze, and Tamar Xazomia, eds. ცხოვრება ვახტანგ გორგასლისა [Life of Vakhtang Gorgasali]. Tbilisi: Mecniereba, 1986.

Sawîrus (Severus) ibn al-Mukaffaʿ. *History of the Patriarchs of the Coptic Church of Alexandria*. Edited and translated by Basil T. A. Evetts. 4 vols. PO 1.2, 1.4, 5.1, 10.5. Paris: Firmin-Didot, 1904–14.

Schöll, Rudolf, and Wilhelm Kroll, eds. *Corpus Juris Civilis*. 6th ed. Berlin: Weidmann, 1954.

Schultze, Karl. *Das Martyrium des heiligen Abo von Tiflis*. TU 28.4b. Leipzig: Hinrichs, 1905.

Schwartz, Eduard, ed. *Acta conciliorum oecumenicorum*. 4 vols. in 17. Berlin: de Gruyter, 1914–.

Seneca. *Epistulae morales*. Richard M. Gummere, ed. *Ad Lucilium epistulae morales*. 3 vols. Cambridge: Harvard University Press; London: Heinemann, 1917.

Severus of Antioch. *Letters*. E. W. Brooks, ed. and trans. *The Sixth Book of the Select Letters of Severus, Patriarch of Antioch, in the Syriac Version of Athanasius of Nisibis*. 2 vols. in 4. London: Williams & Norgate, 1902–4. Repr., Westmead, Eng.: Gregg, 1969.

Smith, Agnes Lewis. *Select Narratives of Holy Women from the Syro-Antiochene or Sinai Palimpsest as Written above the Old Syriac Gospels by John the Stylite, of Beth-Mari-Qanun in A.D. 778*. Studia Sinaitica 9–10. London: Clay, 1900.

Socrates Scholasticus. *Ecclesiastical History*. Günther Hansen and Manja Širinjan, eds. *Sokrates: Kirchengeschichte*. GCS NS 1. Berlin: Akademie, 1995.

———. *Ecclesiastical History*. A. C. Zenos, trans. "The Ecclesiastical History of Socrates Scholasticus." *NPNF* 2/2:1–178.

Sozomen. *Historia ecclesiastica*. Joseph Bidez and Günther Christian Hansen, eds. *Sozomenus: Kirchengeschichte*. GCS 50. Berlin: Akademie, 1960.

———. *Historia ecclesiastica*. Chester D. Hartranft, trans. "The Ecclesiastical History of Sozomen, Comprising a History of the Church." *NPNF* 2/2:239–427.

Stephen of Heracleopolis. *Panegyric on Apollo*. Karl Heinz Kuhn, ed. and trans. *A Panegyric on Apollo, Archimandrite of the Monastery of Isaac, by Stephen, Bishop of Heracleopolis Magna*. 2 vols. CSCO 394–395. Scriptores Coptici 39–40. Leuven: Secrétariat du CorpusSCO, 1978.

Strabo. *Geographica*. Horace Leonard Jones, ed. and trans. *The Geography of Strabo*. 8 vols. LCL. Cambridge: Harvard University Press, 1960–70.

Tanner, Norman P., ed. *Decrees of the Ecumenical Councils*. London: Sheed & Ward; Washington, D.C.: Georgetown University Press, 1990.

Tarchnišvili, Michel, ed and trans. *Le Grand Lectionnaire de l'Église de Jérusalem (v^e^–viiie siècles)*. 2 vols. CSCO 188–89, 204–5. Scriptores Iberici 9–10, 13–14. Leuven: Secrétariat du CorpusSCO, 1959–60.

Theodore Lector. *Historia ecclesiastica*. Günther Christian Hansen, ed. *Theodoros Anagnostes Kirchengeschichte*. 2nd ed. GCS NS 3. Berlin: Akademie, 1995.

Theodoret of Cyrus. *Interpretatio in Danielem*. Robert C. Hill, trans. *Theodoret of Cyrus: Commentary on Daniel*. SBLWGRW 7. Atlanta: Society of Biblical Literature, 2006.

Theodosius. *De situ terrae sanctae*. Paul Geyer, ed. Pages 115–25 in *Itineraria et Alia Geographica*. CCSL 175. Turnholt: Brepols, 1965.

Theophanes. *Chronographia*. Carl de Boor, ed. *Theophanis Chronographia*. 2 vols. Leipzig: Teubner, 1883–85. Repr., Hildesheim: Olms, 1980.

——. *Chronographia*. Cyril Mango and Roger Scott, trans. *The Chronicle of Theophanes Confessor: Byzantine and Near Eastern History AD 284–813*. Oxford: Clarendon, 1997.

Theopistus. *Vita Dioscori*. François Nau, ed. and trans. "Histoire de Dioscore, patriarche d'Alexandrie, écrite par son disciple Théopiste." *JA* 10.1 (1903): 5–108, 241–310.

Thomson, Robert W. *Rewriting Caucasian History: The Medieval Armenian Adaptation of the Georgian Chronicles*. Oxford Oriental Monographs. Oxford: Clarendon, 1996.

Tobler, Titus, and Augustus Molinier, eds. *Itinera Hierosolymitana et descriptiones Terrae Sanctae bellis sacris anteriora et latina lingua exarata sumptibus Societatis illustrandis Orientis latini monumentis*. 2. vols. Geneva: Fick, 1880.

Ward, Benedicta, trans. *The Sayings of the Desert Fathers: The Alphabetical Collection*. Rev. ed. Kalamazoo, Mich.: Cistercian, 1984.

Wardrop, Margery, and James O. Wardrop. "Life of St. Nino." *Studia Biblica et Ecclesiastica* 5 (1903): 1–88.

Zachariah Rhetor. *Chronicle*. E. W. Brooks, ed. and trans. *Historia ecclesiastica Zachariae Rhetori vulgo adscripta*. 4 vols. CSCO 83–84, 87–88. Scriptores Syri 3/5–6. Paris: E Typographeo Reipublicae, 1919–24. Repr., Leuven: Durbecq, 1953.

——. *Chronicle*. F. J. Hamilton and E. W. Brooks, trans. *The Syriac Chronicle, Known as That of Zachariah of Mitylene*. London: Methuen, 1899.

——. *Vita Isaiae*. E. W. Brooks, ed. Pages 3–16 (Syriac) in vol.–1 and 3–10 (Latin) in vol.–2 of *Vitae virorum apud Monophysitas celeberrimorum*. 2 vols. CSCO 7–8. Scriptores Syri 3/25. Paris: E Typographeo Reipublicae; Leipzig: Harrassowitz, 1907.

——. *Vita Severi*. Marc-Antoine Kugener, ed. and trans. *Vie de Sévère par Zacharie le Scholastique*. PO 2.1. Paris: Firmin-Didot, 1907.

Ziegler, Joseph ed. *Sapientia Salomonis*. Septuaginta Vetus Testamentum Graecum 12.1. Göttingen: Vandenhoeck & Ruprecht, 1962.

SECONDARY SOURCES AND REFERENCE WORKS

Abel, F. M. "Saint Cyrille d'Alexandrie dans ses rapports avec la Palestine." Pages 203–30 in *Kyrilliana: Spicilegia edita Sancti Cyrilli Alexandrini XV recurrente saeculo: Études variées à l'occasion du XVe centenaire de Saint Cyrille d'Alexandrie (444–1944)*. Cairo: Editions du Scribe Egyptien S.A.E., 1947.

AbouZayd, Shafiq. *Iḥidayutha: A Study of the Life of Singleness in the Syrian Orient: From Ignatius of Antioch to Chalcedon 451 A.D.* Oxford: ARAM Society for Syro-Mesopotamian Studies, 1993.

Abramowski, Luise. "Was hat das Nicaeno-Constantinopolitanum (C) mit dem Konzil von Konstantinopel (381) zu tun?" *Theologie und Philosophie* 67 (1992): 481–513.

Adshead, Katherine. "Justinian and Aphthartodocetism." Pages 331–36 in *Ethnicity and Culture in Late Antiquity*. Edited by Stephen Mitchell and Geoffrey Greatrex. London: Duckworth; Swansea: Classical Press of Wales, 2000.

Aland, Kurt. *Did the Early Church Baptize Infants?* Philadelphia: Westminster, 1963.

Alishan, L. "Les LXX couvents arméniens de Jérusalem." *AOL* 2 [B] (1884): 394–99.

Alissandratos, Julia. "The Structure of the Funeral Oration in John Chrysostom's 'Eulogy of Meletius.' " *Byzantine Studies* 7 (1980): 182–98.

Anderson, Robert T. "Samaritans." *ABD* 5:940–47.

Ashtor, Eliyahu. "Tyre." *EncJud* 15:1488–90.

Aßfalg, Julius, and David Marshall Lang. "Georgien." *TRE* 12:389–96.

Athanassiadi-Fowden, Polymnia. *Julian and Hellenism: An Intellectual Biography*. Oxford: Clarendon, 1981.

Atiya, Aziz S. "Catechetical School of Alexandria." *CE* 2:469–73.

———. "Cyril I, Saint." *CE* 3:671–75.

———. "Origenist Controversies." *CE* 6:1855–56.

Aune, David E. *The Westminster Dictionary of New Testament and Early Christian Literature and Rhetoric*. Louisville: Westminster John Knox, 2003.

Avi-Yonah, Michael. "The Economics of Byzantine Palestine." *IEJ* 8 (1958): 39–51.

Bagnall, Roger S. *Egypt in Late Antiquity*. Princeton: Princeton University Press, 1993.

Bartelink, G. J. M. "Quelques observations sur παρρησία dans la littérature paléo-chrétienne." Pages 7–57 in vol.–3 of *Græcitas et latinitas christianorum primæva: Studia ad sermonem christianum primævum pertinentia: Supplementa*. Nijmegen: Dekker & van de Vegt, 1968.

Baruch, Rosen. "משומרת מצור בארץ־ישראל בתחילת המאת השישית לספירה [A Convert from Tyre in the Land of Israel at the Beginning of the Sixth Century AD]." *Cathedra* 16 (1991): 54–66.

Baum, Wilhelm, and Dietmar W. Winkler. *The Church of the East: A Concise History*. London: Routledge, 2003.

Beck, Edmund. "Symbolum-Mysterium bei Aphrahat und Ephräm." *OrChr* 42 (1958): 19–40.

Becker, E. "Konstantin der Grosse, der 'neue Moses.'" *ZKG* 31 (1910): 161–71.

Berthold, George C. "History and Exegesis in Evagrius and Maximus." Pages 390–404 in *Origeniana Quarta*. Edited by Robert J. Daley. Innsbruck: Tyrolia, 1987.

Beyer, Hermann Wolfgang, and Heinrich Karpp. "Bischof." *RAC* 2:394–407.

Bieberstein, Klaus, and Hanswulf Bloedhorn. *Jerusalem: Grundzüge der Baugeschichte vom Chalkolithikum bis zur Frühzeit der osmanischen Herrschaft*. 3 vols. BTAVO B/100.1–3. Wiesbaden: Reichert, 1994.

Bitton-Ashkelony, Brouria. "פטרוס האיברי עולה לרגל [The Pilgrim Peter the Iberian]." *Cathedra* 91 (1999): 97–112.

———. "*Imitatio Mosis* and Pilgrimage in the Life of Peter the Iberian." Pages 108–131 in *Christian Gaza in Late Antiquity*. Edited by Brouria Bitton-Ashkelony and Arieh Kofsky. Jerusalem Studies in Religion and Culture 3. Leiden and Boston: Brill, 2004.

Bitton-Ashkelony, Brouria, and Aryeh Kofsky. "Gazan Monasticism in the Fourth-Sixth Centuries: From Anchoritic to Cenobitic." *Proche-Orient Chrétien* 50 (2000): 14–62.

Black, C. Clifton. *The Rhetoric of the Gospel: Theological Artistry in the Gospels and Acts*. St. Louis: Chalice, 2001.

Blazquez, José M. "Las posesiones de Melania la Joven." Pages 67–80 in *Historiam Pictura Refert: Miscellanea in onore di Padre Alejandro Recio Veganzones, OFM*. Edited by Josep Marti-i-Aixala, Eugenio Alliata, and Fabrizio Bisconti. Rome: Pontificio Istituto Archeologia Cristiana, 1994.

Bovini, Giuseppe. *Ravenna Mosaics*. Greenwich, Conn.: New York Graphic Society, 1956.

Bowersock, Glen W. *Julian the Apostate*. Cambridge: Harvard University Press, 1978.

Brock, Sebastian P. "Aspects of Translation Technique in Antiquity." *GRBS* 20 (1979): 69–87. Repr. as ch. 3 in Sebastian P. Brock, *Syriac Perspectives on Late Antiquity*. London: Variorum, 1984.

——. "Christians in the Sasanian Empire: A Case of Divided Loyalties." Pages 1–19 in *Religion and National Identity: Papers Read at the Nineteenth Summer Meeting and the Twentieth Winter Meeting of the Ecclesiastical History Society*. Edited by Stuart Mews. Studies in Church History 18. Oxford: Blackwell, 1982. Repr. as ch. 6 in Sebastian Brock, *Syriac Perspectives on Late Antiquity*. London: Variorum, 1984.

——. "Greek Words in Syriac: Some General Features." *Scripta Classica Israelica* 15 (1996): 251–262. Repr. as ch. 15 in Sebastian Brock, *From Ephrem to Romanos: Interactions between Syriac and Greek in Late Antiquity*. Aldershot: Ashgate, 1999.

——. "The Holy Spirit as Feminine in Early Syriac Literature." Pages 73–88 in *After Eve: Women, Theology and the Christian Tradition*. Edited by J. Martin Soskice. London: Marshall Pickering, 1990.

——. "A Martyr at the Sasanid Court under Vahran II: Candida." *AnBoll* 96 (1978): 167–81. Repr. as ch. 9 in Sebastian P. Brock, *Syriac Perspectives on Late Antiquity*. London: Variorum, 1984.

——. "Syriac Culture, 337–425." Pages 708–19 in *The Late Empire, A.D. 337–425*. Vol. 13 of *The Cambridge Ancient History*. Edited by Averil Cameron and Peter Garnsey. Cambridge: Cambridge University Press, 1998.

——. "Towards a History of Syriac Translation Technique." Pages 1–14 in *III. Symposium Syriacum, 1980: Les contacts du monde syriaque avec les autres cultures, Goslar 7–11 Septembre 1980*. Edited by René Lavenant. OCA 221. Rome: Pontificium Institutum Studiorum Orientalium, 1983. Repr. as ch. 10 in Sebastian Brock, *Studies in Syriac Christianity: History, Literature, and Theology*. Hampshire, Great Britain: Variorum, 1992.

——. "Translating the New Testament into Syriac (Classical and Modern)." Pages 371–85 in *Interpretation of the Bible: The International Symposium in Slovenia*. Edited by Joze Krasovec. JSOTSup 289. Sheffield: Sheffield Academic Press, 1998.

Brockelmann, Carl. *Lexicon Syriacum*. 2nd ed. Halle: Niemeyer, 1928.

Brown, Peter. *The Body and Society: Men, Women and Sexual Renunciation in Early Christianity*. LHR 13. New York: Columbia University Press, 1988.

——. *The Making of Late Antiquity*. Cambridge: Harvard University Press, 1978.

Browning, Robert. *The Emperor Julian*. Berkeley and Los Angeles: University of California Press, 1975.

Bruns, Peter. "John of Apamea." *DECL*, 326.

———. *Den Menschen mit dem Himmel verbinden: Eine Studie zu den katechetischen Homilien des Theodor von Mopsuestia*. CSCO 549. Subsidia 89. Leuven: Peeters, 1995.

———. "Theodotus of Ancyra." *DECL*, 570.

———. "Zum Offenbarungsverständnis des Theodor von Mopsuestia im Zwölfprophetenkommentar." Pages 272–77 in *Athanasius and His Opponents, Cappadocian Fathers, Other Greek Writers after Nicaea*. Vol. 4 of *Studia patristica: Papers Presented at the Twelfth International Conference on Patristic Studies Held in Oxford, 1995*. Edited by Elizabeth A. Livingstone. StPatr 32. Leuven: Peeters, 1997.

Bucci, Onorato. *Il corespiscopato nella storia della chiesa*. Rome: Editrice universitaria di Roma-la Goliardica, 1993.

Burney, Charles Allen, and David Marshall Lang. *The Peoples of the Hills: Ancient Ararat and Caucasus*. History of Civilization. London: Weidenfeld & Nicolson, 1971.

Burridge, Richard A. "The Gospels and Acts." Pages 507–53 in *Handbook of Classical Rhetoric in the Hellenistic Period, 330 BC–AD 400*. Edited by Stanley E. Porter. Leiden: Brill, 1997.

———. "Biography." Pages 371–91 in *Handbook of Classical Rhetoric in the Hellenistic Period, 330 BC–AD 400*. Edited by Stanley E. Porter. Leiden: Brill, 1997.

Callam, Daniel. "The Frequency of Mass in the Latin Church ca. 400." *TS* 45 (1984): 613–50.

Calzolari, V. "La Versione Armena del *Martirio di Andrea* e il suo rapporto con la tradizione manoscritta dell'originale Greco." *Mus* 111 (1998): 139–56.

Caner, Daniel. *Wandering, Begging Monks: Spiritual Authority and the Promotion of Monasticism in Late Antiquity*. Berkeley and Los Angeles: University of California Press, 2002.

Cartlidge, David R. "Transfigurations of Metamorphosis Traditions in the Acts of John, Thomas, and Peter." *Semeia* 38 (1986): 53–66.

Chadwick, Henry. "Eucharist and Christology in the Nestorian Controversy." *JTS* NS 2 (1951): 145–64.

Chilton, Bruce, and Craig A. Evans, eds. *James the Just and Christian Origins*. NovTSup 98. Leiden: Brill, 1999.

Chilton, Bruce, and Jacob Neusner, eds. *The Brother of Jesus: James the Just and His Mission*. Louisville: Westminster John Knox, 2001.

Chitty, Derwas. "Abba Isaiah." *JTS* 22 (1971): 47–72.

Choksy, Jarnsheed K. *Evil, Good and Gender: Facets of the Feminine in Zoroastrian Religious History*. Toronto Studies in Religion 28. New York: Lang, 2002.

———. "Zoroaster." Pages 754–55 in *Late Antiquity: A Guide to the Postclassical World*. Edited by G. W. Bowersock, Peter Brown, and Oleg Grabar. Cambridge: Harvard University Press, 1999.

———. "Zoroastrianism." Pages 755–57 in *Late Antiquity: A Guide to the Postclassical World*. Edited by G. W. Bowersock, Peter Brown, and Oleg Grabar. Cambridge: Harvard University Press, 1999.

Chryssavgis, John. "Abba Isaiah of Scetis: Aspects of Spiritual Direction." Pages 30–40 in *Ascetica, Gnostica, Liturgica, Orientalia*. Vol. 2 of *Studia patristica: Papers Presented at the Thirteenth International Conference on Patristic Studies Held in Oxford, 1999*. Edited by M. F. Miles and E. J. Yarnold. StPatr 35. Leuven: Peeters, 2001.

Clamer, Christa. "The Hot Springs of Kallirrhoe and Baarou." Pages 221–25 in *The Madaba Map Centenary 1897–1997: Travelling through the Byzantine Umayyad Period*. Edited by Michele Piccirillo and Eugenio Alliata. Collectio maior 40. Jerusalem: Studium Biblicum Franciscanum, 1999.

Clark, Donald Lemen. *Rhetoric in Greco-Roman Education*. New York: Columbia University Press, 1957.

Clark, Elizabeth A. *The Origenist Controversy: The Cultural Construction of an Early Christian Debate*. Princeton: Princeton University Press, 1992.

Clark, Gillian. *Women in Late Antiquity: Pagan and Christian Lifestyles*. Oxford: Oxford University Press, 1994.

Clermont-Ganneau, Charles. "Sur quelques localités de Palestine mentionnées dans la Vie de Pierre l'Ibère." Pages 1–22 in vol.–2 of idem, *Études d'archéologie orientale*. 2 vols. BEHE 44, 113. Paris: Bouillon, 1895–97.

Cody, Aelred. "Calendar, Coptic." *CE* 2:433–36.

Cole, Thomas. *The Origins of Rhetoric in Ancient Greece*. Baltimore: Johns Hopkins University Press, 1991.

Collinet, Paul. *Histoire de l'École de Droit de Beyrouth*. Études historiques sur le droit de Justinien 3. Paris: Société anonyme du recueil Sirey, 1925.

Constas, Nicholas P. "Four Christological Homilies of Proclus of Constantinople: Introduction, Critical Edition, Translation, and Commentary." Ph. D. diss. Washington, D.C.: The Catholic University of America, 1994.

———. *Proclus of Constantinople and the Cult of the Virgin in Late Antiquity: Homilies 1–5, Texts and Translations*. VCSup 66. Leiden: Brill, 2003

———. "Weaving the Body of God: Proclus of Constantinople, the Theotokos, and the Loom of the Flesh." *JECS* 3 (1995): 169–94.

Coquin, René-Georges. "Ṣaʿīd." *CE* 7:2080.

Corsaro, Francesco. "Elementi romanzeschi e aretalogia negli Atti apocrifi di Paolo e Tecla: codici e strutture formali." Pages 77–90 in *La narrativa cristiana antica: Codici narrativi, strutture formali, schemi retorici: XXIII Incontro di studiosi dell'antichità cristiana, Roma, 5–7 maggio 1994*. Edited by Salvatore Pricoco, Paolo Siniscalco, and Gianna Dareggi. SEAug 50. Rome: Institutum Patristicum Augustinianum, 1995.

Courth, Franz. *Trinität in der Schrift und Patristik*. Handbuch der Dogmengeschichte 2.1a. Freiburg: Herder, 1988.

Croke, Brian. "Famine." *ODB* 2:777–78.

Dassmann, Ernst. "Entstehung und theologische Begründung der kirchlichen Ämter in der Alten Kirche." *IKZ* 22 (1993): 350–62.

———. "Zur Entstehung des Monepiskopats." *JAC* 17 (1974): 74–90.

Dauphin, Claudine M. *La Palestine byzantine: Peuplement et Populations*. 3 vols. BAR International Series 726. Oxford: Archaeopress, 1998.

Delekat, L. "Ein frühbyzantinischer Fischteich bei Jerusalem." *ZDPV* 84 (1968): 185–86.

Delmas, F. "St. Passarion." *EO* 3 (1899): 162–63.

Devos, Paul. "L'année de la dédicace de Saint-Étienne à Jérusalem: 439." *AnBoll* 105 (1987): 265–79.

———. "Cyrille de Scythopolis: Influences littéraires—Vêtement de l'évêque de Jérusalem—Passarion et Pierre l'Ibère." *AnBoll* 98 (1980): 25–38.

———. "Quand Pierre l'Ibère vint-il à Jérusalem." *AnBoll* 86 (1968): 337–50.

———. "La 'Servante de Dieu' Poemenia d'après Pallade, la tradition Copte et Jean Rufus." *AnBoll* 87 (1969): 189–208.

Dixon, Suzanne. *The Roman Family*. Baltimore: Johns Hopkins University Press, 1992.

———. *The Roman Mother*. Norman: Oklahoma University Press, 1988.

Donner, Herbert. *The Mosaic Map of Madaba: An Introductory Guide*. Kampen: Kok Pharos, 1992.

Dovere, E. "L'*Ἐγκύκλιον Βασιλίσκου*: Un caso di normativa imperiale in Oriente su temi di dogmatica teologica." *Studia et documenta historiae et juris* 51 (1985): 153–88.

Draguet, René. *Julien d'Halicarnasse et sa controverse avec Sévère d'Antioche sur l'incorruptibilité du corps du Christ: Étude d'histoire littéraire et doctrinale suivie des Fragments dogmatiques de Julien*. Leuven: Smeesters, 1924.

Drijvers, Jan Willem. *Helena Augusta: The Mother of Constantine the Great and the Legend of Her Finding of the True Cross*. Leiden: Brill, 1992.

Duval, Rubens, ed. *Lexion Syriacum auctore Hassano bar Bahlule voces syriacas graecasque cum glossis syriacis et arabicis complectens ex multis operas scientificis biblicis et philosophicis compilatum saeculo X*. Paris: E Reipublicae typographaeo, 1888–1901.

Dvorjetski, Estée. "Medicinal Hot Springs in Eretz-Israel and in the Decapolis during the Hellenistic, Roman, and Byzantine Periods." *ARAM* 4.1–2 (1992): 425–49.

Dvornik, Francis. *The Idea of Apostolicity in Byzantium and the Legend of the Apostle Andrew*. Dumbarton Oaks Studies 4. Cambridge: Harvard University Press, 1958.

Dysinger, Luke. "The Logoi of Providence and Judgement in the Exegetical Writings of Evagrius Ponticus." Pages 462–71 in *Cappadocian Writers, Other Greek Writers*. Vol. 4 of *Studia patristica: Papers Presented at the Thirteenth International Conference on Patristic Studies Held in Oxford, 1999*. Edited by M. F. Miles and E. J. Yarnold. StPatr 37. Leuven: Peeters, 2001.

———. "The Significance of Psalmody in the Mystical Theology of Evagrius of Pontus." 176–82 in *Biblica et Apocrypha, Ascetica, Liturgica*. Vol. 2 of *Studia patristica: Papers Presented at the Twelfth International Conference on Patristic Studies Held in Oxford, 1995*. Edited by Elizabeth A. Livingstone. StPatr 30. Leuven: Peeters, 1997.

Ebied, Rifaat T., and Lionel R. Wickham. "A Collection of Unpublished Syriac Letters of Timothy Aelurus." *JTS* NS 21 (1970): 321–69.

———. "Timothy Aelurus: Against the Definition of the Council of Chalcedon." Pages 115–66 in *After Chalcedon: Studies in Theology and Church History Offered to Professor Albert Van Roey for His Seventieth Birthday*. Edited by Carl Laga, Joseph A. Munitiz, and Lucas Van Rompay. OLA 18. Leuven: Departement Oriëntalistiek; Peeters, 1985.

Eßlin, W. "Petrus (95)." PW19.2:1330.

Esbroeck, Michel van. "Victor Stratelates, Saint. Coptic Tradition." *CE* 7:2303–5.

Evelyn-White, Hugh Gerard. *The History of the Monasteries of Nitria and Scetis*. Edited by Walter Hauser. Vol. 2 of *The Monasteries of the Wâdi ʿn Natrûn*. 3 vols. New York: Metropolitan Museum of Art, Egyptian Expedition, 1932.

——. *New Coptic Texts from the Monastery of Saint Macarius*. Part 1 of *The Monasteries of the Wadi ʿn Natrûn*. New York: Metropolitan Museum of Art, 1926.

Fauth, Wolfgang. "Pythagoras, Jesus von Nazareth und der Helios-Apollon des Julianus Apostata: zu Eigentümlichkeiten der spätantiken Pythagoras-Aretalogie." *ZNW* 78 (1987): 24–48.

Ferch, Arthur J. "Abarim." *ABD* 1:6–7.

Ferguson, Everett. "Inscriptions and the Origin of Infant Baptism." *JTS* NS 30 (1979): 37–46.

Festugière, André Jean. *Antioche païenne et chrétienne: Libanius, Chrysostome et les moines de Syries*. BEFAR 194. Paris: de Boccard, 1959.

Fiey, Jean-Maurice "Un grand sanctuaire perdu? Le martyrion de St. Léonce à Tripoli." *Mus* 95 (1982): 77–78.

Fitzgerald, John T. "Christian Friendship: John, Paul, and the Philippians." *Int* 61 (2007): 284–96.

——. "Gadara: Philodemus' Native City." Pages 343–97 in *Philodemus and the New Testament World*. Edited by John T. Fitzgerald, Dirk Obbink, and Glenn S. Holland. NovTSup 111. Leiden: Brill, 2004.

——. "Last Wills and Testaments in Graeco-Roman Perspective." Pages 637–72 in *Early Christianity and Classical Culture*. Edited by John T. Fitzgerald, Thomas H. Olbricht, and L. Michael White. NovTSup 110. Leiden: Brill, 2003. Repr., Atlanta: Society of Biblical Literature: 2005.

Fowden, Elizabeth Key. *The Barbarian Plain: Saint Sergius between Rome and Iran*. The Transformation of the Classical Heritage 28. Berkeley and Los Angeles: University of California Press, 1999.

Fraser, P. M. *Ptolemaic Alexandria*. Oxford: Clarendon, 1972.

Freeman, Kathleen. *The Murder of Herodes*. New York: Norton, 1963.

Frend, William H. C. *The Rise of Christianity*. Philadelphia: Fortress, 1984.

——. *The Rise of the Monophysite Movement: Chapters in the History of the Church in the Fifth and Sixth Centuries*. Cambridge: Cambridge University Press, 1972.

Fuchs, Vinzenz. *Der Ordinationstitel von seiner Entstehung bis auf Innozenz III: Eine Untersuchung zur kirchlichen Rechtsgeschichte, mit besonderer Berücksichtigung auf Anschauungen Rudolph Sohms*. Bonn: Schroeder, 1930. Repr., Amsterdam: Schippers, 1963.

Galtier, Paul. "Saint Cyril et Apollinaire." *Greg* 37 (1956): 584–609.

Garitte, Gérard. *Le Calendrier Palestino-Géorgien du Sinaiticus 34 (xe siècle)*. Subsidia hagiographica 30. Brussels: Société des Bollandistes, 1958.

———. "Textes hagiographiques orientaux relatifs à Saint Léonce de Tripoli." *Mus* 78 (1965): 313–48; 79 (1966): 335–86; and 81 (1968): 415–40.

Gascou, Jean "Eikoston." *CE* 3:951.

———. "Enaton." *CE* 3:954–58.

———. "Oktokaidekaton." *CE* 6:1826–27.

Gessel, Wilhelm. "Das Öl der Märtyrer: Zur Funktion und Interpretation der Ölsarkophage von Apamea in Syrien." *OrChr* 72 (1988): 183–202.

Geva, Hillel, and Michael Avi-Yonah. "Jerusalem. The Byzantine Period." *NEAEHL* 2:768–85.

Gibson, Craig A. "The Agenda of Libanius' Hypotheses to Demosthenes." *GRBS* 40 (1999): 171–202.

Gillman, Florence Morgan. "James, Brother of the Lord." *ABD* 3:620–21.

Gillmann, Franz. *Das Institut der Chorbischöfe im Orient*. Munich: Lentner, 1903.

Glad, Clarence E. "Frank Speech, Flattery, and Friendship in Philodemus." Pages 21–59 in *Friendship, Flattery, and Frankness of Speech: Studies on Friendship in the New Testament World*. Edited by John T. Fitzgerald. NovTSup 82. Leiden: Brill, 1996.

Gottlob, Theodor. *Der abendländische Chorepiskopat*. Bonn: Schroeder, 1928. Repr., Amsterdam: Schippers, 1968.

Green, Judith, and Yoram Tsafrir. "Greek Inscriptions from Hammat Gader: A Poem by the Empress Eudocia and Two Building Inscriptions." *IEJ* 32 (1982): 77–96.

Gregory, Timothy E. "Basiliskos." *ODB* 1:267.

———. "Heracleia." *ODB* 2:915.

Gregory, Timothy E., and Anthony Cutler. "Constantine the Great." *ODB* 1:498–500.

———. "Theodosios II." *ODB* 3:2051–52.

Griffith, Sidney H. "Asceticism in the Church of Syria: The Hermeneutics of Early Syrian Monasticism." Pages 220–45 in *Asceticism*. Edited by Vincent L. Wimbush and Richard Valantasis. New York: Oxford University Press, 1995.

Grossmann, Peter. "Abūṣīr." *CE* 1:34–36.

Grubbs, Judith Evans. "Divorce." Page 414 in *Late Antiquity: A Guide to the Postclassical World*. Edited by Glen W. Bowersock, Peter Brown, and Oleg Grabar. Cambridge: Harvard University Press, 1999.

Guillaumont, Antoine. "Le dépaysement comme forme d'ascèse dans le monachisme ancien." *Annuaire de l'École Pratique des Hautes Études, Section des Sciences Religieuses* 76 (1968–69): 31–58. Repr. as pages 89–116 in idem, *Aux origines du monachisme chrétien: Pour une phénoménologie du monachisme.* Spiritualité Orientale 30. Paris: Abbaye de Bellefontaine, 1979.

———. "Historia Monachorum in Aegypto." *CE* 4:1237–38.

Habas (Rubin), Ephrat. "A Poem by the Empress Eudocia: A Note on the Patriarch." *IEJ* 46 (1996): 108–19.

Haefeli, Leo. *Stilmittel bei Afrahat dem persischen Weisen.* Leipziger semitistische Studien NS 4. Leipzig: Hinrichs, 1932. Repr., Leipzig: Zentralantiquariat der DDR, 1968.

Hage, Wolfgang. "Armenien I. Alte Kirche und Mittelalter." *TRE* 4:40–57.

Hägg, Thomas. *The Novel in Antiquity*. Oxford: Blackwell, 1983.

Hainthaler, Theresia. "Ephraem von Antiochien und sein Neuchalcedonismus." Pages 524–29 in *Augustine and His Opponents, Jerome, Other Latin Fathers after Nicaea, Orientalia.* Vol. 5 of *Studia patristica: Papers Presented at the Twelfth International Conference on Patristic Studies Held in Oxford, 1995.* Edited by Elizabeth A. Livingstone. StPatr 33. Leuven: Peeters, 1997.

Halkin, F. "Passions et miracle posthume de St. Léonce martyr à Tripoli en Phénicie." *AnBoll* 82 (1964): 319–40.

Hall, Linda Jones. "Berytus, 'Mother of Laws': Studies in the Social History of Beirut from the Third to the Sixth Centuries A.D." Ph.D. diss., The Ohio State University, 1996.

———. *Roman Berytus: Beirut in Late Antiquity.* London: Routledge, 2004.

———. ed. *Confrontation in Late Antiquity: Imperial Presentation and Regional Adaptation.* Cambridge: Orchard Academic Press, 2003.

Hannestad, Knud. "Les relations de Byzance avec la Transcaucasie et l'Asie Centrale aux ve et vi[e] siècles." *Byzantion* 25–27 (1955–57): 421–56.

Hanson, R. P. C. *The Search for the Christian Doctrine of God: The Arian Controversy 318–381.* Edinburgh: T&T Clark, 1988.

Hartin, Patrick J. *James of Jerusalem: Heir to Jesus of Nazareth.* Collegeville, Minn.: Liturgical Press, 2004.

Harvey, Susan A. "The Sense of a Stylite: Perspectives on Simeon the Elder." *VC* 42 (1988): 376–94.

Hausherr, Irénée. *The Name of Jesus.* Translated by Charles Cummings. CSS 44. Kalamazoo, Mich.: Cistercian, 1978.

———. *Penthos: The Doctrine of Compunction in the Christian East.* Translated by Anselm Hufstader. CSS 53. Kalamazoo, Mich.: Cistercian, 1982.

Heinen, Heinz. "Persecutions." *CE* 6:1935–38.

Hevelone-Harper, Jennifer. *Disciples of the Desert: Monks, Laity, and Spiritual Authority in Sixth-Century Gaza.* Baltimore: Johns Hopkins University Press, 2005.

———. "Letters to the Great Old Man: Monks, Laity, and Spiritual Authority in Sixth-Century Gaza." Ph. D. diss. Princeton University, 2000.

Hirschfeld, Yizhar. *The Judean Desert Monasteries in the Byzantine Period.* New Haven: Yale University Press, 1992.

Holisky, Dee Ann. "The Georgian Alphabet." Pages 364–69 in *The World's Writing Systems.* Edited by Peter T. Daniels and William Bright. New York: Oxford University Press, 1996.

Holum, Kenneth G. "Hadrian and St Helena: Imperial Travel and the Origins of Christian Holy Land Pilgrimage." Pages 66–81 in *The Blessings of Pilgrimage.* Edited by Robert Ousterhout. Illinois Byzantine Studies. Urbana: University of Illinois Press, 1990.

———. *Theodosian Empresses: Women and Imperial Dominion in Late Antiquity.* Berkeley and Los Angeles: University of California Press, 1982.

Hombergen, Daniël. *The Second Origenist Controversy: A New Perspective on Cyril of Scythopolis' Monastic Biographies as Historical Sources for Sixth-Century Origenism.* SA 132. Rome: Pontificio Ateneo S. Anselmo, 2001.

Honigmann, Ernest. *Le couvent de Barsauma et le patriarcat Jacobite d'Antioche et de Syrie.* CSCO 146. Subsidia 7. Leuven: Durbecq, 1967.

———. *Évêques et évêchés monophysites d'Asie antérieure au* VIe *siècle.* CSCO 127, Subsidia 2. Leuven: Durbecq, 1951.

———. "Juvenal of Jerusalem." *DOP* 5 (1950): 211–79.

———. "Libanos." PW 13.1:1–11.

———. *Die Ostgrenze des byzantinischen Reiches: von 363 bis 1071, nach griechischen, arabischen, syrischen und armenischen Quellen.* Corpus Bruxellense Historiae Byzantinae 3. Brussels: Éditions de l'Institut de Philologie et d'Histoire Orientales, 1935.

Horn, Cornelia B. "Anti-Jewish Polemic and Conversion of Jews to Anti-Chalcedonian Asceticism in the Holy Land: The Case of Eugenia of Tyre." *ARAM* 18 (2006): 33–48.

———. "The Lives and Literary Roles of Children in Advancing Conversion to Christianity: Hagiography from the Caucasus in Late Antiquity and the Middle Ages." *CH* 76.2 (2007), 262–297.

——. *Asceticism and Christological Controversy in Fifth-Century Palestine: The Career of Peter the Iberian.* Oxford: Oxford University Press, 2006.

——. "Beyond Theology: The Career of Peter the Iberian in the Christological Controversies of Fifth- and Sixth-Century Palestine." Ph. D. diss. The Catholic University of America, 2001.

——. "A Chapter in the Pre-history of the Christological Controversies in Arabic: Readings from the Works of John Rufus." *ParOr* 30 (2005): 133–56.

——. "Empress Eudocia and the Monk Peter the Iberian: Patronage, Pilgrimage, and the Love of a Foster-Mother in Fifth-Century Palestine." *ByzF* 28 (2004): 197–213.

——. "Eugenia, a Fifth-Century Jewish Convert to Anti-Chalcedonian Asceticism in Palestine." Paper presented at the Upper Midwest Regional Meeting of the American Academy of Religion/Society of Biblical Literature. St. Paul, Minnesota, 2002.

——. "'Fathers and Mothers Shall Rise Up against Their Children and Kill Them': Martyrdom and Children in the Early Church." Paper presented at the American Academy of Religion/Society of Biblical Literature Annual Meeting, Toronto, Canada, November 2002.

——. "Fighting with the Devil: The Central Function of Women in John Rufus's Anti-Chalcedonian Polemics." Paper presented at the Annual Meeting of the North American Patristics Society. Chicago, 2002.

——. "Peter the Iberian and Monastic Settlement of the Herodian Fortress of Kypros." Work in progress.

——. "Peter the Iberian and Palestinian Anti-Chalcedonian Monasticism in Fifth- and Early Sixth-Century Gaza." *ARAM* 15 (2003): 109–28.

——. "St. Nino and the Christianization of Pagan Georgia." *Medieval Encounters* 4 (1998): 242–64.

——. "Towards a Feminist Ecumenical Reconstruction of the Social History of Anti-Chalcedonian Monasticism in Syria-Palestine in the Fifth and Sixth Centuries." Paper delivered at the American Academy of Religion/Society of Biblical Literature Annual Meeting. Toronto, 2002.

———. "Transgressing Claims to Sacred Space: the Advantage of Portable Relics in the Christological Conflicts in Syria-Palestine in the Fifth and Sixth Centuries A.D." Paper delivered at the American Academy of Religion/Society of Biblical Literature Annual Meeting. Atlanta, November 2003.

———. "Weaving the Pilgrim's Crown: John Rufus's View of Peter the Iberian's Journeys in Late Antique Palestine." *Journal of Eastern Christian Studies* 56 (2004): 171–90.

Horn, Cornelia B., and John W. Martens. *"Let the Little Children Come to Me": Childhood and Children in the Early Christian Community*. Washington, D.C.: The Catholic University of America Press, forthcoming.

Hoss, Stefanie. *Baths and Bathing: The Culture of Bathing and the Baths and Thermae in Palestine from the Hasmoneans to the Moslem Conquest*. BAR International Series 1346. Oxford: Archaeopress, 2005.

Hübner, Reinhard M. "Die Anfänge von Diakonat, Presbyterat und Episkopat in der frühen Kirche." Pages 45–89 in *Das Priestertum in der Einen Kirche: Diakonat, Presbyterat und Episkopat*. Edited by Albert Rauch and Paul Imhof. Aschaffenburg: Kaffke-Verlag, 1987.

Hunt, E. D. *Holy Land Pilgrimage in the Later Roman Empire AD 312–460*. Oxford: Clarendon, 1982.

Hunter, David G. "Borrowings from Libanius in the *Comparatio Regis et monachi* of St. John Chrysostom." *JTS* NS 39 (1988): 525–31.

———. "Libanius and John Chrysostom: New Thoughts on an Old Problem." Pages 129–35 in *Cappadocian Fathers, Chrysostom and His Greek Contemporaries, Augustine, Donatism, and Pelagianism*. Vol. 4 of *Papers Presented to the Tenth International Conference on Patristic Studies Held in Oxford, 1987*. Edited by Elizabeth A. Livingstone. StPatr 22. Leuven: Peeters, 1989.

———. "Preaching and Propaganda in Fourth Century Antioch: John Chrysostom's Homilies on the Statues." Pages 119–38 in *Preaching in the Patristic Age: Studies in Honour of Walter J. Burghardt*. Edited by David G. Hunter. New York: Paulist, 1989.

Jalland, Trevor. *The Life and Times of Leo the Great*. London: SPCK, 1941.

Jeremias, Joachim. *Infant Baptism in the First Four Centuries*. London: SCM, 1960.

Johnson, Mark J. "Bema." *ODB* 1:281.

Jones, A. H. M. "Were Ancient Heresies National or Social Movements in Disguise?" *JTS* 10 (1959): 280–98.

Jones, Brian W. "Hadrian." *ABD* 3:17–18.

Jugie, Martin. *Julien d'Halicarnasse et Sévère d'Antioche (controverse sur la passibilité du corps de Jésus-Christ): La doctrine du péché original chez les pères grecs*. Paris: Feron-Vrau, 1925.

———. "9. Anatole." *DHGE* 2:1497–1500.

Kaplan, Jacob. "Ashdod-Yam." *NEAEHL* 1:102–3.

Kaswalder, Pietro A. *Onomastica Biblica: Fonti scritte e ricerca archeologica*. CMSBF 40. Jerusalem: Franciscan Printing Press, 2002.

Kazhdan, Alexander Petrovich. "Encyclical." *ODB* 1:696.

———. "Quaestor." *ODB* 3:1765.

———. "Tripolis." *ODB* 3:2119–20.

Kazhdan, Alexander Petrovich, and Nancy Patterson Ševčenko. "Forty Martyrs of Sebasteia." *ODB* 2:799–800.

———. "Phokas." *ODB* 3:1666–67.

———. "Sergius and Bakchos." *ODB* 3:1879.

Kelhoffer, James A. *The Diet of John the Baptist: "Locusts and Wild Honey" in Synoptic and Patristic Interpretation*. WUNT 176. Tübingen: Mohr Siebeck, 2005.

———. "'Locusts and Wild Honey' (Mk 1.6c and Mt. 3.4c): The *Status Quaestionis* concerning the Diet of John the Baptist." *CurBR* 2.1 (2003): 104–27.

Kennedy, George A. *The Art of Persuasion in Greece*. Princeton: Princeton University Press, 1963.

———. *Classical Rhetoric and Its Christian and Secular Traditions from Ancient to Modern Times*. 2nd ed. Chapel Hill: University of North Carolina Press, 1999.

———. *Greek Rhetoric under Christian Emperors*. Princeton: Princeton University Press, 1983.

———. *A New History of Classical Rhetoric*. Princeton: Princeton University Press, 1994.

Kirsten, E. "Chorbischof." *RAC* 2:1105–14.

Kloner, Amos. "Beth Guvrin." *NEAEHL* 1:195–201.

Kofsky, Aryeh. "Mamre: A Case of a Regional Cult?" Pages 19–30 in *Sharing the Sacred: Religious Contacts and Conflicts in the Holy Land: First–Fifteenth Centuries CE*. Edited by Arieh Kofsky and Guy G. Stroumsa. Jerusalem: Yad Izhak Ben Zvi, 1998.

———. "Peter the Iberian: Pilgrimage, Monasticism and Ecclesiastical Politics in Byzantine Palestine." *Liber Annuus* 47 (1997): 209–22.

Kraeling, Carl H. *The Synagogue*. New Haven: Yale University Press, 1956. Repr., New York: Ktav, 1979.

Lampe, G. W. H., ed. *A Patristic Greek Lexicon*. Oxford: Clarendon, 1961.

Lanczkowski, Günter. "Iranische Religionen." *TRE* 16:247–58.

Lang, David Marshall. "Peter the Iberian and His Biographers." *JEH* 2 (1951): 158–68.
Leclercq, Henri. "Flabellum." *DACL* 5:1610–25.
———. "Jacques le Mineur." *DACL* 7.2:2109–16.
Leduc, Francis. "Penthos et larmes dans l'œuvre de saint Jean Chrysostome." *POC* 41 (1991): 220–57.
Lefrançois, J. A. "James (Son of Alphaeus), St." *NCE* 7:700–701.
Licheli, Vakhtang. "St Andrew in Samtskhe—Archaeological Proof?" Pages 25–37 in *Ancient Christianity in the Caucasus*. Edited by Tamila Mgaloblishvili. Iberica Caucasica 1. Surrey, U.K.: Curzon, 1998.
Liddell, Henry George, Robert Scott, and Henry Stuart Jones. *A Greek-English Lexicon*. 9th ed. with revised supplement. Oxford: Clarendon, 1996.
Lietzmann, Hans. *Apollinaris von Laodicea und seine Schule: Texte und Untersuchungen*. Tübingen: Mohr Siebeck, 1904.
Lightman, Marjorie, and William Zeisel. "Univira: An Example of Continuity and Change in Roman Society." *CH* 46 (1977): 19–32.
Lilienfeld, Fairy von. "Amt und geistliche Vollmacht der heiligen Nino, 'Apostel und Evangelist' von Ostgeorgien, nach den ältesten georgischen Quellen." Pages 224–49 in *Horizonte der Christenheit: Festschrift für Friedrich Heyer zu seinem 85. Geburtstag*. Edited by Michael Kohlbacher and Markus Lesinski. Oikonomia 34. Erlangen: Lehrstuhl für Geschichte und Theologie des Christlichen Ostens, 1994.
Lordkipanidse, Otar, and Heinzgerd Brakmann. "Iberia II (Georgien)." *RAC* 17:12–106.
Lott, Jeffrey K. "Gerizim, Mount." *ABD* 2:993.
Luker, Lamontte M. "Rachel's Tomb," *ABD* 5:608–9
MacLennan, Hugh. *Oxyrhynchus: An Economic and Social Study*. Amsterdam: Hakkert, 1968.
Magdalino, Paul. "The Maritime Neighborhoods of Constantinople: Commercial and Residential Functions, Sixth to Twelfth Centuries." *DOP* 54 (2000): 209–26.
———. "Prosmonarios." *ODB* 3:1739.
Magen, Itzhak. "Gerizim, Mount." *NEAHL* 2:484–92.
Malherbe, Abraham J. *Paul and the Thessalonians: The Philosophic Tradition of Pastoral Care*. Philadelphia: Fortress, 1987.
Mango, Cyril. "Galata." *ODB* 2:815–16.
Mango, Marlia M. "Rhipidion." *ODB* 3:1790–91.
Manvelichvili, Alexandre. *Histoire de Géorgie*. Paris: Nouvelles Éditions de la Toison d'Or, 1951.

Mare, W. Harold. *The Archaeology of the Jerusalem Area*. Grand Rapids: Baker, 1987.

———. "Siloam, Pool of." *ABD* 6:24–26.

Martindale, J. R.. *The Prosopography of the Later Roman Empire*. Vol. 2: *AD 395–527*. Cambridge: Cambridge University Press, 1980.

Mathisen, Ralph W. "Senate." Pages 689–699 in *Late Antiquity: A Guide to the Postclassical World*. Edited by G. W. Bowersock, Peter Brown, and Oleg Grabar. Cambridge: Harvard University Press, 1999.

Matt, Leonard von, and Giuseppe Bovini. *Ravenna*. New York: Abrams, 1973.

Mattingly, Gerald L. "Pisgah." *ABD* 5:373–74.

Mayerson, Philip. *Monks, Martyrs, Soldiers and Saracens: Papers on the Near East in Late Antiquity (1962–1993)*. Jerusalem: Israel Exploration Society in association with New York University, 1994.

———. "The Wine and Vineyards of Gaza in the Byzantine Period." *BASOR* 257 (1985): 75–80.

McGovern, Leo J. *The Ecclesiology of Saint Leo the Great*. Rome: Pontificia Università Gregoriana, 1957.

McGuckin, John A. *St. Cyril of Alexandria: The Christological Controversy: Its History, Theology, and Texts*. VCSup 23. Leiden: Brill, 1994.

McLeod, Frederick G. *The Roles of Christ's Humanity in Salvation: Insights from Theodore of Mopsuestia*. Washington, D.C.: Catholic University of America Press, 2005.

———. "Theodore of Mopsuestia Revisited." *TS* 61 (2000): 447–80.

McVey, Kathleen. "Ephrem the Syrian's Use of Female Metaphors to Describe the Deity." *ZAC* 5 (2001): 261–88.

Melling, David J. "Archimandrite." *BDEC*, 42.

Menze, Volker. "The Making of a Church: the Syrian Orthodox in the Shadow of Byzantium and the Papacy." Ph.D. thesis. Princeton University, 2004.

Mgaloblishvili, Tamila. "An Unknown Georgian Monastery in the Holy Land," *ARAM* 18–19 (2006–2007): 527–539.

Mingana, A. *Syriac and Garshūni Manuscripts*. Vol. 1 of *Catalogue of the Mingana Collection of Manuscripts*. Cambridge: Heffer & Sons, 1933.

Mlasowski, Alexander. "Denarius." *BNP* 4:301–2.

Moffett, Samuel Hugh. *A History of Christianity in Asia*. 2 vols. San Francisco: HarperSanFrancisco, 1992.

Möhle, Hannes. "Jakobus, Bruder Jesu." *LTK* 5:720–21.

Mühlenberg, Ekkehard. "Apollinaris." *TRE* 3:362–71.

———. *Apollinaris von Laodicea*. Göttingen: Vandenhoeck & Ruprecht, 1969.

Müller, Barbara. "Die Tränen der Wüstenväter: Das Penthos in den *Apophthegmata Patrum*." *OS* 46 (1997): 281–313.

Müller-Abels, S. "John of Antioch." *DECL*, 326.

Murphy, James J., and Richard A. Katula, with Forbes I. Hill and Donovan J. Ochs. *A Synoptic History of Classical Rhetoric*. 3rd ed. Mahwah, N.J.: Hermagoras, 2003.

Murphy-O'Connor, Jerome. *The Holy Land: An Oxford Archaeological Guide from Earliest Times to 1700*. Oxford: Oxford University Press, 1998.

Murray, Robert. "The Theory of Symbolism in St. Ephrem's Theology." *ParOr* 6 (1975): 1–20.

Nedungatt, George. "Archimandrit." *LTK* 1:948.

Neumann, Johannes. "Bischof I." *TRE* 6:653–682.

Neusner, Jacob, and William Scott Green, eds. *Dictionary of Judaism in the Biblical Period 450 B.C.E. to 600 C.E.* Peabody, Mass.: Hendrickson, 1999.

Neyrey, Jerome H. "Josephus' Vita and the *Encomium*: A Native Model of Personality." *JSJ* 25 (1994): 177–206.

Oberlinner, Lorenz. "Jakobus der Jüngere, Apostel." *LTK* 5:719–20.

O'Keefe, John. "'A Letter That Killeth': Toward a Reassessment of Antiochene Exegesis, or Diodore, Theodore, and Theodoret on the Psalms." *JECS* 8 (2000): 83–104.

Orlandi, Tito. "John Chrysostom, Saint." *CE* 5:1357–59.

Painter, John. *Just James: The Brother of Jesus in History and Tradition*. Columbia: University of South Carolina Press, 2004.

Papadakis, Aristeides, and Alexander Kazhdan. "Patriarchates." *ODB* 3:1599–1600.

Paradze, Gregor. "Probleme der ältesten Kirchengeschichte Georgiens." *OrChr* 29 (1932): 153–71.

Patrich, Joseph. *Sabas, Leader of Palestinian Monasticism: A Comparative Study in Eastern Monasticism, Fourth to Seventh Centuries*. Dumbarton Oaks Studies 32. Washington, D.C.: Dumbarton Oaks Research Library and Collection, 1995.

Payne Smith, Robert. *A Compendious Syriac Dictionary*. Edited by J. Payne Smith (Mrs. Margoliouth). Oxford: Clarendon, 1903. Repr., Oxford: Clarendon, 1994.

Peeters, Paulus. "Les débuts du christianisme en Géorgie d'après les sources hagiographiques." *AnBoll* 50 (1932): 5–58.

Perrone, Lorenzo. *La chiesa di Palestina e le controversie cristologiche: Dal concilio di Efeso (431) al secondo concilio di Costantinopoli (553)*. TRSR 18. Brescia: Paideia, 1980.

Pervo, Richard I. "Rhetoric in the Christian Apocrypha." Pages 793–805 in *Handbook of Classical Rhetoric in the Hellenistic Period*. Edited by Stanley E. Porter. Leiden: Brill, 1997.

Peterson, Erik. "Zur Bedeutungsgeschichte von παρρησία." Pages 283–97 in vol.–1 of *Reinhold Seeberg Festschrift*. Edited by Wilhelm Koepp. Leipzig: Scholl, 1929.

Pétridès, S. "Le Monastère des Spoudaei à Jérusalem et les Spoudaei de Constantinople." *EO* 4 (1900–1901): 225–31.

———. "Spoudaei et Philopones." *EO* 7 (1904): 341–48.

Phenix, Robert R., Jr. "A Critical Investigation of Twelve Syriac Verse Homilies on Joseph (Genesis 37–50) Attributed to Balai (Fifth-Century A.D.)." Ph.D. diss. Eberhard-Karls University, Tübingen, Germany, 2005. Forthcoming in STAC. Tübingen: Mohr Siebeck, 2008.

———. "Kunstprosaische Elemente in der *Vita Rabbulae*: Ein Blick auf das Encomium an den Helden." Pages 281–93 in *Die Suryoye und ihre Umwelt: Viertes Deutsches Syrologen-Symposium in Trier 2004: Festgabe Wolfgang Hage zum 70. Geburtstag*. Edited by Martin Tamcke and Andreas Heinz. Studien zur Orientalischen Kirchengeschichte 36. Münster: LIT, 2005.

Piccirillo, Michele. *Chiese e mosaici di Madaba*. Collectio maior 34. Jerusalem: Franciscan Printing Press, 1989.

Piccirillo, Michele, and Eugenio Alliata, eds. *The Madaba Map Centenary 1897–1997: Travelling Through the Byzantine Umayyad Period*. Collectio maior 40. Jerusalem: Studium Biblicum Franciscanum, 1999.

Pinggéra, Karl. "Johannes von Apamea." *BBKL* 23:737–41.

Pottmeyer, Hermann J. "Bischof. II Historisch-Theologisch." *LTK* 2:482–86.

Pratscher, Wilhelm. "Jakobus (Herrenbruder)." *RAC* 16:1227–43.

Prestige, G. L. *God in Patristic Thought*. 2nd ed. London: SPCK, 1952.

Rahner, Hugo. "Die Gottesgeburt: Die Lehre der Kirchenväter von der Geburt Christi im Herzen der Gläubigen." *ZKT* 59 (1935): 333–418.

Rahner, Karl. *Theological Investigations, 15: Penance in the Early Church*. New York: Crossroad, 1982.

Regnault, Lucien. "Les Apophthegmes des Pères en Palestine aux Ve-VIe siècles." *Irén* 54 (1981): 320–30.

Rich, Anthony. *Dictionnaire des Antiquités Romaines et Grecques*. Paris: Firmin-Didot, 1873. Repr., Paris: Payot & Rivages, 1995.

Rist, Josef "Theodotus von Ankyra." *BBKL* 11:997–99.

———. "Die Verfolgung der Christen im spätantiken Sasanidenreich: Ursachen, Verlauf und Folgen." *OrChr* 80 (1996): 17–42.

Roncaglia, Martiniano P. "Dioscorus I." *CE* 3:912–15.

Rubenson, Samuel. "The Egyptian Relations of Early Palestinian Monasticism." Pages 35–46 in *The Christian Heritage in the Holy Land*. Edited by A. G. O'Mahony, G. Gunner, and K. Hintlian. London: Scorpion Cavendish, 1995.

Ruckstuhl, Eugen. "Jakobus." *TRE* 16:485–88.

Russell, James A. *Zoroastrianism in Armenia*. Harvard Iranian Series 5. Cambridge: Harvard University Press, 1987.

Ryan, P. J. "Chrysostom: A Derived Stylist?" *VC* 36 (1982): 5–14.

Sachau, Eduard. *Verzeichniss der syrischen Handschriften*. 2 parts. Vol. 23 of *Die Handschriften-Verzeichnisse der Königlichen Bibliothek zu Berlin*. Berlin: Ascher, 1899.

Saller, Sylvester J. *The Memorial of Moses on Mount Nebo*. 3 vols. PSBF 1. Jerusalem: Franciscan Printing Press, 1941.

Saller, Sylvester, and Bellarmino Bagatti. *The Town of Nebo (Khirbet el-Mekhayyat): With a Brief Survey of Other Ancient Christian Monuments in Transjordan*. Jerusalem: Franciscan Printing Press, 1949.

Samir, Khalil. "Victor Stratelates, Saint. The Copto-Arabic Tradition." *CE* 7:2305–8.

Sanjian, Avedis Krikor. "Anastas Vardapet's List of Armenian Monasteries in Seventh-Century Jerusalem: A Critical Examination." *Mus* 82 (1969): 265–92.

Sauget, J.-M., and T. Orlandi. "John of Maiuma (John Rufus)." *EECh*, 445–46.

Scharf, R. "Die 'Apfel-Affäre' oder gab es einen Kaiser Arcadius II?" *ByzZ* 83 (1990): 435–50.

Scheiber, Alexander. "Parallels to a Topos in Eudocia's Poem." *IEJ* 34 (1984): 180–81.

Schneider, A. M. "Bema." *RAC* 2:129–30.

Schneider, Hilary. *The Memorial of Moses on Mount Nebo*. Jerusalem: Franciscan Printing Press, 1950.

Schöllgen, G. "Flucht vor dem Bischofamt: Anlässe und Motive." Paper delivered at the Fourteenth International Conference on Patristic Studies, Oxford, August 2003.

Schur, Nathan. *History of the Samaritans*. BEATAJ 18. Frankfurt am Main: Lang, 1989.

Schwartz, Eduard. *Johannes Rufus, ein monophysitischer Schriftsteller*. Sitzungsberichte der Heidelberger Akademie der Wissenschaften, Philosophisch-Historische Klasse 16. Heidelberg: Winter, 1912.

Siegert, Folker. "Homily and Panegyrical Sermon." Pages 421–43 in *Handbook of Classical Rhetoric in the Hellenistic Period*. Edited by Stanley E. Porter. Leiden: Brill, 1997.

Sigal, Phillip. "Manifestations of Hellenistic Historiography in Select Judaic Literature." Pages 161–85 in *Society of Biblical Literature 1984 Seminar Papers*. SBLSP 23. Chico, Calif.: Scholars Press, 1984.

Smith, William, and Samuel Cheetham. *A Dictionary of Christian Antiquities*. London: Murray, 1876.

Spanel, Donald B. "Theophilus." *CE* 7:2247–53.

———. "Timothy II Aelurus." *CE* 7:2263–68.

Spanel, Donald B., and Tim Vivian. "Peter I." *CE* 6:1943–47.

Stager, Lawrence E. "Ashkelon." *NEAEHL* 1:103–12.

Stathakopoulos, Dionysios Ch. *Famine and Pestilence in the Late Roman and Early Byzantine Empire: A Systematic Survey of Subsistence Crises and Epidemics*. Birmingham Byzantine and Ottoman Monographs 9. Aldershot, U.K.: Ashgate, 2004.

Steppa, Jan-Eric. *John Rufus and the World Vision of Anti-Chalcedonian Culture*. Gorgias Dissertations: Ancient Christian Studies 1. Piscataway, N.J.: Gorgias, 2002.

Stewart, Columba. "Evagrius Ponticus on Prayer and Anger." Pages 65–81 in *Religions of Late Antiquity in Practice*. Edited by Richard Valantasis. Princeton: Princeton University Press, 2000.

Stewart, Randall. "Atrīb." *CE* 1:307.

Stramara, Daniel F. "Double Monasticism in the Greek East, Fourth through Eighth Centuries." *JECS* 6 (1998): 269–312.

Studer, Basil. *Gott und unsere Erlösung im Glauben der Alten Kirche*. Düsseldorf: Patmos, 1985.

———. "Leo der Grosse und der Primat des römischen Bischofs." Pages 617–30 in *Unterwegs zur Einheit: Festschrift für Heinrich Stirnimann*. Edited by Johannes Brantschen and Pietro Selvatico. Fribourg: Universitätsverlag, 1980.

Suermann, Harald. *Die Gründungsgeschichte der Maronitischen Kirche*. OBC 10. Wiesbaden: Harrassowitz, 1998.

———. "Die Übersetzung des Probus und eine Theorie zur Geschichte der syrischen Übersetzung griechischer Texte." *OrChr* 74 (1990): 103–14.

Taft, Robert F., William Loerke, and Mark J. Johnson. "Pastophoria." *ODB* 3:1594.

Tarchnishvili, Michel. "Le iscrizioni musive del monastero di Bir el-Qutt." Pages 135–39 in Virgilio Corbo, *Gli scavi di Kh. Siyar El Ghanam (Campo dei Pastori) e i monasteri dei dintorni*. Pubblicazioni dello Studium Biblicum Franciscanum 11. Jerusalem: Francescani, 1955.

Toumanoff, Cyril. "Christian Caucasia between Byzantium and Iran." *Traditio: Studies in Ancient Medieval Thought and Religion* 10 (1954): 109–89.

———. *Les Maisons princières géorgiennes de l'Empire de Russie*. Rome: Toumanoff, 1983.

———. "The Princely Nobility of Georgia." Pages 37–46 in *From Byzantium to Iran: Armenian Studies in Honour of Nina G. Garsoïan*. Edited by Jean Pierre Mahé and Robert W. Thomson. Atlanta: Scholars Press, 1997.

———. *Studies in Christian Caucasian History*. Washington, D.C.: Georgetown University Press, 1963.

Trombley, Frank R. "Mithraism." *ODB* 2:1385–86.

Tsafrir, Yoram, Leah Di Segni, and Judith Green. *Tabula Imperii Romani: Iudaea-Palaestina: Eretz Israel in the Hellenistic, Roman and Byzantine Periods*. Jerusalem: Israel Academy of Sciences and Humanities, 1994.

Ullmann, Walter. "Leo I and the Theme of Papal Primacy." *JTS* 11 (1960): 25–51.

Vailhé, Siméon. "Les Philopones d'Oxyrhynque au IVe siècle." *EO* 14 (1911): 277–78.

Van Parys, Michel. "Abba Silvain et ses disciples, une famille monastique entre Scété et la Palestine à la fin du IVe et dans la premiere moitié du Ve siècles." *Irén* 61 (1988): 315–31, 451–80.

Vivian, Tim. *St. Peter of Alexandria, Bishop and Martyr*. Philadelphia: Fortress, 1988.

Vorst, Charles van de, and Paulus Peeters. "Saint Phocas." *AnBoll* 30 (1911): 252–95.

Vryonis, Speros, and Alexander Kazhdan. "Sasanians." *ODB* 3:1845–46.

———. "Zoroastrianism." *ODB* 3:2230–31.

Ward, Benedicta. *Harlots of the Desert: A Study of Repentance in Early Monastic Sources*. CSS 106. Kalamazoo, Mich.: Cistercian, 1987.

Ward, R. B. "James of Jerusalem in the First Two Centuries." *ANRW* 2.26. 1:779–812.

Weinandy, Thomas G., and Daniel A. Keating, eds. *The Theology of St. Cyril of Alexandria: A Critical Appreciation*. London: T&T Clark, 2003.

Wenning, Robert. "Schiloach." *LTK* 9:145.

White, L. Michael. "A Measure of Frank Speech: The State of the Manuscript of PHerc. 1471." Pages 103–30 in *Philodemus and the New Testament World*. Edited by John T. Fitzgerald, Dirk Obbink, and Glenn S. Holland. NovTSup 111. Leiden: Brill, 2004.
Wickham, Lionel R. "Translation Techniques Greek/Syriac and Syriac/English." Pages 345–53 in *V. Symposium Syriacum, 1988, Katholieke Universiteit, Leuven, 29–31 Août 1988*. Edited by René Lavenant. OCA 236. Rome: Pontificium Institutum Studiorum Orientalium, 1988.
Wiemer, Hans-Ulrich. *Libanios und Julian: Studien zum Verhältnis von Rhetorik und Politik im vierten Jahrhundert n. Chr.* Vestigia 46. Munich: Beck, 1995.
Wilder, Amos N. *Early Christian Rhetoric: The Language of the Gospel.* Peabody, Mass.: Hendrickson, 1999.
Wilken, Robert L. "Heiliges Land." *TRE* 14:684–94.
———. *The Land Called Holy: Palestine in Christian History and Thought.* New Haven: Yale University Press, 1992.
Williams, A. V. "Zoroastrians and Christians in Sasanian Iran." *BJRL* 78 (1996): 37–53.
Wright, David F. "How Controversial Was the Development of Infant Baptism in the Early Church?" Pages 45–63 in *Church, Word and Spirit: Historical and Theological Essays in Honor of Geoffrey W. Bromiley*. Edited by James E. Bradley and Richard A. Muller. Grand Rapids: Eerdmans, 1987.
———. "Infant Dedication in the Early Church." Pages 352–78 in *Baptism, the New Testament and the Church: Historical and Contemporary Studies in Honour of R. E. O White*. Edited by Stanley E. Porter and Anthony R. Cross. JSNTSup 171. Sheffield: Sheffield Academic Press, 1999.
———. "The Origins of Infant Baptism—Child Believers' Baptism?" *SJT* 40 (1987): 1–23.
Wright, William. *Catalogue of the Syriac Manuscripts in the British Museum*. 3 vols. London: British Museum, 1870–72.
Yarnold, Edward. "Who Planned the Churches at the Christian Holy Places in the Holy Land?" Pages 105–9 in *Historica, theologica, gnostica, biblica*. Vol. 1 of *Papers of the Ninth International Conference on Patristic Studies, Oxford, 1983*. Edited by Elizabeth A. Livingstone. StPatr 18.1. Kalamazoo, Mich.: Cistercian, 1985.
Yavaȟišvili, Ivane Alek'sandres. *ქართველის ერის ისტორია* [*History of the Georgian People*]. 4 vols. Tibilisi: Stalinis saxelobis T'bilisis saxelmcip'o universitetis gamomc'emloba, 1941–51.

Index of Biblical References

HEBREW BIBLE

Genesis

1:14 15
7 25
15 29
16 10
18:1-8 96

Exodus

3:8 41
3:17 41
8:31 185
11:2-3 49
12:3-13 81
13:5 41
13:21 43
13:25 24
17 181
17:1-7 184
17:11-12 184
19:6 5
20:25 81
23:22 5
25:10-22 47
28:30 149
32:4 19
32:6 19
33:3 41
33:11 155
34:29-35 91
34:30 171, 179
34:35 179
37:1-9 47

Leviticus

19:2 232
20:24 41

Numbers

6 38
13:27 41
32:3 178
32:38 178

Deuteronomy

11:2 41
27:5-6 81
31:4 172
32:10 50
32:11 49, 50
32:12 49
32:13 50
32:39 134
34:5-6 178

Joshua

1:2 30

Judges

13:4-7 38
15:1-8 22
16:17 38

1 Samuel

2:26 30
3:3 35
30:16 19

2 Samuel

6:5 20

1 Kings
18 181

2 Kings
5:14 87

Isaiah
10 23
10:24 134
11:1 12, 23
11:10 12
15:2 178
27:1 132, 134
31:9 19
33:20 51
40:3 224, 278
58:9 75, 184
61:3 47
65:1 28

Jeremiah
30:16 296

Ezekiel
1:1 88
33:11 155

Joel
2:10 88

Amos
2:11-12 38
3:7 191

Jonah
3:5-8 13

Habakkuk
3:11 134

Psalms
4:2 238
5:7 232
5:8 224, 278
10:7 250
14:5 5
18:2 25
43:3 252
45:13-15 228
73:23-24 272
75:3 21
78:65 134
84:5 39
89:10 144
103:8 167
105:1-5 82
108:16 235
112:2 5
118:16-17 272
118:97 70
118:99 70
119:21 144
119:35 4
119:76-77 252
120-134 39
121:3-4 153
135:12 41
140:5 132
140:11 143
141:9 128
141:9-10 132
143:10 278

Proverbs
5:2-4 129
16:25 144
24:20 69

Job
9:6 21
21:7 149
21:30 144

26:11 21
26:13 132
36:16 238
40:11 144

Lamentations

1:1 156

Daniel

1:12 33

3:16-18 15
3:50 183
7 89

Ezra

1:1 88
1:6 49
2:63 149

DEUTEROCANONICAL/APOCRYPHAL BOOKS

Wisdom

1:7 154
1:7-10 155

Sirach

45:1 250

Bel and the Dragon

23-27 132

NEW TESTAMENT

Matthew

1:1 5
2:13 105
3:1-7 70
3:3 278
3:4c 246
3:17 41
4:5-6 115
4:8-9 74
4:19 24
5:47 228
6:5-13 88
6:9 127
6:9-13 127
6:12b 3
6:20 27
6:21 27
6:24 53
9:1-8 248
9:13 167, 229
9:24 150
10:3 292
10:32 23
11:29-30 55, 224
12:18 41
12:36 155
13:18-30 225
13:55 293
16:6-12 161
16:18-19 7
17:2 88
17:5 41, 88
18:20 111
19:11 233
19:12 119
19:16-22 74
19:21 103
20:1-16 230

24:13 234
24:30 89
25:1-13 227
25:31-46 90
26:14-16 65, 110
26:20-25 110
26:21-25 65
26:45-50 65
26:47-50 110
26:51-55 114
26:67 95
27:3-5 110
27:3-10 65
27:56 292
28:20 230

Mark

1:2-8 70
1:3 278
1:6c 246
1:10 88
1:17 24, 226
2:1-12 248
2:17 167, 229
3:18 292
4:3-20 225
4:21-23 225
5:40 150
6:3 293
6:45-52 25
8:15 161
9:3 88
10:17-22 74
10:21 103
13:1-2 79
13:13 234
14:10 65
14:10-11 110
14:17-21 65
14:18-21 110
14:28-1 25
14:42-45 110
14:43-46 65
14:47-49 114
15:40 292
16:1 292

Luke

1:31 30
1:80 39
2:29 243, 254
2:40 39
2:42 30
2:53 25
3:3-14 70
3:4 278
4:7-8 74
4:9-10 115
4:30 139
4:37 28
5:32 167, 229
6:15 292
8:4-15 225
8:16-18 225
9:29 88
10:19 227
10:42 102
11:2-4 127
12:1 161
12:8 23
14:33 103
15:5 168
16:9-13 53
18:18-25 74
21:5-6 79
22:3-6 65, 110
22:21-23 65, 110
22:47-48 65, 110
22:49-53 114
23:43 126
24:10 292

John

1:6-9 70
1:23 278

1:36 81
2:1-11 200
6:15-21 25
8:44 208, 232
10:1-18 284
10:11 4
10:14 4, 284
10:19-21 285
13:2 65
13:8 116
13:18 65
13:21-30 65
15:13ff 138
18:2-5 65
18:4-11 114
20:28 38
20:30-31 169
21:15-17 116, 153
21:24-25 169
21:25 92

Acts

1:13 292
1:16-20 65
1:25 65
2:37 235
7:54-60 66
7:56 88
8:9-24 110
8:26-40 139
12:17 292
13-14 43
15:13 292
15:36-41 43
19:38 223
20:34-35 56
21:14 255
21:18 292

Romans

2:11 260
6:19 234
8:10-12 27
8:23 271
8:26 271
8:7a 69
8:7b 69
10:20 28
12:1 198
14:11 4
15:9 4
15:12 12, 23
15:19 26

1 Corinthians

1:18 47
2:15 198
3:16 33
3:19 295
4:12 56
5:3-4 199
5:7 81
7:2 233
7:5 12
7:9 233
8:2-3 27
9:13-15 56
9:18 56
9:22 147
9:25 14
10:7 19
10:13 165
14:12 28
15:7 292
15:52 88

2 Corinthians

5:18-20 104
5:20 69
6:4-5 26, 164
6:8 26
6:9 26
6:10 27
7:1 33

11:6 170
11:29 147
12:2 227
12:4 258
12:7 286

Galatians

1:19 293
2:9 292
2:12 292
2:16 5
2:20 171
3:28 230
4:9 27
5:15 235
5:17 69
6:10 228

Ephesians

2:9 5
3:7 91
3:10 89
4:25 232
5:19 264
5:29 227
6:12 26, 89
6:16 69

Philippians

2:17 199
3:8 54
3:14 251

Colossians

1:16 89
2:4 199
2:13 27
3:20 3

1 Thessalonians

2:4 3
2:9 56
2:19 14
4:3-5 233
4:16-17 90

2 Thessalonians

3:7-9 56

1 Timothy

1:5 260
2:15 228
3:7 5
4:12 24
5:4 5
6:10 53
6:11 43, 158
6:12 133, 164

2 Timothy

2:19 23
2:21 23
3:2 53
3:15 27
3:16 262
4:7 55, 160, 163, 299
4:8 14

Titus

2:14 4
3:8 230

Philemon

1:22 5

Hebrews

1:1 25
2:11 228
3:1 104
3:12 3
4:15 104
4:16 104
5:3 104
11:6 232
11:12 5
11:39 5

12:13 278
12:14 232
13:4 233
13:5 53
13:7 2-3

James

1:12 14
2:23 139
3:2 69

1 Peter

1:18-19 111
1:19 81
2:9 5
2:25 4, 29
4:17 228
5:4 4, 14

2 Peter

2:20 39
3:10 88
3:12 88

1 John

1:1-3 119
4:15 4

Revelation

4:1 88
4:1-5:14 81
7:11 254
7:14 81
11:16 89
12:10 70
20:4 89

Index of Names, Places, and Concepts

The index covers the introduction, translated text, and all footnotes but not the timeline. Qualifiers for any entries have been placed in parentheses, as have the names of authors of ancient texts that are listed, when these are known. Monastic fathers are generally listed under "Abba."

ʿAbbasid lviii
"one nature made flesh," xxxviii
"one nature of the logos made flesh," xxxviii n. 69
A(nno) M(artyrum) xli
Aaron (monk) lxxxii
Aaron (of Ptolemaïs) 235
Abarim Mountain range 172 n. 2
Abba Abraham of Athrib lxxxiii, 273
Abba Anthony 24 n. 7
Abba Arsenius 100 n. 7. See also *Apophthegmata Patrum*
Abba Gerontios 6 n. 3
Abba Hilarion 24 n. 7
Abba Irenion l n. 121, 107, 117
Abba Isaiah the Egyptian: biography lix; death lxxxii; father of monks 111 n. 11, 243; news of his death 243–45; place in conflict lvi (also n. 138); seclusion 139 n. 11; spiritual companion of Peter lxxx–lxxxi; 201–3
Abba Maxos lxxxiii, 269–73
Abba Peter (priest) lxxxii, 247
Abba Poemen 98 n. 4. See also *Apophthegmata Patrum*
Abba Romanus 123 n. 3, 283
Abba Sana lxxxii, 253
Abba Silvanus l, 98–99
abbot (title) 60 n. 8
Abram (Abraham) 10 n. 1
Abūṣīr—*see* Taposiris Magna
Acacian schism xlvii
Acacius of Constantinople 162 n. 3, 165 n. 9
Acts of the Apostles (apocryphal) lxviii
Adhur 15 n. 7
Aelia Eudoxia—*see* Eudoxia (empress)
Aelia 115 n. 5. *See also* Jerusalem
Aeneas of Gaza l
Ahriman—*see* Angra Mainyu
Ahura Mazda 15 n. 7. *See also* Zoroastrianism
Akoimetai 73 n. 4
Albania xxi, 6 n. 1
Albina lxxvi, 53
Alexandria xl–xli, 133–35
alms (giving) 13, 129
Alphabeticon 261 n. 7
altar 81, 89–91
Amos (prophet) 191

Anahid xxviii n. 37
Anastasis—*see* Church of the Holy Anastasis
Anastasius (Bysantine emperor) lvii
Anastasius (monk) 72 n. 2
Anatolios (brother to Timothy Aelurus) 137, 141
Anatolius of Constantinople xlv–xlvi
Andrew (apostle) xxv, lxxxi, 207 (also n. 8)
Andrew (disciple) 259
Angel: apparition 155–56; hierarchy, 89; likeness, 91
Anglican Christ Church 94 n. 1
Angra Mainyu 15 n. 7. *See also* Zoroastrianism
Anthemius 30 n. 8
anti-Chalcedonian bishops lvii, lxxviii–lxxix, 111, 122–23, 137: in Egypt liii; peripatetic li–lii, 257. *See also* Dioscorus of Alexander, Peter II of Antioch, Peter the Iberian, Timothy Aelurus
anti-Chalcedonian Christology xxxii, 81
anti-Chalcedonian community: as Orthodox church xxxiv, lii, 76 n. 2, 113; Caesarea 236 n. 1; Egypt 139 n. 5, 147 n. 6; inner conflicts 284 n. 1; Palestine xlviii, xlix, li, liv–lv, lxii, lxxviii, 25 n. 9; support network 187 n. 8
anti-Chalcedonian family 199 (also n. 7)
anti-Chalcedonian ordination 111–25, 137–39
anti-Chalcedonian patriarchates xxxv
anti-Chalcedonian holy places 198 n. 1: competing sanctuaries 243 n. 3; maintenance, li–lii; movable relics 214 n. 1; service to 13, 35, 219, 257; shared with Jews 197 n. 4, 266 n. 2; shrines 35, 43; Tomb of Christ 81; veneration 197
anti-Chalcedonian success lviii
anti-Chalcedonianism xxxii–xxxiii
anti-Chalcedonianism; confirmation through miracles 29, 90 n. 2, 121, 159; as Fear of God 5, 109, 121–23, 137, 147 (also n. 8), 239, 295–97; as Orthodoxy lii, 29, 93, 113, 121, 161, 257, 261,
Anti-Encyclikon (Emperor Basiliscus) 163
anti-Judaism xlii, 110 n. 5, 111
Antioch xliv, 285, 287, 295–97
Antiochus IV Epiphanes 60 n. 2
Antiquitates Judaicae (Josephus) 60 n. 2
anti-Samaritan polemic 60 n. 2
Antoninus Martyr 118 n. 1
Antoninus Placentinus—*see Itinerarium*
Antony of Choziba—see *Vita Sancti Georgii Chozebitae*
Apamea lxv
apocalyptic expectation 25 (also n. 9)
Apollinaris of Laodicea xxxviii (also n. 67)

Apophthegmata Patrum: Abba Isaiah 201 n. 1; Abba Hilarion 24 n. 7; Abba Poemen 99 n. 4; Abba Zeno 98 n. 1; Arsenius 100 n. 7, 223 n. 7; Longinus 136 n. 2; Silvanus l, 98 n. 2
apostolic authority 24 n. 2
apostolic sees xlvi
apostolicity xl
approval (divine) lxvii
Apringius (*comes*) lxxxi, 217
Apronius 58 n. 3
Arab conquest xxxiv, lviii
Arabia lxii, lxxix, 159, 169, 183 n. 1
Aramaic language lxxv
Arca (Caesarea) lxxxi, 207
Arcadius (Byzantine emperor) 9, 222 n. 7
archaeology: Constantinople 82 n. 6; destruction of Jerusalem 78 n. 5; Georgian monasteries in Jerusalem xxiii n. 16; Iberia xxv n. 25; inscriptions xxiii–xxiv, 69, 127, 242 n. 1; literature 66 n. 4; Mount Nebo 172 n. 4; Samaria 60 n. 4
Archimandrite (title) 60 n. 8, 283 n. 7
Arčil 9 n. 7
Ardashir xxvii
aretalogy lxvii–lxviii
Arius xxxviii
Armazi (city) xxiii
Armenia xx, xxx–xxxii, 6 n. 1. *See also* Christianity: Armenia
Armenian Kingdom xxiii
Arnon River 183
Arsacid dynasty (Armenia) xxii
Arsenius 222 n. 7, 223
Arsilios lxxxiv, 9, 17–21
ascetic way of life: alms 13, 53; cleaning holy sites 13, 35, 219, 257; fasting 15, 23; for all Christians 230 (also n. 6), 233; labor 55–57; model 19, 25; prayer 15, 23; service 23, 73
ascetic: identity 56 n. 1; philosopher 17; stranger 53, 97, 213, 239; temple 33
asceticism: anti-Chalcedonian 103 n. 9; as way of life 3 (also n. 4), 13; athleticism and war 70 n. 3, 71; battling the devil 71; concerns about food 246 n. 3; effects 71, 171, 203; flight from the world 41–45; hair shirt 33; knowledge 37 n. 7; outer sign 17 (also n. 6), 71, 171; Palestinian 94 n. 2; purification 33; separation xxxi, 23 (also n. 5), 39, 55; teacher-disciple 94 n. 2, 105; testing lxxvi. *See also* Spiritual athleticism, Nazarite asceticism
Asceticon (Abba Isaiah) 203 nn. 10–11
Ashdod lxxxii, 237
Ashkelon lxxix, 157, 193, 201 n. 4
Asia Minor 45
Asianism lxix n. 178
Aspacures III (Varaz-Bakʾar) xxiv, xxx, 8 n. 2

Aspar 122 n. 2
Asterius of Amaseia—*see Homily 9*
Assassins 127
Assyrian Apostolic Church of the East xxx, lviii
Athanasius of Alexandria xxxviii. *See also Vita Antonii*
Athanasius of Egypt lxxxiii, 253, 263, 269
Athenagoras lxviii n. 173. *See also Legatio pro Christianis*
Athenais 30 n. 8. *See also* Eudocia (empress)
Athrib lxxxiii, 273
Atticism lxix n. 178
Augustamnica xlix
Augustine of Hippo lxv. *See also De opere monachorum*
Austrian Academy of Science 82 n. 6
autocracy lxiv
Avita 58 n. 3

Ba'ar lxxix–lxxx, 173, 181
Bacchus (martyr) 215 (also n. 6)
Baghdād lviii
Bahrām V (Persian emperor) 34 n. 3
Bakur III xxxii
Bakurdukhtia lxxxv, 7, 23
Bakurios xxiv, xxix, 7, 13–17, 35 n. 9
baptism of infants 127
baptism 57–59
baptistry as the River Jordan 141
Bar Kokhba letters 79 n. 5
Bar Kokhba Revolt (Second Jewish War) 78 n. 5
Bara 183 n. 1
Bardelios lxxxv, 11
barrenness and sterility 187 (also n. 5). *See also* Miracles: children
Barsanuphius 261 n. 7
Basil (deacon) 37 n. 6
Basil of Caesarea 175 n. 4, 223. *See also In quadraginta martyres Sebastenses, Rules*
Basilides lxxxi, 221
Basiliscus (Byzantine emperor) lxii, lxxix, 161, 163.
Batmin lxxx, 187 n. 3, 191
Beirut lvii, lxxxi, 73 n. 4, 167, 225
Bellum Judaicum (Josephus) 92 n. 6
Bema 263
Benjamin (place) 197 n. 4
Besa—*see Vita Sinuthii Archimandritae*
Beth Daltha lxxx, 203
Beth Guvrin 298 n. 1. *See also* Eleutheropolis
Beth Lāpat (Khorramabad, Iran) 34 n. 3
Beth Pe'or 179
Beth Tafsha lxxx, 195, 197
Bethlehem 197 (also n. 4)
biblical citations lxix
biblical interpretation—*see* exegesis (patristic)
biography lxvi nn. 169–70, lxxiv
Birkat Silwan—*see* Pool of Shiloah
bishops: chorbishop 286 n. 6; influenced by demons 145; martyrs and preachers 113; Palestine 157

blessing: authorities lxxxii, 189, 229, 243; believers 237; deathbed 265; disciples lxxxiii; from the dead 267; hosts 199–201, 235; kiss 177, 193; rain 181; the people 187; vineyards lxxx, 201

Blue Mosque 82 n. 6

Bomirosparia lxxxv, 11

Bosmarios (Peter's father) xxx, xxxii, lxxvi, lxxxv, 7, 29–31

Bosmarios (Peter's grandfather) xxiii, lxxxv, 7

Bostra lxii

Botnia 191 n. 8. *See also* Batmin

Bozrah 183 n. 1

British Museum in London lxxi

Brock, Sebastian viii

Brooks, Ernest W. lx, lxxi

Buzmarios—*see* Bosmarios (Peter's father)

Buzmihr—*see* Bosmarios (Peter's father)

Byzantine patriotism xxxiii

Caesarea Libani—*see* Arca (Caesarea)

Caesarea Maritima xlvi n. 108, liv, lxxxii, 159 (also n. 5), 235

calendar: Coptic xli; Julian 67 n. 6

calendar months: Ab 119, 243; Elul 133; Hator 264 n. 2; Iyor 67, 215; Kanon (first) 259, 279, 293; Nisan 143; Teshrin (first) 240 n. 5, 249; Teshrin (second) 240 n. 5, 279, 301

Calendion of Antioch lxxix, 165

Caliph Hārūn ar-Rašīd 67 n. 4

calques lxx

Candida xxviii n. 37

Cankurtaran 82 n. 6

Canon 1 of Constantinople xxxix

Canon 10 of Antioch (341)

Canon 3 of Constantinople I xxxix–xli, xlvi

Canons of Chalcedon liv

Canons of Constantinople I xxxix–xl

Canons of Nicaea 116 n. 2

Canons of Seleucia-Ctesiphon xxx

Canopis 257

Cappadocian theology 175 n. 4

captatio benevolentiae lxxvi

Carolingian reforms 287 n. 6

carrying the Cross of Christ 25, 47, 55, 159, 235

Cassius Dio 79 n. 5

Castra Arnonensia 183 n. 1

Catholicos of Georgia xxxi

Caucasus xx, xxii, 6 n. 1

Chalcedonian heresies lxxxiii

Chalcedonian rebellion 91

Chalcedonian Schism xxxii, lvii–lviii, lxii

Chalcedonian success liv–lv, lviii

Chalcedonians: as Jews 249 n. 6; as rebels 121

chastity lxxxiii: conversation with women, 203; in marriage 13

children: martyrdom xxvi

Chreiae lxviii n. 174

Christianity: Armenia xxv, xxx–xxxii; Egypt xli; Georgia xxv–xxvi, xxx, lviii; Palestine xlii–xliii, xlvi–xlvii, xlviii, 103 n. 10; Persia xxvii–xxix; under the Arabs lviii
Christianization xxvi
christological formula of Cyril xxxix n. 68, xlvii
christological formula of Leo I xlvii
Christology (Antiochene) xxxix
Christotokos xxxix
Chronicle (Zachariah Rhetor) lix, 110 n. 3, 111 n. 7, 116 n. 5, 141 n. 5, 143 n. 8, 158 n. 3, 160 n. 4, 191 n. 4, 204 nn. 3–4, 287–88, 290 n. 7
Chronographia (Theophanes) 143 n. 8, 282 n. 2, 289 n. 6, 298 n. 4, 300 n. 4
chronology lxvii
Chrysaphius 30 n. 8
Chrysotriclinium 82 n. 6
church autonomy xxv, xxix
church conflicts xlii: violence, 141
church government xxxiv–xxxv
church in Eleona 51 n. 8, 55 n. 4. *See also* Church of the Pater Noster
church in Jerusalem xxvi
church jurisdiction xxxiv, xxxix, xlii, xlvi (also n. 108)
church of Leontius 219
church of Maiuma 119
church of Pontius Pilate 197
church of Saint Hilarion lxxx, 201
church of Saint Stephen 66 n. 4, 196 n. 1, 243
church of Saint Victor 107 n. 3
Church of San Vitale 86 n. 1
Church of Shiloah 118–19, 197
Church of the Cross 51
Church of the East—*see* Assyrian Apostolic Church of the East
Church of the Holy Anastasis 51, 53, 85
Church of the Holy Ascension lxxvi, 51, 55 (also n. 4), 59, 80 n. 4, 197
Church of the Holy Sepulcher 51 n. 7, 81 n. 5. *See also* Church of the Holy Anastasis
Church of the Holy Zion 93, 101
Church of the Nativity 80 n. 4
Church of the Paralytic 197
Church of the Pater Noster 51 n. 8. *See also* church in Eleona
Church of the Probatike—*see* Church of the Paralytic
Church of the Prophet Zachariah lxxxiv
Church of the Resurrection 50 n. 7, 85 n. 9. *See also* Church of the Holy Anastasis
Church of Zion 72 n. 3, 197
church on Mount Nebo 173 (also n. 4), 177–79
church relations xxix, xliv
churches called temples 67–69, 75, 173, 177–79, 197, 201, 219, 243, 267, 273, 293, 299, 301
Cicero lxiv. *See also De amicitia*, *De finibus*

Clement of Alexandria—*see Stromateis*
Codex Encyclicus 291 n. 11
Codex Theodosianus 30 n. 8
Colchis xxi, xxv, xxviii, 6 n. 1. *See also* Lazica
commemoration: James the brother of the Lord 294 n. 1; John the Eunuch 249; of the dead 11 n. 6; Passarion 301; Peter of Alexandria 263; Peter the Iberian 275, 279, 301; Peter's family 11; Romanus 301. *See also* remembrance
communion between patriarchates xlvi–xlvii, lvi
communion, politically motivated liv–lv
companionship: cell-mates 95, 105, 177, 203, 245, 249, 259; in spirit lvi, lxxx–lxxxi, 205, 217–19; in virtue 301
condemnation: Apollinaris xxxix; Arius xxxix ; Nestorius xliii–xliv
confession: public 18 n. 2; penitence 19
consecration of bishops lviii
Constantine I (Byzantine emperor) xl, xlii, lv: co-emperors 65 n. 9, 93; government administration 188 n. 3, 193 n. 5
Constantinople xli, 57, 175 n. 4, 287. *See also* New Rome
Constantius Chlorus (Roman emperor) 79 n. 7
Constantius III (Byzantine emperor) 57 n. 8
contemplation 71
Contra Apionem (Josephus) 225 n. 15
Contra Julianum (Cyril of Alexandria) 151 n. 4
controversies: beginning of Chalcedonian xxxv; effects xxxiv; Trinitarian xxxix; Origenist xxxv (also n. 55), 59 n. 4; *theotokos* xxxv;
conversion of Jews 248 n. 1
Conversion of K'art'li by Nino xxii, 8 n. 2
conversion of Samaritans 243, 247–49
Coptic church xli
Corpus Dionysiacum authorship, 76 n. 1. *See also* Pseudo-Dionysian corpus
correspondence xxxi, lix
Cosmas the Eunuch 205
Council of Chalcedon xliv–xlvii: anathematized, 145; bishops deposed 108 n. 3; bishops restored 109 nn. 6–7; Christology 108 n. 3; Emperor Marcian 122 n. 2; evil opinion 147, 289; foretold lxxvii, lxxx; heresy 261; imperial condemnation 161; imperial support 163; in Armenia xxxi; in Egypt 129; in Georgia xxxi–xxxii; in Palestine xlviii, lxxviii; persuasion 289; portents of lxxvii; quaternian concept of God xxxiv n. 51; transgression

63, 107; ungodly 107–9, 289; work of Satan 121
Council of Constantinople I xxxiv n. 51, xxxix
Council of Constantinople II xxxvi n. 59, 109 n. 7
Council of Ephesus I xxx, xliv, 38 n. 5, 66 n. 1, 108–9
Council of Ephesus II xlv–xlvi, 285 n. 7. *See also Latrocinium*
Council of Nicaea I xxxiv n. 51, xxxvii–xxxviii
Council of Seleucia-Ctesiphon (410) xxix–xxx
Creed of Nicaea (anathemas) xxxviii n. 64
cross 47, 81, 83
crown: of confessorship 14–15, 127, 147, 291; of glory 4 n. 7, 163; of good pilgrimage 239; of the high calling of God 251
Crusades xxv
curses 17, 21–23
cursus honorum 192 n. 5
customs: political 35; reversal of 49; transformation of 19–21
Cyprus (fortress)—*see* Kypros
Cyprus (island) lxxxiv, 22 n. 4, 293
Cyril of Alexandria xl, xliii–xliv, 66–67, 109 n. 6, 160 n. 4, 137 n. 6. *See also Contra Julianum, Twelve Anathemas*
Cyril of Jerusalem 80 n. 2, 93 n. 8
Cyril of Scythopolis—*see Life of Sabas, Vita Cyriaci, Vita Euthymii, Vita Sabae, Vita Theodosii*
Damascus Gate 66–67
Daric 200 n. 3
Darius Hystaspes 200 n. 3
De amicitia (Cicero) 138 n. 4
De finibus (Cicero) 138 n. 4
De martyribus Palestinae (Eusebius of Caesarea) 211 n. 7
De obitu Theodosii (John Rufus): anti-Chalcedonian leaders 123 n. 3; authorship 131 n. 11; imperial persecution 123 n. 7; introduction liii–liv; outline lxxxiv–lxxxv; Romanos 111 n. 11; Theodosius 111 n. 12; visions 126 n. 9
De opere monachorum (Augustine of Hippo) 57 n. 3
De pauperibus amandis (Gregory of Nyssa) 57 n. 3
De situ terrae sanctae (Theodosius) 103 n. 8
Dead Sea 172 n. 2, 183 n. 3, 186 n. 3
Death of Theodosius—see De obitu Theodosii
demons: apparition 151; influencing bishops 145; knowledge 41
deposing bishops xliv–xlvi
destruction of idols 61
diakonikon 215
Diary (Egeria) 170 n. 2, 181 n. 4
Didache 127 n. 6
Dio Cassius 223 n. 8
Diocletian (Roman emperor) xli
Diocletian persecution xli
Diodore of Tarsus xxxvi n. 59, xxxix

Dionysius 141
Dionysius (lawyer) lxxx, 199
Dios (Saint) 288 n. 6
Dioscorus of Alexandria: death in exile 133, 147; doctrine 160 n. 4; xli n. 83 xlv–xlvi, lxxviii, 108 n. 3
disease 85 (also n. 7), 87. *See also* Illness
disguise 45
divorce 188 n. 3
Dominican Fathers 67 n. 4
Domnus of Antioch xlv
Dorotheus of Gaza 261 n. 7
drought 181, 297
Duktia lxxxv, 7, 13–15

École Biblique Française 67 n. 4
Edict of Milan xxvii–xxix
Egeria (pilgrim) 51 n. 8. *See also Diary*
Egypt 58 n. 4, 123, 173 n. 7, 200 n. 2
Egyptian influence xlix
Elath 183 n. 1
Eleutheropolis 114 n. 5, 298 n. 2
Elias of Jerusalem 133 n. 1. *See also Life of John of Tella*
Elijah (tribune) lxxx, 193, 241
Eliseus of Sardis 289 n. 6
Elisha the Lycian 225
Elpidius 61 n. 8, 72 n. 2
Encaenia 241
Encomium in xl martyres 1 and 2 (Gregory of Nyssa) 65 n. 9
encomium xlvi (also nn. 169–70)
Encyclikon (Emperor Basiliscus) 161–63
Ephraem the Syrian 64 n. 2. *See also Hymns against Julian*
Ephrem of Antioch lvii
epikephalaion 129 n. 6
epiklesis 120 n. 3. *See also* Eucharist: Holy Spirit
Epiphany 35
Epistle 28 (Leo I of Rome)—*see Tome of Leo*
Epistulae (Pliny the Younger) 138 n. 4
Epistulae morales (Seneca) 138 n. 4
eschatology (realized) 53 n. 4
Eternal City 58 n. 4. *See also* Rome
Eucharist: celebration 117–21; Holy Spirit 121; purity 157; violence 119. *See also epiklesis*
Eudocia (empress): background 30–32; burial 67 n. 4; disciple lxxvii; household 193; illness 241–43; patronage liv–lv, 67–69, 118 n. 1, 243, 299; petition for Romanus lxxxiv, 297; piety xxxiii, 33; pilgrimage 101
Eudoxia (empress) xxxvi, 9
Eugenia of Tyre lxxxii, 158 n. 5, 227–29, 237
Eunuch of Candace 139
Euphrosius (disciple) 265
Eusebius of Caesarea 21 n. 3. *See also Historia ecclesiastica, Vita Constantini, Onomasticon, De martyribus Palestinae*
Eusebius of Pelusium lxxviii, 137 (also n. 9)

Eutyches xlv, 108 n. 1, 160 n. 4, 163 n. 3; followers of 284 n. 1; heresy of 285
Evagrius of Pontus xxxvii n. 61. *See also Praktikos*
Evagrius Scholasticus—*see Historia ecclesiastica*
excommunication between churches xxxii
exegesis (patristic) xxxvi–xxxvii, 81 n. 9

fantastic voyages lxviii
Fars Province xxvii
Feast of the Ascension 186–87
Feast of the cross 241
Flavian of Constantinople xlv–xlvi, 108–9
flight from ministry 119, 175
forced conversion xxviii
Forma 123
Formula of Reunion xliv
Forty Martyrs of Sebaste 65
Frend William, liv
friendship with God 167

Gad (tribe) 191 n. 8
Gaianos (Chorbishop) 287
Gaiseric lv n. 137
Galla Placidia 57 n. 8
Gangra (Colchis) lxxviii, 108 n. 3, 133, 146–47
Gaza xix, xlviii–li, lvi, lix, lxv, lxxvii–lxxxii, 77, 199, 201 n. 4
genealogical tables lxxxv
genealogy: ancestors xix; of Peter 5–11; *vitaxas* xxiii n. 15
Gennadios of Constantinople 145 n. 7
genres lxiii, lxvi–lxix, lxxiv
Geographica (Strabo) 6 n. 1, 9 n. 8
George Ourṭāyā (bishop) 287 n. 9
Georgia (Eastern) xxi. *See also* Iberia (*and* Albania)
Georgia (Western) xxi, xxv. *See also* Colchis
Georgian Alphabet xxi
Georgian Chronicle (Qauxč'išvili) 9 n. 7
Georgian church xx
Georgian kingdoms—*see* Iberia Albania *and* Colchis
Georgian religion xx
Gerontius lxxvi, 61 (also nn. 8–9), 65, 72 n. 2. *See also Vita S. Melaniae Junioris*
Gethsemane 197
Gišra 217
Gogarene xxii–xxiii
Golgotha 53, 62 n. 2, 81, 85, 195, 197. *See also* Holy Rock
Gospel of John 47
Gospel of the Hebrews 293 n. 8
Gospels lxv, xlvii
Great Harbor 137 n. 8
Great Palace (Constantinople) 82 n. 6
Greek influence on Syriac lxiii, lxix–lxx, lxxiii–lxxiv
Greek language lxxv
Gregory of Aphthoria (abbot) lxxxii–lxxxiii, 237, 263, 265
Gregory of Nazianzen lx
Gregory of Nyssa—see *De pauperibus amandis*, *Encomium in xl martyres 1 and 2*

Griffith Sidney, 15 n. 4, 21 n. 4, 35 n. 8, 39 n. 5, 92 n. 1
guesthouses 22–23, 73, 97
guidance (divine) lxxviii

Hadrian (Roman emperor) 60 n. 2
Hagar 10 n. 1
hagiography xxv–xxvii, lxviii–lxix
Hammat Gader: baths 242 n. 1
healing lxxx, lxxxii, 15, 19, 85–87, 149–51, 217
Hegesippus 293 n. 8
Helena (empress) xlii, 51 n. 8, 79 (also n. 7): churches, 81; cross 81; pilgrimage to Jerusalem 79–81
Helenopolis (Drepanum) 79 n. 7
Henotikon lvi–lvii, 162 n. 3, 165 n. 7. *See also* Zeno (Byzantine emperor)
Hephtalites—*see* White Huns
Heracleia xl
heretics (list) xxxix
heroic deeds of Bakurios 15–17
Hibernia (Spain)—*see Iberia prima*
Hilarion xlix, 111 n. 11
Hippolytus—*see Traditio Apostolica*
Historia Apollonii Regis Tyri—*see History of Apollonius*
Historia ecclesiastica: Eusebius of Caesarea 8 n. 4, 37 n. 5, 46 n. 2, 112 n. 6, 256 n. 1, 293 nn. 8–9; Evagrius Scholasticus lvi n. 139, lix, lxxiv n. 193, 137 n. 9, 143 n. 8, 160 n. 4, 296 n. 4; Rufinus of Aquileia 16 n. 2; Socrates Scholasticus 31 n. 8, 33 n. 6; Sozomen l, 65 n. 9, 98 n. 2, 101 n. 9; Theodore Lector 143 n. 8
Historia Lausiaca (Palladius) 55 n. 4, 58–59
Historia Monarchorum in Aegypto 128 n. 3
History of Apollonius lxvii n. 173
History of the Armenians (Moses of Khoren) 9 n. 7
History of the Kings of K'art'li xxi–xxii
Holiness as gift 63
Holy City 19, 55, 111, 195: ordinations, 113–15; vision 197. *See also* Jerusalem
Holy Family: flight to Egypt xli
Holy Land xlii, 51
Holy Rock 61–63. *See also* Golgotha
Holy Sepulcher 61, 195, 197
Holy Spirit: feminine 47; guide 237; herald lxxvi, 47; writing 263
Holy Sunday 63
homily (exegetical) xlix
Homily 9 (Asterius of Amaseia) 211 n. 6
homoousios xxxvii–xxxviii
Honorius (Byzantine emperor) 223 n. 7
hospitality for pilgrims 97–99. *See also* guesthouses
hospitality 152–53
hospitals 23, 73
house of Lazarus 197
humility 33
Hymns against Julian (Ephraem the Syrian) 64 n. 2

Hypatia xl
Hypatios (martyr) 217 n. 9

I Apologia (Justin Martyr) 12 n. 8
Ibas of Edessa 109 (also nn. 6–7)
Iberia xx–xxi, 5–7
Iberia prima 6 n. 1. *See also* Hibernia (Spain)
Iberia secunda 6 n. 1
Iberian monarchy xx n. 4, 16 n. 2
Ignatius of Antioch—*see To the Philadelphians, To the Magnesians*
illness lxxvii, 74 n. 1. *See also* Disease Peter the Iberian: illness
Imbomon 51 n. 8. *See also* Anastasis
In quadraginta martyres Sebastenses (Basil of Caesarea) 65 n. 9
independence: church xxxi; state xxix, xxxi
Institutio oratoria—see Quintillian
Instructions (Dorotheus of Gaza) 261 n. 7
Itinerarium (Antoninus Placentinus) 118 n. 1
Isaac 10 n. 1
Isaiah of Gaza—*see* Abba Isaiah
Ishmael 10 n. 1
Isidore of Pelusium 137 n. 9
Islamic tradition 56 n. 1
Israelites 38 n. 2
Italy 53 n. 6

Jacobus Intercissus (St. James the Cut-Up) 34 n. 3
James son of Alphaeus 292 n. 7
James the brother of the Lord 131 n. 8, 294–95
Jamnia (fortress of) lxxxii–lxxxiii, 241, 247
Jerome 59 n. 4. *See also Life of Hilarion, Viris illustribus*
Jerusalem (anti) xlii, xlvi n. 108
Jerusalem northern gates—*see* Damascus Gate
Jerusalem lxxx, 175 n. 4: departure, 77; destroyed 78–9, 92–93; liturgy 117; ministry 159; Old City 196 n. 1; patriarchate xlvi, liv; pilgrimage xlii, lii, 51–53, 101; return 193; settlement 79 n. 5, 93; stronghold 51. *See also* Holy City
Jesus Christ: name 75, 99; personal 53 (also n. 4), 99 (also n. 11); present 111, 133
Jesus Prayer 20 n. 2
Jewish fisherman lxxxii, 249
Jews and Christ's death 79
Jews in Palestine xliii, li, lv
John Chrysostom xxxv–xxxvii, lxv, 223
John of Antioch xliv
John of Apamea lxv
John of Ephesus—see *Life of John of Tella*
John of Jerusalem 93 n. 8
John of Tella lviii
John Rufus lxii–lxiii: disciple of Zeno, l; law training lxiii, 166 n. 4; works xix, xliv n. 92, lviii. *See also Life of Peter the Iberian, De obitu Theodosii* and *Plerophoriae*
John Sabanidze xxv

John the Baptist 71, 246 n. 3
John the Canopite 257
John the Eunuch: abbot 158–59; baptized Peter 42 n. 3; burial 91 n. 6, 273; commemoration 249; illness 85–87; monasticism 61, 69, 101; naming 65; ordination lxii n. 161, 89; Peter's companion lxxxii–lxxxiii, 43, 95, 175–77; visions 89–91. *See also* Mithridatos
John the Forerunner—*see* John the Baptist
Jordan River lxii, 172 n. 2, 183 n. 3
Joseph (monk) 301 n. 5
Josephus—see *Antiquitates Judaicae*, *Bellum Judaicum*, *Contra Apionem*
Judaism as a form of heathenism 227 (also n. 5)
Judas Iscariot 65 n. 4. *See also* Typology: Judas
Judean Desert xlviii, 22 n. 4, 71
Julian II (Byzantine emperor) 64 n. 2, 79 n. 5, 150 n. 4, 188 n. 3, 282 n. 4
Julian of Halicarnassus xxxii (also n. 47)
Julian the Apostate—*see* Julian II
Justin I (Byzantine emperor) lvii, lxii
Justin Martyr—*see I Apologia*
Justinian I (Byzantine emperor) xlvi n. 106, 109 n. 6, 164 n. 4
Juvenal of Jerusalem: and Romanus lxxxiv, 297; apostate 64 n. 2, 65, 283, 297; bishop 93 n. 8; opposition lv, 111; Chalcedon xlvi, lxxviii, 109–11; communion with lii, lv n. 137, 61 n. 9; ordination of Peter lxxvi, 105–7; return to Jerusalem xlviii, 287 n. 10

K'art'li xx–xxii
Kaisarion 137 (also n. 8), 139
Karaiatha 183 n. 1
Karkha deBeth Ṣelokh 34 n. 3
Kefar Gamala 66 n. 4, 298 n. 4
Kefar Sheʿartha 105
Kefar Turban 299
Khorramabad Iran—*see* Beth Lāpat
Khuranios lxxxv, 11
kingdom of God xlii
kings of Iberia xxi–xxii
Kypros (fortress) 22–23
Kyrion II (Catholicos) xxxii, lviii

land ownership xliii, li
Latrocinium (Robber Synod) xlv n. 99. *See also* Council of Ephesus II
Lavrai li (also n. 128), lv–lvi
law school lvii, 166 n. 4
law students lxiii, lxxxi, 223, 225
laying on of hands 14–15
Lazica xxxi, 42–43. *See also* Colchis
Legatio pro Christianis (Athenagoras) 13 n. 8.
Lent 11 n. 6

Leo I (Byzantine emperor) liv, lxxviii, lxxxiv, 131 n. 6, 143, 291 (also n. 11)
Leo I of Rome xlii n. 83, xliv–xlv, 108 n. 1, 145 (also n. 8). See also *Tome of Leo*
Leontius (martyr) 217 (also n. 9)
Leontius of Ashkelon 123 n. 3
Leontius of Ruisi (Mroveli) xxi, xxiv
Letter to Cosmas xxxvi
Libanius xxxvi n. 59, lxiv
Licinia Eudocia (empress) 57 n. 9
Licinius (Roman emperor) 65 n. 9
Life of Anthony—see *Vita Antonii*
Life of Dioscorus (Theopistus) 108 n. 3
Life of Hilarion—see *Vita Hilarionis*
Life of John of Lycopolis 59 n. 5
Life of John of Tella lviii n. 146. *See also* Elias John of Ephesus
Life of Longinus 136 n. 1, 143 n. 8
Life of Melania the Younger—see Vita Sanctae Melaniae Junioris
Life of Peter the Iberian: as Scripture 29; authorship lviii–lxi; citations in other works 75 n. 8; compare *Life of Rabulla* lxiii, lxvii; context xix; Coptic versions lxxiii; fear of God motifs 122 n. 1, 137; flight motifs 119 n. 5, 139; framework lxvii; genealogy xix, xxiii, xxxiii, lxvi, lxxv; genres lxiii, lxvi–lxix, lxxiv; geography lxii; Georgian versions lx–lxi, lxvi n. 171, lxxiii, 71 n. 10; literary analysis lxiii–lxxi; manuscripts lxxi–lxxiii; oral tradition 29 n. 13, 92 n. 3, 105 n. 7, 138 n. 4, 216 n. 1, 270 n. 1; pilgrimage lii; politics xxix; rhetoric lxiii, lxv, lxx; *Sitz im Leben* lxiii; synopsis lxxv–lxxxiv; Syriac translation lxiii, lxix–lxxiv. *See also* John Rufus
Life of Rabbula of Edessa lxiii, lxvii; ascetics as soldiers 69 n. 5; framework lxvii; genealogy lxxv n. 196; monasticism 235 n. 8; original Syriac lxiii, lxxiv
Life of Sabas—see Vita Sabae
Life of St. Nino xxv–xxvi
Life of Timothy Aelurus lxxiii
liturgical fans 269
liturgy (divine) 35, 63
Livias lxxviii, 153 n. 3, 169, 171
Long Village lxxxi, 221, 225
Longinus lxxviii, 111 n. 11, 136–37
Lucas (martyr) lxxxi, 211–13
Lucian priest, 66 n. 4
Lydia 122 n. 2

Macedonian Empire xxii
Madeba Map lxxix n. 197, 106 n. 3, 118 n. 1, 171 n. 10
Madeba lxxix–lxxx, 171–73, 180, 183 n. 1, 187, 189
Magdal Tutha lxxx, 200–201

Maiuma l, 103, 113, 159, 200 n. 2
Makarios (monk) lxi
Mamre 266 n. 2
Marcian (Byzantine emperor) xlvi, liv, 122 n. 2, 283: death, 135, 291; Theodosius and Romanus lxxxiv, 287–89
Marcionite canon 129 n. 7
Mareotis (lake) 135 n. 12, 141 n. 5
Mari (Persian Bishop) 109 n. 7
Maria (ascetic) 18 n. 3
Mark (apostle) 81 n. 8, 91
Mark the Deacon—*see Vita Porphyrii Gazensis*
marriage 12 n. 8, 22 n. 2
Martha xxviii n. 37
Martyrdom of Shushanik xxvii
Martyrdom of the Children of Kola xxvi
Martyrdom of Abo xxv
martyrdom: as witness 35; children xxvi; confessorship 15, 63, 131, 137, 147; in Persia xxix
Martyrion: Saint Stephen 196–97; Sergius and Bacchus lxxxi
Martyrius (*quaestor*) 165
martyrs: close to God 218 n. 1; companions 41; guides 43–45; revelation lxxxi; Persian lxxvii, 35, 67; protomartyr 196 n. 1; rebuke 49; women xxviii n. 37
Maximian (Roman emperor) 79 n. 7
Maximus (magistrate) lxxxi, 207
Mazda—*see* Ahura Mazda
Mazdaism—*see* Zoroastrianism
Maziks 173–74
Mc'xet'a: dynasty xxii
Mc'xet'a xx, xxiii
Mediterranean Sea 135 n. 12
Melania the Elder lxxvi, 55 n. 4, 58–59
Melania the Younger: a mother 60 n. 7; influence 101; journey to Constantinople 57–59; labor 55–57; reception of Peter lxxvi, 53 (also n. 6), 61; Rufinus 128 n. 3
Messiah xlii
metaphors lxiii
Migdol Thavatha—*see* Magdal Tutha
Mihrān Dynasty (Iberia) xxii
Miqa of Ashkelon 70 n. 6, 75 n. 8, 158 n. 5
miracles: belief 189; and children lxxx, 33, 151, 187, 189, 217–19; curse 17, 21–23; divine approval lxvii; environment lxxx, 21, 181–85, 249–51, 301; Eucharist 121, 151; exorcism 151, 219; faith 19, 189; for nonbelievers 247–49; healing lxxx, lxxxi, 15, 85–87, 149–51, 217; judgment 95–97, 151; liturgical 36–37, 47; obedience 189; oil 47 (of gladness), 151; preservation lxxx; protection 49, 151, 185; provision 97, 249–51; purpose 81–83; sign of divine grace 179–81; summons lxxxi; through blessing 189; through

martyrs 219; through prayer 19–23, 85–87, 217; through relics lxxxi, 21; transformation 37, 83–85; Wedding of Cana 200 n. 4; witness lxxvii, 29
Mirian (Murabanes) III xxii, xxiv, xxvi
Mithras (god) xxiii, 15 n. 7, 57 n. 4
Mithridatos 52 n. 4, 57, 65 n. 5. *See also* John the Eunuch
Moab 179
monastery (unnamed) lxxxiii
Monastery of Abū Ghālib 302 n. 5
Monastery of Aphthoria 237
Monastery of Beth Mar Bazai 287 (also n. 9)
Monastery of Birru-l Qutt (Georgian) xxiv
Monastery of Buzmihr (Georgian) xxiv
Monastery of Eikoston 135
Monastery of Eleutheropolis liv, lxxxiv
Monastery of Enaton 135
Monastery of Galata and Pera 291 n. 12. *See also* Monastery of Sykai
Monastery of Hypatios 123 n. 3
Monastery of Kefar Turban 299
Monastery of Maiuma l, lxxxiii, 19 n. 3, 91 n. 6, 93, 123 n. 3, 159, 169 n. 8, 267, 273, 275
Monastery of Mar Barsauma lxxii
Monastery of Oktokaidekaton 135
Monastery of Passarion (founding) 73
Monastery of Sabas lvi
Monastery of St. Dios liv, 289
Monastery of Sykai liv, lxxxiv
Monastery of Tekoa lxxxiv, 123 n. 3, 298 n. 2
Monastery of the Holy Cross 93 n. 11
Monastery of the Iberians 93
Monastery on the Mount of Olives lxxvi
monastery: academic centers l; construction 277, 299; double 55, 237; for women 229; palace 33; patronage xliii li, liv–lvi; renovation lxxxiii; solitary lxxvii
monastic foundations in Palestine xliii, xlviii–l, xlix
monastic habit: sacred garment 61–63; straw 55; wool 56 n. 1
monasticism: anchoritic 60 n. 8; carrying the cross of Christ 159, 235; cenobitic l, 60 n. 8, 99; eremitic l; Gaza l; journey to heaven 235; labor 203; master-disciple model l–li; minimum age 69 n. 4; Palestine xlix, li; renunciation of the world 235; three gifts 63; urban proximity xlviii. *See also* Asceticism
monks: from Cappadocia 175; from Egypt and Syria xlix; Greek speaking lxiii; Palestine 111;

father of the 111 (also n. 11), 137, 243
Moses of Khoren—see *History of the Armenians*
Moses (magistrate) 129, 187
Moses liii, lxviii, lxxix, lxxx, 47, 49, 81, 95, 153 n. 3, 169, 173, 177, 179; see also Peter the Iberian (typology)
Mount Gerizim 61, 242 n. 2
Mount Lebanon 211 n. 8
Mount Nebo 172 n. 4, 173, 175 n. 4, 177–79
Mount of Olives 55, 61, 63
Mount Pisgah lxviii, lxxix, 172 n. 4
Mountain of Moses (Abarim) 173. *See also* Mount Pisgah
MS BM Add 12,174 liii, lxxii–lxxiii
MS Sachau 321 lx, lxxi–lxxiii
Muratorian Canon 129 n. 7
Murgaqis lxxv, 11
Murvanos xxiv, lxi. *See also* Peter the Iberian
mystagogy (Pseudo-Dionysius) 89 n. 14

Nabarnugios lxi, lxxxv, 7, 17, 52 n. 4, 57, 65 n. 5, 175. *See also* Peter the Iberian
Nana xxvi
Narcissus of Jerusalem 36 n. 5
Nazarite (term) 38 n. 2
Nazarite habit 39
Nazariteship: asceticism 25, 55, 69, 99; John the Baptist 246 n. 3; self-torture 203
Nestabus 259
Nestorianism 160 n. 4
Nestorius of Constantinople xxxvi–xxxviii, xliv–xlv, 38 n. 5, 66 n. 1, 108 n. 2, 162 n. 3
New Rome xxxiv, xxxix, xl, xlvii, 51. *See also* Constantinople
Nino xxvi
North Africa 53 n. 6, 122 n. 2

Ohrmazd—*see* Ahura Mazda
oil 47, 176 n. 4, 151
On Frank Criticism (Philodemus of Gadara) 261 n. 6
"one nature made flesh," xxxviii
"one nature of the logos made flesh," xxxix 68
Onomasticon (Eusebius of Caesarea) 114 n. 5, 182 n. 1, 191 n. 8
oral tradition 28 n. 3
ordination: forced 107, 115, 137–39; from God 113, 117; from the dead 267
Origen xxxvi
Orthosias lxxx, 209
Osduktia lxxxv, 9, 21
Ota lxxxv, 11, 23
Oxyrhynchos lxxviii, 128 nn. 2–3, 131

P‘arsman 8 n. 2
P‘eroz xxii–xxiv, 8 n. 2
Palaea 157
Palestine and Palestina xlii–xliii xlvi–xlvii, xlix, lxxviii. *See also* Promised Land
Palladius—see *Historia Lausiaca*
Panegyric on Apollo (Stephen of Heracleopolis) 3 n. 4, 95 n. 3
Paphlagonia 108 n. 3, 133
Paramonarius 207

parents 189
Parthian Empire xxii, xxvii
Pascha lxxxi, 237 n. 6
Passarion lxxvi, 60 n. 8, 72 n. 3, 73
Passio of Jacobus Intercissus 34 n. 3
patriarch as high priest xxxi
patriarchal jurisdiction xxxiv: Georgia, xxv; Persia xxx–xxxi
patriarchal system xlvi (also n. 107)
Patriarchate of Antioch xxv, xxix
patronage: Byzantine emperor 80 n. 5; dependence on li, liv–lv; of churches 243; of monasteries xliii, li–lv, 55; of Peter lvi, lxxx
Paul (apostle) liii, 3, 43, 199, 216 n. 2, 232 n. 6
Paul of Ephesus 165
Paul of Gaza (or Maiuma) lxxvii, 107, 116 n. 6
Paul of Samosata 296
Paul the steward 213
penitence in liturgy 63
Pentateuch lxviii
Pentecost lxvii, lxxx, lxxxi, 193, 211, 217, 237 n. 6
perfection before or in death 231, 239, 291
persecution (Chalcedonian) lvii, lxii, lxxvii, lxxx: in Egypt, 133; rebellion 91–93, 105–7; Theodosius 123
persecution: Decian 286 n. 6; for orthodoxy 93; Persian xxviii–xxx; Roman xxx, xli
Persian hegemony xxv, xxvii
Persian martyrs lxxv–lxxvi
Persians xx
personal rivalry xl
Pešitta 149 n. 5
Peter (apostle) lxxv, 7, 167, 216 n. 2, 256 n. 2
Peter II of Antioch lxii, 165, 291 n. 11
Peter Mongus 162 n. 3
Peter of Alexandria 255 (also n. 4), 263
Peter the Fuller—*see* Peter II of Antioch
Peter the Iberian (typology): apostle Peter 7; Christ 139, 239; Elijah 181; Moses 147, 181, 185, 249; Noah 25; Paul 147
Peter the Iberian (visions): concealed 189–91; foreshadowing lxxx, 191; Jesus 39, 75, 121; law students lxiii, 233; Leontius 217; martyrs 35, 43; new monastery 75–77; Peter of Alexandria 255, 257; Peter's final vision lxxxiii; Satan 75; Theodosius lxxxiii, 131, 291–93
Peter the Iberian: after death 279; Alexandria 123–25; as monk 7; ascetic life 11 n. 7, 69–71; authority xx, lii, lxvii, 112 n. 1, 190 n. 1; biography overview lxxv–lxxxiv; birth 31; blessing lxxxii, 221, 235, 237, 243; burial lxxxii; curse against apostasy 261; death lxxxiii, 195, 265; authorship of *Areopagitica* 76 n. 1,

88–89, 162 n. 2, 254 n. 1; discernment 257; disciple of Zeno li; disciples lxxxi–lxxxiii, 37; divine election 79; exile in Egypt lv n. 137, lxxvii, 123–25; exile in Palestine lii; family 5–25; flight from Constantinople 43–45; foreknowledge 194 n. 1, 243, 245 n. 3, 251, 255, 257; founding a monastery 73; genealogical table lxxxv; good shepherd 5, 29, 169, 269, 275; habit 65; heirs lxxxiii, 257, 269, 273, 275; Hilarion's successor l; hostage xxxi, lxxvi, 10 n. 2, 31–33, 41; hot springs 169–73; humility 33; illness lxxvii, lxxix, 75, 169–71, 241; imitator of the apostles 25; imperial summons lxxx; in a vision 279; in Palestine lii, lxxvi–lxxix; in Phoenicia lxxxi, 207; in the desert 71; influence lvii, lviii; influenced by 59; Jerusalem 51–55, 93–95; life as example 3; liturgy 117–19; Magdal Tutha lxxx, 199–201; ministry 5, 11 n. 7, 29, 105, 147, 157–61, 199, 239; miracles 149–51, 193, 247–49; monastery 73, 93, 101, 277; name lxi, lxxxv, 7; old man 243, 249; ordaining bishops lxxviii, 139; ordination lxxvii, 105–7, 113–17; petitioning the Emperor lxxxi, 207; pilgrimage to Jerusalem lxxvi, 51–53; promise to God 205–6; public confrontation 131–33; relics lxxxiii; return to Palestine lxxix, 157; saint 221; teaching lxxxiii, 231–33, 237, 259–63; three commandments lxxxii, 231–33; will lxxxii–lxxxiii, 241, 257. *See also Life of Peter the Iberian*

Pharnabazus I xxii

Pharsamanios xxx, lxxxv, 8–9

Philip (apostle) 139

Philip (prefect of Egypt) 228 n. 8

Philodemus of Gadara—*see On Frank Criticism*

Philoponoi 73 nn. 4 and 6

philosopher (ascetic) 37, 149–51

philosophy 17 (also n. 4), 148 n. 3

Phocas of Sinope (the gardner) lxxxi, 210 n. 11

Phoenicia lxxxi

pilgrimage: as virtue 39–41; in Palestine xlii, lii, liv–lv, 41–53; Jerusalem xliii, lii, 51–53, 101; Leontius's shrine 216 n. 2; meaning lii; Peter's tomb lxxxiii; Promised Land 41; route 197; weaving crown 239

pilgrims lii, 53, 97–99

Pinianus lxxvi, 53 (also n. 6), 55–57

Plato—*see Symposium*

Pleriphoriae (John Rufus) viii, xix n. 1, xxxv n. 53, xliii–xlvi, l n. 125, lv nn. 135 and 137, lviii, lxii (also n. 160), 25 n. 9, 28 n. 3, 37 n. 6, 42 n. 3, 44 n. 3, 52 n. 2, 61 n. 9, 64 n. 2, 70 n. 6, 71 n. 11, 74–75, 77 n. 4, 82 nn. 1 and 3, 88 n. 3, 98 n. 1, 109–12, 123–26, 134 n. 7, 143 n. 8, 146 n. 3, 151 n. 6, 158 nn. 2–3 and 5, 160 n. 4, 162 n. 2, 190 n. 1, 198–99, 228 n. 1, 236 n. 2, 251 n. 6, 257 n. 9, 268 n. 2, 277 n. 8, 282–85, 290–92, 293–95
Pliny the Younger—see *Epistulae*
Poemenia lxxvi, 51 n. 8, 59 (also nn. 5–6)
political alliance xxix–xxxii, 7, 15, 31
political conflict: Byzantines and Persians 10 n. 2
political diplomacy xx, xxix–xxxi
political hostage xxix–xxxi, lxxvi, 10 n. 2, 31, 41
political influence: Hellenistic xxi; Iranian xxi, xxiii
Pool of Shiloah 118–19
Porphyry of Gaza lxv
possession 123
Poteein 191 n. 8. *See also* Batmin
power of God lxviii
Praktikos (Evagrius of Pontus) 36 n. 3, 69 n. 11, 90 n. 3
prayer: monastic order 77; house of 35, 277, 279; miracles lxxx, 19, 21, 36 n. 5, 223; of the saints 5, 169, 185, 189, 217, 239, 277; pre-Christian religion xxvii; prophetic 175; standing 105; thanksgiving 100 n. 6, 173; transforming anger 37; unceasing lxxvii
primacy: Jerusalem 293–95; patriarchal xxxix, xliv–xlv; Rome xliv, xlvii
Primary History of K'art'li xxii
Proclus of Constantinople 39 (also nn. 5–6)
Proclus of Cyzicus xxxv n. 53
Proclus 39
Promised Land 41, 167
prophecy: birth 31; ordination 107
prosōpon xxxix
Proterius of Alexandria lxxviii, 123, 125–29, 133, 135 n. 10, 141, 143, 166 n. 1
Pseudo-Dionysian corpus (authorship) 76 n. 1, 88–89
Pseudo-Dionysius—*see Mystagogy*
Ptolemaïs lxxxii, 235
Publicola 53 n. 6
Pulcheria (Byzantine empress) xxxv–xxxvii, xliv–xlv, 30 n. 8, 122 n. 3

Qaiuma 187
Qata lxxxiv, 11
Qauxč'išvili—*see Georgian Chronicle*
Quaestor 164–65
Questions of the Brethren—see *Rules* (Basil of Caesarea)
quicklime 290 n. 3
Quintillian *Institutio oratoria* lxiv

Raabe Richard: commentary, 9 n. 8, 37 n. 5, 43 n. 7, 45 n. 6, 67 n. 6, 70 n. 1, 104 n. 1, 135 n. 11, 138 n. 3, 200 n. 1, 215 n. 6, 223 n. 8, 246 n. 3, 256 n. 1; conjectures 48 n. 1; emendations lxix–lxx, 28 n. 2, 30 n. 1, 42 n. 4; errors 170 n. 1; textual criticism lxxi–lxxiv, 7 n. 6, 19 n. 5, 52 n. 1, 58 n. 1, 100 n. 3, 224 n. 1
Rachel's Tomb 197 (also n. 4)
Rasapha (Augusta Euphratesia) 215 n. 6
Ravenna 86 n .1
rebellions: Jews and Samaritans xliii (also n. 88); Samaritan lv
Reisefabulistik—*see* fantastic voyages
relics: cross 47, 81, 83; deposition 65–67, 215, 279–81; miracles lxxxi, 21; Persian martyrs lxxvi–lxxvii, 35, 43, 65–67; Peter lxxxiii; discovery lxxxi, 211; Stephen 67, 298 n. 4; tokens 83 n. 7; unifying 267; Zachariah 298 n. 4
religious art: Abel and Melchizidek 86 n. 1
reliquary 47
remembrance of leaders 3–5, 265. *See also* commemoration
repentance: a path 169; gift of tears 63; house of healing 229; new beginning 233–35; through affliction 19
Reuben sons of, 182 n. 1
rhetoric: Asianic style xlviii (also n. 179); centers lxv–lxvi; Greek lxiii, lxviii; humility 148 n. 1; *Life of Peter* lxi, lxviii–lxix; Roman lxiv
Robber Council xlv–xlvi, 108–9. *See also* Council of Ephesus II *Latrocinium*
Roman education lxiv
Roman Empire xx, xxii, 53
Roman hegemony xxv, xxviii
Roman measurement 50 n. 5
Romanus (father of Victor) 106 n. 3
Romanus (martyr) lxxxi, 211–13
Romanus (monk) liii–liv, lxxxiv, 111
Romanus of Caesarea 211 n. 7. *See also* Romanus (martyr)
Rome xli, xliv
royal city 131, 173 *See also* Constantinople
Royal Lists xxii
Rufinus of Aquileia 59 n. 4, 128 n. 3. *See also Historia ecclesiastica*
Rules (Basil of Caesarea) 261–63

Sabas 132 n. 1, 247 n. 5
Sabina (abbess) lxxxii, 237
Sachau Edward, lxxi
Saint Stephen Gate—*see* Damascus Gate

saints: alms given to 129; ascetics 171; blessing 153; characteristics 253; escorted to heaven 247, 255; in a contest 163; monastic company 149; patron xxvi; Peter and John lix, lxxvi, 27, 47, 59, 61, 167, 279; prayers 37, 217; Scetian 173; transvestite 229 n. 8; visions 91, 259. *See also* relics
Sallustius of Jerusalem lvi
salvation guarantee of, 233
Samaritans xliii, li, lv, 242 n. 2, 269
Samson 38 n. 2
Sapientia Salomonis 154 n. 2
sarcophagus lxxxiii, 196–97, 275
Sassanian government administration xxvii–xxix
Sassanian religion 15 n. 7. *See also* Persians, Zoroastrianism
Sassanid Empire (Persian) xx, xxii
Satan: causing speech 37; dragon 133; frustrating plans 41; persecuting the saints 287; possession 121; promoting Chalcedon 131, 161–63
Scetis 98 n. 4, 173–74
schism (Acacian) xlvii, 163 n. 3
schism in Palestine xlviii
schism of 1054 xlvii
Sebaste Armenia, 65 (also n. 9)
Second Jewish War (Bar Kokhba Revolt) 78 n. 5
Seleucid Empire xxii
Senate 193 n. 5
senators 35, 53
Seneca—*see Epistulae morales*
Serapeum 149
Sergius (martyr) 215 (also n. 6)
settlement in Palestine: ascetics xliii, 58 n. 4; imperial policy xlii, li, liv, 93; Christian 79 n. 5
Seven Great Houses xxii
Severianus of Scythopolis 122 n. 3
Severus of Antioch: biography lix; exile lvii; *Letters* lvi n. 143; Peter as model lvii; Peter's disciples lxiii; rivals xxxii
Shapur II (Persian emperor) 15 n. 3
Shiloah 118–19
Shushanik xxvii–xxviii
signs—*see* miracles
Simeon Stylites liii, lxxxiv, 285
Simon the Magician 110–11
Sitz im Leben lxiii, 92 n. 3
Socrates Scholasticus—*see Historia ecclesiastica*
Sokha (Khirbet Shuwaikah) 114–15
Sokkheth—*see* Sokha
Solon's legal reform lxiv
Sophronius 39
Sozomen—see *Historia ecclesiastica*
spiritual athleticism xxxiv, lxxvii, 70–71. *See also* asceticism
spiritual guidance lxxvii, lxxviii, 49, 259
spiritual instruction lxxxii–lxxxiii, 37, 199, 259–61
spiritual wealth 27, 53

Spoudaioi 73 nn. 4 and 6
Spring of Moses 153 n. 3, 169–71
springs in Baʾar 181–83, 186 n. 3
Staatsbibliothek zu Berlin lxxi
Stadia 51
statue of Julian II lxviii, 151
Stephen (apostle) 67, 196 n. 1
Stephen (archdeacon) 257–59
Stephen of Heracleopolis—*see Panegyric on Apollo*
Strabo—see *Geographica*
Straits of the Bosporus 45 (also n. 6)
Stromateis (Clement of Alexandria) 13 n. 8
Sufi mystics 56 n. 1
sun worship 15
Symposium (Plato) 234 n. 7
Synaxarion of Constantinople 288 n. 6
Synod of Dvin xxxii
Syriac dialect lxxv
Syriac Life of Simeon Stylites 285 n. 6
Syriac literature 7 n. 4: Greek influence, lxiii, lxix–lxx, lxxiii–lxxv

Taposiris Magna 141 (nn. 5–6). *See also* Abūṣīr
Tarabulus (Lebanon)—*see* Tripoli
Tarbo xxviii n. 37
Tarsia lxvii n. 173
Tbilisi xxxi
tears: at holy sites 85; compassion 19; in liturgy 121; Jesus prayer 21; joy 217; mourning 265, 271; prayer 75; repentance 63; response to a vision 39, 153, 191; spiritual gift 63
temple (Christian)—*see* churches called temples
temple (Samaritan) 60 n. 2
temple of Augustus 137 n. 8. *See also Kaisarion*
temple of Zeus 60 n. 2
temptation lxxvi–lxxvii, 71, 152 n. 3: devil's attack, 74 n. 1; sexual 99, 101
Thagaste 53 n. 6
Thebaid lxxvii, 128–29
Thekla xxviii n. 37
Theodora (Byzantine empress) 79 n. 7
Theodore (aquaintence) lix
Theodore Lector—see *Historia ecclesiastica*
Theodore of Ashkelon (lawyer) lxxix, lxxxiv, 158–59, 166–67, 259, 277
Theodore of Mopsuestia xxxvi, xxxix, 109 n. 6
Theodoret of Cyrrhus 109 (also n. 6), 285 (also n. 7)
Theodosius: anti-Chalcedonian bishop liii; at Sykai 291; before Marcian 287–89; burial 293, 301; exile in Egypt liii, lxxxiv, 283; in a vision 131; in Constantinople 287; journey to Antioch 285; ordaining clergy lviii; rival bishop of Jerusalem xlviii, 61 nn. 8–9, 113;

selection 111; successor of James 294 n. 1. *See also De obitu Theodosii*, *De situ terrae sanctae*
Theodosius I (Byzantine emperor) xxxix
Theodosius II (Byzantine emperor) xlii, li, 30–32, 188 n. 3; daughter 57 (also n. 9); edict li; government administration 188 n. 3; Peter as hostage xxx–xxxii, lxxv, 10 n. 2, 31, 41; *spoudaioi* 73 n. 4
Theodotus of Ancyra 38–39
Theodotus of Ioppe 123 n. 3
Theodotus 39
Theodoulos (martyr) 217 n. 9
Theophanes—see *Chronographia*
Theophilus of Alexandria xl
Theopistus—*see Life of Dioscorus*
Theotokos controversy xxxv (also n. 53), xxxvii, xxxix
Thomas of Harkel 135 n. 11
Three Chapters 109 nn. 6–7
Timothy (opponent of Romanus) lxxxiv
Timothy Aelurus of Alexandria: exile 141, 144–45, 288 n. 1, 291 n. 11; ordination lxxviii, 137–41; other names 136 n. 4; return from exile lxxix, 161, 163
Timothy (archimandrite) 283–85
Timothy Salophaciolus of Alexandria lxxviii, 146–47
Timothy (bishop) 123 n. 3
Titus (Roman emperor) 78 n. 5
To the Magnesians (Ignatius of Antioch) 208 n. 3
To the Philadelphians (Ignatius of Antioch) 208 n. 3
Tome of Leo (Leo I of Rome) xlvii, 107–9, 111, 163 n. 3, 261
torture liv
Tower of David lxxvii, 73 n. 4, 93–94
Traditio Apostolica (Hippolytus) 151 n. 6
Transcaucasia xix–xx
Transjordan 172 n. 2, 183 n. 1
translation into Syriac lxiii, lxx–lxxiv
Tribunus 192–93
Tripoli lxxxi, 216–17, 219
Trisagion for the Dead 275 n. 4
Twelve Anathemas (Cyril of Alexandria) xliii, 163 n. 3, 285 n. 7
Twelve Syriac Hymns (Balai) lxx n. 183
Typikon 35 n. 7
typology: Abraham 97; apostles 195; Caiaphas 125; cloud or pillar of fire 43; Daniel 15; fishing 227; five wise virgins 227; furnace of the Chaldeans 183; holy of holies 81; Isaiah 201; Israel 41; Isaac 29; James 131; Joseph 41; Judas Iscariot xliv n. 93, 65, 111, 125, 261; Mary 7 n. 4; Moses 47, 95, 147, 181, 185, 249; Noah 25; Paul and Barnabas 43; Peter 7; Pharaoh 287; Samuel 41; Scripture 29; servant of Caiaphas

95; the ark 47; thief on the cross 127; three youths in Daniel 183. *See also* Peter the Iberian (typology)
Tyre lxxxi, 159 n. 5, 225 (also n. 15)

Umm Lisan (*also* Leison) xxiii n. 16
univira 22–23
upper room 197
Urim and Thummim 149 n. 5

Valentinian III (Byzantine emperor) 57 (also n. 8)
Vandals 53 n. 6
Varaz-Bakhʾar (*also* Varaz Bakur)—*see* Aspacures III
Vardan Marmikonean xxviii
Varsken xxviii
Vaxtʻang Gorgasali xxxi
Victor Stratelates 106 n. 3
Victor (saint) 107
Vigil: burial lxxxiii, 265, 275; martyr 35; monasticism 27; miracle 37
virgin xxvi, 17, 227
Viris illustribus (Jerome) 293 n. 8
visions: Abba Abraham 273; Abba Maxos lxxxiii, 269–71; Abba Peter 195, 245–47; angelic court 255; ascension of souls 125–27, Athanasius of Egypt, 253, 279; audible 117, 153; demonstrate worth 271; eschatological 89; interpretation 223; of martyrs 211–13, 213–45; of Lucas, Phocas and Romanus, 211–13; of Saint Andrew 207; of Trinity 44 n. 3; Stephen (archdeacon) 259. *See also* Peter the Iberian (visions)
Vita Antonii Athanasius of Alexandria (Latin), xlix
Vita Antonii Athanasius of Alexandria, 70 n. 3
Vita Constantini (Eusebius of Caesarea) 50–51, 80 nn. 1, 4, and 5,
Vita Cyriaci (Cyril of Scythopolis) 18 n. 3
Vita Euthymii (Cyril of Scythopolis) 61 nn. 8–9, 72 n. 2, 285 n. 6, 297 n. 12, 300 n. 4
Vita Hilarionis (Jerome) xlix (also n. 116–17), 200 n. 2
Vita Isaiae (Zachariah Rhetor) lix–lx, 201 n. 5, 202 n. 5, 245 n. 4, 277 n. 8
Vita Petri Iberi—see Life of Peter the Iberian
Vita Porphyrii Gazensis (Mark the Deacon) 103 n. 10
Vita Sabae (Cyril of Scythopolis) xliii n. 88, lv–lvi, 61 n. 9, 132 n. 1, 297 n. 12, 300 n. 4
Vita Sanctae Melaniae Junioris (Gerontius) 54 n. 1, 57 n. 9, 60 n. 7
Vita Sancti Georgii Chozebitae (Antony of Choziba) 37 n. 5
Vita Severi (Zachariah Rhetor) lix nn. 151–52, lxii n. 160, 43 n. 7, 53 n. 7, 123 n. 8, 158 n. 3, 224–25, 243 n. 5, 257 n. 6, 277 n. 8
Vita Severi (John of Beth Aphthonia) 123 n. 8

Vita Sinuthii Archimandritae (Besa) 97 n. 10
Vita Theodosii (Cyril of Scythopolis) 61 nn. 8–9, 73 n. 4
vitaxas xxiii–xxiv
voice (divine)—*see* visions: audible

Wadi Kidron lvi
wars: Iberia 7; Macedonia and Iberia xxii; Rome and Arabs xxxiv, lviii; Rome and Persia xx, xxx, lviii
weaving: metaphor for the incarnation 56 n. 1; crown of confessorship 15, 63, 127, 291; crown of good pilgrimage 239
White Huns (Hephtalites) 9 (also n. 6)
widows 22–23, 58 n. 4
will as enemy of God 69

xenodocheion xliii

Yazdegerd II (Persian emperor) xxviii

Zachariah (disciple) 245
Zachariah of Melitene—*see* Zachariah Rhetor
Zachariah Rhetor xlvi n. 108, lix–lxi. *See also Chronicle*, *Vita Isaiae*, *Vita Severi*
Zeno (Byzantine emperor) lv–lvi, lxxix, 162–63: dealings with Peter, lxxxi, 205. *See also Henotikon*
Zeno (abbot) xxvii–xxviii, xxix, l–li, lxxvii, 99–107
Zoroastrianism xx, xxvii, 15 n. 7. *See also* Ahura Mazda, Angra Mainyu, Adhur Mithra
Zosimus 261 n. 7
Zuzo lxxxv, 11, 21–23

www.ingramcontent.com/pod-product-compliance
Lightning Source LLC
Chambersburg PA
CBHW021350290426
44108CB00010B/182